Interpersonal Communication

THE WHOLE STORY

Kory Floyd

Arizona State University

Boston   Burr Ridge, IL   Dubuque, IA   Madison, WI   New York
San Francisco   St. Louis   Bangkok   Bogotá   Caracas   Kuala Lumpur
Lisbon   London   Madrid   Mexico City   Milan   Montreal   New Delhi
Santiago   Seoul   Singapore   Sydney   Taipei   Toronto

Higher Education

Published by McGraw-Hill, an imprint of The McGraw-Hill Companies, Inc., 1221 Avenue of the Americas, New York, NY 10020. Copyright © 2009. All rights reserved. No part of this publication may be reproduced or distributed in any form or by any means, or stored in a database or retrieval system, without the prior written consent of The McGraw-Hill Companies, Inc., including, but not limited to, in any network or other electronic storage or transmission, or broadcast for distance learning.

3 4 5 6 7 8 9 0 VNH/VNH 0 9

ISBN: 978-0-07-325877-5 (Instructor's Edition)
MHID: 0-07-325877-6
ISBN: 978-0-07-340664-0 (Student's Edition)
MHID: 0-07-340664-3

Editor-in-Chief: *Michael Ryan*
Publisher: *Frank Mortimer*
Executive Editor: *Katie Stevens*
Director of Development: *Rhona Robbin*
Senior Development Editors: *Nanette Giles and Jennie Katsaros*
Executive Marketing Manager: *Leslie Oberhuber*
Senior Production Editor: *Anne Fuzellier*
Art Director: *Preston Thomas*
Art Manager: *Robin Mouat*
Design Manager and Cover Designer: *Andrei Pasternak*
Interior Designer: *Jeanne Calabrese*
Senior Photo Research Coordinator: *Natalia Peschiera*
Photo Researcher: *Romy Charlesworth*
Senior Production Supervisor: *Tandra Jorgensen*
Composition: *10/12 Celeste by Thompson Type*
Printing: *45# Pub Matte Plus by Quebecor World*

Cover images: ThinkStock/SuperStock

Credits: *The credits section for this book begins on page C-1 and is considered an extension of the copyright page.*

Library of Congress Cataloging-in-Publication Data
Floyd, Kory.
   Interpersonal communication / Kory Floyd. — 1st ed.
      p. cm.
   Includes bibliographical references and index.
   ISBN-13: 978-0-07-340664-0 (alk. paper)
   ISBN-10: 0-07-340664-3 (alk. paper)
   1. Interpersonal communication.   I. Title.
BF637.C45F56   2009
153.6—dc22

                                                          2008038146

The Internet addresses listed in the text were accurate at the time of publication. The inclusion of a Web site does not indicate an endorsement by the authors or McGraw-Hill, and McGraw-Hill does not guarantee the accuracy of the information presented at these sites.

www.mhhe.com

To Luke, Abby, Megan,
and Ben

} Brief Contents {

} Contents {

4 Interpersonal Perception 121

5 Language 163

6 Nonverbal Communication 207

} Meet Kory Floyd {

Kory Floyd's research focuses on the communication of affection in personal relationships, and on the interplay between communication, physiology, and health. He has studied affectionate communication in a host of family relationships, as well as between romantic partners, friends, and even new acquaintances. His work in the Communication Sciences Laboratory at Arizona State University demonstrates how affectionate behavior can alter stress hormones, lower blood sugar, reduce cholesterol, and improve immune system parameters. His most recent project, funded by the National Institutes of Health, investigated the role of oxytocin in the stress-alleviating effects of affectionate communication.

Dr. Floyd is past chair of the family communication division of the National Communication Association, and is also immediate past editor of the Journal of Family Communication. He was the 2006 recipient of the Gerald R. Miller Award for Early Career Achievement from the International Association for Relationship Research. His most recent book, *Communicating Affection: Interpersonal Behavior and Social Context,* was published in 2006 by Cambridge University Press.

} From Me to You {

I can still recall how my family reacted when I said I wanted to study communication. *You already know how to communicate,* I remember one relative saying. Communication seemed like common sense to my family members, so they weren't entirely sure why I needed a PhD just to understand it.

As it turns out, my relatives are like a lot of other people in this regard. Since each of us communicates in some form nearly every day of our lives, it's hard not to think of communication as completely intuitive.

This is especially true for interpersonal communication, since forming and maintaining relationships with others is such a pervasive human activity. What can we learn from research and formal study that we don't already know from our lived experience? Aren't we all experts in interpersonal communication? Just for the sake of argument, let's say we were. Why, then, would we so often misunderstand each other? Why would our divorce rate be as high as it is? How come it would seem like women and men speak different languages? What would explain the popularity of self-help books, relationship counselors, and afternoon talk shows? If we're all experts at communicating interpersonally, why do we often find it so challenging? Maybe communication isn't as intuitive as one might think.

My goal for *Interpersonal Communication: The Whole Story* was to craft a text to help students see how interpersonal communication not only affects their relationships but also influences their health, happiness, and quality of life. I wanted to guide students to go beyond common-sense notions about communication and help them see the value of investigating interpersonal processes systematically. I wanted to meet these priorities while speaking to students in a way that interests them and encourages them to use both the content and the cognitive tools to relate theories and concepts to their own experiences.

Ideally, a good textbook will not only interest and excite students; it will also provide relevant, contemporary, and high-quality support for instructors. *Interpersonal Communication: The Whole Story* offers instructors their own edition of the text, with annotations in the margins, and a thoughtfully designed instructor's Web site and test bank that should help make the interpersonal communication course come alive in their classrooms. I hope you will find the result of these efforts to be a well-integrated package of engaging and contemporary materials for the study of interpersonal communication.

Kory Floyd

} Interview with the Author {

In this interview, Professor **Dawn Braithwaite,** the Willa Cather Professor of Communication Studies at the University of Nebraska, talks to **Kory Floyd** about his textbook. Professor Braithwaite is currently the Second Vice President of the National Communication Association and will serve as its President in 2010.

DB: What motivated you to spend the last several years writing an interpersonal communication textbook for college students?

KF: What's motivated me is the chance to show students how interpersonal communication can better their lives. So many exciting developments in teaching and research are helping us understand communication better than we ever have before. As a discipline, we're continually exploring innovative research questions and methods for instruction. These innovations are only useful, however, if they can help people communicate in more effective ways in their relationships. I see this book as a real opportunity to benefit students' lives by giving them the most contemporary tools for understanding and improving their interpersonal communication. Toward that end, the book includes many applied activities, self-assessments via the "Getting to Know You" feature, and exercises aimed at helping students develop and practice the communication skills most relevant to their relationships.

DB: Over the years I have read through quite a few textbooks for the interpersonal communication course. You describe your text as different from the others because it tells "The Whole Story" of interpersonal communication. What do you mean by that?

KF: Every textbook must be selective in what it covers, but many texts tell only part of the story when it comes to interpersonal communication. I've tried to present a more complete story in this book, in three specific ways. First, although all texts acknowledge the importance of diversity in interpersonal communication, their treatment is often highly skewed toward ethnic and cultural diversity. Diversity in religious background, economic status, sexual identity, and physical and mental abilities can also affect how people interact, however. This book incorporates a focus on these and other diversity factors in the research presented, the examples offered, and the activities suggested for students. We must examine a broader range of human diversity if we are to tell the whole story of interpersonal communication.

Second, telling the whole story means paying more attention to the challenges of interpersonal communication. Every textbook speaks to the "bright side" of managing personal relationships, including topics such as intimacy, affection, humor, and self-disclosure. In recent years, however, research has also illuminated the "dark side" of interpersonal communication by examining topics such as deception, jealousy, harassment, and grief. Many students struggle to deal with these and similar issues in their own relationships. To help them develop the communication skills they need to do so, this book offers a dedicated "Dark Side of IPC" box in each chapter that addresses a specific dark side issue and provides suggestions for managing it in everyday life.

Finally, although every text discusses social and cultural influences on communication, most give little attention to biological influences. Cutting-edge research in several disciplines has identified connections between communication and biology and described their implications for our well-being. By examining biological as well as social and cultural influences, this book presents a more complete picture of interpersonal communication.

DB: How do you help instructors address "the conundrum of the intuitive" that many students have in this course?

KF: Many instructors have had the experience of confronting students' intuitive knowledge when teaching interpersonal communication. When students encounter research results they find intuitive, such as "women are more nonverbally sensitive than men," they often question the value of such research because they believe the result is self-evident. But when they encounter results they find counterintuitive, such as "lack of eye contact is not a good indicator of deception," they often refuse to believe them, deferring instead to their own experience. This creates what I call a "conundrum of the intuitive" for instructors, whereby many students believe intuitive results are self-evident and counterintuitive results are wrong. Early in the book, I point out that although intuition often leads us to an accurate understanding of interpersonal communication, it occasionally does not. To reiterate the point, every chapter offers a "Fact or Fiction?" text box that examines the accuracy of one intuitive notion about communication. This feature will help instructors demonstrate to students how their understanding of interpersonal communication benefits from systematic research.

DB: In what ways will today's college students find your textbook meaningful to their lives? How will it support their goals and needs at home, at school, and in the workplace? In other words, what's in it for students?

KF: I think this book speaks to the types of interpersonal challenges college students face these days. During their college years, many students are negotiating friendships and romantic relationships, managing with their families, and forming their first professional relationships. At the same time, they're formulating their adult self-concepts, learning how to manage their emotions, dealing with interpersonal conflict, and discovering how their worldview is influenced by their gender and culture. To aid in these efforts, this book frequently asks students to reflect on their own beliefs and behaviors and to consider myriad ways of thinking about interpersonal relationships. It also uses research in an active, applied way by teaching students practical skills for person perception, conflict management, and emotional communication. By giving students knowledge and tools that are based on research and contemporary examples with which they'll relate, this book meets students where they are and helps them move forward in their interpersonal relationships.

DB: How do you incorporate your own research about the interplay of interpersonal communication and health into your textbook and make it relevant to college students?

KF: In my own work, I've been fascinated by how intimately the body is connected to interpersonal behavior. When we argue with people, our blood pressure goes up. When we receive a warm embrace from a loved one, our stress hormones go down. When other people surprise or frighten or disappoint us, our bodies react in patterned and predictable ways. The link between interpersonal behavior and physiology implies that some ways of communicating are better for our health than others. Throughout the book, I explain how communication behaviors are related to health and suggest ways of communicating that will enhance well-being.

DB: What do you hope instructors will gain by using your textbook for their interpersonal communication classes?

KF: In this book, instructors will find a perspective on interpersonal communication that is fresh, contemporary, and solidly grounded in research yet easily applicable to students' lives. They'll find a personable, engaging writing style that makes the book user friendly for students. Instructors will also find an annotated instructors' edition of the book filled with additional details, provocative discussion questions, and examples to share in class. Moreover, they'll be provided with many suggestions for in-class and out-of-class activities that will help students apply interpersonal communication principles to their daily lives. Suggestions for activities are included in "Learn It, Try It, Reflect on It" located at the end of every major section in every chapter, in the online instructor's manual, and also in the annotated instructors' edition. All of these features will enrich instructors' abilities to connect the material to their students and make it relevant to their lives.

DB: How well do you believe your textbook reflects the present state of interpersonal communication?

KF: This book introduces students to the core principles of interpersonal behavior by drawing both on classic sources and on the most contemporary research. Cutting-edge work on topics such as emotion, communication technology, persuasion, and health is described within the framework of existing communication theories and perspectives. The up-to-date material and examples will give students a solid foundation in interpersonal communication, while also encouraging them to consider how communication practices are evolving over time.

} List of Supplements {

For Instructors

Our support material provides instructors with fresh ideas about teaching the interpersonal course and offers numerous activity suggestions in the Annotated Instructor's Edition, the Instructor's Manual, and within each chapter.

Interpersonal Communication: The Whole Story supports teachers with an Annotated Instructor's Edition (AIE) written by the author. The AIE features a set of marginal notes for each section of every chapter that will help instructors enrich the material for their students. The marginal notes are organized by function, and include:

- *Outside of Class*—offers suggestions for out-of-class activities.
- *Talking Point*—provides examples or extensions of a particular point in the chapter.
- *Focus on Ethics*—raises ethical questions regarding a specific issue.
- *Focus on Scholarship*—gives examples of specific studies or program of research for instructors to describe to students.
- *In Everyday Life*—provides examples of how a specific concept can be observed in mundane interaction.
- *Writing Note*—offers examples of short writing assignments instructors can assign.
- *Media Note*—offers examples of how instructors can use the book's media tools or other media to illustrate concepts.

In addition to the AIE, *Interpersonal Communication: The Whole Story* offers a robust instructor's Web site and test bank written by the author.

- The instructor can go online to find chapter outlines, discussion questions, key terms and definitions, learning objectives. and numerous ready-to-use in-class and out-of-class activities and assignments for every chapter.
- The test bank offers multiple-choice questions, true/false questions, and essay questions for each chapter. The preparation of all of these materials by the book's author ensures that every assignment, test question, key term, and learning objective directly reflects the book's content.
- Ready-made PowerPoints for each chapter are available online. Created by Jacob Arndt of Kalamazoo Valley Community College, they include lecture outlines, video clips, and photographs to enliven the classroom experience.
- An outstanding video series to accompany *Interpersonal Communication: The Whole Story* offers 30 video clips that illustrate the core concepts in the text. Topics include cultural differences, social construction of gender roles, nonverbal communication, listening, interpersonal conflict and clash of power, harassment, and self-disclosure. These videos provide a foundation for lively classroom discussions. They are available online; for DVD format, please contact your local rep.

For Students

Interpersonal Communication: The Whole Story Online Learning Center provides students with relevant instructional aids to help them review course concepts. These include interactive chapter quizzes, glossary flash cards, and chapter specific videos. (http://www.mhhe.com/floydipc1e)

Acknowledgments and Reviewers

One of my favorite parts about writing books is that so many people play key roles in helping a new book come together. This one was no exception, and it's my pleasure to acknowledge the support of those who were most instrumental in bringing this book to fruition.

First and foremost, my sincere thanks go to the entire team at McGraw-Hill Higher Education. I have had the pleasure of working with them for the past four years as this book has taken shape, and they have consistently been encouraging, inspiring, creative, professional, and a true joy to know. I look forward to many years of working together in the future.

The relationship between author and editor is much like a marriage: often positive, occasionally rocky, but always greater than the sum of its parts. This is an apt simile for my relationship with Nanette Giles who, more than any other person, has been my working partner in this project. I have so appreciated her encouragement, her wit, her fierce intelligence, and her unfailing belief in what we have tried to accomplish with this text. Rhona Robbin, Leslie Oberhuber, and Suzanne Earth have also been a constant source of inspiration, energy, humor, and warmth, and I value immensely my relationship with each of them.

Many interpersonal communication instructors around the country took time from their busy schedules to serve as reviewers for the book, and I am deeply grateful for their feedback. These people are the experts in teaching interpersonal communication and helping students connect with the material, and they provided many excellent critiques and suggestions that I incorporated into the text. To all of the following who reviewed this book, a hearty thank-you for sharing your ideas and recommendations with me.

Judy Carter, Amarillo College

Tasha Davis, Austin Community College–Northridge

Kelly Petkus, Austin Community College–Northridge

Greg Feeney, Bluegrass Community and Technical College

Jack Byer, Bucks County Community College

Gary Kuhn, Chemeketa Community College

Cameron Basquiat, College of Southern Nevada

James McCoy, College of Southern Nevada

Shirlee Levin, College of Southern Maryland

Lisa Kusko, Gateway Technical College

Sheryl Friedley, George Mason University

Victoria Howitt, Grossmont College

Jacob Isaacs, Ivy Technical Community College of Indiana

Terry Helmick, Johnson County Community College

Rebecca Anderson, Johnson County Community College

Jacob Arndt, Kalamazoo Valley Community College

Sarah Miller, KCTCS–Jefferson Community and Technical College

Lyman Hunt, Louisiana State University–Baton Rouge

Hilary Altman, Merritt College

Karen Lollar, Metropolitan State College of Denver

Delois Medhin, Milwaukee Area Technical College

E. David Moss, Mt. San Jacinto College

Michael Reiter, Nova Southeastern University

Anne Ferguson, Oregon State University

Ann Marie Jablonowski, Owens Community College

Eric Reed, Owens Community College

Susan Richardson, Prince Georges Community College

Anneliese Harper, Scottsdale Community College

Heidi Arnold, Sinclair Community College

Kent Zimmerman, Sinclair Community College

Daniel Paulnock, St. Paul College

M. Harry Daniels, University of Florida–Gainesville

Todd Lee Goen, University of Georgia

Leighanne Heisel, University of Missouri–St. Louis

Joseph Valenzano, University of Nevada–Las Vegas

Karin Tidgewell, University of Nevada, Las Vegas

Lindsay Timmerman, University of Wisconsin–Milwaukee

Carol Benton, University of Central Missouri

Alan Shiller, Southern Illinois University, Edwardsville

Elizabeth Grant, Southern Illinois University, Edwardsville

Anissa Moore, Nassau Community College

Robert Hunter, Monroe Community College

Virginia Hamilton, University of California, Davis

Craig Parmley, Ivy Technical Community College of Indiana

Terri Main, Reedley College

Cynthia Marroquin-Baldwin, South Texas College

George Nagel, Ferris State University

Cami Sanderson, Ferris State University

Stephanie Thomson, Ferris State University

Leah Bryant, DePaul University

Keith Griffin, Southern Illinois University, Carbondale

Justin Braxton-Brown, Hopkinsville Community College

Paul Schrodt, Texas Christian University

Mark Morman, Baylor University

Sherry Rhodes, Collin County Community College, Plano

Debra Deitering-Maddox, Asheville Buncombe Technical Community College

Kevin Mitchell, University of Nevada, Las Vegas

Adrianne Kunkel, University of Kansas

Mary Claire Morr Serewicz, University of Denver

Professors Mark Morman, Leah Bryant, and Paul Schrodt served as this book's editorial advisory board.

On this project, I was truly blessed to have a top-notch advisory board helping me during the revision process. We met and carefully considered suggestions about every chapter, and during those discussions I was grateful for the advisors' experience and knowledge, as well as their humor and humanity. Professors Mark Morman, Leah Bryant, and Paul Schrodt will always have my sincere gratitude for their friendship and their contributions to this book.

At several points during the development of this book, I was grateful for the help of Perry Pauley, one of my doctoral students who served as my research assistant. Perry was instrumental in compiling up-to-date research, photo concepts, and contemporary examples to use in the text. He also assisted with the creation and accuracy of the test bank. Most important, he has been a tremendous source of support, encouragement, and friendship, and for that I am truly appreciative.

Finally, the support of my family and friends has been irreplaceable. A project of this size requires long hours of working in relative isolation, and that requires relatives and friends who are genuinely patient and understanding. I will be ever grateful for the support of my family—Diane, Myron, Gary, Pat, Julie, Seth, Tim, and Dawn—and my closest friends—Brian, Valerie, Mac, Jody, Colin, Alan, Belle, Dan, Angela, Jason, Linda, Tim, the Smiths, the Buehlers, Ed, and Josh. Each of you is so loved.

1

About Communication

Why do people communicate?

How does communication affect our relationships with others?

What makes someone a competent interpersonal communicator?

Amiya and Natalie

Amiya's boyfriend, Tyler, had been drinking a lot lately, even for him. Amiya was worried about him but was afraid to say something because he got angry so easily. She tried talking to her sister Sara about it, but Sara was completely self-absorbed and never seemed to listen. On top of that, Amiya's dad had just been diagnosed with lung cancer, and she suspected he was downplaying how serious it was. One day when Amiya was feeling completely overwhelmed, she called her best friend, Natalie, and broke down on the phone. During their two-hour conversation, Natalie listened to her problems and said, "I'm so sorry to hear about what you're going through." Even though they'd had many such conversations over the years, Amiya was still amazed at how much better she felt after talking with Natalie. No matter what was going badly in her life, she could always count on Natalie to lift her spirits and help her put her problems in perspective. Natalie didn't necessarily solve Amiya's problems for her, but she always listened nonjudgmentally, provided feedback, and allowed Amiya to talk through her feelings and frustrations with someone who cared. "Thank goodness for friends," Amiya thought.

We all have relationships, and we all know how challenging they can be. Sometimes even our closest friends can get under our skin. Sometimes our family members aren't completely honest with us. Sometimes we don't quite know how to reach out to others when they need our help.

At the same time, relationships are wonderful, amazing things. Our friends can make us laugh, keep us sane, and pick us up when we're feeling down. Our relatives can give us the kind of unconditional love that lets us know we'll never be alone. Our romantic partners can make us feel as though we're the only person in the world who really matters.

When you think about it, it's quite remarkable that human relationships can be the source of such heartache *and* such joy. What makes the difference between a relationship that's going well and one that's going poorly? One of the biggest factors is *how we communicate.* Many of Amiya's relational problems involved communication: She was unsure of how to talk to Tyler, Sara didn't really listen to her, and she felt her dad wasn't being forthright about his condition. By contrast, the open, supportive communication she had with Natalie made that friendship very positive. It's tough to have good relationships without good communication—and because relationships are so important to us, learning about communication can greatly benefit our lives.

In this chapter, you'll learn:

1} What types of needs communication helps us meet

2} How communication functions in our relationships

3} What makes communication interpersonal

4} How we can become more competent communicators

1} Why Do We Communicate?

Asking why we communicate may seem about as useful as asking why we breathe. After all, could you imagine your life without communication? We all have times, of course, when we prefer to be alone. Nevertheless, most of us would find it nearly impossible—and very unsatisfying—to go through life without the chance to interact with others. As we'll see in this section, communication touches many aspects of our lives, from our physical and other everyday needs to our experiences with relationships, spirituality, and identity.

> *Good communication is as stimulating as black coffee, and just as hard to sleep after.*
> —Anne Morrow Lindbergh (1906–2001) U.S. American writer

Communication Meets Physical Needs

You might be surprised to hear it, but communication keeps us healthy. Humans are such inherently social beings that when we are denied the opportunity for interaction, our mental and physical health can suffer as a result. This is a major reason why solitary confinement is considered such a harsh punishment. Several studies have shown that when people are cut off from others for an extended period of time, their health can quickly deteriorate.[1] Similarly, individuals who feel socially isolated because of poverty, homelessness, mental illness, or other stigmatizing situations can also suffer from a lack of quality interaction with others.[2]

It may sound like an exaggeration to say that we can't survive without human contact, but that statement isn't far from the truth, as a bizarre experiment in the thirteenth century helped to show. German emperor Frederick II wanted to know what language humans would

Most of us would find it nearly impossible and very unsatisfying to go through life without the chance to communicate with others.

{ Fact or Fiction?
Communication Is Affected by Biology }

You're likely to encounter a number of intuitive research findings as you study interpersonal communication, and your intuition is probably right most of the time. Intuition fails us on occasion, however, which is one reason why the systematic study of communication is so useful. In the "Fact or Fiction?" boxes, we'll take a look at some common ideas about communication to determine whether they're as true as we think they are.

For instance, you've probably heard of the "nature versus nurture" debate. This is an ongoing discussion about why people are the way they are and why they do the things they do. Is it because of the way they were raised—the *nurture* side—or because of factors such as genes or hormones—the *nature* side? It's easy to see how communication might be affected by nurture. For example, when children are raised in different cultures or different religions, they often communicate differently. Is communication also influenced by genetic or biological factors?

As we'll note throughout this book, the answer is a resounding yes. Research shows us, for instance, that communication traits such as shyness or argumentativeness are largely inherited genetically. There is also evidence that changes in the balance of hormones or other chemicals in a person's body can greatly alter the way that person behaves. Communication behavior in turn seems to affect biology. For example, when we express affection to a loved one, the levels of our stress hormones are reduced.

As we talk about the relationship between biology and communication in this book, it's important to keep one thing in mind: Saying that a behavior is influenced by biology doesn't mean that the behavior is uncontrollable. People may inherit a tendency toward shyness, for example, but that doesn't mean they can't learn to become more outgoing. By understanding how the body affects—and is affected by—our communication behaviors, we can gain a better appreciation of the roles that *both* nature *and* nurture play in shaping who we are.

Ask Yourself:

- Which aspects of communication do you think are primarily learned? Which do you think are primarily biological?

- In what ways might people use communication behaviors to improve their health?

Sources: Beatty, M. J., Heisel, A. D., Hall, A. E., Levine, T. R., & La France, B. H. (2002). What can we learn from the study of twins about genetic and environmental influences on interpersonal affiliation, aggressiveness, and social anxiety? A meta-analytic study. *Communication Monographs, 69,* 1–18; Floyd, K., Mikkelson, A. C., Tafoya, M. A., Farinelli, L., La Valley, A. G., Judd, J., Haynes, M. T., Davis, K. L., & Wilson, J. (2007). Human affection exchange: XIII. Affectionate communication accelerates neuroendocrine stress recovery. *Health Communication, 22,* 123–132; Keller, M. B., Kocsis, J. H., Thase, M. E., Gelenberg, A. J., Rush, A. J., Koran, L., Schatzberg, A., Russell, J., Hirschfeld, R., Klein, D., McCullough, J. P., Fawcett, J. A., Kornstein, S., La Vange, L., & Harrison, W. (1999). Maintenance phase efficacy of sertraline for chronic depression: A randomized controlled trial. *Journal of the American Medical Association, 282,* 323–324.

speak naturally if they weren't taught any particular language. To find out, he placed 50 newborns in the care of nurses who were instructed only to feed and bathe them but not to speak to them or hold them. The emperor never discovered the answer to his question because all the infants died.[3] This experiment was clearly unethical and, fortunately, wouldn't be repeated today, but more recent studies conducted in orphanages and adoption centers have convincingly shown that human interaction, especially touch, is critical for infants' survival and healthy development.[4]

Social interaction keeps adults healthy too. Research shows that people without strong social ties, such as close friendships and family relationships, are more likely to suffer major ailments, such as heart disease and high blood pressure, and to die prematurely than people who have close, satisfying relationships.[5] They are also more likely to suffer basic ailments, such as colds, and they often take longer to recover from illnesses or injuries.[6] As Anne Morrow Lindbergh noted in the quote at the start of this section, good communication stimulates us and makes us feel alive.

The importance of social interaction is often particularly evident to people who are stigmatized. A **stigma** is a characteristic that discredits a person, causing him or her to be seen as abnormal or undesirable.[7] It isn't the attribute itself that stigmatizes a person, however, but the way that attribute is viewed by others in that person's society. In the United States, for instance, being HIV-positive is widely stigmatized because of its association with two marginalized populations—gay men and intravenous drug users—even though many people with the disease do not belong to either group.[8] Note that U.S. Americans don't tend to stigmatize people with asthma or diabetes or even cancer to the same extent as they do people with HIV, even though these other illnesses can also be serious or even life-threatening.

Stigma A characteristic that discredits a person, making him or her be seen as abnormal or undesirable.

Being stigmatized leads people in many marginalized groups to feel disrespected and shamed about their conditions. In U.S. American society, there are stigmas associated with being homeless, poor, old, disabled, lesbian or gay, alcoholic, mentally ill, and, in some circles, divorced, even though a person may have no choice about belonging to any of these groups.[9]

People who are stigmatized might say they frequently feel like outsiders who "don't fit in" with those around them. As a result, they may be more likely to suffer the negative physical effects of limited social interaction. Going further, the less social interaction they have, the more they are likely to continue feeling stigmatized. Although not everyone needs the same amount of interaction to stay healthy, communication plays an important role in maintaining our health and well-being. To understand more about how communication and biology are interrelated, take a look at the "Fact or Fiction" box on page 6.

Communication Meets Relational Needs

Besides our physical needs, we have several relational needs, such as needs for companionship and affection, relaxation, and escape.[10] We don't necessarily have the same needs in all our relationships—you probably value your friends for somewhat different reasons than you value your relatives, for instance. The bottom line, though, is that we need relationships, and communication is a large part of how we build and keep those relationships.[11]

Think about how many structures in our lives are designed to promote social interaction. Neighborhoods, schools, workplaces, malls, theaters, and restaurants are all social experiences in which we almost always interact with people in some way. In addition, the Internet has opened up multiple ways of connecting with others, and many people have met new friends or romantic partners online.[12] Imagine how challenging it would be to form and maintain strong social relationships if you lacked the ability to communicate with others. This is a common experience for many immigrants, who often struggle to acculturate and learn the language of their new environments and may feel lonely or overlooked by others during that process.[13]

A more extreme example of the challenges of forming relationships without the ability to communicate involves Victor of Aveyron, a child found in France in the late eighteenth century after apparently spending his entire childhood alone in the woods.

Imagine how challenging it would be to communicate if you couldn't speak the language everyone else was using. This is a common experience for many immigrants.

After twice being captured and escaping, he eventually emerged from the forest on his own and was cared for by a local biologist and later by a young medical student. Because he had not acquired language, however, it was quite challenging for Victor—who later became known as "the Wild Boy of Aveyron"—to form strong emotional relationships with his caretakers.[14]

Some scholars believe our need for relationships is so fundamental that we can hardly get by without them.[15] For example, research has shown that having a rich social life is one of the most powerful predictors of a person's overall happiness.[16] In fact, the most important predictor of happiness in life—by far—is how happy you are in your marriage.[17] Marital happiness is more important than income, job status, education, leisure time, or anything else in accounting for how happy people are with their lives. On the negative side, people in distressed marriages are much more likely to suffer major depression, and they even report being in worse physical health than their happily married counterparts.[18]

Of course, the cause-and-effect relationship between marriage and happiness isn't a simple one. It may be that strong marriages promote happiness and well-being, or it may be that happy, healthy people are more likely than others to be married. Whatever the association, personal relationships clearly play an important role in our lives, and communication helps us form and maintain them.

Communication Fills Identity Needs

Are you energetic? trustworthy? intelligent? withdrawn? Each of us can probably come up with a long list of adjectives to describe ourselves, but here's the critical question: How do you *know* you are these things? In other words, how do you form an identity?

The ways we communicate with others—and the ways others communicate with us—play a major role in shaping the way we see ourselves.[19] As you'll learn in Chapter 3, people form their identities partly by comparing themselves with others. If you consider yourself intelligent, for instance, what that really means is that you see yourself as more intelligent than most other people. If you think you're shy, you see most other people as more outgoing than you are. If you think of yourself as attractive, it's because you think you're better looking than most other people.

One way we learn how we compare with others is through our communication with those around us. If people treat you as intelligent, shy, or attractive, chances are you'll begin to believe you are those things. In other words, those qualities will become part of how you see yourself. As you'll see in Chapter 3, your identity develops over the course of your life, and communication plays a critical role in driving that process. Good communicators also have the ability to emphasize different aspects of their identities in different situations. For example, during a job interview it might be

How we communicate with others, and how others communicate with us, play a big role in shaping how we see ourselves—whether it's as intelligent, as popular, or as altruistic.

most important for you to portray your organized, efficient side, whereas when you're on a date you might choose to emphasize your fun-loving nature and sense of humor.

Communication Meets Spiritual Needs

An important aspect of identity for many people is their spirituality. Spirituality includes the principles someone values in life (for example, "I value loyalty" or "I value equal treatment for all people"). It also encompasses people's morals, or their notions about right and wrong (for instance, "It's never okay to steal, no matter what the circumstances" or "I would lie in order to save a life, because life is more important than honesty"). Finally, spirituality involves people's beliefs about the meaning of life, which often include personal philosophies, an awe of nature, a belief in a higher purpose, and religious beliefs and practices (such as "I believe in God" or "I believe I will reap what I sow in life").

Communication enables many people to express their faith and spirituality.

A recent survey of more than 112,000 U.S. college students found that many students consider some form of spirituality to be an important part of their identity.[20] About 75% of those surveyed said they search for meaning and purpose in life and have discussions about the meaning of life with their friends. In addition, more than 60% claimed their spirituality was a source of joy in their lives, and almost 50% affirmed that they seek out opportunities to grow spiritually. For people who include spirituality as a part of their identity, communication provides a means of expressing and sharing spiritual ideas and practices with one another.

Communication Serves Instrumental Needs

Instrumental needs Practical, everyday needs.

Finally, people communicate to meet their practical, everyday needs. Researchers refer to these needs as **instrumental needs.** Instrumental needs include short-term tasks such as ordering a drink in a bar, scheduling a haircut on the telephone, filling

At a Glance: Five Needs Served by Communication

Throughout this book, you will find "At a Glance" boxes that give you a brief look at important content. In this case, we'll take a glance at five types of needs that are served by communication:

Physical needs	Communication helps us maintain physical and mental well-being.
Relational needs	Communication helps us form social and personal relationships.
Identity needs	Communication helps us figure out who we are and who we want to be.
Spiritual needs	Communication lets us share our beliefs and values with others.
Instrumental needs	Communication helps us accomplish many day-to-day tasks.

out a rebate card, and raising your hand when you want to speak in class. They also include longer-term goals such as getting a job and earning a promotion. These communicative behaviors may not always contribute much to our health, our relationships, our identity, or our spirituality. Each behavior is valuable, however, because it serves a need that helps us get through our daily lives.

Meeting instrumental needs probably doesn't seem as interesting as forging new relationships or as meaningful as expressing spiritual beliefs. It's important for two reasons, though. The first reason is simply that we have many instrumental needs. In fact, most of the communication you engage in on a day-to-day basis is probably mundane and routine—not heavy, emotionally charged conversation, but instrumental interaction such as talking to professors about assignments or taking orders from customers at work. A second reason meeting instrumental needs is so important is that many of them—such as buying food at the store or ordering clothes online—really have to be met before other needs—such as maintaining quality relationships or finding career fulfillment—become relevant.[21]

The "At a Glance" box above provides a quick look at five types of needs that communication helps to meet.

Learn It: How is communication related to our physical well-being? What relational needs does communication help us fill? In what ways do communication behaviors meet our identity needs? How does communication help us express spirituality? What are some of the instrumental needs served by communication?

Try It: Recall a recent conversation you had, and identify how your communication behavior contributed to your physical, relational, identity, spiritual, and instrumental needs, if at all. Which need or needs took precedence? Why?

Reflect on It: Can you identify ways in which your own communication meets your relational or spiritual needs? Do you communicate for any reasons that are not discussed in this section?

2} The Nature of Communication

Communication is so much a part of life that it's easy to take it for granted. In one way or another, you've communicated practically every day you've been alive, so you may be wondering what you could possibly have left to learn about communication. In fact, researchers still have many questions about how people communicate, how we make sense of one another's behaviors, and what effects communication has on our lives and our relationships.

> *The most important thing in communication is to hear what isn't being said.*
>
> —Peter F. Drucker (1909–2005)
> Austrian-born professor of management

We begin this section by looking at different ways to understand the communication process. Next, we'll look at some important characteristics of communication, and we'll discuss various ways to think about communication in social interaction. Finally, we'll tackle some common myths about communication. Even though you communicate all the time, you'll probably find there are still many interesting things to learn about the role of communication in our lives.

Three Models of Human Communication

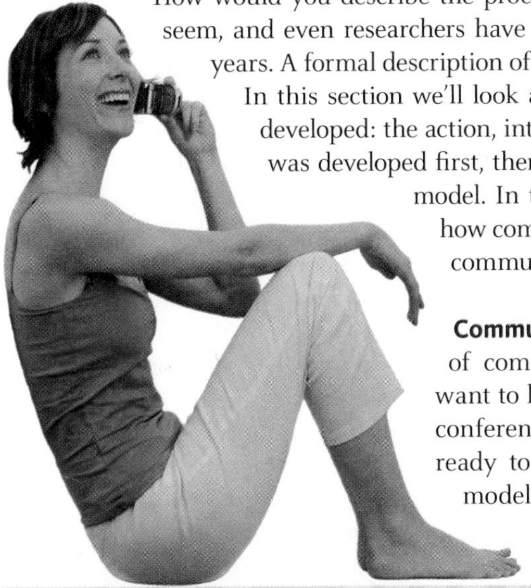

How would you describe the process of communicating? It's not as easy as it might seem, and even researchers have answered this question in different ways over the years. A formal description of a process such as communication is called a **model.** In this section we'll look at three models that communication scholars have developed: the action, interaction, and transaction models. The action model was developed first, then the interaction model, and finally the transaction model. In this sense, these models represent the evolution of how communication researchers have defined and described communication over the years.

Model A formal description of a process.

Communication as action. In the action model, we think of communication as a one-way process. Let's say you want to leave work early one day to attend a parent-teacher conference at your daughter's school, and you're getting ready to ask your supervisor for permission. The action model starts with a **source**—you—who comes up with a thought or an idea you wish to communicate. To convey the idea that you'd like to leave early, you must **encode** it; that is, you must put your idea into the form of language or a gesture that your supervisor can understand. Through this process, you create a **message,** which consists of the verbal and/or nonverbal elements of communication to which people give meaning. In

Source The originator of a thought or an idea.

Encode To put an idea into language or gesture.

Message Verbal and nonverbal elements of communication to which people give meaning.

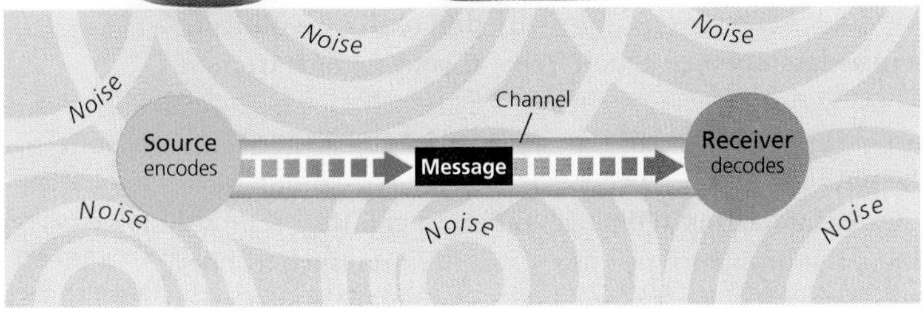

FIGURE 1.1 **The Action Model** In the action model of communication, a sender encodes a message and conveys it through a communication channel for a receiver to decode. Leaving someone a voice mail message illustrates the one-way process of the action model.

this example, your message might be the question "Would it be all right if I left work a couple of hours early today?"

According to the action model, you then send your message through a communication **channel,** which is a type of pathway. For example, you can pose your question to your supervisor face-to-face. Alternatively, you can send your question by e-mail, through a text message, or by calling your supervisor on the phone. These are all channels of communication. Your supervisor acts as the **receiver** of the message; that is, the person who will **decode** or interpret it.

During the communication process, there is also likely to be some **noise,** which is anything that interferes with a receiver's ability to attend to your message. The major types of noise are *physical noise* (such as background conversation in the classroom or static on the telephone line), *psychological noise* (such as other concerns your supervisor is dealing with that day), and *physiological noise* (such as fatigue or hunger). Experiencing any of these forms of noise could prevent your supervisor from paying full attention to your question.

You can see that the action model is very linear: A source sends a message through some channel to a receiver, and noise interferes with the message somehow. Many people talk and think about the communication process in this linear manner. For example, when you ask someone "Did you get my message?" you are implying that communication is a one-way process. The problem is that human communication is rarely that simple. It is usually more of a back-and-forth exchange than a one-way process—more similar to tennis than to bowling. Over time, this criticism of the action model of communication gave rise to an updated model known as the interaction model.

Communication as interaction. The interaction model takes up where the action model leaves off. It includes all the same elements: source, message, channel, receiver, noise, encoding, and decoding. However, it differs from the action model in two basic ways. First, it recognizes that communication is a two-way process. Second, it adds two elements to the mix: feedback and context.

If you've ever taken a physics class, you probably learned that every action has a reaction. That rule also applies to communication. Let's say you're telling your friend Julio about a person you find attractive at the hospital where you volunteer. As you tell your story, Julio probably nods and says "uh-huh" to show you he's listening (or maybe he yawns because he worked late the night before). He might also ask you questions about how you met this person or tell you that he or she sounds nice. In other words, Julio *reacts* to your story by giving you **feedback,** or various verbal and nonverbal responses to your message. In this way, Julio is not just a passive receiver of your message. Instead, he is actively involved in creating your conversation.

Now let's imagine you're sharing your story with Julio while you're having coffee in a crowded employee cafe. Would you tell your story any differently if you were alone? How about if you were in a classroom at school? What if your parents were in the same room?

All these situations are part of the **context,** or the environment that you're in. This environment includes both the physical and the psychological context. The *physical context* is where you are physically interacting with each other. In contrast, the *psychological context* involves factors that influence people's states of mind, such as how formal the situation is, how much privacy you have, and how emotionally charged the situation is. According to the interaction model, we take context into account when we engage in conversation. That is, we realize that what is appropriate in certain contexts may be inappropriate in others, so we adapt our behaviors accordingly.

By taking account of feedback and context, the interaction model presents the communication process more realistically than the action model does. In the case of your tell-

Channel A pathway through which messages are conveyed.
Decode To interpret or give meaning to a message.

Receiver The party who interprets a message.
Noise Anything that interferes with the encoding or decoding of a message.

Feedback Verbal and nonverbal responses to a message.

Context The physical or psychological environment in which communication occurs.

ing Julio about your new romantic interest, for instance, your story and Julio's feedback would probably be affected by where you were speaking, how many other people could overhear you (if any), and whether those people were co-workers, classmates, family members, or strangers.

Although the interaction model is more realistic than the action model, it still has limitations. One drawback is that it doesn't really represent how complex communication can be. Often during conversations, it seems as though two people are sending and receiving information at the same time rather than simply communicating back and forth one message at a time. The interaction model doesn't really account for that process, however. To understand this aspect of communication, we turn to the transaction model, currently the most complete and widely used of the three models discussed in this chapter.

FIGURE 1.2 The Interaction Model The interaction model of communication explains that our messages are shaped by the feedback we receive from others and by the context in which we are interacting. Here we see speakers paying attention to their friends' feedback and communicating in a way that is appropriate for a public restaurant.

Communication as transaction. Unlike the action and interaction models, the transaction model of communication doesn't distinguish between the roles of source and receiver. Nor does it represent communication as a series of messages going back and forth. Rather, it maintains that both people in a conversation are simultaneously sources *and* receivers. In addition, it argues that the conversation flows in both directions at the same time.

To understand the transaction model, imagine you're a medical technician at a community clinic and you're explaining to an elderly patient how to apply a prescription cream to his skin. You notice a confused look on his face, and perhaps a worried one as well. According to the interaction model, those facial expressions constitute feedback to your message. In contrast, the transaction model recognizes that you will interpret those expressions as a message in and of itself, making the patient a source and you a receiver. Note that this process occurs while you're giving the patient your instructions. In other words, you are both sending messages to and receiving messages from the other at the same time.

Not only does the transaction model reflect the complex nature of communication, but it also leads us to think about context a little more broadly. It suggests that our communication is affected not only by the physical or psychological environment but also by our culture, experience, gender, and social class, and even the history of our relationship with the person to whom we're talking.

Let's go back to our previous example. If you have a history with the elderly patient, you might help him understand your directions by referring back to products you have prescribed for him in the past. If he isn't a native English speaker, you might have to demonstrate the use of the cream, rather than just describing it verbally. If he comes from a markedly different socioeconomic class from yours, then your instructions might take for granted that he can afford the medication. Sometimes it's harder to consider how these aspects of context might affect how we communicate. According to the transaction model, however, they are always with us.

Clearly, then, researchers have many different ways of understanding the communication process. Instead of debating which model is *right,* it's often more helpful to look at the useful ideas each model offers. When we do that, we find that each model fits certain situations better than others. For instance, sending a text message to your professor is a good example of the action model. You're the source, and you convey your message through a written channel to a receiver (your professor). Noise includes any difficulty your professor experiences in opening up the message or understanding the intent of your message because of the language you have used.

A good example of the interaction model occurs when you submit a report at your job and the co-workers on your team comment on your recommendations in writing. You (the source) have conveyed your message through your report, and your co-workers (the receivers) have provided written feedback within the context of the activity. Noise in this example includes any difficulties either you or your co-workers experience in understanding what the other has said.

As we've seen, most conversations are good examples of the transaction model, because both parties are sending and receiving messages simultaneously. This process occurs, for instance, when you strike up a conversation with someone while standing in an airport security line. You might make small talk about where each of you is traveling that day or how annoying but necessary the security screening process is. As you do so, each of you is sending verbal and nonverbal messages to the other and is simultaneously receiving and interpreting such messages from the other. Your conversation is affected by the context, in that you may be communicating only

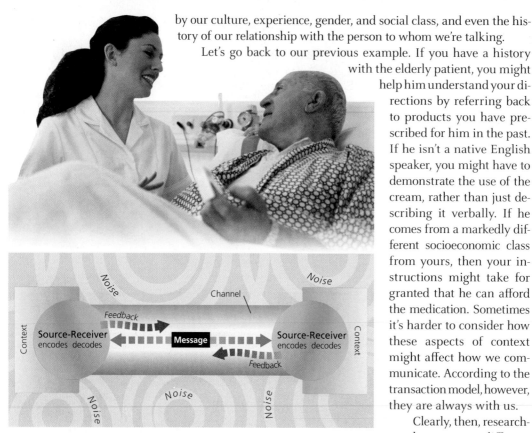

FIGURE 1.3 The Transaction Model The transaction model recognizes that both people in a conversation are simultaneously senders and receivers. The doctor encodes messages that her patient decodes, but the patient also encodes messages for the doctor to decode.

to pass the time until one of you passes through the screening. It is also affected by noise, including the sound of the screeners' instructions.

Each model, then, is useful in some situations but not in others. The action model is too simplistic to describe a face-to-face conversation, for instance, but when you're just leaving a note for someone, it describes the situation quite well. As you come across examples of different communication situations in this book, you might ask yourself how well each model fits them.

Recall that these communication models were developed by communication researchers over time. As scholars came to appreciate the limitations of the action model, they developed the interaction model to take its place. Likewise, the shortcomings of the interaction model gave rise to the transaction model, which many researchers consider the most comprehensive description of communication. As our understanding of communication continues to grow, it is likely that researchers will develop new models that will represent the communication process even more accurately. Now that we've looked at some different ways of modeling the communication process, let's consider some of communication's most important characteristics.

Six Characteristics of Communication

Describing the communication process requires more than just mapping out how it takes place. We also need to catalog its important features. In this section, we'll discover that:

- Communication relies on multiple channels
- Communication passes through perceptual filters
- People give communication its meaning
- Communication has literal meanings and relational implications
- Communication sends messages, whether intentional or unintentional
- Communication is governed by rules

Communication relies on multiple channels. In how many different ways do people communicate with one another? Facial expressions communicate how a person is feeling. A person's gestures and tone of voice help others interpret his or her messages. Touch can signal feelings such as affection or aggression. Even a person's clothing and physical appearance communicate messages about that person to others.

Some interpersonal communication contexts are channel-rich, such as a face-to-face conversation between friends. Other interpersonal communication contexts are channel-lean, such as sending and receiving text messages.

Channel-rich context A communication context involving many channels at once.

Some situations are **channel-rich contexts,** meaning that they involve many different communication channels at once. In face-to-face conversations, for instance, you can pay attention to your partners' words, see their expressions and gestures, hear their tone of voice, and feel them touch you. That is, you experience multiple communication channels at once, and you can evaluate the information you receive from all the channels simultaneously. Other situations are **channel-lean contexts,** with a smaller number of channels.[22] Text messaging, for example, relies almost entirely on text, so we don't experience a person's voice or gestures. As a consequence, we pay more attention to that person's words, because that's all we have to go on.

Channel-lean context A communication context involving few channels at once.

Communication passes through perceptual filters. Anything you put through a filter—such as air, water, or light—comes out a little differently from the way it went in. The same thing happens when we communicate: What one person says is not always exactly what the other person hears. We all "filter" incoming communication through our perceptions, experiences, biases, and beliefs.

Let's say you're listening to a senator speak on television. The way you process and make sense of the speech probably depends on how much you agree with the senator's ideas or whether you belong to the same political party as he or she does. Two people with different political viewpoints may listen to the same speech but hear something very different. I may hear a set of logical, well thought-out ideas, whereas you may hear nothing but lies and empty promises.

Perceptual filters can also influence how two people understand their own words. In an episode of the television show *Friends,* Rachel (played by Jennifer Aniston) and her boyfriend, Ross (played by David Schwimmer), have a big fight and decide to go "on a break" from their relationship. They quickly learn that they perceive the meaning of being "on a break" quite differently. To Rachel, it simply means not seeing each other for a while but keeping their relationship intact in the meantime. To Ross, being on a break means his relationship with Rachel is over. Thus, in the wake of their conflict, Ross has sex with someone else. Rachel feels completely betrayed when she finds out. As a result, she and Ross end their relationship officially. It is important to note that Ross and Rachel agreed that they

were "on a break" when Ross slept with someone else but that they had very different perceptions of what "on a break" meant.

Many aspects of our lives can influence our perception of communication. Whether we're aware of it or not, our ethnic and cultural background, gender, religious beliefs, socioeconomic status, intelligence and education, level of physical attractiveness, and experiences with illness, disease, and death can all act as filters, coloring the way we see the world and the way we make sense of communication. For example, you might listen sympathetically to someone describing her experiences of homelessness based on those and other characteristics. In contrast, other people might blame this person for her homelessness because they have different perceptual filters from yours.

People give communication its meaning. When we write or speak, we choose our words deliberately so we can say what we *mean*. Where does that meaning come from? By itself, a word has no meaning; it's just a sound or a set of marks on a piece of paper or a monitor. A word is a **symbol,** or a representation of an idea, but the word itself isn't the idea or the meaning. The meaning of words—and many other forms of communication—comes from the people and groups who use them.

Almost all language is arbitrary in the sense that words mean whatever groups of people decide they mean. As a result, we can't assume that other people understand the meanings we intend to communicate just because we ourselves understand what we mean. For instance, what is a mouse? If you had asked that question 40 years ago, the obvious answer would have been that a mouse is a small rodent that likes cheese and is chased by cats. Today, however, many people know it as a pointing device for navigating within a computer screen. As another example, what is a robot? In the United States, it's a humanlike machine that performs mechanical tasks. In South Africa, however, it's a traffic light.

Those are just two examples of how the meaning of a word depends on who is using it and how meanings can vary over time and across cultures. How do you define each of the following words? What other meanings might they have, depending on who is using them?

pot	crack
flat	gay
cell	biscuit

You might know that in some countries a *flat* is an apartment and a *biscuit* is a cookie. How have the meanings of words such as *pot, cell, crack,* and *gay* changed within U.S. society over time?

Communication has literal meanings and relational implications. Nearly every verbal statement has a **content dimension,** which consists of the literal information being communicated about the subject of the message.[23] When you say to your friend, "I'm kind of down today," the content dimension of your message is that you're feeling unhappy, bored, or depressed. When your roommate says, "We're out of detergent again," the content dimension of the message is that you have no detergent left.

There's more to messages than their literal content, though. Many messages also carry signals about the nature of the relationship in which they're shared. These sig-

THE NATURE OF COMMUNICATION 17

nals make up the **relational dimension** of the message. For example, by telling your friend you're feeling down, you may also be sending the message "I feel comfortable enough with you to share my feelings"; or, you may be signaling "I want you to help me feel better."

Likewise, you might interpret your roommate's statement that you're out of detergent as also saying "I'm sure you're aware of this but I'm just reminding you," or you might take it as meaning "I'm irritated that you never replace household items when they are empty." Even though these messages were never actually spoken, we often infer meanings about our relationships from the tone and manner in which the statements are made.

One way in which people distinguish between content and relational dimensions is through the use of **meta-communication,** which is communication about communication. Let's say that Ethan asks his stepdad, Daniel, to read over his senior thesis before Ethan submits it to his undergraduate advisor. Daniel reads the manuscript and marks it up with critical comments such as "this argument isn't convincing," "awkward wording," and "I can't tell what you're trying to say." After reading Daniel's comments, Ethan is crushed.

> **Daniel:** I thought you wanted my feedback. I was just trying to help you make your thesis better; that's what you asked for. Why are you taking my comments so personally?
>
> **Ethan:** It's not so much what you said, it's how you said it.

By focusing his attention on Ethan's request for feedback, Daniel is attending to the content dimension of their conversation. He can't understand why Ethan is upset, because Ethan had asked him for his feedback. To Ethan, however, Daniel's comments were overly harsh and insensitive, and they made him feel that Daniel didn't care about his feelings. Therefore, Ethan's focus is on the relational dimension of their conversation. To highlight this distinction, Ethan meta-communicates with Daniel by explaining that his hurt feelings were not caused by what Daniel said but by the way in which he said it. This phrase conveys Ethan's thoughts about his communication with Daniel; thus it is meta-communicative.

Communication sends a message, whether intentional or unintentional. Much of what we communicate to others is deliberate. When you set up a job interview, for instance, you do so intentionally, having thought about why you want the job and how you will respond to the interviewer's questions. Very rarely do you schedule an interview by accident.

You might, however, communicate a number of other things without meaning to. For example, have you ever tried hard to stay awake in an important meeting? Despite your efforts to look engaged and interested, you might not have been aware that your slouched posture and droopy eyelids were signaling the fatigue you were feeling, perhaps after a long day of working at a part-time job and attending several classes. In this instance, your behavior was sending unintentional messages.

Whether unintentional messages should qualify as communication has been a source of debate among communication scholars for many years. Some researchers believe that only deliberate, intentional messages are actually a part of communication, and that if you don't intend to communicate, then you aren't.[24] Others subscribe to the belief that "you cannot *not* communicate," meaning absolutely everything you do has communicative value.[25]

My own position lies somewhere in between: Although I don't believe every possible behavior is a form of communication, neither do I think behaviors must be intentional to have communicative value.[26] I would suggest that even unintended messages—such as the ones you might have expressed while trying to stay awake during a meeting—are forms of communication, because even if they're unintentional, they still convey meaning.[27] Many aspects of appearance illustrate this. For instance, seeing someone in a wheelchair probably leads you to different conclusions than seeing someone in a white lab coat or an orange prison jumpsuit, yet those messages might not be intentional on that person's part.

Communication is governed by rules. Rules tell us what behaviors are required, preferred, or prohibited in various social contexts.[28] Some rules for communication are **explicit rules**, meaning that someone has clearly articulated them. Perhaps your parents used to say, "Don't talk with your mouth full." Maybe the library or hospital posts a sign that reads "No cell phones allowed." Many universities have explicit rules banning hate speech at campus events or in school publications. Social network applications such as Facebook and MySpace enforce specific guidelines regarding the content of text and photos. These are explicit communication rules because they express direct expectations for communicative behavior.

Explicit rule A rule about behavior that has been clearly articulated.

Explicit communication rules can also relate to personal appearance and modes of interacting with others in a group. In the 2004 movie *Mean Girls,* for instance, Cady Heron (played by Lindsay Lohan) enrolls in a public high school for the first time, where she meets a group of teenage girls known as "The Plastics." One member, Gretchen Wieners (played by Lacey Chabert), instructs her on some of the group's rules:

Gretchen: You can't wear a tank top two days in a row and you can only wear your hair in a pony tail once a week, so I guess you picked today. Oh, and we only wear jeans or track pants on Fridays. If you break any of these rules, you can't sit with us at lunch. I mean, not just you . . . any of us. Okay look, if I was wearing jeans today, I'd be sitting over there with the art freaks. Oh, we always vote before we ask someone to eat lunch with us, because you have to be considerate of the rest of the group. I mean, you wouldn't buy a skirt without asking your friends first if it looks good on you.

Cady: I wouldn't?

Gretchen: Right. Oh, and it's the same with guys. I mean, you may think you like someone, but you could be wrong.

In this scene, Gretchen communicates explicit rules about how to dress and how to interact with others in the group that all members of The Plastics are expected to observe. Many communication rules, however, are **implicit rules.** These are rules that almost everyone in a certain social group knows and follows even though no one has formally articulated and expressed them.

In North American cultures, for instance, there are implicit rules about riding in an elevator, such as "Don't get on if it's already full" and "Don't make eye contact with others while you're riding." There are also implicit rules about taking turns when you are waiting for some type of service, such as at a bank or a grocery store, including "Get into an orderly line" and "Don't cut ahead of someone else."

Most people seem to know and accept these rules, even though they usually aren't posted anywhere—they're just a part of everyone's cultural knowledge. Because they're implicit, though, they are likely to vary more from person to person than explicit rules do. For example, some people might believe it's an implicit rule that you shouldn't talk on your cell phone while in a crowded environment (for example, on a public bus during rush hour), whereas other people don't see this behavior as inappropriate.

Now that we know more about the basic characteristics of communication, let's take a look at some common beliefs about communication that are not as valid as they might seem.

Implicit rule A rule about behavior that has not been clearly articulated but is nonetheless understood.

Dispelling Some Communication Myths

Perhaps because communication is such an important part of life, people have many different ideas about it, some of which are not very accurate. We'll take a look at five common communication myths in this section so that you'll be better able to separate fact from fiction. These myths are:

- Everyone is an expert in communication.
- Communication will solve any problem.
- Communication can break down.
- Communication is inherently good.
- More communication is always better.

Myth: Everyone is an expert in communication. People communicate constantly in their day-to-day lives, so it's easy to believe that just about everyone is an expert in communication. Indeed, in a nationwide survey of U.S. American adults conducted by the National Communication Association, fully 91% of participants rated their communication skills as above average.[29] It's important to remember, though, that having experience with something is not the same as having *expertise* in it. Many people drive, but that doesn't make them expert drivers. Many people have children, but that doesn't make them experts at parenting. Experience can be invaluable, but expertise requires the development of knowledge and ability that goes beyond personal experience. Thus, experts in driving, parenting, or communication have training in their fields and a level of understanding that most people who drive, parent, or communicate don't have.

The information you'll read in this book is based on expertise and scientific research, not just personal experience, and from time to time it may not match your own experiences as a communicator. That doesn't mean there's anything wrong with your experience. At the same time, it also doesn't mean that the research is wrong. Remember that all of us, even the experts, can learn more about communication if we keep an open mind. In fact, multiple studies in the U.S. workplace have shown that a large majority of workers could stand to improve their communication skills.[30]

Myth: Communication will solve any problem. In 1967, the classic Paul Newman movie *Cool Hand Luke* featured a prison warden who had his own special way of dealing with inmates. Whenever things went wrong, he would say, "What we've got here is a failure to communicate," after which he would beat the inmate unconscious and send him to solitary confinement. Sometimes it seems as though we could solve almost any problem, especially in our relationships, if only we could communicate better. It's easy to blame a lack of communication when things go wrong. The fact is, however, that poor communication isn't the cause of every problem.[31]

To understand why this is true, let's go back to the opening vignette involving Amiya and her boyfriend, Tyler. Suppose they have been drifting apart for a while and Amiya decides they need to communicate better to save their relationship. When they finally sit down to talk, however, Tyler says very clearly that his feelings have changed and that he is no longer attracted to Amiya.

Did communication save their relationship? No; in fact it caused Amiya to realize that the relationship was probably already over. This might be better for both of them in the long run, so we could say that communication helped them come to that realization. Nevertheless, it didn't solve the problem of their drifting apart in the first place. Therefore, we must be careful not to assume that better communication can resolve any problem we might face in our relationships.

Myth: Communication can break down. Just as we sometimes blame our problems on a lack of communication, many of us also point to a "breakdown in communication" as the cause of our relationship challenges. After months of trying to help his adult stepdaughter overcome her addiction to prescription painkillers, for instance, Justin feels that she is pushing him away. "Things were going fine for a while and she was really making progress," he explains, "but then we had a complete communication breakdown."

This metaphor makes intuitive sense to many of us. After all, our progress on a journey is halted if our car breaks down, so it's easy to think that our progress in a relationship is halted because our communication has broken down. The problem is that communication isn't a mechanical object like a car, or a dishwasher, or an iPod. Instead, communication is a process that unfolds between and among people over time.

It's sometimes easy to blame a "breakdown" in communication for the problems we face in our relationships, as Justin did when he felt he was no longer getting through to his stepdaughter. What's really happening in these situations is that we are no longer communicating effectively. In other words, the problem lies not with communication itself but with the way we're using it. This is one reason why learning about communication—as you are doing in this class—can be of such benefit to your relationships.

Myth: Communication is inherently good. Watch almost any talk show and you'll hear people say they no longer communicate with their romantic partners, parents, or others who are important to them. "Sure, we talk all the time," someone might say, "but we don't really *communicate* anymore." Reflected in this kind of statement is the idea that "talking" means just producing words, but "communicating" means sharing meaning with another person in an open, supportive, and inherently positive manner.[32]

Thinking that communication is inherently good is similar to thinking that money is inherently good. Sometimes money can be put to positive uses, such as providing

When spending time with people you care about, put your cell phone away. Give your energy and attention to the person you are with, and let that person know he or she is more important to you than your phone.

a home for your family or donating to a worthy charity. At other times it can be put to negative uses, such as providing funding for a terrorist group. In either case, however, it isn't the money itself that's good or bad—it's how it is used.

We can make the same observation regarding communication. We can use communication for positive purposes, such as expressing love for our parents or providing comfort to a grieving friend. We can also use it for negative purposes, such as intimidating or deceiving people. Like money, communication itself is neither inherently good nor inherently bad; instead, it can most accurately be described as amoral. It's how we *use* communication that makes it positive or negative.

Myth: More communication is always better. Antonio is the kind of person who thinks that if people don't agree with him, it's only because they don't understand him. Therefore, he talks on and on, figuring that others will eventually see things his way if he just gives them enough information. Maybe you know someone like that. Is it really the case, though, that more communication always produces a better outcome?

When people have genuine disagreements, more talk doesn't always help. In some cases it can just lead to frustration and anger. In fact, a recent study of consultations between doctors and patients found that the more doctors talked, the more likely they were to get off track and forget about the patients' problems, which can translate into worse care for the patient.[33]

The Dark Side of Interpersonal Communication
Cell Phones and Stressed-Out Families

Interpersonal communication has many positive aspects, but it isn't all rosy. We also have to deal sometimes with feelings and events that are negative. Even though these things aren't fun to think about, they deserve our attention so that we can learn to handle them constructively. In each of the "Dark Side" boxes, we will examine one negative issue that people commonly confront. In this instance, we'll talk about stress.

Cell phones are so commonplace these days that some people find it hard to imagine life without them. Like other communication technologies, such as e-mail, text messaging, and instant messaging, cell phones have certainly made it easier for people to keep in touch. You can call people with a cell phone—and they can call you—from just about anywhere.

One of the downsides of being so easy to reach, however, is that keeping work and family lives separate is becoming increasingly difficult. A dad might find himself reassuring the babysitter while he's running an office meeting. A mom might have to take a call from an irate customer while she's watching her daughter's soccer game. These and other examples led sociologist Noelle Chesley to wonder whether cell phone use has affected how happy people are with their lives and how satisfied they are with their families.

Using data collected from more than 1,300 working adults, Chesley determined that the more people used cell phones, the less happy they were, the less satisfied they were with their families, and the more likely they were to say their work lives "spilled over" into their family lives. Some of those patterns were particularly true for women, whereas others were equally true for both sexes. Chesley thinks that communication technologies, such as cell phones, can blur the boundaries between our personal and professional lives, making it tougher for people to concentrate on their families when they're away from work.

Ask Yourself:

- If people are less satisfied with their lives the more they use cell phones, why do so many of us consider cell phones necessary?

- What are some of the ways in which you handle stress in your day-to-day life?

In some of the text boxes in this book, I will include a personal hint about improving your interpersonal communication. These additions will be called *From Me to You*, and here's the first:

From Me to You

- When spending time with people you care about, put your cell phone away; if it rings, let the caller leave a message. Unless you are expecting a specific and urgent call, don't allow your cell phone to determine where you spend your energy and attention. Instead, give your energy and attention to the person you're with, and let that person know that he or she is more important to you than your phone.

Source: Chesley, N. (2005). Blurring boundaries? Linking technology use, spillover, individual distress, and family satisfaction. *Journal of Marriage and Family, 67*, 1237–1248.

We've already pointed out that communication can't solve every problem, so it shouldn't surprise you to learn that more communication isn't always preferred. Indeed, sometimes it seems that the less said, the better. As you'll learn in this book, it's often the *effectiveness* of our communication, rather than the *amount* of communication, that matters, which is why learning to be a competent communicator is so advantageous.

One way to appreciate the difference between more communication and better communication is to examine communication technologies. For instance, cell phones and the Internet let us communicate with others almost whenever we want to. Does this actually make us happier, though? Take a look at the "Dark Side" box on page 23 to read about one study that has addressed this question.

Learn It: What are the primary differences among the actional, interactional, and transactional models of communication? What does it mean to say that communication has literal and relational implications? What is the difference between having experience and having expertise?

Try It: Talk with a friend or a classmate about a topic that is very important to you. Experiment with talking less and caring less about getting your point across than you usually would. What happens when you talk less than you normally would? How do the transactional features of the conversation change?

Reflect on It: What are some implicit communication rules that you can recall? Why do you suppose we so often think communication can solve any problem?

3} How Do We Communicate Interpersonally?

Communication takes place in many contexts. Sometimes it involves one person talking to a large audience, such as when the president gives a speech on TV or a reporter writes an article in the newspaper. At other times it involves a small group of people communicating with one another, as in a college seminar, a team of surgeons in an operating room, or a football huddle. Communication occurs in families, in business organizations, in political institutions, in schools, and through the media. And, as you are probably aware, it often differs from one context to another. For example, few of us would talk to a grandparent the same way we would to a television reporter or a group of customers.

We communicate in many ways—so how do we know whether we're communicating *interpersonally*? In this section, we'll look at what makes communication interpersonal, and we'll learn how interpersonal communication is unique among forms of communication in the effects it has on people and their relationships.

> *Kind words can be short and easy to speak, but their echoes are truly endless.*
>
> —Mother Teresa of Calcutta (1910–1997)
> Indian missionary and Nobel Peace Prize winner

What Makes Communication Interpersonal?

After Jakob had finished taking part in his Alcoholics Anonymous group meeting, all he wanted to do was talk with his sponsor one-on-one. There was something about these person-to-person conversations that he found more comforting and more engaging than the group discussions. Without necessarily realizing it, Jakob was taking note of the uniqueness of interpersonal communication.

Interpersonal communication consists of *communication that occurs between two people within the context of their relationship and that, as it evolves, helps them to*

Interpersonal communication Communication that occurs between two people within the context of their relationship and that, as it evolves, helps them to negotiate and define their relationship.

negotiate and define their relationship. The content of an interpersonal conversation is sometimes highly intimate, as when two romantic partners discuss the details of a sensitive health issue that one of them is experiencing. Interpersonal conversations can also focus on more mundane, impersonal content, as when the same romantic partners talk about what they need to buy at the grocery store. The content of yet other interpersonal conversations falls somewhere along the continuum between intimate and mundane topics. Each of these conversations is interpersonal, however, to the extent that it helps people negotiate and define their relationships.

Interpersonal communication takes place between two people in the context of a relationship. Over time, it helps people negotiate and define their relationships.

As Jakob noticed, interpersonal communication is different from many other forms of communication. To understand how, let's take a look at some of its most important characteristics.

Interpersonal communication occurs between two people. The word *interpersonal* means "between people," and interpersonal communication involves interaction between two people at once. If only one is person involved—as when you talk to yourself—that is **intrapersonal communication.** Communication that is being transmitted to large numbers of people is known as **mass communication.** Most research on interpersonal communication, by contrast, focuses on interaction within a **dyad,** which is a pair of people. Communication that occurs in small groups of three or more people, as in a family, on a committee, or in a support group, is called **small group communication.**

Interpersonal communication takes place within a relationship. People who communicate interpersonally share some sort of relationship. To some people, the word *relationship* implies an intimate bond, such as between spouses or romantic partners. The truth, however, is that we have relationships with many different people in our lives. Some relationships, such as those with relatives or close friends, tend to be close, significant relationships that may last for many years. Others, such as those with classmates, acquaintances, and co-workers, may not be as close and may last only as long as people live or work near one another.

In general, we communicate with each person on the basis of the expectations we have for that relationship. For instance, we might reveal private information, such as news about a family member's marital problems or serious health issues, to a friend but not to a co-worker, because we expect friendship to be a closer relationship.

Interpersonal communication evolves within relationships. Long-distance friends sometimes say that when they see each other, they pick up their conversation right where they left off, as if no time had passed. Interpersonal communication in these friendships, and in all relationships, unfolds over time as people get to know each other better and have new experiences. In fact, people in long-term relationships can

Intrapersonal communication Communication with oneself.

Small group communication Communication occurring within small groups of three or more people.

Mass communication Communication from one source to a large audience.

Dyad A pair of people.

How we communicate with others defines our relationship with them. In what ways does your interpersonal communication differ with friends, co-workers, and romantic partners? In what ways is it similar across these relationships?

often recall how their communication has changed over the course of their relationship.[34] In the early stages of a romantic relationship, for instance, people may spend hours at a time talking and disclosing facts about their lives, such as where they grew up or what their career goals are. As they get to know each other better, their communication might become more instrumental, focusing on tasks such as where they're going to spend the holidays or who's going to pick up the children, instead of sharing deep disclosures. They might even start to experience conflicts. In any case, interpersonal communication is something that occurs over time. It's not a one-shot deal but something that is continually evolving within relationships.

Interpersonal communication negotiates and defines relationships. Every relationship has its own identity. When you think about all your friends, for example, you can probably group them into friendship "types," such as very close friends, casual friends, work friends, and school friends. Within every group, each friendship is probably a little different from the others.

How does each relationship get its own "personality" like this? The answer is that you negotiate the relationship over time using interpersonal communication. The way you talk to people you know, the things you talk (or don't talk) about, and the kinds of nonverbal behaviors you use around one another all help to define what kind of relationship you have with each person. You can also use interpersonal communication to *change* the nature of a relationship, as when friends disclose feelings of romantic interest in each other.

So, what makes communication interpersonal? Interpersonal communication evolves over time between people in some type of dyadic relationship and helps to define the nature of their relationship. You might notice we haven't said anything about how intimate the communication is. Some people think interpersonal communication means only sharing secrets and other private information, but that isn't the case. It includes all communication behaviors, verbal as well as nonverbal, that unfold over time to form and maintain relationships, whether those relationships are casual or intimate.

As Jakob discovered, his interpersonal communication with his sponsor was different from—and in many ways better than—communication within his group. Now that we understand what interpersonal communication is, let's look at some of the reasons why we often find it to be so important.

Why Interpersonal Communication Matters

You can probably think of many reasons why interpersonal communication is important to you. For example, you engage in it almost every day, you use it to maintain your current relationships and form new relationships, and you find it to be engaging and enjoyable. Those are only some of the many reasons why interpersonal communication matters to people. All those reasons fall within three general categories: pervasiveness, relational benefits, and health benefits. We'll take a brief look at each of these categories in this section.

Interpersonal communication is pervasive. We all have relationships, so we all engage in interpersonal communication. For most of us, interpersonal communication is as much a part of everyday life as sleeping or eating or putting on clothes. Sometimes we take part in face-to-face interpersonal communication with the people with whom we live or work. At other times interpersonal communication takes place over the telephone, such as when we talk to relatives or friends we don't see regularly. At still other times we communicate interpersonally via the Internet, as when we share e-mails or instant messages with people in our social circles. No matter how we do it, however, nearly all of us engage in some form of interpersonal communication almost every day.

Interpersonal communication can improve our relationships. We've seen that not every problem in relationships can be traced back to communication. Nevertheless, many of these problems stem from poor communication. In fact, in a nationwide survey conducted by the National Communication Association, respondents indicated that a "lack of effective communication" is the *number one reason* why relationships, including marriages, end.[35] Therefore, improving our interpersonal communication skills will also help us to improve our relationships. Significantly, this observation is not true only for intimate relationships. Research shows that effective interpersonal communication can improve a host of relationships, including those between and among friends, physicians and patients, parents and children, and businesspeople and customers.[36]

Interpersonal communication can improve our health. As we saw earlier in this chapter, we communicate partly to meet our physical needs for social contact. Close personal relationships are very important to our health. As we discussed, one of the best examples is marriage: Several studies have shown that married people live longer, healthier, and more satisfying lives than people who are single, divorced, or widowed.[37] Even having close friendships and other supportive relationships helps us manage stress and stay healthy.[38]

This finding is especially important for people who tend to be socially isolated. Among senior citizens, for instance, communication with close friends not only reduces feelings of loneliness and depression but also is actually associated with a longer life expectancy. (See the "How Do We Know" box on page 28.) As Mother Teresa's quote suggests, kind words can have important and long-lasting benefits.

{ How Do We Know?

People with Friends Live Longer }

Just in case you need another reason to hang onto your friends, research shows they may extend your life span. How do we know? The purpose of the "How Do We Know?" boxes is to introduce you to some of the research methods by which scholars learn about the processes and importance of interpersonal communication.

An Australian research team recently examined data from a 10-year survey of 1,477 senior citizens, each of whom reported on face-to-face and telephone contact with children, other relatives, casual friends, and confidants (closer friends with whom participants shared personal information). The researchers also measured several variables that they believed affect survival, including age, income, number of serious medical conditions, cognitive function, patterns of tobacco and alcohol use, and exercise behaviors. After controlling statistically for all these other factors, the researchers found that communication with friends and confidants increased participants' life expectancies over the period of the study. Moreover, they found that communication with friends and confidants was more important for survival than communication with children or other relatives was. Friendships, the scientists explained, provide a level of social support that helps people deal effectively with stress and avoid depression, a common problem for many seniors.

Ask Yourself:

- Why do you think friends were more beneficial than family members to the seniors in the study?

- What communication difficulties do you think older people might face that could reduce the potential benefits of close friendships?

From Me to You:

- Using the Internet to help you, look up a friend you've lost touch with, and make contact with that person again. Even if you don't communicate with long-term friends often, they are worth holding onto, because of the history and the good times you have shared with them.

Source: Giles, L. C., Glonek, G. F., Luszcz, M. A., & Andrews, G. R. (2005). Effects of social networks on 10-year survival in very old Australians: The Australian Longitudinal Study of Aging. *Journal of Epidemiology and Community Health, 59,* 574–579.

Learn It: What are the features of communication that determine whether it is interpersonal? How and why is interpersonal communication important for health?

Try It: Compose an e-mail to a friend or a family member to whom you have been close for a long time, and tell him or her about your day: what you did, whom you saw, where you ate, and so on. Before sending your message, describe to yourself the personality of your relationship and how your e-mail reflects it by the information you reveal or don't reveal and the kind of language you use.

Reflect on It: In what ways do your close relationships improve your life? What are some of the challenges involved in maintaining those relationships?

4} Building Your Communication Competence

No one is born a competent communicator. Rather, as with driving a car, playing a musical instrument, or writing a computer program, communicating competently requires skills that we have to learn and practice. That doesn't mean nature doesn't give some people a head start. Research shows that some of our communication traits—for example, how sociable, aggressive, or shy we are—are partly determined by our genes.[39] No matter which traits we're born with, though, we still have to learn how to communicate competently. In this section, we'll look at what communication competence is, which skills are necessary for competent communication, and how we learn those skills.

What Does Communicating Competently Mean?

Think about five people you consider to be really good communicators. Who's on your list? Any of your friends or relatives? teachers? co-workers? politicians or celebrities? yourself? You probably recognize that identifying good communicators means first asking yourself what a good communicator is. Even communication scholars find that a tricky question. Nevertheless, most scholars seem to agree that **communication competence** means communicating in ways that are *effective* and *appropriate* in a given situation.[40] Let's take a closer look at what it means to communicate effectively and appropriately.

Communica-tion compe-tence Communicating in ways that are effective and appropriate for a given situation.

Communicating effectively. Effectiveness describes how well your communication achieves its goals.[41] Suppose you want to persuade your housemate to lend you $50. There are many ways you might go about achieving that goal. You could say you really need the money and will pay it back as soon as you get paid next month. You could remind your housemate of favors you've done for him or her in the past. You could even threaten to move out if you don't get the loan. Some of these strategies probably seem more ethical than others, and some may seem more realistic than others.

Your choice of strategy may depend in part on what other goals you are trying to achieve at the same time. If maintaining a good relationship with your housemate is also important to you, then asking politely may be the most effective course of action. If all you want is the money, and your housemate's feelings are unimportant to you, then making your housemate feel guilty or threatening to leave may help you achieve your goal, even though it may not be as ethical.

The point here is that no single communication strategy will be effective in all situations. Because we often pursue more than one goal at a time, being an effective communicator means using behaviors that meet all the goals you have in the specific context in which you have them.

Communicating appropriately. Besides being effective, competent communication should also be appropriate. That means attending to the rules and expectations that apply in a social situation. As we saw earlier in this chapter, communication is governed by rules. A competent communicator takes those rules into account when deciding how to act. For instance, when an acquaintance asks, "How are you?" we know it's appropriate to say, "Fine, how are you?" in return. The acquaintance isn't expecting

Besides being effective, competent communication should also be appropriate. Behavior that's appropriate at home might not be appropriate at work, and vice versa.

a long, detailed description of how our day is going, so if you launch into one, he or she may find that response inappropriate. Similarly, it's appropriate in most classrooms to raise your hand and wait to be called on before speaking, so it would be inappropriate in those cases simply to blurt out your comments.

Communicating appropriately can be especially challenging when you're interacting with people from other cultures. As we noted earlier, many communication rules are culture-specific, so what might be perfectly appropriate in one culture could be seen as inappropriate or even offensive in another.[42] As one example, if you're visiting a Canadian household and your hosts offer you food, it's appropriate to accept the food if you're hungry. In many Japanese households, however, it is inappropriate to accept the food, even if you're hungry, until you decline it twice and your hosts offer it a third time.

Even within a specific culture, expectations for appropriate communication can vary according to the social situation. For example, behavior that's appropriate at home might not be appropriate at work, and vice versa. Moreover, behavior that's appropriate for a powerful person is not necessarily appropriate for less powerful people. For this reason you might not consider it out of line for your boss to arrive late for a meeting, even though engaging in the same behavior yourself would be considered inappropriate.

Communication competence, then, implies both effectiveness and appropriateness. Note that these are aspects of communication, not aspects of people. Thus, the next question we need to consider is whether competent *communicators* share common characteristics. The answer is they share many traits. We'll take a brief look at several of these characteristics in this section.

Characteristics of Competent Communicators

Look again at your list of five competent communicators. What do they have in common? Competence itself is situation-specific, so what works in one context may not work in another. Good communicators, however, tend to have certain characteristics that help them behave competently in most situations. Here we examine five of these characteristics, beginning with self-awareness.

Self-awareness. Good communicators are aware of their own behavior and how it affects others.[43] Researchers call this awareness **self-monitoring.** People who are "high self-monitors" pay close attention to the way they look, sound, and act in social situations. By contrast, people who are "low self-monitors" often seem oblivious to both their own behaviors and how other people are reacting to them. For instance, you may know someone who never seems to notice that he dominates the conversation or who

Self-monitoring Awareness of one's behavior and how it affects others.

seems unaware that she speaks louder than anyone around her.

Self-monitoring usually makes people more competent communicators because it enables them to see how their behavior fits or doesn't fit in a given social setting. In addition, high self-monitors often have high levels of social and emotional intelligence, which allow them to understand people's emotions and social behaviors accurately.[44]

Do you believe this woman is practicing appropriate communication behavior? Why or why not?

Adaptability. It's one thing to be aware of your own behavior; it's quite another to be able to adapt it to different situations. Competent communicators are able to assess what is going to be appropriate and effective in a given context and then modify their behaviors accordingly.[45] This ability is important because what works in one situation might be ineffective in another. Part of delivering a good speech, for instance, is being aware of the audience and adapting your behavior accordingly. A competent communicator would speak differently to a group of senior executives than to a group of new hires, because what works with one audience would probably not work with the other.

Empathy. Good communicators practice **empathy,** or the ability to be "other-oriented" and understand other people's thoughts and feelings.[46] When people say "Put yourself in my shoes," they are asking you to consider a situation from *their* perspective rather than your own. Empathy is an important skill because people often think and feel differently than you do about the same situation.

Empathy The ability to think and feel as others do.

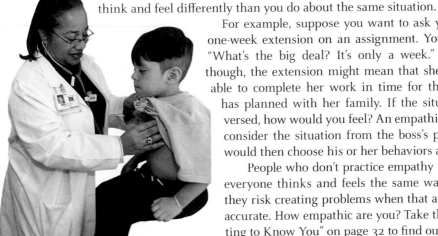

Empathy is an important part of any caregiving relationship, such as the relationship between a patient and a health care provider. An empathic health care provider will sense and respond to a patient's emotional needs as well as his or her physical needs.

For example, suppose you want to ask your boss for a one-week extension on an assignment. You might think, "What's the big deal? It's only a week." To your boss, though, the extension might mean that she would be unable to complete her work in time for the vacation she has planned with her family. If the situation were reversed, how would you feel? An empathic person would consider the situation from the boss's perspective and would then choose his or her behaviors accordingly.

People who don't practice empathy tend to assume everyone thinks and feels the same way they do, and they risk creating problems when that assumption isn't accurate. How empathic are you? Take the quiz in "Getting to Know You" on page 32 to find out.

Empathy is a particular challenge for individuals with conditions such as autism and Asperger's disorder, both of which impair a person's ability to interpret other people's nonverbal behaviors. For instance, you may have little difficulty judging when a friend is being sarcastic, because you infer that from his facial expres-

Getting to Know You
How Empathic Are You?

One of the ways to improve your communication ability is to think about how you communicate now. Each "Getting to Know You" box will help you do this by presenting one self-assessment of a communication skill or tendency. For instance, we have seen that empathy is one of the characteristics of competent communicators. How empathic are you? Read each of the following statements, and indicate how much it describes you by assigning a number between 1 ("not at all") and 7 ("very strongly").

1. _____ It makes me sad to see a lonely stranger in a group.

2. _____ I become nervous if others around me seem nervous.

3. _____ I tend to get emotionally involved with a friend's problems.

4. _____ Sometimes the words of a love song can move me deeply.

5. _____ The people around me have a great influence on my moods.

6. _____ Seeing people cry upsets me.

7. _____ I get very angry when I see someone being ill-treated.

8. _____ I cannot continue to feel okay if people around me are depressed.

9. _____ I am very upset when I see an animal in pain.

10. _____ It upsets me to see helpless elderly people.

When you're finished, add up your scores. Your total score should fall between 10 and 70. A score of 10–25 suggests that empathy is a skill you can work on. Learning more about empathy, as you are doing in this class, might help you become more empathic. If you scored between 25 and 55, you are already moderately empathic, and you have a good ability to understand other people's emotions. Continued practice can improve this skill even more. If you scored above 55, you are a highly empathic person. Chances are that this ability helps you to communicate effectively in interpersonal situations.

Remember that your score on this quiz—and on all the "Getting to Know You" quizzes in this book—reflects only how you see yourself at this time. If your score surprised you, take the quiz again later in the course to see how studying interpersonal communication might have changed the way you assess your communication abilities.

Source: Items adapted from Mehrabian, A., & Epstein, N. (1972). A measure of emotional empathy. *Journal of Personality, 40,* 525–543.

sions and tone of voice. For people with these disorders, however, those nonverbal signals may not be as evident, making it more challenging to understand and adopt another person's perspective.

Cognitive complexity. Let's say you see your friend Tony coming toward you in the hallway. You smile and get ready to say hi, but he walks right by as if you're not even there. How would you explain that? Maybe he's mad at you. Maybe he was concentrating on something and didn't notice anyone around him. Maybe he actually did smile at you and you just didn't see it. The ability to consider a variety of explanations and to understand a given situation in multiple ways is called **cognitive complexity.** Cognitive complexity is a valuable skill because it keeps you from jumping to the wrong

Cognitive complexity
The ability to understand a given situation in multiple ways.

conclusion and responding inappropriately.[47]

Ethics. Finally, competent communicators are ethical communicators. **Ethics** guides us in judging whether something is morally right or wrong. Ethical communication, then, generally dictates treating people fairly, communicating honestly, and avoiding immoral or unethical behavior. This can be easier said than done, because people often have very different ideas about right and wrong. What may be morally justified to one person or one culture may be considered completely unethical to another.

At a Glance: Five Characteristics of Competent Communicators

People who are competent communicators tend to share several characteristics. These include:

Self-awareness	Awareness of how your behavior is affecting others
Adaptability	Ability to modify your behaviors as the situation demands
Empathy	Skill at identifying and feeling what others around you are feeling
Cognitive complexity	Ability to understand a given situation in multiple ways
Ethics	Tendency to behave in morally correct ways

Ethical considerations are often particularly important when we're engaged in compliance-gaining strategies, trying to change the way another person thinks or behaves. Referring back to a previous example, is it ethical to threaten to move out unless your housemate lends you $50? To many people, this compliance-gaining strategy would seem unduly harsh and potentially unfair, because it may give the housemate no choice but to make the loan. Depending on why you need the money, however, or how your housemate has treated you in the past, you might not consider this strategy to be unethical, even if others do. Competent communicators are aware that people's ideas about ethics vary. However, they are also aware of their own ethical beliefs, and they communicate in ways that are consistent with those beliefs.

Take one last look at your list of five good communicators. Are they generally aware of their own behaviors and able to adapt those behaviors to different contexts? Can they adopt other people's perspectives on things and consider various ways of explaining situations? Do they behave ethically? These aren't the only things that make someone a competent communicator, but they are among the most important. A brief review of these skills appears in the "At a Glance" box above. To the extent that we can develop and practice these skills, we can all become better at the process of communication.

Learn It: What is the difference between effectiveness and appropriateness? How is cognitive complexity defined?

Try It: Choose your favorite "reality TV" show, and think about the characters and their communication behaviors. On the basis of the things you've learned in this section, how would you rate each character in communication competence? What makes some characters more competent than others? Try to identify specific skills, such as empathy or cognitive complexity, that differentiate the characters from one another. Consider how each person might improve his or her communication competencies.

Reflect on It: How would you describe your own level of self-monitoring? Where do your ideas about ethics come from?

Section 1} Why Do We Communicate? (p. 5)

I. Why Do We Communicate?

    A. Communication meets physical needs

- Communication meets physical needs, such as helping us to stay healthy.

    B. Communication meets relational needs

- Communication meets relational needs by helping us form and maintain important relationships.

    C. Communication fills identity needs

- Communication fills identity needs by helping us see how others think of us.

    D. Communication meets spiritual needs

- Communication meets spiritual needs by letting us express our beliefs and values.

    E. Communication serves instrumental needs

- Communication serves instrumental needs, such as helping us to schedule a meeting or order a meal.

Section 2} The Nature of Communication (p. 11)

II. The Nature of Communication

    A. Three models of human communication

        1. Communication as action

        2. Communication as interaction

        3. Communication as transaction

- Communication scholars have viewed communication as action, as interaction, and most recently as transaction.

    B. Six characteristics of communication

        1. Communication relies on multiple channels

        2. Communication passes through perceptual filters

        3. People give communication its meaning

        4. Communication has literal meanings and relational implications

        5. Communication sends messages, whether intentional or unintentional

        6. Communication is governed by rules

- Communication relies on multiple channels, passes through perceptual filters, is given its meaning by the people who use it, has literal and relational implications, sends intentional and unintentional messages, and is governed by rules.

    C. Dispelling some communication myths

        1. Myth: Everyone is an expert in communication

        2. Myth: Communication will solve any problem

        3. Myth: Communication can break down

        4. Myth: Communication is inherently good

        5. Myth: More communication is always better

- Five myths about communication are (1) everyone is an expert in communication, (2) communication can solve any problem, (3) communication can break down, (4) communication is inherently good, and (5) more communication is always better.

III. How Do We Communicate Interpersonally?

    A. **What makes communication interpersonal?**

        1. Interpersonal communication occurs between two people

        2. Interpersonal communication takes place within a relationship

        3. Interpersonal communication evolves within relationships

        4. Interpersonal communication negotiates and defines relationships

- Interpersonal communication occurs between two people, evolves over time within their relationship, and helps them to negotiate and define their relationship.

    B. **Why interpersonal communication matters**

        1. Interpersonal communication is pervasive

        2. Interpersonal communication can improve our relationships

        3. Interpersonal communication can improve our health

- Interpersonal communication is pervasive, has benefits for our relationships, and has benefits for our health.

IV. Building Your Communication Competence

    A. **What does communicating competently mean?**

        1. Communicating effectively

        2. Communicating appropriately

- Communicating competently means communicating effectively and appropriately.

    B. **Characteristics of competent communicators**

        1. Self-awareness

        2. Adaptability

        3. Empathy

        4. Cognitive complexity

        5. Ethics

- Competent communicators typically have high self-awareness, adaptability, empathy, cognitive complexity, and ethics.

Key Terms

Channel	Encode	Meta-communication
Channel-lean context	Ethics	Model
Channel-rich context	Explicit rule	Noise
Cognitive complexity	Feedback	Receiver
Communication competence	Implicit rule	Relational dimension
Content dimension	Instrumental needs	Self-monitoring
Context	Interpersonal communication	Small group communication
Decode	Intrapersonal communication	Source
Dyad	Mass communication	Stigma
Empathy	Message	Symbol

Discussion Questions

1. In what ways do we negotiate our own identities through communication? How do we do this as individuals? as families? as societies?
2. Of all the various needs served by communication, which ones do you attend to the most? How often do you feel you are trying to meet more than one need at once?
3. Why do you suppose communication scholars prefer the transaction model? Do you think the model is sufficiently complex to describe the communication process? Is it too complex?
4. Suppose your mom says to you, "I love it when you call me." What are some ways you could describe the relational dimension of that message?

5. Implicit communication rules are never taught or verbalized, yet people seem to know and follow them anyway. How do you think we learn implicit rules?
6. People often mistakenly believe that more communication, or better communication, will solve any problem. What are some relational problems that cannot be solved by more or better communication?
7. How does a relationship get negotiated and defined by interpersonal communication? In what ways are relationships being constantly negotiated?
8. Why is it important to communicate ethically, when people often have such different ideas about ethics?

Practice Quiz

Multiple Choice

1. Which of the following is *not* a type of noise that might inhibit communication?
   a. Physical noise
   b. Psychological noise
   c. Psychonormative noise
   d. Physiological noise
2. Ethical communication generally involves:
   a. Treating people fairly
   b. Honesty in communication
   c. Avoiding immoral behavior
   d. All of these
3. An example of a perceptual filter is:
   a. Personal experiences
   b. Personal bias or prejudice
   c. Personal beliefs
   d. All of these
4. When entering a movie theater, Paul notices a large sign that says "Turn off your cell phone before taking your seat!" This is an example of a/an:
   a. Explicit rule of communication
   b. Implicit rule of communication
   c. Semantic rule of communication
   d. Psycho-social rule of communication
5. Empathy is best defined as:
   a. Feeling sorry for someone else
   b. An ability to identify, feel, and relate to what others are feeling
   c. The ability to keep other people's feelings separated from your feelings
   d. Paying attention to how others are evaluating your social skills
6. Which of the following is *not* an example of a physical context?
   a. Temperature—how hot/cold it is
   b. Size—how large/small a room is
   c. Light—how bright/dark it is
   d. Emotion—how happy/sad you are

7. An example of a channel-lean communication context would be:
   a. Having a face-to-face conversation with your mom
   b. Sending a text message to your roommate
   c. Taking a long walk with your romantic partner
   d. Going deer hunting with your dad and brothers
8. The spiritual identity of an individual is best associated with:
   a. The ability to accomplish day-to-day tasks
   b. The ability to form and maintain personal relationships
   c. The ability to develop a core set of beliefs, values, and morals
   d. The ability to be empathic with another person
9. Research has found that communication with friends and confidants actually:
   a. Decreases a person's physical and mental health
   b. Increases a person's self-monitoring skills
   c. Increases a person's life expectancy
   d. Decreases a person's ability to relate to his or her family members
10. Awareness of your behavior and how it affects others is called:
    a. Self-monitoring
    b. Stigma
    c. Empathy
    d. Meta-communication

True/False

11. Research has found that people with strong, close relationships are more likely to avoid suffering major health ailments such as heart disease and high blood pressure than are people without strong social ties.
12. The most powerful predictor of a person's overall happiness is satisfaction with his or her marriage.
13. Most personal communication is best described as linear in nature.
14. Feedback is mainly determined by two key factors: channel and context.
15. In the transaction model of communication, messages are encoded and decoded at the same time.

Fill in the Blank

16. The tendency to behave in morally correct ways is a characteristic of a/an _____ person.

17. Most people believe that _____ is the number one reason that relationships are ended.

18. The blurring of the boundaries between people's personal and professional lives is known as _____.

19. The most contemporary model of human communication is the _____ model.

20. A _____ is a characteristic that discredits a person, making him or her to be seen as abnormal or undesirable.

Research Library

Movies

Legally Blonde (Comedy; 2005; PG-13)

Legally Blonde *is a comedy focusing on a college sorority president, Elle Woods, who decides to attend Harvard Law School to win back the affections of a former boyfriend. In several places, the film illustrates explicit and implicit communication rules. While assisting her law professor in preparation for a murder trial, for instance, Elle discovers that the defendant is a former member of her sorority. After learning the defendant's alibi but promising to keep it secret, she is pressured by her professor and colleagues to disclose it, but she refuses to do so on the grounds that she cannot "break the bonds of sisterhood," which is a rule about keeping confidences among sorority sisters.*

Love Actually (Comedy; 2003; R)

Love Actually *is a British romantic comedy that chronicles the week-by-week lives of several characters. A recurring theme is how interpersonal communication negotiates and defines relationships. Many of the characters—particularly Juliet and Mark, Jamie and Aurélia, and David and Natalie—use communication behaviors to define the nature of their relationships. These story lines also illustrate the idea that communication helps people meet their relational needs.*

You've Got Mail (Comedy; 1998; PG)

You've Got Mail *is a romantic comedy depicting the development of a romantic relationship between Joe and Kathleen, who meet and (for the majority of the movie) communicate entirely online. Because online communication is a channel-lean context, the characters rely heavily on their e-mail texts to understand each other, which often leads to challenges in interpreting each other's meanings.*

Books

Andersen, P. A. (2004). *The complete idiot's guide to body language.* New York: Penguin.

Baxter, L. A., & Braithwaite, D. O. (2008). *Engaging theories in interpersonal communication: Multiple perspectives.* Thousand Oaks, CA: Sage.

Knapp, M. L., & Daly, J. A. (2002). *The handbook of interpersonal communication* (3rd ed.). Thousand Oaks, CA: Sage.

Spitzberg, B. H., & Cupach, W. R. (Eds.). (2007). *The dark side of interpersonal communication* (2nd ed.). Mahwah, NJ: Lawrence Erlbaum Associates.

Journal Articles

Baumeister, R. F., & Leary, M. R. (1995). The need to belong: Desire for interpersonal attachments as a fundamental human motivation. *Psychological Bulletin, 117,* 497–529.

Buck, R., & Van Lear, C. A. (2002). Verbal and nonverbal communication: Distinguishing symbolic, spontaneous and pseudo-spontaneous nonverbal behavior. *Journal of Communication, 52,* 522–541.

Motley, M. T. (1990). On whether one can(not) not communicate: An examination via traditional communication postulates. *Western Journal of Communication, 54,* 1–20.

Web Sites

www.natcom.org/research/Roper/how_americans_communicate.htm

This Web site reports results from a survey of U.S. American adults about their communication behaviors and perceptions. The survey was commissioned by the National Communication Association, the largest academic association for communication scholars and students in the world.

www.icahdq.org

This is the main Web site for the International Communication Association, an academic association for communication scholars and students with members from 70 countries.

mocracy, free enterprise, and individual choice.[10] When you travel to other countries, you might find that their cultural values are dramatically different from yours.

Norms. Finally, norms are rules or expectations that guide people's behavior in a culture. As an example, consider the norms for greeting people. In North American countries people shake hands and say "Nice to meet you." In other cultures it's normal to hug, kiss on both cheeks, or even kiss on the lips. Cultures also vary in their norms for politeness. Therefore a behavior that would be considered very polite in one culture may be frowned upon in another.

U.S. American culture values freedom, opportunity, choice, and material comfort. These values are epitomized in the media by scenes such as this—where two people are driving a sports car on a spacious open road with the sun on their face and the wind in their hair.

Cultures and Co-Cultures

When you think about culture as shared language, beliefs, and customs, it may seem as though you belong to many different cultures at once. If you grew up in the United States, for example, then you likely feel a part of the U.S. American culture. At the same time, if you're really into computers, or music, or skateboarding, you may notice that the people who share those interests appear to have their own ways of speaking and acting. Or perhaps you notice that people in your generation have different values and customs than people who are older than you—or that different ethnic or religious groups at your school seem to have their own traditions and beliefs. Does each of these groups have a culture of its own? In a manner of speaking, the answer is yes.

What are co-cultures? Within many "large" cultures, such as the Italian, Vietnamese, or U.S. American cultures, are a host of "smaller" cultural groups that researchers call co-cultures. **Co-cultures** are groups of people who share values, customs, and norms related to mutual interests or characteristics besides their national citizenship. Your co-culture isn't based on the country you were born in or the national society in which you were raised. Instead, it is composed of smaller groups of people with whom you identify.

Co-cultures
Groups of people who share values, customs, and norms related to a mutual interest or characteristic.

The bases of co-cultures. Some co-cultures are based on shared activities or beliefs. If you're into fly-fishing, organic gardening, or political activism, for example, then there are co-cultures for those interests. Similarly, Buddhists have beliefs and traditions that distinguish them from Baptists, regardless of where they grew up.

Some co-cultures are based on differences in mental and physical abilities. If you're deaf, for instance, you've probably noticed that many deaf populations have certain values and customs that differ from those of hearing populations.[11] Even if they don't share the same language, political positions, or religious beliefs, people who are deaf often share social customs that are distinctive.

For instance, whereas many people would be uncomfortable having constant eye contact with another person while talking, deaf people frequently maintain steady mutual gaze while communicating through sign language. In addition, they often make it a point to notify others in the group if they are leaving the room, even if just for a few moments. Because they cannot hear one another call out from another room, this practice helps avoid frantic searches for the person who has left. Among hearing people, however, it would be considered annoying at the very least to announce your every departure. Sharing these and other customs, then, helps deaf people interact with one another as members of a shared co-culture.[12]

The deaf co-culture also places strong emphasis on the distinction between in-group and out-group members. People who are deaf may point out that a person really can't understand the physical experience of deafness—or the social experience of being treated as deaf—unless he or she is, in fact, deaf. As a result, deaf individuals often express a strong preference for interacting with other deaf individuals. They may treat sign language interpreters and hearing parents of deaf children as "honorary deaf people," but they are frequently hesitant to accept hearing people as part of the deaf co-culture.[13]

As one illustration of this tendency, students at Gallaudet University in Washington, D.C., whose undergraduate student body consists entirely of deaf people, staged an eight-day protest in 1988 demanding the appointment of a deaf president for the university. The board of trustees responded by appointing the first deaf president in the university's 130-year history.

Can you belong to multiple co-cultures? Many people identify with several co-cultures at once. For example, you might relate to co-cultures for your age group, your ethnicity, your religion, your sexual orientation, your musical tastes, your athletic interests, and even your college major. Every one of those groups probably has its own values, beliefs, traditions, customs, and even ways of using language that distinguish it from other groups. Going further, some co-cultures have smaller co-cultures within them. For example, the deaf co-culture consists of people who advocate using only sign language and others who advocate the use of cochlear implants, which may help a person hear.

Communicating with Cultural Awareness

People with different cultural backgrounds don't just communicate differently; in many cases they also truly *think* differently. As you might imagine, those differences can present some real challenges when people from different cultures interact.

The same thing can happen even when people from different co-cultures communicate. For instance, teenagers and senior citizens may have difficulty getting along because their customs and values are so different. Adolescents often enjoy the most contemporary music and fashions, whereas seniors frequently prefer songs and clothing that they enjoyed as younger adults. Teenagers may value independence and individuality; older people may value loyalty, family, and community.

Young and elderly people might speak the same language, but they don't necessarily use language in the

People from different cultures and co-cultures don't just communicate differently. They often *think* differently. How would you characterize the ways in which younger people and elderly people might think differently?

same ways. Teenagers may have no problem understanding one another when they talk about "blogging" or "IMing," for example, but their grandparents may have no idea what they mean. Maybe you've experienced this kind of situation, or perhaps you've seen other co-cultures have difficulty understanding each other, such as Democrats and Republicans, or gay and straight people.

To complicate this problem, not only do people from different cultures (and co-cultures) differ in how they think and behave, but they're also often unaware of *how* they differ. For instance, a U.S. American college professor might think a Japanese student is being dishonest because the student doesn't look her in the eyes. In the United States this behavior can suggest dishonesty. Within the Japanese culture, however, it signals respect for the teacher. If neither the professor nor the student is aware of how the other is likely to interpret the behavior, then it's easy to see how a misunderstanding could arise.

Communicating effectively with people from other cultures and co-cultures requires us to be aware of how their behaviors and ways of thinking are likely to differ from our own. Unfortunately, this is easier said than done. Many of us operate on what researchers call a "similarity assumption"—that is, we presume that most people think the same way we do, without asking ourselves whether that's true.[14] In the preceding example, the professor thought the student was being dishonest because she assumed the lack of eye contact meant the same thing to the student that it did to her. The student assumed the professor would interpret his lack of eye contact as a sign of respect, because that's how he understood and intended it.

Questioning our cultural assumptions can be a real challenge because we're often unaware that we hold them in the first place. At the same time, however, it is one of the basic ways in which studying interpersonal communication and learning about the influences of culture can make you a more competent communicator.

Learn It: What is a culture, and how is it different from a society? How do societies use symbols, language, values, and norms to reflect their cultures? What are some examples of co-cultures? What is the similarity assumption, and how does it influence our ability to communicate with cultural awareness?

Try It: Choose two of your close friends, and make a list of the co-cultures that each friend belongs to. Remember to include co-cultures for age, ethnicity, disability, religion, and activities or interests, if they are relevant. Next to each co-culture that you list, write down one statement about how you think it affects your friend's personality or communication style. What did you learn about each friend by going through this exercise?

Reflect on It: Which in-groups do you identify the most strongly with? When have you noticed your own cultural awareness being challenged? How did you respond when that happened?

2} How Culture Affects Communication {

If you've ever had difficulty communicating with someone from a different cultural background, you've experienced the challenge of overcoming cultural differences in communication. Dutch social psychologist Geert Hofstede and American anthropologist Edward T. Hall have pioneered the study of cultures and cultural differences. Their work and the work of others suggest that seven cultural differences, in particular, influence how people interact with one another. In this section, we'll discuss:

- Individualism and collectivism, or whether a culture focuses more on the needs of the individual or the needs of the group
- High-context and low-context cultures, which refers to how explicit people expect one another's language use to be
- Power distances, a measure of how equally power is distributed within a society
- Cultural masculinity or femininity, which refers to whether traditionally masculine or feminine values are promoted
- Monochronic and polychronic cultures, a distinction based on how a culture thinks about the importance of time
- Uncertainty avoidance, or how important certainty is within a given culture
- Communication codes, meaning those words or gestures that have particular meaning only to people within a given culture

> *Color makes a difference. Gender makes a difference. Ethnicity makes a difference. Acting as if they don't will create more problems than it will solve.*
>
> —James Jones (1921–1977)
> U.S. American novelist

Individualism and Collectivism

Individualistic culture
A culture that emphasizes individuality and responsibility to oneself.

One way cultures differ is in how much they emphasize individuals rather than groups. In an **individualistic culture,** people believe that their primary responsibility is to themselves. Children in individualistic cultures are raised hearing messages such as "Be yourself," "You're special," and "There's no one else in the world who's just like you." Those messages emphasize the importance of knowing yourself, being self-sufficient, and being true to what you want in life.[15] Indeed, the motto in an individualistic culture might be "I gotta be me!" People in individualistic societies also value self-reliance and the idea that people should "pull themselves up by their own bootstraps," or help themselves when they need it, instead of waiting for others

Cultural values are often expressed through personal appearance. Among the Maori of New Zealand, tattoos are commonly used to reflect collectivism, their shared sense of heritage and community. When people in the U.S. adopt similar, tribal-style tattoos, it's often to express their individuality rather than their connection to a group or community.

to help them. Research shows that the United States, Canada, Great Britain, and Australia are among the most individualistic societies in the world.[16]

By contrast, people in a **collectivistic culture** are taught that their primary responsibility is to their families, their communities, and the companies they work for. Instead of emphasizing the importance of being an individual, collectivistic cultures focus on the importance of taking care of the needs of the group. People in these cultures place a high value on duty and loyalty, and they see themselves not as unique or special but as a part of the groups to which they belong. Among the Kabre of Togo, for instance, people try to give away many of their material possessions to build relationships and benefit their social groups.[17] The motto in a collectivistic culture might be "I am my family and my family is me." Collectivistic cultures include Korea, Japan, and many countries in Africa and Latin America.[18]

Collectivistic culture A culture that places greater emphasis on loyalty to the family, workplace, or community than on the needs of the individual.

How individualistic or collectivistic a culture is can affect communication behavior in several ways. When people in individualistic cultures experience conflict with one another, for instance, they are expected to express it and work toward resolving it. In contrast, people in collectivistic cultures are taught to be much more indirect in the way they handle disagreements, to preserve social harmony.[19]

Another difference involves people's comfort level with public speaking. Many people experience anxiety when they have to give a speech, but this is especially true in collectivistic societies, where people are taught to "blend in" rather than to "stand out." Being assertive and "standing up for yourself" are valued in individualistic cultures, but they can cause embarrassment or shame for a collectivistic culture.

Some researchers have gone so far as to suggest that the individualistic-collectivistic distinction is the most fundamental way that cultures differ from one another. Other researchers disagree, maintaining that this distinction by itself can't adequately characterize cultures.[20]

High- and Low-Context Cultures

Low-context culture A culture in which verbal communication is expected to be explicit and is often interpreted literally.

If you've traveled much, you may have noticed that people in various parts of the world differ in how direct and explicit their language is. In a **low-context culture,** people are expected to be direct, say what they mean, and not "beat around the bush." Low-context cultures value expressing yourself, sharing your opinions, and even trying to persuade others to see things your way.[21] As you might have guessed, the United States is an example of a low-context society, as are Canada, Israel, and most northern European countries.

High-context culture A culture in which verbal communication is often ambiguous and meaning is drawn from contextual cues, such as facial expressions and tone of voice.

In contrast, people in a **high-context culture,** such as Korea, the Maori of New Zealand, and Native Americans, are taught to speak in a much less direct way. In these societies, maintaining harmony and avoiding offending people are more important than expressing your true feelings.[22] As a result, people speak in a less direct, more ambiguous manner, and they convey much more of the meaning through subtle behaviors and contextual cues such as facial expressions and tone of voice.

One example of how this cultural difference affects communication is the way in which people handle criticism and disagreement. In a low-context culture, a supervisor might reprimand an irresponsible employee openly, to make an example of him or her. The supervisor would probably be very direct and explicit about what the employee was doing wrong, what the expectations for improvement were, and what the consequences would be for failing to meet them.

In a high-context culture, however, the supervisor probably wouldn't reprimand the employee publicly for fear that it would put the employee to shame or cause him or her to "lose face." Criticism in high-context cultures is more likely to take place in private.

The supervisor would also likely use more ambiguous language to convey what the employee was doing wrong, "talking around" the issue instead of confronting it directly. To reprimand an employee for repeated absences, for example, a supervisor might point out that responsibility to one's co-workers is important and that "letting down the team" would be cause for shame. The supervisor may never actually say that the employee needs to improve his or her attendance record. Instead, the employee would be expected to understand the message by listening to what the supervisor says and paying attention to the supervisor's body language, tone of voice, and facial expressions.

As you may have guessed, when people from low- and high-context cultures communicate with each other, the potential for misunderstanding is great. To illustrate this point, imagine that you have asked two of your friends if they'd like to meet you tomorrow evening for a coffee tasting at a popular bookstore cafe. Your friend Tina, who's from a low-context culture, says, "No, I've got a lot of studying to do, but thanks anyway." Lee, who grew up in a high-context culture, nods his head and says, "That sounds like fun." Thus, you're surprised later when he doesn't show up.

How can you account for these different behaviors? The answer is that people raised in high-context cultures are often reluctant to say no—even when they mean no—for fear of causing offense. Another person from Lee's culture might have understood from Lee's facial expression or tone of voice that he didn't intend to go to the coffee tasting with you. Because you grew up in a low-context society, however, you interpreted his answer and his nodding his head to mean he was accepting your invitation.

Low- and High-Power Distance

A third way cultures differ from one another is in how evenly power is distributed within the society. Several things can give someone power, including money or other valuable resources, education or expertise, age, popularity, talent, intelligence, and experience. In democracies such as the United States, people believe in the value of equality—that all men and women are created equal and that no one person or group should have excessive power. This belief is characteristic of **low-power-distance cultures.** The United States and Canada belong to this category, as do Israel, New Zealand, Denmark, and Austria.[23] People in these societies are raised to believe that even though some individuals are born with more advantages (such as wealth or fame), no one is inherently better than anyone else. This doesn't necessarily mean that people in these societies *are* treated equally, only that they value the idea that they should be.

Low-power-distance culture A culture in which power is not highly concentrated in specific groups of people.

High-power-distance culture A culture in which much or most of the power is concentrated in a few people, such as royalty or a ruling political party.

In **high-power-distance cultures** power is distributed less evenly. Certain groups, such as royalty or the ruling political party, have great power, and the average citizen has much less. People in these societies are taught that certain people or groups deserve to have more power than others and that respecting power is more important than respecting equality. Mexico, Brazil, India, Singapore, and the Philippines are all examples of high-power-distance societies.[24]

Power distance affects many aspects of interpersonal communication. For example, people in low-power-distance cultures usually expect friendships and romantic relationships to be based on love rather than social status. In contrast, people in high-power-distance cultures are expected to choose friends or mates from within their social class.[25]

Another difference involves the way people think about authority. High-power-distance societies place great emphasis on obedience and respect for those in power. People are taught to obey their parents and teachers without question.[26] In contrast,

people in low-power-distance societies are more often taught that it's their right—even their responsibility—to question authority. In these cultures it's not unexpected for people to ask "Why?" when their parents or teachers tell them to do something.

This difference is also seen in the relationships and communication patterns people have with their employers. Workers in low-power-distance cultures value autonomy, the ability to make choices about the way they do their jobs, and the ability to have input into decisions that affect them. Such workers might provide their input through unions or employee satisfaction surveys. By contrast, employees in high-power-distance cultures are used to having little or no say about how to do their jobs. Instead, they expect their employers to make the decisions and are more likely to follow those decisions without question.

Masculine and Feminine Cultures

As you'll see later in this chapter, we usually use the terms "masculine" and "feminine" when we're referring to people. Hofstede has suggested that we can also apply these terms to cultures.[27] In a highly masculine culture, people tend to cherish traditionally masculine values, such as ambition, achievement, and the acquisition of material goods. They also value sex-specific roles for women and men, preferring that men hold the wage-earning and decision-making positions (such as corporate executive) while women occupy the nurturing positions (such as homemaker). Examples of masculine cultures are Austria, Japan, and Mexico.

In contrast, in a highly feminine culture, people tend to value nurturance, quality of life, and service to others, all of which are stereotypically feminine qualities. They also tend *not* to believe that men's and women's roles should be strongly differentiated. Compared with masculine cultures, therefore, it would not be as unusual for a man to care for children or a woman to be her family's primary wage earner. Examples of feminine cultures are Sweden, Chile, and The Netherlands.

According to Hofstede's research, the United States has a moderately masculine culture. U.S. Americans tend to value sex-differentiated roles—although not as strongly as Austrians, Japanese, or Mexicans do—and they place a fairly high value on stereotypically masculine qualities such as achievement and the acquisition of resources.[28]

Monochronic and Polychronic Cultures

Monochronic
A concept that treats time as a finite commodity that can be earned, saved, spent, and wasted.

Cultures also vary with respect to their norms and expectations concerning the use of time. Societies that have a **monochronic** concept of time, such as Swiss, Germans, and most U.S. Americans, view time as a commodity. We save time, spend time, fill time, invest time, and waste time, as though time were tangible. We treat time as valuable, believe that "time is money," and talk about making time and losing time.[29]

A monochronic orientation toward time influences several social behaviors. Because people in monochronic cultures think of time as valuable, they hate to waste it. Therefore, they expect meetings and classes to start on time (within a minute or so), and when that doesn't happen, they are willing to wait only so long before leaving. They also expect others to show up when they say they will. Perhaps you can think of situations when you've felt frustrated by a co-worker or a classmate who wasn't punctual.

By comparison, societies with a **polychronic** orientation—which include Latin America, the Arab part of the Middle East, and much of sub-Saharan Africa—conceive of time as more holistic and fluid and less structured. Instead of treating time as a finite commodity that must be managed properly to avoid being wasted, people in polychronic cultures perceive it more like a never-ending river, flowing infinitely into the future.[30]

Polychronic
A concept that treats time as an infinite resource rather than a finite commodity.

One result of this orientation is that schedules are more fluid and flexible than they are in monochronic cultures. In Pakistan, for instance, if you're invited to a wedding that begins at 4:30 and you arrive at 4:30, you will most likely find yourself the first one there. A bank or a restaurant may not open at a specified time—as it would be expected to do in a monochronic society—but whenever the owner or manager decides. Students would not expect their professors to begin class at an appointed time. Instead, students would arrive over a period of time, and the class would begin whenever the professor was ready. People in a polychronic culture don't prioritize efficiency and punctuality. Instead, they attach greater value to the quality of their lives and their relationships with others.

Uncertainty Avoidance

Uncertainty avoidance
The degree to which people find novel, unfamiliar situations problematic.

Humans have a natural tendency to avoid situations that are unfamiliar or that make them feel uncomfortable. In other words, we dislike uncertainty: In fact, uncertainty causes many of us a good deal of stress.[31] Not all cultures find uncertainty to be equally problematic, however. Cultures vary in what Hofstede called **uncertainty avoidance**, or the extent to which people try to avoid situations that are unstructured, unclear, or unpredictable.[32] Individuals from cultures that are highly uncertainty avoidant are drawn to people and situations that are familiar, and they are relatively unlikely to take risks, for fear of failure. They are also uncomfortable with differences of opinion, and they tend to favor rules and laws that maximize security and reduce ambiguity wherever possible. Argentina, Portugal, and Uruguay are among the countries whose cultures are the most uncertainty avoidant.

By contrast, people in uncertainty-accepting cultures are more open to new situations, and they are more accepting of people and ideas that are different from their own. They take a "live and let live" approach, preferring as few rules as possible that would restrict their behaviors. Societies with cultures that are highly accepting of uncertainty include Hong Kong, Jamaica, and New Zealand. Hofstede has determined that the U.S. culture is more accepting than avoidant of uncertainty, but it is closer to the midpoint of the scale than many countries are.

Cultural Communication Codes

Communication codes
Verbal and nonverbal behaviors, such as idioms and gestures, that characterize a culture and distinguish it from other cultures.

Finally, cultures differ from one another in their use of **communication codes,** those verbal and nonverbal behaviors whose meanings are often understood only by people from the same culture. Three kinds of communication codes—idioms, jargon, and gestures—differ greatly from society to society and can make intercultural communication especially challenging.

Idioms. An idiom is a phrase whose meaning is purely *figurative;* that is, you can't understand the meaning by interpreting the words literally. For example, most U.S. American adults know the phrase "kicking the bucket" has nothing to do with kicking a bucket. In U.S. American culture, this is an idiom that means "to die." If you grew up in the United States, you can probably think of several other U.S. American idioms. For example, if something is "a dime a dozen," then it is very common or is nothing special. Having "two left feet" means you're not a very good dancer. Finally, "shaking a leg" means you're hurrying, but "pulling someone's leg" means you're joking.

Every society has its own idioms whose meanings are not necessarily obvious to people from other cultures. In Portugal, for instance, a person who "doesn't give one for the box" is someone who can't say or do anything right. In Finland, if something "becomes gingerbread," that means it goes completely wrong. If someone in Brazil says "Fish don't pull wagons," he is encouraging you to eat red meat. Likewise, if an Australian is "as flash as a rat with a gold tooth," she's very pleased with herself. When you interact with people from other cultures, it's helpful to be aware that they may use phrases you're unfamiliar with.[33]

Cultural differences in language use can also make it hard to translate phrases or slogans from one culture to the next, and this has made for some humorous examples of mistranslated signs and advertisements:

- Sign in a Bangkok dry cleaner: "Drop your trousers here for best results!"
- Sign in a Copenhagen airline ticket office: "We take your bags and send them in all directions."
- Sign in a Hong Kong tailor shop: "Ladies may have a fit upstairs."
- Sign in an Acapulco restaurant: "The manager has personally passed all the water served here."
- Sign in a Moscow hotel room: "If this is your first visit to the USSR, you are welcome to it."

Jargon. A specific form of idiomatic communication that often separates co-cultures is jargon, or language whose technical meaning is understood by people within that co-culture but not necessarily by those outside it. Physicians, for instance, use precise medical terminology— what we might think of as "Doctorspeak"—to communicate among themselves about medical conditions and treatments. In most cases, this technical jargon is used only with people in the same co-culture. Therefore, although your doctor might tell her nurse that you have "ecchymosis on a distal phalange," she'd probably just tell you that you have a bruise on your fingertip. Similarly, if your dentist orders a "periapical radiograph," he just wants an X-ray of the roots of one of your teeth.

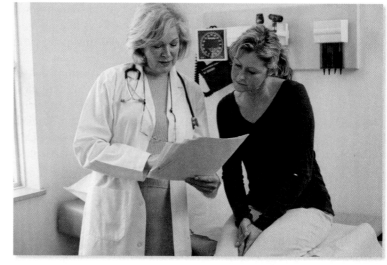

When others use jargon you don't understand, you can feel like an outsider. Good communicators use language that others can understand.

Not understanding jargon such as this can make you feel like an outsider. In addition, you might get the impression that doctors and dentists talk this way just to reinforce their in-group status. Jargon can serve an important function, however, by allowing people who use it to communicate with one another in ways that are very specific, efficient, and accurate.

Gestures. Cultures also differ a great deal in their use of gestures, which are movements, usually of the hand or the arm, that express ideas. The same gesture can have different meanings from society to society. For instance, U.S. American parents sometimes play the game "I've got your nose!" with infants by putting a thumb between the index and middle finger. This gesture means good luck in Brazil, but it is an obscene gesture in Russia and Indonesia. Similarly, holding up the index and pinky finger while holding down the middle and ring finger is a common gesture for fans of the University of Texas Longhorns. In Italy, however, this gesture is used to suggest that a man's wife has been unfaithful.[34]

The "At a Glance" box on page 55 provides a quick summary of the seven aspects of culture we have discussed here.

Communicating cross-culturally can be a challenge. If we're aware of cultural differences, however, those differences can help us to understand one another better. Do you ever feel that men and women don't speak quite the same language? In the next section, we examine several reasons why that may sometimes be the case.

At a Glance: Seven Aspects of Culture

Cultures differ along a number of dimensions. Here's a glance at the seven dimensions we have discussed.

Individualism and Collectivism	Whether a culture emphasizes the needs of the individual or the group
High- and Low-Context	Whether language is expected to be explicit or subtle
High- and Low-Power Distance	Whether power is widely or narrowly distributed among people
Masculine and Feminine	Whether traditionally masculine or feminine values are promoted
Monochronic and Polychronic	Whether time is seen as a finite commodity or an infinite resource
Uncertainty Avoidance	Whether people welcome or shy away from uncertainty
Communication Codes	How idioms, jargon, and gestures reflect cultural values

Learn It: In what ways do people from individualistic and collectivitistic cultures differ in their communication behaviors? Do people use more explicit language in high- or low-context cultures? Is power more evenly distributed in a low- or a high-power-distance culture? What makes a culture feminine, as opposed to masculine? How do people from monochronic and polychronic cultures differ in their use of time? In what ways does a culture's uncertainty avoidance affect the communication behaviors of its members? Why are idioms and gestures considered examples of cultural communication codes?

Try It: How sensitive are you to other cultures? Fill out the Intercultural Sensitivity Scale in the "Getting to Know You" box on page 56 to find out. If your score is lower than you'd like, remember that the first step to becoming more culturally sensitive is learning as much as you can about what culture is and how cultures vary, as you've read about in this chapter.

Reflect on It: How are culture's effects on communication learned and reinforced? What challenges have you experienced when communicating with people from other cultures?

3} Understanding Gender and Communication {

Gender has a profound influence on how we live our lives. What's the first thing you ask about a new baby? *"Is it a boy or a girl?"* Our gender is a defining feature of our identity, shaping the way we think, look, and communicate.

Although gender is powerful, it is far from simple or straightforward. The concept of gender includes many influences, such as psychological gender roles, biological sex, and sexual orientation. As we'll see, some interpersonal behaviors are strongly influenced by psychological gender roles, and others are more strongly influenced by biological sex or sexual orientation. In this section, we'll take a look at these components of gender, and we'll critique one of the most common explanations for why communicating across gender lines can be so challenging.

To reduce potential confusion, I will use the term "gender" as a broad term encompassing the influences of gender roles, biological sex, and sexual orientation in places where I'm not drawing specific distinctions among those terms. Otherwise, I will use "gender roles" in reference to masculinity, femininity, and androgyny. When addressing the differences between females and males, I'll use the term "biological sex" (or simply "sex"), and I'll use "sexual orientation" when discussing how one's sexuality influences behavior. See Figure 2.1 for an illustration of how I'm using these various terms.

> *The great renewal of the world will perhaps consist in this, that man and maid, freed of all false feelings and reluctances, will seek each other not as opposites, but as brother and sister, as neighbors, and will come together as human beings.*
>
> —Rainer Maria Rilke (1875–1926) Austro-German poet

Gender Roles and Communication

A role is a set of behaviors expected of someone in a particular social position. Expectations for male and female behavior make up a culture's **gender roles,** or norms for how women and men are supposed to act. In U.S. American society, for instance, men have traditionally been expected to be the breadwinners and women the homemakers. Men are supposed to be interested in cars, sports, and guns, whereas women are supposed to like shopping, cooking, and childrearing.[35] That doesn't mean men and women always *are* interested in those things, only that traditional gender roles suggest that they ought to be. Similarly, in many cultures, men are expected to make the decisions and occupy the positions of power, although this is not always the case.[36]

These and other expectations reflect our culturally influenced ideas about what it means to be a woman or a man. We can think of gender roles as falling into three specific categories: masculinity, femininity, and androgyny.

Gender role
A set of expectations for appropriate behavior that a culture typically assigns to an individual based on his or her biological sex.

The masculine gender role. When used in reference to people rather than cultures, the term **masculinity** refers to the set of gender role expectations a society typically

Masculinity
A gender role, typically assigned to men, that emphasizes strength, dominance, competition, and logical thinking.

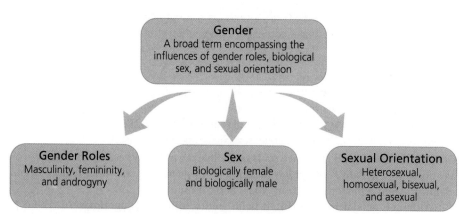

FIGURE 2.1 Diagram explaining gender, biological sex, and sexual orientation
Communication research has examined effects of gender roles, biological sex, and sexual orientation on interpersonal communication behavior.

assigns to men, although anyone can have masculine characteristics and communication behavior patterns. Specific masculine qualities might differ from one culture to the next, but the masculine role usually emphasizes strength, competition, independence, sexual aggressiveness, risk taking, logical thinking, and the acquisition of resources. Traditional masculinity also tends to reject weakness, emotional expressiveness, and any characteristic or behavior that resembles those of women.[37] In childhood, masculine behavior includes playing with toy guns and cars and competing in sports, since those activities emphasize strength, dominance, and winning.

The first thing many of us want to know about a new baby is its sex. Whether we do it consciously or not, many of us interact differently with male and female infants.

Masculine behavior in adulthood includes being a leader, being a breadwinner, and focusing more on action than on talk.

Like most things, masculinity has its good and bad points. For instance, the emphasis on strength and dominance can motivate and enable men to protect themselves and their families against threats. Thinking logically can help solve problems, and being willing to take risks can help someone achieve things he or she didn't believe were possible.

Masculine role expectations can also pose problems, however. For example, the emphasis on independence may keep men from asking for help—such as medical care—when they need it.[38] Focusing on competition and aggression can put men in harm's way and may account for the fact that men are more likely than women to be victims in every type of violent crime except rape.[39] Men are also much more likely than women to commit violent crimes. Masculinity also emphasizes risk taking; therefore, men are more likely than women to smoke, drink excessively, drink and drive, and fail to use seatbelts and sunscreen, and also more likely not to exercise, all of which increase their chances of illness, injury, and premature death.[40]

The feminine gender role. The set of role expectations a society typically assigns to women is called **femininity**, although this term can characterize either sex.[41] Like masculinity, femininity varies somewhat from culture to culture. In general, the feminine gender role typically emphasizes empathy and emotional expressiveness, a focus on relationships and relational maintenance, an interest in bearing and raising children, and attentiveness to appearance. Traditional femininity also emphasizes cooperation and submissiveness and tends to downplay intellectual achievement and career ambition.

Like masculinity, femininity has its pros and cons. The focus on caregiving has helped to ensure the survival of countless generations of children and families. The emphasis on empathy and relationships has allowed women to build strong, intimate friendships with one another and to excel at careers that require interpersonal sensitivity, such as teaching and counseling. Emphasizing cooperation instead of competition has probably also helped women to solve interpersonal problems in mutually beneficial ways.

Traditional femininity can also impose limits on the choices and options available to women. In the past it has discouraged many women from pursuing their education and achieving their career goals out of the belief that a woman's proper place is in the home. In addition, the emphasis on appearance has placed tremendous pressures on many women to achieve certain body types. As a result, women are far more likely than men to develop depression and eating disorders.[42] The focus on submissiveness has also made it difficult for some women to leave abusive relationships.[43]

The androgynous gender role. Masculinity and femininity are, to a large extent, opposing concepts; that is, part of what makes a trait masculine is that it is not feminine, and vice versa. Not everyone is best described as either feminine or masculine, however. Rather, some people seem to have both characteristics. For example, a woman might love children yet be very assertive, logical, and unemotional in her job. Similarly, a man may be strong and independent while still being sensitive and caring deeply and expressively for his friends. **Androgyny** is the term used to describe the combination of masculine and feminine characteristics. When a person strongly identifies with both gender roles, we say that he or she is psychologically androgynous.[44]

Being androgynous does not mean that a person is homosexual or bisexual, or that he or she wants to be of the other sex. Instead, it means the person identifies

Femininity
A gender role, typically assigned to women, that emphasizes expressive, nurturant behavior.

Androgyny
A gender role characterized by a combination of masculine and feminine traits.

strongly with aspects of both femininity and masculinity. As a result, an androgynous person is often less concerned about behaving in gender-appropriate ways than someone who is more strongly masculine or feminine would be.

For instance, an androgynous man would be unlikely to consider working as a nurse to be a threat to his gender identity. Likewise, an androgynous woman probably wouldn't be uncomfortable serving as her family's primary breadwinner. In 1994, British journalist Mark Simpson coined the term "meterosexual" to refer to a man, usually heterosexual, who has adopted the more feminine behavior of paying a great deal of attention to his appearance and grooming, making him an example of an androgynous person.[45]

How gender roles change and vary. Gender roles are never set in stone. Like most roles, they change over time, and they vary from culture to culture. Let's look at media representations of masculinity and femininity for some examples.

In the United States, images of women and men in movies, television shows, and advertisements have changed dramatically, even within the last few decades. In the 1950s, for instance, TV shows such as *Leave It to Beaver* and *Father Knows Best* depicted men, women, and children in very gender-specific ways. Fathers were strong, authoritative, and the sole breadwinners for their families. Mothers were homemakers whose concerns centered on their husbands, their children, and their housework. Boys were interested in masculine activities, such as fishing or playing with cars, and girls were portrayed doing feminine activities, such as playing with dolls or baking cakes. Later television shows, such as *Grey's Anatomy*, *Entourage*, and *Sex and the City*, have featured more flexible portrayals of femininity and masculinity in which women work outside the home, sometimes in traditionally masculine professions such as surgery, and men are demonstrative of their feelings, even with other men.

Androgyny is a term used to describe the combination of masculine and feminine characteristics. The ancient Hindu deity Ardhanari is masculine on one side and feminine on the other, symbolizing androgyny.

Gender roles also differ by culture. For example, in nomadic societies, where people move from place to place to hunt and forage, there is little difference in the way girls and boys are brought up. This may be because everyone's daily tasks are similar—to find food and water—so there is little need to differentiate the roles of girls and boys. By contrast, agricultural societies that rely on farming and herding for their food usually socialize boys and girls very differently, raising girls to tend to the children and home, and boys to tend to the livestock and crops.[46]

As we saw earlier, researchers have even applied the terms "masculine" and "feminine" to cultures themselves. In highly masculine cultures, such as Japan, Italy, and Mexico, men are admired for their strength, material success, and aggressiveness, whereas women are valued for their sensitivity and modesty. In feminine cultures, such as Sweden, Costa Rica, and Thailand, modesty, tenderness, and a concern for relationships are highly valued in both women and men.[47]

There's no question that gender role expectations influence our lives, but being masculine or feminine is not the same thing as being physically male or female. In the next section, we'll explore the meaning of biological sex and how it can affect communication behavior.

Biological Sex and Communication

The term "biological sex" refers to being female or male rather than feminine or masculine. Before we examine how biological sex influences communication behavior, let's take a closer look at what biological sex is and how it differs from gender roles.

When you were conceived you were neither male nor female. About seven weeks later, though, your genes activated your biological sex. Each of us has 23 pairs of chromosomes, which are strands of DNA, in the cells in our body. The 23rd pair is made up of the sex hormones that determine whether you're female or male. Human sex chromosomes are called X and Y, and we inherit one from each of our parents. Mothers supply us with one X chromosome. Fathers give us either a second X or a Y, depending on which one their sperm is carrying. If we get another X, then we grow up female. If we get a Y, then we become male.

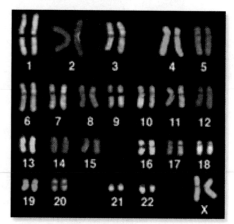

You have 23 pairs of chromosomes in nearly every cell of your body. The 23rd pair determines your biological sex. You are biologically male if you have an X and a Y chromosome. If you have a pair of X chromosomes, as illustrated here, you are biologically female.

We tend to think of "male" and "female" as the only categories of biological sex, but some people have difficulty fitting into one or the other group. There are at least three reasons for this difficulty—psychological, genetic, and anatomical—and we'll take a brief look at each one. Understanding the diversity in forms of biological sex will help us appreciate why studying sex differences in communication behavior is often more complex than it may seem to be at first.

Psychological differences affect biological sex. Some people experience conflict between the sex they were born into and the sex they feel they should be. For instance, a person may see herself as male even though she was born female. The term "transgendered people" is used to describe individuals who experience this type of conflict.[48] Emotional distress and depression are common among transgendered people, who may struggle with the feeling of being "trapped in the wrong body."[49] Some transgendered people undergo hormone therapy or sex-reassignment surgery to bring their physical bodies in line with their images of themselves. We often refer to people who have undergone these procedures as "transsexual people."[50]

Genetic differences affect biological sex. Not everyone is born with either XX (female) or XY (male) chromosomes. Women with Turner's syndrome, for example, have an X chromosome only (XO), and those with trisomy X have an extra X chromosome (XXX). Men with Klinefelter syndrome also have an extra X chromosome (XXY).

Other combinations are also possible, such as XXXX or XXYY. People with these disorders are prone to behavioral and developmental problems, which can influence how they interact with others. Researchers estimate that about 1 in 1,700 people is born with some type of chromosomal disorder.[51]

Anatomical differences affect biological sex. Finally, some people have internal sexual organs that don't match their external appearance. For instance, a child might be born with a penis but have ovaries instead of testicles. Doctors call this condition "intersex," and it can be caused by delayed physical development or by hormonal problems.[52] People with this condition are often able to lead normal, healthy lives, although questions about their correct biological sex may make it difficult for others in their social environments to accept them.[53]

Like gender roles, biological sex is a fundamental part of a person's identity. No matter what a person's biological sex and gender role are, however, his or her interpersonal behavior can also be influenced by a third aspect of gender, sexual orientation. We will examine this aspect next.

Sexual Orientation and Communication

Sexual orientation describes the sex or sexes we are sexually attracted to. Scientists disagree concerning the extent to which sexual orientation is determined by genetics (the way biological sex is) or by socialization (the way gender roles are). Sexual orientation isn't always considered an aspect of gender, but a growing body of research suggests that it influences communication behavior just as gender roles and biological sex do. We'll look briefly at four patterns of sexual orientation: heterosexuality, homosexuality, bisexuality, and asexuality.

Sexual orientation A characteristic determining the sex or sexes to which someone is sexually attracted.

Heterosexuality. **Heterosexuality** refers to being physically and romantically attracted to people of the other sex. Several studies have confirmed that the majority of adults in most societies have experienced mostly heterosexual attraction and have engaged in primarily heterosexual behavior.[54] One possible reason for this tendency is that heterosexual interaction has the potential to support reproduction, whereas other forms of sexual interaction don't. Another reason is that, in most cultures, heterosexuality is the most socially approved form of sexuality. Therefore, heterosexual people in those cultures enjoy a level of social support that others often do not.[55]

Heterosexuality A sexual orientation characterized by sexual interest in members of the other sex.

Homosexuality. The term **homosexuality** refers to romantic and sexual attraction to members of one's own sex. Homosexual males are commonly referred to as "gay" and female homosexuals are typically called "lesbian." Although sexual contact between members of the same sex has been common across cultures and time periods, homosexuality did not really become a recognized part of a person's identity until the 1800s.[56] Before that point, it was not uncommon for adults of the same sex to sleep in the same bed or to write love letters to each other. Such behaviors were interpreted as expressions of affection rather than markers of sexual orientation.[57]

Homosexuality A sexual orientation characterized by sexual interest in members of one's own sex.

Researchers have come up with many different theories to explain homosexuality. Some studies have focused on the social influences of parents and other role models, whereas others have emphasized physiological or genetic explanations.[58] According to a national survey conducted by the Centers for Disease Control and Prevention (CDC), 2.3% of U.S. American men aged 15–44 identified themselves as homosexual, although 6.5% reported having had sexual interaction with another man. Similarly, 1.3% of U.S. American women identified themselves as homosexual, although 11% reported having had sexual interaction with another woman.[59]

Fact or Fiction?
Heterosexual Relationships Are More Stable and Satisfying Than Gay or Lesbian Relationships

There's a great deal of disagreement these days about whether homosexual adults should be allowed to marry. At present, same-sex marriage is only legal in a few U.S. states. By contrast, 17 states have constitutional provisions banning it. Opponents of same-sex marriage have long claimed that gay and lesbian relationships are less stable and more dysfunctional than heterosexual relationships. Is that argument true?

At this point the answer appears to be no. In fact, several studies have shown that same-sex romantic relationships are just as stable and satisfying, on average, as opposite-sex relationships. For example, one study matched samples of heterosexual and homosexual men and women who were in serious romantic relationships. After ruling out any differences in the participants' age, education level, ethnicity, and length of relationship, the researchers found no differences between the heterosexual and homosexual samples in how close or satisfying their relationships were.

These findings don't suggest that all gay and lesbian couples are happy and problem-free. They indicate, however, that same-sex relationships can be just as stable and satisfying as heterosexual relationships. Whatever your individual beliefs about the morality of homosexual relationships, the argument that they are prone to dysfunction simply does not stand up to the evidence.

Ask Yourself:

- Where do you stand on this issue? What type of evidence is the most persuasive to you?

- What do you think contributes to relationship stability and satisfaction?

Sources: Kurdek, L. A. (1992). Relationship stability and relationship satisfaction in cohabiting gay and lesbian couples: A prospective longitudinal test of the contextual and interdependence models. *Journal of Social and Personal Relationships, 9*, 125–142; Kurdek, L. A. (1998). Relationship outcomes and their predictors: Longitudinal evidence from heterosexual married, gay cohabiting, and lesbian cohabiting couples. *Journal of Marriage and the Family, 60*, 553–568; Peplau, L. A., & Cochra, S. D. (1980, August). *Sex differences in values concerning love relationships.* Paper presented at annual meeting of the American Psychological Association, Montreal, Quebec, Canada.

Between 1% and 3% of the U.S. American adult population self-identifies as homosexual. Many societies throughout history have persecuted homosexual women and men for interacting in ways those societies deem abnormal or immoral.

As you probably know, the issue of whether homosexual adults should be allowed to marry or form legal domestic partnerships has been contentious in the United States for some time. The argument against formalizing homosexual romantic relationships often implies that such relationships are inherently less stable than heterosexual marriages. Is this true? Check out the "Fact or Fiction?" box above to find out.

At a Glance: Three Components of Gender

In this section, we discussed three primary components that make up the experience of gender:

Gender Roles	Psychological orientation toward masculinity, femininity, or androgyny
Biological Sex	Genetic characteristics that distinguish females from males
Sexual Orientation	Sexual attraction toward members of the other sex, the same sex, both sexes, or neither sex

Bisexuality. **Bisexuality** refers to having romantic and/or sexual attraction to both women and men. Although bisexuals have some level of attraction to both sexes, they are not necessarily attracted to both sexes equally.[60] Moreover, bisexual people don't usually maintain long-term romantic relationships with members of both sexes. Rather, they often have a romantic relationship with a partner of one sex while engaging in or thinking about sexual interaction with people of the other sex.[61] According to the CDC survey mentioned earlier, 1.8% of men and 2.8% of women in the United States identify themselves as bisexual.[62]

Bisexuality
A sexual orientation characterized by sexual interest in both women and men.

Asexuality. The term **asexuality** is used to describe people who have very little interest in sex. As you might imagine, this orientation is fairly uncommon. In one British study, for example, only 1% of respondents indicated they had never really been sexually attracted to anyone.[63] Researchers aren't sure whether asexuality is a type of disorder or whether it simply represents another sexual orientation. Asexuality is not the same as celibacy, which is the practice of abstaining from sex. In fact, some asexual people do have sex, and most celibate people are not asexual.

Asexuality
A sexual orientation characterized by a general lack of interest in sex.

A quick summary of the three primary components of gender appears in the "At a Glance" box above.

Some Explanations for Gendered Communication

These days, it's a cliché to say that women and men have different styles of communicating. Moreover, based on the complexities we've just discussed, it doesn't seem very accurate to approach men and women as definitively masculine or feminine. From time to time, maybe you feel as though talking with a person of the other sex is like talking to someone from another planet. Popular author John Gray captured this sentiment in his highly successful book *Men Are from Mars, Women Are from Venus*.[64] According to Gray, "Men and women differ in all areas of their lives. Not only do men and women communicate differently but they think, feel, perceive, react, respond, love, need, and appreciate differently. They almost seem to be from different planets, speaking different languages and needing different nourishment."[65]

In contrast to Gray, communication experts don't believe that men and women are from different planets. Nevertheless, some researchers, including communication scholar Julia Wood and linguist Deborah Tannen, do argue that men and women constitute different "gender cultures."[66] Their thesis is that each sex constitutes its own culture, with its own rules and values. The fundamental difference between the two cultures is that each sex values different components of relationships. Specifically, women are taught to value the communicating of intimacy and emotional support, whereas men are taught to value the sharing of activities.

When Zach and his friend Sergio get together, for instance, their time is likely to revolve around a mutual activity, such as going for a hike or watching car racing on

> *From my perspective, the best scientific evidence tells us that sex, gender, and sexual orientation all play a part in how people communicate, but not as large a part as we might believe. When it comes to communication, people are more alike than different.*

TV, because for them, sharing activities is a means of bonding. Sometimes they talk about personal topics, but to them, their conversation is of lesser importance than the shared activity. For Zach's wife Aisha and her friend Thérèse, however, time together is more likely to revolve around conversation. Whatever shared activity they may be doing is often of lesser importance than the conversation itself.

The concept of gender cultures further maintains that when women and men communicate with each other, they each bring their own rules and values to the table. Because these rules and values differ, the result is often gender clash, or the experience of each sex not understanding the other.[67] For instance, when Sergio's daughter was undergoing treatment for leukemia, Aisha couldn't understand why Zach didn't invite him over "just to talk," but instead invited him to a baseball game. This action seemed insensitive to Aisha, who thought Zach should be a better friend to Sergio by getting him to open up about his feelings. As Zach explained, however, going to a ball game and just "hanging out" with no expectation of a deep conversation was his way of letting Sergio know he cared. He also assured Aisha that Sergio would interpret it that way.

There's little question that communicating across genders can be challenging and that several communicative behaviors appear to be affected by sex, gender roles, and/or sexual orientation, as we'll discuss in the next section. Some scholars disagree, however, that the sexes actually constitute different cultures. For example, communication scientists Brant Burleson and Adrianne Kunkel have pointed out that even though the "different cultures" idea seems intuitive, it has not been well supported by the data.[68] In fact, several studies have demonstrated that women and men are more similar than different in the forms of communication they value.[69]

In their analysis of supportive communication, for instance, Burleson and Kunkel reported substantial similarity—not difference—in the value both sexes place on supportive communication skills, such as comforting and listening. They also reported that women and men have similar goals in support situations and consider the same types of messages to be supportive. Interestingly, both women and men prefer to seek support from women instead of men.[70]

In U.S. American culture, women often practice expressive talk, treating communication as a way to establish closeness.

In each of these outcomes, men and women behave as though they are from the same culture, not different cultures. Indeed, the lack of scientific evidence for the gender cultures idea has led communication researcher Kathryn Dindia to suggest a more modest metaphor for gendered communication: "Men are from North Dakota, women are from South Dakota."[71]

Each of these three perspectives—the sexes come from different planets, the sexes comprise different cultures, and the sexes are more similar than different—is intuitively appealing in its own way. In fact, it's easy for many of us to "see" sex differences in communication behavior almost anywhere we look. For instance, you might have a disagreement with a supervisor of the other sex and chalk it up to a sex difference, even if it really wasn't. Societies also find humor in sex differences, making them the focus of jokes and comedic movies and television shows. This practice probably adds to our tendency to see sex differences as large and pervasive.

Just because an idea is intuitive or seems to reflect your personal experience doesn't mean the idea is accurate, however. This is an example of why scientific tests are so important: They allow us to subject our ideas to rigorous scrutiny. From my perspective, the best scientific evidence tells us that sex, gender roles, and sexual orientation all play a part in how people communicate, but not as large a part as we might think. Women and men differ from each other in many ways—as do masculine, feminine, and androgynous people, and heterosexual, homosexual, bisexual, and asexual people. When it comes to communication behavior, however, we are more alike than different. The research tells us that John Gray's claim that women and men "differ in all areas of their lives" may be an exaggeration. It's true that our differences are often more apparent to us than our similarities, but the scientific evidence suggests that, as communicators, we are not as different as we often think we are.

Learn It: How do masculinity, femininity, and androgyny compare with one another? In what ways do psychological, genetic, and anatomical differences influence one's biological sex? What is a sexual orientation? What are the principal ways of explaining gendered communication, and how well are those explanations supported by scientific evidence?

Try It: What gender role best describes you? Fill out the questionnaire in the "Getting to Know You" box on page 66 to find out if you are highly masculine, highly feminine, or androgynous.

Reflect on It: How do you feel about people whose sexual orientation is different from yours? How do you think those feelings affect your communication with them? What are the biggest challenges you have noticed in male-female communication?

Try It Activity

Below is a list of personality characteristics. How well does each characteristic describe you? Using a 1–5 scale, write a number next to each item indicating how well you think it describes you. A score of 1 means it doesn't describe you at all, and 5 means it describes you very well.

1. _____ Affectionate
2. _____ Athletic
3. _____ Feminine
4. _____ Forceful
5. _____ Sympathetic
6. _____ Willing to take risks
7. _____ Sensitive to the needs of others
8. _____ Dominant
9. _____ Eager to soothe hurt feelings
10. _____ Aggressive
11. _____ Loves children
12. _____ Masculine

When you're done, add up all your scores on the odd-numbered items (1, 3, 5, etc.). This is your *femininity* score. Next, add up all your scores on the even-numbered items (2, 4, 6, etc.). This is your *masculinity* score. Each score should be between 6 and 30. If your femininity score is much higher than your masculinity score, then you are highly feminine. If the opposite is true, then you are highly masculine. Finally, if you scored high (say, above 25) on both scales, this indicates that you are *androgynous*.

Sources: Bem, S. L. (1974). The measurement of psychological androgyny. *Journal of Consulting and Clinical Psychology, 42,* 155–162; see also Ballard-Reisch, D., & Elton, M. (1992). Gender orientation and the Bem Sex Role Inventory: A psychological construct revisited. *Sex Roles, 27,* 291–306.

4} How Gender Affects Communication {

Our gender roles, biological sex, and sexual orientation all play a part in how we communicate with others. Whether you think of the sexes as coming from different planets, constituting different cultures, or just plain being different, you can probably appreciate the influence of gender roles, biological sex, and sexual orientation on several types of communicative behaviors. In this section, we'll look at differences in language (the use of spoken and written words) and nonverbal behavior (the ways we communicate without words) to better understand how these various aspects of gender affect our interactions with others. We will also learn more about language in Chapter 5 and nonverbal behavior in Chapter 6.

> *When men and women agree, it is only in their conclusions; their reasons are always different.*
>
> —George Santayana (1863–1952)
> U.S. American philosopher

Before we go on, we need to consider two important points. First, even though gender includes the influences of biological sex, gender roles, and sexual orientation, most of the research we're going to discuss has simply compared the communication behaviors of men and women. As a result, we know quite a bit about sex differences but comparatively little about the effects of gender roles or sexual orientation on communication.

Second, although some behaviors differ between the sexes, other behaviors do not. In addition, some sex differences are large, but many others are fairly small. In recent years, several scholars have encouraged communication researchers and students to be cautious when looking at sex differences in behavior so that we don't exaggerate them beyond the findings that the evidence actually supports.[72]

Men often practice instrumental talk, treating communication as a way to solve problems.

Gender and Verbal Communication

Research shows that gender influences both the content and the style of our speech. In this section, we'll take a closer look at three gender effects:

- Expressive and instrumental talk
- Language and power
- Gendered linguistic styles

Expressive and instrumental talk. Some communication scholars have argued that women and men grow up in different "speech communities," meaning they have different norms and beliefs concerning the purpose of communication.[73] This idea is similar to the "gender cultures" theory, but it focuses more specifically on differences in speech and communication behaviors. In particular, these researchers believe that women are socialized to practice **expressive talk,** which means they are taught to view communication as the primary way to establish closeness and intimacy in relationships. In contrast, men are taught to practice **instrumental talk,** or to see communication as a means to solve problems and accomplish things.[74]

Expressive talk Verbal communication whose purpose is to express emotions and build relationships.

Instrumental talk Verbal communication whose purpose is to convey information.

To understand these different approaches to communication, consider the following scenario. Shannon has noticed that whenever she talks to her co-worker Max about a problem, he always responds by telling her what she should do to fix it. The following exchange illustrates this point.

> **Shannon:** My boss is totally blaming me for losing one of our biggest accounts—but it's completely his fault! He's the one who never returns their calls and wouldn't let me help them last year when one of their shipments was delayed.

> **Max:** You should call your regional manager and tell her what's going on. Show her the paperwork from the order that got delayed so she'll see that you tried to help.

Max's response is a good example of instrumental talk. When Shannon explained her problem, Max viewed it as a request for help, and he offered his suggestions for how to make the situation better. Contrast Max's response with the response Shannon got when she shared the same problem with her sister Sabrina:

> **Sabrina:** That's so unfair! I'm sorry he's blaming you—you must be so frustrated, especially since it's his fault in the first place.

Sabrina's response is an example of expressive talk. Instead of suggesting how Shannon might solve the problem, Sabrina acknowledged Shannon's feelings and expressed her own unhappiness at Shannon's frustration. According to communication scholars such as Julia Wood, this is a common difference between women and men. That is, for women the purpose of sharing problems is to express your feelings. From this perspective, a good friend should listen and empathize. For men, though, the purpose of sharing problems is to get advice on how to solve them. From this perspective, a good friend should offer his opinions about what to do.[75]

How do women and men become socialized into different speech communities? One of the earliest influences seems to be the games they are encouraged to play as children. If you think back to your own childhood, you probably remember that at an early age most children played only with other children of their same sex[76] and that boys and girls played very different games. Boys' games, such as football or building models, tend to emphasize structure, rules, and competition. In contrast, girls' games, such as playing house or jumping rope, emphasize cooperation, sensitivity, and flexibility. One possible result of these patterns is that girls learn to use language to express their feelings and to build camaraderie, whereas boys learn to use language to give instructions and share information.[77]

With respect to sexual orientation, the common stereotype of gay men as feminine and lesbians as masculine would suggest that gay men engage in more expressive and less instrumental talk than heterosexual men, whereas lesbians engage in more instrumental and less expressive talk than heterosexual women. Research indicates that both of these predictions are accurate.[78] Importantly, this observation doesn't mean that gay men talk like women or that lesbian women talk like men. Rather, it suggests only that gay men's speech patterns are more expressive and less instrumental than those of heterosexual men, and that lesbian women's speech is more instrumental and less expressive than that of heterosexual women.

Language and power. For years, researchers have noticed that men and women talk to each other in a style that reflects how superiors and subordinates to talk each other.[79] Powerful forms of speech, such as those used by superiors, include behaviors such as talking more, interrupting more frequently, giving more directions, and expressing more opinions. Less powerful forms of speech, such as those used by subordinates, include asking more questions, using more hedges ("sort of," "might be") and disclaimers ("I could be wrong, but . . ."), and speaking less overall.

In an extensive review of the current research, communication scholars Pam Kalbfleisch and Anita Herold found that, on average, men use more powerful forms of speech than

Language is described as more powerful or less powerful based on communication behaviors such as interrupting, giving directions, expressing opinions, asking questions, using disclaimers, and speaking more or speaking less. From the perspective of language and power, how would you characterize the speaking styles of the three judges on *American Idol*?

How Do We Know?
Women Are Not More Talkative Than Men

In this section, you learned that women and men speak approximately the same number of words per day—roughly 16,000 on average—which is contrary to the stereotype that women are more talkative than men. How do we know this?

The study that identified this finding took place between 1998 and 2005 and involved almost 400 students from universities in the United States and Mexico. Each participant wore a device called an electronically activated recorder, or EAR. The EAR is a digital voice recorder that unobtrusively tracks a person's real-world interactions with others by recording 30-second snippets of sound every 12.5 minutes while the person is awake. The researchers then transcribed each recording and counted the number of words spoken, analyzing them as a function of the percentage of waking time the EAR recorded.

When the researchers compared the results by sex, they found that women and men spoke, on average, 16,215 and 15,669 words per day, respectively. These totals were not significantly different, suggesting that the stereotype that women are more talkative than men isn't accurate.

Ask Yourself:

- How valid is the use of the EAR to measure how talkative people are? What other methods might be used to measure talkativeness?

- Why do you think the stereotype of women as talkative exists? Do you see this perception changing at all?

From Me to You:

- One reason why this study is so important is that it provides scientific evidence that a common stereotype about women and men isn't true. That doesn't mean all stereotypes are false—they aren't—but it does illustrate that some of our commonsense notions about communication may be inaccurate. When you encounter a stereotype, take a minute to think about how accurate it is before you use it to guide your behavior.

Source: Mehl, M. R., Vazire, S., Ramírez-Esparza, N., Slatcher, R. B., & Pennebaker, J. W. (2007). Are women really more talkative than men? *Science, 317*, 82.

women do.[80] For instance, contrary to the commonly held stereotype, women are not more talkative than men. Rather, both men and women speak approximately 16,000 words in an average day.[81]

In fact, men often talk more than women do, particularly about impersonal topics such as money or work.[82] Men also interrupt more frequently, give more directions, and express more opinions—all characteristics of powerful speech.[83] By contrast, women's language use is more attentive to others.[84] Compared with men, women ask more questions and use more disclaimers and hedges in their speech.[85] The following exchange between two colleagues at an advertising firm illustrates more powerful and less powerful forms of communication.

> **Emelie:** I don't know if this is a good idea, but I sort of think we should keep the new ad slogans secret until we launch the marketing campaign, don't you?

> **Stefan:** Find out what the client wants and then we'll decide. The slogans aren't that great anyway. We need to bring some new account reps in on this project and get some fresh ideas in here.

In this exchange, Emelie starts off with a disclaimer ("I don't know if this is a good idea"); she then hedges her opinion ("I sort of think"); and she concludes with a question that seeks validation from others ("don't you?"). By contrast, Stefan's words are directive ("Find out what the client wants") and opinionated ("The slogans aren't that great"). Also, unlike Emelie, Stefan doesn't end his statement by asking if others agree with him. These are examples of less powerful (Emelie) and more powerful (Stefan) forms of speech.

Although these research findings are important, keep in mind two critical points. First, the findings don't apply equally to every woman and man. You can probably think of women who use very powerful styles of speaking and men whose language styles are less powerful. Whenever we compare groups (such as women and men) with each other, we're focusing specifically on *average* differences. Clearly, there can be many individual exceptions to whatever differences we discover. Second, even if a man uses more powerful speech patterns than a woman does, that doesn't necessarily mean that he *is* more powerful. Rather, he is simply using the speech patterns that are typical for men in our society.

A particularly troubling example of the difference between powerful and powerless speech is the use of linguistic violence, which is language that degrades and dehumanizes a group of people.[86] One way the more powerful nature of men's speech is expressed, for instance, is through terms that objectify and degrade women.[87] You can probably think of words that have this effect. Using language to put down other people can constitute a type of emotional violence in the same way that hitting can constitute a type of physical violence.

Unfortunately, linguistic violence is frequently directed not only against women but also against people who are homosexual, bisexual, and/or transgendered. These communities are frequently marginalized, meaning they are subjected to unfair discrimination and prejudice on the basis of their sexual orientation or gender identity.[88] One way marginalization manifests itself is in the form of linguistic violence against members of these communities. Just as you can likely think of some derogatory terms used to put down women, you can probably think of similar terms used to degrade gay, lesbian, bisexual, and/or transgendered people.

Gendered linguistic styles. Thus far, we have looked at gender differences in the purpose of speech (expressive versus instrumental) and in how powerful speech sounds. Research suggests that men and women differ in still other aspects of their speech patterns, or linguistic styles.

For example, women are more likely than men to use second- and third-person pronouns ("we," "they") and to make references to emotions ("hurt," "scared") when they talk. They also use more intensive adverbs, such as describing someone as *really* tall or *so* smart. Women also speak in longer sentences than men do, on average.[89] As an example, Carmen might describe her new house in this way:

> We love our new home! It has a really big yard where the neighborhood children can play, and two very large guestrooms on the ground floor for when we have company. We also have a really nice kitchen, and the master suite is so spacious!

Men's linguistic style makes greater use of self-references ("I" statements) and judgmental adjectives such as "good" or "worthless." Compared with women, men also use more references to quantity, such as informing other people that something "costs four hundred fifty dollars" or someone "is six feet, eight inches tall." Men are also more likely than women to use location statements ("It's in the back") and incomplete sentences ("Nice job.").[90] For example, Carmen's husband Diego might describe their new home in this way:

> The house is great. It's got twenty-two hundred square feet, plus a three-car detached garage. There's about an acre and a half of land. I got a good deal on the mortgage, too. Five point one percent for thirty years.

In these examples, Carmen uses the pronoun "we" whereas Diego uses the pronoun "I." Carmen also uses intensive adverbs ("really big yard," "very large guestroom"), whereas Diego makes several references to quantity ("twenty-two hundred square feet," "acre and a half of land"). Carmen's sentences are also longer than Diego's, on average, and Diego uses an incomplete sentence ("Five point one percent for thirty years"), whereas Carmen does not. Only a few studies have examined whether these patterns are influenced by sexual orientation, and most of the results indicate that they are not.[91] Whether gender role affects the use of these linguistic styles is still unclear.

Gender and Nonverbal Communication

At the beginning of this section on gender, we explained that nonverbal communication is communication that occurs without the use of words. We use several nonverbal behaviors to communicate, including gestures, facial expressions, tone of voice, and the use of personal space. To understand gender and nonverbal communication, let's look at three specific examples:

- Touch and body movement
- Emotional communication
- Affectionate behavior

Touch and body movement. Touch is an important form of nonverbal communication because it can express warmth and intimacy as well as power and dominance (as we'll see in Chapter 6). Many studies have shown that women and men exhibit different patterns of touch behavior. In an analysis of several of these studies, one research team discovered that sex differences in touch depend on whether the touch involves two adults or an adult and a child.[92] When only adults are interacting, the researchers found that:

- Men are more likely to touch women than women are to touch men, unless the touch is occurring as part of a greeting (such as a handshake).
- Other-sex touch is more common than same-sex touch.
- In same-sex pairs, women touch each other more than men do, but this difference is smaller in close friendships than among acquaintances.

In general, these results show that men do more touching than women in other-sex relationships, whereas women do more touching than men in same-sex relationships. The patterns are quite different when one of the parties is a child, however:

- Same-sex touch is more common than other-sex touch.
- Women are more likely than men to initiate touch.
- Boys and girls are about equally likely to be touched.

These patterns may also be affected by culture. In feminine cultures, for instance, women and men may behave more similarly than in masculine cultures.

In addition to touch, sex appears to affect other forms of body movement. Compared with women, men use more body movement in general, they prefer a greater amount of personal space around them, and they try harder to preserve their personal space when it is violated.[93] They also use more relaxed body movements. Both men and women appear to be more relaxed in their posture and gesturing when talking to men than to women.[94]

With respect to personal space, however, some evidence suggests that gender role, rather than biological sex (or sexual orientation), is the most influential factor. For instance, one experiment found that masculine people (whether male or female) maintained a greater amount of personal distance from others than did feminine people (whether male or female).[95]

Emotional communication. Common stereotypes would have us believe that women are more "emotional" than men. We often expect women to cry more than men at sad movies, for instance, or to be more expressive of their feelings for one another than men are. Indeed, a 2001 Gallup Poll found that adults in the United States are significantly more likely to use the term *emotional* to describe women than men.[96]

Even if women are more emotional than men, what does that mean, exactly? Does it mean that women *experience* more emotion than men or just that they're more willing to *express* the emotions they feel? Going further, if women are more expressive than men, does that difference apply to every kind of emotion or just to certain ones? In this section, we'll look at what research tells us about the effects of sex on emotional communication.

To begin with, women generally express more positive emotions—such as happiness or joy—than men do.[97] The most basic behavior we use to communicate positive emotions is smiling, and several studies have found that women smile more than men.[98] Women also use more affiliation behaviors than men do. Affiliation behaviors demonstrate feelings of closeness or attachment to someone else. Common affiliation behaviors include eye contact, head nods, pleasant facial expressions, and warm vocal tones.[99] Research even suggests that women are more likely than men to express positive emotions in e-mail messages through the use of "smileys".[100]

When it comes to negative emotions, though, sex differences appear to vary according to which emotion we consider. Some studies have found that men are more likely than women to express anger, but other studies haven't found a difference.[101] Men do appear to express jealousy in more intense forms than women do, by engaging in dangerous, aggressive behaviors such as getting drunk, confronting the romantic rival, or becoming sexually involved with someone else.[102] Women are more likely than men to express the emotions of sadness and depression, however.[103]

Do women actually experience more emotion than men, or are they just more likely to express it? In a pair of studies, researchers Ann Kring and Albert Gordon found that although women were more expressive than men, they didn't report actually experiencing any more emotion than men did. Rather, men and women reported experiencing the same amount of emotion. Women simply expressed their emotions more frequently and openly, whereas men were more likely to mask their feelings.[104]

Although most research on gender and emotion has focused on biological sex, some studies have examined the influence of gender roles or sexual orientation. In one study, participants reported on their psychological gender roles, using the same instrument that appeared in the "Getting to Know You" box on page 66. Afterward, they watched film clips that were emotionally arousing while researchers videotaped and subsequently coded their facial expressions. The researchers found that both women and men were more emotionally expressive if they were androgynous than if they were primarily masculine or feminine.[105]

In another experiment, lesbian and gay romantic couples took part in conflict discussions in a laboratory while their facial expressions were videotaped. The researchers found that, compared with gay men, lesbians were more expressive of both positive and negative emotion. This finding suggests that the biological sex difference in expression—meaning that women are more expressive than men—is not really affected by sexual orientation.[106]

Affectionate behavior. Affectionate communication includes those behaviors we use to express our love and appreciation for people we care about. As you might have expected, several studies have shown that women use more nonverbal affection behaviors—such as hugging, kissing, and handholding—than men do.[107] This observation appears to be especially true in same-sex relationships. That is, the sex differences in nonverbal affection behaviors are even greater when women and men are interacting with same-sex friends or relatives than when they are interacting with members of the other sex.[108]

Why are women more affectionate than men? Researchers have offered several explanations. One theory is that because girls receive more affection than boys do, they are more likely to grow up perceiving interpersonal interactions as opportunities for communicating affection.[109] Another explanation is that men are more likely than women to see affectionate communication as a feminine behavior, so they avoid expressing affection out of a fear of appearing feminine.[110] A third possible reason is that the different balances of hormones typically found in men and women make women more likely to behave affectionately.[111] Any or all of these factors may play a part in making women more affectionate than men.

Masculinity and femininity are also related to affectionate behavior, although not in the way you might guess. Because affection is often thought of as a "feminine" way of behaving—at least in North American cultures—you might expect that the more feminine people are, the more affectionate they are. Several studies have found this to be the case. The same studies have shown, however, that the more *masculine* people are, the more affectionate they are.[112] As with emotional expressiveness (which we discussed above), it appears that people who score highly on both femininity and masculinity are particularly affectionate.

Only a small number of studies have examined the influence of sexual orientation on affectionate communication. One large national U.S. survey reported that both gay men and lesbian women were more expressive of affection and positive emotion within their romantic relationships than were heterosexual spouses with children. They were not more expressive than heterosexual spouses without children or heterosexual unmarried partners, however.[113]

Two other studies looked specifically at affectionate behavior between adult men and their fathers. The results indicated that fathers are most affectionate with heterosexual sons, less affectionate if they are unsure of their sons' sexual orientation, and least affectionate with sons who are homosexual or bisexual.[114]

Considered together, these studies present a complex picture of how gender roles, biological sex, and sexual orientation influence verbal and nonverbal communication behaviors. Sometimes these factors make a difference, other times they don't, and in some cases they matter in unexpected ways, as when masculinity is positively related to affectionate communication. In addition, as we discussed earlier, even when we do find differences—for example, women use longer sentences than men, or lesbian women use more instrumental speech than heterosexual women—we must keep in mind that these are average differences. Thus, not every woman speaks in longer sentences than every man. Rather, women use longer sentences than men do *on average*.

As students of interpersonal communication, we should take care not to exaggerate or oversimplify the influence of gender roles, sex, or sexual orientation on communication behavior. These features often influence how we behave, but they do not affect every aspect of our lives at all times, as John Gray suggests. Human communication is more nuanced than that. In addition, our interpersonal interaction is affected by many influences besides the gender role, biological sex, or sexual orientation with which we identify.

Learn It: What is the difference between expressive and instrumental talk? How do gender roles, biological sex, and sexual orientation influence the experience and expression of emotion?

Try It: The next time you talk to an adult of the other sex, pay attention to your language style. Is your speech more instrumental or more expressive? Are you using powerful or powerless speech? Think about how your language style influences how effectively you are communicating.

Reflect on It: How would you characterize your verbal and nonverbal behavior? What role do you think your biological sex, gender role, and sexual orientation play in how you communicate with others?

} Master the Chapter {

Section 1} Understanding Culture and Communication (p. 41)

I. **Understanding Culture and Communication**
   A. **What is culture?**
      1. Distinguishing between in-groups and out-groups
      2. Acquiring a culture

   - Culture consists of the learned, shared symbols, language, values, and norms that distinguish one group of people from another.

   B. **The components of culture**
      1. Symbols
      2. Language
      3. Values
      4. Norms

   - Cultures vary in their symbols, language, values, and norms.

   C. **Cultures and co-cultures**
      1. What are co-cultures?
      2. The bases of co-cultures
      3. Can you belong to multiple co-cultures?

   - Co-cultures are groups of people who share values, customs, and norms related to a mutual interest or characteristic.

   D. **Communicating with cultural awareness**

   - Communicating with cultural awareness means paying attention to your cultural values and biases and remembering that others don't always share them.

Section 2} How Culture Affects Communication (p. 47)

II. **How Culture Affects Communication**
   A. **Individualism and collectivism**

   - Individualistic cultures emphasize the importance of individuality and personal achievement, whereas collectivistic cultures emphasize the needs of the family and community.

   B. **High- and low-context cultures**

   - People in low-context cultures expect language to be direct and explicit; those in high-context cultures rely more on contextual cues to interpret verbal statements.

   C. **Low- and high-power distance**

   - In a high-power-distance culture, most of the power is held by relatively few people; in a low-power-distance culture, power is more equitably distributed among people.

   D. **Masculine and feminine cultures**

   - Masculine cultures value competition and achievement and maintain largely different expectations for women and men. In contrast, feminine cultures value nurturant behavior and do not enforce rigidly different expectations for women and men.

E. Monochronic and polychronic cultures	• Time is considered to be a finite commodity in a monochronic culture; it is considered to be more infinite in a polychronic culture.
F. Uncertainty avoidance	• Cultures vary in their uncertainty avoidance, or their aversion to novelty and uncertainty.

G. Cultural communication codes
  1. Idioms
  2. Jargon
  3. Gestures
	• Cultures differ in their use of communication codes, such as idioms and gestures, which often have meaning only to people in a given culture.

Section 3} Understanding Gender and Communication (p. 55)

III. Understanding Gender and Communication	

A. Gender roles and communication
  1. The masculine gender role
  2. The feminine gender role
  3. The androgynous gender role
  4. How gender roles change and vary
	• Gender roles include masculinity, femininity, and androgyny, the meanings of which evolve over time.

B. Biological sex and communication
  1. Psychological differences affect biological sex
  2. Genetic differences affect biological sex
  3. Anatomical differences affect biological sex
	• Biological sex differentiates men and women but is influenced by psychological, genetic, and anatomical factors.

C. Sexual orientation and communication
  1. Heterosexuality
  2. Homosexuality
  3. Bisexuality
  4. Asexuality
	• Sexual orientations include heterosexuality, homosexuality, bisexuality, and asexuality.

D. Some explanations for gendered communication	• Some writers have argued that women and men communicate as though they come from different planets, or at least, different cultures. Others have asserted that those metaphors are exaggerations.

Section 4} How Gender Affects Communication (p. 66)

IV. How Gender Affects Communication	

A. Gender and verbal communication
  1. Expressive and instrumental talk
  2. Language and power
  3. Gendered linguistic styles
	• Gender influences verbal communication, such as expressive and instrumental talk, power, and linguistic styles.

B. Gender and nonverbal communication
  1. Touch and body movement
  2. Emotional communication
  3. Affectionate behavior
	• Gender influences nonverbal communication, including touch and body movement, emotional communication, and nonverbal affection.

Key Terms

Androgyny
Asexuality
Bisexuality
Co-cultures
Collectivistic culture
Communication codes
Culture
Expressive talk
Femininity

Gender role
Heterosexuality
High-context culture
High-power-distance culture
Homosexuality
Individualistic culture
In-groups
Instrumental talk
Low-context culture

Low-power-distance culture
Masculinity
Monochronic
Out-groups
Polychronic
Sexual orientation
Societies
Uncertainty avoidance

Discussion Questions

1. Culture is something that we often assume only other people have. In what ways are you aware of the cultural influences on your own behavior?
2. What co-cultures do you belong to or identify with? What are some ways that your co-cultures influence how you communicate interpersonally?
3. The United States is sometimes criticized for being as individualistic as it is. What are some good things about growing up in an individualistic culture? In what ways would growing up in a collectivistic culture be better?
4. What things does your culture value highly? Achievement? Equality? Respect? Authority? Honesty? Loyalty? How do you see your cultural values being transmitted and reinforced in your society?
5. Many researchers believe that all behavioral differences between women and men (apart from reproductive behaviors) are socially constructed. Do you think that's true? Can you think of any behavioral differences that might be biological or genetic in origin?
6. Are masculinity and femininity different cultures? What are some reasons to think they are?
7. Why do you suppose that men's style of talk is more instrumental than women's, whereas women's is more expressive than men's? What are some various ways to explain those differences?
8. Gay men are stereotyped as communicating more like women than men, whereas lesbian women are often seen as communicating more like men than women. Which do you think is a more powerful influence on behavior—biological sex or sexual orientation?

Practice Quiz

Multiple Choice

1. People from the southern United States often use the word "y'all" when referring to others; however, people from other parts of the United States do not typically use this term. For people from the South, this is an example of:
   a. In-group language use
   b. Out-group language use
   c. Psychonormative language use
   d. Gendered language use
2. Researchers Ann Kring and Albert Gordon have found that when it comes to sex differences and emotion:
   a. Men and women reported expressing equal amounts of emotion.
   b. Men and women reported experiencing equal amounts of emotion.
   c. Men and women were equally likely to limit or mask their emotional expressions.
   d. Men and women varied greatly in their emotional experiences.
3. Presuming that most people think, perceive, and believe the same way you do is the primary point behind the:
   a. Gender assumption
   b. Androgyny assumption
   c. Similarity assumption
   d. Polychronic assumption
4. People raised in this type of culture are taught to believe that all people are equal and that no one person or group should have excessive power:
   a. High-power-distance culture
   b. Low-power-distance culture
   c. Expressive cultures
   d. High-context culture
5. Highly feminine cultures value this characteristic more so than highly masculine cultures:
   a. Ambition
   b. Competition
   c. Achievement
   d. Nurturance

6. Mark hates to be late to anything; he gets anxious at even the thought of being late, especially to events he believes are important. For people like Mark, time is a valuable, tangible commodity that should not be wasted. This orientation toward time is known as:
   a. Monochronic
   b. Polychronic
   c. Androgynous
   d. Instrumental
7. The U.S. American phrase "a dime a dozen," is an example of a cultural:
   a. Norm
   b. Jargon
   c. Idiom
   d. Code
8. Which of the following is *not* a sexual orientation?
   a. Heterosexuality
   b. Homosexuality
   c. Bisexuality
   d. Transsexuality
9. Which of the following is the best example of expressive talk?
   a. "If I were you, this is how I would fix your problem."
   b. "I think you and Sally should just break up; I mean, what's the point in hanging on?"
   c. "I love you and I am so thankful for your support during this rough time for me."
   d. "You're crazy! You need to get into therapy and fast!"
10. With respect to sex differences in talk, research has found that:
    a. Men and women speak about the same amount of words in an average day

    b. Men interrupt women more than women interrupt men
    c. Women ask more questions than men
    d. All of these

True/False

11. A person's culture is determined by his or her ethnicity.
12. In a high-context culture, people are expected to be direct, clear, and explicit in their communication with others.
13. Sex is biological and genetic, whereas gender is social and cultural.
14. Gender roles are fairly stable and enduring; they rarely change and are consistent across most all cultures.
15. Research has found that, on average, same-sex romantic relationships are just as stable and satisfying as opposite-sex romantic relationships.

Fill in the Blank

16. Within many large cultures are a host of smaller groups of people researchers refer to as _____.
17. The phrase "looking out for number one" is reflective of the _____ cultural viewpoint.
18. People in high _____ cultures are raised to believe that certain people or groups deserve to have more power than others.
19. The perception of time as holistic, fluid, and unstructured is associated with the _____ orientation toward time.
20. A person who is both highly masculine and highly feminine would be described as _____.

Research Library

Movies

Bread and Roses (Drama; 2000; R)

Bread and Roses *portrays the struggles of immigrant workers who take part in a 1999 janitors' strike in Los Angeles to protest unfair working conditions. It dramatically illustrates the division in power and resources between citizens and illegal immigrants. Many countries, including the United States, are currently dealing with the challenge of determining fair immigration policies, and this film provides a thought-provoking look at one group for whom this issue matters most.*

My Big Fat Greek Wedding (Comedy; 2002; PG)

My Big Fat Greek Wedding *is a romantic comedy depicting the cultural challenges faced by Toula, a Greek-American woman from a very traditional Greek-American family, and Ian, the non-Greek American man to whom she is engaged to be married. The film provides many examples of how symbols, language, values, and norms differ between cultural groups.*

Transamerica (Drama; 2005; R)

Transamerica *is a drama in which Bree, a male-to-female transsexual, learns she has an adolescent son who was recently released from jail. The two undertake a cross-country road trip together, visiting family members along the way. The film portrays many of Bree's struggles and triumphs related to her transsexual conversion, illustrating the point that biological sex has psychological, genetic, and anatomical characteristics that are not always aligned.*

Books

Dindia, K., & Canary, D. J. (Eds.). (2006). *Sex differences and similarities in communication* (2nd ed.). Mahwah, NJ: Lawrence Erlbaum Associates.

Hofstede, G. (2003). *Culture's consequences: Comparing values, behaviors, institutions, and organizations across nations* (2nd ed.). Thousand Oaks, CA: Sage.

Moran, R. T., Harris, P. R., & Moran, S. V. (2007). *Managing cultural differences: Global leadership strategies for the 21st Century* (7th ed.). Oxford, England: Butterworth-Heinemann.

Wood, J. T. (2007). *Gendered lives: Communication, gender, and culture* (7th ed.). Belmont, CA: Wadsworth.

Journal Articles and Book Chapters

Burleson, B. R., & Kunkel, A. (2006). Revisiting the different cultures thesis: An assessment of sex differences and similarities in supportive communication. In K. Dindia & D. J. Canary (Eds.), *Sex differences and similarities in communication* (2nd ed., pp. 137–159). Mahwah, NJ: Lawrence Erlbaum Associates.

Lee, W. S. (1994). On not missing the boat: A processual method for intercultural understanding of idioms and lifeworld. *Journal of Applied Communication Research, 22,* 141–161.

McConnell, A. R., & Leibold, J. M. (2001). Relations among the Implicit Association Test, discriminatory behavior, and explicit measures of racial attitudes. *Journal of Experimental Social Psychology, 37,* 435–442.

Wood, J. (2002). A critical response to John Gray's Mars and Venus portrayals of men and women. *Southern Communication Journal, 67,* 201–210.

Web Sites

www.un.org

This is the principal Web site of the United Nations, an international organization of 192 countries that works to facilitate human rights, social progress, economic development, and security in societies around the world.

www. trinity.edu/~mkearl/gender.html

This Web site offers discussion, statistics, and numerous links related to sex and gender equality.

3

Communication and the Self

What is the self?

How do we manage our identities in interpersonal interaction?

For what reasons do we share our thoughts and feelings with others?

Simon and Brooke

Simon was one of the most popular guys at his school. He had a reputation for always hanging out with the best-looking girls, so when Brooke transferred into his class, Simon befriended her right away. One Friday after school, they made plans to hang out at Simon's house. The only problem was that Simon's family didn't treat him like the popular kid his friends knew. His dad nagged him about feeding the dog, his mom complained about his overloaded schedule, and his little sister kept asking Brooke whether she was Simon's girlfriend. The longer they were there, the more embarrassed Simon became. He was trying to act the way he usually did around Brooke, but he found he couldn't really do that at home. All he could think was, "Why can't my family be cool?"

Many of us have gone through something very similar to Simon's ordeal, when two of our "selves" clash and we are left to feel uncomfortable and unsure. In his case, there was the Simon his friends knew: the popular kid who attracted the good-looking girls. Then there was the Simon his family knew: the son they had raised and the older brother they had grown up with. Adolescence and early adulthood are times in life when many of us try to break away from our early self-concepts—that is, our ideas of who we *used to* be—and figure out who we really *want* to be as individuals. As a result, it's not at all uncommon for people like Simon to find their "home identities" and their "social identities" in conflict.

This chapter is devoted to the topic of the self and its central role in how we relate to others. We'll explore:

1} What a self-concept is, how it forms, and some of the ways it can affect our communication behavior

2} Why self-esteem influences our communication behavior, and what it does and does not do for us

3} How we enact the images we want others to have of us, and what it means when those images are threatened

4} The ways we use self-disclosure to share information about ourselves with others

1} Understanding the Self: Your Self-Concept   {

Your interpersonal communication begins with you and your understanding of yourself. Who are you? How do you relate to others? What is the *self* in *myself*? Answering those questions is challenging, but it allows us to communicate and form relationships with a solid understanding of who we are and what we have to offer.

This section begins by describing the self-concept and its important attributes. Next, it presents some of the influences on the development of a person's self-concept. Finally, it discusses some of the ways we manage our identities in day-to-day life and how our communication with others reflects our self-concepts.

> *The self is not something one finds, it is something one creates.*
>
> —Thomas Szász (1920–)
> Hungarian-born physician

What Is a Self-Concept?

Let's say you were asked to come up with ten ways to answer the question "Who am I?" What words would you pick? Which answers are the most important? Each of us has a set of ideas about who we are that isn't influenced by moment-to-moment events (such as "I'm happy right now") but is fairly stable over the course of our lives (such as "I'm a happy person"). Your **self-concept** is composed of those stable ideas about who you are. It is your **identity,** your understanding of who you are. Self-concepts have three fundamental characteristics:

Self-concept The set of perceptions a person has about who he or she is; also known as *identity.*

Identity See *Self-concept.*

- Self-concepts are multifaceted
- Self-concepts are partly subjective
- Self-concepts are enduring but changeable

Self-concepts are multifaceted. We define ourselves in many ways. Some ways rely on our name: "I'm Michaela"; "I am Bill." Some rely on physical or social categories: "I am a woman"; "I'm Australian." Others make use of our skills or interests: "I'm artistic"; "I'm a good cook." Still others are based on our relationships to other people: "I am an uncle"; "I do volunteer work with homeless children." Finally, some rely on our evaluations of ourselves: "I am an honest person"; "I am an impatient person." You can probably think of several other ways to describe who you are; but, which of these descriptions is the *real* you?

The answer is that your self-concept is made up of several parts, and each of your descriptions taps into one or more of those parts. What we call *The Self* is actually a collection of smaller *selves,* as Figure 3.1 depicts. If you're female, that's a part of who you are, but it isn't everything you are. If you're Asian, or athletic, or agnostic, or asthmatic, these may all be parts of your self-concept, but none of these terms defines you completely. All the different ways you would describe yourself are pieces of your overall self-concept.

Johari Window A visual representation of components of the self that are known or unknown to the self and to others.

One way to think about your self-concept is to distinguish between aspects of yourself that are known to others and aspects that are known only to you. In 1955, American psychologists Joseph Luft and Harry Ingham created the **Johari Window,** a visual representation of the self as composed of four parts.[1] According to the model, which appears in Figure 3.2, the *open area* consists of characteristics that are known both to the self and to others. This probably includes your name, sex, hobbies, and academic major, and other aspects of your self-concept that you are aware of and freely share with others. In contrast, the *hidden area* consists of characteristics that you

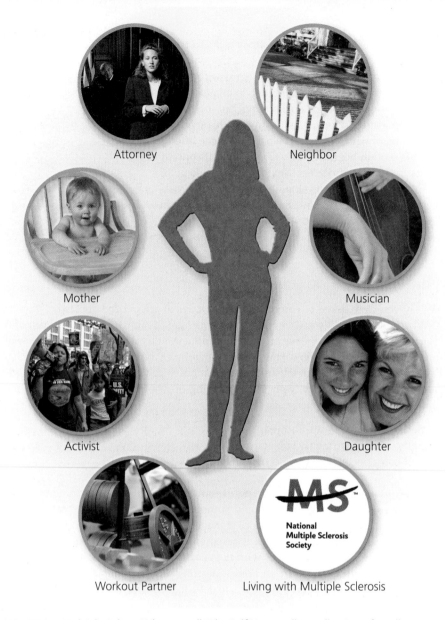

FIGURE 3.1 Multiple Selves What we call "The Self" is actually a collection of smaller "selves," each representing only one aspect of who a person is.

know about yourself but choose not to reveal to others, such as emotional insecurities or traumas from your past that you elect to keep hidden.

One of the innovative aspects of the Johari Window is that it recognizes there are dimensions to our self-concept that we may not be aware of. For instance, others might see us as impatient or volatile, even if we don't recognize those traits in ourselves. These characteristics make up the third part of the model, the *blind area.* Finally, the *unknown area* comprises aspects of our self-concept that are not known either to ourselves or to others. For example, no one—including you—can know what kind of parent you will be until you actually become a parent. Likewise, no one knows how we would handle sudden wealth or a devastating loss until those things happen to us.

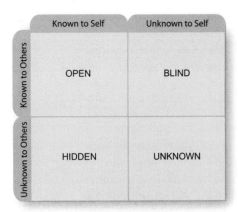

	Known to Self	Unknown to Self
Known to Others	OPEN	BLIND
Unknown to Others	HIDDEN	UNKNOWN

FIGURE 3.2 The Johari Window In the Johari Window, the open area represents what you know and choose to reveal to others, and the hidden area depicts what you know but choose not to reveal. The blind area reflects what others know about you but you don't recognize in yourself, and the unknown area comprises the dimensions of yourself that no one knows.

These four parts of the Johari Window—open, hidden, blind, and unknown—are not necessarily of equal importance for each individual. For example, Raisa keeps many aspects of her self-concept to herself, so her hidden area is much larger than the other parts of her Johari Window. By contrast, people describe Aaron as an "open book," meaning that he keeps very little about his self-concept private. Thus, for him, the open area is the largest area. The areas can also change in importance as a person's experiences change. For instance, when Renae was diagnosed with terminal cancer, she discovered emotional strength, compassion, and a sense of humor that she and others never knew she had. This experience moved those aspects of her self-concept from her unknown area to her open area.

Self-concepts are partly subjective. Some of the things we know about ourselves are based on objective facts. For instance, I'm 5'8" tall and have brown hair, I was born in Seattle but now live in Phoenix, and I teach at a college for a living. These aspects of my self-concept are objective, which means they're based on fact and not just on someone's opinion. That doesn't mean I have no choice about them. I chose to move to Arizona and get a teaching job, and although I was born with brown hair, I could change my hair color if I wanted to. Referring to these personal characteristics as "objective" simply means that they are factually true.

Many aspects of our self-concept are subjective rather than objective, however. By "subjective" I mean that they're based on the impressions we have of ourselves rather than on objective facts. Keep in mind that it's often difficult for people to judge themselves accurately or objectively.

Sometimes our self-assessments are unreasonably positive. For instance, you might know people who have unrealistic ideas about their intelligence, special talents, or understanding of the world or other people. In one study, the College Board (the company that administers the SAT college entrance examination) asked almost a million U.S. American high school seniors to rate their ability to get along with others. *Every single student* in the study responded that he or she was "above average," which is mathematically impossible! Moreover, 60% claimed their ability to get along with others was in the top 10%, and a whopping 25% rated themselves in the top 1%, both of which are highly improbable.[2]

By contrast, sometimes our judgments of ourselves are unreasonably negative. This is especially true for people with low self-esteem. Several studies have shown that such people tend to magnify the importance of their failures.[3] They often underestimate their abilities, and when they get negative feedback, such as a bad evaluation at work or a disrespectful remark from someone they know, they are likely to believe that it accurately reflects their self-worth. Several studies have also suggested that people with low self-esteem have a higher-than-average risk of being clinically depressed, a condition that impairs not only an individual's mental and emotional well-being but also his or her physical health and the quality of his or her social relationships.[4]

In contrast, people with high self-esteem tend to minimize the importance of negative feedback, treating it as a fluke or a random event. We'll look more closely at how self-esteem influences our interpersonal communication behaviors later in the chapter.

Self-concepts are enduring but changeable. We don't come up with our self-concepts on a whim. For the most part, a self-concept is something that develops slowly, over the course of a person's lifetime. As we'll see, many factors affect how your self-concept develops, including your biological makeup, how and where you were raised, and the kinds of people you spend time with.

These and other influences create an understanding of the self that is not easily changed. In fact, several studies have shown that once we develop a self-concept, we tend to seek out others who will confirm it by treating us as we see ourselves.[5] If you're someone with a positive self-concept, for instance, you'll likely associate with friends, co-workers, classmates, and relatives who also have a positive impression of you. By contrast, if your self-concept is negative, you may be more likely to surround yourself with people whose impression of you is also negative.[6] When we associate with people who see us as we see ourselves, our self-concept is continually reinforced, and it becomes even more resistant to change.

Self-concepts do change, however, in response to developmental changes and significant life events. As we go through developmental changes in life, for instance, many of us grow to feel more positive or less positive about ourselves. One study reported that between the ages of 14 to 23—a period when changes in self-concept are often the most pronounced—both men and women go through shifts in their level of confidence and self-esteem. Child psychologists Jack Block and Richard Robins found that approximately 80% of people experienced either an increase or a decrease in their self-esteem during this period.[7]

People can also undergo changes in their self-concept as a result of significant events in their lives, such as undergoing a religious conversion or battling a serious illness.[8] After being widowed and losing her job, for instance, Sherry found herself homeless and living in her car. The more she adapted to the routines of homelessness, the more she came to think of herself as homeless and shunned by society—and the more distrustful she became of people she was once close to. Friends and relatives offered their help, but Sherry felt too ashamed and embarrassed to accept it. Over time, she actually began to prefer the company of other homeless people because she felt she could relate to them more easily.

A healthy self-concept is flexible and can change as life circumstances evolve. That doesn't mean that every significant event changes a person's self-concept, but it does suggest that shifts in a person's self-concept are frequently associated with noteworthy events in his or her developmental stage. Undergoing extensive therapy can also help a person change his or her self-concept, usually for the better. Overall, however, most people's self-concepts don't change very dramatically over the course of their adult lives.[9]

How a Self-Concept Develops

None of us is born with a self-concept.[10] In this section, we explore how factors such as personality and biology, culture and gender roles, reflected appraisal, and social comparison play a role in helping each of us determine who we are.

Personality
The pattern of behaviors and ways of thinking that characterize a person.

Personality and biology. An important part of your self-concept is your **personality,** which consists of the ways

Battling cancer or another serious illness can significantly affect a person's self concept.

you tend to think and act across most situations. Are you usually talkative and outgoing, or shy and reserved? Are you a worrier, or happy-go-lucky? Are your interests broad or narrow? Do you tend to be suspicious or trusting of others? Each of these questions relates to a different personality trait, a characteristic that describes you in most circumstances. If you have an outgoing personality, for instance, that doesn't mean you're friendly and talkative once in a while. Rather, it means you behave that way most of the time.

Some aspects of our personality are undoubtedly affected by where we grow up or how we are raised. Research suggests, however, that biology also plays a role in shaping personality.[11] For instance, several studies have shown that identical twins, who share 100% of their genes, are much more similar in their personality than fraternal twins, who share only 50% of their genes, the same as regular siblings.[12] Even identical twins who were separated at birth and raised apart show substantial similarity in their personalities, as the next How Do We Know? box details on page 88.

Other research shows that children start displaying certain personality traits early in life, before the effects of culture or upbringing are likely to be influential, and that those traits often remain as the children grow up. Toddlers who act shy around strangers, for example, are likely to continue being shy as adolescents and adults. Although personality is strongly affected by biology, however, with concerted effort many people can change their personality traits if they choose.[13]

Most children begin displaying signs of their personality early in life.

Culture and gender roles. The way we see ourselves is also strongly affected by the culture we grow up in and the gender roles we enact. We saw in Chapter 2 that cultures differ from one another in how individualistic they are: Some are highly individualistic, some are highly collectivistic, and some are in the middle. People in highly collectivistic cultures tend to think of their identities as embedded within their families and communities. In other words, they define the "self" in terms of the groups to which the person belongs, and they place more emphasis on the group than on the individual. By contrast, people in highly individualistic cultures think of themselves as independent and unique and not as strongly defined by the families or communities they came from.[14]

Gender also matters when it comes to the self-concept. As we saw in Chapter 2, gender roles are socially constructed ideas about how women and men should think and behave. Most cultures expect men to exhibit more stereotypically masculine traits, such as assertiveness and self-sufficiency, than women. Conversely, they expect women to exhibit more traits that are stereotypically feminine, such as empathy and emotional expressiveness, than men.

These observations don't suggest that all men are assertive or that all women are emotionally expressive. Rather, they are general tendencies that can significantly affect the self-concepts that women and men develop. For instance, competition and achievement may be more important to the self-concept of a masculine person, whereas a feminine person may place a greater emphasis on having strong, equitable relationships.

Reflected appraisal. As we grow up, one of the ways we figure out who we are is by considering who other people think we are. Perhaps you can recall someone important from your childhood who made you feel especially loved and appreciated. This

How Do We Know?
Personality Similarities Among Identical Twins

One influence on your self-concept is your personality. Although your personality is affected by how you were raised, evidence suggests that it is more strongly affected by your genetic makeup. How do we know this?

One way to evaluate the relative influences of biology and environment is to compare identical twins who were separated at birth and raised apart (who share 100% of their genetic material but none of their home environments) with identical twins who were raised together (who share 100% of their genes and a high proportion of their home environments). If personality is determined primarily by how a person is raised, then twins raised together should be substantially more similar than twins raised apart. If personality is primarily genetic, however, then twins raised together and twins raised apart should be much more similar than different.

Since 1979, a group of researchers in the United States and the United Kingdom has been studying more than 100 sets of twins raised together and twins raised apart in those countries, as well as several others. Participants in this ongoing study complete approximately 50 hours of assessments during which researchers measure a broad range of personality characteristics and physiological activities. Researchers also analyze the home environments in which the participants were raised with respect to the parents' education, economic status, material possessions, cultural interests, and methods of childrearing.

After controlling statistically for similarities in home environment, the researchers found that twins are highly similar in several aspects of their personalities, including their interests, dispositions, and mental abilities. What's more, twins raised together and twins raised apart scored so similarly to each other that the influence of home environment on personality was shown to be minimal. This is not the only method researchers have for studying the influences of genetics and environment on personality, but it is a useful one, given that identical twins are genetically identical yet may share none of their home environments. The message from this study is that personality—which is one influence on the self-concept—is more strongly affected by your genes than by how or where you were raised.

Ask Yourself:

- Do these findings surprise you? Why or why not?

- Even if your personality is primarily influenced by your genetic makeup, can you change aspects of your personality if you try? What are some examples?

From Me to You:

- The idea that personality is largely based on genetics is difficult for some people to accept, because it seems to suggest that how parents raise their children doesn't matter. Research such as the study described here does indicate that a child's home environment—which includes the parents' methods of childrearing—has only a negligible effect on the development of her or his personality. That doesn't mean that parents are inconsequential, though. How parents raise their children matters in *many* ways. Parents give their children attention, discipline, and material resources because they love them and because they have moral, ethical, and legal responsibilities to care for them. Parents help ensure their children's safety, health, and emotional comfort, and they often develop close personal relationships with them that last for the rest of their lives.

Source: Bouchard, T. J., Lykken, D. T., McGue, M., Segal, N. L., & Tellegen, A. (1990). Sources of human psychological differences: The Minnesota Study of Twins Reared Apart. *Science* (October 12), 223–228.

Personality is strongly influenced by genetics, but how parents raise their children matters in many ways.

individual may have been a favorite teacher who encouraged you to pursue your interests or an aunt or uncle who always listened to you talk about your favorite music. It's also possible that you were influenced in negative ways by people who were important to you, such as a careless older sibling who teased you in front of your friends or a neighbor who was indifferent or insensitive.

These types of positive or negative messages help us form a mental picture of what others think of us. In turn, this mental picture often affects the image we form of ourselves. The process whereby our self-concept is influenced by how we think other people see us is called **reflected appraisal.**[15] When other people treat us with love and appreciation, we may come to think of ourselves as lovable and worthy. In the same way, when other people tease, ignore, or physically or verbally abuse us, we may begin to perceive ourselves as inadequate or unimportant.

In the early 1900s, sociologist Charles Horton Cooley conceived of what he called the "looking-glass self" to explain how reflected appraisal works. In his model, each of us imagines how we appear to others. For instance, you might believe that others see you as caring and compassionate. Next, we imagine how others evaluate their image of us. For example, if people see care and compassion as positive traits, you would likely imagine they would evaluate you positively. Finally, we develop our self-concepts based on those evaluations. For example, if people seem to think positively of you, then you would think positively of yourself.[16]

Reflected appraisal
The process whereby people's self-concept is influenced by their beliefs concerning what other people think of them.

Our self-concept is influenced by the way we believe others see us. This process is called reflected appraisal.

As you might imagine, not everyone in our lives has the same level of influence over our self-concept. In general, the more important someone is to us, the more his or her judgments will affect the way we see ourselves. Parents, friends, teachers, coaches, and others who play a significant role in our lives are usually the ones whose opinions we care about most.[17] As a result, their appraisals often exert more influence on the development of our self-concept than other people's appraisals.

The effects of reflected appraisal aren't confined to childhood. For example, after years of being told by his father that he's "no good," Jerome finds it hard to have confidence in his abilities, even though he is highly intelligent. This problem has made it difficult for him to hold down a job for more than a couple of years at a time. He also finds it hard to develop a lasting romantic relationship. Because his father's behavior led him to feel unworthy of love, Jerome has a tough time believing that any romantic partner will ever want to stay with him. As a result, his relationships are fleeting.[18] In Jerome's case, the reflected appraisal he received from his father while growing up continues to shape his self-concept as a "no good" adult.

Social comparison. Besides taking note of what other people think of us, we also notice how we compare with the people around us. Maybe you're the least athletic of all your friends. Maybe you noticed while growing up that some of your classmates seemed smarter than you, and others didn't. Perhaps you find that you're funnier, or better looking, or more musically talented than most of the people with whom you interact. A large part of the way we form a self-concept is through this type of **social comparison;** that is, by seeing how we compare with others. Thus, if you're more attractive than most of the people you know, then attractiveness is likely to be a part of your self-concept.

Social comparison The process of comparing oneself with others.

With social comparison, as with reflected appraisal, some people influence our self-concept more than others. For that reason, a key element in social comparison is the individuals or groups with whom we compare ourselves. The people we use to evaluate our characteristics are called **reference groups.** In most cases, our reference groups are our peers. You're more likely to consider yourself a smart person, for instance, if your reference group consists of your classmates than a group of Nobel Prize winners. Similarly, you'll probably feel wealthier if you compare yourself with your friends than with Bill Gates, the founder of Microsoft and one of the world's wealthiest people.

Reference groups The groups of people with whom one compares oneself in the process of social comparison.

Those are extreme examples, but research shows that people sometimes pick unreasonable reference groups when they evaluate themselves. Unfortunately, comparing yourself with unreasonable reference groups can be very frustrating. Even worse, it can also be dangerous. For example, both men and women are likely to develop negative images of their bodies when they compare themselves with movie stars or models. In response, they often put pressure on themselves to achieve an unrealistic

body. In some cases this pressure leads to eating disorders, which can be very serious, or even life-threatening.[19] In 2006, for example, Brazilian model Ana Carolina Reston and Uruguayan model Luisel Ramos both died of complications from the eating disorder anorexia.

In light of these issues, the fashion industry has begun to de-emphasize the unrealistically thin figure that has long been common for female models. For example, following the deaths of Reston and Ramos, the city of Madrid, Spain, banned models from appearing on runways if they were too thin.[20] Officials in other fashion centers, including New York City and Milan, Italy, are considering enacting similar policies.[21]

Social comparison can also be problematic for people with serious weight problems. In the United States, more than 50% of adults are currently classified as either overweight or obese, a figure that has increased sharply in recent years.[22] To the extent that social comparison causes us to see overweight and obese people as different from ourselves, it can lead us to discriminate against them interpersonally, even if we do so unintentionally.

For example, a recent national survey of more than 3,000 U.S. American adults found that overweight and obese adults were significantly more likely than people of normal weight to report employment discrimination, such as not being hired for a job, not being promoted, and being fired. They were also more likely to report instances of interpersonal maltreatment, such as being insulted or harassed, receiving poor service in restaurants or stores, and being treated as though they were dishonest or unintelligent.[23]

The influences we've just discussed—personality and biology, culture and gender roles, reflected appraisal,

Brazilian model Ana Carolina Reston died in 2006 due to complications from anorexia. The quest for attractiveness and acceptance can lead both men and women to develop dangerous eating disorders.

and social comparison—can all significantly affect your self-concept. It is important to realize, however, that none of these factors operates on self-concept by itself. Rather, they all come into play as you develop a sense of who you are. In the next section, we'll take a look at some of the effects your self-concept can have on your communication behaviors.

Awareness and Management of the Self-Concept

Part of being a competent, skilled communicator is being aware of your self-concept and managing its influences on your behavior. Two pathways through which self-concept can shape communicative behavior are self-monitoring and the self-fulfilling prophecy.

Self-monitoring. In Chapter 1, we defined self-monitoring as an awareness of how you look, how you sound, and

People who are significantly overweight routinely suffer discrimination in many societies.

how your behavior is affecting those around you. The tendency toward self-monitoring ranges along a continuum from high to low. People on the high end of the scale pay attention to how others are reacting to their own behaviors, and they have the ability to adjust their communication as needed. Conversely, people on the low end express whatever they are thinking or feeling without paying attention to the kind of impression they're creating.

To understand how self-monitoring operates, imagine that you've fixed up your friends Jin and Katie to go on a blind date. As a high self-monitor, Jin pays a great deal of attention to his clothes and grooming to make sure he looks and smells good. In contrast, as a low self-monitor, Katie doesn't spend much time thinking about those things. During their date, Jin is aware of what he's saying, so he comes across as nice, easygoing, and funny. Katie, however, says whatever is on her mind, without really considering what Jin might think. Jin notices if his behavior seems to make Katie uncomfortable, and he adjusts his actions accordingly. By contrast, Katie doesn't really pay attention to what she's doing and how she's affecting Jin.

From this example, you might get the impression that it's best to be a high self-monitor. Self-monitoring certainly has its advantages. High self-monitors tend to be better at making whatever kind of impression they want to make, because they are aware of their behaviors and how others respond to them. They often find it easier than low self-monitors to put other people at ease in social situations. High self-monitors also tend to be good at figuring out what other people are thinking and feeling, which gives them a clear advantage in many social settings.

Being a high self-monitor also has its drawbacks. Because high self-monitors are constantly aware of themselves and others, they may have a hard time relaxing and "living in the moment." Also, the fact that they can adjust their behaviors to create a certain impression can make it difficult to tell what they are genuinely thinking or feeling. Their motto might be "What you see is what I want you to see."[24]

Being a low self-monitor also has its advantages and disadvantages. On the positive side, low self-monitors spend less time and energy thinking about their appearance and behavior, so they are probably more relaxed than high self-monitors in many situations. Indeed, their motto might be "What you see is what you get." In addition, because they are less aware of, or concerned with, the impressions they make, they are often more straightforward communicators. In fact, they may even be seen as more genuine and trustworthy.

At the same time, however, because low self-monitors are less skilled than high self-monitors in adjusting their behaviors to the demands of the situation, they frequently appear unsophisticated or socially awkward. As a result, they are more likely to make a poor first impression.[25]

Significantly, some medical conditions can inhibit self-monitoring ability. Autism, for instance, is a developmental disorder that impairs a person's capability for social interaction. A 2007 report from the Centers for Disease Control and Prevention found that approximately 1 in 150 U.S. American children has some form of autism.[26] People with autism are often unresponsive to others. They frequently avoid eye contact, and they have difficulty understanding what others are thinking or feeling. This limits their ability to notice how others are reacting to them and to adjust their behaviors accordingly, two hallmarks of self-monitoring. Despite these challenges, however, it is possible for many people with autism to lead relatively independent, productive lives.

Heather Kuzmich, a top contender on the reality show "America's Next Top Model," has been diagnosed with Asperger's syndrome, a version of autism that can limit a person's self-monitoring ability.

Self-fulfilling prophecy. You've probably had the experience of waking up in a bad mood and saying to yourself it was going to be an awful day. After that, everything seems to go wrong. Because you're in a bad mood, you get cranky and speak impatiently to people, and they treat you poorly in return. You think to yourself, "See? I *knew* everyone would treat me badly today." When you have to give a speech in class that afternoon, you figure it's not worth putting much effort into it, because you're just going to get a mediocre grade anyway. When that happens, you think, "See? I *knew* this speech would go badly." Soon you start to feel as though you shouldn't even have gotten out of bed that morning.

Self-fulfilling prophecy
An expectation that gives rise to behaviors that cause the expectation to come true.

Why did your predictions about a lousy day come true? Most likely, it's due to a phenomenon called a **self-fulfilling prophecy.** This term refers to situations in which an expectation causes you to act and communicate in ways that make that expectation come true.

As another example, let's say you volunteer at an afterschool literacy program, and everyone is talking about how much they like the new program director. Because everyone else seems to like him, you expect that you will too. You therefore communicate in a positive, outgoing way when you meet him. You introduce yourself to him in the hallway, and you listen with interest when he tells you a bit about his background. In return, he treats you in a friendly manner. And lo and behold, you *do* like him! What has happened here is that your expectation ("I will like this person") led you to behave in a certain way (talking in a friendly way toward him; not interrupting him) that caused your expectation to be fulfilled (he acted friendly toward you, and therefore you liked him).

How do self-fulfilling prophecies affect how we communicate? Sometimes our expectations influence our communication behavior, as when you think it's going to be a bad day and you then have a bad day. Similarly, when we expect our relationships to fail, we behave in ways that sabotage them, and when we expect to be socially rejected, we perceive and react to rejection even when it isn't really there.[27] Finally, as you may have experienced, when we expect to do poorly on an assignment, we often act in ways that cause the assignment to go badly.[28]

Just as our expectations can influence our behavior, so can other people's expectations. Let's say that your professor believes you're particularly smart. She may therefore treat you as if you are by giving you more attention, demanding higher-quality work from you, and so on. Because you're getting extra attention and having more success demanded of you, you actually learn more in the class and get an "A" on the final exam. In turn, these accomplishments confirm your professor's expectation that you're very smart. In this case, it was someone else's expectation, rather than your own, that influenced your behavior.

A classic experiment by psychologists Robert Rosenthal and Lenore Jacobson demonstrated exactly this pattern: Teachers who believed certain students were intellectually gifted treated those students in ways that actually increased their scores on IQ tests.[29]

In another study, some college men were informed that a certain woman was attracted to them, and other men were told she wasn't. After each man had a conversation with the woman, the researchers found a self-fulfilling prophecy: When the man believed the woman was attracted to him, she was more likely to behave as if she was.[30]

Why would this occur? The most likely explanation is that the men who thought the woman was attracted to them communicated in a friendly, outgoing way toward her, causing her to reciprocate those communication behaviors and thus behave as though she was attracted to them. Research has shown that other people's expectations cause us to behave in expectancy-confirming ways across a range of situations, including the management of our relationships, our ability to heal from illness, and even our productivity on the job.[31]

There is one very important clarification about self-fulfilling prophecies. For a prophecy to be self-fulfilling, it's not enough that you expect something to happen and then it does. Rather, it has to be your expectation that *causes* it to happen. To illustrate this point, let's say you expected it to rain yesterday, and it did. That isn't a self-fulfilling prophecy, because your expectation didn't cause the rain. It would have rained whether you thought it would or not. In other words, your expectation was fulfilled, but it was not *self*-fulfilled. A self-fulfilling prophecy is one in which the expectation itself causes the behaviors that make it come true.

Learn It: What does it mean to say that self-concepts are partly subjective? Compare and contrast reflected appraisal and social comparison as influences on the development of a self-concept. What are the advantages and disadvantages of being a low self-monitor?

Try It: Create a version of Figure 3.1 for yourself. Around the figure in the middle, draw 6–8 small images that represent your different "selves." Then, draw 3–4 new "selves" that represent not the person you are but the person you would like to become. Next to each of these "ideal selves," write one statement describing something you can do to become more like that ideal self.

Reflect on It: How do your friends and relatives affirm and reinforce your perceptions of yourself? If you had to create a time capsule to describe yourself to future generations and could include only five things, what things would you choose, and why?

2} Valuing the Self: Self-Esteem

Knowing your self-concept and being happy with your self-concept are two different things. How do you feel about yourself? Are you satisfied with your looks? your accomplishments? your personality? your relationships? Do you feel confident and proud of who you are? All these questions ask you to think about your **self-esteem**, which is your subjective evaluation of your value and worth as a person.

Self-esteem One's subjective evaluation of one's value and worth as a person.

Many people have speculated about the value of having high self-esteem, but the research results have been mixed. As we'll see, some behaviors and characteristics do appear to be enhanced by high self-esteem. Others *seem* as though they would be, but they really aren't. In this section, we'll look at what it means to have higher or lower self-esteem, and we'll determine how characteristics such as sex and culture affect our self-esteem. We will also describe three interpersonal needs that interact with self-esteem to influence the way we communicate with others.

> *Know yourself. Don't accept your dog's admiration as conclusive evidence that you are wonderful.*
>
> —Ann Landers (1918–2002)
> U.S. American advice columnist

Benefits and Drawbacks of Self-Esteem

Turn on any talk show or browse the self-help aisle of any bookstore and you'll find plenty of discussion about the importance of self-esteem. High self-esteem is often

Getting to Know You

How High Is Your Self-Esteem?

How much do you agree with each of the following statements? On the line before each statement, record your level of agreement on a 1–7 scale. A higher number means you agree more; a lower number means you agree less.

1. _____ On the whole, I am satisfied with myself.
2. _____ Most of the time, I think I'm a good person.
3. _____ I feel I have a number of good qualities.
4. _____ I am able to do things as well as most other people.
5. _____ I feel I have much to be proud of.
6. _____ I rarely, if ever, feel useless.
7. _____ I feel that I'm a person of worth, at least on an equal plane with others.
8. _____ I have a good deal of respect for myself.
9. _____ All in all, I am inclined to feel I am a success.
10. _____ I take a positive attitude toward myself.

When you're done, add all your scores together. Your result should be between 10 and 70. This is your total self-esteem score. If your score is between 10 and 30, your self-esteem is relatively low right now. A score of 31 to 50 indicates a moderate level of self-esteem. A score between 51 and 70 suggests that you have a relatively high level of self-esteem.

Source: Rosenberg, M. (1965). *Society and the adolescent self-image.* Princeton, NJ: Princeton University Press.

believed to boost academic performance and shield people from stress, whereas low self-esteem is frequently blamed as the underlying cause of juvenile delinquency and antisocial behavior. These beliefs have led many parents, educators, and government agencies to pay more attention to improving children's self-esteem as a way to help them grow into more successful adults.

Why do these ideas seem to make good sense? One reason is that they're very intuitively appealing. It's easy to believe that if you feel good about yourself, you'll be more successful in school, work, and relationships. Although research shows that high self-esteem does have some important benefits, it also suggests that we might be giving self-esteem more credit than it's due.

Self-esteem and social behavior. Maintaining a positive image of ourselves does appear to have its advantages when it comes to behavior. Compared with people with lower self-esteem, those with higher self-esteem are generally more outgoing and more willing to communicate.[32] After trying and failing at a difficult task, they try harder to accomplish it a second time.[33] They are more comfortable initiating relationships, and they're more likely to believe that their partners' expressions of love and support are genuine.[34] They don't necessarily have more friends than people with lower self-esteem, however. Moreover, when their relationships have problems, they are more likely to end those relationships and seek out new ones.[35]

Several researchers have speculated that lower self-esteem is related to antisocial behavior, especially among adolescents and young adults. They suggest that people

Adolescents with high self-esteem are more outgoing than those with low self-esteem. They are also sexually active at younger ages and more likely to engage in risky sexual behaviors.

who view themselves negatively are more likely to act aggressively toward others, to abuse drugs or alcohol, and to become sexually active at a young age than people with a more positive self-image. The research hasn't really supported these ideas, however. In fact, aggressive people tend to have higher self-esteem, not lower.[36] In addition, the evidence suggests that self-esteem is not related to drinking or drug use, at least among teenagers.[37]

A similar scenario occurs with teenage sexuality: Adolescents with higher self-esteem are more prone to be sexually active and to engage in risky sexual behaviors than teens with lower self-esteem are.[38] One explanation for these conclusions is that high self-esteem gives some adolescents confidence in their ability to win a fight, attract a sexual partner, or escape the problems of risky sexual behaviors, making them more prone to engage in those types of interactions. By contrast, low self-esteem might lead other adolescents to avoid those situations.

Self-esteem and how we see ourselves and others. As you might imagine, people who have high self-esteem are happier with their lives than people with low self-esteem.[39] This is true around the world, although there is a stronger relationship between happiness and self-esteem in some countries with individualistic cultures—which emphasize the importance of the self—than in others with collectivistic cultures—which emphasize the needs of the group or community (see Table 3.1).[40] In addition, people with high self-esteem have a lower risk of depression[41] and an enhanced ability to recognize and manage emotions, a skill that researchers call "emotional intelligence."[42] Overall, it appears that people who

Table 3.1: The relationship between self-esteem and happiness in various parts of the world

Country	Self-Esteem/Happiness Correlation
United States	.58
New Zealand	.59
Germany	.50
Spain	.39
Brazil	.36
Jordan	.34
Bangladesh	.16

Note: The countries shown are listed from most individualistic to most collectivistic. As you can see, self-esteem generally has a stronger relationship to happiness in individualistic societies than in collectivistic ones. This relationship is not perfect; for instance, the United States is more individualistic than New Zealand, but the New Zealand correlation is slightly stronger. Rather, the relationship is general. These correlations are averaged for women and men.

Source: Diener, E., & Diener, M. (1995). Cross-cultural correlates of life satisfaction and self-esteem. *Journal of Personality and Social Psychology, 68,* 653–663.

Even among adults, self-esteem has little effect on work performance.

feel positive about themselves are also generally satisfied with their lives.

By contrast, people who have a poorer image of themselves adopt more negative emotions and ways of looking at situations. They tend to be more judgmental of others than people with higher self-esteem.[43] They're also more likely to speak poorly of others and to express racial prejudices.[44] When others put them down, they often respond by being excessively critical of others, so as to appear more impressive.[45] Some research has also shown that having low self-esteem in childhood is a predictor of having thoughts of suicide[46] and of making actual suicide attempts[47] in adolescence or young adulthood.

Self-esteem and performance. Much emphasis has been placed on self-esteem in schools and its effects on students' academic performance. Many people have assumed that having high self-esteem would give students the confidence to work hard in school and achieve academic success. They have also maintained that low self-esteem is often the root cause of poor grades.

Those beliefs have led parents and educators to design and implement policies to boost students' self-esteem. One fairly common approach has been to reduce or eliminate opportunities for competition among students, particularly competition based on academic achievement. Many schools now refuse to publish an honor roll, for instance, fearing that it will diminish the self-esteem of students who didn't earn the grades to qualify. Other schools have gone so far as to eliminate grades altogether.[48] In 2005, one U.S. school district even decided to stop participating in the Spelling Bee—a national student spelling competition—because only one child in each grade can win in any given year, which might harm the self-esteem of other children.[49] These and similar efforts are based on the notion that competition is problematic because students who don't win will suffer a loss of self-esteem, and that in turn will impair their academic performance.

The research shows that these efforts have had little effect, however. In fact, several studies suggest that students' self-esteem has very little association with their academic performance.[50] For instance, some studies have found no correlation between students' self-esteem and their scores on standardized tests.[51] Going further, at least one study has shown that attempting to boost students' self-esteem can actually backfire, causing the students to perform more poorly.[52] That may be because inflating student' self-esteem causes the students to have such a degree of confidence in their natural abilities that they study less than they otherwise would.

Significantly, these conclusions are not true just for students. The evidence suggests that self-esteem is also largely unrelated to performance on the job.[53] Research has shown, for instance, that high self-esteem provides no advantage when performing arithmetic tasks[54] or tasks that require sensitivity to nonverbal behaviors,[55] two common components of many jobs.

As you've probably gathered from this review, having high self-esteem is a real benefit in some ways, such as making us happier. In other ways, such as preventing delinquency or improving our academic performance, it isn't. These mixed results don't mean we shouldn't care about the self-esteem of those around us. Rather, they suggest that the benefits of high self-esteem are largely limited to social and emotional areas and may not be as broad as people once thought.

Many people have suggested that self-esteem differs according to a person's sex and cultural background. We'll examine the extent to which that is true in the next section.

Culture, Sex, and Self-Esteem

Sex and culture are such powerful influences in our lives that it's easy to assume they affect almost everything about who we are and how we communicate. The effects are not always what we might guess, however.

Culture and self-esteem. For instance, many people might assume that ethnic minorities in the United States would have lower self-esteem than Caucasians—who form the majority ethnic group—because of the social stigmas that minorities often face.[56] In fact, the research tells a slightly different story. According to psychologists Jean Twenge and Jennifer Crocker, Hispanic Americans, Native Americans, and Asian Americans do tend to rate themselves lower than Caucasians in self-esteem.[57] Beginning in the 1980s, however, African Americans have reported the highest self-esteem of all ethnic groups, including Caucasians.[58] The differences among these groups aren't substantial, but they have been relatively consistent over the past few decades.

If ethnic minorities experience discrimination and social stigma, then how do they maintain their self-esteem? Researchers believe that socially marginalized groups— a category that can also include sexual minorities and people with disabilities—use three general strategies. First, they value the things at which they excel. To the extent that one group excels academically, athletically, or artistically, for instance, that group will emphasize those activities more heavily than activities in which they perform less impressively. Second, they tend to attribute their problems to prejudices in society rather than to their own behaviors or decisions. Third, like most people, they compare themselves with others in their own group more than with people from other groups.[59]

Sex and self-esteem. Unlike culture, sex does not appear to affect self-esteem by itself. Despite alarming reports that girls suffer from a shortage of self-esteem,[60] there is no scientific evidence to support that belief, either among children or among adults. In fact, among ethnic minorities, self-esteem is actually higher for females than for males. There is no sex difference among Caucasians, however.[61] Some experts have suggested that for ethnic minorities, experiences of racial discrimination are more damaging to the self-esteem of males than of females. This theory might explain why males have lower self-esteem than females among ethnic minorities but not among Caucasians, at least in the United States.[62]

We've seen that self-esteem benefits us in some ways and not in others, and that it varies by culture and sex, but not always in the ways we might expect. In the next section, we'll tie self-esteem more directly to interpersonal communication by examining three fundamental interpersonal needs that appear to be facilitated by self-esteem.

The Self and Interpersonal Needs

Self-esteem doesn't just reflect our feelings about ourselves; it can also influence how we communicate with other people. Social psychologist Will Schutz proposed that self-esteem interacts with three important interpersonal needs to affect our communication with others: the need for control, the need for inclusion, and the need for affection. As we'll see, each of these needs motivates us to interact with others in particular ways.

Need for Control. We all have a **need for control**, which is our motivation to maintain some degree of influence in our relationships. As infants, we relied almost completely

Need for control
One's need to maintain a degree of influence in one's relationships.

Affection is one of our most fundamental human needs.

on our caregivers to make decisions for us. As we grew up, however, we needed to play a more decisive role in determining the course of our relationships. In many relationships, people share control, so that each person has some say in what happens. We're often less satisfied in relationships when we feel we have no control.[63]

Research shows that the higher a person's self-esteem, the more she or he feels in control of the events in her or his life.[64] By the same token, many of us also have a need to relinquish control from time to time. Just as we're dissatisfied with having too little control, we can also feel overwhelmed by the responsibility of having too much control. Allowing others to exert influence over us is an important part of the interdependent nature of personal relationships. We're often most satisfied, therefore, with a moderate amount of control.

Need for inclusion
One's need to belong to a social group and be included in the activities of others.

Need for Inclusion. Our **need for inclusion** is our need to belong, to be included in the activities of others, and to have positive human contact. Some of us have a stronger need for inclusion than others, but even people you'd describe as loners need some interaction with others. Studies have shown that people can experience mental and physical distress when their need for inclusion is not met.[65] For people with a high need for inclusion, then, the opportunities to form and maintain interpersonal relationships probably contribute to their self-esteem.

From a different perspective, people with higher self-esteem tend to be more outgoing and extraverted than people with lower self-esteem. For that reason they might be more motivated to seek out relationships that will meet their need for inclusion.[66] For example, they may be more likely to join social groups, religious organizations, or sports teams to meet others. Nevertheless, even people with a high need for inclusion can also enjoy periods of solitude from time to time.

Need for affection
One's need to give and receive expressions of love and appreciation.

Need for Affection. Finally, each of us also has a **need for affection.** We need to have people in our lives who love and appreciate us and who communicate their affection to us. We also need to give love and intimacy to others. Some researchers believe that people are born with the capacity for affection, and studies have shown that the more affection people give and receive, the healthier and happier they are.[67] People with higher self-esteem also tend to be more expressive of their affectionate feelings than people with lower self-esteem.[68] The "At a Glance" box provides a summary of Schutz's three interpersonal needs.

At a Glance: Schutz's Interpersonal Needs

Schutz believed that self-esteem interacts with three important interpersonal needs to affect our communication with others: control, inclusion, and affection.

Need for Control	Our need to maintain some degree of control in a relationship
Need for Inclusion	Our need to belong to a social group and have positive contact with others
Need for Affection	Our need to feel loved and appreciated by others

Schutz believed that all three of these needs were fundamental, meaning that everyone has them to some degree. The greater these needs are, he argued, the more motivated we are to seek and form relationships with people who can help us meet these needs. People with high self-esteem don't necessarily have stronger needs for inclusion, affection, and control than others do, but they appear to be more successful at meeting these needs through their communication with other people.

Learn It: What social behaviors are enhanced by having high self-esteem? How does self-esteem differ between the sexes or among various ethnic groups? What three interpersonal needs did Schutz propose were fundamental?

Try It: How high is your self-esteem? Fill out the scale in the "Getting to Know You" box on page 95 to find out. Is your score close to what you expected?

Reflect on It: When do you feel better or worse about yourself? What things, besides gender and culture, do you think influence self-esteem?

3} Presenting the Self: Image Management {

As you've learned, your self-concept is related to *the way you see yourself*. When we communicate interpersonally, however, we are also concerned with *the way we want others to see us*. In some situations, you might want others to see you as friendly, outgoing, and fun. In other situations, you might want people to look at you as reliable, competent, and serious. And perhaps there are circumstances when you'd like others to think of you as independent and open-minded.

When we consider how we want others to perceive us, we're considering the kind of **image** we want to project. In this section, we'll see that managing your image is a collaborative, multidimensional, and complex process. We'll also consider the contributions of communication researcher Myra Goldschmidt, sociologist Erving Goffman, and other scholars whose work has helped us understand the process of image management.

In search of my mother's garden, I found my own.

—Alice Walker (1944–)
U.S. American novelist

Image
The way one wishes to be seen or perceived by others.

Principles of Image Management

In the 2000 comedy *Meet the Parents,* Greg Focker (played by Ben Stiller) plans to propose to his girlfriend during a weekend trip to her parents' house and finds him-self working hard to make a good impression on her distrusting father (played by Robert De Niro). In sit-uations like these, when the goal is to make a positive first impression on others, you've probably heard that it's best to "just be yourself." Indeed, many people try to project an image that ac-curately reflects their self-concept. As you can prob-ably imagine, though, there are many times when the way we act reflects a specific image we wish to project, and we adjust our behav-ior accordingly. That pro-jection might be "you just being yourself," or it might be an image that suits the occasion or the outcome you desire. This is the pro-cess of **image management.** In this section we will ex-plore three fundamental principles of this process:

In many situations, we consider carefully how we want others to perceive us. This is the process of image management.

Image management
The process of projecting one's desired public image.

- Image management is collaborative.
- We manage multiple identities.
- Image management is complex.

Image management is collaborative. To some extent, managing your image is an in-dividual process. After all, your image is yours. We also get a lot of help managing our image, however, from the people around us. As psychologist Dan McAdams has suggested, each of us develops a "life story," or a way of presenting ourselves to oth-ers, that is based on our self-concept but is also influenced by other people.[69]

If others accept the image you portray, they'll tend to behave in ways that en-courage that image. Let's say you see yourself as a confident person, and you project that image when you interact with others. If other people see you as confident, they'll treat you as though you are—and this will strengthen that part of your identity in your own mind. If others don't accept the image of yourself that you portray, how-ever, they may see you as less credible or trustworthy. Perhaps you have encountered people who are "trying to be someone they aren't," or are portraying an image that you don't accept as genuine. Many of us find it hard to take such people seriously.

We manage multiple identities. Remember Simon, from the story at the beginning of this chapter? The main reason he felt so uncomfortable bringing home his friend Brooke is that it forced him to manage two very different identities. There was the Simon that his parents and sister knew, and then there was the Simon that Brooke knew from school, and he found it hard to enact those two identities at the same time.

Many people have similar experiences. If you think of all the people you know, for instance, you'll probably realize that most of them know you only in a certain context. You have your circle of friends, who know you as a friend. You have your family members, who know you as a mother, son, aunt, brother, cousin, or grandchild. Your boss and co-workers know you as an employee. Your doctor and your dentist know you as a patient, your professors know you as a student, and your landlord knows you as a tenant. Others might know you as a neighbor, a client, or a parishioner.

Significantly, each of these contexts carries its own distinctive role expectations, so you probably enact a somewhat different identity in each one. You likely communicate differently at work than at home, for instance, and your friends probably know you differently than your professors do. We all manage multiple identities; that is, we show different parts of ourselves to different people in our lives.

On occasion, people enact images of themselves that are inaccurate or dishonest. In the 2002 movie *Catch Me If You Can,* actor Leonardo DiCaprio plays Frank Abagnale, a man who, in real life, fraudulently portrayed himself as a substitute teacher, a lawyer, a doctor, and

an airline pilot before being captured and imprisoned by the U.S. government in the 1960s. Although their experiences are usually less dramatic, many people present images of themselves that are not entirely accurate, such as a job applicant who exaggerates her work experience on her resume or a person who describes himself in a personal ad as younger or thinner than he really is.

The challenge of managing multiple identities is especially pronounced for people with "invisible" medical conditions, which are illnesses or disorders that are not necessarily apparent to others. Conditions such as Down syndrome, stuttering, developmental disabilities, and confinement to a wheelchair are relatively "visible," because many people will notice those conditions after seeing or listening to someone who has them. By contrast, people can, to varying degrees, hide the fact that they have conditions such as cancer, diabetes, asthma, and depression if they don't want others to know. Most people can't identify a person with diabetes or asthma, for example, simply by looking at him or her.

For that reason, people with those and other invisible conditions have both the ability and the responsibility to determine how to incorporate their conditions into the image they project to others. For instance, many people with such conditions must continually decide whom to tell about their conditions, when to make those disclosures, and how to do so. That decision can be particularly agonizing for individuals suffering from invisible illnesses that are also socially stigmatized, such as having a mental health disorder or being HIV-positive, because of the fear of how others will react to their disclosures. The "Dark Side of Interpersonal Communication" box addresses this issue as it pertains to people who are HIV-positive.

Image management is similarly challenging for many sexual minorities. Like an invisible medical condition, a person's sexual orientation is not always evident in the way he or she looks, sounds, or communicates. This gives lesbian, gay, and bisexual people the ability to choose to whom to reveal their sexual orientation. Many

{ The Dark Side of Interpersonal Communication }
Risks of Disclosing HIV-Positive Status

Discovering they are infected with HIV is a traumatic experience for many people. Being HIV-positive puts people at risk for developing AIDS, a terminal disease with no known cure. It also requires people to choose whom they're going to share the news of their infection with. Many people with HIV may feel in a bind when deciding whether to disclose their condition to others. On the one hand, disclosing the illness may help people acquire both medical and emotional support, and it may encourage others to adopt healthier sexual or drug-use behaviors themselves. On the other hand, it can be risky. Psychologists Valerian Derlega and Barbara Winstead explain that HIV-positive people may have several reasons for choosing not to disclose their illness:

- Privacy: It's no one else's business but their own.

- Self-blame: They feel guilty for being HIV-positive.

- Communication difficulties: They feel they don't know how to tell others about it.

- Fear of rejection: They worry about others rejecting or even hurting them.

- Fear of discrimination: They fear that employers, landlords, or others will discriminate against them.

- Protection of others: They don't want others to worry about them.

- Superficial relationships: They don't feel close enough to others to trust them with this information.

Despite these risks, Derlega and Winstead emphasize that disclosing HIV status can be useful in many ways. Not only can it help secure needed medical attention and emotional support, but it can also help to strengthen relationships, particularly with others who are also HIV-positive. It is also extremely important for the health and safety of a romantic or sexual partner. To protect potential partners, in fact, several U.S. states have enacted laws making it a felony to knowingly expose someone else to HIV without that person's consent, which an HIV-positive person would do by engaging in sexual behavior with a partner who has not been informed of the person's status.

Ask Yourself:

- Have you heard people make disparaging remarks about HIV-positive individuals? How do you feel when you hear those comments?

- Do you agree with laws making it a crime to expose someone to HIV without the person's knowledge?

From Me to You:

- HIV is a topic that many of us find uncomfortable to discuss. In the United States, being HIV-positive is widely stigmatized because of its association with two marginalized groups, gay men and intravenous drug users. The stigma makes it easier to believe that if you don't belong to either of those groups, you can't or won't develop HIV. The truth, however, is that HIV infects people from all walks of life—homosexual and heterosexual, rich and poor, female and male, adult and child.

Source: Derlega, V. J., & Winstead, B. A. (2001). HIV-infected persons' attributions for the disclosure and nondisclosure of the seropositive diagnosis to significant others. In V. Manusov & J. H. Harvey (Eds.), *Attribution, communication behavior, and close relationships* (pp. 266–284). New York: Cambridge University Press.

find this to be a consequential decision, because sexual minorities are discriminated against in many parts of world, including much of the United States.[70] To avoid prejudice, many sexual minorities choose to "stay in the closet" and keep their sexual orientation a secret, even from their closest friends and relatives.

A person's decision to disclose his or her sexual orientation has some important health consequences. To begin with, long-term concealment of such a fundamental aspect of an individual's identity is stressful.[71] Over time, such stress can elevate the risks for cancer and infectious diseases,[72] rapid progression of HIV[73], and suicide.[74] There is some evidence that these problems are magnified for lesbian, gay, and bisexual adolescents, who, in contrast to adults, may lack the social support and emotional maturity to manage the stress of concealing their sexual orientation.[75]

Although concealing one's sexual orientation can be problematic for health, so can disclosing it. For instance, a study of gay and bisexual men found that those who had disclosed their sexual orientation in their workplace experienced more daily stress and negative moods than did those who kept their orientation secret.[76] Other research has found that lesbians and gay men are at elevated risk for depression and stress even if they are open about their sexual orientations.[77]

Image management is complex. If image management sounds complicated, that's because it often is. For instance, we may have competing goals in our interactions with others. Let's say you've been offered a prestigious internship at a start-up company in California's Silicon Valley, and you ask your older sister and her husband, who live close to that area, if you can move in with them for the semester. You probably want your sister to think of you as a mature, responsible adult, rather than as the carefree teenager you were when she moved out of your parents' house. As a result, you will have to present your request in a way that preserves your image as a responsible person. At the same time, you want to persuade your sister and brother-in-law that you really need a place to stay and you can't afford to rent one on your own, because the internship pays poorly and rents there are so expensive. This may cause you to project the image that you need help. Thus, you may find your image needs in conflict: You want to appear responsible but also in need of assistance. How to manage these competing image needs—while still persuading your sister to let you move in—can be complex.

Communication researcher Myra Goldschmidt found that when people ask others for favors, they often create narratives that help to maintain their images while still being persuasive.[78] To your sister, you might say things like "I only need a place to stay for a couple of months while I do this internship," and "I promise to help around the house." Strategies like this can help preserve your image as a responsible individual even in a situation when that image might be threatened.

We've seen that managing your image is a collaborative process that often requires you to negotiate several identities in a complex way. How do we determine what our image needs are in the first place?

Managing Face Needs

Maybe you've heard the term "saving face." Helping someone save face means helping that person to avoid embarrassment and maintain her or his dignity in a situation that threatens it. The very reason we hate getting embarrassed is that it threatens

Helping others maintain their dignity, especially in situations that threaten it, is an important part of saving face.

the image of ourselves we're trying to project, and this threat is a function of our need to save face. Sometimes we associate the concept of "face saving" with collectivistic cultures such as Korea or Japan. In reality, saving face is important to people in many cultures.[79] Let's take a look at what happens when our desired public image is threatened.

Face and face needs. Each of us has a desired public image—a certain way that we want others to see and think of us—and we work to maintain that image. For instance, if you want others to see you as intelligent and competent, you will likely behave in ways that give that impression and will try to avoid situations that will make you look incompetent or uninformed. Sociologist Erving Goffman coined the term **face** to describe our desired public image and the term **facework** to describe the behaviors we use to project that image to others.[80]

Researchers believe that our face is actually made up of three **face needs,** or important components of our desired public image.[81] You might find it easy to remember these face needs by noting that the first letters of their names—fellowship, autonomy, and competence—constitute the first three letters in the word "face."

Fellowship face refers to the need to have others like and accept us. This is the part of our identity that motivates us to make friends, join clubs or social groups, and behave in a pleasant way around other people. **Autonomy face** refers to our need to avoid being imposed upon by others. It's our autonomy face that motivates us to be in control of our time and resources and to avoid having other people make decisions for us. Finally, **competence face** is our need to be respected, to have others acknowledge our abilities and our intelligence. This need drives us to seek careers and hobbies that we're good at and to avoid situations in which we will embarrass ourselves. A quick summary of these three face needs appears in the "At a Glance" box on page 106.

Face threats. Each of us has a different desired public image, and so our face needs vary. Fellowship, autonomy, and competence are largely independent face needs, so having a high level of one need does not necessarily affect your levels of the other two needs. For instance, some people have a very strong fellowship face need, meaning it is extremely important that others like them. Other people much prefer to be respected than liked. Similarly, one person may have a very high need for autonomy, whereas another person doesn't mind having decisions made for him or her. These differences are part of what makes everyone's identity unique.

Although we all have our own face needs, we often become consciously aware of them only when they're threatened. Let's say you applied to join an honor society but were not accepted. The decision not to include you could threaten your fellowship face. It could also threaten your competence face by making you feel you weren't smart enough to get into the group. The rejection of your application, therefore, is a **face-threatening act** because it fails to meet one or more of your face needs.

Face-threatening acts often lead people to behave in ways that help restore their face. In the case of the honor society, you could say "I didn't really want to be in that society anyway."[82] Making such a statement doesn't mean you actually believe it. Indeed, you probably *did* want to be in the honor society, or you wouldn't have bothered

Face needs Components of one's desired public image.

Fellowship face The need to have others like and accept you.

Competence face The need to be respected and viewed as competent and intelligent.

Face A person's desired public image.

Facework The behaviors we use to maintain our desired public image to others.

Autonomy face The need to avoid being imposed upon by others.

Face-threatening act Any behavior that threatens one or more face needs.

At a Glance: Three Types of Face

Researchers have suggested that each of us has three specific face needs: fellowship, autonomy, and competence.

Fellowship Face	Our need to have others like and accept us
Autonomy Face	Our need not to be imposed upon by others
Competence Face	Our need to be respected for our intelligence and abilities

applying. Rather, you would likely say this to manage your image with others by making it appear as though your face needs weren't threatened. This response, therefore, is a type of "defense mechanism" that helps minimize the effects of a face-threatening act on you.

Face threats are, unfortunately, common experiences for members of many marginalized populations. For example, if people in some marginalized groups have to rely on others to meet their material needs or if they feel they don't have a voice in decisions that affect them, they may experience threats to their autonomy face. For example, elderly people frequently experience losses of autonomy as a result of physical and cognitive limitations associated with aging.[83] People with certain disabilities may also perceive threats to their autonomy if they are unable to do certain things that others can do, such as driving a car or going on a hike. Still other groups may feel their autonomy is threatened when they don't have the ability to make certain decisions for themselves, such as lesbian or gay adults who (in most states) cannot choose to marry their romantic partners.

Being marginalized also leads many people to feel disrespected and shamed about being in a stigmatized group, which can threaten both their fellowship face and their competence face. U.S. American society has stigmas associated with being homeless, poor, old, disabled, lesbian or gay, mentally ill, and, in some circles, even divorced, even though a person may have no choice about belonging to any of those groups.[84] Stigmatized people might feel like outsiders who "don't fit in" with those around them, which threatens their fellowship face by leading them to feel unaccepted. They may also perceive that others judge them not on the basis of their intelligence or abilities but simply because of their stigmatized condition, which threatens their competence face by leading them to feel disrespected.

Learn It: What does it mean to say that image management is collaborative? How are fellowship face, autonomy face, and competence face similar? How are they different?

Try It: The next time you have to ask someone in your family for a favor, think about the types of images you want to project to that person. With those images in mind, write out the words you would use to make your request.

Reflect on It: When do you notice that you have to manage multiple identities? What strategies do you use to do that? How do you usually react when your face needs are threatened?

Self-disclosure
The act of giving others information about one-self that one believes they do not already have.

Now that we have explored how we form a self-concept and how we manage our image, let's look at how we communicate about ourselves, or self-disclose. **Self-disclosure** is the act of intentionally giving others information about ourselves that we believe to be true but that we think they don't already have. From highly intimate conversations with romantic partners about your hopes and dreams to mundane chats with a co-worker about where you dined last evening, self-disclosure involves sharing a part of yourself with someone else.

In this section, we're going to look at several principles of self-disclosure and discuss some of the benefits that self-disclosure can bring to us and to our relationships. Finally, we'll take a look at some of the risks of self-disclosing so that we can also contemplate its downsides.

> *If you reveal your secrets to the wind, you should not blame the wind for revealing them to the trees.*
>
> —Kahlil Gibran (1883–1931)
> Lebanese-born essayist

Principles of Self-Disclosure

Most of us engage in self-disclosure, in one form or another, on a fairly ongoing basis. As we'll see in this section, self-disclosure has several important attributes.

Self-disclosure is intentional and truthful. For an act of communication to qualify as self-disclosure, it must meet two conditions: (1) we must deliberately share information about ourselves, and (2) we must believe that information is true. Let's say that, through a momentary lapse in attention, your friend Dean mentions his financial problems to you without meaning to. That wouldn't constitute an act of self-disclosure according to the definition just given, because he didn't share the information deliberately. Perhaps you can think of instances when you've unintentionally told another person something about yourself. Those instances are examples of verbal "leakage," which is information unintentionally shared with others.

Similarly, self-disclosing means sharing information that we believe is true. If you tell a co-worker that you've never traveled outside your home country, for instance, that qualifies as self-disclosure if you believe it to be true. It's your belief in the truth of the information that matters, not the absolute truth of the information. Perhaps you traveled outside the country when you were an infant and were too young to remember. If you believe the information you're providing is true, however, then it qualifies as self-disclosure. Intentionally giving people information about ourselves that we believe to be false is an act of deception, as we'll see in Chapter 11, "Deceptive Communication."

Self-disclosure varies in breadth and depth. The process of getting to know someone often involves self-disclosures that vary along two fundamental dimensions: breadth and depth. **Social penetration theory,** developed by social psychologists Irwin Altman and Dalmas Taylor and depicted in Figure 3.3, illustrates how self-disclosure over time is like peeling away the layers

Social penetration theory A theory, developed by Irwin Altman and Dalmas Taylor, that predicts that as relationships develop, communication increases in breadth and depth.

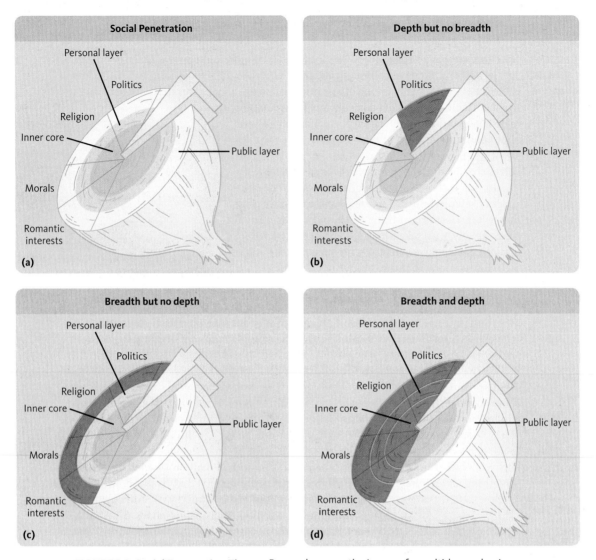

FIGURE 3.3 Social Penetration Theory Researchers use the image of a multi-layered onion to represent the process of social penetration in a relationship. The outer layer of the onion represents breadth of self disclosure. This layer is referred to as the "Public Layer" because it reflects details you would share with most people. The inner layers of the onion reflect depth of self disclosure. We call these the "Personal Layers" because they represent details you would only share with people you know quite well. If you share personal details about your political ideas with someone, but nothing else, then your relationship has depth but not breadth. If you tell someone only superficial information about your political, religious, moral, and romantic experiences but do not provide more personal details on any of those topics, then your relationship has breadth but not depth. In our closest relationships, we usually disclose both superficial and private information about many issues, so those relationships have both breadth and depth.

of an onion: Each self-disclosure helps us learn more and more about a person we're getting to know.

The animated character Shrek, voiced by Mike Meyers in the 2001 movie of the same name, explained to his friend the Donkey how ogres—like people—have "layers" that we "peel away" when we get to know them:

Shrek: For your information, there's a lot more to ogres than people think.

Donkey: Example?

Shrek: Example? Okay, er . . . ogres . . . are . . . like onions.

Donkey *[Sniffs onion]:* They stink?

Shrek: Yes . . . NO!

Donkey: Or they make you cry.

Shrek: No!

Donkey: Oh, you leave them out in the sun and they turn brown and start sproutin' little white hairs.

Shrek: NO! LAYERS! Onions have layers. OGRES have layers. Onions have layers . . . you get it. We both have layers!

According to social penetration theory, peeling away the layers to get to know someone requires sharing disclosures that have both breadth and depth. **Breadth** describes the range of topics you discuss with various people. With some people, you might disclose about only certain aspects of your life. For instance, you might tell your doctor all about your health but not about other aspects of your life. You might disclose only about your professional life with a co-worker, or only about your academic life with a professor. In these relationships, your self-disclosure has little breadth, because you disclose only about a limited range of topics.

In contrast, with your relatives, close friends, and romantic partner you probably talk about several different aspects of your life, such as your work and school experiences, your financial concerns, your professional ambitions, your health, your spiritual or religious beliefs, your political opinions, and your desires for the future. Your disclosure in these relationships is characterized by greater breadth, because you disclose about a wider range of topics.

The second dimension, **depth,** measures how personal or intimate your disclosures are. The depth of our self-disclosures is largely a function of how carefully we feel we must guard the information in the disclosures. Let's say Maya and her romantic partner are having problems. Maya might describe her problems in detail to her mother, not only because she values her opinion, but also because she trusts her mother to keep the information private. Because she doesn't feel the need to guard this information from her mother, Maya can engage in disclosure that has great depth. With her secretary, by contrast, Maya discloses that she is having difficulty, but she doesn't go into detail because she doesn't feel comfortable entrusting her secretary with the specifics. In this instance, Maya engages in self-disclosure of lesser depth.

Self-disclosure varies among relationships. Not every relationship is characterized by the same breadth and depth of self-disclosure. Some relationships involve depth of disclosure but very little breadth. With your accountant, for instance, you might disclose in depth about financial matters but not about anything else. Likewise, you might tell your doctor intimate details about your health but very little about other issues in your life. As you saw in Figure 3.3b, this type of relationship is depicted by coloring one wedge of the circle from the outermost ring to the innermost but leaving the other circles untouched.

Other relationships are characterized by breadth of disclosure but very little depth. With casual friends at school or work, for example, you might disclose a little about several areas of your life—family, hobbies, political ideas, career ambitions—but not provide intimate details about any of them. As Figure 3.3c indicates, you would depict this type of relationship by coloring in several of the wedges on the circle, but only on the outermost ring, leaving the smaller internal rings untouched.

Self-disclosure often progresses quickly in relationships formed online.

Still other relationships, such as romantic relationships and close friendships, often involve high degrees of both breadth and depth. In these relationships, people typically share both public and private information about multiple aspects of their lives. You can see this type of relationship depicted in Figure 3.3d by coloring in several of the wedges around the circle—some of which extend all the way to the center—to illustrate both the breadth and the depth of self-disclosure.

Self-disclosure follows a process. Even our closest relationships usually aren't close right away. Closeness develops over time as people get to know each other and reveal more and more information about themselves. In new relationships, people often disclose slowly, sharing only a few details at first, and offering more personal information only if they like and trust each other.[85]

When they started becoming friends, for instance, Deepak and Prasad shared mostly routine information with each other, such as where they grew up, what their favorite teams were, and what they did for a living. As they got to know and trust each other more, they started sharing their opinions on things such as politics, relationships, and religion. Only after they had known each other for quite a while did they feel comfortable talking about more personal things, such as Prasad's health problems or the challenges in Deepak's marriage. Although people in some relationships begin sharing intimate information very quickly, self-disclosure usually moves in small increments.

One exception to that general pattern involves relationships formed online, such as through e-mail, in a chat room, or on a Weblog.[86] At first thought, you might predict that people would be less disclosive in computer-mediated contexts than in face-to-face settings, because they may not feel as engaged with online conversational partners or as comfortable sharing personal information. Just the opposite appears to be true, however. Research shows that the lack of face-to-face interaction in computer-mediated contexts *encourages* self-disclosure, so that people are often more disclosive at the start of an online relationship than in a face-to-face one.[87] For example, a study of new romantic relationships discovered that couples disclose personal information earlier in their relationship via computer-mediated communication than in person.[88]

How do researchers account for this behavior? Communication scholar Joseph Walther explains that the computer-mediated environment encourages not just personal communication but also communication that is "hyperpersonal," meaning that it contains more private information than people would typically share face-to-face.[89] Walther believes that hyperpersonal communication occurs partly because we see communication partners in a more positive light online than face-to-face, so we feel less inhibited about disclosing highly personal information. This hyperpersonal nature of online disclosure can accelerate feelings of closeness between people. As we will see, however, it also involves certain risks.

Self-disclosure is usually reciprocal. You may have heard the phrase "One good turn deserves another." This saying suggests that when someone gives you some type of gift or resource, you are expected to return the favor. Sociologist Alvin Gouldner called this expectation the **norm of reciprocity.**[90] In North American cultures, at least, the norm of reciprocity usually extends to self-disclosure; that is, when we disclose things to other people, we typically expect them to disclose things to us in return.[91]

Norm of reciprocity
A social expectation, articulated by Alvin Gouldner, that resources and favors provided to one person in a relationship should be reciprocated by that person.

There are some exceptions to this rule. For example, when we disclose to a physician or a counselor, we don't expect her or him to disclose back to us. In our friendships and other personal relationships, however, we generally expect that others will share information with us as we share it with them.

Self-disclosure can serve many purposes. People self-disclose to one another for many reasons. Let's say you have been laid off from your job and you're debating whether to tell your roommates. Disclosing this information to them might serve several purposes. One purpose is simply to share the information. Another might be to signal to your roommates that you could use their support or that you might be late with your share of the rent that month. Your disclosure might also remind your roommates that you trust them, and this act of trust may help strengthen your friendships with them.

Although self-disclosure can serve multiple functions, it isn't appropriate in every case. There are times when it is more important to be discreet and to keep information to yourself. It's often important to maintain professional relationships with colleagues or customers, for instance, because of the business you transact with them. In these relationships, you may find it best to keep personal information to yourself and to focus your communication on the business you're conducting.

One reason discretion is often advisable in professional relationships is that information a person self-discloses can later be used against him or her. Let's say that Gena asks the construction company you work for to bid on a large demolition job and that you are in charge of providing an estimate for the costs of the work. In the course of your many conversations with Gena, she discloses to you that her family is having severe financial problems. Because of the norm of reciprocity, you feel as though you ought to disclose something equally personal to her. As a result, you tell her you have been having financial problems, too, and are considering looking for a new job to improve your situation—something you have not yet shared with your current employer.

After Gena receives your company's bid, she

In formal settings, such as a business luncheon, discretion is often more appropriate than self-disclosure.

calls you to ask if you can lower the price. When you reply that you have offered the lowest estimate you can reasonably provide, Gena asks you to reconsider, saying, "I'm sure you wouldn't want your boss to know you're thinking of looking for a new job." At that point, you realize that Gena self-disclosed to you only to elicit a disclosure back from you that she could later use as leverage when negotiating the demolition bid. This example doesn't suggest you shouldn't trust others, but it illustrates the fact that some people use self-disclosure only as a means of serving their own needs.

Self-disclosure is influenced by cultural and gender roles. Many factors affect how much information we are willing to disclose to other people, such as the type of relationship we have with them and how long we've known them. Self-disclosure is also affected by the norms for our sex and culture.[92] Regarding gender, many people probably believe that women self-disclose more than men, because disclosure and emotional expressiveness are a bigger part of the feminine gender role than of the masculine gender role, especially in North America.[93] Is this generalization true? In fact, the evidence suggests that women, on average, do self-disclose more than men. One reason for this difference may be that they are expected to. However, as the "Fact or Fiction?" box illustrates, this difference isn't as large as many people believe it is.

Self-disclosure is also affected by the norms for the culture in which we grow up. In some cultures, such as those in North America and Northern Europe, people are often encouraged to express themselves and self-disclose to their friends and family. By contrast, other cultures, such as most Asian and Middle Eastern cultures, value discretion and encourage people to disclose only under more limited circumstances. For instance, people in those cultures may be inclined to disclose personal information only within their families or romantic relationships, rather than with social or professional acquaintances.[94]

Benefits of Self-Disclosure

There are many ways that self-disclosure can be good for us and for our relationships. In this section, we will take a brief look at four key benefits of self-disclosure:

- Enhancement of relationships and trust
- Reciprocity
- Emotional release
- Assistance to others

Enhancement of relationships and trust. One benefit of self-disclosure is that it often helps us maintain high-quality relationships. We tend to disclose the most to people we like, and we also tend to like people who disclose to us.[95] Sharing appropriate self-disclosure with friends, relatives, or romantic partners helps us to maintain those relationships and reinforce the trust we share with those individuals.[96] Conversely, a lack of self-disclosure in a long-term relationship such as a marriage or a close friendship can be a sign of distress in the relationship.[97] Can you think of times when this has happened to you?

Reciprocity. As we noted earlier, many people follow a norm of reciprocity when it comes to self-disclosure: When we disclose to others, they tend to disclose back to us.[98] Thus, one way to get to know other people is to tell them things about yourself. When you share personal information with others, they may feel more comfortable doing the same in return.

Emotional release. Sometimes the best part of self-disclosing is just the feeling of getting something "off your chest." Perhaps you've had the experience of holding on

Over the years, many researchers and popular authors have advanced the idea that women self-disclose more than men do. One writer even went so far as to call women "blabbermouths" and men "clams"! Is it a fact that women disclose more than men do, or is it simply an untrue stereotype?

To find out, communication researchers Kathryn Dindia and Mike Allen conducted a meta-analysis, meaning they looked across several studies to see what conclusions the research would support. Using academic search engines, Dindia and Allen collected more than 250 studies about sex differences in self-disclosure. Altogether, those studies included almost 24,000 women and men. After compiling all the results from each study and analyzing them statistically, Dindia and Allen found that women do, indeed, self-disclose more than men. The difference was relatively small, however—not nearly as large as some researchers have suggested.

Dindia and Allen also found that the sex of the person receiving the disclosure made a difference. Specifically, women are more likely than men to disclose to females, but women and men are equally likely to disclose to males.

Ask Yourself:

• Why do many people believe that women are substantially more disclosive than men? How is that stereotype reinforced?

• Are you generally more comfortable self-disclosing to members of one sex than to members of the other, or do you feel equally comfortable disclosing to both women and men?

Sources: Dindia, K., & Allen, M. (1992). Sex differences in self-disclosure: A meta-analysis. *Psychological Bulletin*, *112*, 106–124; Hacker, H. M. (1981). Blabbermouths and clams: Sex differences in self-disclosure in same-sex and cross-sex friendship dyads. *Psychology of Women Quarterly*, *5*, 384–402.

to a secret that you felt you just had to talk to someone about. Let's say that Caryn borrowed her sister Amy's car and accidentally put a small dent in the fender. Instead of telling Amy about the dent, Caryn hoped she wouldn't notice. Pretty soon, Caryn started feeling so guilty that she was having trouble sleeping. Thus, when she finally disclosed the accident to Amy and apologized, she felt a sense of relief. Appropriate self-disclosures such as this one can often provide a feeling of emotional release.[99] Several studies have also shown that they can reduce the stress of holding on to a secret. This is an important benefit, because reducing stress can improve both your mental and your physical health.[100]

Assistance to others. Finally, you can self-disclose in ways that help other people, particularly when you're consoling people who are going through hard times. If your friend is having difficulty handling his parents' divorce, for instance, you might disclose how you managed traumatic situations in your own family. This disclosure can provide comfort and signal to your friend that he's not alone.

Many self-help programs, such as Alcoholics Anonymous, use this principle to help their members realize they are all going through a similar struggle.[101] Some disclosures even have the effect of protecting others against threats to their health. One example

Inappropriate disclosure can be hurtful to others, but appropriate disclosure often provides needed emotional release.

is HIV-positive people disclosing their status to health care providers and potential sexual partners.[102]

Enhancing relationships, reciprocity, emotional release, and assisting others are not the only benefits provided by self-disclosure, but they're among the most important for interpersonal communication. Before we conclude that self-disclosure is *always* a positive behavior, however, let's take a look at some of its most notable risks.

Risks of Self-Disclosure

Like many interpersonal behaviors, self-disclosure has its good and its bad aspects. Communication scholar Malcolm Parks has argued that we spend so much time thinking about the benefits of disclosure that we tend to ignore the risks it involves for both the people who make the disclosures and those who receive them.[103] Here we'll look at five potential risks:

- Rejection
- Chance of obligating others
- Hurt to others
- Violation of other people's privacy
- Risks of disclosing online

Rejection. When we self-disclose, we allow others to know information about us that they didn't know before. As we've seen, this can lead to some very good outcomes, such as emotional release and enhancing trust. It also involves some serious risks, however.[104] For instance, what if the people to whom we're disclosing don't like what we tell them? Let's say your brother decides to confide in you that he's gay. His disclosure might bring you closer together. If his sexuality is a problem for you, however, then his disclosure could lead you to reject him. Often, the way a person reacts to a disclosure will determine whether its outcome is positive or negative.

Chance of obligating others. The reciprocity of self-disclosure can be a very good thing if you are trying to get to know someone better. It can also lead the other person to feel "put on the spot" to disclose something back to you, however, when he or she might not be comfortable doing so. This may cause awkward silences and feelings of discomfort. Even worse, it could encourage the person to avoid you.

Hurt to others. Beyond making someone uncomfortable, it's possible to hurt others with disclosures that are too critical or too personal. Despite the idea that "honesty is the best policy," uncensored honesty can lead to wounded feelings and even resentment. Imagine that your wife has asked you what you think of a childhood friend with whom she recently reunited over the Internet. You have never been a big fan of Sonya, but you find yourself torn between wanting to be honest and wanting to be nice, because their renewed friendship seems to be lifting your wife's spirits. Indeed, you may have been taught that if you can't say something nice, you shouldn't say anything at all. This rule for politeness is meant to reduce the chances that someone will be hurt by a self-disclosure that's too critical.

Violation of other people's privacy. Inappropriate disclosures can even hurt people who aren't participating in the conversation. Let's say that while playing poker with his buddies, Miguel discloses information about his girlfriend that she trusted him to keep private. Miguel's disclosure doesn't hurt his friends, but it would be very hurtful to his girlfriend if she were to find out.

People in many relationships, including families, friendships, and workplace relationships, share private information with one another that is not meant to be shared with others. When we disclose this information to third parties without permission—a behavior we call **gossip**—we risk hurting our loved ones and damaging their trust in us.

Gossip The sharing of an individual's personal information with a third party without the individual's consent.

Risks of disclosing online. Earlier in this chapter, we discussed how disclosures made in online environments are often hyperpersonal, or of a more personal nature than they would be if they were shared face-to-face. The tendency to be hyperpersonal makes disclosing online particularly vulnerable to the risks discussed in this section. As we will see in Chapter 10, researchers believe that communicating online has a "disinhibition effect," encouraging people to say or do things that they wouldn't if they were in face-to-face settings.[105] For instance, you might not feel comfortable talking about the intimate details of your health while sitting with a friend in a restaurant, but you might describe them in explicit detail to members of an online support group.

The disinhibition associated with computer-mediated communication can be liberating, because it helps people to feel free to express themselves in ways they normally wouldn't. We have to be careful, however, that we don't disclose inappropriate information about ourselves or others. Because nearly all computer-mediated communication is written, recipients can save disclosures made online and even forward them to third parties. Consider the case of Lanny, who self-disclosed to an online chat room about his impatience with his boss's speech impediment. Another person in the chat room recognized Lanny's screen name and forwarded his postings to his boss, who found them personally offensive.

Many people have experienced regret or distress about information that they or others disclosed online, a phenomenon known as "postcyberdisclosure panic."[106] Because disclosures are usually made online in the form of written text, and because people often feel uninhibited about disclosing online, it's a good idea to be especially careful about what you disclose in computer-mediated environments.

Learn It: What are breadth and depth of self-disclosure? In what ways can self-disclosure enhance relationships? What are the primary risks of self-disclosure?

Try It: Choose one friend, one family member, and one school or work relationship. For each one, recreate the drawing in Figure 3.3, specifying both the depth and the breadth of disclosure that you typically share with that person. Notice the similarities and differences in breadth and depth across these three relationships.

Reflect on It: In what ways do you benefit from disclosing to other people? How do you feel when people share inappropriate disclosures with you?

} Master the Chapter {

Section 1} Understanding the Self: Your Self-Concept (p. 83)

I. **Understanding the Self: Your Self-Concept**
   A. **What is a self-concept?**
      1. Self-concepts are multifaceted
      2. Self-concepts are partly subjective
      3. Self-concepts are enduring but changeable

   • Your self-concept consists of your perceptions about who you are. It is multifaceted, partly subjective, and enduring but changeable.

   B. **How a self-concept develops**
      1. Personality and biology
      2. Culture and gender roles
      3. Reflected appraisal
      4. Social comparison

   • Personality, cultural and gender roles, reflected appraisal, and social comparison all influence the development of your self-concept.

   C. **Awareness and management of the self-concept**
      1. Self-monitoring
      2. Self-fulfilling prophecy

   • Self-monitoring and the self-fulfilling prophecy are two pathways through which self-concept can shape communicative behavior.

Section 2} Valuing the Self: Self-Esteem (p. 94)

II. **Valuing the Self: Self-Esteem**
   A. **Benefits and drawbacks of self-esteem**
      1. Self-esteem and social behavior
      2. Self-esteem and how we see ourselves and others
      3. Self-esteem and performance

   • Self-esteem is your subjective evaluation of your value and worth as a person. Having high self-esteem is a benefit in some ways and a liability in others.

B. Culture, sex, and self-esteem
   1. Culture and self-esteem
   2. Sex and self-esteem

C. The self and interpersonal needs
   1. Need for control
   2. Need for inclusion
   3. Need for affection

- Ethnic groups appear to differ somewhat in their self-esteem. In the United States, women report higher self-esteem than men among ethnic minorities but not among Caucasians.

- Humans have fundamental needs for control, inclusion, and affection, and self-esteem is affected by the extent to which those needs are met.

Section 3} Presenting the Self: Image Management (p. 100)

III. Presenting the Self: Image Management
   A. Principles of image management
      1. Image management is collaborative
      2. We manage multiple identities
      3. Image management is complex

- Your image consists of the way you want others to perceive you. Most of us manage multiple images in collaborative and complex ways.

   B. Managing face needs
      1. Face and face needs
      2. Face threats

- Humans have three kinds of face needs: fellowship face, autonomy face, and competence face. Behaviors that impinge on face needs are called face-threatening acts.

Section 4} Communicating the Self: Self-Disclosure (p. 107)

IV. Communicating the Self: Self-Disclosure
   A. Principles of self-disclosure
      1. Self-disclosure is intentional and truthful
      2. Self-disclosure varies in breadth and depth
      3. Self-disclosure varies among relationships
      4. Self-disclosure follows a process
      5. Self-disclosure is usually reciprocal
      6. Self-disclosure can serve many purposes
      7. Self-disclosure is influenced by culture and gender roles

- Self-disclosure is the deliberate act of giving others information about ourselves that we believe to be true and think they don't already have. It is intentional and involves true information, varies in breadth and depth, varies among relationships, usually follows a process, is usually reciprocal, serves many purposes, and is influenced by sex and culture.

   B. Benefits of self-disclosure
      1. Enhancement of relationships and trust
      2. Reciprocity
      3. Emotional release
      4. Assistance to others

- Benefits of self-disclosure include the enhancement of relationships and trust, the probability of reciprocity, emotional release, and the provision of assistance to others.

   C. Risks of self-disclosure
      1. Rejection
      2. Chance of obligating others
      3. Hurt to others
      4. Violation of other people's privacy
      5. Risks of disclosing online

- Risks of self-disclosure include rejection, the chance of obligating others, provision of hurt to hurting others, and violation of another person's privacy. Some of these risks are made more likely when self-disclosure takes place online.

Key Terms

Autonomy face
Breadth
Competence face
Depth
Face
Face needs
Face-threatening act
Facework
Fellowship face

Gossip
Identity
Image
Image management
Johari Window
Need for affection
Need for control
Need for inclusion
Norm of reciprocity

Personality
Reference groups
Reflected appraisal
Self-concept
Self-disclosure
Self-esteem
Self-fulfilling prophecy
Social comparison
Social penetration theory

Discussion Questions

1. In what ways has your self-concept changed over the course of your adolescent and adult life? What parts of your self-concept have remained relatively constant?

2. When it comes to social comparison, what reference groups are particularly relevant to you?

3. What are examples of the multiple identities that you manage on an ongoing basis?

4. Of the three types of face needs—fellowship face, competence face, autonomy face—which is the most important to you? Under what circumstances do the others become more important?

5. Can you think of a situation in which you have been the recipient of inappropriate self-disclosures? How did you feel in that situation? In what ways were the self-disclosures inappropriate?

6. What's good about gossip? In what ways can gossip produce positive relational outcomes?

7. Why do you suppose parents and teachers pay so much attention to the self-esteem of children? What's especially good about having high self-esteem?

8. What are some situations that threaten our need for inclusion? our need for affection? our need for control? How do you generally react in those situations?

Practice Quiz

Multiple Choice

1. The Johari Window is a visual representation of self that consists of all *except* which of the following parts?
   a. Open
   b. Hidden
   c. Visual
   d. Unknown

2. The motivation to maintain some degree of influence in our relationships is known as which of the followings needs?
   a. Need for belonging
   b. Need for control
   c. Need for inclusion
   d. Need for autonomy

3. When we compare ourselves with others, we engage in which of the following to help us form our self-concept?
   a. Social mimicry
   b. Impression management
   c. Reflected concept
   d. Social comparison

4. When expectations cause people to act and communicate in ways that make the expectations come true, this is known as what?
   a. Self-fulfilling prophecy
   b. Self-serving bias
   c. Expectancy outcome theory
   d. Social comparison

5. Individuals in socially marginalized groups tend to engage in three general strategies to help them maintain their self-esteem. Which of the following is *not* one of the strategies?
   a. Valuing things at which they excel
   b. Attributing problems to prejudice in society rather than their own behavior
   c. Comparing themselves with others in their own group more than people in other groups
   d. Maintaining contact primarily with similarly marginalized individuals

6. Which of the following is *not* one of the interpersonal needs articulated by Schutz?
   a. Inclusion
   b. Affection
   c. Similarity
   d. Control

7. Which of the following is *not* one of the three fundamental principles of image management?
   a. Image management is collaborative.
   b. Image management is deceptive.
   c. Multiple identities are managed.
   d. Image management is complex.

8. The need to avoid being imposed upon by others is known as what?
   a. Fellowship face
   b. Competence face
   c. Connectedness face
   d. Autonomy face

9. After Frances shares with James her intense fear of public speaking, James then feels compelled to share with Frances something personal about himself. This example illustrates that self-disclosure usually occurs incrementally and is guided by which of the following?
    a. Norm of reciprocity
    b. Rule of reciprocation
    c. Disclosure rules
    d. The idea that more is better
10. Social penetration theory is characterized by which of the following aspects of self-disclosure?
    a. Breadth and depth
    b. Honesty and intimacy
    c. Quantity and quality
    d. Good and bad

True/False

11. Individuals with low self-esteem overestimate the importance of their failures, whereas people with high self-esteem have a tendency to minimize their failures.

12. Our reference group is usually our peers.
13. People in highly collectivistic cultures tend to think of themselves as independent and unique.
14. High self-monitors have a tendency to state what they are thinking or feeling without paying much attention to the impression they make.
15. Individuals with high self-esteem tend to be happier than individuals with low self-esteem.

Fill in the Blank

16. Your _____ consists of ways you tend to think and act across most situations.
17. Through _____ our self-concept is influenced by how we think other people see us.
18. The subjective evaluation of one's value and worth as a person is known as one's _____.
19. A behavior that threatens one's face need is known as a _____.
20. Disclosures made in an online environment would be described as _____ when they are more personal in nature than they would be face-to-face.

Research Library

Movies

Catch Me If You Can (Drama; 2002; PG-13)
> This film portrays the life of Frank Abagnale, a former con-man who fraudulently portrayed himself as a doctor, an attorney, a substitute teacher, and an airline pilot before being captured. It illustrates in a dramatic fashion the extent to which people can adopt and manage multiple identities.

Meet the Parents (Comedy; 2000; PG-13)
> In this comedy, Greg Focker tries hard to make a good first impression on the parents of his fiancée. Despite his best efforts, however, he makes several poor impressions before finally being accepted by his fiancée's parents. In a humorous way, this film illustrates many of the challenges of eliciting positive impressions from others.

Sweet Home Alabama (Comedy; 2002; PG-13)
> Sweet Home Alabama *is a romantic comedy starring Reese Witherspoon, whose character gets herself into a tangled web by misrepresenting her life to so many friends and family members to achieve her agenda that she just about loses all of them. It portrays the complexity of negotiating multiple "selves" at once.*

Books

Baumeister, R. F. (Ed.). (1993). *Self-esteem: The puzzle of low self-regard.* New York: Plenum.

Cupach, W. R., & Metts, S. (1994). *Facework.* Thousand Oaks, CA: Sage.

Derlega, V. J., Metts, S., Petronio, S., & Margulis, S. T. (1993). *Self-disclosure.* Newbury Park, CA: Sage.

Wright, W. (1998). *Born that way: Genes, behavior, personality.* New York: Knopf.

Journal Articles

Baumgardner, A. H., Kaufman, C. M., & Levy, P. E. (1989). Regulating affect interpersonally: When low esteem leads to greater enhancement. *Journal of Personality and Social Psychology, 56,* 907–921.

Goldschmidt, M. M. (2004). Good person stories: The favor narrative as a self-presentation strategy. *Qualitative Research Reports in Communication, 5,* 28–33.

Kelly, A. E., Klusas, J. A., von-Weiss, R. T., & Kenny, C. (2001). What is it about revealing secrets that is beneficial? *Personality and Social Psychology Bulletin, 27,* 651–665.

Web Sites

www.utexas.edu/student/cmhc/booklets/selfesteem/selfest.html
> This Web site, from the University of Texas Counseling and Mental Health Center, focuses on the benefits of self-esteem and offers suggestions for improving low self-esteem.

kevan.org/johari
> This site allows you to create an interactive Johari Window by selecting characteristics that you feel describe you and then by asking your friends and relatives to nominate their characteristics of you.

4

Interpersonal Perception

What is interpersonal perception?

Why are we prone to perceptual errors?

How can we improve our perception-making ability?

Lisa and Ed

Lisa and her husband, Ed, had been arguing for months about where to send their twins to school. Ed wanted them to go to a private school, but Lisa was concerned about the tuition costs. The conflict was starting to take a toll on their marriage. Lisa thought Ed was being unrealistic about their finances; Ed thought Lisa cared more about money than about their children. One day while Ed was at work, Lisa e-mailed him to remind him to pick up dinner on the way home. Ed never replied, and by the time he got home, Lisa was furious. "So you're just ignoring me now?" she said when he walked through the door, no dinner in hand. When Ed said he didn't get the e-mail and Lisa didn't believe him, it set off yet another evening of conflict, accusations, and sleeping in separate rooms. When Lisa got online the next morning she saw that her e-mail had been returned to her. Only then did she notice that her e-mail to Ed had bounced back because his inbox was full.

Getting along in our social world depends a great deal on our ability to make meaning out of other people's behaviors. When we talk about making meaning, we're talking about the process of perception. Our minds and our senses help us understand the world around us, but they can also lead us to make mistakes, such as misinterpreting other people's behaviors. Lisa's perception of Ed's behavior—that he had reached the point of ignoring her altogether—was off base. Unfortunately, such misunderstandings between people happen all the time. The more we learn about our perception-making abilities, the better we know ourselves, one another, and our world. We can all learn to perceive things more accurately, and this chapter will help show you how. Specifically, you'll learn:

1 } What interpersonal perception is and what factors influence our ability to understand the world around us

2 } Which perception-making tendencies are common

3 } How we form explanations for our own and other people's behaviors

4 } What we can do to improve our perception-making ability

1} Perception Is a Process   {

Despite being one of the most productive marketing managers at her publishing company, Gisele has a hard time earning favor from her supervisor, Dale. She enthusiastically presents new products and innovative marketing plans at her weekly meetings with Dale, but all he ever seems interested in is the bottom line. Instead of sharing Gisele's excitement about fresh ideas, his concerns always center on how much a new product will cost and how much profit it will generate. Gisele has come to perceive Dale as an uninspired manager who is simply biding his time until retirement. Dale concedes that Gisele is energetic and smart, but he perceives her as naïve concerning the way business works.

> *To perceive means to immobilize . . . we seize, in the act of perception, something which outruns perception itself.*
> —Henri Louis Bergson (1859–1941) French scientist

Part of what makes Gisele and Dale's relationship so challenging is the differences in their interpersonal perceptions. In this section, we will examine the process of perception by focusing on:

- What interpersonal perception is
- What the stages of the perception-making process are
- What factors influence the accuracy of our perceptions of others

What Is Interpersonal Perception?

Perception
The process of making meaning from the things we experience in the environment.

It's probably an understatement to say that Gisele and Dale have quite different perceptions of each other, but what does that mean, exactly? **Perception** is the process of making meaning from the things we experience in our environment. When we apply this process to people and relationships, we are engaged in *interpersonal* perception.[1]

We engage in interpersonal perception constantly. Lisa notices that Ed didn't reply to her e-mail, and she makes meaning from it ("he is ignoring me"). Gisele experiences Dale's repeated references to costs and profits, and she makes meaning from it ("he has no enthusiasm for anything except the bottom line"). You notice what your friends, colleagues, relatives, and co-workers do and say, and their words and actions have meaning to you based on the way you interpret them.

Three Stages of the Perception Process

Our minds usually select, organize, and interpret information so quickly and so subconsciously that we think our perceptions are objective, factual reflections of the world. Lisa might say she perceived that Ed was ignoring her because he *was* ignoring her. In fact, she created her perception on the basis of the information she *selected* for attention (he didn't bring home dinner), the way she *organized* that information (this was yet another example of his deliberately being inconsiderate), and the way she *interpreted* it ("he's ignoring me").[2]

Selection, organization, and interpretation are the three basic stages of the perception process. We examine each one in this section.

Selection. The process of perception begins when one or more of your senses is stimulated. You pass a construction site and hear two workers talking about the foundation they're pouring. You see one of your classmates smile at you. A co-worker bumps you on the shoulder as he walks past. If you notice these sensory experiences of hearing, seeing, and being bumped, then they can initiate your process of forming perceptions.

In truth, your senses are constantly stimulated by things in your environment. It's simply impossible, though, to pay attention to everything you're seeing, hearing, smelling, tasting, and feeling at any given moment.[3] When you're walking past the construction site, for instance, you're probably no longer hearing the sounds of traffic going by.

Selection
The process of attending to a stimulus.

Rather than pay attention to all the stimuli in your environment, you engage in **selection,** which means your mind and body help you select certain stimuli to attend to. For example, you notice your classmate smiling at you without paying attention to what others in the classroom are saying or doing. You notice that your spouse failed to bring home dinner, but you ignore the fact that he got the car washed and picked up your dry cleaning. Clearly, the information we attend to influences the perceptions we form.

A key point here is that we don't necessarily make conscious decisions about which stimuli to notice and which to ignore. How, then, does selection occur? Research indicates that three characteristics especially make a particular stimulus more likely to be selected for attention.

First, being unusual or unexpected makes a stimulus stand out.[4] For instance, you might not pay attention to people talking loudly while walking across campus, but hearing the same conversation in the library would probably spark your attention, because it would be unusual in that environment. Perhaps you're walking back to your car after a night class and you don't take particular notice of other students walking along the same sidewalk, but you do notice an older, poorly dressed man pushing a shopping cart. His presence on the sidewalk stands out to you because you aren't used to seeing people on campus who look like him.

Second, repetition, or how frequently you're exposed to a stimulus, makes it stand out.[5] For example, you're more likely to remember radio ads you've heard repeatedly than ones you've heard only once. Similarly, we tend to notice more characteristics about the people we see frequently than about the people we don't see very often, such as their physical appearance or patterns of behavior.

Third, the intensity of a stimulus affects how much we take notice of it. We notice strong odors more than weak ones, for instance, and bright and flashy colors more than dull and muted ones.[6]

Organization The process of categorizing information that has been selected for attention.

Organization. Once you've noticed a particular stimulus, the next step in the perception process is to classify it in some way. This is the task called **organization,** and it helps you make sense of the information by understanding how it is similar to, and different from, other things you know about. To classify a stimulus, your mind applies a *perceptual schema* to it, or a mental framework for organizing information. According to communication researcher Peter Andersen, we use four types of schema to classify information we notice about other people: physical constructs, role constructs, interaction constructs, and psychological constructs.[7]

- *Physical constructs* emphasize people's appearance, causing us to notice objective characteristics such as a person's height, age, ethnicity, or body shape, and

People use physical, role, interaction, and psychological constructs to classify information about others. How would you describe Ryan Seacrest according to each of these schema?

subjective characteristics such as a person's physical attractiveness.

- *Role constructs* emphasize people's social or professional position, so we notice that a person is a teacher, an accountant, a father, a community leader, and so on.[8]
- *Interaction constructs* emphasize people's behavior, so we notice that a person is outgoing, aggressive, shy, sarcastic, or considerate.
- *Psychological constructs* emphasize people's thoughts and feelings, causing us to notice that a person is angry, self-assured, insecure, envious, or worried.

Think about the first time you met your interpersonal communication instructor. What sensory information did you notice about him or her, and which schema did you apply to that information? Perhaps you paid attention to your instructor's age, ethnicity, and choice of clothing. If so, you probably organized those pieces of information as *physical constructs,* meaning you recognized that they all dealt with your instructor as a physical being. If you paid attention to how friendly or how demanding your instructor is, you probably organized those pieces of information as *interaction constructs,* recognizing that they all dealt with how your instructor behaves or communicates. If your focus was on how well your instructor taught, you were emphasizing *role constructs* by attending to your instructor's professional role in the classroom. Finally, if you took note of how happy or self-confident your instructor seemed, you focused on *psychological constructs* by paying attention to his or her disposition or mood.

Whichever schema we use to organize information about people—and we may use more than one at a time—the process of organization helps us determine the ways in which various pieces of information that we select for attention are related to one another.[9] If you notice that your neighbor is a Little League softball coach and the father of three children, for example, then those two pieces of information go together because they both relate to the roles he plays. If you notice that he seems irritated and angry, those pieces of information go together as examples of his psychological state. In addition, you recognize them as being different from information about his roles, physical characteristics, or behaviors.

Perceptual schemas can also help us determine how other people are similar to us and how they're different. If your dentist is female, for instance, that's one way in which she is similar to (or different from) you. If she is very friendly and outgoing, that's another similarity (or difference). Perceptual schemas help us organize sensory information in some meaningful way so we can move forward with the process of perception.[10]

Interpretation The process of assigning meaning to information that has been selected for attention and organized.

Interpretation. After noticing and classifying a stimulus, you have to assign it an **interpretation** to figure out what it means for you. Let's say one of your co-workers has been acting especially friendly toward you for the last week. She smiles at you all the time, brings you little gifts, and offers to run errands for you over her lunch break. Her behavior is definitely noticeable, and you've probably classified it as a psychological construct, because it relates to her thoughts and feelings about you.

What does her behavior *mean*, though? That is, how do you interpret it? Is she being nice to you because she's getting ready to ask you for a big favor? Does she want to look good in front of her boss? Or does she like you? If she does like you, does she like you as a friend, or is she making a romantic gesture?

To address those questions, you likely will pay attention to three factors to interpret her behavior: your personal experience, your knowledge of her, and the closeness of your relationship with her. Your personal experience helps you assign meaning to behavior. If co-workers have been nice to you in the past just to get favors from you later, then you might be suspicious of this co-worker's behavior.[11]

Your knowledge of the person helps you interpret her actions. If you know she's friendly and nice to everyone, you might interpret her behavior differently than if you notice that she's being nice only to you.[12] Finally, the closeness of your relationship influences how you interpret a person's behavior. When your best friend does you an unexpected favor, you probably interpret it as a sincere sign of friendship. In contrast, when a co-worker does you a favor, you're more likely to wonder whether he or she has an ulterior motive.[13]

Experience, knowledge, and closeness can all affect how you interpret something that you perceive, but these factors don't necessarily suggest the *same* interpretation. Think back to the example of seeing a poorly dressed man pushing a shopping cart on campus at night. Perhaps you have had experiences dealing with panhandlers and homeless people in the city where you grew up, so you interpret his appearance and behavior as suggesting that he is a transient. Let's say you also know, however, that the drama department at your school is currently rehearsing a play about the challenges of homelessness. This knowledge leads you to interpret his appearance and behavior as suggesting that he is part of the drama production.

In this instance, your experience and knowledge lead you to quite different interpretations of the same situation. Because you don't know this man personally, the closeness of your relationship with him doesn't provide you with any additional clues to aid your interpretation.

We've said that perception is a process, which means it happens in stages. That doesn't necessarily mean the process is always linear, however. The three stages of perception—selecting, organizing, and interpreting information—all overlap.[14] How we interpret a behavior depends on what we notice about it, for example, but what we notice can also depend on the way we interpret it.

Let's assume, for example, that you're listening to a speech by a politician. If you find her ideas and proposals favorable, then you might interpret her demeanor and speaking style as examples of her intelligence and confidence. In contrast, if you oppose her ideas, then you might interpret her demeanor and speaking style as examples of arrogance or incompetence. Either interpretation, in turn, might lead you to select for attention only those behaviors or characteristics that support your interpretation and to ignore those that don't. Therefore, even though perception happens in stages, the stages don't always take place in the same order. The "At a Glance" box provides a brief summary of the three stages of perception.

At a Glance: Stages of the Perception Process

Interpersonal perception involves three different but interrelated stages: selection, organization, and interpretation.

Selection	We select certain sensory information for attention.
Organization	We categorize each piece of information to determine how it is similar to, and different from, other pieces of information.
Interpretation	We assign meaning to each piece of information.

We're constantly noticing, organizing, and interpreting things around us, including other people's be-haviors. Like other skills, perception takes practice, and our perceptions are more accurate on some occasions than others.

What Influences Our Perceptual Accuracy?

Because we constantly make perceptions, you might think we'd all be experts at it by now. As you've probably noticed from your own experience, however, perceptual mistakes are often easy to make. For example, perhaps your sister calls to check on you out of concern when you're feeling ill. Because your illness makes you short-tempered and grumpy, however, you perceive that she is calling only because she feels obligated to. As another example, on your overseas trip you perceive that two adults you see in a restaurant are having a heated argument, when in fact they are engaging in behaviors that signify interest and involvement in that culture.

Why do we continue to make perceptual errors despite our accumulated experience? Three factors in particular influence the accuracy of our perceptions and can lead to errors: our physiology, our cultural and co-cultural backgrounds, and our social roles.

Physiological states and traits. Physiology is the study of the mechanical and biochemical ways in which our bodies work. Many aspects of our physiology influence the way we perceive the world.[15] In this section, we focus specifically on physiological states and traits.

Physiological *states* are conditions that are temporary. We enter and leave various physiological states, meaning that their influence comes and goes over time. For instance, the physiological state of feeling tired alters our perception of time and can make us anxious. Therefore, the five minutes we're waiting in line at the grocery store might seem much longer.[16] Similarly, being hungry or sick seems to sap our energy and make us grumpy and impatient, reducing our ability to get along with others.[17] You can probably think of personal experiences that demonstrate how those or other aspects of your physiology have influenced your perceptual accuracy.

If you're not a morning person but your romantic partner is, this difference in your biological rhythms can create conflict in the relationship.

In contrast, our physiological *traits* are conditions that affect us on an ongoing basis. Compared with states, which are continually changing, traits are more enduring. For example, perception relies a great deal on our senses—our abilities to see, hear, touch, taste, and smell. A voice that sounds just right to a hearing-impaired person may seem too loud to others. A food you find too spicy might seem bland to someone else.[18] You might think a room is too hot, another person might think it's too cold, and a third person might think it's just right. Our senses help us perceive and understand the world around us. So, when our sensory abilities differ, our perceptions often do, as well.

Another physiological trait is your biological rhythm, or the cycle of daily changes in body temperature, alertness, and mood that you go through.[19] As levels of various hormones rise and fall throughout the day, your energy level and susceptibility to stress change as well. Consequently, there are times during the day when you interact positively with people, and other times when you feel cranky and are more easily annoyed.

Everyone's biological rhythm is a little different. You might be refreshed and alert first thing in the morning, whereas your roommate is more of a night owl who doesn't really get going until later in the day. Most of the time, these differences aren't a huge problem. Research shows, however, that when romantic partners have very different biological rhythms, they report more conflict and less intimacy than partners whose rhythms are more closely matched.[20]

Consider the case of Aida and her partner, Luca. Aida wakes up around 6 a.m. every day. Her biological rhythm gives her the most energy early in the morning, but by early evening she is drowsy and ready for bed. In contrast, Luca likes to sleep until 8 or 9 in the morning. He gets energized late at night and will often stay up until well past midnight. As a result of their different rhythms, Luca is grumpy whenever they both have to be up early, such as when they have to catch a morning flight. Similarly, Aida is unhappy whenever they both have to stay up late, such as when they babysit their nephews.

Because either Aida or Luca is always cranky during these times, they frequently get on each other's nerves. They also interpret each other's behavior in negative ways. For instance, when Luca forgets to put his clothes in the washing machine, Aida's short temper leads her to interpret his behavior as a deliberate attempt to annoy her instead of as an innocent oversight. Similarly, if Aida speaks impatiently to Luca, his own crankiness causes him to interpret her speaking tone as condescending rather than to consider that she may just be tired. Their tendency to interpret each other's behaviors negatively causes Aida and Luca to let even small annoyances turn into arguments. If their biological rhythms were more similar, however, they would feel energized and drowsy at the same times, making them more understanding of each other and less likely to feel "out of sync" with each other.

Culture and co-culture. Another powerful influence on the accuracy of our perceptions is the culture and co-cultures with which we identify. Cultural values and norms have many different effects on the way we communicate interpersonally. In addition to affecting our behavior, culture influences our perceptions and interpretations of other people's behaviors.[21]

Let's say that Jason, an American, is meeting Rosella, an Italian, at their company's international sales meeting. Right away, Jason notices that Rosella stands very close to him and touches him frequently, which makes him a little uncomfortable. He might perceive that she's being dominant and aggressive, because in the United States people usually maintain more personal space and touch new acquaintances less often. Noticing Jason's discomfort, Rosella might perceive that he's shy or socially awkward, because Italians are used to closer interpersonal distances and more frequent touch.[22] In this situation, Rosella and Jason's cultural norms affect not only their own behavior but also their perceptions of each other's behaviors.

Co-cultural differences can also influence perceptions. Teenagers might perceive their parents' advice as outdated or irrelevant, for instance, whereas parents might perceive their teenagers' indifference to their advice as naïve.[23] Some middle-class people might perceive that wealthy people are constantly taking advantage of them, whereas wealthy people may see lower-class people as lazy or ungrateful.[24] Liberals and conservatives might each perceive the others' behaviors as rooted in ignorance.[25]

Each of us has multiple "lenses" through which we perceive the world around us. Some of these lenses are products of our cultural background. Many others are

Each of us has multiple "lenses" through which we perceive the world around us.

influenced by our age, social class, political orientation, education, religion, and hobbies, and by other elements of our co-cultures.

Unfortunately, for people in many socially marginalized populations, the experience of feeling misunderstood by others is common. For instance, Hasani is a high school teacher who has struggled with clinical depression for most of his adult life. Much of the time, he controls his depression adequately with medication. Occasionally, however, he has a severe depressive episode, during which he becomes physically and mentally immobilized. His illness causes him to miss work more frequently than normal, often requiring his principal to find a substitute for him at the last minute.

Some of Hasani's colleagues and even some of his students perceive that he is merely taking advantage of a system that allows him to miss work without penalty. Because the disabling nature of depression isn't outwardly visible—in contrast to being in a wheelchair, for instance—it can be easy for others to perceive that Hasani is simply taking a day off whenever he is in a bad mood. This inaccurate perception is fueled by people's misunderstandings about depression.

Like people with mental illnesses, people in many other marginalized populations frequently find that others have inaccurate perceptions of them that are rooted in misunderstanding.[26] As the "Dark Side" box on page 130 details, these inaccurate perceptions often lead to prejudice and discrimination against members of socially marginalized groups.

Social roles. A social role is a set of behaviors that is expected of someone in a particular social situation. Each of us plays several social roles, and these roles can also influence the accuracy of our perceptions. One example is gender roles. Gender and biological sex affect a range of communication behaviors, so it's not surprising that they influence the perceptions we form of others.[27]

After years of hard work and consistently high performance ratings, for example, Karin has finally been promoted to senior manager at the telecommunications company where she works. She now supervises a staff of 12 managers, 7 male and 5 female. Karin is experienced, highly motivated, and very straightforward in her dealings with others. The women on her staff see her as powerful, assertive, and an excellent role model for female executives. To the

The Dark Side of Interpersonal Communication
Misperceptions About Marginalized Populations

Marginalized populations live outside the "mainstream" in a given society. Some people are born into a marginalized group, such as ethnic minorities and children born into poverty. In other cases people become marginalized through events that happen in their lives, such as developing a mental illness or acquiring AIDS. Every marginalized group is distinctive in some ways. One common experience, however, is being misperceived by people outside the group. These misperceptions are problematic because they can lead to prejudice and discrimination.

Prejudice means, literally, "pre-judging," or making up your mind about someone before you know him or her. It often involves suspicion or hatred of members of a particular group, based on that group's ethnicity, religion, sexual orientation, or other factors. Being prejudiced against a certain group means you are more likely to treat people from that group negatively or unfairly, even if you don't know anything else about them as individuals.

Marginalized populations aren't the only ones who experience prejudice. It's possible, in fact, to be prejudiced against almost any group of people, despite its characteristics. Research indicates, however, that prejudices against traditionally marginalized groups—such as ethnic minorities and elderly people—are common, even among individuals who perceive themselves as being free of prejudice. Some activities that emphasize empathy and role playing appear to help reduce people's prejudices against one another.

We sometimes use the terms "prejudice" and "discrimination" interchangeably, but they're actually different things. By itself, discrimination isn't a bad thing. To *discriminate* simply means to make a choice or distinction between or among options. You discriminate whenever you decide what to wear, what to eat for dinner, which classes to take, or whom to hang out with on a Friday night. In truth, each of us discriminates on an ongoing basis. What, then, makes discrimination so bad when it is applied to marginalized populations?

men, however, she seems domineering, aggressive, and pushy, because they perceive her behavior as unfeminine. In this instance, women and men who otherwise have much in common (they are all managers under the same boss) perceive the same pattern of behaviors in completely different ways.

Our experience and occupational roles can also influence our perceptions of other people's behaviors.[28] As a first-time mother, for instance, Charlotte was terrified when her infant son began jerking and convulsing while she was holding him one day. She was certain he was having a seizure, so she rushed him to the emergency room. Derek, an experienced pediatric nurse, recognized the problem immediately: The baby simply had the hiccups. He explained to Charlotte that newborns often don't make the "hiccup" sound, so it's easy to mistake the baby's jerking motion for something more serious. Because of the differences in their training and experience with babies, Derek and Charlotte perceived the same behavior quite differently.

Though it seems almost reflexive, perception is actually a complex process susceptible to many different biases and patterns. We'll examine some of these biases in the next section.

The answer is that people don't always discriminate for the right reasons. Let's say you have to choose who should be hired for a job. There's nothing wrong with discriminating among candidates on the basis of their skills, their education, or their experience. In fact, most of us would want to hire the most qualified person for the job. Discriminating against people because of their skin color, sexual orientation, disability, economic status, or sex is a different issue, however, because these factors are often irrelevant to a person's ability to work. Each of these cases is an example of *unfair discrimination,* and people from many marginalized populations report having been victims of unfair discrimination when it comes to finding housing, getting a job, securing a bank loan, and even dating or marrying the person they love.

Ask Yourself:

- What perceptions do you have of sexual minorities; people who are homeless, hearing impaired, or overweight; and other marginalized groups? Where do these perceptions come from?

- How do you feel when others hold mistaken perceptions of you? What might you do to reduce your chances of misperceiving others?

From Me to You:

- People sometimes get nervous when talking to members of marginalized populations. Concerned that they might say or do something offensive, many people find themselves becoming rigid or hyperpolite around minorities or other marginalized groups. This pattern of behavior, in itself, can serve to reinforce divisions among people. It's hard for others to feel comfortable around you if you don't seem to feel comfortable around them. People in many marginalized groups will tell you that they don't expect any kind of special treatment. Indeed, what they often want the most is simply to be treated like anyone else. So relax! When you talk to people, try not to see them as members of a particular group, but simply as people.

Sources: Aboud, F. E., & Levy, S. R. (2000). Interventions to reduce prejudice and discrimination in children and adolescents. In S. Oskamp (Ed.), *Reducing prejudice and discrimination* (pp. 269–293). Mahwah, NJ: Lawrence Erlbaum Associates; Burstein, P. (1985). *Discrimination, jobs, and politics: The struggle for equal employment opportunity in the United States since the New Deal.* Chicago: University of Chicago Press; Greenwald, A. G., McGhee, D. E., & Schwartz, J. L. K. (1998). Measuring individual differences in implicit cognition: The implicit association test. *Journal of Personality and Social Psychology, 74,* 1464–1480.

Learn It: What does it mean to engage in interpersonal perception? How are selection, organization, and interpretation related to one another? How do physiological states or traits, culture, co-culture, and social roles affect our perception-making ability?

Try It: Think of a perception you recently made of someone else's behavior. In writing, describe what the person did and what your perception was. Given what you now know about the effects of physiology, culture, and social roles on perception making, formulate at least two alternative perceptions that you might have made about the same behavior.

Reflect on It: What sensory information are you attending to right now? How do your co-cultures influence the perceptions you make of others?

People in many marginalized groups will tell you that they don't expect any kind of special treatment. What they often want the most is simply to be treated like anyone else.

2} Fundamental Forces in Interpersonal Perception {

Most of the time we believe we're seeing things as they really are. Karin's male managers saw her as aggressive and domineering, but is that because she actually *was*, or simply because they disliked having a female boss? Charlotte believed her son was having convulsions, but is that because he was, or simply because she didn't recognize that he merely had the hiccups? Even though we rely a great deal on our perceptions, research shows that those perceptions are vulnerable to a number of biases, many of which operate outside our conscious awareness. In this section, we examine seven fundamental forces that affect our perceptions:

- Stereotyping
- Primacy
- Recency
- Perceptual set
- Egocentrism
- Positivity bias
- Negativity bias

> *What we see depends mainly on what we look for.*
>
> —Sir John Lubbock (1834–1913) British statesman

Stereotyping Relies on Generalizations

Stereotypes

Generalizations about groups of people that are applied to individual members of those groups.

We're probably all familiar with **stereotypes**, which are generalizations about a group or category of people that can have powerful influences on how we perceive other people.[29] Stereotyping is a three-part process:

- First, we identify a group we believe another person belongs to ("you are a blonde").
- Second, we recall some generalization others often make about the people in that group ("blondes have more fun").
- Finally, we apply that generalization to the person ("therefore, you must have more fun").

You can probably think of stereotypes for many groups.[30] What stereotypes come to mind when you think about elderly people, for instance? How about people with physical or mental disabilities? Wealthy people? Homeless people? Gays and lesbians? Science fiction fans? Immigrants? Athletes? What stereotypes come to mind when you think about yourself?

Many people find stereotyping to be distasteful or unethical, particularly when stereotypes have to do with characteristics such as sex, race, or sexual orientation.[31] There's no question that stereotyping can lead us to some inaccurate, even offensive, evaluations of other people. The reason for this is that stereotypes underestimate the differences among individuals in a group. It may be true, for instance, that elderly people are more conservative than other age groups, but that doesn't

Stereotyping means classifying a person as part of a group, making a generalization about that group, then applying the generalization to that person. What stereotypes come to your mind for this person?

mean that *every* elderly person is conservative or that all elderly people are conservative to the same extent. Similarly, people of Asian descent are sometimes stereotyped as being more studious than those in other ethnic groups, but that doesn't mean every Asian person is a good student or that all Asians do equally well at school.[32]

There is variation in almost every group. Stereotypes focus our attention only on the generalizations, however. In fact, we have a tendency to engage in *selective memory bias,* remembering information that supports our stereotypes but forgetting information that doesn't.[33] During interpersonal conflicts, for instance, both women and men tend to remember only their partners' stereotypical behaviors.[34] Let's take a look at a conflict between Carmen and her boyfriend, Nick, regarding their division of household labor:

Carmen: You were supposed to vacuum and put in a load of laundry when you got home; instead you're just sitting there watching TV. Why am I the one who has to do everything around here?

Nick: Look, I'm sorry. I've had a long day, and all I want to do is sit here for a while and de-stress.

Carmen: I understand that, Nick, but I've also had a long day; I'd like to just sit around doing nothing too, but this stuff has to get done, and it shouldn't be my responsibility to do it all.

Nick: Whatever. Can't we talk about this later?

What do you think Carmen and Nick will remember most about this conflict after it's over? Nick may recall that Carmen nagged and criticized him without remembering that she also listened to what he was saying. Likewise, Carmen may report that Nick "tuned her out" without noting that he also offered an apology. In other words, they both may remember only the other person's behaviors that conformed to stereotypes for female and male behavior.

That is one reason why it's so important to check our perceptions before we act on them. After an argument like Nick and Carmen's, for instance, ask yourself what communication behaviors the other person engaged in that were *not* necessarily stereotypical. That may help you form a more accurate memory of the conflict; it may also help you to treat the other person as an individual and not simply as a representative of his or her sex.[35]

We have to remember, though, that perceptions about an individual made on the basis of a stereotype are not always inaccurate.[36] For example, consider the stereotype that *women love being around children.* If you met a woman and assumed (on the basis of this stereotype) that she enjoyed being around children, you might be wrong—however, you also might be right. Not every woman enjoys spending time with children, but some do. By the same token, not every elderly person is conservative, but some are. Not every sorority sister likes to party, but some do. Not every male florist is gay, but some are.

The point is that just because your perception of someone is consistent with a stereotype, it isn't necessarily inaccurate. Just as we shouldn't assume a stereotypical judgment is true, neither should we assume it's false.

At this point, you might expect me to recommend that you abandon stereotyping altogether. Actually, that advice would be unrealistic. A more productive way of dealing with stereotypes involves two elements: awareness and communication. First, be aware of the stereotypical perceptions you make. What assumptions do you make, for instance, when you meet an elderly Asian woman, an African American teenage boy, or an adult in a wheelchair? It's natural to form perceptions of these people based on what you believe to be true about the groups they belong to. Try to be aware of when you do this, however, and also to remember that your perceptions may not be accurate.

Second, instead of assuming your perceptions of other people are correct, get to know these people, and let your perceptions be guided by what you learn about them as individuals. By communicating interpersonally, you can begin to discover how well other people fit or don't fit the stereotypical perceptions you formed of them.

To deal productively with stereotypes, we must first be aware of how they influence our perceptions and behavior. What stereotypes would you apply to this person?

The Primacy Effect Governs First Impressions

As the saying goes, you only get one chance to make a good first impression. There's no shortage of advice available on how to accomplish this, from picking the right clothes to polishing your conversational skills. Have you ever noticed that no one talks about the importance of making a good *second* impression? What's so special about first impressions anyway?

Primacy effect The tendency to emphasize the first impression over later impressions when forming a perception.

According to a principle called the **primacy effect,** first impressions are critical because they set the tone for all future interactions.[37] Our first impressions of someone seem to stick in our mind more than our second, third, or fourth impressions do. In an early study of the primacy effect, psychologist Solomon Asch found that a person described as "intelligent, industrious, impulsive, critical, stubborn, and envious" was evaluated more favorably than one described as "envious, stubborn, critical, impulsive, industrious, and intelligent."[38] Notice that most of those adjectives are negative, but when the description begins with a positive one (intelligent), the effects of the more negative ones that follow it are diminished.

Asch's study illustrates that the first information we learn about someone tends to have a stronger effect on how we perceive that person than information we receive later on.[39] That's why we work so hard to make a good first impression in a job interview, on a date, or in other important situations. When people evaluate us favorably at first, they're more likely to perceive us in a positive light from then on.[40]

As an example of first impressions, take a look at the following conversation between Gina, a mortgage officer, and Lee, a new client who is deaf and communicates with Gina through a sign language interpreter. In this situation, Lee has just arrived with his interpreter for his first meeting with Gina.

Lee: Thank you for meeting with me. I'm interested in refinancing my mortgage and wanted to look at some different options with you.

Gina [speaking to the interpreter]: Uh, tell him I can show him some options, but this could take a while if everything has to go through you. Doesn't he read lips?

Lee: You can speak directly to me. I don't read lips, but I can communicate with you just fine.

Gina [laughing nervously, unsure of whom to speak to]: Sorry, this is just a little too weird; I'm not used to talking to people like this.

Lee: Just talk to me like you would anyone else, please.

Gina is making a poor first impression, because by speaking only to Lee's interpreter, she is treating Lee as if he weren't even there. When you speak to a deaf person through a sign language interpreter, it's appropriate to direct your attention to the person, not to the interpreter. As someone who has been deaf since birth, Lee is used to interacting with people who don't know this, and he doesn't mind educating others about it.

By commenting on how long the refinance application process is going to take through an interpreter, asking if Lee can read lips, and saying "this is just a little too weird," Gina is giving the impression that she considers Lee's hearing impairment to be an inconvenience to her. Her actions likely create a perception in Lee's mind that Gina is somewhat self-centered and not very professional.

Because of the primacy effect, Lee will probably leave Gina's office with a poor impression of her, even if she communicates more professionally during the rest of the meeting. In other words, her negative first impression will be more memorable to Lee than the impressions she makes later in the conversation.

Now, let's look at what Gina might have done differently:

Lee: Thank you for meeting with me. I'm interested in refinancing my mortgage and wanted to look at some different options with you.

Gina [speaking directly to Lee]: I'd be happy to help you with that. Before we start, can I get either of you a cup of coffee?

Lee: No, thank you. I would take a glass of water, though.

Gina: Absolutely. Let me get that for you, and then we'll go over some options for your refinance.

Lee: I appreciate it, thanks.

In this instance, Gina has made a much better first impression. Not only does she look at Lee when she speaks to him, but she also focuses on making him feel comfortable by offering him coffee and saying that she will be glad to help him with his plans to refinance. Although she acknowledges the interpreter's presence by offering coffee to him as well as Lee, her focus is clearly on Lee. This gives Lee the impression that Gina is professional and considerate. Because Gina has made a good first impression, Lee is likely to feel positively about her even after their meeting has ended.

Although first impressions are powerful, they aren't necessarily permanent.[41] For example, when Suzette first met her hairstylist, Trey, she didn't like him at all. At the time, he had just come from a contentious visit with the manager of his salon, and he was in a bad mood when Suzette sat down in his chair. As a result, he seemed distant and uninterested while he cut her hair. His behavior made a poor impression on Suzette, and she decided to switch to another stylist at the same salon after that. As she continued to see Trey on her subsequent visits, however, he would always greet her warmly and ask her about her family. Over time, Suzette began to realize that her initial negative impression of Trey was inaccurate and that he is actually a nice, caring person.

You can probably think of at least one good friend whom you didn't especially like when you first met. The primacy effect means that first impressions are powerful, not that they are unchangeable. By communicating with someone in more positive ways than we might have initially, as Trey did with Suzette, we can sometimes overcome negative first impressions.

The Recency Effect Influences Impressions

Stand-up comedians will tell you that the two most important jokes in a show are the first and the last. We've already discussed how important it is to make a good first impression. As most entertainers know, however, it's equally important to make a good *final* impression, because that's what the audience will remember after leaving. This advice follows a principle known as the **recency effect,** which says that the most recent impression we have of someone is more powerful than our earlier impressions.[42]

Recency effect The tendency to emphasize the most recent impression over earlier impressions when forming a perception.

As an example, let's say that Diego has been diagnosed with testicular cancer and has made appointments with two doctors, Dr. Tan and Dr. Meyer, to discuss his treatment options. The doctors made equally good first impressions by listening to Diego and asking him questions about his symptoms and his overall health. At the end of their visit, Dr. Tan explained the specifics of surgery, radiation therapy, and chemotherapy to Diego and asked him how he felt about each option before ul-

The recency effect says we are most influenced by our most recent impression of someone. Diego formed a positive impression of Dr. Tan, in part because of how positively their interaction ended.

timately recommending surgery. Diego left the first appointment with a positive impression of Dr. Tan.

At Diego's other appointment, however, Dr. Meyer ended by telling him that he definitely needed surgery and that any doctor who said otherwise was wrong. To Diego, this approach made Dr. Meyer seem as though he was pushy and didn't care about Diego's feelings or his treatment preferences. As you might guess, Diego left the second appointment with a negative impression of Dr. Meyer. Significantly, Diego didn't form this negative impression because their visit had started poorly. On the contrary, he felt good about both doctors at the beginning of his appointments. Rather, the last impression Diego formed of Dr. Meyer before he left was negative, and that impression remained with him after the visit.

At first glance, it might seem as though the recency effect and the primacy effect contradict each other. Which is the more important impression—the first one or the most recent one? The answer is that both appear to be more important than any impressions that we form in between.[43] To fully understand this point, consider the last movie you saw. You probably have a better recollection of how the movie started and how it ended than you do of all the events that happened in between.

The same observation applies to our perceptions of other people. Diego's impressions of Dr. Tan and Dr. Meyer weren't based on his perceptions of everything that happened during his appointments. What he remembered was how they started (positively for both doctors) and how they ended (positively for Dr. Tan, negatively for Dr. Meyer). Figure 4.1 illustrates the relationship between the primacy effect and the recency effect.

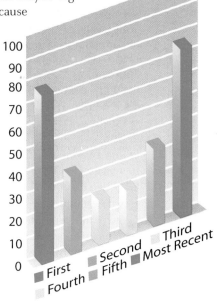

FIGURE 4.1 Our first impressions and our most recent impressions are more important than those that come in between.

Our Perceptual Set Limits What We Perceive

"I'll believe it when I see it," people often say. Our perception of reality is influenced not only by what we see, however, but also by our biases, our expectations, and our desires. These elements can create what psychologists call a **perceptual set,** or a predisposition to perceive only what we want or expect to perceive.[44] An equally valid motto, therefore, might be "I'll see it when I believe it."

For example, our perceptual set regarding gender guides the way we perceive and interact with newborns. Without the help of contextual cues such as blue or pink baby clothes, we sometimes have a hard time telling whether an infant is male or female. However, if we're told the infant's name is David, we perceive that child to be stronger and bigger than if the same infant is called Diana.[45] Our perceptual set tells us that male infants are usually bigger and stronger than female ones, so we "see" a bigger, stronger baby when we're told it's a boy.

A dramatic example of perceptual set occurred after the publication of a photo taken of the surface of Mars. In 1976, while surveying the Martian topography, Viking Orbiter 1 captured what many observers believed to be the unmistakable image of a human face. (See Figure 4.2, photograph a.) This perception fueled the public's imagination about the existence of intelligent life on our neighbor planet. A

Perceptual set A predisposition to perceive only what we want or expect to perceive.

FIGURE 4.2 These two photos are of the same place on the Martian landscape. Picture a, taken in 1976, shows what to most people looks like a human face. When Picture b was taken in 2001, it revealed that the "face" was just an optical illusion created by light and shadow. The reason we "see" a face in the first place is because our perceptual set leads us to recognize faces in anything that resembles them—including rocks on Mars!

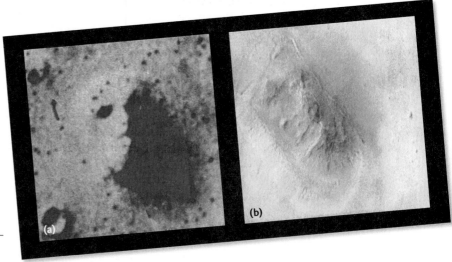

quarter century later, however, the Mars Global Surveyor captured a higher-resolution photo of the same site (see Figure 4.2, photograph b) that proved that the "face" in the 1976 picture was simply an optical illusion created by light and shadow.

It was our perceptual set that led us to "see" the face to begin with. Indeed, the face is such a fundamental tool for interpersonal recognition and communication that we are led to recognize it in nearly any pattern that resembles it. Research has shown that even newborns stare longer at figures that resemble faces than at similar figures that do not (see Figure 4.3).[46]

FIGURE 4.3 Research suggests that humans are attuned to recognizing faces at a remarkably early age. Studies show that newborns—some less than an hour old—stare significantly longer at drawings that loosely resemble faces (such as the picture on the left) than at similar drawings that do not (such as the picture on the right). Sources: Monloch, C. J., Lewis, T. L., Budreau, D. R., Maurer, D., Dannemiller, J. L., Stephens, B. R., & Kleiner-Gathercoal, K. A. (1991). Face perception during early infancy. *Psychological Science, 10*, 419–422; Morton, J., & Johnson, M. H. (1991). CONSPEC and CONLERN: A two-process theory of infant face recognition. *Psychological Review, 98*, 164–181.

Our perceptual set also influences how we make sense of people and circumstances. People who are deeply religious may perceive medical healings as miracles or answers to prayer, whereas others see them as natural responses to medication.[47] People who are highly homophobic are more likely than others to perceive affectionate behavior between men as sexual in nature.[48]

Our cultural experiences often influence our perceptual set. Take a look at the family in Figure 4.4. What do you see? Westerners tend to see a family sitting indoors, with a window above the woman's head. When this drawing was shown to people from East Africa, however, nearly all of them said the family was sitting under a tree and that the woman was balancing a metal box on her head.[49]

The reason for the different interpretations is that people see what they are used to seeing. People in Western societies are used to houses and other buildings in which walls are at right angles to one another, with windows embedded in them. This can create a perceptual set that causes them to interpret the box in the drawing as a window and the vertical image in the middle of the drawing as the corner of a room.

FIGURE 4.4 **What do you see depicted in this picture?**

Source: Deregowski, J. B. (1973). Illusion and culture. In R. L. Gregory & E. H. Gombrich (Eds.) *Illusion in nature and art* (pp. 1690–191). London: Gerald Duckworth & Co.

In many African societies, however, homes have rounded walls. As a result, people in these societies are less likely than Westerners to see the vertical image in the middle of the drawing as the corner of a room. In addition, women in some African societies commonly carry boxes or baskets by balancing them on their heads. Consequently, when people from these societies look at the drawing, they are more likely to see a box balancing on the young woman's head.

Neither way of interpreting the drawing is necessarily correct or incorrect. Although you might be amused by what people in other cultures "see" in the picture, remember that you are interpreting the picture according to your own perceptual set as well.

Perceptual set is relevant for interpersonal communication because it can shape the way we interpret social situations. Suppose, for instance, that Ryan, Emilio, and Kerry are all sitting around a café table eating ice cream when a married couple enters the café and walks up to the cash register to place an order. The man seems irritated, the woman looks as if she has recently been crying, and neither spouse talks to—or even looks at—the other. They order two coffees and walk to an outdoor patio behind the café, leaving Ryan, Emilio, and Kerry to form their own perceptions of the situation.

Having grown up with an abusive, alcoholic father, Kerry perceives that the spouses had recently been fighting and that the woman was probably crying because of something her husband had said or done. Her perceptual set, therefore, causes her to "see" the aftermath of a conflict that was the man's fault. In contrast, Emilio, who has lost several relatives to chronic illness in the past few years, isn't primed to perceive conflict the way Kerry is. Instead, his perceptual set leads him to perceive that the couple must be worried about something, such as the failing health of one of their children. Finally, Ryan is madly in love with his new romantic partner, which puts him in such an elated mood that he doesn't notice there is anything wrong with the spouses in the first place.

All three friends witnessed the same couple walk into the café, place an order, and then leave. Their distinctive perceptual sets, however, led them to form different perceptions about the situation.

Egocentrism Narrows Our Perspective

If you've spent any time around preschoolers, you've probably noticed that they often behave in ways that, to adults, seem selfish or inconsiderate. Timmy stands right in front of the TV, blocking your view. Susie asks you questions while you're on the phone. These types of behaviors can be frustrating for parents, but in reality, the children aren't being selfish or inconsiderate at all. Instead, they are **egocentric,** meaning they lack the ability to take another person's perspective.[50]

According to developmental psychologist Jean Piaget, egocentrism is a normal part of development for children ages 2 to 6.[51] Timmy doesn't understand that he is blocking your view because he assumes you can see what he sees. Susie assumes you can hear only what she hears, so she doesn't know she is interrupting your phone conversation.

Although most people grow out of the egocentric stage by mid-childhood, even adults can behave egocentrically from time to time.[52] More important, our egocentrism can influence our perceptions of others. This happens when we assume that other people experience the world the same way we do.

Let's say, for example, that Paul and Marty are new roommates who don't know each other very well. Marty is very sociable and outgoing; Paul is very quiet and somewhat shy. The night of Paul's 20th birthday, Marty organizes a big get-together and invites everyone in their residence hall to the surprise party. Paul is surprised, all right, but not in a good way. It turns out that the *last* thing he wanted to do was spend his birthday at a loud, crowded party making conversation with people he hardly knew. So, he spends 30 minutes at the party and then leaves. The next day, Marty is angry because Paul didn't appreciate any of the trouble he took to arrange the party. Paul is angry because he hates parties and that wasn't how he wanted to spend his birthday.

Paul and Marty are both being egocentric here, because each is assuming that the other should react to the situation the way *he* would. Marty loves parties, so it doesn't even occur to him that Paul doesn't; he just thinks Paul is being ungrateful. Paul hates being in crowds, so he doesn't even consider that Marty was trying to do something nice for him.

The opposite of being egocentric is being "altercentric," or focused on the perspective of another person instead of your own. To what extent do you communicate in altercentric ways? Take a look at the "Getting to Know You" box to find out.

Positivity and Negativity Biases Affect Perception

Sometimes our perceptions are influenced more by positive or negative information than by neutral information. When we pay the most attention to positive information, we are exhibiting what researchers call a **positivity bias.**[53]

One form of the positivity bias is the tendency of people in love to look at each other "through rose-colored glasses," overestimating the partner's positive qualities while underestimating or ignoring his or her faults or shortcomings.[54] Perhaps you've been around people who have seen their love interests in this way. Research suggests this is a normal stage of relationship development, and that a certain amount of "idealizing" is actually healthy for new relationships.[55] Most relationships eventually grow out of this stage, however. People who cling to an idealized view of their romantic partners may experience disappointment when they realize the person is not as perfect as they thought.

The opposite of the positivity bias is the **negativity bias,** or the tendency to weigh negative information more heavily than positive.[56] According to the negativity bias, even one piece of negative information can taint your perception of someone you

Egocentric Unable to take another person's perspective.

Positivity bias The tendency to focus heavily on a person's positive attributes when forming a perception.

Negativity bias The tendency to focus heavily on a person's negative attributes when forming a perception.

Getting to Know You
Being Altercentric

How much would you say you agree with each of the following statements? On the line before each statement, record your level of agreement on a 1–5 scale: Higher numbers mean you agree more, and lower numbers mean you agree less.

In conversations with other people, I usually:

2 1. _____ Try to see things from their point of view.

4 2. _____ Don't assume they think the same way I do.

2 3. _____ Focus mostly on their ideas or opinions.

5 4. _____ Pay attention to their facial expressions and body language to figure out how they feel.

4 5. _____ Try to "put myself in their shoes."

2 6. _____ Attempt to avoid making assumptions about what they think or feel.

3 7. _____ Don't assume they're thinking whatever I'm thinking.

4 8. _____ Try to focus more on them than on myself.

When you're done, add all your scores together. Your result should be between 8 and 40. This score represents the extent to which you try to be altercentric, rather than egocentric, when communicating with others. If you scored between 8 and 18, your conversation style is primarily egocentric. A score between 19 and 29 suggests that you strike a balance between egocentrism and altercentrism. If your score was 30 or higher, you're fairly altercentric.

It's difficult to assess exactly how altercentric you are with questions such as these, because we might believe ourselves to be more altercentric than we actually are. So, don't interpret your score as necessarily being a scientifically valid assessment of your altercentrism. Rather, consider this assessment an exercise in reflecting on how altercentric you try to be with others.

would otherwise like. As you might have guessed, the negativity bias is particularly strong in competitive situations, such as a job interview or graduate school admissions.[57] When many people are competing for a limited number of opportunities, even seemingly minor pieces of negative information can ruin an otherwise positive impression.

Let's say you're calling references to check up on a person you have just interviewed for a key position on your work team. If the candidate is described as "innovative," you'll probably form a positive impression of her. If she's described as "rigid," your impression will probably be negative. What happens, however, if the candidate is described as both "innovative" and "rigid"? The answer is that you, like most people, will still form a negative impression. In other words, the negative information will override the positive.[58]

Positivity and negativity biases are particularly influential for communication and satisfaction in long-term relationships, such as marriages. People in almost any significant relationship will encounter positive events, such as the birth of a new child or a long-anticipated vacation. They will also encounter negative events, such as a prolonged conflict or an unexpected job loss. When they consider their relationship as a whole, however, satisfied couples tend to emphasize its positive characteristics;

The positivity bias leads us to emphasize an event's positive characteristics. For instance, we might think more positively about a distressing event, such as a conflict, if it occurs in the wake of an enjoyable vacation.

in other words, they are biased toward the positive. Dissatisfied couples, by contrast, tend to emphasize the negative characteristics.[59]

Stereotyping, primacy, recency, perceptual set, egocentrism, positivity, and negativity are all powerful influences, and simply knowing about them doesn't shield us from their effects. The more we know about perceptual errors, however, the better we can think critically and question our judgments to form more accurate perceptions of the people around us.

Learn It: What are the three stages of the stereotyping process? How are the primacy and recency effects related to each other? How does a perceptual set influence interpersonal perception? What does it mean to be egocentric? What are the effects of the positivity and negativity biases?

Try It: Watch the 2005 movie *Crash*, which highlights numerous cultural stereotypes. Identify as many stereotyped beliefs as you can from the movie, and take note of the ways in which each character's stereotyped beliefs influenced his or her behaviors toward other characters. Also, look for examples of other perceptual influences, particularly egocentrism or negativity bias, that affected the characters' behaviors.

Reflect on It: What is one inaccurate stereotype that someone might have of you? When are you most likely to make egocentric perceptions of others?

We humans have an almost constant need to make sense of the world around us. It's not enough just to notice someone's behavior, for instance—we are also driven to figure out why it happened. Why did Paul leave his party so soon? Why did Ed fail to respond to Lisa's e-mail? We want to know.

We Explain Behavior Through Attributions

Attribution
An explanation for an observed behavior.

An **attribution** is simply an explanation, the answer to a "why" question.[60] You notice your brother ignoring his girlfriend, for instance, and you wonder what to attribute his behavior to. Your adviser asks you why you failed your history midterm, and you decide what to attribute your behavior to. Attributions for behavior vary along three important dimensions—locus, stability, and controllability.[61]

> *We don't see things as they are—we see them as we are.*
>
> —Anaïs Nin (1903–1977) French-born author

Locus. Locus refers to where the cause of a behavior is "located," whether within ourselves or outside ourselves.[62] Some of our behaviors have *internal* causes, which means they're caused by a characteristic of ourselves. Other behaviors have *external* causes, meaning they're caused by something outside ourselves.

Let's say your boss is late to a lunch meeting, and you're trying to figure out why. Some internal attributions are that he has lost track of time, he's rarely punctual, and he's making you wait on purpose. Those attributions are all different, but they all identify some internal characteristic of your boss as the cause of his lateness. External attributions are that traffic is really heavy, that your boss has a long way to walk, and that his employees always have numerous questions for him in the morning. Again, those are all different attributions, but each one points to something in your boss's external environment—not within him personally—as the cause of his behavior.

Stability. A second dimension of attributions is whether the cause of a behavior is stable or unstable.[63] A *stable* cause is one that is permanent, semipermanent, or at least not easily changed. Why was your boss late for lunch? Rush-hour traffic would be a stable cause for lateness, because it's a permanent feature of many people's morning commutes. By contrast, a traffic accident would be an *unstable* cause for lateness, because accidents occur only from time to time in unpredictable places with unpredictable effects.

Notice that these are both external attributions. Internal causes for behavior also can be either stable or unstable, however. Imagine that you are trying to understand why your roommate snapped at you this morning. If you claim the reason is that she's a mean person, that would be a stable attribution, because most people's personalities don't change dramatically over the course of their lives. If you conclude that she snapped at you because she has the flu and is feeling tired, however, that's an unstable attribution, because having the flu is a temporary condition.

Controllability. Finally, causes for behavior also vary in how controllable they are.[64] If you make a *controllable* attribution for someone's behavior, then you believe that the cause of that behavior was under the person's control. In contrast, an *uncontrollable* attribution identifies a cause that was outside the person's control.

Let's say your brother is supposed to pick you up from the airport, but he isn't there when you arrive. You might assume he failed to show because he spent too much time hanging out with his friends beforehand and is now running late. This is a controllable attribution, because the cause of his lateness (spending time with friends) is within his control. Alternatively, you might assume he got into a car accident. This is an uncontrollable attribution because he couldn't help but be late if he wrecked his car.

Locus, stability, and controllability are all related to one another. However, different attributions can reflect different combinations of these dimensions. In fact, any combination of locus, stability, and controllability is possible.

For example, just because an attribution is internal doesn't necessarily mean it's also stable or uncontrollable. Referring back to an earlier example, one attribution for why your roommate snapped at you this morning is that she's not a "morning person." This is an internal attribution (she's not a morning person) that is stable (she's probably never been a morning person) and relatively uncontrollable (it probably has to do with her biological rhythm).

A different attribution is that she was grumpy because she got only two hours of sleep, having been out partying most of the night before. This attribution is also internal (she's grumpy), but it is probably unstable (she isn't grumpy every morning) and controllable (she chose to stay up late the night before). Table 4.1 provides eight different attributions for a single behavior that represent all the possible combinations of locus, stability, and controllability.

Although most of us probably try to come up with accurate attributions for other people's behaviors, we are still vulnerable to making attribution mistakes.[65] These errors can create problems for us because our response to other people's behaviors is often based on the attributions we make for those behaviors.

Attribution errors can create problems because our response to other people's behaviors—such as not doing the dishes—is based on the attributions we make for those behaviors.

Let's say that Adina and her 14-year-old son, Craig, get into an argument one night about whether Craig can go on a school-sponsored overseas trip. After their argument, they both go to bed angry. When Adina gets up the following morning, she finds that Craig hasn't done the dishes or taken out the trash, two chores he is responsible for doing every night before bed. Craig had been so flustered by the previous night's conflict that doing his chores had completely slipped his mind. Adina made a different attribution, however: She perceived that Craig didn't do the chores because he was deliberately disobeying her. On the basis of that attribution, she told Craig he was grounded for a week and was definitely not going on the school trip. Her actions only prolonged and intensified the conflict between them.

Had Adina attributed Craig's behavior to an honest oversight, she might have been able to overlook it instead of making it the basis for additional conflict. As we'll see in the next section, learning how to recognize common attribution errors will best equip us to avoid making mistakes that, as in the case of Adina and Craig, transform a bad situation into a worse one.

How to Recognize Common Attribution Errors

We might think we always explain behavior in an objective, rational way, but the truth is that we're all prone to taking mental "shortcuts" when coming up with attributions. As a result, our attributions are often less accurate than they ideally should be. Three of the most common attribution errors are the self-serving bias, the fundamental attribution error, and overattribution.

Table 4.1: Eight Attributions for Rudeness

We generally expect social interaction to be pleasant, so when someone is rude to us, we usually wonder why. Let's say Ricardo, the cashier at your grocery store, was especially rude today, and you're crafting an attribution for his behavior. Below are eight attributions representing every possible combination of locus, stability, and controllability.

Internal, Stable, and Controllable

| *He's a jerk.* | Personality traits (such as being a jerk) are internal and usually stable, but he should be able to control whether he acts like a jerk. |

Internal, Stable, and Uncontrollable

| *He's mentally challenged and he doesn't always understand politeness.* | Although being mentally challenged is internal and stable, he can't help being mentally challenged. |

Internal, Unstable, and Controllable

| *He's hung over.* | Physical states such as being hung over are internal, but they aren't stable (because they will go away), and they are controllable (he didn't have to drink). |

Internal, Unstable, and Uncontrollable

| *He's got the flu.* | Illness is internal but unstable (because he'll get better). Presumably he didn't choose to get sick, so it's also uncontrollable. |

External, Stable, and Controllable

| *He's got a girlfriend who picks a fight with him every single morning; he needs to get out of that relationship.* | The source is external (a girlfriend); her influence is stable (they interact every day) but controllable (he can end the relationship if he wants). |

External, Stable, and Uncontrollable

| *The medication he takes to control his heart condition makes him impatient.* | Medication is an external source; it's stable (because it's for an ongoing condition) and uncontrollable (because he has to take it). |

External, Unstable, and Controllable

| *He's cranky because the air-conditioning in his apartment isn't working; he should get that fixed.* | The air-conditioning is an external cause; it's unstable (because it will eventually get fixed), and controllable (because he can get it fixed). |

External, Unstable, and Uncontrollable

| *Someone rear-ended his truck this morning, so he's upset.* | The source is external (another driver); it's unstable (it was a one-time accident) and uncontrollable (it was an accident). |

Self-serving bias The tendency to attribute one's successes to internal causes and one's failures to external causes.

Self-serving bias. The **self-serving bias** refers to our tendency to attribute our successes to stable, internal causes while attributing our failures to unstable, external causes.[66] For example, if you got an "A" on your test, it's because you're smart, but if you got an "F," it's because the test was unfair or because you work so much to keep up with tuition payments that you didn't have time to study. These attributions are called *self-serving* because they suggest that our successes are deserved but our failures are not our fault.

The self-serving bias deals primarily with attributions that we make for our own behaviors. Research shows, however, that we often extend this tendency to other important people in our lives.[67] In a happy marriage, for instance, people tend to attribute their spouse's positive behaviors to internal causes ("She remembered my birthday because she's a thoughtful person") and negative behaviors to external causes ("He forgot my birthday because he's been very distracted at work"). In distressed relationships, however, the reverse is often true: People attribute negative behavior to internal causes ("She forgot my birthday because she's completely self-absorbed") and positive behavior to external causes ("He remembered my birthday only because I reminded him five times").

The self-serving bias is a natural, self-protective tendency, although it is a form of self-delusion.[68] Virtually none of us is responsible for *all* our successes and *none* of our failures. If we're being honest, most of us would agree that our failures are sometimes our fault (you got an "F" because you didn't study). Similarly, most of us would admit that our successes sometimes result from factors outside our control (you got an "A" because of the curve, not because of your performance).

We often extend the self-serving bias to our relationships. Why did your partner remember your birthday? Was it because your partner is a thoughtful person, or because you reminded him or her repeatedly?

These observations also apply to communication in relationships. We might like to think, for instance, that we are responsible for everything that is going well in our relationships but are not responsible for anything that is going poorly. Again, this attitude is unrealistic. As you've probably learned from your own experience, both people in an interpersonal relationship contribute to its positive *and* negative aspects. When you commit the self-serving bias and act as though you're responsible only for successes but not for failures, your actions are likely to cause resentment from others. For those reasons, it's important to be aware of our self-serving biases and to be honest about the attributions we make for our behavior.

Fundamental attribution error. Think about how you reacted the last time someone cut you off in traffic. Specifically, what attribution did you make for the driver's behavior? You might have said to yourself, "She must be late for something important," or "He must have a car full of noisy children," but you probably didn't. "That driver is a jerk!" is probably closer to the reaction most of us would have.

The reason for that response isn't that we're cranky. Rather, it's our tendency to commit what scientists call the **fundamental attribution error,** in which we attribute other people's behaviors to internal rather than external causes.[69] The high school student ran the pledge drive because she's a caring, giving person, not because she earned extra credit for doing so. The cashier gave you the wrong change because he doesn't know how to count, not because he was distracted by an announcement being made over the loudspeaker. That driver cut you off because he or she is a jerk, not because of the noisy children or any other external factor that might have motivated that behavior.

The fundamental attribution error is so strong, in fact, that we commit it even when we know better. For instance, you can probably think of at least one actor you

Fundamental attribution error The tendency to attribute others' behaviors to internal rather than external causes.

dislike simply because you don't like the characters he plays. Now, most of us understand that acting involves playing a role and pretending to be a character that someone else has created; an actor's words and behaviors clearly aren't his own. However, we often commit the fundamental attribution error by assuming (even subconsciously) that an actor's behavior reflects who he is as a person.

Just how strong is the fundamental attribution error? Consider that in one study people explained a person's behavior in terms of internal factors even after they were specifically told that it was caused by external factors.[70] In the study, college students talked with a young woman whose behavior was either friendly or unfriendly. Before their conversations, half the students were told the woman's behavior would be spontaneous, but the other half were told she had been instructed to act either friendly or unfriendly.

How did this information influence the students' attributions for the woman's behavior? The answer is that it had no effect at all. When the woman acted friendly, the students maintained it was because she is a friendly person, and when she acted unfriendly, they maintained it was because she is an unfriendly person. In both cases, students attributed the woman's behavior to her personality, *even when they were specifically told that she was only behaving as instructed.*

As interpersonal communicators, we should bear in mind that people's behaviors—including our own—are often responses to external forces. For instance, when the new doctor you're seeing spends only three minutes diagnosing your condition and prescribing a treatment before moving on to the next patient, you might conclude that she's not a very caring person. This would be an internal attribution for her behavior, which the fundamental attribution error increases your likelihood of making. If you think your doctor rushed through your consultation because she's uncaring, that attribution might lead you to give her a poor evaluation to your friends and co-workers or to switch to another doctor altogether.

Was your attribution correct, however? Ask yourself what external forces might have motivated her behavior. For example, she might have rushed through your consultation simply because another doctor's absence that day forced her to see twice as many patients as usual, not because she's an uncaring person. If that's the case, then you might have switched to another doctor for no reason, forgoing your opportunity to form a positive professional relationship with her. To the extent that we base our decisions on inaccurate attributions, we run the risk of needlessly damaging our relationships in the process.

Overattribution. A third common attribution error is **overattribution,** in which we single out one or two obvious characteristics of a person and then attribute everything he or she does to those characteristics.[71] Let's use the example of Fatima, who is an only child. When you see her being impatient or acting selfishly, you might say to yourself, "That's typical of an only child." Maybe you notice that she pushes herself to make good grades, she is very conservative with her money, or she doesn't seem to enjoy the holidays. "Well, she *is* an only child!" you might say to yourself, as if that one characteristic is the underlying cause of everything she does.[72]

Overattribution is a form of mental laziness. Instead of trying to understand why Fatima might push herself so hard in school, we pick something obvious about her (she's an only child) and conclude that it must have something to do with that.

Although this example might seem inconsequential, overattribution can contribute to problematic behavior in some contexts. For instance, psychologists William Schweinle, William Ickes, and Ira Bernstein have studied overattribution in the context of marital aggression. On the basis of the principle of overattribution, the researchers predicted that when women communicate in a certain way, such as by

Overattribution
The tendency to attribute a range of behaviors to a single characteristic of a person.

Overattribution can be easy to do with people in socially marginalized groups, such as immigrants—especially when interaction with them is limited. Humans are complex social beings, though. We cannot understand people simply by characterizing their most obvious qualities.

being critical, men sometimes explain the behavior as being typical of women in general. In other words, they focus on one aspect of a person ("she's a woman") as the cause of her behavior ("because she's a woman, that's why she's criticizing").

Schweinle and his colleagues found that the more men engage in this form of overattribution with women in general, the more likely they are to be verbally abusive with their own wives.[73] These researchers noted that engaging in this form of overattribution causes men to perceive their wives as being critical even when they aren't, simply because they are women. As one result, men form defensive thoughts that provoke their verbal aggression.[74] You can read more about the research from Schweinle and his colleagues in the "How Do We Know?" box.

Overattribution is particularly easy to do with marginalized groups such as sexual minorities, homeless people, and people with disabilities.[75] Because members of these groups are marginalized, some people don't have much experience interacting with them. This lack of communication might make it easier to believe that the group a person belongs to is the primary cause of his or her behaviors. For that reason, it's important to remember that being homeless or gay might be one characteristic of a person, but it doesn't define the person completely, and it's not the cause of everything that person says or does.[76]

Humans are complex social beings. So, if we want to understand the reasons behind another person's behaviors, we need to look past his or her outward characteristics and consider what aspects of his or her physical or social environment might be motivating his or her behavior.

Like other forms of perception, attributions are important but prone to error. This observation doesn't imply that we *never* make accurate attributions for other people's behavior. It simply acknowledges that the self-serving bias, the fundamental attribution error, and overattribution are easy mistakes to commit. The more we know about these processes, the better able we'll be to examine the attributions we make. A summary of three common attribution errors appears in the "At a Glance" box on page 150.

Learn It: What does it mean to say that attributions vary according to locus, stability, and controllability? How are the self-serving bias, the fundamental attribution error, and overattribution examples of attribution errors?

Try It: For one week, keep a list of all the attributions you give to someone else about something you have done. At the end of the week, go back through your list, and evaluate each attribution for accuracy. How many attributions fit the self-serving bias? How many were accurate? Were any of your attributions overly negative?

Reflect on It: When do you commit the fundamental attribution error? With which group(s) of people would you be most likely to make overattributions?

How Do We Know?

Overattribution Is Related to Verbal Aggression Against Women

You learned in this section that the more men overattribute women's criticism to their sex, the more verbally aggressive they are with their wives. How do we know this? In an important study, psychologists William Schweinle, William Ickes, and Ira Bernstein recruited 86 married men to report on their tendencies to communicate in verbally aggressive ways with their wives. They then had each participant watch three videotapes depicting a female patient discussing her relationship with her former husband during a psychotherapy session with a male therapist.

As each man watched the videotapes, a researcher paused the tapes every 15 seconds and asked the man to write a single sentence indicating what he believed the patient was thinking or feeling right before the tape was paused. After writing each sentence, the participant was asked to categorize the patient's thoughts or feelings as being either critical with respect to

her former husband, not critical, or ambiguous.

Once each experimental session was finished, eight trained raters independently viewed each of the participant's written comments regarding the female patient to look for evidence of overattribution bias. In particular, the raters looked to see how well each written statement about the patient's thoughts or feelings (e.g., "she feels that her former husband was never attentive enough") corresponded to the category the participant put it in (critical, not critical, or ambiguous). The researchers reasoned that men who are biased toward overattributing criticism to women would be likely to categorize a statement as critical even if the content of the statement didn't reflect criticism.

Using this method, the researchers calculated a score representing each man's overattribution tendency. They then looked to see whether this score was correlated with each man's report of verbal aggressiveness toward his wife. As predicted, they found that the more a man overattributed criticism to women, the more verbally aggressive he was with his wife. This result doesn't necessarily mean that the overattribution tendency *causes* verbal aggression.

It does indicate, however, that the two are related.

Ask Yourself:

- How would you explain this finding? Why do you suppose overattribution of criticism is related to how verbally aggressive a man is?

- What behavioral tendencies do you overattribute to women? to men?

From Me to You:

- This study focused on communication within marriages, so we can't be certain whether its findings apply to other types of relationships. It's possible that the connection between overattribution and verbal aggression also occurs in friendships, workplace relationships, or parent-child pairs. Overattribution is easy to do because it relies on a person's most obvious characteristics and doesn't require much in-depth thought. Conclusions you draw on the basis of overattribution are often incorrect, though. When you notice yourself attributing several of a person's behaviors to a single characteristic, ask yourself whether you are making the mistake of overattribution.

Source: Schweinle, W. E., Ickes, W., & Bernstein, I. H. (2002). Empathic inaccuracy in husband to wife aggression: The overattribution bias. *Personal Relationships, 9,* 141–158.

At a Glance: Three Common Attribution Errors

Research shows we have a tendency to make errors when forming attributions about behavior. Here are three common errors:

Self-serving bias	We attribute our successes to internal causes and our failures to external causes.
Fundamental attribution error	We attribute other people's behaviors to internal causes more often than to external causes.
Overattribution	We focus on one characteristic of a person and attribute a wide variety of behaviors to that characteristic.

4} Improving Your Perceptual Abilities

We've talked about how easy it is to make perceptual mistakes. We stereotype people. We assume they think the same ways we do. We attribute all their behaviors to one or two characteristics. If you've concluded that perception making is hard work, you're correct. On the positive side, however, despite all those limitations, we can do a better job of it if we know how. Improving our perceptual ability starts with being mindful of what our perceptions are and what influences them. Next, it involves checking the accuracy of our perceptions. Before we examine these steps, though, imagine yourself in the following situation.

> *Most of the mistakes in thinking are inadequacies of perception rather than mistakes of logic.*
>
> —Edward de Bono (1933–)
> British psychologist

Let's say you have just started working at a store that sells and services swimming pools. You've noticed that the social atmosphere at the store seems playful and fun, but you're starting to sense tension between the store manager, Dmitri, and one of the salespeople, Min. Dmitri grew up in Greece, went to college in Canada, and has been living in the United States since he graduated. Min's parents emigrated from South Korea when she was an infant and raised Min and her older brother in the Pacific Northwest.

From what you've observed, Dmitri is friendly and informal with almost everyone, including his employees. Min is also friendly, but she communicates with others in a more formal, reserved manner. On a couple of occasions, you have seen Dmitri put his arm around Min and act flirtatious with her. You have seen him do the same with several other people as well; Dmitri is a very gregarious person. You've also heard from another employee, however, that Min has asked Dmitri not to behave that way toward her at work, although you don't know for certain if that's true.

Then, one morning while you're working in the showroom, you overhear what sounds like an argument in Dmitri's office. You recognize the voices as Dmitri's and Min's, and although you can't hear everything they're saying, you hear enough to figure out that Min is upset because Dmitri promoted another employee instead of her to the position of lead salesperson. Eventually you see Min walk out of Dmitri's office looking visibly upset. By that afternoon, you start hearing a rumor that Min has filed a harassment complaint against Dmitri.

We'll use this scenario throughout this section to understand how we can improve our perception-making abilities. As you imagine yourself in this scenario, consider what perceptions you'd form. Has Dmitri harassed Min by denying her a promotion because she expressed discomfort at his flirtatious behavior? Alternatively, is Min falsely accusing Dmitri of harassment because she is angry at not getting the promotion? Or are both parties at fault? Arriving at an accurate perception of the situation will be difficult given the limited information you have. Nevertheless, as we have already observed, we can all work to improve our perceptual ability. This process begins with being mindful of the perceptions we form.

Being Mindful of Your Perceptions

We form perceptions of people and situations constantly—so often, in fact, that we're sometimes unaware that we're doing it. We can improve our perceptual abilities, however, only when we're *mindful* of our perceptions. In other words, we must be aware of what our perceptions are and how they might be affected by our own characteristics and the characteristics of the people we're perceiving and of the context in which we're perceiving them.

Know yourself. How can several people observe the same event and form different, even contradictory, perceptions of it? As we've seen in this chapter, the reason is that our individual characteristics often shape the way we perceive people and situations. One part of being mindful of your perceptions, therefore, is to ask yourself how they are influenced by your personal attributes.

For instance, how might your perception of Dmitri and Min's situation be affected by your sex? Perhaps you identify more with Min if you're female because you are projecting how you would feel in the same situation. Likewise, you might identify more with Dmitri if you're male. In the same vein, your cultural values and expectations might also influence your perception of the situation. If you grew up in a low-power-distance culture that values equality and workers' rights, you might be predisposed to perceive that Dmitri is abusing his power and victimizing Min. Conversely, if you were raised in a high-power-distance culture that values hierarchy and discourages the questioning of authority, you might be more likely to perceive that Min is overreacting and needlessly causing problems.

Remember that your physiological states and traits can also shape your perceptions. If you were tired or hungry when you overheard Dmitri and Min's exchange, for example, you might have felt short-tempered and been more likely than usual to rush to judgment one way or the other. That could lead you to select, organize, and interpret only those clues that support your initial perception and to ignore any information that does not.

Your experiences with previous jobs could also bias your perceptions of Dmitri and Min by creating a perceptual set. Let's say that one of your closest friends at your last job was the victim of harassment. Noticing the pain and frustration she went through may have sensitized you to instances of harassment, leading you to "see" a situation as an example of harassment because that's what you expect to see.

Now let's take the opposite approach and imagine that your friend was wrongfully accused of harassment by a disgruntled employee. That experience might sensitize you to "see" even legitimate victims of harassment as simply vindictive and dishonest, because that's what you expect to see. In either case, your experiences would have created a perceptual set that shaped the perceptions you formed.

We can't always change these influences on our perception-making ability. Try as we might, for example, we can't just choose to think like someone of a different gender or cultural background. But what we *can* do is ask ourselves how factors such as our experiences, our sex and cultural background, and our physiological states and traits might affect the perceptions we make. Acknowledging those influences is one of the first steps in improving our perceptual ability.

Focus on other people's characteristics. Being mindful of our perceptions also means acknowledging how they are influenced by characteristics of the people we're perceiving. For instance, are you more inclined to believe Dmitri and Min's situation is an example of harassment because the supervisor is male and the employee is female? What if the situation involved a male employee accusing a female supervisor of harassment: Might that change your perception of the accusation's merit? You might think the sex of the people involved wouldn't matter—legally and ethically, it shouldn't—but several studies have shown that people are more likely to perceive harassment when the supervisor is male as opposed to female.[77]

Another characteristic of Min and Dmitri that may affect your perceptions of their situation is their cultural backgrounds. Culture has a strong influence on how we behave and communicate, so it should come as no surprise that it also influences the way we *perceive* behavior. When we observe interactions between people from our own culture, our shared knowledge about cultural norms enables us to perceive and interpret their behaviors with relative ease. When we observe interactions between people from other cultures, however, we are more likely to misinterpret their behaviors. One reason why this is true is that people's cultural backgrounds can activate stereotypes in our minds that can influence our perceptions.

For example, perhaps you stereotype Greek men as being naturally gregarious, so you see Dmitri's friendly behavior toward his employees merely as an expression of his nature, not as harassment. Or perhaps you stereotype Asian women (even those raised in the United States) as being accommodating and respectful of authority. If so, then you would likely perceive that Min wouldn't have argued with her supervisor unless she truly felt victimized. Neither of those stereotypes may actually be valid. Nevertheless, to the extent that you hold stereotyped beliefs that are relevant to Dmitri or Min, those beliefs can color the way you perceive the situation.

Consider the context. The last step in being mindful of your perceptions is to consider how the context itself influenced them. In the example of Dmitri and Min, the context includes not only the argument you overheard but also the observations you made of Dmitri's and Min's communication behaviors before the argument. Let's say that when you started working at the store, your first impression of Dmitri was that he was inappropriately affectionate toward his employees. Because of the primacy effect, that first impression might encourage you to perceive his behavior toward Min as harassment. Conversely, let's say that you recently observed Min communicating in an unprofessional manner with two customers. Because of the recency effect, that recent negative impression might encourage you to perceive that she is accusing Dmitri unfairly.

Positivity and negativity biases can also shape your perceptions. If you really like Min and have always gotten along well with her, then you might be inclined to believe only positive things about her. This inclination could easily bias you toward believing her side of the story and concluding that Dmitri had, in fact, harassed her. From the opposite perspective, if you and Min don't get along, then you might be inclined to believe the worst about her, which could bias you against believing her accusations.

Don't forget, too, that you heard only bits and pieces of Dmitri and Min's argument. It's possible, then, that your limited ability to hear the conversation caused you to miss parts of the argument that would have changed your perception of the situation. In other words, the context itself limited the information that you could select for attention. An important part of being mindful of your perceptions, therefore, is to ask yourself what pieces of information you *didn't* have access to.

These three clues—knowing yourself, focusing on the characteristics of others, and considering the context—can all help you think critically about your perceptions by acknowledging the range of factors that can influence them.

Checking Your Perceptions

Being mindful of your perceptions is an important step toward improving your perceptual abilities, but it is only the first step. After you have considered which factors led you to form a particular perception, the next step is to check the accuracy of that perception. Let's continue with the example of Dmitri and Min to see how we can check our perceptions.

Separate interpretations from facts. *Dragnet* was a radio and television police drama that debuted in the early 1950s. Its main character, Sgt. Joe Friday, was a detective best known for requesting "just the facts, ma'am." This phrase implies that objective facts are different from our interpretations of those facts. Let's say you saw Dmitri put his arm around a customer and kiss her on the cheek. If you were asked to describe the scene, you might say that "Dmitri was acting friendly with that woman," or "he was flirting with her," or even "he was coming on to her."

Which of those reports is factual? Technically, none of them is. Rather, they are all interpretations, because they all assign *meaning* to what you observed. You witnessed Dmitri's behavior and interpreted it as friendliness, as flirtation, or as a sign of sexual interest, so you described it in those ways. In fact, if you and two co-workers had witnessed the behavior, you could easily have interpreted it in three different ways.

If all three of your perceptions were subjective interpretations, then what are the facts here? The essential fact is that you saw Dmitri put his arm around the woman and kiss her on the cheek. That's what you objectively observed. Perhaps you also noticed other clues that helped you arrive at your interpretation, such as what occurred right before or how the customer reacted. The point is that *describing* what you actually saw or heard is not the same thing as *interpreting* it. If we are to check the accuracy of our perceptions, we must start by separating what we heard or saw from the interpretation we assigned it.

Generate alternative perceptions. Once you have assigned meaning to an event, ask yourself what other meanings or interpretations you might have come up with. As we discussed earlier, most people arrive at a perception and then pay attention only to information that supports their perception, ignoring any information that doesn't. A better approach is to look for alternative ways of perceiving the situation, even if they contradict your initial perception.

Your observations of Dmitri and Min, for example, might lead you to perceive that Min is accusing Dmitri of harassment only out of anger at not getting the promotion. What are alternative ways of perceiving the situation? One alternative we have already identified is that Dmitri has actually harassed Min. Are there others? Perhaps Dmitri feels threatened by Min and worries that he might put his own job in jeopardy by promoting her. Perhaps Min and Dmitri have had a contentious relationship for a long time. In that case, the conflict you witnessed wasn't really about Min's promotion at all but, instead, reflected longer-standing grudges that both individuals hold.

The practice of generating alternative perceptions is important for two reasons. First, it requires you to look at information about the situation that doesn't match your original perception. For example, if you initially perceived that Min accused Dmitri of harassment only out of anger at not getting the promotion, then it would be easy for you to ignore your observations of Min's discomfort with Dmitri's overly friendly behavior because those observations don't support your perception. In contrast, to generate an alternative perception, you would have to take those observations into account.

Second, generating alternative perceptions encourages you to ask yourself what information you don't have that might be relevant to the situation. How much do you know about Dmitri and Min's history with each other, for instance? If you knew they used to be a romantic couple but had an emotional breakup just a few months before you started working at the store, that information might give you a more accurate context for interpreting their behaviors toward each other.

Keep in mind, however, that even if you are able to generate alternative perceptions, that doesn't necessarily mean your initial perception was inaccurate or should be discarded. In fact, looking at alternatives will sometimes make you even more convinced that your first perception was accurate. The purpose of considering alternative perceptions is to make certain you aren't ignoring or discounting clues from the situation simply because they are inconsistent with the perception you formed.

Once you have separated interpretations from facts and have considered alternative ways of perceiving the situation, you can engage in direct and indirect forms of perception checking.

Engage in perception-checking behaviors. Perception checking is the process of testing your perceptions for accuracy. This is an important step toward improving your perceptual abilities because when you act on the basis of inaccurate perceptions, you run the risk of turning a situation from bad to worse, as you saw Adina do with Craig earlier in this chapter. You can engage in either direct or indirect means of perception checking.

Direct perception checking involves simply asking other people if your perception of a situation is accurate. If you perceive that Min is angry at Dmitri, for instance, one way to find out if you're right is to ask her. Direct perception checking involves three elements:

1. Acknowledging the behavior you witnessed
2. Interpreting that behavior
3. Asking whether your interpretation was correct

Here's an example of how you might directly check your perception that Min is angry with Dmitri:

> "I heard you talking to Dmitri in his office [*acknowledging behavior*]. It sounded like you were pretty mad at Dmitri [*offering an interpretation*]. Is that true?" [*asking about your interpretation*]

Depending on your relationship with Min, she may feel comfortable telling you how she feels: "Yeah, I'm *furious* with him!" Or she might downplay her feelings if she doesn't feel comfortable disclosing them to you: "I'm just a little upset about not getting the promotion, that's all." If your perception is wrong, she might tell you that: "No, I'm not mad at Dmitri at all; why would you think that?" She might even choose not to respond to your question: "I'd appreciate it if you could just leave me alone for a little while." Direct perception checking will be the most useful, therefore, when you approach people who are willing either to confirm your perceptions or to correct them.

By contrast, *indirect perception checking* involves listening and observing in order to seek additional information about the situation. Instead of asking Min if she is angry, for example, you might observe her facial expressions, listen to how she talks to others, and watch her body language when she's around Dmitri. If you notice that Min looks and sounds angry, this gives you additional confidence in the accuracy of your perception. If she seems to interact with Dmitri in a calm, pleasant manner, however, this might suggest that your perception was off base.

Neither direct nor indirect perception checking will provide foolproof results every time. As we saw, asking people if your perceptions are correct is useful only if they are willing to tell you. Indirect perception checking can fail, too, because your initial perception ("Min is angry") might lead you to pay attention only to clues that reinforce that perception. For instance, you might notice Min's distressed tone of voice without also noticing that her facial expression appears calm. Another danger of indirect perception checking is that you might pay attention to information that isn't relevant. To determine whether Min is angry, for example, you might take careful note of the way she's sitting at her desk and how she's looking at others, even though these behaviors might not be affected by her emotion. Although we might think that gathering more information will always lead us to make more accurate perceptions, there are instances when having more information actually makes our perceptions *less* accurate, as the "Fact or Fiction" box on page 156 details. For those reasons, it's often in your best interests to engage in both direct and indirect forms of perception checking, so that each strategy can compensate for the shortcomings of the other.

The process of perception checking will increase your confidence in the accuracy of your perceptions in some cases and will give you reason to question them in other cases. The last step in improving your perceptual ability is to make use of this information by revisiting your perceptions and revising them, if necessary.

Fact or Fiction?

When It Comes to Perception Checking, More Information Is Always Better

People sometimes criticize others for making "snap judgments," or arriving at their perceptions on the basis of limited information. After listening to one speech, for example, you decide to vote for a political candidate without learning anything else about her. Or a customer comes into your store, and after taking one look at him, you perceive that he's trouble. It's easy to see how these on-the-spot judgments about people can be misleading and how our perceptions might be more accurate if we had additional information.

In many cases, this observation is true: When forming perceptions of others, we should remember that first im-pressions can be misleading. That candidate might *sound* good, but you may have a different perception of her when you learn that she has no experience. That customer might *look* suspicious, but you might think differently when you find out he's a youth minister just home from a long and tiring retreat. In many situations, the more information we can gather to check our perceptions, the more accurate our perceptions will be.

Research shows, however, that in certain cases our snap judgments are surprisingly accurate. Going further, gathering additional information about someone, such as through indirect perception checking, *can* make our per-ceptions more accurate, but it doesn't *always* make them more accurate.

You might think, for instance, that friends you have known for a long time would describe you more accurately than strangers would. An interesting experiment in 2002 proved otherwise, though. Participants in the study described themselves on personality inventories and then asked their close friends to describe them on the same inventories. Not surprisingly, the friends' reports matched the participants' self-reports fairly well. The researchers then asked complete strangers to walk through the partici-pants' dorm rooms and then describe the participants' per-

Revise your perceptions as necessary. Although many of us don't like to admit when we're wrong, good communicators will use what they learn from perception checking to modify their perceptions of a situation. Sometimes you'll find that your percep-tions were accurate from the start. At other times, however, you'll realize that they were not very accurate, for any of the reasons we've considered: (1) They were limited by characteristics of yourself, of the people involved, or of the situation; (2) you were confusing facts and interpretations; or (3) you didn't consider any alternative percep-tions. As one example, perhaps you initially perceived that Min was being dishonest and vindictive by accusing Dmitri of harassment, but after you dug a little deeper into the situation, you discovered that Dmitri did, in fact, harass Min. When the re-sults of perception checking give us reason to believe our perceptions are inaccurate, it's our responsibility as communicators to revise them.

Improving our perceptual ability, therefore, involves two major strategies. First, we have to be mindful of the factors that influence what perception we form of a situ-ation. Second, we have to check that perception by separating facts from interpreta-tions, considering alternative perceptions, engaging in direct and indirect perception checking, and revising our perception if necessary. With practice, these skills, which are represented in Figure 4.5, will help you improve your perceptions of people in interpersonal contexts.

sonalities. That is, they filled out descriptions of the participants without even meeting them—just on the basis of the limited information they got from browsing around the participants' dorm rooms.

Interestingly—and perhaps surprisingly—the strangers were more accurate than the close friends in describing three of five dimensions of participants' personalities. This experiment illustrates that having more information about a person—the way you would if you had known that person for years—does not necessarily make your perceptions of him or her more accurate. More information is sometimes better, but not always.

Ask Yourself:

- How do you suppose people can sometimes form perceptions on the basis of very limited information (i.e., snap judgments) that are accurate? What clues might we be picking up on subconsciously that help us interpret a situation?

- When have you made a snap judgment that turned out to be accurate? What led you to form that perception?

From Me to You:

- The observation that more information is not always better might leave you feeling a little torn. On the one hand, it's useful to check your perceptions by gathering additional information; on the other hand, additional information can sometimes make your perceptions less accurate, rather than more accurate. The trick to solving this paradox is to learn which pieces of information to pay attention to and which ones to ignore. That's a difficult skill to teach, and most of us learn it simply by our experience at forming and checking perceptions. Just knowing that more information isn't always better gives you an advantage. When you engage in indirect perception checking, you can ask yourself whether each new clue you gather about a situation is relevant to your perception. Over time, this practice should improve your perceptual accuracy.

Source: Gosling, S. D., Ko, S. J., Mannarelli, T., & Morris, M. E. (2002). A room with a cue: Personality judgments based on offices and bedrooms. *Journal of Personality and Social Psychology, 82,* 379–398.

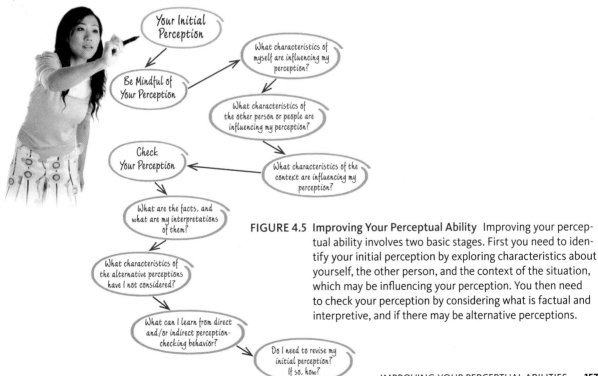

FIGURE 4.5 **Improving Your Perceptual Ability** Improving your perceptual ability involves two basic stages. First you need to identify your initial perception by exploring characteristics about yourself, the other person, and the context of the situation, which may be influencing your perception. You then need to check your perception by considering what is factual and interpretive, and if there may be alternative perceptions.

} Master the Chapter {

Section 1} Perception Is a Process (p. 123)

I. Perception Is a Process

   A. What is interpersonal perception?

- Interpersonal perception is the process of making meaning from the people and the relationships we encounter.

   B. Three stages of the perception process
1. Selection
2. Organization
3. Interpretation

- The process of perception includes selecting stimuli for attention, organizing them into relevant categories, and interpreting their meaning.

   C. What influences our perceptual accuracy?
1. Physiological states and traits
2. Culture and co-culture
3. Social roles

- Physiological states and traits, cultures, co-cultures, and social roles all influence the accuracy of our perceptions.

Section 2} Fundamental Forces in Interpersonal Perception (p. 132)

II. Fundamental Forces in Interpersonal Perception

   A. Stereotyping relies on generalizations

- Stereotyping is the process of applying generalizations about a group to a person we perceive to belong to that group.

B. The primacy effect governs first impressions

- According to the primacy effect, our first impressions are more powerful than any of our later impressions.

C. The recency effect influences impressions

- The recency effect maintains that the most recent impression we have formed will overshadow the impressions that came before it.

D. Our perceptual set limits what we perceive

- Our perceptual set causes us to perceive only what we want or expect to perceive.

E. Egocentrism narrows our perspective

- When we are egocentric, we lack the ability to adopt another person's perspective.

F. Positivity and negativity biases affect perception

- The positivity bias encourages us to focus on a person's positive aspects; the negativity bias encourages us to focus on his or her negative aspects.

Section 3} How We Explain What We Perceive (p. 143)

III. How we Explain What We Perceive

A. We explain behavior through attributions
  1. Locus
  2. Stability
  3. Controllability

- Attributions, or explanations for behavior, vary according to their locus, stability, and controllability.

B. How to recognize common attribution errors
  1. Self-serving bias
  2. Fundamental attribution error
  3. Overattribution

- The self-serving bias, the fundamental attribution error, and overattribution are common attribution mistakes.

Section 4} Improving Your Perceptual Abilities (p. 151)

IV. Improving Your Perceptual Abilities

A. Being mindful of your perceptions
  1. Know yourself
  2. Focus on other people's characteristics
  3. Consider the context

- Being mindful of your perceptions involves focusing on the aspects of yourself, others, and the context that are influencing what you perceive.

B. Checking your perceptions
  1. Separate interpretations from facts
  2. Generate alternative perceptions
  3. Engage in perception-checking behaviors
  4. Revise your perceptions as necessary

- Checking the accuracy of your perceptions involves separating interpretation from fact, generating alternative perceptions, engaging in direct and indirect perception checking, and revising your perceptions as necessary.

Key Terms

Attribution
Egocentric
Fundamental attribution error
Interpretation
Negativity bias

Organization
Overattribution
Perception
Perceptual set
Positivity bias

Primacy effect
Recency effect
Selection
Self-serving bias
Stereotypes

Discussion Questions

1. What inaccurate perceptions do people often have of you? Why are people prone to making these perceptual mistakes? What perceptual mistakes concerning other people do you find yourself making?
2. How do hunger, fatigue, and illness affect your perception-making abilities? Are their effects different?
3. Why is the idea of stereotyping so distasteful to many people?
4. In what situations have your "eyes played tricks on you"? When have you noticed that your perceptual set caused you to "see" something that wasn't really there (or not to see something that was)?

5. Why do you think people are so motivated to come up with attributions for behavior?
6. Can you think of a situation when you have committed the error of overattribution with someone? What characteristic of that person did you overattribute his or her behavior to? How did you realize you were overattributing?
7. If we recognize that our perceptions are always limited, what can we do to improve our perception making? How can we make our perceptions *less* limited?
8. What is the difference between a fact and an interpretation? How can you tell the difference?

Practice Quiz

Multiple Choice

1. Which of the following does *not* make a particular stimulus more likely to be selected for attention?
   a. It is unusual.
   b. It is expected.
   c. You are frequently exposed to it.
   d. It is of high intensity.
2. Noticing that someone is a college student is an example of which schema used to classify information about people?
   a. Physical
   b. Interaction
   c. Psychological
   d. Role
3. Which of the following is *not* one of the factors used to interpret people's behavior?
   a. Personal experience
   b. Knowledge of the person
   c. Closenesss of the relationship
   d. Biofeedback
4. Which of the following is *not* one of the stages of perception?
   a. Selection
   b. Reaction
   c. Organization
   d. Interpretation
5. The process of stereotyping occurs in which order?
   I. Generalization are applied to a person.
   II. A person is identified as being part of a particular group.
   III. Some generalizations are made about people in a particular group.

   a. I, II, III
   b. I, III, II
   c. III, II, I
   d. II, III, I
6. Lacking the ability to take another person's perspective is known as which of the following?
   a. Egocentrism
   b. Id
   c. Superego
   d. Cultural relativism
7. Michaela sees her new partner as perfect, although her friends can see many flaws. Michaela is experiencing which of the following?
   a. Negativity bias
   b. Positivity bias
   c. Perceptual set
   d. Egocentrism
8. Which of the following is *not* a dimension of behavioral attributions?
   a. Locus
   b. Stability
   c. Controllability
   d. Egocentrism
9. Frankie believes that he got into graduate school at The University because he is a good student. Jolie believes that she was not accepted for admission to The University because she is an out-of-state student. Frankie and Jolie are both engaging in which of the following?

a. Halo and horn effect
b. Attributional reasoning
c. Self-serving bias
d. Errors in judgment

10. The predisposition to perceive only what we want or expect to perceive is known as which of the following?
a. Interpretation
b. Organization
c. Attribution
d. Perceptual set

True/False

11. Perception is the ongoing process of making meaning from the things we experience in our environment.
12. Selective memory bias occurs when we do not remember information that supports our stereotypes.
13. Having a perceptual set means that everyone has a predisposition to perceive only what he or she wants to perceive.

14. You think your classmate turned in his paper late because he's careless and not able to complete his work on time. This is an example of an external attribution.
15. The fundamental attribution error occurs when we attribute other people's behavior to internal causes rather than external ones more often than we should.

Fill in the Blank

16. The first of the three stages of perception is the _____ stage.
17. A _____ is a set of behaviors that is expected of someone in a particular social situation.
18. According to the _____, first impressions are crucial because they set the tone for future interactions.
19. The _____ posits that the most recent impression we have of someone is more powerful than our earlier impressions.
20. Singling out one or two obvious characteristics of a person and attributing everything he or she does to those characteristics is known as _____.

Answers
Multiple Choice: 1 (b); 2 (d); 3 (d); 4 (b); 5 (d); 6 (a); 7 (b); 8 (d); 9 (c); 10 (d); **True/False:** 11 (T); 12 (F); 13 (F); 14 (T); 15 (T); **Fill in the Blank:** 16 (selection); 17 (social role); 18 (primacy effect); 19 (recency effect); 20 (overattribution)

Research Library

Movies

An Ideal Husband (Comedy; 1999; PG-13)

In his youth, Sir Robert Chiltern is paid for providing a foreign official with sensitive government information. Years later, after an otherwise impeccable government career, he is blackmailed by a mysterious woman who is an acquaintance of his wife. When Chiltern seeks his best friend's advice, he is told to confess everything to his wife and seek her support against the blackmailer. Because he doesn't want to tarnish his wife's perception of him, he refuses, which has severe consequences. In a comedic way, the film illustrates the extent to which we will protect others' perceptions of us.

Crash (Drama; 2004; R)

This drama illustrates tensions fueled by stereotypes among characters living in Los Angeles. The story portrays tense interactions involving an African American television director and his wife, a Mexican locksmith, a middle-aged Korean couple, a Caucasian district attorney and his wife, a Persian store owner, two carjackers, and others, each of whom acts on his or her stereotypes about ethnicity, age, and social class. The film is a powerful illustration of the ease with which we recall stereotypes and the extent to which they can affect our behavior.

Primal Fear (Drama; 1996; R)

Primal Fear stars Richard Gere as an attorney defending a young man charged with murdering a prominent Catholic archbishop. Although the defendant's guilt is fairly evident, the defense is complicated by his mental limitations and by allegations of abuse at the archbishop's hands. Gere's character is consumed with the need to control others' perceptions to win the case. In the end, though, he learns that his own perceptions are profoundly misinformed.

Books

Goldstein, E. B. (2007). *Sensation and perception* (7th ed.). Pacific Grove, CA: Wadsworth.

Kenny, D. A. (1994). *Interpersonal perception: A social relations analysis.* New York: Guilford.

Manusov, V., & Harvey, J. H. (Eds.). (2001). *Attribution, communication behavior, and close relationships.* Cambridge, England: Cambridge University Press.

Journal Articles

Hughes, P. C., & Baldwin, J. R. (2002). Communication and stereotypical impressions. *Howard Journal of Communication, 13,* 113–128.

Kellerman, K. (1989). The negativity effect in interaction: It's all in your point of view. *Human Communication Research, 16,* 147–183.

Manusov, V. (1990). An application of attribution principles to nonverbal behavior in romantic dyads. *Communication Monographs, 57,* 104–118.

Web Sites

https://implicit.harvard.edu/implicit/demo/

This site describes the Implicit Association Test, an assessment of your prejudices toward others, and allows you to take the test for yourself.

http://changingminds.org/explanations/theories/stereotypes.htm

This Web site describes the process of stereotyping and provides additional detail not only on how people use stereotypes but also on how we can change our stereotypes.

5

Language

What are the characteristics
of language?

In what ways does language affect
interpersonal communication?

How can we become better
verbal communicators?

CHAPTER OUTLINE

Darren and Maria

Darren answered the phone at 3 a.m. to find his friend Maria sobbing on the other end of the line. "What's wrong?" he kept asking, but Maria was so upset she could barely speak. Only after several tries was she able to get out the words that her sister had been killed in an accident. The message hit Darren like a bag of bricks, and he was immediately aware that he had no idea of what to say to Maria. Instead, he just let her cry on the phone, offering only "I'm so sorry" every few minutes until she thanked him for listening and they agreed to meet the next day. After hanging up, Darren thought about Maria and wished he'd had the words to comfort and console her, as she had done for him on many occasions. He knew she appreciated him for just listening to her, but he wanted to help her even more. He just didn't know what to say.

Finding the right words can be challenging under the most ordinary of circumstances, let alone during extraordinary ones. We may not always know what to say to make someone feel comforted, informed, entertained, motivated, or persuaded. If we know how to use language effectively, however, then we can employ it to accomplish those and many other goals in our personal relationships.

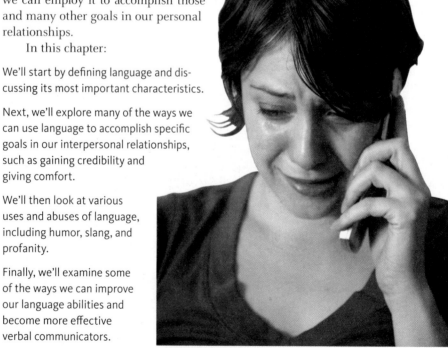

In this chapter:

1} We'll start by defining language and discussing its most important characteristics.

2} Next, we'll explore many of the ways we can use language to accomplish specific goals in our interpersonal relationships, such as gaining credibility and giving comfort.

3} We'll then look at various uses and abuses of language, including humor, slang, and profanity.

4} Finally, we'll examine some of the ways we can improve our language abilities and become more effective verbal communicators.

Many species communicate in one form or another, but we humans are the only creatures on the planet who use language. Although most of us are born with verbal ability, we have to learn the specific languages we use; and, like most learned skills, our language abilities improve as we practice and learn about them.

In the opening scene, Darren felt inadequate because he didn't know what to say to Maria to help her feel better. Maybe you've had a similar experience. If so, then you already understand that we use language as a way to represent or symbolize our thoughts and feelings. We can provide comfort to others without talking, but we still try to find the right words to be helpful. Darren felt bad for Maria, but he wasn't able to represent his feelings through words; that is, he couldn't translate them into language.

> *Language shapes the way we think, and determines what we can think about.*
>
> —Benjamin Lee Whorf (1897–1941)
> U.S. American linguist

Language
A structured system of symbols used for communicating meaning.

We can understand **language** as *a structured system of symbols used for communicating meaning.* Many scientists believe that language evolved from early humans' use of gestures to communicate.[1] For instance, many of us hold out our hands when we ask for something. We share this gesture with other primates, such as chimpanzees. The human brain, however, appears to have a specific capacity for learning and using language that is not shared by other species. Researchers in the field of biolinguistics have proposed that our advanced cognitive capacity has allowed humans to develop the symbolic system we know as language.[2]

You can probably think of many behaviors and items that represent or symbolize some type of meaning. A smile often symbolizes happiness, for instance; a red traffic light symbolizes the need to stop. Many gestures also have symbolic meaning, in that they represent a particular concept or idea. For example, you probably wave to say "hello" or shrug your shoulders to say "I don't know." Significantly, although traffic lights, gestures, and facial expressions all symbolize meaning, none of those behaviors or items qualifies as a language. Instead, a language is characterized by the use of a specific type of symbol: words.

Words are the building blocks of verbal communication. As we'll see in this chapter, we use words to represent ideas, observations, feelings, and thoughts. Words have a profound influence on how we relate to others. One key point here is that the power of verbal

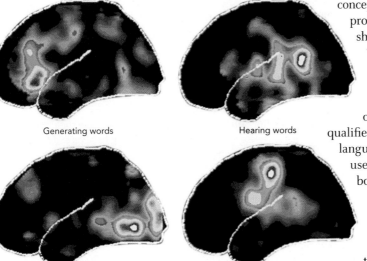

Generating words

Hearing words

Seeing words

Speaking words

The human brain seems to have a specific capacity for learning and using language that is not shared by other species. This PET scan of the left half of the human brain contrasts the different areas used in aspects of language activity, including generating words, hearing words, seeing words and speaking words.

communication isn't limited to the words we speak; it also includes the words we write. When we hear the term *verbal,* we sometimes think only of spoken language. In fact, written messages are also verbal, because they also use words. Keep that in mind as we take a look at some of the most important features of language.

Language Is Symbolic

Language is *symbolic.* This statement means that each word represents a particular object or idea, but it does not constitute the object or idea itself. For example, the word *barn* represents a structure often used for storing hay, grain, or livestock. The word itself is not the structure; rather, it merely symbolizes it. Similarly, the word *five* represents a specific quantity of something (one more than four and one fewer than six), but the word itself is not the quantity; it simply represents it.

One way to understand the symbolic nature of language is to remember that different languages have different words for the same thing. The English word *barn,* for instance, is *schuur* in Dutch, *celeiro* in Portuguese, 축사 in Korean, and σιταποθήκη in Greek. These are completely different symbols, but they all represent the same object or idea. If you were to invent your own language, you could create any term you wanted to represent the concept of a barn.

As an illustration of the use of different symbols to represent the same idea, Figure 5.1 displays the word "speak" as represented in five different alphabets. These include (1) the Roman alphabet, with which you are already familiar; (2) Braille, an alphabet consisting of raised dots used by people who are blind to read and write; (3) Morse code, a system of long and short sounds used to communicate by means of a telegraph machine; (4) American Sign Language, a system of gestures and body language used to communicate with people who have hearing impairments; and (5) Gregg shorthand, a symbolic alphabet used for rapid note taking. Notice how different these symbols look, even though they are all symbolizing the same idea.

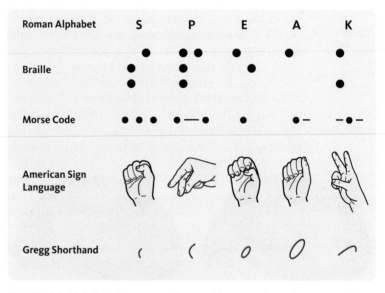

FIGURE 5.1 Alphabet Soup Many forms of language have their own alphabets. Here's the word SPEAK according to several different language systems.

We saw in Chapter 1 that the meaning of words—that is, what they symbolize— can change over time. You might not realize it, but *awful* used to mean "full of awe," and *neck* used to mean "a parcel of land" (as in "my neck of the woods"). Those terms now symbolize something different, and it is entirely possible that they will represent something different in the future. This example illustrates the important point that the symbolic nature of language is never static. Rather, it changes and evolves as words take on new meanings.

Language Is Arbitrary (Mostly)

Why do words symbolize the particular things they do? For the most part, words have only an arbitrary connection to their meanings.[3] Think of the word "car," for instance. The actual word doesn't look like a car or sound like a car, so why does it make you think of one? The only reason is that speakers of English have agreed to give the word "car" that particular meaning. We could just as easily call cars "whickles" or "geps" or "mumqualls." Those words don't mean anything, but they would if we assigned them a meaning. The point is that the meaning of almost all words is arbitrary: Words literally mean whatever we, as users of a language, choose for them to mean.

Language can be arbitrary precisely *because* it is symbolic. As we saw earlier, words only symbolize their meanings; they don't constitute their meanings themselves. For that reason, we can assign almost any word to symbolize a particular meaning, making the connection between language and meaning arbitrary.

Onomatopoeia A word formed by imitating the sound associated with its meaning.

One major exception to this rule is **onomatopoeia,** a word formed by imitating the sound associated with its meaning. Words such as "buzz," "meow," "splash," and "click" are all onomatopoetic words because their sounds reflect their meanings. For that reason, we can say that these types of words have an *iconic* connection to their meanings—that is, they serve as an icon or a representation of the meaning they symbolize—rather than an arbitrary one.

It's worth noting, however, that even onomatopoeia varies by language. To a U.S. American speaker of English, a dog goes "bowwow," but to an Indonesian, it says "gong gong." A sheep says "baa" to an English speaker, but "me'e'e" to the Navajo. The sound of a gunshot is "bang" in the United States but "pum" to the Spanish, "peng" to the Germans, and "pan" to the French.[4]

Language Is Governed by Rules

We have said that language is symbolic and that the meaning of most words is arbitrary. That assertion leads to an obvious question: How is it that we all understand one another? The answer is that every language is governed by rules.

You already know many of the rules that frame your native language. Even if you can't articulate them, you generally notice them when they're violated. To a native speaker of English, for instance, the statement "I filled the tub with water" sounds correct, but the phrase "I filled water into the tub" does not. Even if you aren't quite sure *why* the second sentence sounds wrong, you probably still recognize that it does. Along these same lines, when you learn a new language, you don't learn just the words; you also learn the rules for how the words work together to convey meaning.

Researchers distinguish among four types of language rules:

- *Phonological rules* deal with the correct pronunciation of a word, and they vary from language to language. If you speak French, for example, you know that the proper way to pronounce *travail* is trah-VYE. In contrast, according to English phonological rules, the word looks as though it should be pronounced trah-VALE.

- *Syntactic rules* govern the ordering of words within phrases. The question "What is your name?" makes sense to an English speaker because the words are in the proper order. To ask the same question in American Sign Language, we would sign "your – name – what?" Signing "what – your – name?" is incorrect.

Pragmatic rules deal with our interpretations of verbal statements. When someone says, "Nice to meet you," do you always think he or she is happy to meet you?

- *Semantic rules* have to do with the meanings of individual words. These meanings may be arbitrary, as we have seen, but they are agreed upon by speakers of a language. When you hear the word "car," for instance, you think of an automobile, not a washing machine or a piano or a lightbulb. It is a semantic rule that connects "car "with "automobile" and not with one of the other meanings.

- *Pragmatic rules* deal with the implications or interpretations of statements. Think of hearing the phrase "Nice to meet you," a common greeting among speakers of English. Depending on the context and the speaker's tone of voice, you might think the speaker really *is* happy to meet you, or you might infer that he or she is just saying so to be polite. If there's a sarcastic tone in the speaker's voice, you might even infer that he or she is actually *unhappy* to meet you. In each instance, it is pragmatic rules that lead you to your conclusion.

The "At a Glance" box below provides a summary of these four types of language rules.

As children acquire a language, they gain an almost intuitive sense of its phonological, syntactic, semantic, and pragmatic rules. That knowledge allows native speakers of a language to speak and write *fluently*. In contrast, people who are less familiar with the language are more prone to violate these rules.[5]

At a Glance: Rules of Language

Languages observe four types of rules: phonological, syntactic, semantic, and pragmatic.

Phonological rules	Deal with the correct pronunciation of words
Syntactic rules	Dictate the proper order of words for the intended meaning
Semantic rules	Govern the meanings of individual words
Pragmatic rules	Deal with the implications or interpretations of statements

Language Has Layers of Meaning

Many words imply certain ideas that differ from their literal meanings. The literal meaning of a word—that is, the way it is defined in a dictionary—is called its **denotative meaning.** Think of the word "home," for instance. Its denotative meaning is "a shelter used as a residence." When you hear the word "home," however, you probably also think of concepts such as "a place where I feel safe, accepted, and loved" or "a space where I am free to do whatever I want." These are examples of the word's **connotative meaning,** the implications that it suggests in addition to its literal meaning.

Denotative meaning A word's literal meaning or dictionary definition.

Connotative meaning A word's implied or secondary meaning, in addition to its literal meaning.

The Semantic Triangle. To illustrate the relationship between words and their denotative and connotative meanings, psychologist Charles Ogden and English professor Ivor Richards developed the *Semantic Triangle* (see Figure 5.2).[6] In its three corners, the Semantic Triangle portrays three necessary elements for identifying the meaning in language. The first element is the *symbol,* which is the word being communicated. In the second corner is the *referent,* which is the word's denotative meaning. Finally, there's the *reference,* which is the connotative meaning.

As the Semantic Triangle illustrates, if several listeners hear the same word, they might attribute the same denotative meaning to it but different connotative meanings. For instance, if I say the word "euthanasia," the word itself is the symbol, and its referent is a medically assisted death. To one listener, the word represents a merciful way to end a person's pain and suffering. To another person, it represents a form of homicide. To still other listeners, it represents an unfortunate—but sometimes justified—component of the death experience. These are all differences in the word's reference, or connotative meaning, rather than in its denotative meaning.

This example illustrates the essential point that the meanings of words are situated in the people who use them and not in the words themselves. Consequently, people may use a word such as "euthanasia" to connote a range of different meanings. As the transaction model of communication, which we discussed in Chapter 1, suggests, most words don't have meanings of their own. Instead, they receive their meanings through the social interaction of the people who use them.

FIGURE 5.2 The Semantic Triangle The Semantic Triangle portrays three necessary elements for identifying the meaning in language. The first element is the *symbol,* which is the word being communicated. In this visual, the symbol is the word "home." In another corner of the Semantic Triangle is the *referent,* which is the word's denotative meaning. In this visual, the upper corner of the triangle features a photo representing the literal, denotative meaning of the word home: "a shelter used as a residence." Finally, there's the *reference,* which is the connotative meaning of the word. In the right corner of this visual, the connotative meaning of the word is depicted by a family sharing breakfast in their kitchen.

Loaded language. Denotations and connotations represent different layers of meaning in language. This is particularly apparent in the case of **loaded language,** which refers to terms that evoke strongly positive or negative connotations. At a denotative level, for instance, the word "cancer" simply refers to a malignant growth or tumor in the body. For many people, however, "cancer" connotes any evil condition that spreads destructively. For example, you might hear someone describe conditions such as poverty or bigotry as "cancers on society." This example illustrates that people can use the term "cancer" as a loaded word when they wish to evoke feelings of fear, disgust, or anger on the part of listeners. People can also use loaded words to evoke positive emotions. Terms such as "mother," "peace," and "freedom" have emotionally positive connotations even though their denotative meanings may be emotionally neutral.[7]

Loaded language
Terms that carry strongly positive or negative connotations.

Words such as "mother" and "marriage" have emotionally positive connotations, even though their denotative meanings are neutral. Whether the term "marriage" should apply to same-sex couples has been a controversial issue for some time.

In some cases, the relationship between a word's denotative and connotative meanings can itself be cause for contention. One current example is the ongoing debate over same-sex marriage. At a denotative level, the word "marriage" implies a legally sanctioned romantic union that, according to the laws of most countries in the world and most states in the United States, must involve one woman and one man. In response to committed same-sex couples who wish to have their relationships legally sanctioned, many U.S. states have instituted laws recognizing "civil unions" or "domestic partnerships." Although these relationships provide many of the same legal rights and protections as marriage, many lesbian and gay adults nonetheless object to civil union and domestic partnership laws because they don't refer to the relationships as "marriages."[8]

This disagreement partly reflects a clash between the denotative and connotative meanings of the word "marriage." If civil unions and domestic partnerships offer the same legal rights as marriage, then the terms "civil union" and "domestic partnership" are equivalent to "marriage" in their denotative meanings. You might argue that if they are equivalent, then it doesn't really matter what the relationship is called.

The term "marriage," however, has connotative meanings that other terms don't necessarily share. For example, to many people the word "marriage" implies stability, acceptance, and normality, whereas "civil union" and "domestic partnership" connote relationships that are less traditional and less legitimate.[9] Because these terms differ from "marriage" in their connotative meanings, many people have argued that calling legal same-sex relationships anything other than "marriages" implies that they are inferior or second-class relationships.

Language Varies in Clarity

Josh is driving his brother Jeremy to an appointment with a new physician, and Jeremy has the directions. As they approach an intersection, they have the following conversation:

Josh: I need to turn left at this next light, don't I?

Jeremy: Right.

Which way should Josh turn? When Jeremy responded to Josh's question by answering "right," was he saying that Josh was correct in thinking he should turn left, or was he correcting Josh by instructing him to turn right? We don't really know, because Jeremy has used **ambiguous language** by making a statement that we can interpret to have more than one meaning. Jeremy's reply was ambiguous because the word "right" could mean either "correct" or "turn right" in this situation.

> **Ambiguous language**
> Having more than one possible meaning.

We might interpret the communication between Josh and Jeremy to suggest that ambiguous language is always a problem. The reality is that a certain amount of ambiguity is inherent in our language. In fact, according to the *Oxford English Dictionary,* the 500 most frequently used words in the English language have an average of 23 meanings each. The word *set* has so many meanings—nearly 200, more than any other English word—that it takes the *Oxford English Dictionary* 60,000 words to define it![10] Obviously these multiple meanings can affect clarity. For example, what would you think if you heard someone say "I saw her duck"? Did you observe her pet water fowl, or did you witness her crouching down? How about the statement, "I'm at the bank"? Is that the financial institution or the side of the river? Sometimes ambiguity arises not because of the words themselves but because of the way we arrange them. Years ago, for example, while discussing a local flood, former California governor Pat Brown said, "This is the worst disaster in California since I was elected." He clearly meant that the flood was the worst disaster that had occurred during his tenure in office. We could, however, interpret his remarks to suggest that his election was itself a disaster. Comedian Groucho Marx was famous for his ambiguous statements; for example, "This morning I shot an elephant in my pajamas. How he got in my pajamas, I'll never know!"

How much ambiguity is acceptable within a language? Perhaps not surprisingly, cultures vary in how precise they expect language to be. In the United States, for example, we generally expect a weather forecast to specify temperatures, sky conditions (clear, cloudy), and the chances of rain or snow. In contrast, an Australian forecaster might report that today's weather will be "fine" and tomorrow's will be "mostly fine." A German woman might say that she has five children, but a woman who speaks Pirahã, an Amazonian tribal language, would simply say that she has "many," because her language includes no words for numbers beyond one and two.

As we saw in the case of Josh and Jeremy, people often use ambiguous language unintentionally. Jeremy probably knew exactly what he meant when he said "right"; he just didn't realize that Josh wouldn't know how to interpret his response. Ambiguity can also be intentional, however. Let's say you've invited your co-worker Simone to spend the weekend with you and your family. In response to your invitation, she smiles and says, "That sounds like a lot of fun." Has she accepted your invitation?

We really can't tell, because Simone's response—although it might sound positive—is actually unclear because she never explicitly answered "yes" or "no." Moreover, she might have used ambiguous language on purpose to keep her options open. Her response might lead you to believe she is planning to join you. If she later decides not to, however, the ambiguity of her response would allow her to claim "I never said I was going to." Research shows that people often use ambiguous language strategically.[11] Can you think of times when you have done so?

Another reason language varies in clarity is that some words are more *concrete* than others. A word that is concrete refers to a specific object in the physical world, such as a particular car, a specific house, or an individual person. By contrast, a word

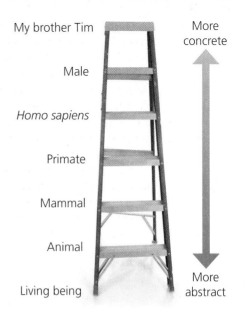

FIGURE 5.3 Ladder of Abstraction One reason language varies in clarity is that some words are more concrete than others. A word that is concrete refers to a specific object in the physical world, such as a particular car, a specific house, or an individual person. By contrast, a word that is abstract refers to a broader category or organizing concept of objects. According to English professor Samuel Hayakawa, words can be arrayed along a "ladder of abstraction," which shows their progression from more abstract to more concrete. In this figure, the bottom of the ladder refers to all living beings, which is a broad, abstract category. Moving upward from there, the concepts become more and more concrete, referencing all animals, then all mammals, all primates, all *Homo sapiens*, and all males, before reaching the most concrete reference to a specific individual.

My brother Tim

Male

Homo sapiens

Primate

Mammal

Animal

Living being

More concrete

More abstract

that is *abstract* refers to a broader category or organizing concept of objects. According to English professor Samuel Hayakawa, words can be arrayed along a "ladder of abstraction," which shows their progression from more abstract to more concrete.[12]

An example of Hayakawa's ladder of abstraction appears in Figure 5.3. At the bottom of the ladder is a reference to all living beings, which is a broad, abstract category. Moving upward from there, the concepts become more and more concrete, referring to all animals, then all mammals, all primates, all *Homo sapiens,* and all males, before reaching the most concrete reference to a specific individual.

Language Is Bound by Context and Culture

Finally, the meaning in language is affected by the social and cultural context in which it is used. Societies and cultures differ in many ways, including their degree of individualism and their use of communication codes. Many of those differences are reflected in people's verbal messages. For instance, when you hear someone say, "I'm looking out for Number One," you're hearing a very individualistic message that would be less common in a collectivistic society. In fact, a common adage in Japan states that "it is the nail that sticks out that gets hammered down," which reflects the collectivistic culture of that nation.[13]

Studies have shown that for individuals who speak more than one language, the choice of language can affect their perceptions.[14] While completing a values test, for instance, students in Hong Kong expressed more traditional Chinese values while speaking Cantonese than while speaking English. Jewish and Arab students in Israel both described themselves as more distinct from outsiders when speaking their native languages than when speaking English. Just as each language is distinctive, the language we use leads us to see the world in a particular way.

In fact, the idea that language shapes our views of reality was proposed by anthropologist Edward Sapir and linguist Benjamin Whorf in what became known as the **Sapir-Whorf hypothesis.** Their notion was that language influences the ways that members of a culture see the world—and that the attitudes and behaviors of a culture's people are reflected in its language.[15]

Sapir-Whorf hypothesis The idea that language influences the ways that members of a culture see and think about the world.

The Sapir-Whorf hypothesis embodies two specific principles. The first, called *linguistic determinism,* suggests that the structure of language determines how we think. In other words, we can conceive of something only if we have a term for it in our vocabulary.[16] Imagine a language, for instance, that includes no word describing the emotion of envy. According to the principle of linguistic determinism, people who speak that language would not experience envy because their experiences of the world would be limited to what their language allowed them to communicate about.

The second principle, called *linguistic relativity,* suggests that because language determines our perceptions of reality, people who speak different languages will see the world differently. In his research, for instance, Whorf discovered that the language of the Hopi Indians makes no distinction between nouns and verbs. Whereas English uses nouns to refer to *things* and verbs to refer to *actions,* the Hopi language describes just about everything as an action or a process. Compared with English speakers, then, the Hopi tend to see the world as being constantly in motion.[17]

Just as English includes words and concepts that have no equivalents in some other languages (such as Hopi), other languages contain words that have no English equivalent. According to the principle of linguistic relativity, we would conclude from this that speakers of these languages would differ from English speakers in their conceptions of these elements of life. Linguist Christopher Moore has identified several such terms:[18]

- *Ilunga:* This word denotes a person who will forgive a transgression once and will tolerate it a second time, but not a third. It is from the Tshiluba language, spoken in the Democratic Republic of the Congo.
- *Taarradhin:* The Arabic language contains no word for "compromise," but this term refers to a "win-win" situation.
- *Litost:* This Czech word refers to a state of emotional torment that would be created by the sight of one's own misery.
- *Meraki:* The Greeks use this term to describe pouring your heart and soul into an activity, such as cooking or fishing.
- *Yoko meshi:* In Japanese, this term refers to the specific stress people feel when they are trying to speak a foreign language.

The Sapir-Whorf hypothesis is provocative, but is it true? We'll examine some of the evidence in the "Fact or Fiction? box on page 174.

Learn It: What does it mean to say that language is symbolic? How is onomatopoeia an exception to the rule that language is arbitrary? How do syntactic rules differ from semantic rules? Describe the difference between a word's denotative meaning and its connotative meaning. When is a word or phrase ambiguous? What is the Sapir-Whorf hypothesis?

Try It: To observe how language evolves, invent a new word or expression. Write out a definition for it, and begin using it in everyday conversation with your friends. Take note of how well your word or expression catches on and whether your friends begin using it in their own conversations.

Reflect on It: In what ways is your language use affected by your culture? Where did you learn all the rules associated with your native language?

Sapir and Whorf proposed that our thoughts are rooted in language, so we can think about something only if we have words for it. This idea implies that if we don't have a word for a particular concept, then we can't experience that concept. It also implies that people who speak different languages will see the world differently *because of the differences in their languages*. Are these ideas fact or fiction?

It's hard to tell for certain, but the Sapir-Whorf hypothesis has been widely criticized by researchers. Three criticisms are common. The first criticism centers on the cause-and-effect relationship between language and thought. The Sapir-Whorf hypothesis proposes that language shapes and constrains how we think. It is equally possible, though, that our thoughts shape and constrain our language. For instance, an experienced fashion designer might look at four jackets and label their colors as scarlet, ruby, crimson, and vermilion. You might look at the same jackets and call them all red. Does the designer think of the four colors as different because she has more terms for them than you do, or does she have more terms because she has more experience thinking about differences among colors? It's difficult to know for sure, but either idea is possible.

Second, even if people don't have a word for a particular experience, such as the stress of trying to speak a foreign language, that doesn't necessarily mean they don't have that experience. Perhaps you can recall feeling stress at learning another language, even if you didn't have a specific term for it. Finally, as linguist Steven Pinker has pointed out, even people who don't acquire language, perhaps because of mental or cognitive deficiencies, are able to think, count, and interact with others, which they wouldn't be able to do if language determines thought.

These criticisms don't necessarily mean that the Sapir-Whorf hypothesis is entirely wrong. They suggest, however, that language doesn't shape and constrain our ways of thinking quite to the extent that Sapir and Whorf believed.

Ask Yourself:

- What did you think of the Sapir-Whorf hypothesis when you first read about it? Did it seem reasonable or unreasonable to you at first?

- Do you think only in words? Do you ever think in numbers or colors or sounds? If you didn't know any languages, would you lack the ability to think?

Source: Pinker, S. (1994). *The language instinct*. New York: Harper-Collins.

2} Appreciating the Power of Words

English writer Rudyard Kipling, author of *The Jungle Book,* once called words "the most powerful drug used by mankind." To understand his point, think about how you feel when someone you love expresses affection to you, or when you have to listen to a speech by a politician you can't stand, or when you have to comfort a grieving friend, as Darren tried to do in the opening scene. Words can literally change a person's day—or a person's life—in positive or negative ways.

Whole books have been written about the power of language. Here we'll focus on five important contexts in which words have special power: naming, persuasion, credibility and power, affection, and comfort.

Naming Defines and Differentiates Us

What's something that belongs to you yet is constantly used by others? The answer to this riddle is: *your name.* A name is simply a linguistic device that identifies something or someone. Your name does more, however, than just differentiate you from others—it's also an important component of your sense of self. From the perspective of interpersonal communication, naming is one way we represent ourselves to others and one way we gain information about other people. Let's examine how names relate to identity and look at some of the most common ways that names come about.

> *Words mean more than what is set down on paper. It takes the human voice to infuse them with shades of deeper meaning.*
>
> —Maya Angelou (1928–)
> U.S. American poet

Naming and identity. As we discussed in an earlier chapter, first impressions are often critical to the perception we form of someone. Although impressions are influenced by factors such as a person's appearance or behaviors, they can also be shaped by his or her name. A person's first name, for instance, frequently suggests information about the person's demographic characteristics. One such characteristic is the person's sex. In Western societies, for instance, we usually assign names such as Jeff, Wesley, and Ian only to males and names such as Kimberly, Laura, and Monique to females.

Names can also provide clues about a person's ethnicity. For example, you might infer that LaKeisha is African American, Huong is Asian, and Santiago is Latino. Some names even suggest a person's age group, so you might assume that Emma, Madison, and Hannah are younger than Edna, Mildred, and Bertha.

Your name portrays your sense of self, and it can evolve as your sense of self develops. Puff Daddy, P. Diddy, and Sean Combs all represent the same person, whose image has evolved over time.

In addition to demographic information, names can suggest information about our disposition and sense of self. For instance, we might perceive an adult man who goes by the name William differently than one who goes by Billy, even though those are two forms of the same name. Indeed, research shows that we do make assumptions about people—whether accurately or not—on the basis of their names.[19]

In one study, for instance, people made more positive evaluations of men named David, Jon, Joshua, and Gregory than they did of men named Oswald, Myron, Reginald, and Edmund, even though they were given no information about the men other than their names.[20] In a similar study, researchers asked college students to vote for one of six women for campus beauty queen after seeing the names and photographs of the "candidates." In reality, the researchers had selected photographs of six women who had been judged to be equivalent in physical attractiveness and had assigned a name to each picture. Although the women were equally attractive, students were significantly more likely to vote for women named Jennifer, Kathy, or Christine than for women named Ethel, Harriet, or Gertrude.[21] As both studies suggest, names can carry implicit meaning about a person's goodness or desirability. It's difficult to know exactly *why* people prefer some names to others, but one possibility is that names that were more common in the past than they are today, such as Oswald or Ethel, suggest the image of someone who is older—and perhaps less vital or attractive—than names that are more contemporary.

Perhaps as a result, people sometimes adopt completely different names to project a different identity. Internet screen names, for instance, allow people to create their own identities for the purpose of interacting online. In a famous example of disassociating with one's name, the U.S. American singer Prince relinquished his name from 1993 to 2000, after a contract dispute with his record label. During that period, he chose to be known instead as ♀, a symbol with no pronounceable equivalent (although he was referred to during this period as "The Artist formerly known as Prince"). After his contract with the record label expired, the singer readopted his name. Perhaps to enhance their distinctiveness, other celebrities have also adopted the practice of being known by a single name, such as Bono, Cher, Madonna, Sting, and Oprah.

Naming practices. In the United States, the Social Security Administration keeps track of the most popular first names given to newborns throughout the country. Some names have remained fashionable for quite some time. Beginning in 1880, for example, Mary and John were the most popular female and male first names nearly every year until 1926, when Robert took over the top spot for boys. Mary dominated the list for girls until 1947, when it was replaced with Linda. As times change, though, so do naming preferences. By 1985, Jessica and Michael were the most popular first names. Emily and Jacob topped the list in 2006.[22] (Incidentally, Jacob and Joshua were the most popular names for twins born that year.) Table 5.1 lists the most popular first names since 1900.

Practices of naming also vary according to culture and religion. In predominantly Catholic communities around the world, for instance, males are often given a feminine middle name, such as Marie or Maria. (In French Catholic families, men often have a compound first name, such as Paul-Marie, to accommodate the same tradition.) These naming practices appear to reflect

Table 5.1: Popular Names over the Last Century

Year	Top Three Boys' Names	Top Three Girls' Names
2006	Jacob	Emily
	Michael	Emma
	Joshua	Madison
1975	Michael	Jennifer
	Jason	Amy
	Christopher	Heather
1950	James	Linda
	Robert	Mary
	John	Patricia
1925	Robert	Mary
	John	Dorothy
	William	Betty
1900	John	Mary
	William	Helen
	James	Anna

Amish naming practices honor both maternal and paternal lineages.

cultural traditions, rather than specific church doctrine. Among the Sikh of India, boys are given the surname *Singh* and girls the surname *Kaur*, although adults of both sexes often take these as middle names instead. This practice of giving common surnames to all boys and girls is meant to symbolize the abolition of class inequalities. Amish children receive their fathers' surname and are commonly given the first letter of their mother's maiden name as their middle name; thus, the son of Mary Jacobs would have the middle name J (with no period). This practice is intended to give honor to both the maternal and the paternal lineages.

In many parts of the world, it is also traditional for women to adopt their husband's last name when they marry, or at least to add his name to hers. So, when marrying George Rogers, Jean Levitt might become Jean Rogers, or Jean Levitt Rogers, or Jean Levitt-Rogers. Alternatively, she might choose to remain Jean Levitt. What factors influence this decision?

In a study by communication researchers Karen Foss and Belle Edson, married women who kept their birth names gave more importance to their personal concerns than to their relationships. By contrast, women who took their husband's names rated their relationships as more important than issues of self. As you might guess, women who hyphenated their last names were in the middle, rating their relationships and personal concerns about equally.[23]

Other research has confirmed that women who retain their birth names at marriage score higher than other women on self-reports of masculinity and feminist attitudes.[24] Name changers and name keepers don't appear to differ from each other in their self-esteem, autonomy, or reports about the balance of control in their marriages, however.[25]

To an extent, then, your name tells your story. Like your clothes or your hairstyle, it is a part of how you present yourself to others and how others relate to you.

We Use Words to Persuade

Persuasion is the process of moving people to think or act in a certain way. Every time you watch a TV commercial, read a billboard, or listen to a political speech, someone is trying to influence what you believe or how you behave. There's no question that we are persuaded by images. When we see an attractive model using a product, for instance, we subconsciously associate the product with the person's attractiveness.[26] Much of our ability to persuade others, however, comes from the language we use.

Let's say that you've decided to run in a 10-kilometer race to benefit your local children's hospital, and you're trying to persuade your relatives, friends, and co-workers to make pledges to sponsor you. What are some ways of asking for their sponsorship that would encourage them to agree?

Anchor-and-contrast. One strategy is to use what researchers call an **anchor-and-contrast** approach. When you adopt this technique, you first craft a request that is so large that few people will agree to do it. This large request is the anchor. After people

Anchor-and-contrast A form of persuasion in which you initially make a large request that is rejected and then follow it with a smaller, more reasonable request.

How would you persuade someone to sponsor you in a 10-K race? You could use anchor-and-contrast by contrasting your request with a larger one. You might use the norm of reciprocity by reminding people of favors you've done for them. Or, you could use the social validation principle by pointing out that most people you have asked have sponsored you.

reject the anchor, you then ask for what you actually want, which, by contrast with the anchor, will seem more reasonable to most people, thus encouraging them to comply. To solicit sponsors for your 10-K run, for instance, you could craft a letter giving people the following sponsorship options:

1. $40 per kilometer, or $400 in total
2. $20 per kilometer, or $200 in total
3. $10 per kilometer, or $100 in total
4. $5 per kilometer, or $50 in total

If you had simply asked people to pledge $50 or even $100 toward your fund-raising efforts, many of them probably would have declined because they felt those amounts were too generous. Fifty dollars doesn't seem quite as unreasonable when it is contrasted with anchors of larger amounts, such as $400. In fact, it seems quite reasonable by comparison, which would likely increase the persuasive success of your appeal.[27]

Norm of reciprocity. A second persuasive strategy is to appeal to the norm of reciprocity. As you might recall from Chapter 3, the norm of reciprocity suggests that we expect people to repay favors they have received from others. When someone has helped you in the past, therefore, the norm of reciprocity predicts that you should feel a sense of duty to help that person in the future.[28] Businesses and organizations appeal to reciprocity any time they offer you free samples of their products. By giving you something for free, they hope to invoke a sense of obligation on your part to return the favor by buying something.

You might employ this persuasive technique when soliciting sponsorships for your race by reminding people of ways in which you have helped them in the past. Sometimes this technique involves direct reciprocity, wherein you ask people to repay the same favor you did for them before. Perhaps you sponsored your brother in a race last year; if so, then you could say to him:

> *I'm so glad I was able to sponsor you last year; would you be able to return the favor and sponsor me this time?*

More often, however, appeals to reciprocity involve indirect reciprocity, wherein you have done some type of favor for people in the past and you are now asking them to repay you with a favor of similar perceived value. Instead of sponsoring your brother in a race last year, let's say that you babysat his children for a three-day weekend so he and his spouse could take a vacation. In this instance, you could say something such as:

> *Remember when you were wondering how to pay me back for babysitting? I have the perfect opportunity: How about sponsoring me for the race?*

Social validation principle. A third persuasive strategy is to invoke the **social validation principle,** which maintains that people will comply with requests if they believe others are also complying.[29] Whenever advertisers say that "four out of five people preferred" a certain brand of car, refrigerator, or chewing gum, they are hoping you

Social validation principle
The prediction that people will comply with requests if they believe others are also complying.

will want to buy the same brand that most people are buying. The idea is that we gain social approval by acting the way others act. So, to the extent that social approval is important to people, the quest for approval can influence the decisions they make.

When soliciting sponsorships for your 10-K race, you could invoke the social validation principle directly, by saying to potential sponsors:

> Almost everyone in your neighborhood has agreed to sponsor me in the race; I hope I can count on your support too.

As with reciprocity, social validation can be either direct or indirect. The preceding example is direct because you have expressed overtly that many other people have already agreed to sponsor you. You could also invoke social validation indirectly, however. For instance, instead of having each potential sponsor fill out a separate pledge form, you might use one master list so that each person you ask to support you can see the names of everyone who has already agreed. This strategy implicitly sends the message that many other people are sponsoring you, so you don't have to make that point overtly.

Choosing a persuasive strategy. Anchor-and-contrast, reciprocity, and social validation are simply three of many persuasive strategies people use in interpersonal situations. Deciding which strategy will be the most influential often relies on your knowledge of the people you are attempting to persuade. If you know that your friend Bailey cares a great deal what others think of him, for instance, he will probably be persuaded by an appeal to social validation. If your neighbor Caryn is very conscientious about repaying favors, she will likely find appeals to reciprocity persuasive. Your co-worker Kris, who is always on the lookout for a good deal, may be most persuaded by an anchor-and-contrast approach.

The point is that no single persuasion strategy is effective for every person or in every situation. To be as persuasive as possible, therefore, you often must adopt more than one strategy at a time.

Credibility Empowers Us

Credibility
The extent to which others find our words and actions trustworthy. Our **credibility** is the extent to which others perceive us to be competent and trustworthy. Some speakers have credibility on certain topics because of their training and expertise. You'll probably have more confidence in medical advice if you hear it from a doctor or a nurse, for instance, than if you hear it from the barista at your local coffee shop. If the advice is about making a great latte, however, you'll probably trust your barista more than your doctor or nurse. In either case, you are assigning credibility on the basis of the speaker's specific expertise.

It might seem as though training and expertise automatically give a person credibility. In fact, however, credibility is a perception that is influenced not only by a person's credentials but also by his or her actions and words. One journalist, for instance, might be perceived as highly credible because she always double-checks her facts and tries to represent all opinions on an issue. In contrast, another journalist with the same training might be perceived as less credible if he has made factual errors in the past or if his writing seems slanted toward a particular point of view. Many people in the public eye, such as politicians, work especially hard to be perceived as credible, knowing they can lose public support if they aren't.

Language is intimately tied to issues of credibility. Irrespective of our training or credentials, our words can portray us as confident, trustworthy communicators, or they can make us appear unsure of ourselves. In either situation, our ability to get what we want out of our interpersonal interactions is affected by the credibility that our use of language gives us.

Political candidates often use clichés, such as calling themselves the "candidate of change." How do you react when you see or hear messages of this sort?

Clichés. Several forms of language have the potential either to enhance or to damage perceptions of a person's credibility. One use of language that can diminish credibility is the use of *clichés,* or phrases that were novel at one time but have lost their effect because of overuse. When politicians talk about "being an agent of change," businesspeople refer to "thinking outside the box," or community leaders talk about "making a difference," for instance, they may lose credibility with their audiences because those phrases are clichés that may make speakers sound uninformed or out-of-touch.

Dialects. People can also affect perceptions of their credibility by using certain *dialects,* which are variations on a language that are shared by people of a certain region or social class. Many U.S. Americans, for example, can tell the difference between a speaker from the South and one from New England on the basis of the words these speakers use. The Southern speaker might use words characteristic of a Southern dialect, such as saying "y'all" to mean "you," whereas the speech of the New Englander might reflect the dialect of that region, perhaps calling something "wicked good" rather than "very good."

According to communication accommodation theory, we may be able to enhance our credibility by speaking in a dialect that is familiar to our audience.[30] By contrast, when we use a dialect that is different from that of our listeners, we can appear as an outsider, which may lead our audience to question our credibility.

Equivocation. Another form of language that sometimes influences a speaker's credibility is *equivocation,* or language that disguises the speaker's true intentions through strategic ambiguity. We often choose to use equivocal language when we're in a dilemma, a situation when none of our options is a good one. Suppose, for example, that you're asked to provide a reference for your friend Dylan, who is applying for a job on the police force in your town. One of the questions you're asked is how well Dylan handles pressure. Even though Dylan's your friend, you can immediately think of several occasions when he hasn't handled pressure well. Now you're caught in a bind. On the one hand, you want Dylan to get the job because he's your friend. On the other hand, you don't want to lie to the police lieutenant who's phoning you for the reference.

Several studies have shown that when we're faced with two unappealing choices such as these, we often use equivocal language to get ourselves out of that bind.[31] In response to the lieutenant's question about how well Dylan handles pressure, for instance, you might say something like this: "Well, that depends; there are lots of different kinds of pressure."

As you can probably tell, that statement doesn't give the lieutenant much information at all. Instead, it might imply that you don't know how well Dylan handles pressure but you don't want to admit that you don't know. It might also imply that you do know how well Dylan handles pressure but don't want to say. In either case, you are likely to come across as less credible than if you had answered the question directly.[32] Researchers John Daly, Carol Diesel, and David Weber have suggested that these sorts of conversational dilemmas are common and that we frequently use equivocal language in such situations.[33]

Weasel words. A form of language related to equivocation is the use of *weasel words:* terms or phrases that are intended to mislead listeners by implying something that they don't actually say. Advertisers commonly use weasel words when making claims about their products. For instance, when you hear that "four out of five dentists prefer" a certain chewing gum, the implication is that 80% of all dentists prefer this brand. That would indeed be impressive—but that isn't what the statement actually said. For all we know, only five dentists were surveyed to begin with, making the support of "four out of five" appear much less impressive.

Another advertisement might claim that a brand of aspirin has been "clinically tested" for its effectiveness against migraine headaches. Sounds impressive—except that we aren't told the *results* of the clinical tests. The implication of the claim is that the aspirin was tested and found to be effective. That claim is only implied, however; it was never actually stated.

One way people use weasel words in interpersonal communication is by making broad, unsupported generalizations. To make herself sound intelligent and informed, for instance, Eva is fond of starting statements with "People say that . . ." or "It's widely known that . . ." These phrases are weasel words because they imply a broad level of agreement with whatever Eva is saying, but they provide no evidence of that agreement. That is, Eva never specifies *which* people say or know whatever she is claiming, or *how many* people say or know it, or why we should trust their beliefs or knowledge in the first place.

Allness statements. One specific form of weasel words is an *allness statement,* or a statement implying that a claim is true without exception. For instance, when you hear somebody claim that "experts agree that corporal punishment is emotionally damaging to children," the implication is that *all* experts agree. Note, however, that the speaker provides no evidence to back up that claim. Likewise, when someone says "there's no known cure for depression," the implication is that no cure exists. All the statement actually means, however, is that no cure is known to the speaker.

Choosing credible language. All the forms of speech we just discussed can make the speaker's words sound imprecise, untrustworthy, and lacking in credibility. As we would expect, that perception can have several negative effects on how other people respond to the speaker. Several studies have shown, for instance, that people perceive speakers who use these forms of language as less competent, less dynamic, and even less attractive than speakers whose language is free of these characteristics.[34] In fact, using even one of these forms is enough to taint someone else's perceptions of the speaker.[35]

More credible forms of speech avoid using weasel words and allness statements. Thus, instead of claiming that what you're saying "is widely believed," simply claim that *you* believe it, unless you actually do have evidence to support it. Instead of saying that "experts

Avoiding weasel words, equivocation, and allness statements are some ways you can make your speech more credible, which is important in many social and professional situations.

agree" with what you're saying, say that "some experts agree," and be prepared to give examples of those who do. These forms of speech have more credibility because they make your claims clearer and more precise.

Language Expresses Affection and Intimacy

Language has a profound ability to communicate affection and create or enhance intimacy in our personal relationships. Although affection and intimacy are closely related, they are not the same thing. *Affection* is an emotional experience that includes feelings of love and appreciation that one person has for another. In contrast, *intimacy* is a characteristic of close, supportive relationships. We humans use language both to convey our affectionate feelings for one another and to strengthen our intimate bonds with those who are most important to us.

Verbal statements can communicate affection or intimacy in many ways. Some statements express our feelings for another person, such as "I like you" or "I'm in love with you." Others reinforce the importance of our relationship with another person, such as "You're my best friend" or "I could never love anyone as much as I love you." Still others convey hopes or dreams for the future of the relationship, including "I can't wait to be married to you" or "I want us to be together forever." Finally, some statements express the value of a relationship by noting how we would feel without it, such as "I can't stand the thought of losing you" or "My life would be empty if I hadn't met you."

We use language to convey affectionate feelings for others and strengthen our intimate bonds.

As you might imagine, statements like those are characteristic of our closest personal relationships. In fact, evidence suggests that communicating intimacy and affection is good both for relationships and for the people in them. For example, family studies researcher Ted Huston and his colleagues found that the more affection spouses communicated to each other during their first 2 years of marriage, the more likely they were still to be married 13 years later.[36] You'll find more information on this study in the "How Do We Know?" box on the next page. Other research has found that the more affection people receive from their parents during childhood, the lower their chances of developing depression, anxiety, and physical health problems later in life.[37]

Although verbal statements of affection and intimacy are probably more precise than nonverbal gestures (such as hugging), they can still be ambiguous. Consider, for instance, how many different things you can mean when you say "I love you" to someone. Do you love that person romantically? as a platonic friend? as a family member? Research shows it's not uncommon for people to misinterpret verbal displays of affection—to think someone is expressing romantic love when he or she means to express platonic love, for instance.[38] Maybe you've even been in that kind of situation yourself. If so, then you know how uncomfortable it can be for both the sender and the receiver.

How Do We Know?

Affectionate Spouses Stay Married Longer

We saw in this section that the more affection spouses communicated to each other in the first years of their marriage, the more likely they were to be married after 13 years. How do we know this?

This finding was identified by a *longitudinal study,* in which data are collected from the same group of people over a period of time. In this particular study, family studies researcher Ted Huston and his colleagues interviewed 168 pairs of newlyweds 2 months after their weddings, then again 1 year and 2 years later. During the interviews, the researchers asked spouses several questions about how they communicated with each other. Some of these questions concerned the extent to which spouses expressed affection to each other verbally, for example, by saying "I love you" or by giving each other compliments.

Approximately 13 years later, the researchers contacted nearly all the original couples again to find out if they were still married. They then examined whether the divorced couples differed from still-married couples in their affectionate communication scores from 13 years earlier. The results indicated that this was the case. Specifically, they showed that couples who reported more affectionate communication early in their marriage were more likely to be married 13 years later than couples who reported less affectionate communication. Only by following the same couples over a period of time can researchers determine which behaviors predict certain outcomes, such as divorce.

Ask Yourself:

- Why do you suppose affectionate communication early in the marriage predicts marital success?

- Does this finding mean that expressing affection *causes* marriages to succeed? Could it be the case that naturally affectionate people are simply better at making relationships succeed than less affectionate people are?

From Me to You:

- You might wonder why the researchers had to follow these couples over such a long period of time. Couldn't they simply have asked happily married couples how affectionate they were toward each other during the early years of their marriage? The answer is that they could have, but that method would be problematic because we often don't remember our own communication behaviors accurately, especially over long periods of time. Suppose I asked you to describe how your parents communicated with you when you were a child. You might have some accurate memories of that time, but your memories are also likely to be influenced by the relationship you have with your parents now. The same thing can happen with married couples. Those who are happily married now might "remember" being more affectionate early in their marriage than they really were; those who are divorced might "remember" being unaffectionate. We often believe our memories are genuine and accurate, but we can't know for sure. That's why it's so useful to see how behaviors measured at one time predict outcomes later, which is the purpose of longitudinal research.

Source: Huston, T. L., Caughlin, J. P., Houts, R. M., Smith, S. E., & George, L. J. (2001). The connubial crucible: Newlywed years as predictors of marital delight, distress, and divorce. *Journal of Personality and Social Psychology, 80,* 237–252.

In many cases, nonverbal behaviors (such as tone of voice or facial expression) and contextual information help to clarify the meaning of an affectionate message. Nevertheless, there's still a risk of misinterpretation, especially when we use affectionate language with new friends or with people we don't know well.[39]

Words Provide Comfort and Healing

Finally, we use our words to comfort people in distress. These exchanges can be mundane, such as a mother comforting a child with a stubbed toe, or they can occur in extraordinary circumstances, such as giving comfort and support to a young man who has lost his romantic partner to cancer. Indeed, you can probably recall times when you have been in distress and another person's comforting words made a major difference.

Recall that verbal communication includes both written and spoken words. To convey support we often use written messages. In fact, the greeting card industry is a $10 billion-a-year business. Although people send cards for a variety of reasons, including to acknowledge birthdays or to celebrate holidays, many greeting cards, such as get-well and sympathy cards, are used to express verbal messages of comfort.[40] There are also cards that express gratitude and ones that convey hope. Bluemountain .com, a Web site from which people can send free electronic greeting cards, offers e-cards in several categories related to comfort and healing, including special cards for the families of deployed military personnel and for the remembrance of September 11 victims.[41]

Using language to comfort other people. As you read in the opening vignette, Darren had a difficult time talking to Maria about her sister's death because he wasn't sure what to say to comfort her. Maybe you've been in similar situations yourself and felt unsure about what to say. According to professional counselors, there are several things Darren might have said to provide support and comfort to Maria, either during their telephone conversation or in the form of a card or a letter:[42]

- *Acknowledge the loss:* "I'm so sorry to hear about your sister's accident. I know that everyone who knew her will miss her greatly."
- *Express sympathy:* "Words can't express how sorry I feel. Please know that my heartfelt sympathies are with you."
- *Offer a positive reflection:* "I will always remember your sister's wonderful sense of humor and her great compassion for others."
- *Offer assistance:* "Please remember I'm here for you, whatever you need. I'll give you a call this weekend to see if there's anything I can do for you."

These sentiments can give comfort and support to someone grieving the loss of a loved one. In addition, many other situations call for words of comfort, such as a divorce, a job loss, or a serious illness. The words we use may be different in each case, but the underlying goals are the same: to acknowledge the person's feelings and to offer your support.

Using language to comfort ourselves. Just as we can use our words to comfort other people, we can also use them to comfort ourselves. Many people find that "journaling," or keeping a diary of their feelings, helps them find comfort and meaning even in traumatic events. In fact, some evidence indicates that writing about our thoughts and

Research by psychologist James Pennebaker demonstrates the health benefits of expressing your thoughts and feelings in a journal.

feelings can improve our health. Psychologist James Pennebaker has conducted many studies showing that when people write about traumas they've gone through—such as physical abuse or the death of a loved one—they often experience reduced levels of stress hormones, strengthened immune systems, and a decrease in doctor visits.[43]

Pennebaker's theory is that holding in negative emotions requires effort that we might otherwise use to support our health. For that reason, expressing those emotions (even on paper) allows us to put that energy to better use. The healing effects of expressive writing can be so strong, in fact, that participants in Pennebaker's studies have seen improvements after only two or three writing sessions of 20 minutes each.

In a similar vein, communication scholars have shown that when people are in distress, writing about their positive feelings for a loved one can accelerate their recovery. In one experiment, for instance, participants were put through a series of stressful tasks, such as mentally solving complicated math problems under time constraints and watching video clips of married couples fighting.[44] These tasks elevated their levels of a hormone called cortisol, which the body produces when people are under stress.

The participants were then assigned to one of three conditions. Participants in the first group were instructed to write a letter expressing their affection to someone they loved. The second group merely thought about a loved one but didn't put their feelings into words. Finally, the third group did nothing for 20 minutes. The researchers found that when people wrote about their affectionate feelings, their cortisol levels returned to normal the most quickly. Putting their affectionate feelings into words, therefore, accelerated their recovery from stress.

Just thinking about a loved one didn't provide any more benefit than doing nothing. Only those participants who translated their feelings into language recovered quickly from their elevated stress. As with Pennebaker's work, this study demonstrated the health benefits of using words to express your feelings.

As we've seen throughout this section, people use language to accomplish a number of important tasks. They assign people names and grant identities to others. They persuade others to adopt certain ideas or behaviors. They gain credibility and power. They convey affection and build intimacy with others. They provide comfort and support, both to others and to themselves. Many interpersonal situations require us to perform one or more of these tasks. Therefore, our understanding of how language serves these functions will help us communicate effectively in those contexts.

Learn It: Which characteristics about a person are often implied by his or her name? How can you use the social validation principle to persuade someone? How is equivocation related to credibility? In what ways do we express affection to others verbally? What types of statements should messages of comfort contain?

Try It: The next time you're feeling stressed, try a version of Pennebaker's emotional writing activity. Sit quietly in a room with a pen and paper, and begin to write about your feelings. Why are you feeling stressed? What else are you feeling? Don't worry about your punctuation or grammar; just write nonstop for at least 20 minutes. Even if you feel a little worse immediately afterward (because you've been thinking so hard about what's bothering you), notice how you feel later in the day. Does putting your feelings into words help your frame of mind?

Reflect on It: If you had to choose a different name for yourself, what would it be? What makes one speaker more credible than another to you?

We've seen that there is a wide variety of purposes we can achieve with language. Now let's look at the ways in which language can also vary in its form. Some forms, such as humor, are generally positive and can produce all sorts of good outcomes, such as entertaining others, strengthening relationships, and even contributing to healing. Others, such as hate speech, are known for the devastating hurt they can cause.

> *Quarrels end, but words once spoken never die.*
> —African proverb

In this section, we explore several forms of language: humor, euphemism, slang, libel and slander, profanity, and hate speech. Many of these forms are neither entirely *good* nor entirely *bad*. Like many human inventions, language can be used well, and it can also be abused. In this section, we will look at examples of both.

Humor: What's So Funny?

A few years ago, psychologist Richard Wiseman designed a study with an ambitious goal: to discover the world's funniest joke. More than 2 million people from around the world visited his Web site and rated some 40,000 jokes for their level of humor. Here was the winning entry—the funniest joke in the world:

> Two hunters are out in the woods when one of them collapses. He doesn't seem to be breathing, and his eyes are glazed. The other guy takes out his phone and calls the emergency services. He gasps: "My friend is dead! What can I do?" The operator says: "Calm down, I can help. First, let's make sure he's dead." There is a silence, then a gunshot is heard. Back on the phone, the guy says: "Okay, now what?"[45]

Whether or not you find that joke funny, you can probably recognize the humor in it. That's because it contains what researchers believe to be the most important aspect of humor: a violation of our expectations. Most of us would interpret the operator's statement ("Let's make sure he's dead") as a suggestion to check the hunter's vital signs, not as a recommendation to shoot him. It's this twist on our expectations that makes the joke funny. In fact, researchers have discovered that specific parts of the brain process humor, and that without the violation of expectations—that is, without the punch line—these neurological structures don't "light up" or provide the mental reward we associate with a good joke.[46]

Humor can enhance our interpersonal interactions in many ways. It can bring us closer to others and make social interaction more pleasant and enjoyable.[47] It can diffuse stress, such as when people are in conflict with one another.[48] Within relationships, "inside jokes" can reinforce people's feelings of intimacy. Humor can provide so many personal and social benefits, in fact, that a good sense of humor is something both women and men strongly seek in a romantic partner.[49]

Not all effects of humor are positive, however. Humor can also be used to demean social or cultural groups, as in the case of racial jokes or jokes about elderly people or persons with disabilities. Moreover, even when they are made without the intention to offend, jokes told at another's expense can cause embarrassment or distress and might even qualify as instances of harassment.[50] When using humor, therefore, it's important to take stock of your audience to make certain that your jokes will amuse rather than offend.

Euphemisms: Soft Talk

Euphemism
A vague, mild expression that symbolizes something more blunt or harsh.

Some topics are difficult or impolite to talk about directly. In these cases, we might use a **euphemism,** which is a vague, mild expression that symbolizes something more blunt or harsh. Instead of saying that someone has died, for instance, we might say that he has "passed away." Rather than mentioning that she is pregnant, a woman might say she's "expecting." You can probably think of many euphemisms, such as "let go" (instead of "fired"), "sleep together" (instead of "have sex"), or "praying at the porcelain altar" (instead of "vomiting in the toilet").

In almost every case, the euphemistic term sounds less harsh or less explicit than the term it stands for, and that's the point. We use euphemisms when we want to talk about sensitive topics without making others feel embarrassed or offended.[51] As you might imagine, however, euphemisms require more than just a technical understanding of the language in which they're made; they also require an understanding of cultural idioms. The reason why this understanding is necessary is that euphemisms often have a literal meaning that differs from their euphemistic meaning. For example, at a literal level, the phrase "sleep together" means just that: to engage in sleep while together. If you didn't realize this is a cultural euphemism for "have sex," then you wouldn't understand the meaning when it is used in that way.

Many euphemisms change over time. What we today call "posttraumatic stress disorder" was called "shell shock" during World War I, "battle fatigue" during World War II, and "operational exhaustion" during the Korean War. Sometimes societies change euphemisms in order to treat the groups of people they refer to with greater dignity. The euphemism "differently abled," for instance, began as "lame," then became "crippled," then "handicapped," and then "disabled" before evolving into its present form. These and other euphemisms may continue to evolve as our culture and cultural ideas develop over time.

Like humor, the use of euphemisms has its good and bad points. As we've seen, euphemisms provide people a way to talk about sensitive topics, such as sexuality, disability, and death, without having to use uncomfortable language. This is beneficial, particularly to the extent that people otherwise would avoid communicating about these important topics. Some researchers have warned, however, that the excessive use of euphemisms can desensitize people, causing them to accept situations they would otherwise find unacceptable.[52]

In line with that idea, communication researchers Matthew McGlone, Gary Beck, and Abigail Pfiester found that when a euphemism becomes conventional or commonplace, people may use it without thinking about what it means.[53] Euphemisms that are common during times of war, for instance, include "friendly fire" (for fir-

Euphemisms are common during times of war. Do you think euphemistic language lessens our sensitivity to the harshness of combat?

ing on one's own troops) and "collateral damage" (for civilians killed inadvertently).[54] When euphemisms are used specifically to disguise or distort meaning, as these euphemisms exemplify, they are referred to as instances of *doublespeak*.[55] Some language experts believe that using doublespeak for horrendous situations such as these can lead people to feel emotionally detached from—or even accepting of—the horrors of war.[56] Using euphemisms competently, therefore, requires us to consider whether "softening" the topic of discussion will facilitate open communication or encourage us to tolerate what we may otherwise find intolerable.[57]

Slang: The Language of Subcultures

Closely related to euphemism is **slang,** which is the use of informal and unconventional words that often are understood only by others in a particular group. If you grew up in Boston, for instance, you probably know that "rhodie" is a slang term for people from nearby Rhode Island. In Australia, "snag" is slang for "sausage." On the Internet, a "blog" is a Web page featuring ongoing news or commentary, and a "hacker" is someone who creates or modifies computer software.

In fact, people have slang terms for all sorts of things. Many slang words are used in games, such as "quads" for four-of-a-kind in poker or "squash" for a one-sided match in professional wrestling. People in the medical community might refer to psychiatrists as the "Freud squad" or urologists as the "stream team." A "gym bunny" is someone who spends excessive amounts of time exercising at the gym; a "mall rat" is someone who spends excessive amounts of time hanging out at a shopping mall.

Slang can serve an important social function by helping people distinguish between those who do and don't belong to their particular social networks. Many social, cultural, and religious groups have their own terminology for certain ideas, and a person's ability to use a group's slang appropriately can "mark" him or her as belonging to that group. For instance, if you don't know what "on the lash" means, you're probably not from Dublin, and if you don't know whether you're in "T Town" or "Big T," chances are you're not a trucker.

A form of informal speech closely related to slang is jargon. As we saw in Chapter 2, jargon is the technical vocabulary of a certain occupation or profession. The purpose of jargon is to allow members of that occupation or profession to communicate with one another precisely and efficiently. For example, many law enforcement officers in North America talk to one another using "ten-code," or number combinations that represent common phrases. In this jargon, "10-4" means you've received another person's message; "10-24" means your assignment is completed. Health care providers also use jargon specific to their profession. For instance, they refer to a heart attack as a "myocardial infarction," a headache as a "cephalalgia," and athlete's foot as "tinea pedis." Other occupations and professions that have their own jargon include attorneys, engineers, dancers, airplane pilots, television producers, and military personnel.

Like humor and euphemisms, slang and jargon are neither inherently good nor inherently bad. As you saw before, we can use these forms of language for positive purposes, such as to reaffirm our membership within a particular social community. Whether you're into surfing or wine tasting, doing calligraphy, or restoring vintage cars, learning and using the slang appropriate to those interests serves as a type of membership badge, allowing you to connect with others like you.

By the same token, however, our use of slang and jargon can also make people feel like outsiders. If you're a police officer, for instance, saying that you're "10-7" instead of "done for the day" might make those around you who are not in law enforce-

Slang Informal, unconventional words that are often understood only by others in a particular subculture.

Whether you're into gardening, political activism, or surfing, slang allows you to connect and identify with others who share your interests.

ment feel excluded from the conversation. For that reason, you should consider how your use of slang and jargon might come across to those around you.

Libel and Slander: Harmful Words

Libel A defamatory statement made in print or some other fixed medium.

Slander A defamatory statement made aloud.

Libel and slander are both forms of *defamation,* language that harms a person's reputation or character. **Libel** refers to defamatory statements made in print or some other fixed medium, such as a photograph or a motion picture. **Slander** is a defamatory statement that is simply made aloud.

For instance, let's say that Aliyah wants to open a day care center in a town where Toni also operates one. To discourage parents from using Aliyah's center, Toni circulates rumors that Aliyah has been charged with child molestation. That statement is defamatory because it would harm Aliyah's reputation and cause her financial damage in the form of lost business.

Does it matter whether Toni's accusation is true? Usually the answer is yes: Under most legal systems, a statement must be false to be considered libel or slander. There are situations, however, when even a true accusation can qualify as slander or libel. These cases often involve public figures, such as politicians or celebrities, and hinge on the importance of the information for the public. Disclosing in print that a senator has tested positive for HIV, for example, might qualify as libel even if it were true, if disclosing it serves no prevailing public interest.

Slander is more common than libel in interpersonal interaction. Although *slander* is a legal term, behaviors we would call *gossiping* or *spreading rumors* often amount to the same thing. If you've ever had someone spread rumors about you, you know how painful that can be. Although gossip can serve some positive functions, such as reinforcing bonds of intimacy among people, the targets of gossip or rumors can experience profound distress.[58]

Profanity: Offensive Language

Profanity is a form of language that is considered vulgar, rude, or obscene in the context in which it is used. We sometimes call profane terms *swear words* or *curse words,* and they come in many forms. Some profane terms are meant to put down certain groups of people, such as calling a woman a "bitch" or a homosexual man a "fag." (Many of these also qualify as instances of hate speech, which we discuss next.) Other terms are attacks on religious beliefs or figures considered sacred by followers of a particular religion. Still others describe sexual acts or refer to people's sexual organs or bodily functions. Finally, some are general expressions of anger or disappointment, such as "damn!"

Like other forms of language, profanity is context-specific: What makes a word profane is that it is considered rude or obscene in the language and context in which it is used. For instance, calling a woman a "bitch" might be profane, but using the same term to describe a female dog is not. In the United States, the word "fag" is a derogatory term for gay men, but to the British, it refers to a cigarette.

Some swear words translate among languages; for example, the expression "damn!" in English is "zut!" in French and "verflucht!" in German and can be profane in all of them. Other expressions appear to be unique to certain languages; for instance, a Dutch speaker might say "krijg de pest!," which translates to "go get infected with the plague!"

Profanity has many different effects on social interaction. Often, it makes people feel uncomfortable or insulted. In recent years, some social groups have recognized that they can reduce the negative effects of certain profane terms themselves by making the terms more commonplace, thus lowering or eliminating their shock value. This practice is called *reclaiming* the term. For instance, when homosexuals call one another "queers," their intent is not to cause insult but, rather, to remove the power to insult from the word.

Not all effects of profanity are negative. In certain contexts, the use of profanity can act as a form of "social lubricant" by maintaining an informal social atmosphere. Profanity is a common element in comedy, for instance, partly because it creates an expectation that nothing is taboo in that context and that ideas can flow freely. In addition, using profanity within your own social network can actually reinforce interpersonal bonds by sending the meta-message that "I feel comfortable enough with you to use profanity in your presence."

Hate Speech: Profanity with a Hurtful Purpose

Hate speech is a specific form of profanity meant to degrade, intimidate, or dehumanize people on the basis of their gender, national origin, sexual orientation, religion, race, disability status, or political or moral views.[59] Calling people derogatory names, intimidating them, and advocating violence against groups of individuals might all qualify as forms of hate speech. For instance, the terms "bitch" and "fag" that we discussed in the previous

Profanity
A form of language considered vulgar, rude, or obscene in the context in which it is used.

Hate speech
A form of profanity meant to degrade, intimidate, or dehumanize groups of people.

section can be used not only as profanity but also as hate speech if they're directed at women or homosexuals with the intent to degrade or intimidate them.

At least two recent incidents have brought widespread public attention to hate speech. First, after being pulled over and detained in July 2006 on suspicion of driving while intoxicated, film actor Mel Gibson reportedly made several derogatory comments to deputies about Jewish people. Four months later, during a stand-up routine at a comedy club in West Hollywood, California, television actor Michael Richards made inflammatory remarks about African Americans, reportedly using the "n-word" more than half a dozen times. Although neither actor was formally charged with committing a hate crime as a result of his statements, these incidents have fueled public debate over whether hate speech should be illegal.

The use of hate speech also appears to be increasingly common online.[60] In 2006, Randall Ashby was arrested by the FBI in Delaware for allegedly sending hate speech by e-mail to the National Association for the Advancement of Colored People (NAACP).[61] In his e-mail message, Ashby told NAACP members "you are no match for our numbers and our power" and suggested that they would be victimized in their sleep. The FBI determined that the e-mail message constituted a violation of a federal law prohibiting the interstate communication of a threat.

Threats and derogatory statements about racial groups are relatively blatant forms of hate speech. Sometimes, however, language can be offensive to a group of people not because of the words being used but because of the way the words are connected to one another. For examples, see the next "Dark Side" box on page 192.

Several laws and regulations exist in North America to restrict hate speech or other acts of intimidation against minority groups and to punish people who engage in them (see Figure 5.4). In fact, many of these restrictions are found in campus speech codes, which dictate the types of statements that students, staff, and faculty can and cannot make on a college campus. There is little question that most, if not all, of the effects of hate speech are negative, which would justify laws and regulations to restrict it.

Despite this fact, these laws and regulations are controversial. Supporters argue that the regulations are necessary to promote civility and to protect people—especially minority-group members—from the discrimination and even violence that hate speech can incite. Opponents counter that it is difficult to determine what qualifies as hate speech and what does not. They also maintain that restricting speech is a form of censorship and a violation of the First Amendment of the U.S. Constitution.[62] Given the complexities of defining hate speech and determining how best to respond to it, these points of contention are likely to be debated for some time.

As we've seen in this section, language comes in many forms, including hu-

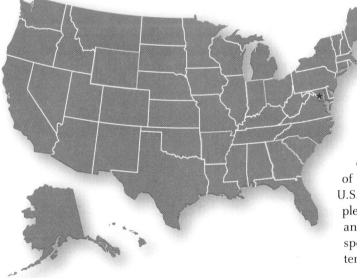

FIGURE 5.4 U.S. States with Hate Crime Laws At present, all U.S. states except Wyoming, Arkansas, Indiana, South Carolina, and Georgia have laws prohibiting hate crimes such as the use of hate speech.

From a strictly linguistic point of view, the only thing different about the terms "person of color" and "colored person" is the use of a preposition. Socially, however, they are worlds apart. In the United States, the term "colored" originally referred to those of mixed African and Caucasian or Native American descent, who were generally afforded higher status than those of strictly African ancestry. Over time it evolved to refer to all black people, and today it is widely considered to be an offensive term. Currently, the preferred phrase is "person of color," which refers to people of nonwhite descent, including African, Chicano/Latino, Asian, and other heritages.

"Person of color" is an example of *person-first terminology* because it identifies the person first and his or her characteristics second. Using person-first forms of language allows us to acknowledge that people are people first, regardless of their attributes. Person-first terminology doesn't ignore a person's characteristics, but it recognizes that they don't define a person completely. Some additional examples of person-first terminology include "person with a disability" instead of "disabled person," "person living with AIDS" instead of "AIDS patient," and "person of European descent" instead of "white person."

The use of person-first terminology is controversial even among those groups it is intended to serve. For instance, many members of the deaf community describe themselves as "deaf persons" rather than "persons with deafness" because they see their hearing impairment as an integral part of who they are. Sociologist C. Edwin Vaughan, who studies the experience of blindness, has also argued that person-first terminology—such as "person with a visual impairment" instead of "blind person"—is often awkward and therefore might actually draw greater atten-

mor, euphemism, slang, libel and slander, profanity, and hate speech. Some of these forms, such as humor, generally have positive effects but can also produce unwanted negative outcomes. Other forms, such as profanity, are generally negative even though they can have positive effects on the people using them. Understanding the positive and negative aspects of these diverse forms of language helps us to appreciate the power and complexity of verbal communication.

Learn It: What makes a joke funny? What are the purposes of using euphemisms? In what ways does the use of slang reflect a person's subcultures? How is libel different from slander? What makes a word or a phrase profane? What is hate speech?

Try It: Many groups of people have their own slang. Talk to some people who have hobbies, interests, or jobs very different from yours, and learn some of the slang common to those groups.

Reflect on It: What euphemisms do you tend to use? Do you feel that prohibiting hate speech is a good idea or a bad one?

tion to a person's disability. He points out, for instance, that we don't use person-first terminology for positive attributes such as intelligence or beauty. We say "smart person" instead of "person with intelligence," and "beautiful person" instead of "person with beauty." Although person-first terminology aims to acknowledge that a person's disability or background is only a part of his or her identity and not all of it, Vaughan suggests that person-first terminology may actually call undue attention to these characteristics. What do you think?

Ask Yourself:

- How much does hate speech or offensive language reside in the words being used? How much does it depend on how others respond to those words?

- Think about your own characteristics. How do you prefer that people refer to you? What forms of reference would cause you to feel offended?

From Me to You:

- Communicating respectfully about people from other social groups can seem challenging, especially if you're trying not to use the wrong terminology. Some people become extremely nervous when they speak with members of other populations. They are so worried they might say or do something offensive that they become rigid or hyper-polite around minorities or other groups. Unfortunately, this pattern of behavior, in itself, can serve to reinforce divisions among people. It's hard for

other people to feel comfortable around you if you don't seem to feel comfortable around them. When you find yourself in such a situation, my advice is simply to relax. When you talk to people, try not to see them as members of this group or that, but simply as people. If you're not sure how someone wishes to be referred to, simply ask the person. Just be yourself, and treat others with the same level of politeness and respect that you would want from them.

Sources: Bolt, D. (2004). Terminology and the psychosocial burden of blindness. *British Journal of Visual Impairment, 22,* 52–54; Moore, R. B. (1985). *Racism in the English language.* New York: Council on Interracial Books for Children; Vaughan, C. E. (1993). *The struggle of blind people for self-determination: The dependency-rehabilitation conflict: Empowerment in the blindness community.* Springfield, IL: Charles C. Thomas.

4} Improving Your Language Use {

Using language is a skill, and it's one that nearly all of us can improve on. In this section, we'll look at four pieces of advice that can help you become a better verbal communicator. Some tips may be more relevant to one situation than another, but each one can assist you in improving your language. These are the four pieces of advice we'll explore in this section:

- Consider the effect you wish to create.
- Separate opinions from factual claims.
- Speak at an appropriate level.
- Own your thoughts and feelings.

> *Language is wine upon the lips.*
>
> —Virginia Wolff (1882–1941)
> English writer

Consider the Effect You Wish to Create

When you speak—whether it's to one person or to several people—consider what you want your words to accomplish. Is your goal to make others feel comfortable around you? to persuade them? to inform them? to entertain them? You might even have multiple goals at once. Regardless of what your goals are, you're more likely to achieve them if you consider how your use of language can help you.

One aspect of creating effective verbal messages is to make certain that what you're saying is appropriate to your audience. Considering your messages from your listeners' point of view will help you avoid three basic mistakes: shared knowledge errors, shared opinion errors, and monopolization errors. Let's take a closer look at all three.

When you speak with others, consider the effect you wish to create. Avoid monopolizing the conversation or assuming that others share your knowledge or opinions.

Shared knowledge error. When you presume your listeners have information that they don't have, you are making the *shared knowledge error*. For example, when Devon is speaking to casual acquaintances, he refers to his friends and relatives by their names without explaining who they are. He also makes reference to events that occurred earlier in his life, before his acquaintances knew him.

We can communicate with close friends and family members this way because they usually know our personalities, our histories, and the other people in our social circles. We shouldn't presume, however, that strangers or casual acquaintances have this information. As competent communicators, therefore, we must consider the perspectives of the people we're talking to and use language that is appropriate to what they do or do not know about us.

Shared opinion error. The mistake known as the *shared opinion error* occurs when you incorrectly assume that your listeners share your opinions. In diverse company, for example, it's often risky to express strong opinions on potentially controversial issues such as politics or religious beliefs, because you might offend people who don't share your positions. It's even riskier, however, to speak as though you assume that everyone present agrees with you. When you communicate in this manner, other people may be more likely to confront you with their different points of view. In some situations, this can lead to a healthy exchange of ideas. It can quickly turn contentious, however, leading you to become defensive about your positions.

Monopolization error. The *monopolization error* occurs when one speaker inappropriately dominates the conversation. No matter with whom she's speaking, for instance, Tara always does the vast majority of the talking. Certainly, there are situations when this behavior is appropriate, such as a classroom discussion being led by an instructor. In interpersonal interaction, however, monopolizing a conversation can make other people feel as though you aren't interested in what they have to say but are interested only in presenting your own ideas. Remember that good inter-

Consider the influence you want your communication to have on others, especially if you are in a position of authority.

personal conversations involve a give-and-take of ideas, opinions, and comments—so don't forget to allow everyone to speak!

As these examples illustrate, the ways we use language influence those around us. Therefore, to communicate competently, it is essential that you consider what influence you want to have. This is particularly important for parents, teachers, supervisors, and others in positions of authority, because they often have a responsibility to set expectations for language use in their homes, classrooms, and work environments. If you don't want your children to use profanity, for instance, you can help set that expectation by not using it yourself—or at least by not using it in their presence. If you value supportive communication in your classroom or workplace, set an example by using appropriate humor and avoiding hate speech. In these ways, you will help ensure that your language use has positive effects on others.

Separate Opinions from Factual Claims

As we pointed out in the last chapter, factual claims ("she hit him") are different from interpretations ("she assaulted him"). Factual claims are also different from opinions. A factual claim makes a claim that we can verify with evidence and show to be true or false in an absolute sense ("I've taken piano lessons for ten years"). An opinion expresses a personal judgment or preference that we could agree or disagree with but that is not true or false in an absolute sense ("I'm a terrific piano player"). Competent communicators know how to keep opinions and factual claims separate in verbal communication.

Unfortunately, distinguishing factual claims from opinions is easier said than done, especially when you're dealing with strong opinions on emotionally heated issues. Let's say, for instance, that you and several friends are discussing an upcoming election in which you're choosing between two candidates. Half of you prefer Candidate C, the conservative, and the other half prefers Candidate L, the liberal. Consider the following statements you might make about these candidates, and indicate which are factual claims and which are opinions.

- "Candidate C has more experience in government." Because we can show this statement to be true or false by looking at the candidates' records, this is a factual claim.

Getting to Know You
How Well Can You Distinguish Opinions from Factual Claims?

As we've seen, the ability to separate opinions from factual claims is an important skill for effective verbal communication. How well can you spot the difference? Read each of the following statements. Assuming nothing more than the statement tells you, indicate whether you think the statement is an opinion or a factual claim by placing a check mark in the appropriate column.

	Opinion	Factual Claim
1. Britney Spears is the best singer in the world.	_____	_____
2. Television was invented in the 1920s.	_____	_____
3. Religious people are happier than nonreligious people.	_____	_____
4. The United States is better off with a Democrat as president.	_____	_____
5. Men talk as much as women do.	_____	_____
6. Same-sex couples should not be allowed to marry.	_____	_____
7. Children should be required to learn a foreign language.	_____	_____
8. Neil Armstrong was the first person to walk on the moon.	_____	_____
9. Dogs have a keener sense of smell than people do.	_____	_____
10. Abortion should be legal in the United States.	_____	_____

Statements 1, 4, 6, 7, and 10 are all opinions. Statements 2, 3, 5, 8, and 9 are all factual claims. How well did you do? If you missed some of the answers, don't worry—distinguishing opinions from factual claims can be harder than it seems.

- "Candidate L is the better choice for our future." This is an opinion, because it expresses a value judgment (this candidate is *better*), which we cannot objectively validate.
- "Candidate C is immoral." This is an opinion, because the truth of this claim depends on what morals you subscribe to. Morals are subjective; therefore, the statement can't be proved true or false in an absolute sense.
- "Candidate L accepted illegal bribes." This is a factual claim, because you can examine the evidence to discover whether it's true.

Opinions and factual claims require different types of responses. Suppose you tell me that "Candidate C has never held an elective office," and I reply by saying "I disagree." This isn't a competent response. You have made a factual claim, which means it is either true or false. Therefore, whether I agree with it is irrelevant. I can agree or disagree with an opinion, but a factual claim is either true or false no matter how I feel about it. Instead, if I had responded to your statement by saying "I think you're incorrect," that would be a competent reply because we would now be discussing the *truth* of your statement, rather than my agreement with it.

As you develop this skill, keep two principles in mind. First, *opinions are opinions, whether you agree with them or not.* If you believe abortion should be legal in the United States, for instance, you might be inclined to call that statement a fact. It isn't, though. It is still a statement of opinion because it expresses an evaluation about what "should be." Second, *factual claims are factual claims whether they are true or not.* If you think it's untrue that religious people are happier than nonreligious people, for instance, you might be inclined to call that statement an opinion. It isn't, though. Even if the statement isn't true, it is still a factual claim because it expresses something that could be verified by evidence.

Separating opinions from factual claims takes practice, but it will help you respond competently to each type of verbal statement. The "Try It" exercise on page 201 suggests some additional ways for you to practice this skill.

As noted earlier, separating opinions from factual claims is especially challenging when we're dealing with emotionally charged issues such as religious values, ethics, and morality. The more strongly we feel about an issue, the more we tend to think of our beliefs as facts rather than opinions. In these cases we are less likely to consider the possibility that other people have opinions that differ from ours but are valid nonetheless.

Consider the heated debate over euthanasia, for example. Euthanasia is the practice of ending the life, in a minimally painful way, of a person or an animal who is terminally ill, as a way of limiting suffering.[63] Supporters perceive euthanasia as an act of selfless mercy, whereas opponents consider it an act of selfish cruelty.[64] People on both sides of the issue feel their position is the *right* one. Some of them probably don't realize, however, that both positions are opinions, not facts. Whether a behavior is merciful or cruel depends on individual beliefs, not on any objective standard.

Although it's probably more difficult to separate opinions from facts when you feel strongly about an issue, that's often when it's most important to do so. Instead of telling others that their positions on sensitive issues are right or wrong, tell them that you agree or disagree with their positions. This language expresses your own position and acknowledges that different—even contradictory—opinions may also exist.

Speak at an Appropriate Level

Efficacious linguistic devices must demonstrate isomorphism with the cerebral aptitude of the assemblage. If the meaning of that statement isn't exactly clear, the reason is that the language is inappropriately complex. What the statement really means, in fact, is that good messages must be understandable to listeners.

Part of being an effective verbal communicator is knowing how simple or how complex your language should be for your audience. A competent teacher, for instance, knows to use simpler language when teaching an introductory course than when teaching an advanced course, because students in each class will have different levels of understanding. When we use language that is too complex for our audience, we are "talking over people's heads." Can you think of situations when that has happened to you? If so, then you know how hard it can be to understand what the speaker is trying to say.

The opposite problem is "talking down" to people, or using language that is inappropriately simple. We often do this by mistake. You might provide unnecessary detail when giving someone driving directions, for example, because you don't realize that she is already familiar with the area. At other times, people use overly simple language on purpose. This behavior can make the listeners feel patronized, disrespected, or even insulted.

Simple and complex language each has its appropriate place. To be a good communicator, you should practice your perspective-taking ability. Put yourself in your listeners' shoes, and then consider how simple or complex your words should be.

Own Your Thoughts and Feelings

People often use language that shifts responsibility for their thoughts and feelings onto others. Perhaps you always dread going to visit your Aunt Alice, because whenever she doesn't understand you, she says, "You're not being clear," but when you don't understand her, she says, "You're not paying attention." By using this pattern of language, Alice blames others for misunderstandings but takes no responsibility for her own role in the communication process. Instead of the other person not being clear, for example, Alice herself might not be paying attention. Instead of the other person not paying attention, Alice might not be using clearly understandable language. Maybe you can think of times when you have encountered people who, like Alice, always seem to make others responsible for how they communicate.

Good communicators take responsibility for their thoughts and feelings by using I-statements rather than you-statements. An **I-statement** claims ownership of what we are feeling or thinking, whereas a **you-statement** shifts that responsibility to the other person. Instead of saying, "You're not being clear," Alice might say, "I'm having a hard time understanding you." Rather than saying, "You make me mad," I might say, "I'm angry right now." Table 5.2 provides several examples of I-statements and you-statements.

I-statements don't ignore the problem; they simply allow the speaker to claim ownership of his or her feelings. This ownership is important because it acknowledges that *we* control how we think and feel. Constructive I-statements include four parts that clearly express that ownership:

- "I feel ____" (this expresses responsibility for your own feelings)
- "when you ____" (this identifies the behavior that is prompting your feelings)
- "because ____" (this points to the characteristic of the behavior that is prompting your feelings)
- "and I would appreciate it if you would ____" (this offers an alternative to the behavior)

Let's say, for instance, that Caleb is frustrated with his officemate, Ji, because she often leaves the door to their office open when neither of them is inside. Let's look at one way he might express those feelings:

You need to stop leaving our door open, because anyone can waltz in here and take whatever they want. You're really starting to make me mad.

This statement rightfully points out that the problematic behavior is Ji's; after all, she is the one who leaves the door open. What it doesn't do, however, is acknowledge

I-statement
A statement that claims ownership of one's thoughts or feelings.

You-statement
A statement that shifts responsibility for one's own thoughts or feelings to the listener.

Table 5.2: Examples of You-Statements and I-Statements

You-Statement	I-Statement
You're making me mad.	I'm mad right now.
You're not listening to me.	I'm feeling ignored.
You don't know what you're doing.	I don't think this task is getting done right.
You hurt my feelings.	My feelings are hurt.
You're not making any sense.	I'm having trouble understanding you.

Finding the right words can be challenging under the most ordinary of circumstances, let alone during extraordinary ones. We may not always know what to say to make someone feel comforted.

that Caleb's feelings of frustration belong to him. Now let's look at a more constructive way of communicating his feelings:

> *I get angry when you leave our office door open, because anyone could come in here and steal my briefcase or your purse. I would really appreciate it you would close the door whenever you step out of the office.*

Notice that this statement doesn't ignore or downplay the problem. Rather, it allows Caleb to take responsibility for his feelings of frustration and to identify clearly how he would like Ji to change her behavior.

The major benefit of using I-statements is that they are less likely than you-statements to cause your listener to become defensive.[65] By saying "You're really starting to make me mad," Caleb sounds as though he is accusing Ji, which would likely cause her to respond defensively. In contrast, by saying "I feel angry when you leave our office door open," Caleb acknowledges that he is responsible for his own feelings, and he is only suggesting a change in Ji's behavior. Ji may still disagree with his assessment, but she will probably be less likely to feel that he is attacking or accusing her.

Learning to use I-statements can be challenging, because we might think that other people really are causing our thoughts and feelings; so it might feel right to say, "You're

Characters in *The Office* differ dramatically in the way they use language. Michael often commits the shared opinion error by assuming everyone thinks the way he does. Pam uses language to create a supportive environment and forge relationships with others. Dwight often speaks in a condescending manner, talking down to his co-workers and giving them more information than is necessary.

At a Glance: Components of Constructive I-Statements

Constructive I-Statements include four parts:

"I feel _____"	Identifies your feeling
"when you _____"	Identifies the behavior that prompts your feeling
"because _____"	Identifies what you find problematic about the behavior
"and I would appreciate it if you would _____"	Suggests a solution

making me mad." Recall that other people can't control our thoughts and feelings unless we let them. Effective communicators speak in ways that acknowledge responsibility for and ownership of the ways they feel and think. A summary of the components of constructive I-statements appears in the "At a Glance" box above.

In summary, there are several ways to become a more effective verbal communicator. Consider the effect you want your language use to have on others around you, and craft your verbal messages accordingly. Separate opinions from facts, particularly for highly sensitive or contentious issues. Use language that is appropriate for your audience. Take ownership of your thoughts and feelings, and let your language reflect that. These are among the most valuable ways of improving your verbal communication ability in interpersonal settings.

Learn It: What is the shared knowledge error? How are opinions distinguished from facts? Why is it important to speak at an appropriate level? What are the four components of a constructive I-statement?

Try It: Separating facts and opinions can be difficult, not only when you're speaking, but also when you're listening to others. Practice this skill by watching a television newscast or reading an Internet blog. For each statement you hear or read, ask yourself if it is a fact, an opinion, or some other type of statement (such as an instruction). Remember that facts make claims that can be verified with evidence, whereas opinions express a person's judgments or evaluations about something. With practice, you'll sharpen your ability to distinguish opinions from facts.

Reflect on It: When someone "talks down to you," what does it make you think about that person? When do you tend to commit the monopolization error?

} Master the Chapter {

Section 1} The Nature of Language (p. 165)

I. The Nature of Language

A. Language is symbolic
- Language consists of words that represent, or symbolize, objects or concepts.

B. Language is arbitrary (mostly)
- The connection between most words and the objects or concepts they symbolize is arbitrary.

C. Language is governed by rules
- Languages are governed by phonological, syntactic, semantic, and pragmatic rules.

D. Language has layers of meaning
- Words have both denotative and connotative meanings.
  1. The Semantic Triangle
  2. Loaded language

E. Language varies in clarity
- Verbal statements vary in how ambiguous they are.

F. Language is bound by context and culture
- The meaning of language is affected by the social and cultural contexts in which it is used.

Section 2} Appreciating the Power of Words (p. 174)

II. Appreciating the Power of Words

A. Naming defines and differentiates us
- Naming is a fundamental way of giving identity to someone or something.
  1. Naming and identity
  2. Naming practices

B. We use words to persuade
   1. Anchor-and-contrast
   2. Norm of reciprocity
   3. Social validation principle
   4. Choosing a persuasive strategy

- Language can be used to persuade others to think or act in a particular way.

C. Credibility empowers us
   1. Clichés
   2. Dialects
   3. Equivocation
   4. Weasel words
   5. Allness statements
   6. Choosing credible language

- Some forms of language are perceived as more credible than others.

D. Language expresses affection and intimacy

- People use verbal behavior in personal relationships to convey affection and create intimacy.

E. Words provide comfort and healing
   1. Using language to comfort other people
   2. Using language to comfort ourselves

- We can use words to provide comfort to others and also to ourselves.

Section 3} How We Use and Abuse Language (p. 186)

III. How We Use and Abuse Language

A. Humor: What's so funny?

- Humor relies on a violation of expectations.

B. Euphemisms: soft talk

- Euphemisms allow us to discuss sensitive topics in a minimally discomforting way.

C. Slang: the language of subcultures

- Many subcultures have their own slang, which serves to mark membership in those groups.

D. Libel and slander: harmful words

- Libel is defamatory language that appears in print; slander is defamatory language that is spoken.

E. Profanity: offensive language

- Profanity is a form of language that is generally considered offensive.

F. Hate speech: profanity with a hurtful purpose

- Hate speech is a form of profanity aimed at degrading or intimidating a specific group of people.

Section 4} Improving Your Language Use (p. 193)

IV. Improving Your Language Use

A. Consider the effect you wish to create
   1. Shared knowledge error
   2. Shared opinion error
   3. Monopolization error

- Avoid shared knowledge, shared opinion, and monopolization errors.

B. Separate opinions from factual claims

- Learn to separate opinions from statements of fact and to respond appropriately to each one.

C. Speak at an appropriate level

- Speak at a level that is appropriate for your audience.

D. Own your thoughts and feelings

- Take ownership of your thoughts and feelings by using I-statements more than you-statements.

Key Terms

Ambiguous

Anchor-and-contrast

Connotative meaning

Credibility

Denotative meaning

Euphemism

Hate speech

I-statement

Language

Libel

Loaded language

Onomatopoeia

Profanity

Sapir-Whorf hypothesis

Slander

Slang

Social validation principle

You-statement

Discussion Questions

1. What do you think of the Sapir-Whorf hypothesis? What examples can you think of that illustrate how your language reflects your culture's behaviors and attitude?

2. In what ways does American Sign Language constitute verbal communication? In what ways is it nonverbal?

3. What perceptions do you have of women who retain their own last names when they marry? How about women who take their husband's name? How about women who take hyphenated names?

4. The more you learn about persuasion, the greater your ability to persuade others. What are the ethical implications of having the ability to persuade?

5. Why do you think so many people laugh at jokes that put down other people? Can a joke be funny even if you find it distasteful?

6. There is much disagreement regarding hate speech laws: Supporters maintain they are necessary to promote civility; critics contend they amount to unconstitutional censorship. What do you think?

7. You've probably encountered people who monopolize conversations. What perceptions do you form of people who do this?

8. Why do many people find it so challenging to separate opinions from factual claims?

Practice Quiz

Multiple Choice

1. The dictionary definition of a word is its _____ meaning, whereas the implication of that word is its _____ meaning.
   a. denotative, connotative
   b. connotative, denotative
   c. denotative, relational
   d. connotative, relational

2. Words can have more than one meaning. This illustrates that language is:
   a. arbitrary
   b. abstract
   c. ambiguous
   d. deterministic

3. Which type of rule governs the ordering of words within phrases?
   a. phonological
   b. syntactic
   c. semantic
   d. pragmatic

4. Which of the following rules relates to the correct pronunciation of a word?
   a. phonological
   b. syntactic
   c. semantic
   d. pragmatic

5. Which of the following is *not* one of the three elements in Ogden and Richard's Semantic Triangle?
   a. symbol
   b. reference
   c. referent
   d. article

6. Which of the following illustrates the idea that language shapes our views of reality by influencing the ways that various cultures see the world?
   a. Ogden and Richard's Semantic Triangle
   b. Shannon and Weaver's Model of Channels
   c. Sapir-Whorf Hypothesis
   d. Hypothetical Rationalism

7. Which of the following terms is defined as a vague, mild expression that symbolizes something more blunt or harsh?
   a. euphemism
   b. equivocation
   c. equating
   d. emphasis

8. The statement "Nine out of ten dentists agree that chewing Brand X gum after a sugary snack helps fight tooth decay" is an example of which of the following persuasion techniques?
   a. anchor-and-contrast
   b. norm of reciprocity
   c. social validation
   d. majority rule

9. Sophie really wants a new bike, so she first asks her mom for a new car, thinking that will increase the likelihood that her mom will buy her a new bike. This strategy is known as which of the following?
   a. anchor-and-contrast
   b. norm of reciprocity
   c. social validation
   d. majority rule

10. Good communicators take responsibility for their own thoughts and feelings by using which of the following?
   a. I-statements
   b. you-statements
   c. we-statements
   d. they-statements

True/False

11. Written messages are not a type of verbal communication.
12. Research indicates that a person's name can carry implicit meaning about his or her goodness or desirability.
13. Equivocation is language that articulates your true intentions without being strategically ambiguous.

14. According to a study by Huston and colleagues, the more affection spouses communicated to each other during their first 2 years of marriage, the more likely they were to still be married 13 years later.
15. Libel refers to defamatory statements made in print or some other fixed medium, such as a photograph or a motion picture, whereas slander is a defamatory statement that is simply made aloud.

Fill in the Blank

16. Because language is _____, each word represents a particular object or idea, but it does not constitute the object or idea itself.
17. A word whose sound imitates its meaning is an example of _____.
18. _____ rules allow an individual to connect the word "laptop" with "computer."
19. The idea that we can only conceive of something if we have a word for it is known as _____.
20. Terms or phrases that are intended to mislead listeners by implying something that they don't actually say are known as _____.

Research Library

Movies

Babel (Drama; 2006; R)

In Babel, *a married couple from California is vacationing in Morocco when the wife is shot while riding a bus. The movie integrates their story with those of their nanny back home in San Diego, a Moroccan man and his teenage sons, and a hearing-impaired teenage girl in Japan. Underlying all four stories is the challenge of understanding—and being understood by—those whose languages are different from our own.*

In the Land of the Deaf (Documentary; 1992; NR)

In the Land of the Deaf *is a French documentary focusing on the world of deaf culture and language in France. The story centers on Jean-Claude Poulain, a deaf teacher. One important theme of the film is that deafness can present challenges—one deaf character is so misunderstood that she is eventually placed in an asylum for the insane—but that such challenges can be overcome. The movie features French sign language and spoken French, with English subtitles for both.*

Windtalkers (Drama; 2002; R)

This movie follows the story of U.S. Marines who are deployed to the Pacific during World War II to intercept and translate Japanese radio transmissions, which the U.S. military had discovered were being communicated using the ancient language of the Navajo. The translators, who are referred to as "code-talkers," are heavily protected because of their value to the U.S. military mission. The story illustrates one direct application of the ability to understand and use language.

Books

Bavelas, J. B., Black, A., Chovil, N., & Mullett, J. (1990). *Equivocal communication.* Newbury Park, CA: Sage.

Bryson, B. (1990). *The mother tongue: English and how it got that way.* New York: William Morrow.

Moore, C. J. (2004). *In other words: A language lover's guide to the most intriguing words around the world.* New York: Walker & Co.

Pinker, S. (2007). *The stuff of thought: Language as a window into human nature.* New York: Viking.

Journal Articles and Book Chapters

Foss, K. A., & Edson, B. A. (1989). What's in a name? Accounts of married women's name choices. *Western Journal of Speech Communication, 53,* 356–373.

Hosman, L. A. (1989). The evaluative consequences of hedges, hesitations, and intensifiers: Powerful and powerless speech styles. *Human Communication Research, 15,* 383–406.

Huston, T. L., Caughlin, J. P., Houts, R. M., Smith, S. E., & George, L. J. (2001). The connubial crucible: Newlywed years as predictors of marital delight, distress, and divorce. *Journal of Personality and Social Psychology, 80,* 237–252.

Paul, J., & Strbiak, C. A. (1997). The ethics of strategic ambiguity. *The Journal of Business Communication, 34,* 149–159.

Web Sites

www.lsadc.org/

This is the home page of the Linguistic Society of America, an organization founded in 1924 to advance the scientific study of language.

www.aclu.org/studentsrights/expression/12808pub19941231.html

This Web page, hosted by the American Civil Liberties Association, defines hate speech and presents an argument against prohibiting it through regulations or laws.

6

Nonverbal Communication

How do we communicate without words?

Why is nonverbal communication powerful?

What behaviors do we use to communicate nonverbally?

Wayan and Jack

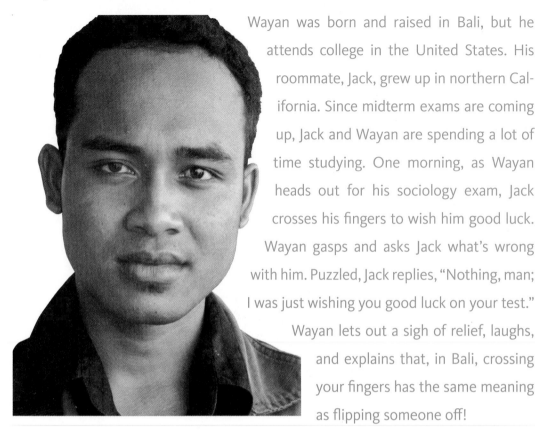

Wayan was born and raised in Bali, but he attends college in the United States. His roommate, Jack, grew up in northern California. Since midterm exams are coming up, Jack and Wayan are spending a lot of time studying. One morning, as Wayan heads out for his sociology exam, Jack crosses his fingers to wish him good luck. Wayan gasps and asks Jack what's wrong with him. Puzzled, Jack replies, "Nothing, man; I was just wishing you good luck on your test." Wayan lets out a sigh of relief, laughs, and explains that, in Bali, crossing your fingers has the same meaning as flipping someone off!

Nonverbal communication is powerful stuff. So much of what we learn about other people's thoughts and feelings comes not through listening to their words but through observing their body language—watching their facial expressions, seeing how they move and gesture, and taking note of their eye contact. These and other behaviors often convey enormous amounts of information about people in efficient and sometimes subtle ways.

In this chapter, we'll explore the uses of nonverbal behavior in various communication contexts. In particular, we'll discuss:

1} What nonverbal communication is and what five of its most important characteristics are

2} How nonverbal communication makes use of ten specific channels

3} The ways we use nonverbal communication to manage conversations, express emotions, maintain relationships, form impressions, influence others, and conceal information

4} How we can become better nonverbal communicators

On the animated television show *The Simpsons*, Marge Simpson is seldom shy about expressing disapproval when her husband, Homer, or son, Bart, misbehaves. She frequently communicates her feelings through her facial expressions, her posture, and the stressful grunting sound she makes with her voice when she's annoyed. These and other nonverbal communication behaviors clearly convey Marge's state of mind to anyone who happens to be around her at the time. What makes nonverbal behavior such an effective form of communication? We'll find out in this section, first by differentiating nonverbal communication from verbal communication and then by examining five of its most important characteristics.

> *The body says what words cannot.*
>
> —Martha Graham (1894–1991)
> Pioneer in dance and choreography

Marge Simpson uses her facial expressions, posture, and tone of voice to communicate her feelings about her husband and children.

What Is Nonverbal Communication?

If we just look at the word "nonverbal," we can tell right away that it means "not verbal." Nonverbal communication requires neither words nor language. How, exactly, do we communicate with one another without using words?

The answer is, in many ways! We can tell a great deal about people by watching their facial expressions or listening to the tone of their voices. When you listen to your doctor tell you the results of your recent blood tests, for instance, you might hear the tension in her voice and determine that something is wrong, or you might see the pleasant look on her face and conclude that everything is fine. We also interpret people's gestures and notice the way they carry themselves. Perhaps you see two people punching each other but you determine from their behaviors that they are playing rather than genuinely fighting.

In addition, we frequently make judgments about people on the basis of their appearance. While scanning a series of personal ads online, for example, you might be more drawn to some people than to others based on their photographs. Sometimes, we also perceive others according to the way they use their time and the space around them. Perhaps you tried talking to your boss about your recent evaluation, but you felt ignored because he kept looking at his new BlackBerry. As we'll see in this chapter, people routinely communicate more information through their nonverbal behaviors than they do through their use of language. When it comes to interpersonal communication, actions often do speak louder than words.

Nonverbal communication Those behaviors and characteristics that convey meaning without the use of words.

We can define **nonverbal communication**, then, as *those behaviors and characteristics that convey meaning without the use of words.* Nonverbal communication behaviors frequently accompany verbal messages to clarify or reinforce them. For instance, if someone asks you for directions to the bookstore and you point and say "It's that way," your nonverbal behavior (pointing) clarifies the meaning of your verbal message. In contrast, if you just say "It's that way" without pointing, then your verbal message is ambiguous—and not very helpful. Likewise, if you're explaining to a nurse where you're feeling pain, you might point to certain areas on your body and say "I'm hurting here." The combination of your words and your nonverbal gestures will help the nurse understand where your pain is located.

At other times, however, nonverbal communication behaviors convey meaning on their own. For example, if you ask me where the bookstore is and I shrug my shoulders, you will probably infer from my behavior that I don't know the answer to your question, even though I never actually said that. Similarly, if you ask your nurse how many times you should take your pain medication each day and she holds up two fingers, you'll probably interpret her behavior to mean that you should take your medication twice a day, even though she didn't tell you that verbally.

Nonverbal behavior is a powerful way of communicating. It also comes naturally to many of us. In fact, we often engage in nonverbal behavior without really thinking about it. Therefore, you might wonder why, if nonverbal behavior is so natural, we need to study it in the first place. The truth is, there's much more to nonverbal communication than meets the eye. Even though we frequently encounter nonverbal behaviors, we often face challenges when trying to interpret them. In a 1993 episode of the television sitcom *Seinfeld*, for instance, characters Jerry, Elaine, and George visit with Jerry's accountant, Barry, who seems to be sniffing frequently. After Barry leaves, Jerry and his friends try to figure out how to interpret Barry's sniffing behavior. Unable to figure it out, Jerry becomes increasingly concerned that Barry is sniffing because he's addicted to cocaine. Only at the end of the episode does Jerry discover that Barry was sniffing because he is allergic to the material in a sweater Jerry was wearing.

Martha Graham

As that example illustrates, interpreting nonverbal communication accurately can be challenging. The more we learn about nonverbal communication, the better we can understand it. In the following section, we'll take a look at five important characteristics of nonverbal behavior, each of which makes this type of communication worth our while to study.

Five Characteristics of Nonverbal Communication

It's difficult to imagine what life would be like if we didn't have nonverbal communication. It's particularly critical for people who lack language skills, such as infants, who can only vocalize without words, and people with certain types of neurological problems, such as a stroke, that limit their language use.

Even people with language abilities, however, rely immensely on nonverbal communication. For example, because Bergitta had only a limited knowledge of Spanish, she relied heavily on nonverbal behaviors while traveling through Bolivia, Uruguay, and Argentina the summer after she graduated from college. She was frequently amazed at how well she could understand others simply by observing their gestures and facial expressions. Her communication was more challenging than it would have been if she had known the language, but she was still able to understand and be understood by others through nonverbal behaviors. Imagine you are traveling through an area where you don't speak the language. How might you use nonverbal behaviors to be understood by others?

Five characteristics of nonverbal communication explain why it plays such an important role in human interaction. We list these characteristics here and then discuss each one in detail.

- Nonverbal communication is present in most interpersonal communication.
- Nonverbal communication often conveys more information than verbal communication.
- Nonverbal communication is usually believed over verbal communication.
- Nonverbal communication is the primary means of communicating emotion.
- Nonverbal communication is meta-communicative.

Nonverbal communication is present in most interpersonal conversations. Whether you talk to people one-on-one or in a group, you have access not only to the words they speak but also to several dimensions of nonverbal communication. Whether you're hosting a party, meeting a new friend, or attending a business lunch, you can watch people's facial expressions for signs of emotion. For example, you might tell from your supervisor's facial expression that she is bored at the business lunch and eager to leave. You can also see from the gestures people use and the posture they adopt whether they're feeling confident or insecure. You might notice your new friend's expressive use of gestures, for instance, and infer that she feels confident and comfortable around you. You can judge from the tone of their voices when people are being serious and when they're kidding. At a party, you might come across a small group of people who are speaking in hushed voices and infer that they are discussing something serious.

Even the way people dress and the way they smell to you can send you information. Glancing around the room at a business lunch, you might be able to guess which people are managers and which are staff members by the formality of their dress. You're also likely to form more positive impressions of those who smell good to you than of those who don't. In these and many other social situations, we are nearly flooded with nonverbal signals.

In other communication contexts, such as talking on the telephone or sending e-mail messages, we don't have access to as many nonverbal cues as we do in face-to-face conversation. We still make use of what's available, however. On the telephone, for instance, even if we haven't met the people to whom we're speaking, we can make judgments about their voices, such as how fast they're talking, how loudly, with what tone, and with what type of accent. In electronically mediated communication, such as e-mail, chat rooms, instant messaging, and text messaging, we can introduce non-verbal cues through the use of emoticons, the familiar textual representations of facial expressions (see Figure 6.1), and through other signals such as pauses and the use of all capital letters. Take a look at the e-mail messages in Figures 6.2a and 6.2b. These two messages are identical verbally, but would you interpret them in the same way?

Most of our interpersonal communication includes at least some form of nonverbal communication. Going further, when we only have a few nonverbal signals to go on, we pay them extra attention. For example, vocal characteristics such as pitch and tone are important nonverbal cues in face-to-face conversation, but they are even more important on the telephone because so many other nonverbal signals, such as facial expressions and gestures, are unavailable to us. By the same token, when people lose the ability to use one of their senses to communicate, they typically compensate by relying more heavily on their remaining senses. Deaf people, for example, pay extra attention to visual cues when communicating with others because they are unable

Communication in computer-mediated formats, such as e-mail, instant messaging, and text messaging, relies heavily on language. Even in these environments, however, people can still introduce nonverbal facial expressions through the use of emoticons (a word that means *emotional icons*). Here are some of the most common emoticons:

Smiles	:)	
Laughs	:D	
Frowns	:(	
Winks	;)	
Kisses	:X	
Confusion	:/	
Sticking out tongue	:P	

FIGURE 6.1 **Emoticons: Nonverbal Communication in Cyberspace** You might be surprised to learn that the first emoticon appeared in an online bulletin board posting more than 25 years ago, on September 19, 1982. Since then, emoticons have been used in computer-mediated communication to simulate the facial expression of various emotions, which helps readers decipher the sender's emotions. Interestingly, there are sex differences in emoticon use that mirror sex differences in facial expressions during face-to-face communication. For instance, women use them more often than men, particularly when they are communicating with other women. In cross-sex communication, though, men tend to match women's use of emotions, but women do not tend to match men's use of them. The sexes also differ in *why* they use emoticons: Women tend to use them primarily to express joy or humor, whereas men are more likely to use them to communicate sarcasm. Sources: Microsoft, Inc. (2006). The first smiley :-). Retrieved January 19, 2006, from http://research.microsoft.com/~mbj/Smiley/Smiley.html; Walther, J. B., & D'Addario, K. (2001). The impacts of emoticons on message interpretation in computer-mediated communication. *Social Science Computer Review, 19*, 324–347; Witmer, D., & Kaztman, S. (1997). On-line smiles: Does gender make a difference in the use of graphic accents? *Journal of Computer-Mediated Communication, 2*(4). Retrieved May 23, 2000, from http://www.ascusc.org/jcmc/vol2/issue4/witmer1.html; Wolf, A. (2000). Emotional expression online: Gender differences in emoticon use. *CyberPsychology & Behavior, 3*, 827–833.

to interpret vocal characteristics. Similarly, blind people often rely more heavily on their senses of hearing and touch to help them communicate, because they are unable to see gestures or facial expressions.

Nonverbal communication often conveys more information than verbal communication. If you browse the self-help section at most bookstores, chances are you'll find at least one book about the power of nonverbal communication. Open up titles such as *How to Read a Person like a Book*[1] or *What You Do Is More Important Than What You Say,*[2] and you'll get the impression that nearly all the information we get by communicating with others comes through nonverbal behavior. In fact, some unreliable but frequently cited studies have estimated that as much as 93% of meaning is transmitted nonverbally, leaving only 7% to be conveyed by the words we use.[3]

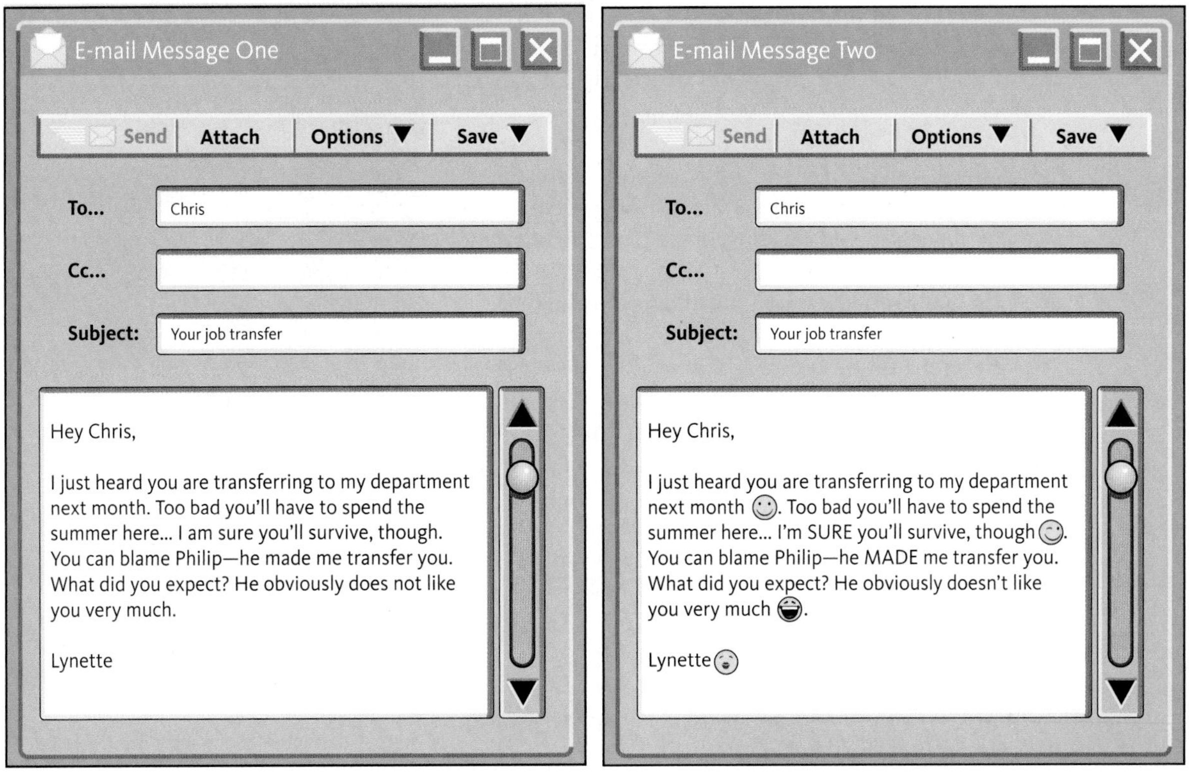

FIGURE 6.2 Two e-mail messages Based on the first email message on the left, how would you describe Lynette's feelings about Chris being transferred to her department? Does she think Chris will enjoy being there during the summer? How does she think Philip feels about Chris? With only the text to go by, many of us would find it difficult to interpret a message such as this. Now read through the email on the right, which is the same text message supplemented by a few nonverbal clues. From the addition of the emoticons and the use of all capital letters for emphasis, we can gather that Lynette actually is happy about Chris's transfer to her department. The wink at the end of the second sentence suggests that Lynette is being sarcastic when she says it's too bad Chris will have to spend the summer there. The laughing emoticon at the end of the last sentence suggests she is also being sarcastic when she says that Philip doesn't like Chris very much. Notice how much these small nonverbal clues reveal the true intent of the message.

Nonverbal communication isn't quite that powerful, however. More realistic estimates from nonverbal communication scholar Judee Burgoon suggest that between 65% and 70% of meaning comes from nonverbal clues, whereas 30% to 35% comes from language.[4] Significantly, even Burgoon's more conservative statistics suggest that we communicate more through our nonverbal behaviors than we do through our words.

The most likely reason why nonverbal communication adds up to such a significant percentage is that it makes use of many **nonverbal channels,** which are the various behavioral forms that nonverbal communication takes. Some of these channels rely on our sense of vision, such as facial expressions, gestures, and personal appearance. Vocal characteristics, such as loudness, pitch, and tone of voice, engage our sense of hearing. We also use our senses of touch and smell to communicate. We often express different messages with a handshake and a hug, and we convey subtle messages about attraction to others through our use of smell.

We sometimes rely on clues from nonverbal channels to make sense of a situation when talking to others isn't a good option. As the son of an alcoholic, for instance, Rick has learned that his mother, Claudia, has very unpredictable mood swings. When Rick visits his mother, he's never really sure how she'll be feeling. Some days, she's

Nonverbal channels
The various forms that nonverbal communication takes.

outgoing and chipper; other days, she's sullen and withdrawn. Occasionally, she'll start yelling at the slightest provocation. Over time, Rick has noticed that he can tell which mood Claudia is in without even talking to her. He only needs to look at her posture and facial expression to tell whether she's feeling cheerful, depressed, or angry that day. Perhaps you also know people whose emotional states you can interpret by paying attention to nonverbal channels.

In many situations, we send and receive multiple signals through multiple channels at once. Imagine you and I were sitting on the sidelines at my sister's soccer game having a conversation about her upcoming deployment to Afghanistan. Not only would you hear my words, but you would also be able to listen to the tone of my voice, watch my facial expressions, interpret any gestures that I use, and see how I was dressed. You could also smell my cologne and you could feel if I touched your arm. In other words, you would have access not only to the verbal channel (the words I'm using) but also to quite a number of nonverbal channels at once (my facial expressions, gestures, posture, appearance, voice, smell, and touch).

Given the number and variety of signals we can receive at one time, you might wonder why we aren't overwhelmed by having to pay attention to this much information at once. The answer is that your nervous system gives you the ability to manage social interaction and process a great deal of information simultaneously. Indeed, you do it every time you talk to someone. The

Nonverbal communication is a part of most interpersonal interactions and it often involves multiple channels at once. During a face-to-face conversation, speakers can attend to facial expressions, eye behaviors, tone of voice, gestures, posture, and touch as sources of information.

important point to remember is that you will learn more about what I'm thinking and feeling by processing all those nonverbal signals than by paying attention only to my words. How do I feel about my sister being deployed? Am I proud? sad? nervous? You might not figure this out just by listening to my words. Language is very important, of course, but nonverbal communication is often even more important.

Nonverbal communication is usually believed over verbal communication. It's not uncommon to get conflicting messages from what a person says versus what he or she does. How do we respond when this occurs? Multiple studies have demonstrated that we believe the nonverbal clues most of the time.[5]

Let's say, for example, that you're meeting your friend Joel at your favorite bookstore. When he walks in, Joel slumps down on the seat next to you, rolls his eyes, and lets out a heavy sigh. You ask him how he's doing, and he says, "It's been a *great* day." In this situation, Joel's verbal behavior is sending you one message ("I'm having a great day"), but his nonverbal behavior is suggesting something quite different ("I'm having a lousy day"). These messages obviously contradict each other, so which one do you believe? Most of us would pay attention to what Joel is *doing* instead of what he is *saying*. In other words, we would believe his nonverbal message.

Why do we put our trust in nonverbal communication? The most likely reason is that we believe people have a harder time controlling nonverbal signals than verbal ones. Thus, we assume that nonverbal behaviors more accurately reflect what a person is really thinking or feeling. It's easy for Joel to *say* he's having a great day, but if he actually feels frustrated or depressed, it's probably tougher for him to *act* as though his day is going well. Therefore, when he slumps in his chair, rolls his eyes, and sighs, you probably would conclude that his day is going poorly, despite his words to the contrary.

Our preference for believing nonverbal signals even when they conflict with words is especially critical for our ability to detect deception, because people often display inconsistent verbal and nonverbal behaviors when they're lying. Imagine that Tawny misses her group study session for the third time because she overslept, yet she tells her study group that she was in the emergency room with a severe migraine. Tawny might feel nervous telling such a lie, especially because she knows she could be kicked out of the group were she to get caught. Chances are that her nervousness will affect her nonverbal behavior. She might perspire, get dry in the mouth, sound unusually tense, and assume an especially rigid posture. In contrast, if she really had been in the hospital, there's probably no reason she would be nervous telling her study group about it. She would be able to explain her medical emergency calmly and apologize for her absence. So, if she looks or sounds nervous, these nonverbal messages will contradict her verbal message and may convince her group that she's not telling the truth.

Nonverbal communication is the primary means of communicating emotion. Although we have a large verbal vocabulary for describing our emotions, our nonverbal behaviors communicate emotion much more efficiently. How many times have you been able to tell how someone is feeling just by looking at him or her? We may not always be right about the emotions we sense—and some of us are better than others at interpreting people's emotions—but research shows that humans are acutely sensitive to nonverbal emotion cues.[6] As we saw in the example of Rick and his mother, Claudia, Rick has developed the ability to interpret Claudia's emotional state accurately with just a glance by paying attention to her facial expressions and posture. Emotion is a powerful influence on our behavior, and our primary way of communicating how we feel is through our nonverbal behaviors.

Two channels of nonverbal behavior that are particularly important in communicating emotion are facial expressions and vocal behaviors. Humans are highly visually oriented beings, meaning that we tend to pay a great deal of attention to people's facial expressions when we want to figure out their emotional state, whether we're talking to them face-to-face, listening to them speak to a group, or even watching them on television. On reality TV shows such as *American Idol, Project Runway,* and *Extreme Makeover: Home Edition,* for instance, producers often shoot close-ups of people's faces during critical moments in the show to capture their facial expressions of emotion. Most of us can easily think of the type of facial expression that connotes happiness, for example: The eyes tend to be wide and bright, and the person tends to be smiling. This expression differs from the expressions we associate with anger, sadness, surprise, and other emotional states. The distinctive patterns associated with each expression help us interpret other people's emotions.

In fact, several studies suggest that facial expressions of these basic emotions are interpreted very similarly across cultures.[7] In a classic study, psychologist Paul Ekman took photographs of people communicating six basic emotions through their facial expressions: happiness, fear, disgust, anger, sadness, and surprise. He then showed the photos to participants in Chile, Brazil, Argentina, Japan, and the United States. Each participant was asked to identify

Nonverbal communication—particularly facial expression—is our primary means of conveying emotion.

the emotion that was being expressed in each photograph. Ekman then compared the participants from different countries and found that they were equally accurate at describing which emotion was displayed in each photograph.[8]

Similar studies have repeated these results using groups from a range of cultures, including Greek, Chinese, Turkish, Malaysian, Ethiopian, Swedish, Italian, Sumatran, Estonian, and Scottish.[9] The degree of similarity in interpretations of emotion displays does differ from culture to culture. It also differs from emotion to emotion, with facial displays of some emotions, such as happiness, being interpreted more consistently than others, such as fear.[10] Overall, however, it appears that facial expressions of our most basic emotions are interpreted similarly around the world.

We also pay attention to vocal cues to understand a person's emotional state. When someone is yelling or screaming and using harsh vocal tones, for example, we usually infer that he or she is angry. In contrast, we interpret laughing and extensive pitch variation to suggest happiness or excitement. It turns out that we may be more accurate at interpreting emotions through vocal cues than through facial expressions.[11] This appears to be particularly true when the vocal channel is the only channel we have access to, such as when we're speaking with someone on the telephone. We don't necessarily get *more* information about their emotional state from their voice than from their facial expressions, but we might get *more accurate* information.

Let's say you're chatting about an upcoming sales meeting with your co-worker Jude, whose desk is in the cubicle next to yours. Although you can't see each other, you can hear each other just fine. You might notice from the sound of Jude's voice that she seems nervous when describing the presentation she will be giving at the meeting. You finally walk into her cubicle, and even though her facial expression doesn't suggest that she's nervous, you have correctly interpreted her emotional state by listening to the sounds of her voice. Just as with facial expressions, the vocal clues to emotion show consistency across cultures.[12] Take a look at the "How Do We Know?" box to learn more.

Nonverbal communication is meta-communicative. As we discussed in Chapter 1, meta-communication is communication *about* communication, and we often meta-communicate verbally. When we use phrases like "Let me tell you what I think" or "Don't take this the wrong way," or "I'm just kidding," we are sending messages related to our other messages; that is, we're communicating about our communication. Usually, we use meta-communication to avoid misunderstandings and to provide listeners with greater clarity about the meaning of our statements.

This is a very important feature of social interaction, and several nonverbal behaviors also help us to achieve this goal. Suppose, for example, that you're sitting at the dinner table with your brother and he leans over to you, lowers his voice to a whisper, and cups his mouth with

Nonverbal behaviors can be meta-communicative. When a friend whispers and covers her mouth with her hand, those behaviors convey that what she's telling you is meant to be a secret.

In the previous section, we explained that people from different cultures interpret vocal expressions of emotion similarly. How do we know this is true?

This finding comes from an experiment in which psychologists Klaus Scherer, Rainer Banse, and Harald Wallbott had professional actors record different speech segments while they were instructed to sound happy, sad, fearful, angry, and disgusted. The researchers then played the recordings for participants in nine countries in Europe, North America, and Asia. Each participant was asked to listen to each speech segment and to identify which emotion was being portrayed.

The researchers found that participants across cultures were able to identify nearly all the emotions with a high degree of accuracy on the basis of the vocal recordings. In contrast to Ekman's studies, however, the most difficult emotion to interpret from the vocal samples was happiness; participants frequently identified the happy sounding voice as emotionally neutral. Overall, however, vocal emotion cues appear to show cross-cultural consistency, just as facial expressions of emotion do.

Ask Yourself:

- How accurately do you think you can identify a person's emotional state just by listening to his or her voice?

- Why do you suppose cultures are more similar than different when it comes to interpreting vocal and facial expressions of emotion?

Source: Scherer, K. R., Banse, R., & Wallbott, H. G. (2001). Emotion inferences from vocal expression correlate across languages and cultures. *Journal of Cross-Cultural Psychology, 32,* 76–92.

his hand, as though he's about to tell you a secret. This combination of nonverbal behaviors sends you the message "What I'm about to say is meant for only you to hear." In other words, his nonverbal behavior meta-communicates his intentions to you.

We often use nonverbal behaviors such as facial expressions or gestures to indicate how someone else should interpret our messages. For instance, we might smile and wink to indicate that we're being sarcastic or raise our eyebrows to signal that what we're saying is very serious. All these behaviors are examples of how we can use nonverbal cues to meta-communicate with those around us.

Learn It: What determines whether a form of communication is verbal or nonverbal? Why are we more likely to believe nonverbal behaviors than words when the two conflict?

Try It: Consider how tone of voice can influence meaning. Take a simple phrase such as "She made me do that." First, say it as though you're angry, then surprised, and, finally, sarcastic. Notice how your voice changes each time, even though the words are the same.

Reflect on It: How accurate do you think you are at interpreting other people's nonverbal behaviors? Why do you suppose that some people are better at "reading" nonverbal behavior than others?

Nonverbal communication engages nearly all our senses, so it's probably no surprise that we experience it in so many different forms, or channels. In this section, we consider ten channels:

- Facial displays
- Eye behaviors
- Movement and gestures
- Touch behaviors
- Vocal behaviors
- The use of smell
- The use of space
- Physical appearance
- The use of time
- The use of artifacts

> *The human body is the best picture of the human soul.*
>
> —Ludwig Wittgenstein (1889–1951)
> Austrian philosopher

Facial Displays

It's hard to overstate the importance of **facial displays,** or facial expressions, in nonverbal communication. Indeed, according to the *principle of facial primacy,* the face communicates more information than any other channel of nonverbal behavior.[13] This principle is especially true for three important functions of facial displays: identity, attractiveness, and emotion. We use the appearance of the face more than any other single cue to identify others. We consider facial attractiveness to be of prime importance when evaluating our attraction to others. Finally, we look to facial displays more than any other channel to provide cues about a person's emotional state.

Facial display The use of facial expression for communication.

Identity. The face is the most important visual clue that humans use to identify one another.[14] We don't usually hang pictures on our walls of people's hands or legs or feet; rather, we hang pictures of their faces because the appearance of the face is our most reliable clue to identity. It's your face that appears on your driver's license and in your passport to help authorities identify you. Likewise, it's your face that appears in your high school yearbook to help your classmates remember you.

Attractiveness. The face also plays a major role in attractiveness. Even though we like to think that "beauty is in the eye of the beholder," there is actually remarkable consistency in what people find attractive in faces, both within and across cultures. Two properties that appear to be especially important in assessing attractiveness are **symmetry** and **proportionality.** Symmetry refers to the similarity between the left and right sides of your face. For most of us, the two sides of our faces look similar, but they aren't *exactly* alike. For both women and men, however, attractive faces have greater symmetry than unattractive faces.[15] Take a look at the photos in Figure 6.3 for an example of symmetric and asymmetric faces.

Symmetry The similarity between left and right sides of the face or body.

Proportionality The size of facial features relative to one another.

Proportionality refers to the relative size of your facial features. Is your nose too big for your face? Are your ears too small? On a proportional face, all the features are of the proper size, not in an absolute sense, but relative to one another. Just as with symmetry, attractive faces have greater proportionality than unattractive ones. Unlike symmetry, which can be objectively measured, proportionality is a subjective judgment we make about a person's face. It makes a difference for the attractive-

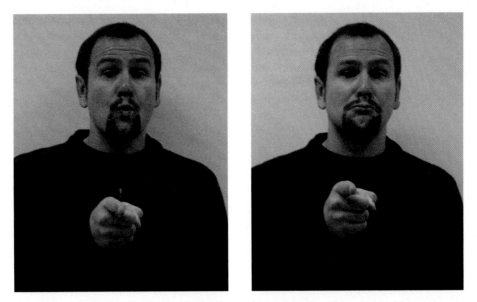

FIGURE 6.4 Facial Expressions in American Sign Language Facial expression plays a vital role in communicating ideas in American Sign Language (ASL). In some instances, the same hand sign is associated with different meanings if it is accompanied by different facial expressions. Both photographs feature the hand sign for "you," for example, but they involve different facial displays. The photo on the left would be interpreted as a question, such as "Are you?" or "Did you?" The photo on the right, however, would be interpreted as an exclamation, such as "It's you!" Although the hand sign is the same in the two photographs, the meaning differs because of the accompanying facial expression.

learn better decoding skills as result.[19] Finally, people who are very outgoing and extroverted tend to be better at interpreting facial emotion displays than people who are shy or introverted.[20]

As a way to convey meaning, facial expressions are also extremely important to people who communicate through sign language. In sign language, facial expressions are sometimes called "non-manual signals" because they work alongside hand signs to help express a particular meaning. For instance, when someone asks a yes-or-no question using sign language, his or her eyes are wide open, the eyebrows are raised, and the head and shoulders are pushed forward. Sometimes a person can change the entire meaning of a sign just by changing the facial expression that goes with it (see Figure 6.4).[21]

Eye Behaviors

Because the eyes are part of the face, it may strike you as odd that researchers study eye behavior separately from facial behavior. However, just as facial behavior communicates more than any other nonverbal channel, the eyes communicate more than any other part of the face. For that reason, we treat **oculesics,** or the study of eye behavior, as a separate nonverbal channel.

When people think about eye behavior, they frequently think first about eye contact, and with good reason. Eye contact plays a role in several important types of relational interaction. The role it plays, however, varies by culture. In Western cultures,

Oculesics
The study of eye behavior.

such as those in North America, Europe, and Australia, we use eye contact to signal attraction to someone and to infer that someone is attracted to us. We use it to gain credibility and to come across as sincere or trustworthy. We use it to persuade others and to signal that we are paying attention and understanding what others are saying. We can even use eye contact when we want to intimidate someone or take a dominant or authoritative position in a conversation or a group discussion. Indeed, there are few times when we feel as connected to other people—in either positive or negative ways—as when we are looking each other in the eyes.

In contrast to Western cultures, some Asian, Latin American, and Middle Eastern cultures discourage eye contact in certain situations. For example, they teach people to avoid making eye contact with authority figures as a sign of deference or respect.[22] In these cultures a young person who maintained eye contact with a teacher or another authority figure would be acting disrespectfully.

In addition to eye contact, researchers also study the communicative value of other eye behaviors, including the *lack* of eye contact. Sometimes, not looking a person in the eyes can send just as strong a message as looking at him or her. Multiple studies have shown that avoiding eye contact—at least, in Western cultures—elicits negative evaluations from others.[23] Let's say, for instance, that Ruben is being interviewed by an admissions committee at the medical school to which he has applied. Early in the interview, the committee members notice that Ruben rarely looks at them when responding to their questions. Instead, he gazes at the floor or out the window. Although he has good grades and excellent recommendations from his undergraduate professors, the committee is reluctant to recommend his admission. His lack of eye contact has caused the committee members to perceive Ruben as untrustworthy and lacking in self-confidence.

Another eye behavior that has communicative value is pupil size. The pupil is the darkest spot right in the center of your eye, which you can see when you look at your eyes in a mirror. Your pupils control how much light enters your eyes; as a result, they continually change in size. In darker environments, they dilate, or open wider, to take in every available amount of light. In brighter environments, they contract, or become smaller, to avoid taking in too much light at once.

What communication researchers find interesting is that your pupils also dilate when you look at someone you find physically attractive and when you feel any kind of arousal. This is true whether your response is positive, such as excitement or sexual arousal, or negative, such as anxiety or fear. Watching how a person's pupils react to different social situations or conversational partners, therefore, tells us something about his or her interest and arousal. Unless it is extreme, however, pupil dilation is not easily noticeable to the naked eye. Rather, researchers use sophisticated video equipment to measure and track changes in a person's pupil size.

Movement and Gestures

Think about the different ways you can walk. When you're feeling confident, you hold your head high and walk with smooth, consistent strides. When you're nervous, you probably walk more timidly, stealing frequent glances at the people around you. Perhaps you walk fast when it's raining, facing downward to avoid the raindrops. Your *gait*, or the way you walk, is one example of how your body movement can commu-

Gestures comprise body movements that have communicative meaning, and we begin to use them when we are young children. How would you interpret the gestures used by each of these people?

Kinesics
The study of movement.

Gesticulation The use of arm and hand movements to communicate.

Emblem A gesture with a direct verbal translation.

Illustrator A gesture that enhances or clarifies a verbal message.

Affect display A gesture that communicates emotion.

nicate various messages about you to others, such as "I feel proud," "I feel scared," or "I don't want to get wet." The study of movement is called **kinesics.**

Now imagine how you use your arms and hands to communicate. Perhaps it's to wave at your neighbor when you see her at the grocery store. Maybe it's to hold up two fingers to signal that you want two hot dogs at the football game concession stand. It might be to point in the direction you want your taxi driver to go. The use of arm and hand movements to communicate is called **gesticulation.** Research indicates that most people—even people who are born blind—start using gestures even before they begin speaking.[24] Communication scholars divide gestures into several forms, including emblems, illustrators, affect displays, regulators, and adaptors. Let's look at some examples of each.

Emblems. An **emblem** is any gesture that has a direct verbal translation. Whenever you see an emblematic gesture, you should be able to translate it into words. Examples are the wave for "hello" or "goodbye," the upright extended palm for "stop," and the shrugged shoulders for "I don't know." As we saw in the opening vignette, the specific words an emblem symbolizes can vary by culture. Although Jack used the crossed-fingers gesture to mean "good luck," his roommate Wayan interpreted the gesture differently, according to the way it is used in his native Bali.

Illustrators. **Illustrators** are gestures that go along with a verbal message to enhance or clarify it. Suppose, for example, you're telling your sister about the salmon you caught on your fishing trip to Alaska. If you hold up your hands a certain distance apart and say that your fish was "this big," your gesture serves as an illustrator to clarify what you mean by "this big." Similarly, when a politician is making a particularly important point in a campaign speech, she or he might raise her or his arms in the air. This gesture would also be an illustrator because it would enhance the importance of what the individual was saying.

Affect displays. **Affect displays** are gestures that communicate emotion. You probably know people who wring their hands when they're nervous or cover their mouths with their hands when they're surprised. Both of these actions are affect displays because they communicate the particular emotions that the person is feeling at the time.

Some affect displays are specific to certain cultures. In China, for example, women express emotional satisfaction by holding their fingertips over their closed mouth. Similarly, a man in Uruguay will hold his fists together and turn them in opposite directions, as if wringing out a wet cloth, to express anger.

Regulators. **Regulators** are gestures that control the flow of conversation. If you're speaking and someone is trying to interrupt, you might hold up your index finger to signal that you're not quite finished talking. When someone is telling a long, drawn-out story and you want that person to get to the point, you might roll your hand in a circle, as if to say "get on with it." One regulator you're probably very familiar with is raising your hand when you're in a group and wish to speak or ask a question. Each of these gestures plays a role in regulating who is speaking, and for how long, so that conversations can flow smoothly.

Regulator A gesture that controls the flow of conversation.

Adaptors. Finally, **adaptors** are gestures you use to satisfy some personal need, such as scratching an itch or picking lint off your shirt. When we do these behaviors to ourselves, we call them *self-adaptors.* When adaptors are directed at others (say, picking lint off someone else's shirt), they're called *other-adaptors.* Although we don't usually engage in adaptors for the purpose of communicating, research shows that they do convey messages about us to others. When people use excessive self-adaptors, for instance, they are often perceived by others as being nervous, aroused, or even deceptive.[25] Moreover, using other-adaptors with someone can signal a high level of familiarity and intimacy with that person. Because other-adaptors often require you to touch or be in close proximity to a person, using these gestures can convey the message that you have a close, familiar relationship with that person.

Adaptor A gesture used to satisfy a personal need.

Touch Behaviors

Touch is the first of our five senses to develop. Therefore, even before an infant can see, hear, taste, or smell, her skin can respond to stimuli in the environment. Touch is the only sense we cannot survive without. No matter how much we may cherish our other senses, it's entirely possible to survive without being able to see, hear, taste, or smell. Without our sense of touch, however, we would constantly be susceptible to burn, frostbite, and other forms of injury that would eventually be life-threatening.

Not only is touch vital to our survival, but it also plays a key role in communication. We call the study of how we use touch to communicate **haptics.** In human communication, there are five major areas in which touch plays a critical role in conveying meaning: affection, caregiving, power and control, aggression, and ritual. Let's take a closer look at each one.

Haptics The study of how we use touch to communicate.

Affectionate touch. Sharing affection is one of the most important functions of touch. Behaviors such as hugging, kissing, and hand-holding communicate love, intimacy, commitment, and safety; they are commonplace in many romantic relationships, parent-child relationships, and friendships.[26] One reason affectionate touch is so important is that it contributes to our physical and mental well-being. Infants who are regularly cuddled ex-

No matter how much we cherish our other senses, touch is the only sense we cannot survive without.

Touch has become a sensitive issue in many grade schools. What are the implications of discouraging touch with children?

perience faster physical development than those who are not.[27]

Just how essential is affectionate touch? In a now-famous set of experiments, psychologist Harry Harlow demonstrated that baby monkeys preferred the touch of a terrycloth-covered artificial "mother" over one made only of wire, even when the wire "mother" was the one who dispensed food.[28] This preference seemed to be especially true when the monkeys were scared. On the basis of his findings, Harlow concluded that affectionate touch was nearly as important for infant monkeys as food or shelter. Although these studies would not be conducted in the same way today, their findings were influential in shaping much of the advice given to human parents about the importance of touching and cuddling their children.

In recent years, concerns over sexual abuse of children have caused many public school districts to adopt strict "no touch" policies that prevent teachers, counselors, or other school staff from touching students in any way unless it is a medical emergency. As educator Tony Del Prete explains, "In an effort to keep one step ahead of sexual offenders, more and more schools are sending the message to adults—hands off! Touching children in schools has become virtually taboo."[29]

Although such zero-tolerance policies are designed to protect children, many experts have wondered whether preventing children from being touched actually does more harm than good. For example, researcher Tiffany Field, an internationally recognized expert on touch, believes that no-touch policies are "not a good idea, because children need touch for survival. Their growth and development thrive on touch. And how will they learn about love and affection if not through touch?"[30]

What's your opinion? Do you think no-touch policies in schools help protect children from abuse? Do they go too far? not far enough? If you were the parent of a young schoolchild, would you want him or her to be touched by a teacher? If so, what types of touch would you consider appropriate?

Caregiving touch. We're often touched by others while receiving some form of care or service. When you get your hair cut, have your teeth cleaned, receive a massage, or work with a personal trainer, you're touched in ways that correspond to those activities. Babysitters touch young children while cleaning or dressing them, and nursing home employees touch elderly residents while changing a bandage or helping them take a medication. Each of these actions is an example of caregiving touch because it is done in the course of providing a specific type of care or service.

Caregiving touch is distinguished from affectionate touch because it doesn't necessarily reflect any affection or positive emotion for the person being touched. When a physician touches you as part of a physical exam, for example, you don't infer from her touch that she has personal feelings for you. Rather, you interpret her touch as task-oriented. As a consequence, we generally expect caregiving touch to be limited to caregiving contexts. Although you allow a dentist to touch your teeth and gums as part of a dental exam, for example, you probably wouldn't be comfortable allowing the same kind of touch if you ran into him at an art fair.

The fact that caregiving touch is task-oriented doesn't mean it isn't beneficial. Indeed, several forms of caregiving touch have important health benefits. For instance, adolescents and adults who receive therapeutic massage show improvement in a host of medical conditions, ranging from depression and stress to asthma, diabetes, cancer, multiple sclerosis, and HIV.[31] Caregiving touch can also induce calm and relieve stress for nursing home residents, as well as patients in a hospital or clinic.[32]

Power and control touch. Still other touches are used to exert power over other people's behavior. We sometimes touch people merely to suggest a certain course of behavior, as when the host of a party puts his hand on a guest's back to lead her in a certain direction. In other instances, we touch people to protect them by restricting their movement, such as when a nursing aide holds the hand of an elderly patient to help him walk without falling.

Although these behaviors involve some degree of control, they are intended to be friendly and helpful. In some cases, however, we touch people to control their behavior against their wishes. This type of touch can constitute a legitimate exercise of power, such as when police officers hold a suspect on the ground while applying handcuffs. It can also embody an illegitimate or unlawful exercise of power, such as when bullies hold an adolescent immobile to steal from him.

Aggressive touch. Behaviors done to inflict physical harm, such as punching, pushing, kicking, slapping, and even stabbing, are all forms of aggressive touch. Using touch behaviors to inflict physical harm on others almost always constitutes a criminal act. In fact, in some U.S. states, even *acting* as though you are going to touch someone to inflict harm, such as raising your hand as if you're about to strike, is a crime, whether you actually touch the person or not. In those states, threatening to hit somebody is called "assault," and actually hitting the person is called "battery."

Despite such laws, however, incidents of violence and abuse using aggressive touch are unfortunately still common, both in North America and in many societies around the world. Research indicates that, although men are more likely than women to be the victims of violence at the hands of a stranger, women are more likely than men to be victimized by a close relational partner, such as a spouse.[33]

Ritualistic touch. Some touches are ritualistic, meaning that we do them as part of a custom or a tradition. In North America, shaking hands is one such example: When we shake hands with people as part of a greeting ritual, we understand that the handshake does not convey any particular meaning about the relationship (the way that, say, holding hands would). By contrast, the greeting ritual in many cultures involves kissing on the lips or on the cheeks; people in those cultures would also understand those touches to be part of a ritual, not necessarily expressions of love or affection. Other ritualistic touches take place in the context of athletics. For example, basketball, wrestling, soccer, water polo, and many other sports involve body-to-body contact between players.[34]

Vocal Behaviors

Vocalics
Characteristics of the voice.

Perhaps you have a high, breathy voice or a deep, booming voice. Maybe you usually talk very fast, or quite loudly. Perhaps you have an accent that indicates where you grew up. Finally, there may be times when you speak with a particular tone in your voice to suggest that you are irritated, amused, or bored. We refer to these and other characteristics of the voice collectively as **vocalics**.

Some people are surprised to learn that the voice is a channel of nonverbal communication. After all, we speak with our voices, and spoken communication is verbal, right? That's true, but the only aspect of spoken communication that's verbal is *what* we say—that is, the words themselves. Everything else about our voices is nonverbal.

Voices are much like fingerprints. Although two voices might sound similar, each voice comprises multiple properties that make it unique. We refer to these properties as *paralinguistic cues.* Calling these cues "paralinguistic" means we use them in conjunction with the words we speak; however, each can also communicate meaning separately from the meaning of the words. In this section we list and then examine some of the most important paralinguistic cues that affect how your voice conveys meaning:

- Pitch
- Inflection
- Volume
- Rate
- Filler words
- Pronunciation
- Articulation
- Accent
- Silence

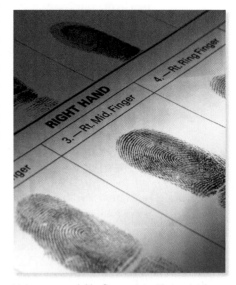

Voices are much like fingerprints. Your voice is composed of multiple properties that make it different from every other voice.

Pitch. The pitch of your voice is an index of how high or deep your voice sounds. Pitch is also called "fundamental frequency." Every person's voice has an average fundamental frequency, which is the pitch your voice hits the most often. On average, women's voices have a higher pitch than men's voices, and adults have deeper voices than children. Several studies have reported that women are more attracted to men with lower vocal pitch than to men with higher voices, particularly when they are seeking short-term romantic partners.[35] Men show the opposite pattern, judging women with higher voices as more attractive than women with lower voices.[36] One possible reason for this sex difference is that low voices are associated with high levels of the male sex hormone testosterone.[37] Having a high level of testosterone gives a person a masculine look, which would tend to make men *more* physically attractive but women *less* attractive.

Inflection. When we talk about the inflection in your voice, we're referring to your variation in pitch. Voices that have a great deal of inflection are usually described as very expressive; those with little inflection are said to be "monotone." Perhaps you have seen the classic comedy *Ferris Bueller's Day Off*, in which the economics teacher, played by Ben Stein, calls attendance in monotone: "Bueller? Bueller?" Research indicates that most of us find monotone voices unattractive, regardless of whether the speaker is female or male.[38] That may be because monotone voices lack variety, so we might find them less interesting than voices with greater inflection.

Volume. Volume is an index of how loud or quiet your voice is. Most of us alter our vocal volume as the social context demands. For instance, we tend to speak more loudly than normal when we are excited or when we are trying to be heard over a long distance. By contrast, we might speak more quietly than normal when sharing a secret or conversing in a library. Each of our voices also has an average volume, meaning that some people generally speak more loudly than others.

An especially quiet voice was the cause of problems in a season five episode of *Seinfeld* called "The Puffy Shirt." Kramer's girlfriend, Leslie, whom Jerry referred to as a "low talker" because of her unusually quiet voice, asked Jerry to wear a puffy pirate shirt she had designed while he was being interviewed on national television. Because he couldn't hear her, Jerry simply nodded his head, unaware of what he was agreeing to. As a result of Leslie's particularly quiet voice, therefore, Jerry ended up having to wear the puffy shirt on television, causing him great embarrassment. Research suggests that we don't find unusually quiet voices to be attractive, but neither are we attracted to unusually loud ones. Instead, people are most attracted to voices with moderate average volume.[39]

Rate. Vocal rate refers to how fast or slowly you speak. The average adult speaks at a rate of approximately 150 words per minute, but there are several instances in which we increase or decrease our rate.[40] For instance, many of us speak faster than usual when we're excited or when we have only a short period of time to talk. By contrast, we might speak more slowly than usual when we're unsure of ourselves, or when we're speaking to children or the elderly, since they may find it challenging to hear or pay attention. Vocal rate doesn't appear to be directly related to how attractive we find a person's voice to be. Research has found, however, that faster speakers are perceived as more physically attractive than slower speakers.[41]

Filler words. Filler words are nonword sounds such as "umm" or "er" that people often use to fill the silence during pauses while they're speaking. Linguists explain that normal conversation consists of a series of back-and-forth speaking turns, and that when one person pauses or is silent, this can signal that the person is ready to give up his or her turn. If we have to pause while speaking—say, to remember the word we want to use or the fact we want to describe—we can use filler words during the pause to indicate that we intend to continue speaking.

The particular sounds we use as filler words vary among languages. Although "umm" and "er" are common filler words for English speakers, the pure sound of the "e" vowel is frequently used by people speaking Latin languages. Moreover, speakers of Chinese often say "zhege zhege zhege"—which translates to "this this this"—as filler words. Although using filler words is common, research indicates that we judge people as less competent and sociable the more they use them.[42]

Pronunciation. Pronunciation reflects how correctly you combine vowel and consonant sounds to say a word. For example, how would you pronounce the word "victuals"? Although it looks as though it should be pronounced VIK-TULES, its correct pronunciation is VITTLES. Some mispronunciations become notorious when they are committed by public figures. For instance, President George W. Bush was frequently parodied for mispronouncing the word "nuclear" as NU-KU-LER instead of NU-KLEE-ER. Many people struggle with pronunciation, however, when they are learning a foreign language, since rules for pronunciation vary among languages.[43]

Articulation. Articulation refers to how clearly you speak. People who mumble their words, or who speak with their mouths full, demonstrate poor articulation. By contrast, people whose words are clear and easily understandable are enacting good articulation. We sometimes refer to articulation as *enunciation.* Poor articulation can make it difficult to identify the words a speaker is speaking. If an adult who normally has good articulation suddenly begins to slur his words, this can be a sign of fatigue, intoxication, or even neurological problems such as a stroke or speech apraxia.[44]

Accent. An accent is a pattern of pronouncing vowel and consonant sounds that is representative of a particular language or geographic area. Everyone speaks with an accent—even you—although we typically notice only those accents that are different from ours. When you encounter accents with which you're familiar, they often provide clues as to where a person grew up. For instance, you might be able to distinguish residents of Brooklyn, Boston, and Biloxi on the basis of their different accents. Likewise, you may be able to tell whether a person's first language was Russian, Italian, or Hindi just by listening to his or her accent.

Silence. Silence is the absence of sound. In a technical sense, therefore, it isn't an attribute of vocalics. Nevertheless, we frequently use silence to convey meaning in conversations.[45] For instance, we often become silent when we are unsure how to respond to a question or when we have said as much as we wish to about a topic. We might also give someone the "silent treatment," ignoring him or her to convey defiance or disdain.[46] Finally, we can use silence to indicate that we do not wish to answer a question, perhaps to avoid embarrassment or offense.[47]

As we've seen, each of these vocal properties—pitch, inflection, volume, rate, filler words, pronunciation, articulation, accent, and silence—can communicate messages that are independent of the words being spoken. This is part of what makes vocalics such a powerful nonverbal channel.

The Use of Smell

Out of all the channels of nonverbal behavior, you might have the hardest time figuring out what smell has to do with human communication. It's relatively easy to describe how movement, gesture, touch, and voice convey meaning. Is it really possible, however, to communicate meaning through smell? The truth is that your sense of smell, which we call **olfactics,** operates in some subtle but powerful ways to influence how you react to other people. In fact, two phenomena that are central to the human experience and how we communicate are profoundly affected and regulated by smell. These are memories and sexual attraction.

Olfactics
The study of the sense of smell.

Memories. Smells can affect our communication behavior by influencing our memories and our moods. Have you ever smelled a particular scent—maybe a certain food or a specific cologne—and instantly remembered a particular person, event, or place? Maybe the smell of banana bread makes you think of your grandmother's kitchen, or the smell of motor oil reminds you of your uncle who used to work on cars in his garage. These are examples of *olfactic association,* which is the tendency of odors to bring to mind specific memories. Many of our other senses evoke memories as well. For instance, hearing a certain song or seeing a certain painting can make us recall specific times or people in our lives. Because of the way that sensory information is processed in the brain, however, none of your senses evokes memories as strongly as your sense of smell.

Why does this connection between smell and memories matter for communication? The answer is that memories are often accompanied by specific emotions. Therefore, when a smell reminds us of a particular person or place, it can affect our mood and our behavior by arousing specific emotions.

To illustrate this process, imagine that you have a job interview for a management position with a major name-brand retailer. When you walk through the door, you notice that the office smells like the place where you worked while you were in high school. That job had been awful because of the cranky, disorganized store manager. Without even realizing why, you suddenly feel anxious and apprehensive, and those feelings come across in the way you interact during your interview. Even though you went into your interview feeling positive and acting upbeat, the olfactic association you experienced brought back a memory—and with it, an emotion—that quickly changed your disposition.

Sexual attraction. Smell also affects our communication by playing a role in determining to whom we are sexually attracted. This may surprise you, because we often think of sexual attraction as being driven mostly by visual cues. That is, when we say that we find someone attractive, this usually means we think he or she *looks* attractive. Whether you realize it or not, though, your judgments about how sexually attractive someone appears are strongly affected by the way that person smells to you. More specifically, research tells us that when we are looking for opposite-sex romantic partners, we are drawn to people whose natural body scent is the most different from our own.

Why is this true? The answer is that if two people smell very similar, that means their genes are very similar. People produce much healthier children when they mate with partners who are dissimilar to them genetically. Therefore, selecting a sexual partner with similar genes can increase the probability of producing genetically abnormal children. It turns out that a person's natural body scent sends a signal to your brain that tells you how similar his or her genes are to yours. The more dissimilar a person's body odor is to yours, therefore, the more sexually attractive you will instinctively judge him or her to be. We don't make these judgments consciously. Rather, our brains are adapted to pick up on these olfactic signals subconsciously.

This point is very important. One of the reasons we may not think of smell as a component of nonverbal communication is that its influence often operates outside our conscious awareness. Smelling a particular odor may evoke a specific memory, for instance, but we may not realize it was the odor that brought the memory to mind. In fact, some researchers argue that because smell often influences us in subconscious ways, it is not a genuine channel of communication. These scholars consider only consciously controlled behaviors to be legitimate elements of communication.

In truth, however, we do intentionally manipulate the way we smell to others. Particularly in Western cultures, people use a number of products, including deodorant, soap, toothpaste, and perfume or cologne, to mask or eliminate their natural body odors. Although we may not always be consciously aware of how smells are influencing our behavior, therefore, we frequently manipulate the way we smell in very intentional ways.

The Use of Space

When we interact socially, we constantly negotiate our use of space. This behavior becomes particularly apparent when our personal space is limited; think of being in a crowded elevator or on a full airplane, for instance. Why do so many of us find situations such as these to be uncomfortable? The scientific study of spatial use, known as **proxemics,** explains that we each have a preferred amount of personal space that

Proxemics
The study of spatial use.

we carry like an invisible bubble around us. How much personal space each of us prefers depends on a number of factors, including our temperament, the type of situation we're in, and how well we know the people around us.

Our culture also plays a large role in the way we negotiate personal space. Researchers refer to some cultures as **high-contact cultures** and others as **low-contact cultures.** People in high-contact cultures usually stand or sit fairly close to one another and touch one another frequently. Many Hispanic, southern European, and Middle Eastern cultures are classified as high-contact. By contrast, people in low-contact cultures keep greater amounts of personal space between themselves and touch one another less frequently. Some Asian and Scandinavian cultures are examples of low-contact cultures.

Many communication researchers also classify the United States as a fairly low-contact culture. In one study involving observations at McDonald's restaurants, touch researcher Tiffany Field found that adolescents in France (a high-contact culture) touched one another substantially more often during a 20-minute period than did adolescents in the United States.[48]

Anthropologist Edward T. Hall discovered that people in Western cultures use four spatial zones, or levels of personal distance, when interacting with one another.[49] "Intimate distance," which ranges from 0 to approximately 1½ feet, is the zone we willingly occupy with only our closest and most intimate friends, family members, and romantic partners. With other friends and relatives, we typically maintain a "personal distance," which Hall defined as extending from 1½ to about 4 feet. With customers, casual acquaintances, or others whom we don't know very well, we occupy a "social distance." Social distance ranges from about 4 to 12 feet and indicates that interactions are more formal and less personal. Finally, we typically use "public distance" when we are giving a speech or performing in front of a large audience. The purpose of public distance is to keep the presenter far enough away from the group that he or she is safe and visible to everyone. Public distances are usually 12 to 25 feet or greater, depending on the circumstance.

The ways in which people *use* space are also important, and this is particularly true in groups. In any group of people, where the group members stand or sit relative to one another affects the flow of conversation and the ways the group interacts. In particular, the more powerful or dominant group members tend to position themselves in a more visible, central location, such as at the front of the room or the end of the conference table. By contrast, people who don't wish to play as big a role in the group's discussions are more likely to position themselves in the sidelines, out of the view of the group leaders.[50]

You might notice this type of pattern in your classroom or in meetings. Most likely, the instructor or the person running the meeting stands or sits at the head of

High-contact culture A culture in which people frequently touch and maintain little personal distance with one another.

Low-contact culture A culture in which people touch infrequently and maintain relatively high levels of personal distance with one another.

This bus is empty now but what if it were filled with passengers? Where would you sit? How much personal space do you prefer when taking public transportation?

the room, with all the chairs or desks facing him or her. People who sit toward the front of the room are probably actively engaged in the class or meeting, whereas others may tend to sit in the back or on the sides of the room.

Another factor that influences physical proximity is a person's disability status. Many people who do not have physical disabilities stand or sit farther away from individuals with physical disabilities than they do from others. In fact, communication scholars Dawn and Charles Braithwaite have suggested that people often shy away from interacting with persons with disabilities in the same way they tend to avoid people from other cultures.[51] Some researchers think this happens because people are inherently cautious around anyone they think of as different from themselves.[52] Why do you think people maintain greater distances from persons with disabilities? What might be done to change that pattern?

Physical Appearance

The importance we place on physical appearance is extraordinary. Whether we intend to or not, we make all sorts of judgments about people on the basis of how they look. Imagine that the two women pictured in Figure 6.5 were both running for office and you had to decide which one to vote for. Now imagine these pictures are the only information you have to go on. Research suggests that most people, if they were being honest, would say they'd vote for the woman on the right because she is more attractive. If we don't know anything about either woman, why would most of us choose the more attractive one?

The reason is the "halo effect," which is the tendency to attribute positive qualities to physically attractive people. In other words, when a person *looks* good, most of us subconsciously assume that he or she *is* good. Indeed, research has shown that we think attractive people are friendlier, more competent, and more socially skilled than less attractive people.[53]

FIGURE 6.5 Which woman would you vote for if she were running for office?

These perceptions translate into some real advantages for attractive people. For instance, they have higher self-esteem and date more frequently than less attractive people.[54] We are also nicer and more cooperative toward attractive people and more lenient toward attractive criminal defendants.[55] Thus, if it seems at times that good-looking people get all the breaks, research tells us this is often the case. Much as we may like to claim otherwise, most of us are strongly influenced by physical appearance when making assessments about other people.

Assessments based only on a person's attractiveness can be strongly misguided, however. In a 2007 episode of the television series *House,* for instance, Dr. Gregory House (played by Hugh Laurie) offers a fellowship to Dr. Samira Terzi (played by Michael Michelle) simply because he is smitten by her good looks. He soon discovers, however, that despite Dr. Terzi's beauty, she is not particularly competent. Before long, he begins to regret hiring her. This story line doesn't imply that highly attractive people *can't* be good doctors. Rather, it illustrates that a person's attractiveness and his or her professional competence are not necessarily related.

The Use of Time

Chronemics
The use of time.

Chronemics is the way we use time. You might not immediately think of our use of time as nonverbal behavior. In fact, the way we give (or refuse to give) our time to others can send them important messages about the way we feel about them. This is particularly true for two important relational messages, one concerning value and the other concerning power.

Messages of value. Let's say that you have saved up for a plane ticket to visit your friend Shelley in California during spring break. The two of you have been planning the trip for months. Once you arrive, however, you find that Shelley hasn't taken any time off from work and has a number of other obligations during the week you're there. Some days you barely see her at all. Even though the time you spend together is enjoyable, you leave with the feeling that your visit wasn't very important to Shelley because of the limited amount of time she set aside for it. Because we tend to spend our time on things that matter to us, Shelly's failure to set aside time for your visit sent the signal—whether accurate or not—that she doesn't really value your relationship.

Messages of power. Our use of time also sends messages about power. When you go to see someone who is in a position of power over you, such as your supervisor, it is not uncommon for her or him to keep you waiting. We would probably consider it in very bad form, however, to keep a more powerful person waiting for us. Indeed, the rule seems to be that the time of powerful people is more valuable than the time of less powerful people. You wait to see the doctor; the doctor does not wait to see you. You might keep a subordinate waiting, but not a superior. Thus, when we are kept waiting to see someone, that use of time can signal or reinforce a power difference between us.

The Use of Artifacts

The first thing Alma did after moving into her new house was to fix it up the way she wanted. She painted her bedroom walls a nice shade of green, made sure there was plenty of light in the kitchen and the hallways, and filled the living room with her favorite pictures, plants, and artwork. Like many of us, Alma wanted her home environment to reflect her tastes and her personality. Without realizing it, she was using artifacts as a nonverbal channel to express herself.

Artifact An object or a visual feature of an environment with communicative value.

Each of us has certain physical environments that we inhabit and control, such as a house or an apartment, a residence-hall room, or an office. **Artifacts** are the objects and visual features within an environment that reflect who we are and what we like. Some offices, for instance, are plush and opulent, with oak desks, leather furniture, soft lighting, and expensive paintings on the walls. Others are decidedly spartan, featuring metal desks and chairs, fluorescent lighting, and bare walls. What messages might these different artifacts convey about the occupants of these two offices?

We can select and arrange artifacts in many ways to send specific nonverbal messages. For instance, some people create an "ego wall" in their home or office, on which they display diplomas, awards, photographs of them with famous people, and other artifacts that signal their status or achievements.[56] Others prefer to cover the walls with photographs of their friends and relatives. Each of these arrangements may send a different signal about the person and what he or she values. Even something as simple as our choice of holiday decorations can convey information concerning our values, beliefs, and sociability.[57]

Artifacts are objects that reflect who we are and what we like. What messages would you infer about the person who owned this chair?

The way we place artifacts such as furniture within an environment can facilitate or inhibit interpersonal interaction. For example, teachers at Phillips Exeter Academy, a private preparatory school in New Hampshire, practice the "Harkness method" of teaching, which involves arranging up to 12 students and a teacher around an oval table. This arrangement is meant to diminish the separation between students and teachers, encouraging everyone to interact in an open, engaging way. By contrast, people who wish to discourage conversation in their offices or work environments might place their desks so that their back is to others.

The color of our environments can also influence nonverbal behavior by affecting our mood and disposition.[58] Specifically, "warm" colors such as red, orange, and yellow tend to be arousing, whereas "cool" colors such as blues and greens have calm-

At a Glance: Ten Channels of Nonverbal Communication

Facial displays	Important for identity, attraction, and emotion.
Eye behaviors	Eye contact and pupil size both have communicative value.
Movement and gestures	Serve as emblems, illustrators, affect displays, regulators, and adaptors.
Touch behaviors	Used for conveying affection, caregiving, power and control, aggression, and ritual.
Vocal behaviors	Voices vary in pitch, inflection, volume, rate, use of filler words, pronunciation, articulation, accent, and silence.
Use of Smell	Important for memory and sexual attraction.
Use of space	Four spatial distances: intimate, personal, social, and public.
Physical appearance	Halo effect maintains we assume attractive people have other positive qualities.
Use of time	Sends messages of value and power.
Use of artifacts	Includes selection and placement of objects, use of light, and use of color.

ing effects on people.[59] Some researchers have suggested that these associations may have been formed early in human history, when humans associated blues and greens with nature and nighttime—and therefore with being passive—and bright colors with sunshine and daytime—and therefore with being active.[60]

The ten channels by which we communicate with others nonverbally encompass almost all our senses, making nonverbal communication a truly engaging experience. A brief summary of these nonverbal channels appears in the "At a Glance" box on the previous page. Although we have addressed the question of *how* we communicate nonverbally, we have yet to discuss *why* we do so. Now that we are familiar with the various forms nonverbal communication can take, let's look at the functions it can serve.

Learn It: What are three primary communicative functions of the face? How is eye behavior affected by culture? When is a gesture an emblem? Why is touch the most important sense for survival? Which aspects of the voice are verbal and which are nonverbal? How does smell affect memory and sexual attraction? What are Hall's four spatial zones? What is the halo effect? How does the use of time communicate messages about value? What is an artifact?

Try It: Dress in conservative business attire, and visit a restaurant, a department store, a bank, or some other business. Take note of how quickly you are helped by the employees and how friendly and eager they are to serve you. Now repeat the experiment in casual or run-down clothing. What differences do you notice in other people's behaviors toward you? What differences do you notice in your own behavior?

Reflect on It: What olfactic associations do you have? Why do you think the halo effect is so powerful?

3} Functions of Nonverbal Communication {

We have seen that nonverbal behaviors come in many forms, or channels. People also use these channels for many reasons. In this section, we will take a look at six common functions that nonverbal communication serves in personal relationships:

- Managing conversations
- Expressing emotions
- Maintaining relationships
- Forming impressions
- Influencing others
- Concealing information

> *What you are speaks so loudly that I cannot hear what you say.*
>
> —Ralph Waldo Emerson (1803–1882)
> U.S. American essayist, poet, philosopher

Managing Conversations

Even though conversations involve the exchange of verbal communication, we use several nonverbal behaviors to help our conversations with others go smoothly. In particular, nonverbal cues assist us in inviting, maintaining, and ending conversations.

Inviting conversations. Imagine you've just arrived at a crowded holiday party being thrown by your partner's company. Your partner is running late, so you're left to interact with others until he arrives. Unfortunately, you can't spot anyone you know very well. How, then, do you decide with whom you'll strike up a conversation?

Research suggests that three nonverbal cues are especially relevant for inviting conversations: proxemics, personal appearance, and eye contact. First, you're most likely to initiate conversations with people who are physically closest to you than with people who are farther away.[61] Therefore, whom you happen to be standing by partly determines whom you'll talk to. Second, you'll be more inclined to initiate conversations with people you find physically attractive.[62] Because attractive people are often sought out as conversational partners, you may not always be successful in striking up conversations with them. Their physical attractiveness, though, will often motive you to try. Finally, you'll be more likely to talk with people who make eye contact with you than with people who don't.[63] Conversely, when people avoid making eye contact with you, they're often signaling that they're unavailable for conversation.

Maintaining conversations. Let's say you've struck up a conversation with Miriam, an accountant in the company's international division. You'll probably use gestures, eye contact, and tone of voice as **turn-taking signals.** Turn-taking signals are nonverbal signs that indicate when each person's speaking turns begin and end. For example, you might raise a finger, a gesture that indicates you have something to say or that signals to Miriam that you're not yet finished with your speaking turn. Eye contact can serve similar turn-taking functions. Research shows that most of us maintain more eye contact with a conversational partner when we're listening than when we're speaking.[64] You can therefore withhold eye contact while you're speaking as a way of signaling that you're not yet done with your turn. When you're ready to give the speaking turn back to Miriam, then you can reestablish eye contact with her.

In addition to using gestures and eye contact to indicate turn taking, we use tone of voice to signal changes in the conversation.[65] When you're talking but want to give the speaking turn back to Miriam, for instance, you can let the pitch of your voice drop at the end of your last statement. This nonverbal cue would indicate that you're about to finish speaking. You might also let your vocal pitch rise at the end of your last statement, as though it were a question, inviting Miriam's response. Using and exchanging these nonverbal turn-taking signals will help your conversation flow smoothly.

Ending conversations. Suppose that while you're talking to Miriam, you notice out of the corner of your eye that your partner has just arrived at the party. You decide, therefore, to wrap up your conversation with Miriam so you can go and greet him. It would be rude simply to walk away in the middle of your conversation. How, then, can you end the conversation politely? One way would be to say, "I see that my partner has just arrived; it's been nice talking with you." If you choose not to be that direct, however, you can also employ nonverbal *leave-taking behaviors,* which are signals that you are ready to end a conversation.

Research suggests that changes in eye behavior and posture are particularly common as strategies for ending a conversation. When communication scholar Mark Knapp and his colleagues induced experimental participants to try to end conversations, the most frequent nonverbal leave-taking behavior was breaking eye contact.[66] As we just discussed, we tend to look at people when we're listening to them. Therefore, one way you could signal to Miriam that you're ready to end your conversation is to break eye contact with her.

A second strategy would be to angle your posture away from Miriam and toward the direction in which you wish to go, which in this case

> **Turn-taking signal** Nonverbal behavior that indicates when a person's speaking turn begins and ends.

would be toward your partner. This behavior is called *left-positioning,* and it signals that you are preparing yourself to leave the site of the conversation.[67]

Expressing Emotions

As you may have observed in this chapter, many nonverbal behaviors communicate information about a person's emotional state. This fact is consequential for interpersonal communication because our emotions can influence our behavior in multiple ways. When we're angry or frustrated, for instance, we may be less patient with others than we usually are. Similarly, when we're nervous or frightened we may be more withdrawn or cautious. Interpreting another person's emotions can therefore give us clues about how best to interact with that person. The two most expressive nonverbal channels for emotion are facial expressions and vocal behaviors.

Facial expressions of emotion. Many of us "wear" our emotions on our face.[68] Facial expression is such a central part of our experience as social beings that we begin signaling our emotions through facial displays very early in life. For instance, studies have shown that infants begin smiling in response to external stimuli, such as a pleasant voice or touch, around the end of the first month of life.[69] By 10 months of age, most infants smile more in the presence of a parent than a stranger, suggesting they are happier when the parent is present.[70] Another indicator of the importance of facial emotion displays is that they show considerable consistency across cultures.[71] If you're happy, therefore, you'll express it in much the same way regardless of whether you grew up in Laos, Chad, Pakistan, Belgium, Estonia, or Costa Rica.

Vocal expressions of emotion. The voice is also remarkably emotionally expressive.[72] We sometimes can tell how a person is feeling not by what he or she says but by the way his or her voice sounds. Experimental research on vocal displays of emotion has shown that many emotions affect the pitch of the voice. Specifically, the emotions of anger, surprise, happiness, fear, and affection tend to cause a higher-than-normal vocal pitch, whereas disgust, boredom, and extreme grief are conveyed by a lower vocal pitch.[73] Sadness, unless it is extreme, typically does not cause the pitch of the voice to change.[74]

Several emotions also influence a person's rate of speech. Research indicates that we speak much faster than normal when we're scared, slightly faster than normal when we're angry, slightly slower than normal when we're sad, and much slower than normal when we're disgusted.[75] With respect to happiness, some studies have shown that we talk faster than normal when we're happy, but others have concluded that we talk slower than normal.[76] One possible explanation for these contradictory results is that our speech becomes faster when we're excited but slower when we're content.

Although facial displays and vocal behaviors are the most emotionally expressive nonverbal channels, other nonverbal behaviors also convey a person's emotional state.[77] For example, hostile emotions, such as anger, disgust, and jealousy, often involve particular movements, such as slamming doors or gritting one's teeth. At other times, we express them by moving toward the other person and touching him or her in an aggressive manner. Finally, they often lead us to spend time apart from the person toward whom we feel angry, disgusted, or jealous.

Going further, we commonly convey sadness and anxiety through slouched posture and slow movement, excessive fidgeting, and frequent use of self-adaptors, such as scratching your head or picking lint off your shirt. Finally, when we feel happy or affectionate we are more likely to spend time with others, to enhance our physical appearance, to give gifts, and to engage in mutual eye contact with those around us.

Maintaining Relationships

Think about the relationships that matter most to you. They might include current or former romantic relationships, your close friendships, work partnerships, and your relationships with family members. How do you maintain each of these important relationships, ensuring that it doesn't end? Communication plays a central role in how most of us maintain our relationships, and nonverbal behaviors are especially important for several key features of relationships. These behaviors include attraction and affiliation, power and dominance, and arousal and relaxation.

Attraction and affiliation. Many nonverbal behaviors send messages of attraction or affiliation. Researchers call these **immediacy behaviors.** When two people flirt, for example, they use their eye contact to signal attraction; they stand or sit close to each other; they touch each other playfully; and they use expressive tones of voice to convey the message that they are interested in each other.[78] People in many cultures use these same types of behaviors in initial interactions to signal that they are attracted to each other and wish to explore the possibility of future interaction.[79]

Immediacy behavior Nonverbal behavior that conveys attraction or affiliation.

In more established relationships, nonverbal behavior is a common means of expressing affection and love. We hug, kiss, and hold hands with the people we love, and we speak to them in softer and higher-pitched tones of voice. These kinds of behaviors help to reinforce feelings of affiliation, intimacy, and love, whether with our romantic partners, our family members, or our friends.[80]

Power and dominance. Power is the potential to affect another person's behavior, and dominance is the actual exercise of that potential. Adults often convey messages about their power and status using nonverbal behavior. For example, supervisors touch subordinates more than subordinates touch superiors, and a powerful person is more likely to keep a less-powerful person waiting than vice versa.[81] As we discussed earlier, many of us also use artifacts as status symbols. For instance, we might hang college diplomas on our office walls to signal our level of education or leave our expensive cars parked conspicuously in the driveway to signal our wealth.

People also use nonverbal behaviors to assert dominance and control over others. Teachers do this anytime they use a certain look to convey disapproval about a child's behavior. Police officers control drivers' behaviors when they hold up a hand to signal "stop." Finally, some of us use silence to stop others from continuing to speak when we're in an uncomfortable conversation. In these and many other ways, one person's nonverbal behavior can be used to control the behavior of other people.

Arousal and relaxation. You may have noticed that some interpersonal interactions are physically and emotionally arousing, such as describing an exciting vacation or a significant health scare to a close friend. Other interactions cause you to feel physically and emotionally calm and relaxed, such as discussing the day's mundane events with your neighbor. Several nonverbal behaviors provide clues to those around us about whether we're feeling aroused or relaxed at any given moment.

Arousal refers simply to an increase in energy. We experience arousal in two fundamentally different ways depending on whether it is accompanied by positive or negative emotions. When it is accompanied by positive emotions, we experience it as excitement. Most of us express excitement through nonverbal cues such as an increase in eye contact with others, more laughter, faster rate of speech, higher vocal pitch and volume, and closer proximity to others.[82] When arousal is accompanied by negative emotions, however, we experience it as anxiety. Feeling anxious tends to cause fidgeting and random movement, nervous smiling or laughter, the use of more gestures and self-adaptors, higher vocal pitch and rate of speech, and the use of more filler words.[83]

The opposite of arousal is relaxation, which we feel in situations of decreased energy. As with arousal, we experience relaxation in two different ways depending on the emotion involved. When relaxation is accompanied by positive emotion, we experience it as contentment. Feeling content leads most of us to smile more than usual, have a more relaxed posture, and increase our eye contact with and proximity to those around us.[84]

In contrast, when relaxation is accompanied by negative emotion, we experience it as depression. Some people suffer from clinical depression, a psychiatric disorder thought to be caused by problems with chemicals called neurotransmitters, which relay signals between neurons and other cells in the brain.[85] Others just feel down from time to time, experiencing some of the symptoms of depression without the underlying psychiatric problems. In either case, feeling depressed often leads people to smile less, make less frequent eye contact, and use fewer gestures and more self-adaptors.[86]

Forming Impressions

Many of us enjoy people-watching. While sitting in a coffee shop, waiting at the airport, or strolling through the mall, we notice other people. We pay attention to what they look like, what they sound like, and how they behave, and we use those pieces of information to form impressions about who they are. Although our impressions are influenced by what people say, they are also strongly affected by their nonverbal

People use touch for many purposes, including showing affection, providing care, and exercising power.

behaviors. In particular, nonverbal cues influence two general types of impressions, those related to a person's demographic characteristics and those related to a person's sociocultural characteristics.

Demographic impressions. A person's demographic characteristics include his or her age, ethnic background, sex, and sexual orientation. Research indicates that, on the basis of visual cues, most of us can accurately classify a person into broad categories for age—such as infant, teenager, or elderly adult—and ethnicity—such as Asian, Hispanic, or white.[87] Making finer distinctions, such as whether a woman is 50 or 60 years old or whether a man is Cambodian or Vietnamese, is often more challenging. Similarly, most people can correctly identify an individual's biological sex by attending to visual cues such as the shape of the face and the body, hairstyle, clothing, jewelry, and cosmetics.[88] These studies don't indicate that we're necessarily going to be right 100% of the time, however. Can you think of instances when you've been unsure of a person's sex, ethnicity, or age on the basis of his or her appearance?

Although patterns in anatomy and physiology provide relatively reliable visual cues about a person's age, ethnicity, and sex, a person's sexual orientation is not as distinguishable using those same cues.[89] Although members of sexual minorities might adopt distinctive styles of clothing that can signal their sexual orientation, homosexual and bisexual women and men don't necessarily differ from heterosexual women and men in any of their physical characteristics.[90] As a result, sexual orientation is not as reliably determined as other demographic characteristics on the basis of visual cues.

The voice is another nonverbal channel that helps us form demographic impressions of others. Vocal behaviors tend to be particularly good clues as to a person's age, sex, and sexual orientation. As people age, for instance, their vocal pitch and rate of speech typically decrease.[91] Consequently, many of us can determine a person's age with relative accuracy by listening to the sound of his or her voice.[92] By the same token, women and men's voices differ from each other in average pitch and vocal quality.[93] As a result, listeners can distinguish between male and female adult voices with nearly perfect accuracy.[94] We tend to be less accurate at determining sex on the basis of children's voices, however, since vocal characteristics don't differ between the sexes as much before puberty as after it.[95]

Several studies have also shown that people can reliably use vocal cues to distinguish heterosexual from homosexual or bisexual adults.[96] Research on the acoustic properties of people's voices has found that lesbian, gay, and bisexual adults articulate the "e," "i," and "u" vowel sounds more clearly than do heterosexual adults.[97] Moreover, gay men's voices articulate the "s" consonant sound more clearly than do heterosexual men's voices,[98] but they do not differ in average pitch or inflection.[99]

Vocal behaviors can suggest a person's age, sex, and sexual orientation, but they do not reliably indicate a person's ethnic background. Some vocal characteristics, such as average pitch, do systematically differ among some ethnic groups.[100] These differences are small, however. Generally speaking, most people cannot accurately discriminate among ethnic groups on the basis of vocal cues unless they are specifically trained to do so.[101]

Sociocultural impressions. When you watch people in restaurants, on public transportation, or in the aisles of the supermarket, you might form an idea about their demographic features, but you're probably more likely to speculate about their sociocultural characteristics. One such characteristic is socioeconomic status, which is an index of how much money and education a person has and how prestigious his or her career is. Another sociocultural feature reflects the cultures and co-cultures to which people belong, such as whether someone is British, Filipino, or Venezuelan, or identifies with surfers, feminists, or bird-watchers.

Personal appearance is usually the most informative nonverbal channel for forming sociocultural impressions. When you see a woman in an expensive, tailored business suit, for instance, you're likely to infer that she is of higher socioeconomic status than a woman wearing torn jeans and a sweatshirt.[102] You may not be accurate in your impression of these particular women, but the quality of a person's clothing is a relatively reliable visual cue to his or her socioeconomic status, for two reasons. First, compared with people with limited economic resources, people with greater resources can usually afford more expensive clothing and may also be more likely to work in occupations in which dressier attire is required. Second, people often use personal appearance cues to signify their socioeconomic status, so higher-status people may wear expensive clothing or jewelry to convey or symbolize their good fortune.[103]

Many organized co-cultural groups, such as those associated with particular sports interests or music preferences, adopt fashions that identify their members. You might infer, therefore, that a young man in a football jersey and tennis shoes is a sports fan, whereas a young woman in black pants and a black shirt featuring a skull and crossbones is into alternative rock. Similarly, studies have shown that we can accurately distinguish between people with conservative and liberal political ideologies on the basis of how conventional their clothing styles are.[104] You might accurately infer, therefore, that a young man in a button-down shirt and cotton pants has more conservative political views than a young man in ripped jeans and a T-shirt denouncing U.S. foreign policy. Unless people are wearing traditional cultural attire, such as the kimono for Japan or the kilt for Scotland, personal appearance generally is not a reliable clue about their cultural backgrounds.

Many people believe they can identify a person's socioeconomic status by the sound of his or her voice. Studies that have tested this idea have found that although people are highly *consistent* in the socioeconomic impressions they form on the basis of vocal cues, they are not very *accurate*.[105] That means people may strongly agree with one another on the socioeconomic status that a particular voice represents, but they will often be incorrect. The voice is also a poor indicator of a person's co-cultural affiliations, making it difficult to identify people's interests, hobbies, or religious orientations on the basis of how their voices sound.[106]

Research does suggest, however, that we may be able to identify a person's cultural background on the basis of his or her vocal accent. As you learned earlier in this chapter, a person's accent is largely determined by the region in which he or she was raised. Speakers native to Taiwan, Finland, Brazil, the Ivory Coast, Mexico, and Australia would therefore speak with distinctive accents that we might be able to identify.[107]

Our ability to identify people's cultural backgrounds diminishes, however, when we try to differentiate people from cultures with similar languages (and thus similar accents). For example, we may not be able to distinguish an Australian accent from a British one, a Korean accent from a Japanese one, or a Finnish accent from a Swedish one unless we have particular familiarity with those accents. In general, however, vocal accents can provide us with cues about a person's cultural background.

Influencing Others

You probably find yourself in many social situations in which you wish to influence other people's behaviors. Perhaps you're trying to persuade your co-workers and friends to sponsor you in a marathon for cancer research. Maybe you're trying to talk your elderly grandfather into considering a move to an assisted care facility. You might just be trying to get the diners on whose table you're waiting to leave you a good tip. In these and many other contexts, you can use nonverbal behaviors to influence others. Nonverbal communication can be persuasive when it is applied as part of several strategies, including creating credibility, promoting affiliation, and maximizing attractiveness.

Creating credibility One of the most effective strategies for influencing other people's behaviors is to project an image of credibility. We often do this by adopting a personal appearance that conveys expertise and authority. Consider uniforms as an example. A judge's black robes, a doctor's white lab coat, and a police officer's badge and uniform all symbolize particular forms of experience and authority.[108] Several studies have shown that we not only consider people in uniform to have more credibility than people in lay clothing but also are actually more likely to comply with their requests.[109] The same is also true of formal business attire, such as suits and dresses. People are more persuaded by requests made by people in business attire than by people dressed in more casual clothing.[110] The most likely reason for this higher rate of compliance is that professional attire projects a higher level of credibility than casual attire does.

There are other nonverbal behaviors you can use to enhance your credibility. For instance, speaking loudly, quickly, and expressively, with a good deal of pitch variation, makes a person sound more credible.[111] Research shows that in the legal profession, attorneys who speak loudly and fluently, with fewer slips of the tongue, not only are seen as highly credible but also earn more favorable decisions.[112] The use of eye contact and illustrator gestures also enhances a person's credibility.[113] In particular, maintaining eye contact with someone while you're speaking, instead of only while you're listening, has been shown to be a powerful influence on persuasiveness.[114]

Promoting affiliation. Suppose you were asking people to help you pack up your belongings and move to a new condo across town. Whom would you ask? Most of us would approach family members and close friends, as opposed to people we hardly know or who dislike us. The reason we would select these individuals is that we are more persuaded by people we like than by people we don't.[115] Nonverbal behaviors that promote a sense of affiliation, closeness, and liking can therefore enhance our persuasive ability.

One behavior that often contributes to a sense of affiliation is touch.[116] Because we share more touch within close relationships than casual ones, being touched in appropriate, familiar ways can make us feel close to others. Several experiments have demonstrated that casual touches—such as a brief touch to the hand, forearm, or shoulder—make people more likely to comply with our requests. In one study, for instance, waitresses received significantly larger tips when they briefly touched customers on the hand or the shoulder as they were returning change.[117] Other studies have concluded that being touched increases our willingness to comply with another person's requests or to help a person in need.[118]

Affiliation is also enhanced by interactional synchrony, which is the convergence of two people's behaviors. When you mirror another person's posture, gestures, facial expressions, or vocal behaviors, you may cause that person subconsciously to perceive you as similar to him or her.[119] This perception is consequential for persuasion, because we like people who are similar to us.[120]

Let's say that you're preparing to make a persuasive appeal to the president of your homeowners' association to allow holiday decorations to be placed on front lawns, which the association's policies currently prohibit. You've noticed that the president usually speaks slowly and deliberately during association meetings. When you visit with him one-on-one, therefore, you intentionally match his slow rate of speech, even though you usually speak more quickly. This strategy puts you in vocal synchrony with your listener. Multiple studies suggest that you will be more persuasive as a result.[121]

Maximizing attractiveness. You may have noticed that models who appear in television commercials and print ads tend to be physically attractive. Advertisers hope that if you see an attractive person using their product, you'll be more persuaded to buy that product. Guess what—they're right![122] Physical attractiveness makes a person more persuasive.

Significantly, this observation isn't limited to models in commercials. Several studies have shown that even in our interpersonal conversations, we are more influenced by attractive than unattractive people.[123] One likely explanation for this behavior is that because we value physical attractiveness, we want to identify with and be liked by attractive people, and this desire leads us to comply with their requests.[124]

Nonverbal behaviors that maximize our physical attractiveness can therefore increase our interpersonal influence. Physical appearance cues, such as dress, hairstyle, use of cosmetics, and use of jewelry, can all be manipulated to make a person look more attractive. Multiple studies have demonstrated that good-looking people are more influential than unattractive people in a variety of contexts, including job interviews,[125] salary negotiations,[126] college admission decisions,[127] and requests for assistance from others.[128]

Although physical appearance is the most relevant nonverbal channel when it comes to perceptions of physical attractiveness, some evidence suggests that other channels affect how attractive we perceive someone to be. One study, for example, explored whether smell would affect the perception of physical attractiveness. In a field experiment, communication researcher Kelly Aune had female research assistants approach male and female undergraduate students to ask if they could be interviewed about their library usage. The assistants explained that they were enrolled in an interviewing class and would be asking the students to evaluate them at the end of the interview. The evaluations included an assessment of the assistants' physical attractiveness. Assistants conducted the interviews while wearing either no perfume, a small amount of perfume, a moderate amount, or a heavy amount.

Aune found that male students rated the assistants as most physically attractive when they wore a small amount of perfume. In contrast, female students claimed the confederates were most attractive when they wore no perfume. Because the assistants were the same women in all conditions, these results indicate that how a person *smells* can affect how attractive other people think she *looks*.[129]

Perceptions of physical attractiveness also appear to be influenced by the attractiveness of the person's voice. Two experiments have demonstrated that the more pleasant a woman's voice sounds, the more physically attractive she is judged to be.[130] Whether these findings extend to the smells and voices of men is still unknown.

Your personal appearance, clothing, and demeanor can give you the credibility to influence others.

All these studies suggest that attractiveness is an advantage for influencing other people's behavior. There's a dark side to this observation, however. Because physical attractiveness is so highly valued, some people go to dangerous extremes to achieve it. As you'll see in the "Dark Side" box, one of the unfortunate effects of the quest for beauty is the prevalence of eating disorders.

Concealing Information

The final function of nonverbal communication is to help people conceal information. Despite the cultural adage that "honesty is the best policy," people frequently decide not to be entirely truthful in their conversations with others. As you'll discover in Chapter 11, "Deceptive Communication," we have many reasons for choosing to conceal information. Sometimes people lie to benefit themselves, such as faking an illness to get out of work. Sometimes they lie to avoid hurting themselves, such as concealing marital infidelity. Often, however, people choose to be deceptive to avoid hurting others—for example, by saying they're happy to receive a gift that they actually dislike.

Whatever our reasons for concealing information, however, research indicates that certain facial, vocal behaviors, and kinesic behaviors are reliably associated with deception. We address these behaviors briefly in this section and then discuss them more fully in Chapter 11.

FASHION PLATE

Stop Starvation Imagery
CREATE AN ABOUT-FACE: DON'T FALL FOR THE MEDIA CIRCUS

measures to achieve thinness. For instance, some people undergo a procedure called vertical banded gastroplasty—better known as "stomach stapling"—which surgically alters the stomach to restrict food intake so that the patient will lose weight. A different procedure called abdomino-plasty—better known as a "tummy tuck"—surgically removes excess skin and fat from a person's abdomen to make her or him appear thinner.

including gastrointestinal disorders, clinical depression, and tooth decay (as a result of frequent purging). About 4% of U.S. females and 0.4% of U.S. males between the ages of 10 and 20 suffer from bulimia.

Even people without eating disorders can take extreme

Ask Yourself:

- Why do you suppose thinness is considered attractive in so many cultures, particularly for women?

- Besides developing eating disorders, what are some other examples of dangerous extremes to which people will go in their quest for attractiveness?

From Me to You:

- If you've never had an eating disorder, it might be easy to dismiss anorexia and bulimia as merely the result of narcissism, an unhealthy obsession with the self. In a similar vein, people who have never experienced clinical depression sometimes wonder why depressed patients can't simply "snap out of it." Eating disorders and depression are illnesses, however. People suffering from these disorders need treatment from the medical community, and they also need compassion and support from their relatives and friends.

Sources: National Institute of Mental Health: http://www.nimh.nih.gov/health/publications/eating-disorders/what-are-eating-disorders.shtml; National Eating Disorders Association: www.nationaleatingdisorders.org.

We begin our discussion by examining facial behaviors. One of the most commonly studied facial behaviors that can indicate deception is smiling. Most research studies have found that people don't differ in *how much* they smile when they're being honest as opposed to being deceptive. Rather, they differ in *how* they smile.[131] When we're telling the truth, we're more likely to use genuine smiles that reflect actual positive emotion. This is the kind of smile we display when we hear really good news or smell a delicious dinner cooking in the oven. When we're being dishonest, however, we're more likely to use false smiles to make it appear as though we're happy even though we aren't. This is the smile you display when you run into a coworker you don't like and are trying to appear happy to see him. Both types of smiles draw the edges of the mouth upward, but genuine smiles also cause the skin around the eyes to wrinkle, whereas false smiles do not.

Attempting to conceal information can also influence certain vocal behaviors, particularly the pitch of the voice. Several studies have demonstrated that people speak with a higher pitch when they are deceiving than when they're telling the truth.[132] In one study, for instance, student nurses were asked to watch either a pleasant nature film or a grotesque film depicting amputations and burns. After viewing each film, the student nurses were told to convince an interviewer that the film they had just watched was pleasant and enjoyable. In one condition, therefore, the students were to be truthful, and in the other they were to be deceptive. By recording the participants' voices and analyzing them later, the researchers determined that the students' vocal

At a Glance: Six Functions of Nonverbal Communication

Managing conversations	Nonverbal cues are used to invite, maintain, and end conversations.
Expressing emotions	Facial and vocal channels are particularly expressive.
Maintaining relationships	Nonverbal behaviors signal attraction and affiliation, power and dominance, arousal and relaxation.
Forming impressions	Nonverbal cues are useful in forming demographic and sociocultural impressions.
Influencing others	Strategies include creating credibility, promoting affiliation, maximizing attractiveness.
Concealing information	Facial behaviors, eye behaviors, vocal behaviors, and kinesic behaviors are most useful.

pitch was significantly higher when they were attempting to deceive the interviewer than when they were telling the truth.[133]

Finally, certain kinesic behaviors indicate that a person is concealing information. Because being deceptive generally makes people feel nervous, you might expect it would also cause an increase in body movements that are commonly associated with anxiety, including gesturing, forward leaning, and random hand and foot movements.[134] You may be surprised to learn, then, that most studies have shown just the opposite. That is, kinesic behavior decreases, rather than increases, when people are being dishonest.[135] In particular, speakers use fewer illustrator gestures, fewer hand and finger movements, fewer foot and leg movements, and fewer forward leans when they are lying than when they are telling the truth.[136]

One explanation for this decreased body movement is that people try too hard to control signs of nervousness when they're being deceptive and they end up looking rigid or tense as a result.[137] An alternative theory suggests that we simply don't think about engaging in body movement when we're deceiving because our minds are so focused on the lie itself.[138] Whatever the reason, decreased kinesic behavior appears to be a reliable cue to deception.

Managing conversations, expressing emotions, maintaining relationships, forming impressions, influencing others, and concealing information are not the only functions of nonverbal behavior, but they are among the most valuable. In its own way, each of these functions helps us to communicate with others in efficient, productive ways. A summary of these functions appears in the "At a Glance" box above.

Learn It: What are leave-taking behaviors? How do people communicate emotion vocally? Which nonverbal behaviors convey power and dominance in personal relationships? How are demographic and sociocultural impressions different? What are three major strategies for influencing others? Which facial and eye behaviors are most reliably associated with deception?

4} Improving Your Nonverbal Communication Skills {

In the NBC television comedy series *The Office,* actor Steve Carell plays Michael Scott, the regional manager of a paper distribution company who can accurately be described as socially awkward. In conversations with employees and customers, he often has difficulty expressing some of his emotions, using inappropriate humor to mask feelings of insecurity or inadequacy. At the same time, he frequently fails to notice when other people react negatively to his communication style. Although he tries to get others to like him and even comes across as a likable character, he is not a particularly skilled nonverbal communicator. In this section, we'll explore some ways you can improve two fundamental communication skills: interpreting nonverbal communication and expressing messages verbally.

> *A body talks.*
>
> —Anne Parillaud (1960–)
> French actress

Interpreting Nonverbal Communication

As you've discovered in this chapter, people use nonverbal communication to express many types of messages, including messages related to emotions and attitudes, power and dominance, persuasion, and deception. An important skill for communicators, therefore, is the ability to decode, or interpret, other people's nonverbal behaviors. This ability requires two separate but interrelated skills: being sensitive to, and deciphering the meaning of, messages.

Be sensitive to nonverbal messages. One skill involved in interpreting nonverbal communication is being sensitive to other people's nonverbal messages. When your daughter grimaces after learning you're having broccoli for dinner or your son has an excited tone in his voice when he describes his last fencing bout, do you notice those nonverbal emotion cues? When a competitor at work intentionally keeps you waiting for an appointment or seems unusually tense during your conversation, do you pick up on those potential signs of dominance or deception?

Sensitivity to nonverbal behaviors is important because we can't interpret messages unless we first take note of them. Although research tells us that some people are more nonverbally sensitive by nature than others, you may be able to increase your own nonverbal sensitivity through mindful awareness.[139] When you're interacting with someone, try these approaches:

- Remind yourself that as much as two-thirds of his or her communication is being conveyed through nonverbal behaviors. It's useful to interpret his or her words, but remember that nonverbal communication is often more important.

Just as facial behavior communicates more than any other nonverbal channel, the eyes communicate more than any other part of the face.

- Pay particular attention to facial expressions for signs of what he or she is feeling. Remember that the face communicates more emotion than other nonverbal channels do.
- Don't forget to take note of his or her tone of voice and body movements, because those behaviors are particularly relevant for signaling dominance and deception.

To the extent that you can remind yourself of these principles when you are interacting with others, you may be able to increase your nonverbal sensitivity. Being aware of others' nonverbal behaviors is only half of the interpretation process, however. As we'll see, to interpret nonverbal communication effectively you must learn to decipher the meaning of the messages you perceive.

Decipher the meaning of nonverbal messages. Nonverbal messages sometimes carry multiple meanings. If you notice a young man smiling, for instance, it might mean he's happy. It might also mean, however, that he's persuading a customer to make a purchase, giving comfort to a relative who has just shared bad news, or flirting with his attractive new neighbor.[140] If you hear him speaking loudly, it might mean he's excited, or it might mean he's angry, or surprised, or talking with someone who's hard of hearing.

An essential part of interpretation, therefore, is deciphering the meaning of the nonverbal behaviors exhibited by the people with whom you're communicating. Accurately deciphering a nonverbal behavior means taking it to mean what the sender intended it to mean.[141] Suppose that while you are describing your grandmother's failing health to your friend Vanessa, she squeezes your hand to convey her support. If you take her behavior as a gesture of support, then you have accurately deciphered her nonverbal message. If you interpret it to mean she's interested in you romantically, however, then you have deciphered her message inaccurately.

To improve your skill at deciphering nonverbal messages, try the following strategies:

Be aware of the situation. Consider both the social situation a person is in and what other nonverbal behaviors he or she is enacting. If you notice a man crying, for instance, your first instinct might be to conclude that he's sad. Perhaps you also notice, however, that he is surrounded by smiling friends and relatives who are hugging him and patting him on the back. You even hear him laugh, although tears are running down his face. When you take these additional pieces of information into consideration, you might take his crying to mean that he is happy or relieved, rather than sad.

Keep culture in mind. Remember that cultural differences sometimes influence the meaning of a nonverbal message. This observation appears to be particularly true for gestures and eye behaviors. We've seen, for instance, that using the thumbs-up gesture or maintaining eye contact while talking with someone can have different meanings in different cultures. The more you learn about cultural variation in nonverbal behaviors, therefore, the more accurately you'll be able to decipher those behaviors.

Keep cultural differences in mind when you interpret nonverbal behavior. Although kissing often conveys romantic feelings in Western cultures, it is a common component of routine social greetings in many parts of the world.

Ask for clarification. When you're unsure of how accurately you've deciphered a person's nonverbal message, it often helps to ask the person. Let's say you're describing the details of a new product to a client, and her facial expression suggests that she's confused. Instead of assuming you've deciphered her expression accurately, you might simply ask her, "Did my description make sense?" If she replies that she found it confusing, then you can explain the product again using simpler language. Instead, however, she may reply that she is developing a headache. In that case the expression you deciphered as confusion was actually one of discomfort.

In sum, then, practicing your sensitivity and deciphering skills should help you to improve your ability to interpret the meaning of nonverbal behaviors.[142]

Expressing Nonverbal Messages

Some of us are good at *interpreting* nonverbal behaviors but are not particularly good at *expressing* ourselves nonverbally. Skill at expressing nonverbal messages is valuable for the same reason that interpretation skill is: because people communicate more information nonverbally than verbally. If you're skilled at expressing nonverbal messages, therefore, you'll be able to communicate with other people more effectively and more efficiently than someone who is less skilled.

Just as with interpretation skills, some people are naturally more expressive, charismatic, and outgoing than others.[143] To improve your own skill at expressing nonverbal messages, however, try the following ideas:

Learn from others. Spend time with people who are highly expressive. Some researchers have suggested that we can learn how to become more nonverbally expressive by being around people who are extroverted and charismatic.[144] Perhaps you have friends or co-workers who fit this description. Research also suggests that certain professions attract highly expressive people. These professions include teachers and lecturers, actors and singers, politicians, salespeople, diplomats, customer service representatives, counselors and therapists, and members of the clergy.[145] To perform effectively in any of these professions an individual must be able to communicate clearly and competently with others. Being nonverbally expressive is a key component of competent communication.

Practice being expressive. Take part in games and activities that exercise your nonverbal expression skills. A good example is playing charades, a popular game in which you act out a word or a phrase without speaking while members of your team try to guess the word based on your depiction. Because success in charades depends on your ability to depict your word or phrase nonverbally, this game can be a good exercise of your expression skill. Another activity that can improve your nonverbal expression skills is role playing, which involves acting out the roles of characters in a specific situation the way you would if you were actually in that situation. Role playing is often used in couples' therapy.[146] The therapist asks a couple to act out an argument that is common in their relationship, for instance, but instructs each partner to take the role of the other in the conversation. Like playing charades, role playing may give you an opportunity to exercise your skills in nonverbal expression and improve through practice.

To become skilled at conveying nonverbal messages you need to do more than simply be expressive. You also must learn to express yourself using nonverbal behaviors that other people can interpret accurately. Spending time with people who are skilled at nonverbal expression may help you learn or improve this ability. Similarly, taking part in activities such as charades and role playing can provide you with an opportunity to exercise your skills.

One key strategy to improve your skills at nonverbal interpretation and expression is to assess how skilled you are now. Take a look at the at the "Getting to Know You" box to reflect on and evaluate your interpretation and expression abilities.

Learn It: What is the difference between being sensitive to a nonverbal message and deciphering its meaning? What are some professions in which you would commonly find highly expressive people?

Try It: Record an episode of one of your favorite television shows, then watch a few minutes of it with the sound turned off. Pay attention to the characters' nonverbal behaviors, and try to figure out what emotions they are experiencing. Once you have an idea of a character's emotion, ask yourself what other conclusions you might have come to with the information available to you. Then, watch the same few minutes again with the sound turned on to determine how accurate you were.

Reflect on It: Which nonverbal behaviors are you the most sensitive to, and which ones are you least likely to notice in others? Why is your ability to express yourself nonverbally important?

Getting to Know You
Your Nonverbal Interpretation and Expression Skills

How much do you agree with each of the following statements? Indicate your level of agreement with each statement on a scale of 1 to 7, wherein 1 means you strongly disagree and 7 means you strongly agree.

1. _____ When I feel depressed, I tend to bring down those around me.
2. _____ It is nearly impossible for people to hide their true feelings from me.
3. _____ I have been told that I have "expressive" eyes.
4. _____ At parties I can instantly tell when someone is interested in me.
5. _____ Quite often I tend to be the "life of the party."
6. _____ People often tell me that I am a sensitive and understanding person.

When you're finished, add up your scores from items 1, 3, and 5. This is your score for expressiveness. Next, add up your scores from items 2, 4, and 6. This is your score for interpretation. Both scores should range from 3 to 21.

If both scores are between 16 and 21, then you are already quite good at nonverbal interpretation and expressiveness. If your scores are between 9 and 15, you have a moderate ability to interpret and express nonverbal behavior, and the suggestions offered in this chapter may help you sharpen these abilities. If your scores are between 3 and 8, then you especially can benefit from the guidance provided in this chapter for improving these skills. You may also find that one of your scores is quite a bit higher than the other. If that's the case, then you know which skill you're already good at and which skill could benefit from more practice.

Source: Riggio, R. E. (1986). Assessment of basic social skills. *Journal of Personality and Social Psychology, 51*, 649–660.

} Master the Chapter {

Section 1} The Nature of Nonverbal Communication (page 209)

I. The Nature of Nonverbal Communication
   A. What is nonverbal communication?

   - Nonverbal communication comprises those behaviors and characteristics that convey meaning without the use of words.

   B. Five characteristics of nonverbal communication
      1. Nonverbal communication is present in most interpersonal conversations
      2. Nonverbal communication often conveys more information than verbal communication
      3. Nonverbal communication is usually believed over verbal communication

   - Nonverbal communication has the following characteristics: (a) It is present in most interpersonal conversations, (b) it usually conveys more information than verbal communication, (c) it is usually believed over verbal communication, (d) it is the primary means of communicating emotion, and (e) it is meta-communicative.

4. Nonverbal communication is the primary means of communicating emotion
5. Nonverbal communication is meta-communicative

Section 2} Ten Channels of Nonverbal Communication (page 218)

II. Ten Channels of Nonverbal Communication

A. **Facial displays**
   1. Identity
   2. Attractiveness
   3. Emotion

   - Facial displays are important for identity, attractiveness, and emotion.

B. **Eye behaviors**
   1. Eye contact
   2. Pupil dilation

   - Eye behaviors include eye contact and pupil dilation.

C. **Movement and gestures**
   1. Emblems
   2. Illustrators
   3. Affect displays
   4. Regulators
   5. Adaptors

   - Movement and gestures include emblems, illustrators, affect displays, regulators, and adaptors.

D. **Touch behaviors**
   1. Affectionate touch
   2. Caregiving touch
   3. Power and control touch
   4. Aggressive touch
   5. Ritualistic touch

   - Touch behaviors include affectionate, caregiving, controlling, aggressive, and ritualistic touch.

E. **Vocal behaviors**
   1. Pitch
   2. Inflection
   3. Volume
   4. Rate
   5. Filler words
   6. Pronunciation
   7. Articulation
   8. Accent
   9. Silence

   - Voices vary in pitch, inflection, volume, speaking rate, use of filler words, pronunciation, articulation, silence, and accent.

F. **The use of smell**
   1. Memories
   2. Sexual attraction

   - Smell is particularly important for memories and sexual attraction.

G. **The use of space**

   - People maintain four levels of space: intimate, personal, social, and public.

H. **Physical appearance**

   - Physical appearance is important because we attribute positive qualities to attractive people, a phenomenon called the halo effect.

I. **The use of time**
   1. Messages of value
   2. Messages of power
J. **The use of artifacts**

- The use of time sends messages of value and power.

- We use artifacts to communicate through the selection and placement of objects, the use of light, and the use of color.

Section 3} Functions of Nonverbal Communication (page 235)

III. **Functions of Nonverbal Communication**
   A. **Managing conversations**
      1. Inviting conversations
      2. Maintaining conversations
      3. Ending conversations

- Nonverbal behaviors allow us to invite, maintain, and end conversations.

   B. **Expressing emotions**
      1. Facial expressions of emotion
      2. Vocal expressions of emotion

- Facial and vocal behaviors, in particular, are emotionally expressive.

   C. **Maintaining relationships**
      1. Attraction and affiliation
      2. Power and dominance
      3. Arousal and relaxation

- To maintain relationships, we use nonverbal messages of attraction and affiliation, power and dominance, and arousal and relaxation.

   D. **Forming impressions**
      1. Demographic impressions
      2. Sociocultural impressions

- Nonverbal behaviors help us form demographic and sociocultural impressions of people.

   E. **Influencing others**
      1. Creating credibility
      2. Promoting affiliation
      3. Maximizing attractiveness

- To influence others, we use nonverbal behaviors to create credibility, promote affiliation, and maximize our attractiveness.

   F. **Concealing information**

- Nonverbal behaviors—particularly facial, eye, vocal, and kinesic behaviors—help us conceal information from others.

Section 4} Improving Your Nonverbal Communication Skills (page 247)

IV. **Improving Your Nonverbal Communication Skills.**
   A. **Interpreting nonverbal communication**
      1. Be sensitive to nonverbal messages
      2. Decipher the meaning of nonverbal messages
         a. be aware of the situation
         b. keep culture in mind
         c. ask for clarification

- The ability to interpret nonverbal messages is a function of being sensitive to these messages and deciphering their meanings.

   B. **Expressing nonverbal messages**
      1. Learn from others
      2. Practice being expressive

- The ability to express nonverbal messages can be enhanced by spending time with expressive people and taking part in activities that exercise your expressiveness.

Key Terms

Adaptor
Affect display
Artifact
Chronemics
Emblem
Facial display
Gesticulation
Haptics

High-contact culture
Illustrator
Immediacy behavior
Kinesics
Low-contact culture
Nonverbal channels
Nonverbal communication
Oculesics

Olfactics
Proportionality
Proxemics
Regulator
Symmetry
Turn-taking signal
Vocalics

Discussion Questions

1. What meanings does the use of space convey? When someone has a larger house, a larger office, or a larger seat on the airplane than yours, what conclusions do you make about that person?

2. In what ways would you alter your personal appearance if you were trying to look friendlier? smarter? more liberal? wealthier? What aspects of personal appearance convey these messages?

3. What scent or odor evokes a specific, positive memory for you, and why? How about a specific, negative memory? Is the pleasantness of your memories related to the pleasantness of the odors?

4. How do you feel when someone keeps you waiting? What messages does someone's use of time send you?

5. Touch is a form of nonverbal communication that is highly affected by social and cultural rules. What are some of the rules of touch that you perceive?

6. Why do you suppose we tend to believe nonverbal cues, even when they contradict what a person is saying? Can you think of a situation in which you would believe the person's verbal message instead?

7. The face is very expressive when it comes to communicating emotion. What are some of the characteristics of a surprised face? an angry face? a confused face? a jealous face?

8. People in certain professions, such as baseball umpires or orchestra conductors, create gestures that only have meaning within that profession. What other examples can you think of?

Practice Quiz

Multiple Choice

1. Which of the following is *not* a characteristic of nonverbal communication?
   a. Nonverbal communication is present in most interpersonal conversations.
   b. Nonverbal communication usually conveys more information than verbal communication.
   c. Nonverbal communication is the secondary means of communicating emotion.
   d. Nonverbal communication is meta-communicative.

2. The two characteristics that contribute most to facial attractiveness are:
   a. Symmetry and proportionality
   b. Symmetry and expressiveness
   c. Proportionality and diameter
   d. Proportionality and expressiveness

3. Which of the following phrases correctly defines oculesics?
   a. The study of smell
   b. The study of attractiveness
   c. The study of emotion
   d. The study of eye behavior

4. When Jorge proposed to Janie, she put her hand on her heart to signal how much she loved him. Which type of gesture was she enacting?
   a. Regulator   c. Affect display
   b. Adaptor   d. Emblem

5. The study of haptics concerns which of the following?
   a. How we use touch
   b. How we interpret taste
   c. How we move our eyes
   d. How we use space

6. Which of the following is *not* a major area in which touch plays a critical role in conveying meaning?
   a. Affection   c. Aggression
   b. Caregiving   d. Argumentation

7. When a manicurist touches Suzi's hands while giving her a manicure, which type of touch is Suzi receiving?
   a. Affectionate   c. Ritual
   b. Caregiving   d. Power and control

8. Which of the following vocal behaviors is an index of how high or low a voice sounds?
   a. Inflection   c. Pitch
   b. Volume   d. Rate

9. According to the text, all of the following influence the messages that artifacts convey *except:*
   a. Use of color   c. Placement of objects
   b. Use of light   d. Number of objects

10. Three behaviors that systematically change when people attempt to deceive are:
    a. Smiling, eye blinking, pupil dilation
    b. Eye blinking, fidgeting, wincing
    c. Pupil dilation, wincing, smiling
    d. None of the above

True/False

11. Verbal communication is usually perceived as more believable than nonverbal communication.
12. We communicate more through nonverbal behavior than we do through our words.
13. Research indicates that facial expressions of our most basic emotions are interpreted similarly around the world.
14. Researchers suggest that attractiveness is judged much differently across cultures. (In other words, beauty is in the eye of the beholder.)
15. The use of time conveys meaning about value and power.

Fill in the Blank

16. _____ is the first of the five senses to develop in humans.
17. The study of smell is called _____.
18. Nonword sounds such as "umm" or "uh" are called _____ words.
19. Turning your posture away from the person you're speaking to, as a signal that you want to end the conversation, is called _____.
20. _____ is the convergence of two people's nonverbal behaviors.

Answers

Multiple Choice: 1 (c); 2 (a); 3 (d); 4 (c); 5 (a); 6 (d); 7 (b); 8 (c); 9 (d); 10 (a); **True/False:** 11 (F); 12 (F); 13 (T); 14 (F); 15 (T); **Fill in the Blank:** 16 (touch); 17 (olfactics); 18 (filler); 19 (left positioning); 20 (synchrony)

Research Library

Movies

Children of a Lesser God (Drama; 1986; R)

In this drama, James (played by William Hurt) is a new teacher at a school for the deaf. He falls in love with Sarah (played by Marlee Matlin), a deaf former student who remained at the school as an employee out of fear of venturing into the hearing world. The movie portrays James and Sarah's communication via sign language and nonverbal behaviors.

Nell (Drama; 1994; PG-13)

This film tells the story of a young woman, Nell, brought up in social isolation in the backwoods of North Carolina. Other than her deceased mother and twin sister, Nell has never met anyone until she is discovered by Jerome, a local doctor, and Paula, a psychologist who wants to study Nell in her laboratory. Because Nell speaks her own language, which is incomprehensible to outsiders, the movie provides many opportunities to witness communication via nonverbal signals.

Two Can Play That Game (Comedy; 2001; R)

Two Can Play That Game is a romantic comedy in which Shanté discovers that boyfriend, Keith, has been keeping company with other women. She decides to lure Keith back to her using various tricks and games, only to discover later that Keith is playing games with her. In several scenes, the characters use nonverbal behaviors (particularly affectionate behaviors) to convey messages to each other.

Books

Andersen, P. A. (2004). *The complete idiot's guide to body language.* New York: Penguin.

Andersen, P. A. (2007). *Nonverbal communication: Forms and functions* (2nd ed.). Long Grove, IL: Waveland Press.

Guerrero, L. K., & Floyd, K. (2006). *Nonverbal communication in close relationships.* Mahwah, NJ: Lawrence Erlbaum Associates.

Manusov, V., & Patterson, M. L. (Eds.). (2006). *The SAGE handbook of nonverbal communication.* Thousand Oaks, CA: Sage.

Journal Articles and Book Chapters

Burgoon, J. K., & Hoobler, G. D. (2002). Nonverbal signals. In M. L. Knapp & J. A. Daly (Eds.), *Handbook of interpersonal communication* (3rd ed., pp. 240–299). Thousand Oaks, CA: Sage.

Eagley, A. E., Ashmore, R. D., Makhijani, M. G., & Longo, L. C. (1991). What is beautiful is good, but . . . : A meta-analytic review of research on the physical attractiveness stereotype. *Psychological Bulletin, 110,* 109–139.

Field, T. M. (1999). American adolescents touch each other less and are more aggressive toward their peers as compared with French adolescents. *Adolescence, 34,* 753–758.

Herz, R. S., & Inzlicht, M. (2002). Sex differences in response to physical and social factors involved in human mate selection: The importance of smell for women. *Evolution and Human Behavior, 23,* 359–364.

Web Sites

www6.miami.edu/touch-research/

This site, from the Touch Research Institute in Miami, describes research demonstrating the many benefits of touch and touch therapy.

www.scienceofsmell.com

This Web site is the home page of the Smell and Taste Treatment and Research Foundation, a research institute in Chicago focusing on the importance of olfactics and taste in perception, relational communication, and health.

7

Listening

What does it mean to listen well?

Why is effective listening so challenging?

How can we improve our listening skills?

Carmen and Shane

When Carmen and Shane's oldest son called to invite them to dinner on Saturday night, Carmen happily accepted his invitation. Later that evening, she mentioned the invitation to Shane. Shane, who was engrossed in the evening news at the time, nodded his head and said "okay." He wasn't really paying attention to Carmen, however, so when their daughter called a few days later to invite them to play cards at her place on Saturday night, Shane answered the phone and said they would be glad to come. "I told you we already made plans," Carmen angrily replied when she found out. "You never listen!"

You've probably had the experience of feeling as though someone was *hearing* you but not really *listening.* Like most people, you probably felt frustrated. As you might imagine, problems with listening are fairly common in interpersonal relationships.[1] These problems arise because listening effectively is more difficult than you might think. Like other aspects of communication, listening is a skill you have to learn and practice. When we do it properly, listening adds a great deal to the quality of our relationships. When we don't, our communication and our relationships both suffer.

In this chapter, you will learn:

1} What listening is, why it is such an important part of interpersonal communication, and how it is influenced by culture

2} What the six components of effective listening are

3} Why listening effectively is often so challenging

4} How you can improve your listening skills

1} The Nature of Listening {

If you're like most people, you probably don't give much thought to how well you listen. You can take classes to become a better speaker or a better writer, but few schools offer courses to improve your listening skills. Nevertheless, most of us spend much more time listening than we do speaking, writing, or engaging in other communicative behaviors. That's one reason why listening effectively is such a valuable skill.

> *Listen or your tongue will keep you deaf.*
> —Native American Proverb

What Is Listening?

Listening is one of the most important concepts in interpersonal communication. Despite this fact, many people find effective listening hard to define. When someone complains "You never listen!" as Carmen did to Shane, what exactly does that mean?

We can define **listening** as the active process of making meaning out of another person's spoken message.[2] Several details about this definition are important to note. First, listening is an active process. That means it isn't automatic; rather, you have to *make* yourself listen to someone. Second, listening isn't just about hearing, or receiving input, but also about creating *meaning* from what you hear. Even if people are hearing the same message, they may construct different meanings for it, which means they are listening differently.

To understand this point, imagine that you are listening to your brother's description of his new officemate and you conclude that he finds her very competent and likable. After listening to the same description, however, your mom concludes that your brother feels threatened by his officemate's intelligence and self-confidence. In this case, the two of you heard the same description, but you listened to it differently.

Finally, listening deals with spoken messages. We certainly pay attention to written messages, and nonverbal messages influence our interpretation of spoken messages. We can perform the act of interpersonal listening, however, only when someone is speaking.

Listening The active process of making meaning out of another person's spoken message.

Just because we're listening to someone, however, that doesn't necessarily mean we're listening *effectively*. Effective listening means listening with the conscious and explicit goal of understanding what the speaker is attempting to communicate. You might never know for certain whether you have understood a speaker's meaning *exactly* as he or she intended. If you're listening with the goal of understanding the speaker's meaning as best you can, however, then you're listening effectively.

As we'll see in this chapter, listening effectively is easier said than done. There are several barriers that make effective listening difficult, and different situations call for different types of listening. Understanding these dimensions of listening can help us improve our ability to listen effectively. That's a worthwhile goal, as we'll see in the next section.

How Do We Know?
College Students Spend More Time Listening Than Doing Any Other Communication Activity

Researchers Kathryn Dindia and Bonnie Kennedy reported that college students spend more time listening than they spend engaging in any other communication activity. How do they know?

This finding came from a study in which Dindia and Kennedy gave each of 143 participants a handheld computer to carry with them during waking hours for seven consecutive days. The computers were programmed to beep at six randomly chosen times between 7 a.m. and 11 p.m. on each of the seven days. Each time their computers beeped, participants completed an electronic questionnaire on what they were doing at the time. When Dindia and Kennedy reviewed participants' reports of what they were doing when they were beeped, they discovered that of all reported communication activities, listening was by far the most commonly cited.

Although these results are enlightening, we must keep two important points in mind. First, the study counted both interpersonal listening and listening to media such as television or music as listening behaviors. Second, the study employed a self-report method, which is open to bias, because some participants may have reported listening when they actually weren't. Despite those limitations, however, the results support findings from earlier studies that show we spend more time listening than engaging in any other communication activity.

Ask Yourself:

- If you had been in this study, what forms of communication would you have been engaged in most often?

- What advantages and disadvantages does the self-report method have compared with alternatives, such as having researchers directly observe participants or having participants keep a diary of their behaviors?

From Me to You:

- This study suggests that many of us spend more of our time listening than we realize. Because listening is such an important part of how we communicate, we should each try to be as good at it as we can. Even though improving our listening skills takes effort, it's well worth it when you consider that you spend half of your communicating time listening.

Source: Dindia, K., & Kennedy, B. L. (2004, November). *Communication in everyday life: A descriptive study using mobile electronic data collection.* Paper presented at the annual conference of the National Communication Association, Chicago, IL.

The Importance of Listening Effectively

One of the reasons it's important to understand listening is that we do it so much of the time. How much of your day do you think you spend listening? In one study, researchers Kathryn Dindia and Bonnie Kennedy found that college students spent more time listening than engaging in any other communication activity. Specifically, participants spent 50% of their waking hours listening.[3] In contrast, they spent only 20% of the time speaking, 13% reading, and 12% writing. Overall, then, they spent as much time listening as they did performing all other communication behaviors *combined*.

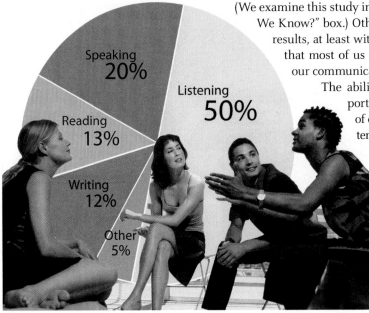

Speaking
20%

Listening
50%

Reading
13%

Writing
12%

Other
5%

FIGURE 7.1 Percentages of Various Communication Activities

(We examine this study in greater detail in the "How Do We Know?" box.) Other studies have found similar results, at least with college students, suggesting that most of us spend a similar percentage of our communication time listening.[4]

The ability to listen effectively is important to our success in a variety of contexts. For example, good listening skills are vital in the workplace, as you can well imagine. Suppose, for instance, that your employees don't listen when you tell them the alarm they will soon be hearing will signal a fire drill, not a real fire. Some of them might panic, and others might injure themselves as they rush frantically from their work spaces. As another example, imagine that your manager at work doesn't listen when her employees warn her about problems with the company's equipment. As a result, a critical production line breaks down, stalling operations for a week.

These examples illustrate how consequential effective listening can be in the workplace. In a recent survey, in fact, one thousand human resource professionals ranked listening as the most important quality of effective managers.[5] The top ten qualities appear in Table 7.1. In other research, listening topped the list of the most important communication skills in families and in personal relationships.[6] Indeed, being a good listener is important to just about every social and personal bond we have.[7]

Listening well doesn't affect just our relationships; it also has implications for our physical health. When a pharmacist gives us instructions about how to take a medication, for instance, we need to listen carefully to avoid taking the medication improperly. When a doctor tells us what foods to avoid or a nurse instructs us as to how to care for a wound, exercising effective listening skills is vital. When a physical therapist or trainer shows us how to exercise properly, we need to be certain we've understood so we get the maximum benefit from our workouts and avoid hurting ourselves.

If listening skills are so valuable, then why don't we work harder to improve them? One reason is that many of us overestimate our actual listening abilities. In one study, for instance, 94% of corporate managers rated themselves as "good" or "very good" at listening, whereas not a single one rated himself or herself as "poor" or "very

Table 7.1 Most Important Attributes of Effective Managers, According to 1,000 Human Resource Professionals Surveyed

1. Ability to listen effectively and counsel

2. Ability to work well with others one-on-one

3. Ability to work well in small groups

4. Ability to gather accurate information from others to make a decision

5. Ability to write effective business reports

6. Ability to give feedback

7. Knowledge of job

8. Ability to present a good public image for the company

9. Ability to use computers

10. Knowledge of finance

Source: Windsor, J. L., Curtis, D. B., & Stephens, R. D. (1997). National preferences in business and communication education: A survey update. *Journal of the Association for Communication Administration, 3*, 170–179. Material is adapted from Table 4, p. 176.

poor." Several of their employees told quite a different story, however: They rated their managers' listening skills as weak.[8] Studies like these indicate that there is little association between how good we think we are at listening and how good other people think we are![9] As we'll see later in the chapter, many obstacles get in the way of our ability to listen well. The good news, though, is that listening is a skill that we can improve. In this chapter, we'll look at some ways to do just that.[10]

Listening skills are particularly important in the workplace. One study, however, found that many employees rated their employers' listening skills as weak.

Some Misconceptions About Listening

Are you surprised to learn that people often overestimate their listening abilities? Here are some other misunderstandings about the listening process.

Myth: Hearing is the same as listening. Some people use the terms *hearing* and *listening* interchangeably, but they aren't really the same activity. Hearing is merely the perception of sound. Most people hear sounds almost continuously—you hear your roommate's music, the neighbor's dogs barking, the television playing in the background, the car alarm that wakes you in the middle of the night. Hearing is a passive process that occurs when sound waves cause the bones in your inner ear to vibrate and send signals to your brain.

Just because we're hearing something, though, doesn't mean we're *listening* to it. Unlike hearing, listening is an active process of paying attention to a sound, assigning meaning to it, and responding to it. Hearing is a part of this process, but listening requires much more than just perceiving the sounds around you.

By the same token, we sometimes listen without hearing, and our understanding can be impaired as a result. This point is illustrated humorously in a series of television ads recently aired by the Cingular/AT&T telephone company. Each ad depicts a cell phone call between two people in which they unknowingly lose their cellular connection halfway through the conversation. In every case, one speaker interprets the other's silence as meaningful, when in fact it is simply the result of the dropped call. For instance, just after telling her husband that she is expecting a baby, one woman's call is dropped without her knowledge. Although her husband is exclaiming his excitement about the pregnancy, all she hears is silence, which she incorrectly interprets as indifference or fear on his part. Even though she was trying to listen, then, she wasn't hearing. As these ads further illustrate, listening and hearing are related but separate processes.

Myth: Listening is natural and effortless. It's easy to think of listening as a completely natural, mindless process, much like breathing. As we've discussed, however, listening is a *learned skill,* and not an innate ability like hearing. We have to acquire our listening abilities. Just as we are taught to speak, we have to be taught to listen, and to listen effectively. Many of us are taught by our experiences. Perhaps you can recall instances when you didn't listen effectively to a supervisor's instructions about how to accomplish a work project and you made poor decisions as a result. Maybe you have been in situations with a romantic partner when you didn't listen as effectively as you could have, which led to an unnecessary argument. Good communicators learn from their mistakes, so these types of experiences have probably taught you how important effective listening is.

We also learn through instruction, such as the instruction you are receiving in your interpersonal communication course. The more you learn about what makes listening effective and what barriers to watch out for, the better equipped you'll be to listen effectively to other people.

The fact that listening is a skill also means that people vary in their listening abilities. Just as some people are better artists, singers, or writers than others, some people are better

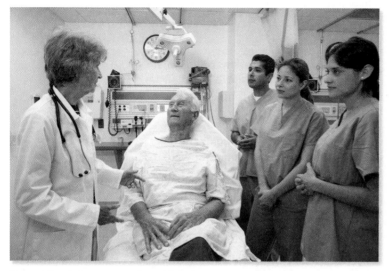

Recognizing the importance of good listening skills in the health care field, several medical schools in the United States have added coursework to teach young doctors how to listen effectively to their patients.

listeners than others. Finally, as with most skills, you can improve your listening ability through education and training.[11] Counselors and social workers, for instance, are trained to listen effectively to clients, a skill that improves the quality of services they provide. In recent years, medical schools around the United States have also added coursework on effective listening and other interpersonal skills to their curricula for training physicians. People in many professions, from education and the ministry to customer service and politics, can benefit from training in effective listening.

Myth: All listeners hear the same thing. We might assume that when several people are listening to the same message, they are all hearing and understanding the message in the same way. As we learned in Chapter 4, however, our perceptions of what we see and hear are always limited. Our experiences, our biases, and even our gender and culture all influence how we create meaning from the information we take in.

The safer assumption is that all listeners are hearing something slightly different, because each of us is filtering the message through our unique sets of experiences and biases. As communication scholar Ben Broome points out, even the most skilled listener can't "step outside" himself or herself entirely.[12] Broome is *not* implying that no one can ever understand another person's meaning. Rather, he is encouraging us to learn to be aware of how different people might interpret and understand the same message differently.

Culture Affects Listening Behavior

Cultural messages shape many communication behaviors, and listening is no exception. In particular, listening behavior appears to be affected by how people in a given culture think about the importance of time. In individualistic cultures, people often think of time as a resource. U.S. Americans, for instance, commonly say that "time is money," and they think of time as a commodity that can be saved, spent, and wasted. People in such cultures typically place a premium on efficiency, and they expect others to do the same. They value direct, straightforward communication, and listeners become impatient with speakers who don't "get to the point."[13] In contrast, collectivistic cultures such as Korea emphasize social harmony over efficiency. As part of their listening behavior, people in these cultures often pay close attention to nonverbal behaviors and contextual cues to determine the meaning of a speaker's message.[14]

Learn It: How is listening different from merely hearing? Approximately how much of a person's communication time is spent listening? Why isn't listening a natural, effortless process? How do people in individualistic and collectivistic cultures listen differently?

Try It: The next time you have a conversation with someone, try to focus your attention on what she or he is saying rather than on how you're going to respond. With practice, you can learn to listen more intently to others.

Reflect on It: In what situations do you find you have difficulty listening effectively? How do you think your own cultural values and experiences influence the way you listen?

2} Ways of Listening

> *How utterly amazing is the general assumption that the ability to listen well is a natural gift for which no training is required.*
>
> —Mortimer Adler (1902–2001)
> U.S. American author

Until now, we've been talking about listening as though it were a single, unified activity. In truth, listening *effectively* consists of several stages, all of which are equally important.

Stages of Effective Listening

Judi Brownell, a professor of organizational communication, is an expert on listening who developed the **HURIER model** to describe the six stages of effective listening: hearing, understanding, remembering, interpreting, evaluating, and responding.[15] (The name "HURIER" is an acronym for these stages.) We don't necessarily have to enact these stages in order; sometimes listening effectively requires us to go back and forth among these stages. When we listen effectively, however, these are the behaviors we adopt. Let's take a closer look at each one.

HURIER model A model of effective listening that involves hearing, understanding, remembering, interpreting, evaluating, and responding.

Hearing. Recall that hearing is the physical process of perceiving sound. This is where the listening process begins. As we discussed, we can hear someone without listening to what he or she is saying. We tend to do this when we're tired, when we're uninterested in what the person is saying, or when we're hearing multiple voices at once, as in a crowded restaurant. In the opening scenario, Shane wasn't listening to Carmen because he was paying attention to the news. Although we sometimes hear without listening, however, we can't really listen to a person unless we can first hear him or her. People with hearing impairments find ways to overcome this challenge, such as reading lips and using sign language. For hearing persons, though, hearing is the first step in effective listening.

Understanding. It's not enough simply to hear what someone is saying—you also have to understand it. To understand means to comprehend the meanings of the words and phrases you're hearing.[16] If someone is speaking in a language you don't understand, you might be able to hear that person, but you won't be able to listen effectively. The same is true when you hear technical language or jargon that you're unfamiliar with—even if the speaker is speaking your language, you can't effectively listen if you don't understand the words. If you're uncertain whether you understand what a speaker is saying, the most effective course of action is usually to ask him or her questions to check your understanding.

Remembering. The third stage of the HURIER model is remembering, or being able to store something in your memory and then retrieve it when needed.[17] Remembering what we hear is important for interpersonal communication because it can help us to avoid getting into awkward situations. In the opening vignette, for instance, Shane probably heard Carmen explain that they were having dinner with their son on Saturday. Because he wasn't paying attention when he heard it, however, he didn't remember that information when he accepted his daughter's invitation, leading Carmen to criticize his listening skills. Similarly, you might have had the embarrassing experience of running into someone whose name you can't remember, even though you have met him or her on several prior occasions. In these and other interpersonal encounters, remembering what we hear can help us communicate with others more effectively.

If you're particularly good at remembering the details of a conversation, you're in the minority. Research shows that most people can recall only 25% of what they hear—and of that portion, they remember only about 20% of it accurately.[18] The average person, therefore, is not especially good at remembering. Fortunately, like listening in general, remembering is a skill you can practice and improve.

Mnemonic devices are tricks that can improve our short- and long-term memory. Such devices come in several forms. If you've ever studied music, for instance, perhaps you learned to recall the lines of the treble staff—EGBDF—by treating the letters as an initialism for a phrase, such as "every good boy does fine." You might also develop rhymes to help you remember certain rules, such as when spelling in English "*i* comes before *e,* except after *c.*" Another mnemonic device is the acronym, a word formed from the first letters or parts of a compound term. If you remember the elements of Brownell's effective listening model by learning the word "HURIER," you are employing this type of mnemonic device. Research suggests that using these and other types of mnemonic devices can significantly enhance memory.[19]

The process of interpreting involves paying attention to a speaker's verbal and nonverbal behaviors so you can assign meaning to what she has said.

Interpreting. Besides hearing, understanding, and remembering, an effective listener must interpret the information he or she receives. The process of interpreting has two parts. The first part is paying attention to all the speaker's verbal and nonverbal behaviors so that you can assign meaning to what he or she has said. Suppose your friend Maya says, "It's a beautiful day outside!" On the basis of her facial expressions and tone of voice, you might interpret this message either as sincere—meaning that Maya thinks today's weather is beautiful—or as sarcastic—meaning she actually thinks the weather is lousy. Notice that these are very different interpretations of Maya's message even though her words are the same.

The second part of interpreting is signaling your interpretation of the message to the speaker. If you interpret Maya's statement as sincere, for instance, you might smile and say you're looking forward to getting outside to enjoy the great weather. In contrast, if you interpret her statement as sarcastic, you might laugh or respond with a sarcastic remark of your own. Signaling not only lets the speaker know you're following along with what he or she is saying but also allows you to confirm your interpretations. Suppose, for instance, that Maya intended her comment about the weather to be sarcastic but you interpreted it as sincere. If you smiled and said you were looking forward to getting outside, this would probably signal to Maya that you have misinterpreted the intent of her statement. She might then say, "I was just kidding," to correct your interpretation.

Evaluating. Several events happen at the evaluation stage. For one, you're judging whether the speaker's statements are accurate and true. You're also separating facts from opinions and trying to determine why the speaker is saying what he or she is saying. Finally, you're considering the speaker's words in the context of other information you have received from that speaker or other sources. All these activities help you to be an active, engaged listener, rather than a passive recipient of information.

Responding. The last stage of effective listening is responding, or indicating to a speaker that you're listening. We sometimes call this process "giving feedback," and we do it both verbally and nonverbally using a variety of strategies.[20] Below are seven types of listening responses, arranged in order from the most passive strategies to the most active ones:

In the HBO series, *The Sopranos*, Tony Soprano (played by James Gandolfini) was a powerful, dangerous man with a large ego and many dark secrets. Counseling him was the daunting task undertaken by Dr. Jennifer Melfi (played by Lorraine Bracco). During therapy sessions, Dr. Melfi used backchanneling, paraphrasing, and analyzing as effective ways of responding. Because of Tony Soprano's involvement in crime, she was often unable to empathize or support and was reluctant to advise.

- *Stonewalling*: Responding with silence and a lack of expression on your face. Stonewalling often signals a lack of interest in what the speaker is saying.
- *Backchanneling*: Nodding your head or using facial expressions, vocalizations such as "uh-huh," and verbal statements such as "I understand" or "That's very interesting" to let the speaker know you're paying attention.
- *Paraphrasing*: Restating in your own words what the speaker has said, to show that you understand.
- *Empathizing*: Conveying to the speaker that you understand and share his or her feelings on the topic being discussed.
- *Supporting*: Expressing your agreement with the speaker's opinion or point of view.
- *Analyzing*: Providing your own perspective on what the speaker has said.
- *Advising*: Communicating advice to the speaker about what he or she should think, feel, or do.

Depending on the situation, some of these responses may be more useful or appropriate than others. For instance, if you're listening to a friend who has just lost her favorite uncle to cancer, empathizing and supporting are probably the most helpful responses. Stonewalling, backchanneling, or paraphrasing might make it seem as though you don't care about your friend, and analyzing or advising might seem in-

At a Glance: HURIER Model of Effective Listening

Brownell's model suggests that effective listening has six elements, represented by the acronym *HURIER:*

Hearing	Physically perceiving sound
Understanding	Comprehending the words we have heard
Remembering	Storing ideas in memory
Interpreting	Assigning meaning to what we've heard
Evaluating	Judging the speaker's credibility and intention
Responding	Indicating that we are listening

sensitive. By contrast, if you're an accountant who is listening to a client who is wondering how she can make the most of her stock portfolio, then analysis and advice are probably called for.

In addition to the specific situation, our cultural expectations influence our ideas concerning appropriate listening responses, particularly with respect to appropriate nonverbal behavior. As we discussed in Chapter 6, for instance, people in U.S. American culture typically expect listeners to maintain eye contact with them while they're speaking. For that reason, they often assume that listeners who look down or away aren't listening. In contrast, in many Native American cultures, looking down or away while listening is a sign of respect.[21]

A brief recap of the HURIER model appears in the "At a Glance" box above. According to Brownell, these six stages characterize effective listening no matter why we happen to be listening in the first place. As you probably know, however, we engage in many types of listening. We'll take a closer look at three of the most common types of listening in the next section.

Three Types of Listening

When we talk about different *types* of listening, we're referring to the different *goals* we have when we listen to other people. Sometimes, we listen to learn, which is called *informational listening.* At other times, our goal is to evaluate, which is called *critical listening.* On still other occasions, our goal is to empathize, so we use *empathic listening.* These goals aren't necessarily distinct; sometimes we listen with more than one of them in mind. When we distinguish among types of listening, therefore, we are considering what our *primary* listening goal is at a given time.

Informational listening. Much of the listening you engage in during class or at work is **informational listening,** or listening to learn. Whenever you watch the news or listen to driving directions or pay attention to a professor's lecture, you're engaged in informational listening.

Informational listening is both very common and extremely helpful. Indeed, it is one of the most important ways we learn. It is also the most passive type of listening. When we're engaged in informational listening, we are simply taking in information. Even though we may be listening effectively and even taking notes, we are listening primarily to learn something new rather than to criticize or support the speaker's information.

Informational listening
Listening to learn something.

Critical listening. When our goal is to evaluate or analyze what we're hearing, we are engaged in **critical listening.** You listen carefully to a commercial to determine whether you want to buy the product it's advertising. You listen to a sales presentation or a political speech and evaluate the merits of what you're hearing. You listen critically to your mother's description of her recent medical appointment to determine how worried she is about the results of her blood test.

A key point here is that the term "critical listening" doesn't necessarily mean disapproving of or finding fault with what you're hearing. Instead, it means analyzing and evaluating the merits of what a speaker is saying. Compared with informational listening, therefore, critical listening is a more active, engaging process. It requires us not only to take in information but also to assess and judge it. In fact, as we will see at the end of this chapter, practicing critical listening skills is one of the best ways of becoming a better listener overall.

Empathic listening. Perhaps the most challenging form of listening is **empathic listening,** which occurs when you are trying to identify with the speaker by understanding and experiencing what he or she is thinking or feeling.[22] When you are talking to a friend who has just lost a loved one or listening to a family member describing the stress of her divorce, you can use empathic listening to give comfort and support.

Effective empathic listening requires two skills. The first, "perspective taking," is the ability to understand a situation from another individual's point of view.[23] The second skill, "empathic concern," is the ability to identify how someone else is feeling and then experience those feelings yourself.[24] When you're listening to a co-worker describing his recent cancer diagnosis, for instance, you can practice perspective taking by trying to think about the situation as he is thinking about it. You can practice empathic concern by imagining how he must feel and then sharing in those emotions.

Empathic listening is different from sympathetic listening, which means feeling sorry for another person. If your neighbors lost their young grandson to leukemia, for instance, you might be able to sympathize with them even if you can't truly understand the feelings they are experiencing. In contrast, the goal of empathic listening is to understand a situation from the speaker's perspective and to feel what he or she is feeling. You might be listening to a friend who didn't get into the graduate school she was hoping to attend and trying to convey that you share her disappointment. Listening empathically is a challenge, because our perceptions can cause us to focus on how *we* would be feeling in the same situation rather than how the *speaker* is feeling.

Informational, critical, and empathic listening aren't the only types of listening in which we engage. For example, we sometimes engage in "inspirational listening," which is listening in order to be inspired. This type of listening is common when we're listening to a sermon or a motivational speech. At other times, we engage in "appreciative listening," which is listening for pure enjoyment. We adopt this style when we're listening to someone telling a funny story or singing one of our favorite songs. When it comes to interpersonal interaction, however, informational, critical, and empathic listening are often the most common and most important types.

Learn It: What are the differences between interpreting a message and responding to it? How are the goals of informational, critical, and empathic listening different?

Try It: What's your listening style? Take a look at the box on page 270 to find out.

Reflect on It: When do you have a hard time understanding a speaker? Which type of listening are you the best at?

3} Common Barriers to Effective Listening {

> *We have two ears and one mouth that we may listen the more and talk the less.*
>
> —Zeno of Citium (335–263 BC)
> Greek philosopher

In the 2006 movie *The Break-Up,* Brooke Meyers (played by Jennifer Aniston) asks her boyfriend, Gary Grobowski (played by Vince Vaughn), to bring home a dozen lemons for a dinner party she is throwing for their families. Gary doesn't listen, and he brings home only three lemons. Brooke finds this distressing because their company is arriving shortly, so she expresses her concern to Gary, who continues to watch television while talking to her:

Brooke: You got three lemons.

Gary: What my baby wants, my baby gets; you know that.

Brooke: I know, but I wanted twelve, baby wanted twelve.

Gary: Why would you want twelve lemons?

Brooke: Because I'm making a twelve-lemon centerpiece.

Gary: So no one's actually even eating them, they're just show lemons?

Brooke: Yeah, they're just show lemons. To go in the center of the table. I'm glad you find that amusing, but I cannot fill a vase with only three lemons.

Brooke isn't upset in this scene just because she doesn't have the right number of lemons. She's also upset because Gary didn't listen to her when she asked him to bring home a dozen lemons, and she gets increasingly frustrated because he continues watching television during their conversation instead of paying attention to her.

This scene raises the question, Why are so few of us good listeners? One answer is that several problems get in our way, acting as barriers to our ability to listen well. In this section, we examine several obstacles to effective listening:

- Noise
- Pseudolistening and selective attention
- Information overload
- Glazing over
- Rebuttal tendency
- Closed-mindedness
- Competitive interruption

Getting to Know You
What Kind of Listener Are You?

We have seen that people listen for various reasons—sometimes to learn, sometimes to evaluate, and sometimes to provide empathy to others. Did you know that each of us also has a primarily listening *style*? A listening style is a set of attitudes and beliefs about listening. Researchers have identified four distinct styles. We can adopt any of these styles as the situation dictates, but research suggests that most of us have one primary style that we use the most often. Which of these styles best describes you?

- *People-oriented style:* This style emphasizes concern for other people's emotions and interests. As the name suggests, someone with a people-oriented style tries to find common interests with others. For instance, when Palik listens to his middle school students, he tries to understand what they are thinking and feeling so he can relate to them effectively.

- *Action-oriented style:* This style emphasizes organization and precision. Someone with this style likes neat, concise, error-free presentations. For example, Monica approves when her interns fill her in on the week's activities in a clear, straightforward way, and gets frustrated when she can't understand them.

- *Content-oriented style:* This style emphasizes intellectual challenges. Someone with a content-oriented style likes to attend to details and think things through. Emma really enjoys listening to political commentators, for instance, because they make her think about her own social and political views.

- *Time-oriented style:* This style emphasizes efficiency. Someone with a time-oriented style prefers conversations that are quick and to-the-point. As an emergency room physician, for example, Ben relies on short and fast reports of a patient's condition from paramedics and nurses, and he gets impatient when they take more of his time than is necessary.

Each of these styles has its distinctive strengths and weaknesses, so none is inherently better than the others. If you're primarily a people-oriented listener, for example, you're likely to get to know other people well but you might not be able to work as efficiently as a time-oriented listener.

Action-oriented listeners might do best in majors that emphasize clarity and precision, such as engineering and computer science, whereas content-oriented listeners might prefer majors that involve greater ambiguity and room for debate, such as art and political science.

Regardless of your primary listening style, however, research demonstrates that we adopt different styles for different situations. For instance, you might prefer a time-oriented style when you're in a rush but a people-oriented style when you're visiting loved ones. Similarly, you might adopt a content-oriented style when listening to your professor give a lecture but an action-oriented style when listening to the evening news.

Which of these four listening styles describes you in most situations? Why did you choose this answer?

Sources: Imhof, M. (2004). Who are we as we listen? Individual listening profiles in varying contexts. *International Journal of Listening, 18,* 36–45; Watson, K. W., Barker, L. L., & Weaver, J. B. (1995). The listening styles profile (LSP-16): Development and validation of an instrument to assess four listening styles. *International Journal of Listening, 9,* 1–13.

Noise

How many stimuli are competing for your attention right now? Or at work, for instance, where your boss, your customers, and your co-workers are all trying to talk to you at once? In the context of listening, noise is anything that distracts you from listening to what you wish to listen to. Most of us find it more difficult to listen to a conversational partner when there are other sounds in the environment, such as a TV or loud music.[25] It isn't just sound that can distract us, though. If we're feeling hungry or tired, or if we're in an environment that is especially cold or hot, those influences can also qualify as noise because they interfere with our ability to listen effectively.[26]

When you're faced with those and other distractions, try to focus your attention on your conversational partner and listen intently to what he or she is saying. To do this you must be conscious of noise in your environment and identify those factors that are drawing your attention away from your conversation. Eliminating or ignoring these sources of noise—for example, turning off your car radio or ignoring your ringing cell phone—will help you focus on your partner. If you're being distracted by noise that you can't ignore or reduce at the time, you might reschedule your conversation for a time when fewer stimuli are competing for your attention.

Pseudolistening and Selective Attention

Pseudolistening
Using feedback behaviors to give the false impression that one is listening.

At one time or another, you've probably pretended to pay attention to someone when you weren't really listening. This behavior is called **pseudolistening.** When you are pseudolistening, you use feedback behaviors that make it *seem* as though you're paying attention, even though your mind is elsewhere. When Carmen told Shane in the opening vignette that they were going to their son's home for dinner, he nodded along and said "okay" as though he were listening. In reality, his attention was focused on the evening news. So, although he seemed to be listening to Carmen, he actually wasn't; instead, he was pseudolistening.

A variation of pseudolistening is **selective attention,** which means listening only to what you want to hear and ignoring the rest.[27] When you engage in selective attention, you are actually listening to some parts of a person's message and pseudolistening to other parts. In her job as an insurance adjuster, for instance, Sue-Ann receives an evaluation from her supervisor every January. Most of her supervisor's comments are usually positive, but some of them suggest ways in which Sue-Ann could improve her performance. The problem is, Sue-Ann doesn't listen to those suggestions. Instead, she listens selectively, paying close attention to her supervisor's praise but only pretending to listen to her critiques.

Selective attention
Listening only to what you want to hear.

We engage in pseudolistening and selective attention for many reasons. Maybe you're bored with what the speaker is saying, but you don't want to seem rude. Maybe you don't understand what you're hearing, but you're too embarrassed to admit it. Maybe you're paying attention to something

Noise is anything that distracts you from listening. When you're faced with noise that you can't eliminate, try intently to ignore it so you can focus your attention on your conversational partner.

else while someone is talking to you, or maybe you simply don't like what the other person is saying. Whatever the reason, pseudolistening and selective attention not only are barriers to effective listening but also can be a source of frustration for the speakers you're pretending to listen to. This frustration arises because people are often aware when others—including us—aren't listening to what they're saying. How do *you* feel when you know someone is only pretending to listen to you or is paying only partial attention to what you're saying?

Information Overload

A third barrier to effective listening is **information overload.** Information overload refers to the huge amount of information that each of us is required to take in every day. We talk to people, we watch television, we listen to the radio, we surf the Internet, and we thumb through magazines, newspapers, and even college textbooks. At times, the sheer volume of information we have to attend to can seem overwhelming. When it does, we find it harder to listen effectively to new information.

As just one example, consider how many advertising messages you see or hear on a daily basis. Many of us see ads on television, in magazines and newspapers, on billboards, on people's clothing, in junk mail, and during the previews before a movie. We receive ads by fax, we hear them on the radio, and we find them in product inserts. We see them at gas pumps, at automated teller machines, on banners flying behind airplanes, and on the stickers we peel off of apples and bananas. We also receive them in the form of e-mail spam and pop-up announcements on the Internet. In fact, researchers have estimated that the average U.S. American is exposed to between 600 and 625 advertising messages each day.[28]

You might conclude from these paragraphs that information overload is a product of the digital age, when overwhelming amounts of information are easily available. In truth, however, the term "information overload" was coined in 1970 by sociologist Alvin Toffler in a book titled *Future Shock,* which discussed the downsides of rapid technological change.[29] Clearly, then, people were experiencing the distracting effects of information overload even before computer-mediated communication was widely used.

Information overload
The state of being overwhelmed by the amount of information one takes in.

Many of us experience information overload in our fast-paced world, where information and sensory stimulation are abundant. When multiple stimuli compete for our attention at once, we can find it difficult to listen to others. You can overcome information overload by finding a quiet place without computers or cell phones where you can listen without distraction.

One of the biggest problems arising from information overload is that it can interrupt our attention. If you're e-mailing with an important client, for instance, your ability to pay attention to her messages can be compromised repeatedly by each new radio advertisement you hear, each new faxed announcement you receive, and each new pop-up ad you see. Those interruptions may seem small and inconsequential, but when you consider their effects on the entire population over time, they become a significant distraction. In fact, a 2007 analysis by a New York–based management research firm estimated the annual cost to U.S. companies of unnecessary interruptions from information overload to be a staggering $650 billion.[30]

Information overload can be particularly troubling for people with attention deficit hyperactivity disorder, or ADHD. People with ADHD are often easily distracted and have trouble focusing their attention for very long. They are often also overly active and restless.[31] ADHD is a developmental disorder whose symptoms usually appear during childhood. A majority of children diagnosed with ADHD will continue to suffer from it during adulthood.[32] Because of their impaired ability to focus and their tendency to become easily distracted, people with ADHD may have an especially difficult time coping with the volume of information most of us encounter every day.

Fortunately, there are several strategies to reduce the distracting effects of information overload. During meetings and important conversations, for instance, turn off the ringer on your cell phone or PDA so you won't be distracted by incoming calls, text messages, or e-mails. Set filters on your e-mail system to reduce spam, and use a pop-up blocker to eliminate pop-up ads when you're online. Contact the Direct Marketing Association to have your address removed from junk-mail lists. Use your VCR or digital video recorder (DVR) to record your favorite TV shows so you can watch them at your convenience and skip through the commercials. Using strategies such as these will help reduce the distractions of information overload, allowing you to focus your attention on more important things, including your conversational partners.

Glazing Over

A fourth reason why effective listening is challenging is that our minds think so much faster than most people talk. Most of us are capable of understanding up to 600 words per minute, but the average person speaks fewer than 150 words per minute.[33] That leaves quite a bit of "spare time" for the mind to wander. We frequently use that time to engage in what researchers call **glazing over,** or daydreaming during the time we aren't actually listening.

Glazing over
Daydreaming with the time not spent listening.

For instance, Rochelle picks up her six-year-old daughter and her nine-year-old son every afternoon, and they describe what they did in school during the drive home. Although she listens to what they say, Rochelle frequently allows her mind to wander during this time. She thinks about the novel she's currently reading, daydreams about taking a Caribbean vacation with her husband, and ponders the next week's grocery list. Because her children speak more slowly than she can listen, and because their reports of their school activities are similar every day, Rochelle often glazes over when she's listening to them.

Glazing over is different from pseudolistening, or only pretending to listen. When you're glazing over, you actually *are* listening to what the speaker is saying—you're just allowing your mind to wander while doing so. Glazing over can lead to at least three problems. First, it can cause you to miss important details in what you're hearing. If you're glazing over while listening to a lecture in your communication theory course, for instance, you might fail to hear a critical piece of information about the term paper assignment. Second, glazing over might lead you to listen less critically than you normally would. For example, if your mind is wandering while you're listening to a salesperson describe the terms of a car loan, you might not realize that the deal isn't really as good as it sounds. Finally, glazing over can make it appear to a speaker that you aren't listening to what he or she is saying, even though you are. In these instances, you can come across as inattentive or dismissive. An effective listener, therefore, will work to keep his or her focus on what the speaker is saying instead of daydreaming or thinking about other topics.

Rebuttal Tendency

Regan has recently started work as a customer service representative for an electronics retailer, but his first two weeks on the job have not gone well. He knows he should listen nonjudgmentally to customers as they describe their frustrations with the products they bought and then offer them his assistance and advice. Instead, Regan begins "arguing" with customers in his mind, even while they're still speaking. Rather than listening carefully to their concerns, Regan jumps to conclusions about what the customers have done wrong and formulates his response even before the customers have stopped talking.

Regan is enacting a **rebuttal tendency,** which is the propensity to debate a speaker's point and formulate your reply while the person is still speaking.[34] According to research by business professor Steven Golen, thinking only of how you're going to respond to a speaker, arguing with the speaker in your mind, and jumping to conclusions before the speaker has finished talking are all barriers to effective listening, for two basic reasons.[35] First, the rebuttal tendency uses mental energy that should be spent paying attention to the speaker. That is, it's difficult to listen effectively when all you're thinking about is how you're going to respond. Second, because you're not paying close attention to the speaker, you can easily miss some of the details that might change how you respond in the first place.

To understand this second point, consider Regan's experience during his second shift. A customer returned a wireless Internet router she was having trouble installing. As usual, Regan was quick to conclude that she hadn't followed the instructions, and was already crafting his response. Consequently, he didn't hear her explain that she'd already had a technician guide her through the installation procedure and inform her that the router was defective. Had he heard this important detail, Regan could have exchanged the product quickly and sent the customer on her way. Instead, he spent 10 minutes telling her to do what she had already done, leaving her frustrated and dissatisfied.

Rebuttal tendency
The tendency to debate a speaker's point and formulate a reply while the person is still speaking.

Closed-Mindedness

Another barrier to effective listening is **closed-mindedness,** or the tendency not to listen to anything with which you disagree.[36] Perhaps you know people you would describe in this way. Closed-minded individuals refuse to consider the merits of a speaker's point if it conflicts with their own beliefs. They also tend to overreact to certain forms of language, such as slang or profanity, and will stop listening to speakers who use them.[37]

Many people are closed-minded only about particular issues, not about everything. As an educator, for instance, Bella prides herself in being open to diverse opinions on a range of topics. When it comes to her religious beliefs, however, she is so

Closed-mindedness
The tendency not to listen to anything with which you disagree.

Aristotle wrote that someone with an educated mind can entertain a thought without necessarily accepting it. Today, we call this ability open-mindedness.

thoroughly convinced of the merits of her position that she refuses even to listen to any religious ideas that she doesn't already accept. For all practical purposes, she closes her mind to the possibility that any religious ideas besides her own could have any value whatsoever. Many of her fellow teachers find this off-putting. Not only does it prevent Bella from learning more about their religious traditions, but it also prevents her from teaching others about her beliefs, because she won't talk about religion with anyone who doesn't already share those beliefs.

Bella should remember that we can listen effectively to people even if we disagree with them. As the Greek philosopher Aristotle (384–322 BC) once wrote, "It is the mark of an educated mind to be able to entertain a thought without accepting it." When we refuse even to listen to ideas we disagree with, we limit our ability to learn from other people and their experiences. If you find yourself feeling closed-minded toward particular ideas, remind yourself that listening to an idea doesn't necessarily mean accepting it.

Competitive Interrupting

Normal conversation is a series of speaking "turns." You speak for a while, then you allow another person to have a turn, and the conversation goes back and forth. Occasionally, though, people talk when it isn't their turn. People interrupt for many reasons. Sometimes, the reason is to express support or enthusiasm for what the other person is saying ("Yeah, I agree!"); sometimes it's to stop the speaker to ask for clarification ("Wait, I'm not sure what you mean"); and sometimes it's even to warn the speaker of some impending danger ("Stop! You're spilling your coffee!").

Competitive interrupting Using interruptions to take control of a conversation.

For some people, however, interrupting is a way to dominate a conversation. Researchers use the term **competitive interrupting** to describe the practice of interjecting yourself when other people are speaking in order to take control of the conversation. The goal in competitive interrupting is to ensure that you get to speak more than the other person does and that your ideas and perspectives take priority. You can probably think of people who engage in this behavior, people with whom you feel you "can't get a word in edgewise."

Research shows that most interruptions *aren't* competitive. As you might imagine, however, talking with a competitive interrupter can be frustrating.[38] Some people respond to constant interruptions by becoming competitive themselves, thereby turning the conversation into a battle of wits. Other people simply withdraw from the interaction.

Studies suggest that, on average, men interrupt others more often than women do.[39] How else do women and men differ in their listening behaviors? Check out the "Fact or Fiction" box on page 276 to find out.

The "At a Glance" box on page 277 provides a summary of the barriers to effective listening. Each of these barriers can be overcome. With some training and practice, most of us can improve our abilities to listen well. We'll look at some strategies for improvement in the next section.

Fact or Fiction?
Men and Women Listen Differently

In this book we examine several stereotypes about how women and men communicate. Some are outright false; others are true; and still others are true but highly exaggerated. One stereotype that relates to listening is that women and men have different listening styles; specifically, women are more interested in people, whereas men are more interested in facts. Is this stereotype true?

Recent research suggests that it is. In a study of adults' listening styles, researchers Stephanie Sargent and James Weaver found that women scored themselves higher on people-oriented listening than men did. These results suggest that women use their listening skills to learn about people and make connections with others. By contrast, men scored themselves higher on content-oriented listening than women did, suggesting that men use their listening skills to take in content and solve intellectual challenges. These results don't mean that women don't engage in content-oriented listening and men don't engage in people-oriented listening—they do. Rather, it shows that women and men—overall—have different approaches to listening, as the stereotype suggests.

You might recall that people often overestimate their listening abilities. If so, you might be wondering how we can have confidence in the results of a study that relies on self-reports. Because virtually every study of listening styles uses a self-report method for collecting data, that's a critical question. The answer is that reporting on *how* you listen is different from reporting on *how well* you listen. Research indicates that although many of us have a tendency to exaggerate how well we listen, we are much more accurate at reporting what our styles of listening are.

How can we use the information about sex differences in listening styles to improve our communication abilities? When we're communicating with members of the other sex, we can consider their listening tendencies and formulate our messages accordingly. Let's say you're describing a recent conflict you had with your romantic partner to different groups of friends. Because you know that men tend to focus on the content of what they're hearing, you might tailor your description to highlight what the conflict was about and what each person's position was. Because you know that women tend to focus on the interpersonal aspects of what they're hearing, you might adapt your description to focus on what the conflict taught you about your relational partner and yourself. It's important to remember

Research shows that women and men have different styles of listening. Women are more likely than men to say they use their listening skills to learn about people and make personal connections. Men are more likely to say they use their listening skills to solve intellectual challenges.

that the sex differences in these listening preferences are just tendencies. Nevertheless, they can give you some clues for how best to communicate with members of each sex.

Ask Yourself:

- How do these general sex differences compare with the behaviors of the women and men you know?

- Is one style of listening better than another? How might women's and men's styles of listening be appropriate in different situations?

Source: Sargent, S. L., & Weaver, J. B. (2003). Listening styles: Sex differences in perceptions of self and others. *International Journal of Listening, 17,* 5–18.

At a Glance: Barriers to Effective Listening

Common barriers to effective listening include:

Noise	Anything that distracts you from listening to what you wish to listen to
Pseudolistening	Using feedback behaviors to give the false impression that you are listening
Selective listening	Listening only to points you want to hear and ignoring all other points
Information overload	The state of being overwhelmed by the large amount of information you must take in every day
Glazing over	Daydreaming when you aren't speaking or listening during a conversation
Rebuttal tendency	Propensity to argue inwardly with a speaker and formulate your conclusions and responses prematurely
Closed-mindedness	Refusal even to listen to ideas or positions with which you disagree
Competitive interrupting	Interrupting others to gain control of a conversation

Learn It: What constitutes noise? What do people do when they pseudolisten? How does information overload affect listening ability? What does it mean to glaze over? When people have a rebuttal tendency, what do they tend to do while they're listening? What does it mean to be closed-minded? When are interruptions competitive?

Try It: For one week, keep a diary of times when you feel that other people haven't listened to you effectively. For each instance, try to identify the barriers to effective listening. After the week is over, read back through your notes, and reflect on times when the same barriers have affected your own listening ability. Assess how you might avoid these barriers to effective listening in the future.

Reflect on It: In what ways do you notice information overload in your own life? What topics do you tend to be closed-minded about, if any?

4} Becoming a Better Listener

We've seen several examples of ineffective listening in this chapter. In the opening vignette, Shane didn't listen to Carmen when she said they were having dinner with their son. In the movie *The Break-Up*, Gary didn't listen to Brooke when she said she needed a dozen lemons. Regan doesn't listen effectively to his customers' complaints, and Rochelle glazes over when she is listening to her children describe their day at school. Listening effectively can be a major challenge. Fortunately, effective listening is a skill rather than an innate ability. Consequently, most of us can become better listeners through education and practice. In this section, we'll

> *Much silence makes a powerful noise.*
> —African proverb

look at some strategies you can use to improve your skills for informational, critical, and empathic listening.

Becoming a Better Informational Listener

When you engage in informational listening, your goal is to understand and learn from the speaker's message. For instance, you might be attending a presentation about saving for retirement, or listening to your CEO talk about a merger your firm has just completed. How can you make the most of these opportunities?

Separate what is and isn't said. One important strategy for improving your informational listening skills is to beware of the tendency to "hear" words or statements that aren't actually said. Think about the last time you saw a television commercial for a pain reliever, for instance. A common tactic for advertisers is to claim that "nothing is more effective" than their product. What do you learn from hearing that statement? In other words, how would you paraphrase it?

The advertisers are hoping you learn that their particular pain reliever is the strongest one available . . . but that's not really what they said, is it? All they said is that nothing is *more* effective, which means there may be several other products that are *just as effective* as theirs. It may also mean that all the products are equally ineffective! If you listened to this ad and concluded that this product is the most effective one available, you arrived at that conclusion on your own (although it was definitely the conclusion the advertiser wanted you to form). When you are engaged in informational listening, be careful to distinguish between what is actually being said and what you are simply inferring.

Perhaps the most effective way to determine whether you have understood a speaker's message is to paraphrase it. As we saw earlier in the chapter, paraphrasing means restating the speaker's message in your own words to clarify the meaning of the message. If you paraphrase a statement in a way that accurately reflects its meaning, speakers tend to reply by confirming your understanding. Let's suppose that while leaving a theater after watching a movie, your roommate and you have the following exchange:

> **Roommate:** I think we should swing by that new barbecue place on the way home.
>
> **You:** You want to pick up some dinner?
>
> **Roommate:** Yeah, I'm starving.

You think your roommate is trying to imply that he's hungry and wants to get some food, but that isn't actually what he said. To check your understanding, therefore, you paraphrase his statement by putting it into your own words. Because you understood your roommate's statement correctly, he replied by confirming your interpretation.

Conversely, if you paraphrase a statement in a way that changes its meaning, speakers generally will correct your misunderstanding. Let's say the exchange with your roommate goes like this:

> **Roommate:** I think we should swing by that new barbecue place on the way home.
>
> **You:** You want to pick up some dinner?
>
> **Roommate:** No, I want to see if my friend Blake is working tonight.

In this instance, your interpretation of your roommate's statement was inaccurate. By paraphrasing his statement, you invited him to correct your understanding, and he did so. Paraphrasing is a simple activity, but it's one of the most efficient ways to determine whether you have correctly distinguished between what a speaker has and has not said.

Confirmation bias The tendency to seek information that supports our values and beliefs while discounting or ignoring information that doesn't.

Avoid the confirmation bias. The **confirmation bias** is the tendency to pay attention only to information that supports our values and beliefs while discounting or ignoring information that doesn't.[40] It becomes a problem for listening when it causes us to make up our minds about an issue without paying attention to all sides.

Let's say your close friend Tim is having a conflict with his girlfriend, Molly. Tim confides in you about the negative things Molly has been saying and doing, and because he's your friend, you're biased toward believing him. When Molly comes to talk to you about the situation, therefore, you tune her out because you've already made up your mind that she's at fault.

In this case, you're falling victim to the confirmation bias. Because you've already made up your mind that Tim is behaving fairly, you will pay attention only to information that confirms your belief and will tune out any information that doesn't. Good informational listeners are aware that their beliefs are not necessarily accurate. Therefore, a strategy for improving your informational listening skills is to ask yourself whether you have listened to all sides of an issue before you form a conclusion, or whether you are simply avoiding information that would lead you to question your beliefs.

Vividness effect The tendency for dramatic, shocking events to distort our perception of reality.

Listen for substance more than for style. The psychological principle called the **vividness effect** refers to the tendency for dramatic, shocking events to distort our perceptions of reality.[41] We watch news coverage of a deadly plane crash, for instance, and we become nervous about getting on a plane, even though the probability of dying in a plane crash is only about one in eight million.[42] Two days after the 1999 massacre at Columbine High School, 63% of Americans surveyed thought a shooting at their own child's school was likely, even though only 10% of all schools report even one experience of violent crime in a year.[43]

Good informational listeners look past what is dramatic and vivid and focus on the substance of what they're hearing.

The same effect can occur within interpersonal situations. If your parents went through a traumatic divorce when you were a child, for instance, that experience may have convinced you that marriage is more prone to fail than is actually the case. Dramatic events are more vivid and memorable than everyday events, so we pay more attention to them.

We can experience much the same problem during informational listening if we focus only on what's most vivid. In class, for instance, you might be more entertained by a lecture with dramatic stories and flashy PowerPoint slides than by one that's dry. That doesn't mean, however, that the flashy presentation contains better information than the dry one or that you'll learn more from it. Similarly, we might love being in classes with engaging, humorous teachers. That doesn't necessarily mean, however, that we'll learn more from them than from teachers who are disengaged and dry.

Being a good informational listener, then, means being able to look past what is dramatic and vivid to focus on the substance of what you're hearing. This process begins with being aware of the vividness effect and remembering that vivid experiences can distort your perceptions. The next time you go through a dramatic event or listen to a particularly engaging speaker, ask yourself whether you are listening and paying attention to accurate information or are being swayed by the drama of the event or the charisma of the speaker.

Becoming a Better Critical Listener

Many interpersonal situations require you to assess the credibility of what you're hearing. Here are three ways to get better at it.

Be a skeptic. Being a good critical listener starts with being skeptical of what you hear. Despite its reputation, **skepticism** isn't about being cynical or finding fault; rather, it's about evaluating the evidence for a claim. Recall from our discussion of the confirmation bias that people often pay attention only to evidence that supports their existing beliefs. Being skeptical means setting aside your biases and being willing to be persuaded by the merits of the argument and the quality of the evidence. A good critical listener doesn't accept claims blindly. Instead, he or she questions them to determine whether they're valid.[44]

In the CBS series, *CSI: Miami*, Horatio Caine (played by David Caruso) is an expert informational listener. As an investigator, he must subordinate his own ideas to whatever the evidence shows. Thus, he is particularly good at avoiding the confirmation bias, or the tendency to pay attention only to information that supports his ideas. He stays open-minded and remembers that he must consider all the evidence, whether it supports his preconceived notions or not.

Skepticism
The practice of evaluating the evidence for a claim.

Consider the following example. Your co-worker Fahid has come up with a business opportunity. He tells you about his plan and asks you to invest in it. If you're a poor critical listener, you may base your decision on how you feel about Fahid or how excited you are at the prospect of making money. In contrast, if you're a good critical listener, you'll set aside your feelings and focus on the merits of Fahid's idea. Does he have a sound business plan? Is there really a market for his product? Has he budgeted sufficient funds for advertising? Did he explain in detail how he would use your investment? Being a critical listener doesn't mean that you automatically criticize his plans; it does mean that you carefully evaluate them to determine whether they make sense.

Evaluate a speaker's credibility. Besides analyzing the merits of an argument, a good critical listener pays attention to the speaker's credibility. Credibility is a measure of how reliable and trustworthy someone is. All other things being equal, you can generally presume that information you hear from a credible source is more believable than information you get from a noncredible source.

Several qualities make a speaker more or less credible. One is expertise. It makes more sense for us to trust medical advice we receive from a physician than to trust medical advice from a professional athlete, for instance, because the doctor is a medical expert and the athlete is not. At the same time, it doesn't make sense to trust a physician for legal or financial advice, because he or she isn't an expert on those topics.

It's sometimes easy to confuse having expertise with having experience. Having experience with something may give a person credibility on that topic, but it doesn't necessarily make him or her an expert. After raising six children, for instance, Hannah is a very experienced parent, which does give her credibility insofar as she can draw on her many experiences to give advice to other moms. Although she's an experienced parent, however, she isn't an expert on parenting, because her only source of credibility is her individual experience. She doesn't have a degree in child development, for instance, and she isn't a recognized authority on parenting issues.

Conversely, people can be experts on topics with which they have no personal experience. As a board-certified obstetrician and gynecologist, for instance, Tyrell is an expert on pregnancy and women's health issues, even though, as a man, he has no direct experience with those topics. Similarly, Young Li is an outstanding marital therapist who has helped countless couples even though she has never been married herself. Why can a man be a good obstetrician and a single person be a good marital therapist? The answer is that they are drawing on their training and expertise to help others and not on their individual experiences.

Another characteristic that affects a speaker's credibility is bias. If the speaker has a special interest in making you believe some idea or claim, that fact tends to reduce his or her credibility. If a tobacco company executive claimed publicly that there were health benefits to smoking, for instance, a good critical listener would be highly skeptical, because the executive is a biased source.

This example might seem obvious, but sometimes you have to dig a bit deeper to investigate the source behind a particular idea to evaluate its credibility. For example, you might be intrigued to hear about a research report claiming that using your cell phone while driving does not increase your risk of being in a collision. The study may have been conducted by a reputable research team at a major university, which would enhance its credibility. After you investigate further, however, perhaps you discover that the study was funded by a group that lobbies on behalf of the telecommunications industry. Given its purpose, such a group would have a vested interest in the study's producing results that are favorable to cell phone use. Simply because a study is funded by a group with a vested interest in its results doesn't necessarily mean the study's conclusions are wrong. It does mean, however, that you should be more skeptical when you are exposed to them.

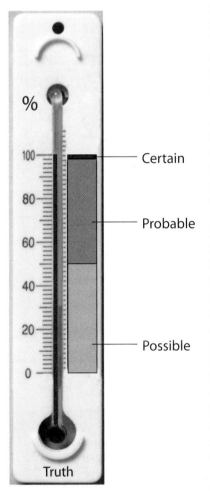

FIGURE 7.2 **Possibility, Probability, and Certainty** A statement is *possible* if its likelihood of being true is between 1% and 50%. It is *probable* if its likelihood of being true is between 51% and 99%. It is *certain* only if its likelihood of being true is 100%.

Understand probability. Evaluating the merits of a claim means speculating about the likelihood that the claim is true. This process can be tricky, because we sometimes confuse what's possible with what's probable, and what's probable with what's certain. An event or a fact is *possible* if there's even the slightest chance, however small, that it might be true. To be *probable,* a statement has to have greater than a 50% chance of being true. A statement is *certain* only if its likelihood of being true is 100%, nothing less. An illustration of the relationship among possibility, probability, and certainty appears in Figure 7.2.

Take a claim such as "I can survive without water for a month." There's a possibility this could be true, but the likelihood is very small. This claim certainly isn't probable, and a good critical listener wouldn't treat it as though it were. In contrast, the statement "I will get married someday" is not only possible, it's probable, because a very large majority of people marry at least once in their lives. Does this fact mean that this claim is certain, therefore? The answer is no, because there's a chance, however small, that it may *not* happen. For a claim to be certain, there can be *absolutely no chance* that it isn't true. A claim such as "I will die someday" is certain, because every living creature eventually dies. People who are good at critical listening understand the difference between possibility, probability, and certainty. They bear in mind that just because a claim is possible, that doesn't mean it's worth believing.

Just as with evaluating a speaker's credibility, determining the probability of claims you hear isn't always easy. Suppose that Manuel visits his uncle Alfredo, who has been a vegetarian for most of his adult life. "If you eat red meat, you'll eventually die of heart disease," he is constantly saying to his nieces and nephews.

How should Manuel evaluate the probability of that claim? He should start by determining whether the claim is possible. In this case, it is, because there is a possibility that people who eat red meat will die of heart disease. He should then ask himself whether the claim is certain. In this case, it isn't, because many people who eat red meat do *not* die of heart disease. Manuel knows, therefore, that the chances that Alfredo's claim is true are between 1% and 100%. Although he cannot accept it as a certainty, therefore, neither can he reject it as an impossibility. What he should do is to consider the probability that the claim is true. To determine probability he needs to research the link between heart disease and the consumption of red meat. With this information, he could assess whether Alfredo's claim is probable—that is, true more often than it is false—or improbable—that is, false more often than it is true.

Becoming a Better Empathic Listener

Within our relationships, a common goal for listening is to provide empathy and support. Being a good empathic listener can be difficult at times, but it's not impossible.

Listen nonjudgmentally. When we listen to learn, and especially when we listen to evaluate, we often make judgments about the information we're taking in. Good empathic listening, however, is about being open-minded and nonjudgmental.

Two strategies are particularly helpful here. The first is to listen without interrupting. Being supportive and empathic means letting the other person say what he or she needs to say without interrupting him or her. Fight the urge to jump into the conversation, and simply listen to the other person. Second, don't offer advice unless you're asked. Often, when we're hearing other people tell us their problems, our tendency is to respond with advice on how to solve those problems.[45] A good empathic listener will remember that people aren't always looking for advice—often, they just want someone to listen to them.

Acknowledge feelings. Empathizing involves understanding how someone else is feeling and trying to relate to those feelings. It's *not* the same thing as sympathizing, which is feeling sorry for the other person. An important strategy for good empathic listening, therefore, is to acknowledge a speaker's feelings and allow him or her to continue expressing them.

We do this by responding to speakers with "continuer statements," which are phrases that identify the emotions a person is experiencing and allow him or her to

When you're listening rather than speaking, your nonverbal behaviors communicate your interest, understanding, and empathy to the speaker.

communicate them further. By contrast, it is important to avoid "terminator statements," which are phrases that fail to acknowledge a speaker's emotions, shutting down his or her opportunity to express them. After listening to a patient describe her concerns about the progress of her illness, for instance, empathic physicians can use continuer statements such as "That must make you feel very uncertain" or "I can imagine how scary this must be" to reassure the patient that they understand and appreciate her feelings. Physicians with less empathic ability are more likely to use terminator statements such as "We're doing everything we can" or "You just need to give this some time." These types of responses imply to the patient that her feelings are unimportant.

In a recent study, researchers examined conversations between advanced cancer patients and their oncologists.[46] With permission, the researchers recorded nearly 400 conversations between patients and oncologists and listened for times when patients expressed negative emotions such as sadness, fear, or anxiety. When those moments arose, the researchers found that oncologists replied with continuer statements only 22 percent of the time. Younger physicians were more likely than older ones to use continuers, and female physicians were more likely than male ones to do so. These findings don't mean that oncologists lack empathy. Rather, the data suggest that they may have trouble *communicating* their empathy through emotionally sup-

Losing a loved one is among the most traumatic experiences in life. When someone you care about has this experience, one of the ways you can be most supportive is to be a good listener. Listening during times of grief often reflects the dark side of interpersonal communication because it involves actively attending to something that is difficult to hear. Here are some specific tips for being an empathic listener during times of grief:

- Remember that everyone grieves differently; there is no "right" or "wrong" way to deal with loss.

- Avoid telling the person "I know exactly how you feel" unless you have experienced the same type of loss yourself.

- Encourage the person to take care of his or her needs (especially physical needs). If you're close to the person and you feel it's appropriate, suggest that the person put off making any major personal, financial, or professional decisions until he or she is in a better frame of mind.

- Don't try to diminish the person's grief by using statements such as "You have to be strong" or "Look how much you still have." These suggestions can unfairly make people feel ashamed of their grief.

- Remind the person that you are willing to listen and to help in any way you can.

Ask Yourself:

- Why is it important to let people experience their grief?

- How do you like others to treat you when you are sad or grieving?

From Me to You:

- Many of us feel uncomfortable communicating with grieving people because we aren't sure what to say or how to help. Sometimes we even tune out conversations that are difficult or upsetting. If you want to be a caring friend, however, you must strive to pay attention and respond appropriately when others share their grief with you. Remember that grief is a normal response to loss, not something to be feared or avoided.

Adapted from St. Mary's College Counseling Center Grief and Loss Guidelines: http://www.stmarys-ca.edu/prospective/undergraduate_admissions/student_life_and_services/student_support/counseling_center/grief.html

portive listening responses. Such responses are particularly important for individuals who are struggling with terminal illnesses.

There are times when it may be difficult to empathize with other people. If you have never lost a parent, for instance, it would be very difficult for you to understand what that experience must be like. When you find yourself in situations like these, resist the urge to tell the speaker "I know how you feel." Unless you really *do* understand the speaker's experience, many people will find this type of statement disrespectful or insincere, even if you mean it as a show of support. (See the "Dark Side" box.) Instead, use your listening skills to try to understand how the person is feeling.

Communicate support nonverbally. One of the most important aspects of being a good empathic listener is to communicate your support nonverbally. When you're listening rather than speaking, your nonverbal behaviors convey your interest, understanding, and empathy to the speaker.

Perhaps the most important nonverbal behavior in this situation is eye contact. Speakers often watch your eye behaviors to see whether you're paying attention to what they're saying. If you allow yourself to be distracted by your environment, you can convey the message that you aren't really listening. Other important behaviors are your use of facial expressions and touch. A reassuring smile and a warm touch can make people feel as though you understand, support, and empathize.[47]

Learn It: What is the vividness effect? When should you question another person's credibility? Why is it important to listen nonjudgmentally?

Try It: Television commercials offer ample opportunity to sharpen your critical listening skills. Spend some time watching advertisements and thinking about the claims they're making. How credible are the sources? How probable are the claims? Do the commercials encourage you to make inferences that aren't supported by evidence? If so, how do they do this?

Reflect on It: In what situations do you find it difficult to engage in informational listening? Whom do you know who is a particularly good empathic listener?

} Master the Chapter {

Section 1} The Nature of Listening (p. 259)

I. The Nature of Listening

  A. What is listening?

- Listening is the active process of making meaning out of another person's spoken message.

  B. The importance of listening effectively

- The ability to listen effectively is important to success in a variety of communicative contexts.

  C. Some misconceptions about listening
    1. Myth: Hearing is the same as listening
    2. Myth: Listening is natural and effortless
    3. Myth: All listeners hear the same thing

- Listening is a learned skill that includes more than merely hearing.

  D. Culture affects listening behavior

- Cultural differences in the directness of verbal communication affect expectations for listening.

Section 2} Ways of Listening (p. 264)

II. Ways of Listening
  A. Stages of effective listening
    1. Hearing
    2. Understanding
    3. Remembering
    4. Interpreting
    5. Evaluating
    6. Responding

- Effective listening has six stages: hearing, understanding, remembering, interpreting, evaluating, and responding.

  B. Three types of listening
    1. Informational listening
    2. Critical listening
    3. Empathic listening

- People engage in informational listening, critical listening, and empathic listening in interpersonal contexts.

Section 3} Common Barriers to Effective Listening (p. 269)

III. Common Barriers to Effective Listening
  A. Noise

- Noise is anything that distracts you from listening to what you wish to listen to.

  B. Pseudolistening and selective attention

- Pseudolistening uses feedback behaviors that make it seem as if you're paying attention even when you aren't; selective attention means listening only to what you want to hear.

  C. Information overload

- Information overload refers to the large amount of information each of us takes in every day.

  D. Glazing over

- Glazing over is daydreaming during the time you aren't spending on listening.

  E. Rebuttal tendency

- The rebuttal tendency is the tendency to debate a speaker's point and formulate your reply while the person is still speaking.

  F. Closed-mindedness

- Being closed-minded means failing to listen to anything with which you disagree.

  G. Competitive interrupting

- Some people engage in competitive interrupting, or interrupting to take control of a conversation.

Section 4} Becoming a Better Listener (p. 277)

IV. Becoming a Better Listener
  A. Becoming a better informational listener
    1. Separate what is and isn't said
    2. Avoid the confirmation bias
    3. Listen for substance more than for style

- Becoming a better informational listener means separating what is and isn't said, avoiding the confirmation bias, and listening for substance.

B. **Becoming a better critical listener**
  1. Be a skeptic
  2. Evaluate a speaker's credibility
  3. Understand probability
C. **Becoming a better empathic listener**
  1. Listen nonjudgmentally
  2. Acknowledge feelings
  3. Communicate support nonverbally

- Becoming a better critical listener means being skeptical, evaluating a speaker's credibility, and understanding probability.

- Becoming a better empathic listener means listening nonjudgmentally, acknowledging feelings, and communicating support nonverbally.

Key Terms

Closed-mindedness	Glazing over	Rebuttal tendency
Competitive interrupting	HURIER model	Selective attention
Confirmation bias	Informational listening	Skepticism
Credibility	Information overload	Vividness effect
Critical listening	Listening	
Empathic listening	Pseudolistening	

Discussion Questions

1. What does it mean to listen? How is it different from merely hearing? In what instances do you hear someone without listening?
2. Why do you suppose people tend to overestimate how good they are at listening?
3. Which stage in the effective listening process do you think is the easiest? Which is the most challenging? Do you think everyone in your class would have the same answers?
4. Which type of listening—informational, critical, empathic— do you engage in the most often? Which type do you enjoy the most? Why?
5. When are you most likely to engage in pseudolistening or glazing over? How can you improve your listening in these situations?
6. What is the difference between interrupting and competitive interrupting? Why do people engage in competitive interrupting?
7. When do you notice yourself falling victim to the confirmation bias? What can you do to prevent it?
8. What does it mean to be skeptical? How does being skeptical help you to be a better listener?

Practice Quiz

Multiple Choice
1. Which of the following is *not* a part of the definition of listening?
   a. It is an active process.
   b. It involves the creation of meaning.
   c. It deals with only spoken messages.
   d. It occurs automatically.
2. Which of the following examples most accurately reflects how culture affects listening behavior?
   a. In individualistic cultures, people tend to think of time as something that can be saved or spent ("time is money") and listeners tend to be impatient when speakers do not get to the point.
   b. In collectivistic cultures, people tend to think of time as something that can be saved or spent ("time is money") and listeners tend to be impatient when speakers do not get to the point.
   c. When listening, people in individualistic cultures pay close attention to nonverbal behaviors to determine the meaning of a speaker's message.
   d. When listening, people in collectivistic cultures pay close attention to nonverbal behaviors to determine the meaning of a speaker's message.
3. Which of the following is the correct order of the listening responses from most active to most passive?
   a. Stonewalling, backchanneling, empathizing, advising
   b. Advising, empathizing, backchanneling, stonewalling
   c. Empathizing, advising, backchanneling, stonewalling
   d. Backchanneling, empathizing, stonewalling, advising

4. Using facial expressions and verbal statements such as "I understand" to let the speaker know you are paying attention is an example of which of the following types of listening responses?
   a. Analyzing
   b. Empathizing
   c. Paraphrasing
   d. Backchanneling
5. Assigning meaning to what we hear illustrates which of the following elements of the HURIER model of effective listening?
   a. Hearing
   b. Remembering
   c. Interpreting
   d. Responding
6. Which type of listening involves trying to understand a situation from the speaker's perspective?
   a. Empathic listening
   b. Informative listening
   c. Critical listening
   d. Persuasive listening
7. Having the attitude or belief that emphasizes organization and precision best describes which of the following listening styles?
   a. People-oriented
   b. Action-oriented
   c. Outcome-oriented
   d. Content-oriented
8. In class, Charyn cannot keep her mind off her problems at work. Instead of skipping class, she attends and pretends to listen to the professor's lecture. Charyn is experiencing which barrier to effective listening?
   a. Information overload
   b. Information underload
   c. Pseudolistening
   d. Glazing over
9. Understanding probability is crucial for being a good critical listener. Evaluate the following messages and identify which one is true.
   a. For a message to be probable, it has to have at least a 1% chance of being true.

b. For a message to be certain, it must be true 99% of the time.
   c. For a message to be possible, it must have only the slightest chance of being true.
   d. For a message to undeniable, it must be denied.
10. To be a good empathic listener when someone is grieving, it is *not* advisable to do which of the following?
    a. Remind the grieving person that she or he must stay strong.
    b. Offer to help the grieving individual in any way possible.
    c. Offer to listen if the grieving person wants to talk.
    d. Encourage the grieving individual to take care of his or her needs.

True/False

11. Research shows that college students spend more time listening than engaging in any other communication activity.
12. Glazing over is the same thing as pseudolistening.
13. The rebuttal tendency is an effective listening strategy because it requires the listener to pay close attention to the speaker's message to formulate a rebuttal.
14. Researchers found that women score themselves higher on people-oriented listening and men score themselves higher on content-oriented listening.
15. To be a good empathic listener, it is important to offer advice, even if you are not asked.

Fill in the Blank

16. Regarding the relationship between hearing and listening, _____ is a passive process, whereas _____ is an active process.
17. _____ occurs when someone listens only to the part of the message that she or he wants to hear and ignores the rest.
18. The _____ occurs when shocking and dramatic events distort an individual's perception of reality.
19. The first stage of effective listening, according to the HURIER model, is _____.
20. _____ is the tendency not to listen to anything with which you disagree.

Answers

Multiple Choice: 1 (d); 2 (a); 3 (b); 4 (d); 5 (c); 6 (a); 7 (b); 8 (c); 9 (c); 10 (a); **True/False:** 11 (T); 12 (F); 13 (F); 14 (T); 15 (F); **Fill in the Blank:** 16 (listening; hearing); 17 (selective attention); 18 (vividness effect); 19 (hearing); 20 (confirmation bias)

Research Library

Movies

Dead Man Walking (Drama; 1995; R)

> This drama depicts the true story of Sister Helen Prejean, a Roman Catholic nun who befriends convicted murderer Matthew Poncelet in the weeks leading up to his execution. By listening empathically, Sister Helen provides comfort to Poncelet before his death and helps his victim's family come to terms with their loss.

Sixteen Candles (Comedy; 1984; PG)

> In this classic teen comedy, Molly Ringwald plays Samantha Baker, whose entire family forgets her 16th birthday in the wake of her older sister's wedding. Samantha feels immense frustration that no one in her family is listening to her. Eventually, she discloses her frustrations to her geeky classmate, who makes her feel better by listening to her.

The Interpreter (Drama; 2005; PG-13)

> In this dramatic thriller, Nicole Kidman portrays Silvia Broome, a foreign-language interpreter at the headquarters of the United Nations in New York. Her job is to listen carefully to what speakers are saying and to interpret their speech into another language simultaneously. While in the building after hours one night, she overhears a threat against a foreign leader made in an obscure African language in which she happens to be fluent. Attempts to verify and protect against the threat rely heavily on the credibility of Broome's skills as a listener.

Books

Burley-Allen, M. (1995). *Listening: The forgotten skill: A self-teaching guide.* New York: Wiley.

Harris, R. M. (2006). *The listening leader: Powerful new strategies for becoming an influential communicator.* Westport, CT: Greenwood.

James, A., & Kratz, D. (1995). *Effective listening skills.* New York: McGraw-Hill.

Wolvin, A., & Coakley, C. (1996). *Listening.* Dubuque, IA: Brown & Benchmark.

Journal Articles

Brownell, J. (1990). Perceptions of effective listeners: A management study. *Journal of Business Communication, 27,* 401–415.

Carrell, L. J., & Willmington, S. C. (1996). A comparison of self-report and performance data in assessing speaking and listening competence. *Communication Reports, 9,* 185–191.

Watson, K. W., Barker, L. L., & Weaver, J. B. (1995). The listening styles profile (LSP-16): Development and validation of an instrument to assess four listening styles. *International Journal of Listening, 9,* 1–13.

Web Sites

www.listen.org

> This Web site is the home page of the International Listening Association, a professional organization promoting research and teaching about the importance of effective listening.

www.cnr.berkeley.edu/ucce50/ag-labor/7article/article40.htm

> This Web site, sponsored by the University of California at Berkeley, focuses on listening skills and offers a free one-hour workshop in effective empathic listening for download.

8

Interpersonal Communication in Social Relationships

Why are friendships and other social ties important?

How do we use interpersonal communication to form and maintain social relationships?

What are the challenges of having social relationships in the workplace?

Julie and Anne

Julie was having a terrible day. She was behind on all her work projects, and her boss wouldn't stop pressuring her about it. Her psychology midterm was less than a week away, and she had barely studied. She forgot to pick up the supplies for her son's birthday party that weekend. Even traffic was a mess as she wound her way through rush hour to meet up with her friend Anne for a late-afternoon coffee. When Julie arrived, Anne was talking to her husband on the phone. The moment Anne saw Julie's face, though, she knew Julie was having a rough day. "I gotta go, honey," Anne said to her husband, "I need to cheer Julie up." Julie started feeling better immediately, just hearing Anne say that.

Imagine what life would be like without friends. Families and romantic relationships are important to us, but our friends and acquaintances contribute significantly to our well-being as well. Sometimes, we look to friends for social and emotional support. At other times, we seek out our friends when we just want to hang out and relax or when we need help making a decision or dealing with a problem. Friends lift our spirits and remind us we're not alone in the world, just as Anne did for Julie.

This chapter illustrates the importance of social relationships, such as those between friends, close acquaintances, and co-workers, and focuses on how we use interpersonal communication to manage those relationships. All relationships are social to some extent. Because romantic and familial relationships often meet different social needs than do friendships, acquaintanceships, and workplace relationships, I will address those relationships in the next chapter. In this chapter, you'll learn:

1} Why social relationships matter so much to us

2} Which communication processes we use to form, maintain, and end social relationships

3} Which characteristics of friendship make it vital to our social experience and well-being

4} How we manage social relationships in the workplace

> *True friendship consists not in the multitude of friends, but in their worth and value.*
>
> —Ben Jonson (1572–1637)
> British writer and dramatist

Julie's experience in the opening story illustrates what many of us probably go through from time to time: really bad days made better by a good friend. Having strong social ties with our friends, our neighbors, our co-workers, and others helps many of us deal better with life's ups and downs. In this section, we'll take a look at:

- Why we form social relationships with others
- What benefits we get from our social relationships
- What costs are associated with maintaining these relationships

We Form Relationships Because We Need to Belong

In his 2007 book, *Personal Relationships and Personal Networks,* communication scholar Mac Parks wrote: "We humans are social animals down to our very cells. Nature did not make us noble loners."[1] He's right. One reason social relationships matter is that it's in our nature to form them. In fact, evolutionary psychologists argue that our motivation toward social relationships is innate, rather than learned.[2] This fundamental human inclination to bond with others is the idea behind psychologist Roy Baumeister's theory called the **need to belong**.[3] Need-to-belong theory posits that each of us is born with a drive to seek, form, maintain, and protect strong social relationships. To fulfill that drive, we use interpersonal communication to form social bonds with others at work, at school, in our neighborhoods, in community and religious organizations, on sports teams, in online communities, and in other social contexts. According to Baumeister's theory, each of these relationships helps us feel as though we aren't alone because we belong to a social community.

The need-to-belong theory also suggests that for us to satisfy our drive for relationships, we need social bonds that are both interactive and emotionally close. For example, most of us wouldn't be satisfied if we had emotionally close relationships with people with whom we never got to communicate. Being cut off from social interaction

Need to belong A hypothesis that says each of us is born with a fundamental drive to seek, form, maintain, and protect strong social relationships.

Deployed military personnel and elderly individuals who live alone often experience intense loneliness when they don't see their relatives or friends for extended periods of time.

can be physically and psychologically devastating. That's one of the reasons why solitary confinement is considered such a harsh punishment.[4] Women and men who are deployed for military service,[5] and many elderly individuals who live alone,[6] also experience loneliness when they don't see their families or friends for extended periods.

By the same token, interacting only with people we have no real feelings for would be largely unrewarding as well. Imagine, for instance, that you moved to a large city where you didn't know anyone. Even though you'd have plenty of interactions with people—taxi drivers, grocery store clerks, your eye doctor, your hair stylist—you wouldn't encounter anyone you felt close to. Although these task-oriented relationships would help us to fulfill various needs, such as getting from one place to another or having our vision checked, they wouldn't fulfill our need to belong because they usually aren't emotionally close.

Many social relationships do, however, fulfill our needs for both interaction and emotional closeness. For instance, you probably have long-time friends to whom you feel very close and with whom you interact regularly. Perhaps you formed some of those friendships during your childhood or adolescence. Others you may have formed through school or work. Still others may be friendships you formed online. Significantly, research indicates that online relationships can be just as emotionally close and involve just as much interaction as face-to-face friendships.[7] Each of these social relationships can help us feel connected to others in a way that we don't experience when we can't interact with people we care about or when we don't care about the people with whom we interact. The natural "need to belong" for humans is not the only reason social relationships matter to us, but the need-to-belong theory suggests it's one of the most important ones.

Social Relationships Bring Rewards

Besides fulfilling our need to belong, social relationships matter because they bring us all sorts of rewards. In this section, we'll take a brief look at three types of rewards: emotional, material, and health rewards. These rewards aren't necessarily independent of one another; rather, they are often intertwined in our social relationships.

Social relationships bring emotional rewards. Friends provide us with at least two types of emotional rewards. One is emotional support, or encouragement during times of emotional turmoil. Whether you're going through a serious crisis or just having a bad day, friends can provide comfort and empathy to help you make it through.[8] When Frank's long-term romantic relationship was falling apart, for instance, his group of close friends made sure he knew they were there to listen to him and support him. Although the experience was difficult for Frank, the emotional support he received from his friends helped him to cope.

The second emotional reward of having friends is happiness. We enjoy interacting with friends because it's fun and relaxing and because our friends entertain us. One of Angel's favorite ways to spend a Friday night, for example, is by inviting her good friends over to cook dinner, watch DVDs, and talk about what's going on in their lives. Hanging out with her close friends always makes Angel feel good. Indeed, many of our happiest times are spent with our close friends around us.[9]

Social relationships bring material rewards. A second way social relationships benefit us is by helping us meet our material needs, such as our needs for money, food, shelter, and transportation. We tend to share these types of resources with people to whom we feel close. When you need someone to help you move, a place to stay for the weekend, or a few dollars to tide you over until payday, you're more likely to have these material needs met if you have strong social relationships to draw on than if

How Do We Know?

Social Relationships Help Keep Us Healthy

In this chapter, we discuss how having positive social relationships improves our ability to fight off the common cold. How do we know this is true?

In a highly regarded study, a team of researchers led by psychologist Sheldon Cohen asked more than 300 women and men to report on how sociable they were, how large their social networks were, and how much social support they received from others. The participants were then quarantined and (with their permission) exposed to one of two viruses known to cause colds. Participants remained quarantined for five days. During this time, the researchers took blood samples to test for presence of the infection and asked participants to self-report on their cold symptoms, such as a runny nose, sneezing, and coughing. They even collected and weighed all the participants' used facial tissues to determine their daily mucus production! After looking at their data, the researchers found that the more positive people's social relationships were, the less susceptible they were to the cold virus.

Ask Yourself

- Why do you suppose having a strong social network helps you stay physically healthy?

- Besides a cold, what other illnesses might the researchers have ethically studied?

Source: Cohen, S., Doyle, W. J., Turner, R., Alper, C. M., & Skoner, D. P. (2003). Sociability and susceptibility to the common cold. *Psychological Science, 14*, 389–395.

you don't. You're also more likely to offer these material rewards to your close friends than to strangers or to people you don't know well.

Social relationships bring health rewards. As we saw in the first chapter, good social relationships keep us healthy. One study found, for instance, that the more social relationships people had, the better able they were to fight off a common cold. This research by psychologist Sheldon Cohen and his colleagues is described in the "How Do We Know?" box above.[10] Another study reported that people with a strong social network were twice as likely as those without strong relationships to survive after a heart attack.[11] In fact, after reviewing more than 60 published studies on the topic, sociologist James House and his colleagues concluded that the lack of strong, positive social relationships is as big a risk factor for premature mortality as cigarette smoking, obesity, and elevated blood pressure.[12]

There are at least two reasons why having good friends may help keep us healthy. One reason is that the happiness and relaxation close friendships provide help us to ward off the negative effects of stress. We all face sources of stress in our daily lives, such as dealing with an illness or worrying if we'll have enough money to pay our rent. Stress can have many negative effects on the body, such as causing sleeping problems or unhealthy weight gain; increasing our risk for heart disease, stroke, and depression; and aggravating conditions such as intestinal disorders and acne.[13] Research shows, however, that having close, satisfying social relationships acts as a buffer, protecting us from overreacting to stressful events.[14] This doesn't mean that we don't experience

stress when we have strong relationships. Rather, having close friends helps us deal with stress in a more effective, optimistic way, so that it doesn't threaten our health as much as it otherwise would.[15]

A second reason why having good friends helps us stay healthy is that friends can look out for our safety and well-being. Friends can encourage us to pursue healthy behaviors, such as wearing a seatbelt while driving or avoiding excessive use of alcohol.[16] They can prompt us to seek medical attention when we need it, and they can encourage us to take preventive measures, such as eating properly or getting the car brakes inspected every six months.[17] They can exercise with us and hold us accountable for maintaining a healthy weight.[18] Finally, if we have chronic health problems such as diabetes or cancer, our friends can help us with the day-to-day tasks of managing those conditions.[19]

Because they help us to manage stress and because they look out for our welfare, close friends and other social relations provide us with health rewards. Indeed, you might even say that having good friends adds years to your life!

Social Relationships Carry Costs as Well as Rewards

It's easy to think of the rewards of social relationships: They bring us emotional support, help us during times of need, and even make us healthier. Friendships and other social relationships carry costs as well as rewards, however. Think about what it "costs" you to be friends with someone. For example, you might have to spend time with your friend that you would prefer to spend doing something rewarding by yourself. In addition, you must make an emotional investment, particularly when your friend needs your support. There can also be material costs associated with doing things together, such as traveling or going out to dinner. Finally, friendships often require physical investments as well. For example, you may not *want* to help your friend move into his new apartment, but you do it anyway because he's your friend.

Much of the time, we decide that the rewards of friendship are worth the costs. We invest our energies and resources in our friends because they benefit us. We spend our time and money with our friends because we feel happy and entertained by their friendship. In some cases, how-

We invest time, emotional energy, and even physical energy in our close friendships.

ever, the costs of staying in the relationship outweigh the rewards. Maybe you've felt that way in one of your friendships before. As we'll discuss later in this chapter, a social exchange orientation suggests that being in this kind of "under-benefited" state can motivate people to end relationships, or at least to find them unsatisfying.

Learn It: What is the need to belong? In what ways do social relationships reward us? What sorts of costs are associated with maintaining a friendship?

Try It: For a week, record the time, the energy, and other resources your friends give you, as well as those you give your friends.

Reflect on It: How do your friendships benefit you emotionally, materially, and with respect to your health? In what ways do you provide these types of benefits in your social relationships?

2} Forming and Maintaining Social Bonds {

We've discussed why social relationships matter and how they reward us. In this section, we'll look at several theories that explain the various interpersonal forces that work to form and develop social relationships. Some of these theories help us to understand whom we choose to form social relationships with. These theories include:

> *It's the friends you can call up at 4 a.m. that matter.*
>
> —Marlene Dietrich (1901–1992)
> German-American entertainer

- Attraction theory, which describes why we are drawn to others
- Uncertainty reduction theory, which indicates why we initially interact with others
- Predicted outcome value theory, which details why we get to know some people and not others

Other theories explain why and how we maintain social relationships once we form them. These theories include:

- Social exchange theories, which indicate how we compare our current relationships with our alternatives and how we count our costs and benefits
- Relational maintenance behaviors, which are the communication behaviors we use to sustain our relationships

Attraction Theory

Interpersonal attraction
Any force that draws people together to form a relationship.
Physical attraction
Attraction to someone's physical appearance.

The process of forming most relationships begins with **interpersonal attraction,** which is the force that draws people together. You're probably already familiar with the concept of **physical attraction,** or being drawn to someone because of his or her looks. There are at least two other ways to be attracted to a person, though. One is **social attraction,** which means being attracted to someone's personality. For example, you might like your new officemate at work because of her positive attitude. Likewise, you might be drawn to a classmate in your communication course because he has a great sense of humor. A third kind of attraction is **task attraction,** or being

Social attraction
Attraction to someone's personality.
Task attraction
Attraction to someone's ability and dependability.

attracted to someone's abilities and dependability.[20] You might feel positively toward
your new carpool partner because he shows
up on time every day, rain or shine. Maybe
you admire your suitemate because of her
excellent karaoke skills. Any or all of these
types of attraction can draw us to others and
make us want to get to know them better.

A variety of qualities in a new acquaintance can spark the forces of interpersonal
attraction, but research suggests that four
factors are especially powerful. These are:

- Personal appearance
- Proximity
- Similarity
- Complementarity

Let's look at each one more closely.

We are attracted by appearance. When we
say a person is attractive, what we often mean
is that he or she *looks* attractive. Humans are
highly visually oriented, so when we find
someone to be physically attractive, we are often motivated to get to know that person better. There are at
least two reasons why we behave this way. One reason
is that we value and appreciate physical attractiveness,
so we want to be around people we consider attractive.[21]

Most relationships are sparked by some type of
attraction. That might include physical attraction
(attraction to one's appearance), social attraction
(attraction to one's personality), and task attraction (attraction to one's abilities).

Another reason is that, throughout history, humans have sought physically attractive others as mates. Because attractive people often have particularly healthy genes,
children produced with attractive people are likely to be healthy, because they will
inherit those genes.[22]

A popular cultural saying is that "beauty is only skin deep." This maxim suggests that physical beauty or attractiveness is superficial, meaning that it reflects only
people's outer appearance but offers no indication of who they are or how they behave. Indeed, perhaps you've heard someone assert that an individual is physically
handsome or beautiful, but "it's what's on the *inside* that really counts." Despite the
popularity of this belief, however, decades of research demonstrate that in reality we
pay an enormous amount of attention to physical appearance when we're forming
social and personal relationships.[23]

What makes one person more physically attractive than another is a combination of social and genetic characteristics. Some notions of beauty vary widely from
culture to culture. Consider weight, for example. In North America and Western Europe, a thin, physically fit body type is generally considered the most attractive. In
many African and Australian tribal cultures, however, an overweight body is considered the most attractive, at least for women.[24]

Cultures also vary in the ways in which they manipulate or mutilate the body
to achieve physical attractiveness. One example is the practice of wearing lip plates.
Girls in the Mursai of southern Ethiopia and the Mebêngôkre Indians of Brazil have
their lips pierced at a young age and a large wooden or clay plate inserted into the
hole. As the girls grow older, their lip plates are increased in size, and those with
the largest plates are considered the most desirable as mates.[25] Similarly, women in

the Padaung tribe of Myanmar often wear metal rings around their necks to make their necks appear longer than they are. Those women with the longest necks are considered the most attractive and most desirable as mates.[26]

Other aspects of physical attractiveness are cross-cultural. For instance, people around the world prefer bodies and faces that are symmetrical—that is, similar on the left and right sides—and have features that are proportional in size to one another. Across cultures, men are also attracted to women who appear healthy and young, because these characteristics signal their ability to produce healthy offspring.[27] Similarly, women across cultures are attracted to men who look powerful and appear to have resources, because these characteristics signal their ability to provide for a family.[28] We may not consider these factors at a conscious level when we're assessing another person's attractiveness, but research demonstrates that people around the world are nonetheless attracted to these qualities in others.[29]

Our preferences for physically attractive people begin early in life. Studies have shown that infants as young as six months prefer looking at images of attractive people,[30] and that through our life span, we place a premium on appearance.[31] Although we often think about physical attractiveness in the context of forming romantic relationships, research also tells us that we even prefer attractive people over unattractive ones in our friendships and work associations.[32]

We are attracted by proximity. Another important predictor of attraction is proximity, which refers to how close together people live or work and how often they interact. We're more likely to form and maintain social relationships with people we see often than with people we don't.[33] For example, we tend to know our next-door neighbors better than the neighbors down the road, and we're more likely to become friends and maintain friendships with our classmates and co-workers than with people we rarely see, such as other students at school or other employees at work.

Some researchers have suggested that the Internet may be reducing the influence of physical proximity on attraction. With chat rooms, instant messaging, and other forms of online interaction, we're now free to develop friendships with virtually anyone, no matter how geographically distant they are. Indeed, research has shown that a vast majority of Internet users have formed social relationships with people they met online.[34] Web sites such as Facebook and MySpace allow us to make friends and communicate with them regularly, even if they live in different cities, in different countries, or on different continents. Although our choices of online friends may still be influenced by physical appearance and our perceived similarity, they need not be bound by physical proximity.

We are attracted by similarity. You've probably had the experience of getting to know someone and marveling at how much you have in common. When we meet people with backgrounds, experiences, beliefs, and interests that are similar to our own, we find them to be comfortable and familiar; sometimes it's almost as if we already know them. It turns out that we find similarity to be very attractive. Research shows we're more likely to form social relationships with people who are similar to, rather than different from, ourselves.[35]

We find similarity to be attractive for at least two reasons. The first reason is that we often find social validation in people who are similar to us. Liking people who are similar to you is, in a way, like liking yourself. You might be especially drawn to people who share your hobbies, your sense of humor, or your way of seeing the world, for instance, because these people make you feel better about who *you* are.[36] We don't necessarily think about this at a conscious level, but it may nonetheless be one of the reasons we find similarity to be attractive.

Although we're attracted to similarity, many of us have friends whose personalities and experiences are different from our own. As long as we see the differences as positive, they can contribute to close and enduring friendships.

The second reason we find similarity attractive is that it is in our genetic interests to do so.[37] For our primitive ancestors, similarity—particularly in physical appearance and behavior—was one of the most reliable ways to distinguish relatives from nonrelatives. This was important, because two people who look and behave similarly are more likely to share genetic material with each other than are two people who look and behave differently. And humans, like many other species, are motivated to help those with whom they share genetic material. This is why, for instance, we love our own children more than we love other people's children, and why we give more of our resources to family members than to strangers.[38] When we help our genetic relatives, we help our own genes survive into future generations.

Again, we don't do this consciously. Rather, researchers believe that, over millennia, humans have developed the motivation to help their genetic relatives because it ensures the survival of their own genes.[39] Similarity in physical appearance is one of the ways we can tell who our genetic relatives are.

We are attracted by complementarity. Of course, no one is *exactly* like you—we all differ from one another in various ways. We may believe that "opposites attract," but, as the "Fact or Fiction?" box on the next page points out, similarity is often more attractive than difference is. Even though we're attracted to similarity, however, we can also be attracted to people who are different from ourselves if we see their differences as *complementary*—that is, if we see the differences as beneficial to ourselves. Some-

Fact or Fiction?

When It Comes to Forming Friendships, Opposites Attract

You've probably heard the expression that "opposites attract." This notion suggests we find difference attractive and will be drawn most strongly to people who are different from us. Is this fact or fiction?

When we're forming friendships, difference *can* be attractive to us, but only if we see the difference as complementary—that is, if it benefits us in some way, such as by reflecting a personality trait that we don't have ourselves. Study after study has shown, however, that we find similarity to be much more attractive.

In one study, the researchers paired college students at the beginning of a semester with strangers of their same sex and ethnicity. Both people in each pair reported on their individual attitudes, personalities, and ways of seeing the world. Over the next eight weeks, they also reported how much they liked each other. The researchers found that having similar attitudes was the strongest predictor of initial attraction. If the students' attitudes were highly dissimilar, the students tended not to like each other. The study also found that having similar personalities and ways of looking at the world was the strongest predictor of whether students remained friends after being initially drawn to one another. The results of this and dozens of other studies suggest that, when it comes to forming friendships, the more accurate statement would be "similars attract."

Ask Yourself

- Why do you suppose so many people believe that opposites attract?

- Why do we find similarity to be rewarding in a friend?

From Me to You

- When it comes to choosing your friends, some forms of similarity are probably more important to you than others. Perhaps you find it very important that your friends have beliefs or moral values similar to your own. Maybe you strive for friends who are similar to you in level of education or physical attractiveness. No friend is like you in every way, so each friend represents a combination of similarity and difference. Consider what types of similarities matter to you the most in the friends you choose.

Source: Neimeyer, R. A., & Mitchell, K. A. (1988). Similarity and attraction: A longitudinal study. *Journal of Social and Personal Relationships, 5,* 131–148.

one who's shy might be drawn to a more outgoing person because this friend can help him become more sociable. Someone with a serious personality might prefer friends who are a little more lighthearted, and a person who prefers to plan activities ahead of time might be attracted to a friend who's more spontaneous.

The key to attraction based on complementarity is that people have to see their differences as positive. We may not be drawn to people with religious beliefs or political orientations that are radically different from our own, for instance. If we are convinced our beliefs and orientations are correct, we may see differences as negative. Because religious beliefs and political orientations often reflect our fundamental ways of viewing the world, we may see opposing viewpoints as threatening to our own, which may decrease our attraction to someone else. If we enjoy engaging in other ways of thinking, however, then we may see differences in beliefs and orientations as complementary, which could make another person seem attractive to us as a friend.[40]

Uncertainty Reduction Theory

A second major theory of why we form relationships focuses not on interpersonal attraction but on the uncertainty we feel when we don't know others very well. Let's say you meet someone and want to get to know him or her better. What does it *mean* to get to know someone? According to communication scholars Charles Berger and Richard Calabrese, it means we're reducing our level of uncertainty about the person.[41]

When you first meet a new co-worker, your uncertainty about her is high. According to uncertainty reduction theory, you'll be motivated to reduce your uncertainty by using communication behaviors to get to know her.

When you first meet a new co-worker, for instance, you don't know much about her, so your uncertainty about her is high. Berger and Calabrese's **uncertainty reduction theory** suggests that you will find uncertainty to be unpleasant, so you'll be motivated to reduce your uncertainty by using communication behaviors to get to know her. At first, you'll probably talk about basic information, such as where she lives or what she likes to do outside work. As you get to know her better, she will probably disclose more personal information about herself. You may also learn about her by paying attention to nonverbal cues, such as her personal appearance, the sound of her voice, or the way she uses gestures. According to uncertainty reduction theory, each new piece of information that you gain reduces your uncertainty even more.

Uncertainty reduction theory A theory suggesting that people are motivated to reduce their uncertainty about others.

Importantly, uncertainty reduction theory also suggests that the less uncertain you are, the more you will like the person. Because we dislike being uncertain about people, we will like people more as our uncertainty about them is decreased. The relationship between liking and uncertainty, as reflected in uncertainty reduction theory, is illustrated in Figure 8.1.

Predicted Outcome Value Theory

We have just read that as your uncertainty about your new co-worker is reduced, you probably will like her more. What happens, however, if you don't like the information you learn about her? Will you still like her more or want to get to know her better? Communication professor Michael Sunnafrank offered a slightly different way to think about how we form relationships. In his **predicted outcome value theory,** he suggested that when we first communicate with others, we try to determine whether continued communication with them will be worth our effort.[42] If we like what we learn about someone during our initial conversations, we predict positive outcomes for future communication with that person, meaning we will want to get to know the person better. By contrast, if

Predicted outcome value theory A theory predicting that we form relationships when we think the effort will be worth it.

FIGURE 8.1 **Relationship between liking and uncertainty, according to uncertainty reduction theory** According to uncertainty reduction theory, as uncertainty about a person goes down, liking for that person goes up.

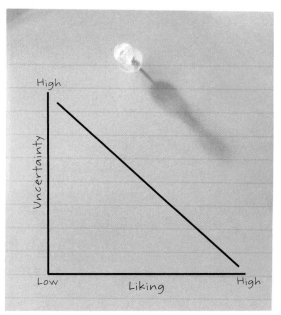

we don't like what we learn about someone during our initial conversations, we predict negative outcomes for future communication, and we won't be motivated to continue to get to know him or her.[43]

There are many reasons we might predict positive outcomes when we first communicate with a particular individual. We might find that we have many things in common with her or that she has a great sense of humor and is fun to be around. We might also find that she is very knowledgeable about something we're interested in, such as kayaking or designing Web pages, so we can learn more about these hobbies by being around her. If we value those qualities, then Sunnafrank's theory predicts that we will engage in communication behaviors aimed at getting to know her better, such as increasing verbal communication and nonverbal immediacy around her.[44]

In other cases, we might predict negative outcomes when we first get to know someone. After spending time with a new acquaintance, for instance, we might discover that she's always criticizing people, she's boring, or she's very defensive. If we dislike those qualities, predicted outcome value theory proposes that we will reduce our verbal and nonverbal communication with her or even avoid her altogether. The process of predicted outcome value theory is displayed in Figure 8.2.

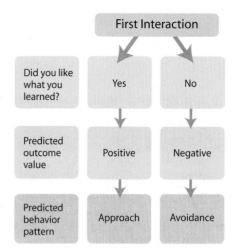

FIGURE 8.2 **Predicted outcome value theory** Predicted outcome value theory says we project how positive our interactions with people will be in the future, and we behave toward them accordingly.

Understanding Relationship Formation

Attraction theory, uncertainty reduction theory, and predicted outcome value theory all help us to understand how, and with whom, we form social relationships. According to attraction theory, we want to get to know people when we feel some measure of physical, social, or task attraction to them. Any of these forms of attraction will motivate us to engage in **approach behaviors,** which are communication behaviors that signal our interest in another person. Approach behaviors include verbal behaviors, such as introducing yourself to someone and asking about him or her. They also include nonverbal behaviors, such as smiling and maintaining eye contact with the person. We use these and other communication behaviors to express our desire to get to know others, and attraction theory predicts that these are the result of physical, social, and/or task attraction.

According to uncertainty reduction theory, the primary purpose of engaging in approach behaviors is to collect information about the other person to reduce our uncertainty about him or her. The more our uncertainty is reduced, the more we will like the person. As we have discussed, this assumption might be true if most of what we learn about the person is positive. What if we find out, however, that he or she is bigoted, or obnoxious, or just plain dull? According to uncertainty reduction theory, we may still like the person more because our uncertainty has been reduced.

According to predicted outcome value theory, however, we should like the person less, because the outcomes we'd predict from knowing him or her would seem less positive. As a result, we should no longer be motivated to engage in approach behaviors with the person. Rather, we would likely engage in **avoidance behaviors,** which are communication behaviors that signal our lack of interest in someone else. As with approach behaviors, avoidance behaviors include both verbal communication behaviors, such as saying "please leave me alone," and nonverbal behaviors, such as

Approach behaviors Communication behaviors that signal your interest in getting to know someone.

Avoidance behaviors Communication behaviors that signal your lack of interest in getting know someone.

Sometimes we like people less the more we learn about them. Predicted outcome value theory suggests we'll use avoidance behaviors to signal our lack of interest in such people.

avoiding eye contact with the person or not spending time with him or her. According to predicted outcome value theory, therefore, we're motivated to form relationships with people only when the initial information we learn about them is positive.

Merely forming a social relationship, however, doesn't necessarily mean we'll want to maintain it. Some friendships start strong but fade over time, for instance, whereas others continue to grow and flourish. Two theoretical traditions, in particular, help us understand why and how we maintain the social relationships we have formed. These are cost/benefit theories and the concept of relational maintenance behaviors. We will look at each of these next.

Theories About Costs and Benefits

Suppose you've been drawn to someone, you've gotten to know her, and the two of you have become friends. At this point, you've completed the process of forming a social relationship. Now the question is, How will you decide whether you want to stay in the relationship? One way to understand why we maintain certain friendships but let others die out is by examining the give-and-take of relational costs and benefits.

Earlier in this chapter, we saw that relationships carry costs as well as rewards. You invest certain things in a friendship, such as your time, your attention, and your money. In return, you receive certain benefits from it, such as emotional support, entertainment, and help. Two specific theories help us understand how these costs and benefits influence which relationships we are most likely to maintain: social exchange theory and equity theory. We discuss both theories in this section. Although these theories take slightly different approaches, they both focus on how we balance the costs and the rewards of maintaining our relationships with others.

Being neighborly has both costs and benefits. According to social exchange theory, we are driven to maintain relationships in which our benefits outweigh our costs.

Social exchange theory A theory predicting that people seek to form and maintain relationships in which the benefits outweigh the costs.

Social exchange theory and relationship formation. The guiding principle of **social exchange theory** is that people seek to maintain relationships in which their benefits outweigh their costs.[45] Think of your relationship with a neighbor, for instance. There are costs involved in being neighborly. For example, you have to be willing to help when needed, and you may experience a loss of privacy if your neighbor is aware of your comings and goings. There are also benefits to a neighborly relationship, such as knowing someone can watch your home when you're away and having someone close by whose company you enjoy. The question, according to social exchange theory, is whether you think the benefits outweigh the costs. If you do, then you're likely to stay in that relationship; if not, then you're less inclined to maintain it.

Comparison level Your realistic expectation of what you think you deserve from a relationship.

An important concept in social exchange theory is your **comparison level,** which is your realistic expectation of what you want and think you deserve from a relationship. Your expectations are based on both your prior experiences with social relationships and the prevailing cultural norms for such relationships. Perhaps you think neighbors should be friendly and should help you out when you need it but otherwise should mind their own business. These ideas would form part of your comparison level for your own neighborly relationships. Similarly, you might believe that friends should care about your well-being, always keep your secrets, and support you even when they disagree with your decisions. These desires and expectations would be part of your comparison level for your own friendships.

Comparison level for alternatives Your assessment of how good your current relationship is, compared with your other options.

Equally important is your **comparison level for alternatives.** This concept refers to your beliefs concerning how good or bad your current relationship is compared with your perceived options. Are you satisfied with your neighborly relationships, for instance, or do you think you could find better neighbors if you moved? Likewise, are you happy with your current friendships, or do you think you'd be better off terminating those relationships and finding new friends? Social exchange theory suggests that we maintain relationships when we believe that doing so is better than our alternatives, such as ending the relationships or finding new ones. By contrast, we're most likely to end relationships if we believe staying in them is worse than our alternatives.

Research suggests that, in some relationships, your comparison level for a particular relationship will strongly influence how satisfied you are in that relationship.[46] Your comparison level for alternatives, however, will more strongly influence whether that relationship will last. Even satisfying friendships can end if the alternatives are more appealing. By contrast, sometimes unsatisfying friendships endure over time. The association between the comparison level and the comparison level for alternatives is depicted in Figure 8.3.

	Comparison Level	
	High	**Low**
High (Comparison Level for Alternatives)	Your relationship is satisfying, but you may be inclined to end it if an even more satisfying relationship looks probable.	You're likely to be dissatisfied with this relationship and will probably look for opportunities to end it.
Low (Comparison Level for Alternatives)	You'll probably be satisfied with this relationship and won't be likely to end it.	Although you won't find your relationship satisfying, you are unlikely to end it.

FIGURE 8.3 Comparison level and comparison level for alternatives in social exchange theory Social exchange theory says four outcomes are possible when we cross our comparison level with our comparison level for alternatives.

Let's say your friend Clarissa has a great sense of humor, enjoys many of the same activities you do, and is always willing to listen when you have a problem. To the extent that you value these characteristics, you would perceive your friendship with her as matching your comparison level for friendships. Let's say, though, that Clarissa also has a tendency to gossip and speak badly of other people when she's around you. Not only do you find this behavior unappealing, but it also makes you wonder what she says about you behind your back. You have also seen Clarissa behave dishonestly, such as when she accused one of her classmates of stealing even when she knew he hadn't. If you find dishonesty and a tendency to gossip to be unattractive qualities, you might perceive that your friendship doesn't meet your comparison level for friendships. Indeed, you might consider ending your friendship with Clarissa after you see her behave in these ways. Social exchange theory, however, argues that you'd first have to consider how attractive your alternatives are.

Suppose you ended your friendship with Clarissa. In that case, you'd no longer have to put up with her gossiping and dishonesty. At the same time, however, you would also lose what you value about her as a friend, including her good humor and her willingness to listen. If you have other friends who provide you with these same benefits—or if you believe you could make such friends—then you might decide it's worth ending your relationship with Clarissa. In this situation, you've decided that your comparison level for alternatives exceeds your comparison level. Because you think you'd be better off without having Clarissa as a friend, you would likely end this relationship, according to social exchange theory.

Conversely, suppose you don't have other friends who benefit you the way that Clarissa does. Maybe you've just moved to the area and she's the only real friend you have, perhaps you're shy and don't feel comfortable trying to make new friends. As a result, you might conclude that even though you dislike some of Clarissa's behaviors, you're still better off maintaining your friendship than ending it. In this situation, you've decided that your comparison level exceeds your comparison level for alternatives. Because you believe you'd be better off keeping Clarissa as a friend, you would likely maintain this relationship.

One major contribution of social exchange theory is that it provides an explanation for why people maintain relationships that appear to be costly. For instance, people frequently wonder why anyone would stay in an abusive friendship. Perhaps you've even thought to yourself, "I'd never remain friends with someone who treated me that way." Any type of abuse—whether physical, psychological, or emotional—represents a cost, rather than a benefit, of being in a relationship. For the person being abused, however, the choice between maintaining or ending the abusive relationship is rarely as simple as it appears to outsiders. Some victims of abuse believe that the other person's positive qualities compensate for his or her negative ones; thus, they have a favorable comparison level. Other victims believe that the costs of ending the relationship—which might include loneliness, loss of other friends, and even

One major contribution of social exchange theory is that it explains why people maintain relationships that appear to be costly.

the threat of violence—exceed the costs of staying in the relationship. In this case, their comparison level exceeds their comparison level for alternatives. They acknowledge that the relationship is bad, but they're convinced that the consequences of ending it would be worse.

Equity theory and relationship formation. If you think of social relationships as having costs and rewards, then it's easy to see that both people in a given relationship might not benefit equally. Imagine your friend Chandra is always text messaging you about her problems but never has time to listen to you about yours. She's getting the benefit of your time and attention without the cost of giving her own time and attention to you. In contrast, you are putting more into the friendship than you're getting from it.

In this situation, Chandra is **over-benefited** and you are **under-benefited.** According to **equity theory,** this arrangement is a recipe for trouble.[47] Equity theory borrows the concepts of cost and reward from social exchange theory and extends them by defining a good relationship as one in which your ratio of costs and rewards is equal to your partner's. It's fine if you're working harder on your relationship than your friend is, as long as you're getting more out of it than she does. For example, if you're doing all the cooking every night but Chandra is letting you share her apartment for free, you're probably getting more out of the friendship than Chandra is, even though you may be putting more effort into it.

If the two of you get the same level of benefit but your costs are greater than your partner's, equity theory predicts you won't want to maintain that relationship. This observation doesn't mean that relationships have to be equitable every moment or in every instance. It does suggest, however, that they must be equitable *in the long run.*

To illustrate this point, let's say you meet your friend Braden regularly for dinner, and he picks up the check almost every time. Assuming you and he derive the same pleasure from each other's company, this would seem to be a friendship in which Braden is under-benefited and you are over-benefited. Let's also say, though, that you bought airplane tickets for his grandparents so they could attend his college graduation ceremony. Monetarily, that one contribution equaled the value of several dinners. Thus, your financial investments in your friendship are equal in the long run.

Many long-term friendships exhibit this type of ebb and flow of investments. Each friend may be over-benefited at some points and under-benefited at others. As long as the two friends experience equal costs and rewards in the long run, however, equity theory predicts that their friendship will be stable. An example of costs and rewards over time in a friendship appears in Figure 8.4.

Our costs and benefits in friendships aren't just a matter of money or other tangible goods. We also invest our time, our attention, and our care in our friends, and in an equitable relationship, we reap these rewards back from them.

Over-benefited The state in which your relational rewards exceed your relational costs.

Under-benefited The state in which your relational costs exceed your relational rewards.

Equity theory A theory predicting that a good relationship is one in which your ratio of costs and rewards is equal to your partner's.

Balance Sheet			
Date	Benefits	Cost	Balance
9/03	Bernard drove me to the airport for a late-night flight	I bought him a nice dinner beforehand	=
3/04		I helped him replace all the tile on his roof	-
12/04	he got me tickets to a sold-out concert for my birthday		=
8/05	he stayed at my house and watched my pets while i was out of town		+
10/05		I gave him the DVD of his favorite television show for his birthday	=
5/06	he helped me cut down excess trees on my property and chop them into firewood	I gave him half of the firewood	=
2/07		I paid the airfare for a trip he and I took to Disneyland	-
6/07	he got me an interview for my current position		=
9/08	he let my aunt and uncle stay at his house while my extended family was in town		

FIGURE 8.4 An example of benefits and costs over time in a friendship The balance column represents whether I am over-benefited (+), under-benefited (−), or equally benefited (=) at the time. As the balance sheet shows, we often cycle through periods of being over-benefited, under-benefited, and equally benefited in our long-term friendships.

In some situations, however, we may go through prolonged periods when our investments far outweigh our returns. One such situation occurs when a friend is dealing with a significant health concern. The A&E television series *Intervention* chronicles stories of adults with addictions to alcohol, drugs, gambling, eating disorders, unprotected sex, and other serious health threats. Each episode includes a real-life intervention, which is a structured conversation in which an addict's family and friends ask him or her to get professional help.

A common component in such interventions is for friends and relatives to tell the addict how his or her addiction has negatively affected them. Often, friends feel as though the addicted person has lied to, manipulated, or taken advantage of them. Although they want the addicted person to receive help, they also frequently inform the person that they are tired of being under-benefited in their friendship and are willing to end the friendship if he or she doesn't enter treatment. That was the situation with Brian, a 24-year-old man addicted to methamphetamines and promiscuous, unprotected sex. After several years of trying to help him with his addictions, his friends and family organized an intervention that was attended by his best friend, Derek. When it came time for Derek to speak, he told Brian:

> I've been in hell for the last three months. I've lost all trust in people, and most of all, you. If you're not willing to take part in this recovery process, our relationship is over.

Such a statement may seem extreme, but the friends and relatives of people suffering from addiction often feel that their relationships with them are inequitable. Like Derek, many friends and family members decide they are no longer willing to be manipulated and used, and they plead with the addicted person to receive professional help.

Relational Maintenance Behaviors

As we've seen, social exchange theory and equity theory both explain *why* we choose to maintain relationships. By contrast, the concept of relational maintenance behaviors explains *how* we maintain them. Let's imagine now that you've made friends with someone and you're both satisfied with the costs and benefits of your friendship. Therefore, you'll want to maintain your relationship so that it continues to grow and thrive. How do you accomplish this? Communication researchers Laura Stafford and Dan Canary have found that we use five primary **relational maintenance behaviors:** positivity, openness, assurances, social networks, and sharing tasks.[48]

Relational maintenance behaviors Behaviors used to maintain and strengthen personal relationships.

Positivity. The first type of relational maintenance behaviors is known as *positivity* behaviors because they make other people feel comfortable around us. Positivity behaviors include acting friendly and cheerful, being courteous, and refraining from criticizing other people. People who engage in positivity behaviors smile frequently, express their affection and appreciation for other people, and don't complain. In other words, they're pleasant and fun to be around. As you might guess, these types of behaviors tend to make people well liked.[49] By contrast, behaviors such as complaining, being critical of others, and pouting when things don't go your way reflect low positivity.

Openness. *Openness* describes your willingness to discuss your relationship with your friend or relational partner. People who use this relational maintenance strategy are likely to disclose their thoughts and feelings, ask how their friend feels about the relationship, and confide in their friend. Although it's possible to have too much openness in a relationship, an optimal amount will help maintain the relationship and keep it strong.[50] When we refuse to share our thoughts and feelings with others

One way people maintain their friendships is by sharing their social networks—such as their families, work relationships, and other friendships—with each other.

or don't reciprocate their disclosures to us, we are displaying low amounts of openness.

Assurances. Stafford and Canary define *assurances* as verbal and nonverbal behaviors that people use to illustrate their faithfulness and commitment to others. A statement such as "Of course I'll help you; you're my best friend" sends the message that we're committed to the relationship, and it reassures the friend or partner that the relationship has a future.[51] By contrast, when we don't acknowledge the importance of our friendships, we convey the message that we aren't very committed to them.

Social networks. The term *social networks* includes all the friendships and family relationships you have. An important relational maintenance behavior is to share your social networks with another person. Two close friends, for instance, are likely to know each other's families, co-workers, and other friends. When this happens, we say that the friends' social networks have converged. Research shows this convergence is an important way to keep relationships stable and strong.[52] We undermine this convergence when we speak poorly of the friends and relatives of our friends or when we actively avoid spending time with them.

Sharing tasks. As the term suggests, *sharing tasks* means performing your fair share of the work in your friendship. If your friend gives you a ride to the airport whenever you need it, for example, then it's only fair that you help her paint her apartment when she asks. If your roommate cooks you dinner, it would be fair for you to do the dishes afterward. As we've discussed, being in a social relationship requires investments of energy and effort. One way of maintaining a relationship, then, is to make certain the two parties are contributing equally.[53] When we expect our friends to do favors for us without reciprocating, we are not sharing tasks equally.

A quick review of these relational maintenance behaviors appears in the "At a Glance" box.

At a Glance: Relational Maintenance Behaviors

According to communication researchers Stafford and Canary, people use five primary behaviors to maintain their social relationships.

Positivity	Acting friendly, being courteous, refraining from criticism
Openness	Being willing to discuss your relationship
Assurances	Expressing and stressing your faithfulness and commitment
Social networks	Introducing one person to your other friends, family members, and co-workers
Sharing tasks	Performing your fair share of the work in your relationship

Understanding Relationship Maintenance

To understand social relationships, we need to examine both *why* people maintain such relationships and *how* they maintain them. Social exchange theory and equity theory both explain why people maintain their relationships by focusing on the rewards and costs of those relationships. As you've seen, your social relationships bring you certain rewards, such as pleasure, safety, and material help, and they also invoke certain costs, such as your time, attention, and financial resources. Are the rewards you get from a particular relationship worth the costs of that relationship? Social exchange theory and equity theory both help you answer that question, although they do it in slightly different ways.

Social exchange theory and relationship maintenance. Social exchange theory leads us to compare the costs and rewards of our current relationships *with those of our alternatives.* Suppose you are deciding whether to maintain a relationship with your friend Betsy. One alternative would be simply to end that friendship. Another option would be to replace her with a different friend. According to social exchange theory, whether you stick with Betsy or adopt one of these alternatives depends on your perception of the costs and rewards associated with each option. From the perspective of this theory, we ultimately will choose the option that benefits us the most.

Equity theory and relationship maintenance. In contrast to social exchange theory, equity theory leads us to compare how much the current relationship costs and rewards ourselves with how much it costs and rewards our partner. If you're debating whether to stay friends with Betsy, therefore, you would consider how your ratio of costs and rewards compares with Betsy's. What you're striving for, according to equity theory, is a balance between your own cost-benefit ratio and Betsy's. From the perspective of this theory, we prefer relationships in which we receive benefits equal to—not greater than or less than—those of our partners.

Shifts in costs and benefits. It's important to realize that some of the characteristics we think of as benefits can turn into costs. In the hit comedy movie *Mrs. Doubtfire,* Miranda Hillard (played by Sally Field) separates from her husband, Daniel (played by Robin Williams). She then hires a housekeeper named Mrs. Doubtfire who, unbeknownst to her, is actually her husband in disguise. In a conversation with Mrs. Doubtfire, Miranda describes Daniel as having a wonderful sense of humor and the ability to make her laugh. Early in their marriage, she regarded this trait as a benefit. Over time, however, Daniel's inability to take himself or his parental responsibilities seriously took its toll on her patience. In other words, his humorous nature, which Miranda had previously considered a benefit, had become a cost.

Of course, the opposite is also true: Costs can turn into benefits. For example, you may regard a friend's political views to be a cost if they are radically different from yours, because you feel irritated and defensive when he expresses them. Over time, you may come to realize that his ideas have expanded your way of thinking and helped you understand certain political issues better. What you first regarded as a cost to your friendship may now seem like a benefit.

Participating together in their shared interests is one way many friends maintain their relationships.

Once we form relationships, we maintain them through our communication behaviors. Some of the most important types of relationship maintenance behaviors are behaving positively, being open, giving our partner assurances, involving our partner in our social networks, and sharing tasks. You may have additional ways of maintaining your social relationships, such as doing favors for a friend or always asking your friend about his or her day. Many friends also maintain their relationships by participating together in their shared interests, such as watching sporting events, going to movies, and trying out new recipes.[54] In various ways, each of these behaviors conveys the message that you appreciate and value your friend and enjoy his or her company. Because friendships are largely voluntary, feeling appreciated and valued can motivate us to stay in them.

Learn It: What is the difference between physical, social, and task attraction? According to uncertainty reduction theory, how is uncertainty related to liking? According to predicted outcome value theory, when we predict positive relational outcomes, what are we motivated to do? What is a comparison level for alternatives? What does it mean to be under-benefited? What behaviors do people enact to maintain their relationships?

Try It: Choose one of your friendships, and make a point of practicing the five relational maintenance behaviors—positivity, openness, assurances, social networks, and sharing tasks—with that friend over the next several weeks.

Reflect on It: Do you feel over-benefited in any of your relationships? Which relational maintenance behaviors are most important in your social relationships?

3} Characteristics of Friendships

Your various friendships are likely as different and individual as your friends themselves. Some of these friendships are probably long-term and seem almost like family ties. Others may be specific to certain contexts, such as work friends, school friends, workout buddies, or friends you volunteer with. Even though each one is unique in some ways, however, nearly all friendships have certain qualities in common. Can you think of what some of those qualities might be? In this section, we take a look at five common characteristics of friendships:

- Friendships are voluntary.
- Friends are usually peers.
- Friendships are governed by rules.
- Friendships differ by sex.
- Friendships have a life span.

> *Friendship is a sheltering tree.*
> —Samuel Taylor Coleridge (1772–1834)
> British poet, critic, and philosopher

Friendships Are Voluntary

One of the defining characteristics of friendship is that it is *voluntary*.[55] We choose our friends and they choose us, and we don't have to be friends with anyone we don't want to be. That's part of what makes a friendship so special: Both friends are in the relationship by choice.

Friends can shield and protect us from many of the stresses of life. With friends, our lives are safer, happier, and more meaningful than they otherwise would be.

Friendship is voluntary, but that doesn't mean we choose our friends *arbitrarily.* Indeed, as we learned in the previous theoretical discussions about relationship formation and maintenance, attraction and the balance of costs and rewards all affect whom we pursue and maintain as friends.

The fact that friendships are voluntary also doesn't mean that they flourish on their own. On the contrary, they require communication behaviors on our part and on the part of our friends. Not only do we have to interact with others to form friendships in the first place, we also have to use relationship maintenance behaviors such as positivity, openness, assurances, network convergence, and sharing tasks to maintain them.

Friends Are Usually Peers

A second important characteristic of friendship is that it is usually a relationship between equals. A **peer** is someone who is similar to you in power or status. Your professors or your boss or your parents aren't your peers because these people all exercise some measure of control over you, at least temporarily. Most of us conceive of friendship as a relationship with peers—that is, people who are our equals, no more or less powerful than we are.

Does that mean we can't become friends with our professors, bosses, or parents? Not at all—in fact, many people consider these people to be very good friends. We can have satisfying friendships with individuals who have some type of power over us.

Peer Someone of similar power or status.

These relationships can also be complicated, however. When a friend exercises power over you, it can cause conflicts between the voluntary nature of your friendship and the involuntary nature of your parent-child, teacher-student, or employer-employee relationship. For instance, a professor may vacillate between giving a friend a good grade and giving him the poorer grade he actually earned. Likewise, a supervisor may want to share news about an upcoming layoff with a friend who works for her but may also feel that she cannot because of her supervisory position. In situations such as these, people may feel that the expectations of their friendships and the expectations of their professional relationships are in conflict. Later in this chapter, we'll discuss strategies for managing these situations.

Friendships Are Governed by Rules

In some ways, a friendship is like a social contract to which both parties agree. By being someone's friend, you acknowledge—at least implicitly—that you expect certain things from that person and that he or she can expect certain things from you. Those expectations are possible because friendships have rules. Even if the rules aren't explicitly stated, most people within a given society usually know and understand them.[56]

As you'll see in the "At a Glance box," researchers have identified and studied many of the underlying rules of friendship. Some of these rules relate to specific behaviors (e.g., standing up for your friends and not publicly criticizing them), whereas others relate to the way you should think or feel about your friends (e.g., trusting them and not being jealous of their other friendships). Perhaps you've been in a friendship in which one or more of these implicit rules was broken. For example, perhaps a friend has been criticizing you behind your back or has consistently failed to show up when you made plans together. Just as with communication rules in general—which we discussed in Chapter 1—friendship rules become explicit only when someone violates them. As research tells us, most people agree there simply are right and wrong ways to treat your friends.[57]

At a Glance: Friendship Rules

One way to understand a relationship is to consider the rules or expectations that govern it. Researchers Michael Argyle and Monika Henderson have confirmed that people have certain rules for friendships. When the parties to the relationship observe these rules, the friendships tend to be stronger. Here are some of the most important friendship rules Argyle and Henderson found. What rules would *you* add to this list?

- ◉ Stand up for your friend in his or her absence.

- ◉ Trust each other.

- ◉ Offer help when your friend needs it.

- ◉ Don't criticize your friend in public.

- ◉ Keep your friend's secrets.

- ◉ Provide emotional support when needed.

- ◉ Respect your friend's privacy.

- ◉ Don't be jealous of his or her other friends.

Source: Argyle, M., & Henderson, M. (1984). The rules of friendship. *Journal of Social and Personal Relationships, 1*, 211–237.

Friendships Differ by Sex

You've probably noticed some differences between the friendships you have with women and the ones you have with men. If you have, then it may not surprise you to learn that researchers have written volumes about sex differences and similarities in friendships and friendship behaviors. In this section, we examine these differences and similarities separately for same-sex and opposite-sex friendships.

Same-sex friends. One of the most consistent findings concerning same-sex friendships is that women and men value different aspects of their respective friendships. Essentially, friendships among women tend to place greater emphasis on conversational and emotional expressiveness, whereas men's friendships focus on shared activities and interests.[58]

Best friends Juanita and Lindsay, for instance, frequently get together just to talk and catch up. Their visits often include sharing their feelings about what's going on in their lives. During these talks, Juanita and Lindsay listen to each other and express their support and affection for each other. Sometimes, they engage in an activity while they talk, such as attending Lindsay's daughter's basketball game or driving to the bus station to pick up Juanita's sister; sometimes, they just talk. Regardless of when their conversations take place, however, Juanita and Lindsay agree that their ability to share, disclose, and express feelings with each other is what makes their friendship satisfying.

In contrast, when Alex thinks about his closest male friends, he thinks of Jake, his golfing buddy, and Davin, his patrol partner on the police force. The time he spends with these friends almost always revolves around some type of activity. With Jake, it's usually playing a round of golf and then having nachos and beer at a sports bar. With Davin, it's working together during the many hours they spend on patrol. Alex feels close to each friend because he enjoys their company when they are engaged in these activities.

Significantly, Alex's time with Davin and Jake allows them to talk about what's happening in their lives. During a long patrol shift, for instance, Alex and Davin frequently talk about their children's activities or their plans for the future. Similarly, during a recent round of golf, Jake told Alex how much he missed his recently deceased father. Most often, though, Alex and his friends simply enjoy the time they spend together doing activities, even if their time together doesn't involve much conversation. For Alex, it's the *doing*, not the *talking*, that makes a friendship close.

Although research has confirmed that these sex differences exist, it has also identified two important qualifications about these differences. First, as with nearly all sex differences in behavior, these differences in same-sex friendships are just averages. They don't characterize all friendships. Some women's friendships focus more on shared activities than on conversation, and some men routinely share personal conversations with their male friends even if they aren't engaged in an activity together.

Second, the fact that women's and men's relationships differ does *not* mean that friendships are more important to one sex than to the other. Some people believe that because women self-disclose more to one another than men do, women's friendships are closer and more satisfying than men's are. In fact, research has demonstrated that women and men report equal levels of closeness in their same-sex friendships.[59] What differs between the sexes is simply the characteristics that make those friendships close. For women, the key characteristic is shared conversation; for men, it's shared activity.

Opposite-sex friends. What do we know about opposite-sex friendships? Research suggests that both men and women value these relationships as a chance to see things from each other's perspective.[60] Opposite-sex friendships can provide opportunities for men to be emotionally expressive and for women to enjoy shared activities that their same-sex friendships do not.[61]

In addition, many opposite-sex friends feel some degree of physical or romantic attraction toward each other,[62] and they often communicate in ways that resemble romantic relationships, such as by flirting with each other[63] and sharing sexual humor.[64] In fact, a study of more than 300 U.S. American college students conducted by com-

Studies show that men's friendships often focus on shared activity, whereas women's friendships often privilege shared conversation. Men and women often value opposite-sex friendships as opportunities to communicate in ways that are important to the other sex.

munication scientists Walid Afifi and Sandra Faulkner found that half of the students reported having engaged in sexual activity with a nonromantic opposite-sex friend.[65] Although some research has suggested that sexual activity changes the fundamental nature of an opposite-sex friendship from platonic to romantic,[66] more than half of the students in Afifi and Faulkner's study who had engaged in sexual activity with an opposite-sex friend reported no such change in the nature of their relationship.

Whether they are attracted to each other or not, many opposite-sex friends have specific reasons for not wanting their friendship to evolve into a romantic relationship. In surveys of more than 600 U.S. American college students, communication scholars Susan Messman, Dan Canary, and Kimberly Hause discovered that people keep their opposite-sex friendships nonromantic for six primary reasons:[67]

· They aren't physically attracted to their friend.
· Their relatives and other friends wouldn't approve of a romantic relationship with the friend.
· They aren't ready to be in a romantic relationship.
· They want to protect their existing friendship.
· They fear being disappointed or hurt.
· They are concerned about a third party, such as a sibling, who is romantically interested in the friend.

Studies show that, overall, both women and men consider their same-sex friends to be more loyal and helpful than their opposite-sex counterparts.[68] At the same time, however, opposite-sex friendships allow women and men to enjoy those aspects of friendship most valued by the other sex. Thus, it appears that same-sex and opposite-sex friendships offer unique rewards.

Friendships Have a Life Span

Important as friendships are to us, the reality is that most friendships are not permanent. Rather, as with most relationships, friendships have a life span: They are initiated, they are maintained, and eventually, many of them end. Communication scholar and friendship expert William Rawlins has proposed that most friendships move through a life span consisting of six stages:[69]

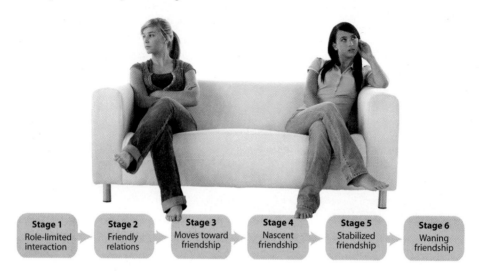

Stage 1	Stage 2	Stage 3	Stage 4	Stage 5	Stage 6
Role-limited interaction	Friendly relations	Moves toward friendship	Nascent friendship	Stabilized friendship	Waning friendship

Suppose Naya and Emily have been called for jury duty on the same day and they meet in the jurors' waiting lounge. Let's see how their relationship might progress through Rawlins's six stages.

Role-limited interaction. At the *role-limited interaction* stage, Naya and Emily meet and interact for the first time. Because they are strangers at this stage, their communication follows social and cultural norms for interaction between strangers. They are civil and polite but share little personal information with each other.

Friendly relations. After chatting for a while, Naya and Emily may enter the *friendly relations* stage. At this point, their conversation becomes friendlier. For example, they may share personal stories or humorous anecdotes. Naya and Emily may intend for this friendly interaction simply to make their wait in the jurors' lounge more enjoyable. It can, however, also be an invitation for friendship.

Moves toward friendship. Suppose Emily e-mails Naya the following week to ask if she'd like to go to an art gallery opening. This invitation can signal progression to the *moves toward friendship* stage. At this stage, Naya and Emily's communication becomes more social and less bound by norms and rules.

Nascent friendship. If Naya and Emily continue getting together and enjoying their interactions, they may enter the *nascent friendship* stage. At this point, they begin to think of themselves as friends. Their communication continues to become more personal and less prescribed.

Stabilized friendship. Over time, Naya and Emily's relationship may progress to the *stabilized friendship* stage. At this point, they consider their friendship to be fully established. They trust each other strongly, and they may even begin to adjust their attitudes and opinions to be more in line with each other's.

Waning friendship. After many years of close friendship, Naya and Emily may enter the *waning friendship* stage. This stage marks the decline of their friendship. Their friendship may simply become more distant and casual during this stage, or it may end altogether.

Early in this chapter, we discussed some of the most typical reasons why friendships form. There also are many reasons why a friendship comes to an end.[70] Research suggests that we can divide these reasons into two general categories: events that cause friends to dislike each other, and changes in life circumstances that decrease opportunities for communication and attention. Let's take a closer look at each situation.

Friends can grow to dislike each other. Some friendships end because the friends no longer like each other. Although friends initially may have become friends because of their perceived similarity or their social attraction to each other, they can develop negative feelings toward each other that cause them to end their friendship. Studies have demonstrated that negative feelings are most likely to arise when one friend:

- Constantly nags or criticizes the other
- Betrays the other's confidence or trust
- Behaves in a hostile or physically violent way around the other
- Begins abusing alcohol or drugs
- Fails to provide help or support when the other friend needs it
- Becomes intolerant of the other friend's romantic partner or other friends
- Feels he or she no longer has anything in common with the other friend

We don't necessarily terminate friendships on the basis of a single negative event. When a friend repeatedly wrongs us, however, we might grow to dislike him or her over time. This change in feelings can lead us to end the friendship.[71] In such cases, we might decide to confront the individual directly and make it clear that we no longer wish to be friends. In other cases, we might decide simply to reduce our communication with the person by avoiding him or her.

Friends' life circumstances can change. Although friendships sometimes end because of negative feelings, some friends simply "drift apart." As our lives change and evolve, we may have less opportunity to interact with particular friends. That doesn't necessarily mean we develop any negative feelings for them. It does mean, however, that some friendships end simply from lack of attention.

According to research, one of the most common life changes that can end a friendship is physical separation.[72] Recall that physical proximity is one of the main reasons we're attracted to potential friends. Friendships are relatively easy to maintain with people you see all the time. If one friend moves away, however, keeping up the friendship becomes much more of a challenge.[73] Friends may keep in touch for a while af-

Physical separation often increases the chances that a friendship will end. Do you think that social networking sites, such as MySpace and Facebook, are changing that?

Getting to Know You
Forms of Attraction in Your Closest Friendship

Close friendships always include one or more forms of interpersonal attraction. We might be attracted to someone's personality; we might find the person physically attractive; we might be drawn to him or her as a work partner. Think about the closest friendship you have right now. On a scale of 1 (strongly disagree) to 7 (strongly agree), how much would you say you agree or disagree with each of the following statements?

Social Attraction

_____ I find this person easy to be around.

_____ I really enjoy his or her personality.

_____ We get along really well with each other.

_____ He or she is the kind of person I like to spend time with.

Physical Attraction

_____ I think this person is good-looking.

_____ He or she has a nice appearance.

_____ Most people would find this person physically attractive.

_____ This person has a nice look.

Task Attraction

_____ This person would be fun to work with.

_____ I can always count on this person.

_____ I would enjoy studying with this person.

_____ This person is very dependable.

Add up your scores for each scale. Each score will range from 4 to 28. For each type of attraction, a score of 4–12 indicates that you don't feel that type of attraction very strongly for your friend. A score of 13–20 suggests you have a moderate level of that form of attraction. A score of 21–28 indicates that you feel a good deal of that form of attraction for your friend. You may find that your scores vary quite a bit. If so, that simply means your friendship is based more heavily on some forms of attraction than on others. In any event, this exercise will give you a chance to reflect on what you find most attractive about one of your closest friendships.

Items adapted from McCroskey, J. C., & McCain, T. A. (1974). The measurement of interpersonal attraction. *Speech Monographs*, *41*, 261–266.

ter being separated, but their communication often declines over time, causing them to lose track of each other. Perhaps you can think of friendships in which you've experienced this.

Other changes in life circumstances can also cause friendships to fade. When one friend gets married or has a baby, for instance, his or her attention is understandably diverted toward the new spouse or child. As a result, he or she has less time and opportunity to interact with friends. The demands of work or school can also make it difficult to spend time with our friends. Experiencing a chronic illness can also limit our opportunities to see friends. This may be particularly true with illnesses that impair our social abilities, such as depression and chronic anxiety.

It is important to note that in these situations we don't necessarily *want* the friendship to end. Rather, we may simply no longer have the necessary time, energy, and attention to maintain it. If the friend is particularly important to us, however, we can use our communication and relational maintenance behaviors to keep the friendship going. Even if you go months or years without seeing a friend, it may take only an occasional phone call or e-mail message to maintain contact and let that friend know you still care about him or her. We can even use the Internet to help us restore communication with friends we've lost touch with.

Learn It: What does it mean to say that friendship is voluntary? What is a peer? Which rules are common for friendships in North America? Do people report feeling greater loyalty to same-sex or opposite-sex friends? Why do friendships come to an end?

Try It: Take stock of your social, physical, and task attraction to your closest friend by completing the questionnaire (see the "Getting to Know You" box on page 318). Acknowledging what you find appealing about your friends will help you to appreciate the important place your friends have in your life.

Reflect on It: Do you have any friendships that you feel are involuntary? What do you value differently about your same-sex and opposite-sex friendships?

4} Social Relationships in the Workplace

Nearly all of us will be employed at some point in our lives, and our jobs will require us to interact with other people. It's realistic to assume, therefore, that most of us will have to relate to and communicate with people we know from work, whether they are co-workers, superiors, subordinates, or customers. In fact, many public agencies and private corporations expect their employees to communicate with one another in well-defined ways. These expectations might include communicating honestly, treating people with dignity, listening to others, and being open to other people's opinions. All these communication behaviors contribute to a civil and respectful work environment. They can also make it easier for employees to form workplace friendships.[74]

> *Even the frankest and bravest of subordinates do not talk with their boss the same way they talk with colleagues.*
>
> —Robert Greenleaf (1904–1990)
> U.S. American essayist

As you may know already from personal experience, friendships at work can be a "dual-edged sword." On the one hand, having friends at work is great, because friends can make the workday pleasant and help and support you when you need it. On the other hand, friendship roles and work roles often conflict. For instance, your workplace friends might wish to chat with you, but if you have tasks to complete by a tight deadline then you might not have time for them.

Workplace friendships can also be more challenging to control than regular friendships. As a part of our job, we are usually required to see and interact with our supervisors, co-workers, and customers, whether we want to or not. Interaction with regular friends, by contrast, is usually voluntary and easier to control. If you have an argument with a regular friend, for example, you can choose to avoid him or her for a period of time while you both cool down. Because of your work responsibilities, however, you may not have this option with workplace friends.

It is important to understand the dynamics of workplace friendships so that we can successfully address some of the challenges they present. In this section, we'll examine these dynamics in three specific workplace relationships: between co-workers, between superiors and subordinates, and with clients.

Social Relationships with Co-Workers

You are probably most likely to form workplace friendships with your immediate co-workers. One reason this is true is that co-workers are usually peers rather than superiors or subordinates, so their levels of power and responsibility are similar to yours.[75] Another reason is that immediate co-workers share with you some common experiences, such as working for the same company, the same department, and the same supervisor. In addition, you probably spend a great deal of time with your co-workers, perhaps even more than you spend with your friends outside work. These characteristics can form a ready-made basis for friendship.[76]

Research has shown that the quality of people's friendships with their co-workers affects their job satisfaction.[77] All other things being equal, the closer you are to your co-workers, the happier you are at work.

Beneficial as friendships with co-workers are, however, they are also very challenging. The reason this is true is that the relationship has both a *social dimension* and a *task dimension,* and these different aspects of the friendship frequently come into conflict. The social dimension is your personal relationship with the co-worker; the task dimension is your professional relationship. Let's say, for example, that you're friends with your co-worker Tonya, who's up for a promotion. As *her friend,* you want her to have the promotion, but as *her co-worker,* you don't believe she has really earned it. It's easy to see how these mixed feelings could be troublesome for your friendship.

Research indicates that having high-quality workplace friendships is important to overall job satisfaction. As beneficial as they are, however, workplace friendships are often challenging to maintain.

Clearly, then, to maintain friendships with your co-workers, you need to balance the personal and professional sides of the relationships at all times. For instance, you might decide it's important to tell Tonya you support her, to voice enthusiasm if she receives the promotion, and to express disappointment if she doesn't, because she's your friend. Even though you don't feel she has earned the promotion, your friendship with Tonya may motivate you to be supportive of her anyway.

Alternatively, you might remind Tonya that the promotion is very competitive, that she is competing with employees who have more experience and seniority than she does, and that she shouldn't be surprised if she doesn't get it. You might even say "I'm telling you this as your co-worker" to make it clear that you are speaking from the perspective of your professional relationship rather than your personal one. Which approach you choose will probably depend on how close your friendship is and on what your experiences with similar situations have been.

Social Relationships Between Superiors and Subordinates

Challenging as friendships among co-workers can be, friendships between superiors and subordinates are considerably more complicated, because they include a power difference that co-worker friendships generally do not.[78] As you learned earlier in this chapter, one of the defining characteristics of friendship is that it's a relationship between equals. So, when two friends are a supervisor and an employee, the power difference between them introduces a task dimension that friendships between co-workers usually don't have.

Genuine friendships between superiors and subordinates certainly aren't impossible to form or maintain. Indeed, research shows that being friends with your boss usually adds to your job satisfaction.[79] That makes sense: If you like your supervisor, you'll probably enjoy working for him or her.

The challenge arises because what's best for the superior-subordinate relationship isn't always what's best for the friendship. If you're the employee, for instance, you might dislike or disagree with your boss's decisions concerning the company's policies or future direction, particularly when those decisions affect you. Conversely, if you're the supervisor, you may agonize about such decisions because you realize that what's best for the company is not always what's best for each individual employee.

To understand these stresses, imagine that your supervisor announces that the company will reduce the clerical staff that you depend on to get your work done. How would that make you feel as an employee? Now imagine that, to accommodate a new business strategy, your boss cancels a promotional campaign you've been developing, including a photo shoot you were looking forward to. In such cases, it can be hard not to take your boss's actions personally, which can strain your friendship.[80] In a study of superior-subordinate friendships, communication scholar Theodore Zorn found that superiors commonly experienced these types of tensions between their work responsibilities and their friendships with subordinates.[81]

Given all these tensions, you may be wondering whether friendships between superiors and subordinates are ultimately doomed. In fact, in spite of all these challenges, such friendships *are* possible to maintain. This is especially true if both parties acknowledge that their friendship and their work relationship might conflict and agree to keep those relationships separate as best they can.

As we have discussed, it's often best if people in power-imbalanced friendships acknowledge the potential conflicts their friendships can entail and discuss them directly, particularly if they started their relationship as peers and one of them was later promoted. A helpful discussion might go something like this:

Supervisor: There will probably be occasions when we have to put our friendship aside and focus on what's best for the company. Sometimes that will mean I'll have to make decisions that you don't like. When that happens, please don't take it personally; remember that I'm just doing my job.

Employee: I will, and I hope you know I'll support you even if I don't agree with you. I hope you'll do the same with me. There may be times when I disappoint you and times when you disappoint me, but let's keep in mind that our friendship and our work relationship are separate.

By acknowledging the potential for conflicts and establishing their expectations for how to address them *before they occur,* this supervisor and employee are laying the groundwork for a successful friendship. That doesn't mean they won't experience the tensions that often accompany this type of relationship. Rather, it means they have agreed on how to handle these tensions so that the tensions don't damage either their professional relationship or their friendship.

One situation that's extremely problematic for superior-subordinate relationships is the case in which the subordinate feels she or he has been sexually harassed. The "Dark Side" box explains what sexual harassment is and how it is related to interpersonal communication.

Social Relationships with Clients

In most professions, you'll interact not only with co-workers, superiors, and subordinates, but also with customers. For instance, you may sell your company's products to the same retail stores or medical offices each month and get to know the buyers there. Likewise, you may work for a financial or technology firm that offers ongoing consulting services to a number of long-term business clients. Depending on the nature of your job, you may have clients you see or talk to on a regular basis, and it's reasonable to expect that you may form social relationships with some of them.[82] These relationships can be highly rewarding personally, and they can also benefit your organization, because they can be a major reason why your customers continue to buy from you or your company.[83] After all, most of us prefer dealing with a salesperson or a service provider with whom we have developed a comfortable and trusting relationship.

At the same time, friendships with customers invoke some of the same task–social tensions that friendships with co-workers, employers, and employees do. Your customers may be your friends, but they still expect you to furnish a high-quality product or service, and you still expect them to provide full and prompt payment. If either party doesn't uphold its end of the bargain, then the customer-provider relationship can be disrupted, and the friendship can suffer as a result.

To avoid some of these tensions, some companies encourage employees not to develop personal friendships with customers. Although it may be very important to treat customers in a friendly way, many businesses recognize that the feelings of loyalty and favor we often have for friends can interfere with the professional relationship.

Social relationships with clients can be highly rewarding if there are clear boundaries distinguishing the personal and professional dimensions of the relationship.

When Deion took a position as a sales representative for a cable television company, for instance, he became close friends with several of his clients. Because he liked them, he began giving them steep discounts on their cable service that other customers didn't receive. Because they liked him, they consistently gave him the highest possible scores on customer satisfaction surveys. These special deals and preferential treatments continued for almost a year before Deion's regional manager realized what was happening. She reprimanded Deion for allowing his friendships with his clients to compromise his professional relationships with them.

The separation of personal and professional relationships is particularly important in the health care setting. In the United States, ethical guidelines issued by the American College of Physicians discourage doctors from treating friends, relatives, intimate partners, and other individuals with whom they have close personal relationships.[84] The reasoning behind these guidelines is that a doctor's professional judgment and objectivity could be compromised by his or her personal feelings for the patient. If this happens, then the doctor may not make proper decisions about the patient's condition or treatment, putting the patient's health at risk.

Like friendships between superiors and subordinates, friendships with customers need to have clear boundaries between personal and professional relationships. While conducting business, treat these friends as you would any other customers, and ask them to treat you as they would any other provider. A personal friendship with customers can be successful if the friends agree that their professional relationship is separate and should be treated professionally.

Whether in our professional or personal lives, having friends and other social relationships enriches us in many ways. In his quote at the beginning of the previous section, Samuel Taylor Coleridge called friendship a "sheltering tree" to point out that friends can shield and protect us from many of the stresses of life. With friends, our lives are safer, happier, and more meaningful than they otherwise would be.

Learn It: What do we mean by the terms *social dimension* and *task dimension* in work friendships? How are superior-subordinate relationships different from co-worker relationships? Why are health care providers discouraged from treating friends?

Try It: Suppose you're good friends with your co-worker Kyle, whose sales figures have been dismal recently. His manager has warned him that another month of poor sales performance will earn him a demotion. In contrast, you're having a successful year. One day Kyle realizes that he is not going to make his sales quota for the month. He comes to you in a panic and asks you to let him take credit for some of your sales. This act would save his position. It would also mean, however, that your sales report would look unimpressive for the first time in many months. You want to help Kyle, but you are also concerned about how your manager will feel about your performance.

With a friend or a classmate, role-play a conversation in which you discuss this situation and try to come to an agreement on how to resolve it. One of you should take your position in the conversation, and the other should take Kyle's. After your role-play, discuss alternative ways of responding to the situation. Identify how you think you would probably react in this situation, and why. Also, identify the ethical issues this situation raises.

Reflect on It: Have you ever experienced tensions in your workplace friendships? If so, how were they resolved, and with what effects?

} Master the Chapter {

Section 1} Why Social Relationships Matter (p. 293)

I. Why Social Relationships Matter

   A. We form relationships because we need to belong

   B. Social relationships bring rewards

      1. Social relationships bring emotional rewards

      2. Social relationships bring material rewards

      3. Social relationships bring health rewards

   C. Social relationships carry costs as well as rewards

- Each of us has a need to belong, which motivates us to seek, form, maintain, and protect strong social relationships.

- Social relationships bring us emotional, material, and health rewards.

- Social relationships incur costs in our time, our energy, and other resources.

Section 2} Forming and Maintaining Social Bonds (p. 297)

II. Forming and Maintaining Social Bonds

   A. Attraction theory

      1. We are attracted by appearance

      2. We are attracted by proximity

      3. We are attracted by similarity

      4. We are attracted by complementarity

   B. Uncertainty reduction theory

   C. Predicted outcome value theory

   D. Understanding relationship formation

   E. Theories about costs and benefits

      1. Social exchange theory and relationship formation

      2. Equity theory and relationship formation

- We value attraction in the form of physical appearance, proximity, similarity, and complementarity.

- Uncertainty reduction theory says we are driven to reduce uncertainty about others by getting to know them.

- According to predicted outcome value theory, we form relationships when we think there is value in doing so.

- Social exchange theory predicts that we form relationships in which the benefits outweigh (or are at least equal to) the costs.

- According to equity theory, a good relationship is one in which your ratio of costs and rewards is the same as your partner's.

F. **Relational maintenance behaviors**
  1. Positivity
  2. Openness
  3. Assurances
  4. Social networks
  5. Sharing tasks

- People use several relational maintenance behaviors, including positivity, openness, assurances, social networks, and shared tasks.

G. **Understanding relationship maintenance**
  1. Social exchange theory and relationship maintenance
  2. Equity theory and relationship maintenance
  3. Shifts in costs and benefits

Section 3} Characteristics of Friendships (p. 311)

III. **Characteristics of Friendships**

A. **Friendships are voluntary**

- We generally expect friendships to be voluntary.

B. **Friends are usually peers**

- Most friendships are between peers, or people of equal status.

C. **Friendships are governed by rules**

- Friendships are governed by rules, many of which are implicit.

D. **Friendships differ by sex**
  1. Same-sex friends
  2. Opposite-sex friends

- Some characteristics of friendship differ according to the sexes of the friends involved.

E. **Friendships have a life span**
  1. Role-limited interaction
  2. Friendly relations
  3. Moves toward friendship
  4. Nascent friendship
  5. Stabilized friendship
  6. Waning friendship

- Friendships have a life span; they develop over time and we don't necessarily expect them to be permanent.

Section 4} Social Relationships in the Workplace (p. 319)

IV. **Social Relationships in the Workplace**

A. **Social relationships with co-workers**

- Having positive social relationships with co-workers increases job satisfaction.

B. **Social relationships between superiors and subordinates**

- Social relationships between superiors and subordinates can be very positive, but they are also complicated by the inherent power difference within them.

C. **Social relationships with clients**

- Positive social relationships with customers can be highly rewarding, both personally and professionally.

Key Terms

Approach behaviors
Avoidance behaviors
Comparison level
Comparison level for alternatives
Equity theory
Interpersonal attraction

Need to belong
Over-benefited
Peer
Physical attraction
Predicted outcome value theory
Relational maintenance behaviors

Social attraction
Social exchange theory
Task attraction
Uncertainty reduction theory
Under-benefited

Discussion Questions

1. How strong is your own need to belong? In what ways do you see your need for social relationships influencing the decisions you make (such as where to live, how to spend your free time)?
2. What are some of the biggest costs associated with maintaining your friendships? Can you think of friendships that have ended because the costs exceeded the rewards?
3. Why do you think physical attraction is so important in forming relationships, even friendships?
4. What would social exchange theory and equity theory have to say about being over-benefited in a friendship?
5. How do you know what the rules of friendship are? How do we learn them?
6. Why do you think friendships differ by gender in the ways they do? What causes these differences?
7. What are the costs and the rewards of having a social relationship with your supervisor?
8. Give examples of the social and task dimensions of a relationship with a co-worker.

Practice Quiz

Multiple Choice

1. Which of the following is *not* one of the rewards associated with being in a social relationship?
   a. egocentric
   b. emotional
   c. material
   d. health
2. Attraction to someone's personality is known as:
   a. task attraction
   b. physical attraction
   c. semantic attraction
   d. social attraction
3. Which of the following characteristics are most salient to interpersonal attraction?
   a. difference, personal appearance, proximity, closeness
   b. personal appearance, proximity, complementarity, similarity
   c. similarity, personal appearance, complementarity, distance
   d. difference, distance, closeness, personal appearance
4. According to the predicted outcome value theory, which of the following is true?
   a. When we do not like what we learn about someone during an initial conversation, we are likely to predict negative outcomes for future interaction and, therefore, will not be motivated to get to know the person better.
   b. When we like someone during initial interaction, we predict positive outcomes and will want to get to know the person better.
   c. Both A and B.
   d. Neither A nor B.
5. Uncertainty reduction theory posits which of the following?
   a. Uncertainty about someone creates mystery and facilitates attraction toward him or her.
   b. We like uncertainty because what we do not know cannot hurt us.
   c. Uncertainty is unpleasant and through communication we seek to reduce uncertainty.
   d. None of the above.
6. According to equity theory, which of the following describes a good relationship?
   a. Rewards outweigh the costs.
   b. Costs outweigh the rewards.
   c. The ratio of costs to rewards is equal for both people.
   d. None of the above.
7. Verbal and nonverbal behaviors that people use to express their faithfulness and commitment to others constitutes which type of relationship maintenance behavior?
   a. positivity
   b. openness
   c. sharing tasks
   d. assurances
8. Which of the following is *not* a characteristic of friendships?
   a. They are voluntary.
   b. They last a lifetime.
   c. They are governed by rules.
   d. They usually are between peers.

9. Friendships between co-workers can be challenging for which of the following reasons?
   a. conflict between social and task dimensions of the relationship
   b. constant competition for resources
   c. repeated and prolonged interaction
   d. none of the above
10. This form of sexual harassment happens when a supervisor offers an employee rewards in exchange for sexual favors:
    a. quid pro quo
    b. hostile work environment
    c. sexual scheming
    d. unlawful demands

True/False

11. Having good friends helps keep us healthy because friends help us manage stress and look out for our welfare.
12. In social relationships, difference is always more attractive than similarity.
13. People seek to maintain relationships that are more beneficial than costly.
14. The realistic expectation of what is wanted and deserved in a relationship is known as the comparison level for alternatives.
15. To maintain relationships, it is important not to share social networks, because that tends to create jealousy.

Fill in the Blank

16. The theory that says that each of us is born with a desire to seek, form, and maintain social relationships is _____.
17. We can be attracted to others who are different from ourselves if their differences are perceived as _____, or beneficial to ourselves.
18. The behaviors that signal our lack of interest in another person are _____.
19. Because friendships are _____, we choose our friends and they choose us.
20. Relationships between superiors and subordinates can be complicated because they include a _____ difference that co-worker relationships generally do not.

Answers
Multiple Choice: 1: (a); 2 (d); 3 (b); 4 (c); 5 (c); 6 (c); 7 (d); 8 (b); 9 (a); 10 (a); **True/False:** 11 (T); 12 (F); 13 (F); 14 (F); 15 (F); **Fill in the Blank:** 16 (need-to-belong theory); 17 (complementary); 18 (avoidance behaviors); 19 (voluntary); 20 (power)

Research Library

Movies

Good Will Hunting (Drama; 1998; R)

This film depicts Matt Damon as Will Hunting, a janitor at the prestigious Massachusetts Institute of Technology, who is discovered to be a math prodigy but is troubled about his past. He begins therapy with psychologist Sean Maguire (played by Robin Williams), and over time, the two develop an unlikely friendship that is aided both by the similarities in their backgrounds and life experiences and also by the complementary nature of their psychologist-client relationship.

In Good Company (Comedy; 2005; PG-13)

In this comedy, Dan Foreman (played by Dennis Quaid) is a senior advertising salesman whose new supervisor, Carter Duryea (played to Topher Grace), is half his age. The film depicts the challenges of negotiating a superior-subordinate relationship with a younger, inexperienced supervisor. When Carter begins dating Dan's daughter, the tension between Carter and Dan's social and professional relationships is amplified.

Stand By Me (Drama; 1986; R)

Based on a short story by Stephen King, this drama depicts the friendship between four 12-year-old boys who set off on a journey to find a dead body they have heard about. Along the way, they encounter circumstances that test their friendships. Sometimes they support one another and sometimes they do not. At the end of the film, we learn that the boys' friendships fell by the wayside when they entered junior high school. The movie illustrates both the importance of friendship and the idea that friendships have a life span.

Books

Blieszner, R., & Adams, R. G. (1992). *Adult friendship.* Newbury Park, CA: Sage.

Bukowski, W. M., & Newcomb, A. F. (Eds.). (1998). *The company they keep: Friendship in childhood and adolescence.* New York: Cambridge University Press.

Parks, M. R. (2007). *Personal relationships and personal networks.* Mahwah, NJ: Lawrence Erlbaum Associates.

Rawlins, W. K. (1992). *Friendship matters: Communication, dialectics, and the life course.* New York: Aldine de Gruyter.

Journal Articles

Argyle, M., & Henderson, M. (1984). The rules of friendship. *Journal of Social and Personal Relationships, 1,* 211–237.

Baumeister, R. F., & Leary, M. R. (1995). The need to belong: Desire for interpersonal attachments as a fundamental human motivation. *Psychological Bulletin, 117,* 497–529.

Parks, M. R., & Floyd, K. (1996). Meanings for closeness and intimacy in friendship. *Journal of Social and Personal Relationships, 15,* 517–537.

Winstead, B. A., Derlega, V. J., Montgomery, M. J., & Pilkington, C. (1995). The quality of friendships at work and job satisfaction. *Journal of Social and Personal Relationships, 12,* 199–215.

Web Sites

www.policylink.org/CHB/SocialRelationships/default.html

This site comments on the associations between social relationships and health, particularly mental health. The site is sponsored by Policy Link, a research and advocacy group promoting economic and social equity.

www.apa.org/monitor/apr07/social.html

This Web site, sponsored by the American Psychological Association, discusses research showing how having social relationships at work contributes to job satisfaction.

9 Intimate Relationships

What distinguishes intimate relationships
from other relationships?

How do people communicate
in their romantic relationships?

What communication issues
do families commonly face?

Ron and Meghan

Even though they had been dating for almost a year, Ron was uncomfortable when Meghan asked him to go with her to her family reunion. He didn't want to go because he wouldn't know many people and wasn't sure exactly what Meghan had told her family about him. As the reunion approached, Ron felt conflicted about how to communicate his feelings to Meghan. He didn't want to insult her family or make her think he was uncomfortable meeting her relatives. He also felt somewhat obligated to go, both because he was her boyfriend and because she had accompanied him to his class reunion two months earlier. Moreover, Meghan was very important to him, and he didn't want to cause any problems in their relationship.

Eventually, Ron decided to keep his concerns to himself and attend the reunion with Meghan. Despite his hesitations, he enjoyed himself. More important, he saw how happy his decision to attend made Meghan. Seeing her happiness made him realize just how important she was to him.

It's hard to overstate the importance of our intimate relationships. We may have many close friends, co-workers, and other acquaintances in our lives, but our relationships with romantic partners and family members are special. These are the people whose lives affect us the most and with whom we share our deepest sorrows and our greatest joys. We usually invest more in, and feel more committed to, these relationships than any others. The intimate relationships we develop with our families and romantic partners truly shape our lives in unique and important ways.

Families and romantic relationships also influence each other. Growing up in a family gives most of us our first exposure to the concept of personal relationships and our first examples of romantic unions. Moreover, the romantic relationships we form in adulthood often serve as the basis for starting new families. Thus, although romantic and familial relationships are different in some important respects, there is often an intimate connection between the two.

In this chapter:

1} We'll begin by examining four features that distinguish these relationships and make them so important to us.

2} We will then look specifically at how we use communication to form, maintain, and dissolve romantic relationships.

3} Next, we'll examine the structure and the function of family relationships and discuss some communication issues that are common within families.

4} Finally, we'll look at some ways to improve communication in our intimate relationships.

1} The Nature of Intimate Relationships {

> *Man is a knot into which relationships are tied.*
>
> —Antoine de Saint-Exupéry (1900–1944)
> French writer

Many people think specifically of romantic relationships when they hear the word "intimate," but intimacy is about more than romance. Several characteristics are common to intimate relationships. As we'll see in this section, intimate relationships:

1. Require deep commitment
2. Foster interdependence
3. Require continuous investment
4. Spark dialectical tensions

Intimate Relationships Require Deep Commitment

Commitment
A desire to stay in a relationship.

Most of us are more committed to our intimate relationships than we are to our other relationships. For instance, we may be more willing to put aside minor differences and make compromises to preserve our intimate relationships. **Commitment** is our desire to stay in a relationship no matter what happens. When people are committed to each other, they assume they have a future together. That assumption is important because most intimate relationships—such as families and romantic relationships—go through periods of conflict and distress. What allows us to deal with those difficult times is the knowledge that our relationship will still be there after those periods have ended.

How do we commit ourselves to others? Intimate relationships usually include some level of *emotional* commitment, or a sense of responsibility for each other's feelings and emotional well-being. For example, it's your emotional commitment to your romantic partner that leads you to listen to his or her problems, even if they seem trivial to you. Your family's emotional commitment to you has probably shaped your desire to do well in your education and your career. We also tend to feel a level of *social* commitment in our intimate relationships, which motivates us to spend time together, to compromise, to be generous with praise, and to avoid petty conflict. Ron really didn't want to go to Meghan's family reunion, for example, but he went anyway because of his commitment to her.

Finally, some intimate relationships are bound by *legal* and *financial* commitments, which are more formal expressions of people's obligations to each other. Spouses, for instance, enter into a legally binding contract when they marry. Parents have a legal responsibility to provide housing, food, clothing, health care, and education for their minor children, and family members often take on financial obligations to care for relatives who are aging or who have specific physical or mental needs. No matter what forms it takes, commitment is one of the foundations of intimate relationships.

Interdependence
A state in which each person's behaviors affect everyone else in the relationship.

Although deep commitment is important for many relationships, people can take commitment too far. At an extreme level, commitment can turn into obsession, a topic explored in the "Dark Side" box on page 334.

Intimate Relationships Foster Interdependence

Another hallmark of intimate relationships is that they include high degrees of **interdependence**. In an interdependent relationship what happens to one person affects everyone else in the relationship. Because people in families or romantic relation-

The Dark Side of Interpersonal Communication
When Commitment Becomes Obsession

Although deep commitment is necessary in intimate relationships, excessive levels of commitment can turn into an unhealthy obsession with another person. According to communication scholars William Cupach and Brian Spitzberg, intimate relationships are healthy and satisfying only if both partners desire approximately the same level of connection and interaction with each other. When one partner expresses a substantially higher level of interest in the relationship than the other, the result can be what Cupach and Spitzberg call "obsessive relational intrusion" (ORI). In some cases ORI occurs between strangers, but it can also occur within the context of an established relationship in which one partner feels substantially more invested than the other.

The reason why ORI is so problematic is that it can lead someone to engage in upsetting or threatening behaviors aimed at increasing intimacy with the target of his or her affections. These behaviors can include spying on the target or invading his or her privacy, sending the target unwelcome expressions of attraction or love, and engaging in sexually harassing behaviors. They can also include demanding that the target curtail communication with others and commit to an exclusive relationship with the pursuer.

Although relational intrusion can occur in face-to-face contexts, it is also becoming increasingly common online. Using the Internet, e-mail, or other electronic devices to intrude on another person's life is called *cyberstalking*. Intrusive behaviors can have several negative effects on their recipients, including physical and psychological stress, disruptions in everyday routines, loss of sleep or appetite, potential physical violence, and impairment in the ability to trust others.

Ask Yourself:

- What other communication behaviors, besides those mentioned, might constitute obsessive relational intrusion?

- Have you ever experienced obsessive relational intrusion? If so, what were the outcomes of that experience?

From Me to You:

- When they find themselves the target of obsessive relational intrusion, many people are inclined to initiate conversation with the pursuer to persuade him or her to stop the intrusive behaviors. Because this approach involves open and direct communication, it might seem to be an effective strategy for dealing with this problem. Experts warn, however, that the pursuer might interpret such communication as positive attention. In these cases it might actually encourage, rather than discourage, his or her pursuit. Often, a more effective strategy is to make yourself as inaccessible to the pursuer as possible, cutting off all communication with the person and asking your family and friends to help shield you from him or her. Many experts believe that, over time, this strategy is the most effective for eroding the pursuer's interest.

Sources: Cupach, W. R., & Spitzberg, B. H. (2004). *The dark side of relationship pursuit: From attraction to obsession and stalking.* Mahwah, NJ: Lawrence Erlbaum Associates; Spitzberg, B. H., & Hoobler, G. (2002). Cyberstalking and the technologies of interpersonal terrorism. *New Media & Society, 4,* 71–92.

ships depend on one another, one person's actions influence others. For instance, how parents use their time and money depends not only on themselves but also on their children's needs. Likewise, how children perform in school and how they treat their siblings also affects their parents. Parents and children, therefore, are interdependent. So are romantic partners: If a woman is offered a job promotion that requires her to relocate, for example, her decision will affect her romantic partner as much as it will affect her. The essence of interdependence is the idea that our actions influence other people's lives as much as they influence our own.

Almost all relationships have some measure of interdependence. What distinguishes intimate relationships is their *degree* of interdependence. You may feel very close to your best friend, but you probably wouldn't sell your house and move if his job were relocated. If your supervisor at work broke her leg, you might send flowers or visit her in the hospital, but you probably wouldn't offer her round-the-clock care. Like most social relationships, friendships and work relationships are interdependent to a degree. What usually sets our romantic and familial relationships apart, however, is their *higher* level of interdependence. This higher degree of interdependence often motivates us to engage in greater relational maintenance behaviors than we do with friends or co-workers.

Intimate Relationships Require Continuous Investment

Investment
The resources we put into our relationships.

Compared with other relationships, intimate relationships usually involve a higher degree of **investment.** We put more of ourselves and our resources into these relationships—particularly resources such as time, energy, and attention. We also expect to benefit from this investment—think of our expectations from financial investments, for instance—but know we cannot retrieve the resources we've dedicated to it if the relationship comes to an end. If we drift apart from our siblings during adulthood, for example, we may retain memories of our relationships, but we cannot retrieve the time, attention, and material resources we invested in them.

People in romantic relationships are often especially aware of how much—and how equally—they are each investing in the relationship. In the opening vignette, for instance, Ron was reluctant to attend Meghan's family reunion, but he reminded himself that she had accompanied him to his class reunion only a couple of months before. Her attendance at his class reunion represented an investment of time and energy that Ron felt obligated to repay by going to Meghan's family reunion.

Friendships generally are strongest when both people feel that each person is investing in the relationship to the same degree. Research shows that this same observation applies to romantic partners.[1] If you think you're putting more time or resources into your relationship than your partner is, it's easy to feel resentful. Meghan, for instance, might have been upset or hurt if Ron hadn't gone to her family reunion because he wasn't repaying her investment of attending his class reunion. From the opposite perspective, if your partner is investing more than you are, then you might feel guilty. Ron would probably have felt guilty had he not accompanied Meghan to her family reunion, for example. The most satisfying intimate relationships, therefore, appear to be those in which all parties are investing equally.

Intimate Relationships Spark Dialectical Tensions

Have you ever felt as though you wanted to be closer to someone, but you also wanted to maintain your individuality? In your relationships, have you wanted to disclose more about yourself but still keep some thoughts private? Maybe you enjoy novelty and surprise in your relationships but you also want those relationships to be stable and predictable. If you can relate to any of these situations, then you have already experienced what relationship researchers call **dialectical tensions.** *Dialectic* refers to conflicts between two important but opposing needs or desires. As the foregoing situations suggest, dialectical tensions are common in intimate relationships.[2]

Dialectical tensions Conflicts between two important but opposing needs or desires.

Within families, romantic relationships, and even friendships, we often find three dialectical tensions, in particular. One is the tension between the desire for *autonomy*—being your own person—and the desire for *connection*—being close to others. People often experience this tension with their children. Particularly as children enter adolescence, it's natural for them to desire greater autonomy. After all, adolescence is the period of life when people begin to develop independent identities and make decisions for themselves.[3] Many adolescents, however, still want to be emotionally close to their parents. Even as they are learning to behave like adults, many teenagers still need and crave the security of family closeness. In fact, it's not uncommon for parents and children to experience this dialectical tension for some time, even as the children grow into adults.

Many relationships invoke dialectical tensions. Perhaps you want to be close to someone but you also want to maintain your autonomy. Maybe you want to disclose to the other person but still keep some of your thoughts private. You might enjoy surprises but also value predictability. These are three tensions that are common in interpersonal relationships.

Consider, for example, the case of Raul. After attending his first year of college out of state, Raul moved back in with his parents for the summer. Because he had become accustomed to coming and going as he chose, he expected to be able to do the same at his parents' house. His parents, however, expected him to follow their house rules, which included letting them know where he was going and when he would be home. This dialectic tension between Raul's desire for autonomy from his parents and his connection to them was a source of conflict early in the summer. (Perhaps you've felt this way with your own parents from time to time.[4]) By discussing the issue, Raul and his parents were able to set aside their own expectations and agree on new rules that honored Raul's autonomy *and* his connection to his parents.

A second common dialectical tension is the conflict between the desire for *openness*—disclosure and honesty—and the desire for *closedness*—keeping certain facts, thoughts, or ideas to yourself. Suppose your brother asks you how your new relationship is going. On one hand, you might want to confide in him as a way of reinforcing your closeness to him. On the other hand, you might feel it's best to keep some of the details to yourself out of respect for your partner's privacy. In this instance, part of you desires openness, and another part of you desires closedness.

Ron negotiated this dialectical tension when he had to decide whether to tell Meghan how he felt about going to her family reunion. He wanted to tell her about his

When choosing a flavor of ice cream, do you stick with your usual favorite or try something new? This decision demonstrates that tension between predictability and novelty that many people experience in their intimate relationships.

concerns. At the same time, he didn't want to insult her or make her feel he didn't care about her. You can probably think of many instances when you have experienced this tension in your own relationships.

Finally, many intimate relationships experience conflict between the desire for *predictability*—consistency and stability—and the desire for *novelty*—fresh and new experiences. After nearly 20 years of marriage, for instance, Pauline and Victor were so settled into their routines that their relationship had become highly predictable. They made the same seven or eight dishes for almost every dinner, for example. They spent every New Year's Eve with Victor's parents, and they always gave each other artwork for their anniversary. Predictability such as this can be very comforting, and Victor and Pauline had grown to enjoy knowing what to expect from their relationship.

At times, however, too much predictability made their marriage feel stale, leaving them longing for new experiences. One year, instead of spending their holidays with Victor's family, they discussed doing something different, such as volunteering at a homeless shelter or taking gifts to elderly patients in a local hospital. Although they were uncertain about trying something new, they were also excited at the possibility. In the end, they spent their holiday creating care packages for deployed military troops and their families. They found the novelty of doing something different to be a refreshing change from the predictability of their lives. They also recognized that predictability gave their lives a sense of order and certainty that they both appreciated.

Although dialectical tensions can present serious challenges, it is important to understand that they aren't necessarily bad for relationships. Rather, researchers believe they are a normal part of any close, interdependent relationship, and they become a problem only when people fail to manage them properly. We'll look at several strategies that relational partners use to manage dialectical tensions at the end of this chapter.

Learn It: What is commitment? What does it mean to be interdependent? How do relational partners invest in each other? What is a dialectical tension?

Try It: Write a letter to your romantic partner, one of your parents, or another person with whom you have a close relationship, and express why you feel so committed to that relationship. Even if you never give the letter to that person, putting your reasons for your commitment in words can help clarify the importance of that relationship for you.

Reflect on It: In which relationships do you feel you invest the most? When do you experience tensions between autonomy and connectedness, openness and closedness, or predictability and novelty?

2} Communicating in Romantic Relationships {

The most intimate of intimate relationships is often the one we share with a romantic partner. Romantic relationships—particularly significant, long-term ones—engage people mentally, emotionally, physically, financially, even spiritually, and they often play a substantial role in people's social experiences. As noted earlier, they are also often the foundation for the beginning of new families. In this section, we'll explore:

- Several characteristics of romantic relationships
- The process by which we form them
- How we manage various communication issues within them
- The process by which we end them

> *Love doesn't make the world go 'round—love is what makes the ride worthwhile.*
>
> —Elizabeth Barrett Browning (1806–1861)
> British poet

Characteristics of Romantic Relationships

Forming romantic relationships is a nearly universal human experience. Some 95% of us, for instance, will get married at least once in our lifetimes, and many of those who don't will have at least one significant, marriagelike romantic relationship.[5]

These relationships aren't just pervasive. They are also very important to our health and well-being. Multiple studies have shown, for instance, that married people live longer[6] and healthier[7] lives than people who never marry. One reason may be that healthy people are more likely than unhealthy people to get married[8] and to stay married.[9] Another possible reason is that being married reduces a person's likelihood of engaging in risky health behaviors. Research demonstrates that, compared with unmarried people, married people drink less[10] and are less likely to use illicit drugs such as marijuana.[11] They are also less likely to suffer from mental illnesses such as depression.[12] Other studies have shown that the health benefits of marriage

Although traditions vary around the world, forming romantic relationships is a practically universal human activity. 95% of us will get married.

are greater for men than for women.[13] Some women are healthier if married rather than single, particularly those who are unemployed and lack the social support and financial resources that employment provides.[14]

People in every known society form romantic unions. Although many romantic relationships share certain characteristics, romantic relationships throughout the world also exhibit a great deal of diversity. In this section, we examine how romantic relationships vary in the extent to which they are:

- Exclusive
- Voluntary
- Based on love
- Composed of opposite-sex partners
- Permanent

Some romantic relationships are exclusive; others are not. One common expectation for romantic relationships is that they are exclusive. Usually, exclusivity takes the form of **monogamy,** which means being in only one romantic relationship at a time and avoiding romantic or sexual involvement with people outside the relationship. Exclusivity is an expression of commitment and faithfulness that romantic partners share with each other and trust each other to uphold. As a result, relational **infidelity,** which means having romantic or sexual interaction with someone outside your romantic relationship, is often an emotionally traumatic experience for the partner who is wronged.

Not all romantic partners expect their relationship to be exclusive, though. Instead, some couples choose to have "open" relationships in which romantic and/or sexual involvement with people outside the relationship is accepted.[15] Although it's difficult to know exactly how common open relationships are, research indicates that open relationships are observed between heterosexuals,[16] bisexuals,[17] gay men,[18] and lesbians alike.[19]

Not only are some romantic relationships not exclusive, but exclusivity isn't always an expectation for marriage. In fact, many countries—primarily in Africa and southern Asia—allow the practice of **polygamy,** in which one person is married to two or more spouses at the same time. Some people in open or polygamous relationships report that they appreciate the closeness and intimacy they share with multiple partners. Others indicate that feelings of jealousy and resentment can lead to increased conflict in such relationships.[20]

Some romantic relationships are voluntary; others are not. Another common expectation for romantic relationships is that they are voluntary. In voluntary relationships people get to choose for themselves whether to become romantically involved. Moreover, if they decide to, they get to choose their romantic partner. This expectation presumes that a strong, satisfying romantic relationship is one in which both partners have freely chosen to participate. One indicator of this expectation in the United States is the abundance of online and in-person dating services, which allow customers to browse the profiles of prospective partners and choose which ones they want to make contact with. In fact, one such service—Match.com—claims more than 15 million registered clients.[21]

In much of the world, however, it is common for other people—usually the parents—to select a person's romantic partner. According to the practice of arranged marriage (which is most common in the Middle East and other parts of Asia and Africa), people are expected to marry the partner their parents select for them. Some-

Monogamy
Being in only one romantic relationship at a time and avoiding romantic or sexual involvement with others outside the relationship.

Infidelity
Sexual involvement with someone other than your spouse.

Polygamy
A practice in which one person is married to two or more spouses at once.

times, children can reject their parents' selection of a spouse, in which case the parents look for someone else. In other cases, children may be pressured to marry the person their parents have chosen for them. In either situation, an arranged marriage is not entirely voluntary.

The fact that arranged marriages aren't voluntary doesn't necessarily mean that people whose marriages are arranged are dissatisfied with the relationship. Indeed, people who expect their marriages to be arranged might prefer this practice to the task of choosing a spouse on their own. For people who expect to choose their own romantic partner, however, the practice of arranged marriage would likely decrease their satisfaction with their relationships.

Some romantic relationships are based on love; others are not. In individualist societies such as the United States and other Western nations, people tend to believe not only that they should choose their romantic partner but also that their choice should be based on love and attraction.[22] The typical American wedding ceremony (whether religious or civil) emphasizes the importance of love in the marital relationship, whereas the lack of love is frequently cited as a reason why relationships fail.[23]

Would you marry someone you didn't love? Many people in collectivistic societies would say yes. In countries such as China or India, for instance, the choice of a spouse has more to do with the wishes and preferences of family and social groups than it does with love, even if the marriage isn't arranged. One study found that only half of the participants in India and Pakistan felt that love was necessary for marriage, whereas 96% of the U.S. American participants did.[24] Sociologist Frances Hsu explained that, when considering marriage, "an American asks, 'How does my heart feel?' A Chinese asks, 'What will other people say?'"[25]

As family studies scholar Stephanie Coontz points out, the connection between love and marriage is a historically recent trend, even in Western cultures.[26] She argues that although romantic love has existed throughout the ages, socie-

Love and marriage, love and marriage
Go together like a horse and carriage
This I tell you brother,
You can't have one without the other.
The sentiments Frank Sinatra expressed in this verse from the song *Love and Marriage* reflect how marriage is typically perceived in the U.S. and other Western countries.

For much of human history, marriage was conceived of as primarily an economic and political arrangement between families with a presentation of a dowry from one family to the other, as shown here. Professor Stephanie Coontz points out that connecting marriage to love is a relatively recent trend, even in Western cultures.

HUMAN RIGHTS
CAMPAIGN®

The Human Rights Campaign advocates equality for same-sex individuals and couples through federal and state laws.

ties began thinking of love as a basis for marriage only within the last three centuries. Coontz explains that before that time, some societies believed that love should develop *after* marriage, and many others thought love had no place at all in marriage. Thinking of marriage primarily as a romantic relationship, therefore, is a recent development in human history.

Some romantic relationships involve opposite-sex partners; others do not. Both heterosexual and homosexual people form romantic relationships. Moreover, people often communicate similarly in same-sex and opposite-sex romantic relationships.[27] People in both types of relationships value intimacy and equality between partners.[28] They both experience conflict,[29] and over similar topics.[30] They both seek emotional support from family members and friends.[31] Finally, they both negotiate how to accomplish instrumental needs, such as everyday household chores.[32] In fact, research indicates that people in same-sex romantic relationships report the same levels of satisfaction with their relationships as opposite-sex couples.[33]

Perhaps the greatest disparity between same-sex and opposite-sex romantic relationships in most parts of the world involves the legal recognition of the relationships. In the United States and abroad, the question of whether same-sex romantic partners should be allowed to marry has been socially and politically controversial for decades. People in many same-sex relationships live as *domestic partners,* often owning joint property and raising children together, so many have questioned why they should not be allowed to legally marry. Proponents of same-sex marriage argue that people should be allowed to marry whomever they love and that denying marriage rights to people based on their partner's sex is an act of unfair discrimination. Opponents argue that marriage is inherently a reproductive relationship and that allowing same-sex couples to marry threatens the sanctity of marriage and the family. This issue is likely to remain controversial for some time.

Federal law in the United States provides many benefits to spouses that are not available to those who aren't legally married.

Some romantic relationships are permanent; others are not. People often conceive of marriage and other long-term romantic relationships as permanent. This expectation is reflected in the fact that traditional wedding vows in many parts of the world emphasize the permanence of marriage. The vow "till death do us part" captures this sentiment by suggesting that once spouses are married, they will stay together for the rest of their lives. The results of a recent survey of 300 marriage license applicants illustrate this idea. Even though respondents correctly noted that a large percentage of new marriages end in divorce, every single respondent said the likelihood that his or her *own* marriage would end in divorce was zero![34]

Many marriages do last for many years, thanks in part to the large number of ways in which societies promote, protect, and reward marriages. In the

United States, for instance, federal law provides spouses a number of benefits that are often denied to couples who are not legally married. Many of these benefits relate to communication and the maintenance of marriage and family relationships.[35] Here are just a few:

- *Spousal privilege.* Communication between spouses is privileged, just like doctor-patient and attorney-client communication.
- *Visitation.* Marriage gives spouses rights of visitation if one spouse is hospitalized or imprisoned.
- *Stepchildren.* Stepparents have legal status with stepchildren only if they are legally married to the children's parent.
- *Cohabitation on controlled properties.* Marriage allows spouses to live together on military bases and other controlled properties.
- *Medical and burial decisions.* Spouses have the ability to make medical decisions for each other and to make burial or cremation decisions when one of them dies.
- *Domestic violence protection.* If one spouse is abusive or violent, the other spouse can request domestic violence protection orders from a court.

Many marriages and romantic relationships don't last, however. After a period of time together, romantic partners often find that they no longer share the same goals or feel the same level of attraction toward each other. They may also have developed romantic feelings for someone else and may choose to end their current relationship to develop a relationship with that person. No matter the cause, many romantic relationships come to an end. We discuss the process of dissolving romantic relationships later in this chapter.

As these characteristics help illustrate, romantic relationships—whatever their form—are among the most significant of all human relationships. To ascertain your own expectations for romantic relationships, take a look at the "Getting to Know You" box on the next page.

Forming Romantic Relationships Is a Process

Romantic relationships don't form overnight. Like many important relationships, they evolve, and researchers have found that people follow some fairly consistent steps when they form romantic relationships with others. Communication scholar Mark Knapp, for instance, has suggested that relationship formation involves five stages: initiating, experimenting, intensifying, integrating, and bonding.[36]

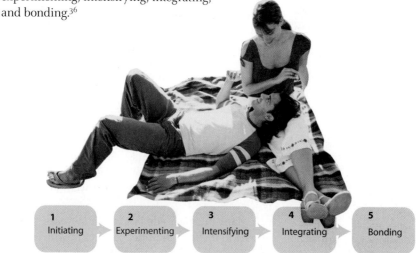

According to Professor Mark Knapp, people form relationships in five stages.

Getting to Know You
My Expectations for Romantic Relationships

As we've seen, people come into romantic relationships with a variety of expectations. What are yours? Read the statements below, and circle the number in front of each statement that you agree with. You can take this quiz whether you are currently in a romantic relationship or not.

1. I expect my romantic partner to be my best friend.
2. I expect my romantic relationship to be only one of several important relationships in my life.
3. I expect my romantic relationship to be problem-free.
4. I expect a romantic relationship to have its share of problems.
5. I think the most important aspects of a good romantic relationship are love and attraction.
6. I think a romantic relationship can be successful and satisfying even without high degrees of love and attraction.
7. I expect that once I get married or enter into a significant relationship, I will remain in that relationship until one of us dies.
8. I don't necessarily expect to spend the rest of my life with the same romantic partner.
9. I think living together before marriage sets up the marriage to fail.
10. I think living together before marriage is realistic and wise.

When you're finished, count the number of odd-numbered statements you circled. Now, count up the number of even-numbered statements you circled. Which number is greater? If you circled more odd-numbered statements, your expectations for romantic relationships are mostly *idealistic*. You believe in the ideal version of romantic relationships, and you want that for yourself. If you circled more even-numbered statements, your expectations are mostly *pragmatic*. You may want a good romantic relationship for yourself, but you don't expect it to be perfect or permanent.

Ask Yourself:

- Where do you think your expectations for relationships come from? Do you have these expectations only about romantic relationships or about all relationships?

- How do you see your expectations reflected in your communication behaviors?

As we explore these stages of relationship formation, bear in mind that this model, like most models of interpersonal communication, simplifies what is actually a complex, dynamic process. Indeed, the purpose of models is generally to simplify complex realities so that people can understand them. It's important, however, to remember that the process of developing relationships isn't necessarily the same for every relationship or in every culture. Nonetheless, research suggests that people experience distinct thoughts, feelings, and behaviors at each stage in the model.[37]

Initiating stage The stage of relationship development when people meet and interact for the first time.

Initiating. The **initiating stage** occurs when people meet and interact for the first time. For instance, you may make eye contact with someone on the first day of class and then decide to introduce yourself, or strike up a conversation. "What's your name?" and "Where are you from?" are among the questions people commonly ask each other at this initial stage.

Relationship initiation traditionally occurred in person. Today, however, it increasingly takes place online. The Internet provides many opportunities to meet new people.[38] These include popular networking sites, such as Facebook.com and MySpace .com, as well as commercial dating sites, such as eHarmony.com and Chemistry.com. Anytime you're interacting with someone for the first time, whether online or face-to-face, you're at the initiating stage.

Experimenting. When you meet someone you're initially interested in, you can move to the **experimenting stage** and have conversations to learn more about that person. At this stage, we may ask questions such as "What movies do you like?" and "What do you do for fun?" to gain some basic information about the other person, and we provide similar information about ourselves. This process, which we sometimes call "having small talk,"[39] serves a very important function: It helps us decide if we have enough in common with the person to move the relationship forward. Often, we decide that we don't. In such cases relationship development ends at this stage and we move on to other prospective partners. In fact, research indicates that most potential relationships end at the experimenting stage, whether they are initiated online or face-to-face.[40] Occasionally, however, we decide we want to continue getting to know the other person. In these cases we progress to the intensifying stage.

Intensifying. During the **intensifying stage,** people move from being acquaintances to being close friends. They spend more time together and might begin to meet each other's friends. They also start to share more intimate information, such as their fears, their goals for the future, and their secrets about the past. They often begin expressing affection for each other and may even develop nicknames or terms of endearment for each other. They increase their commitment to the relationship and may express their commitment verbally, through statements such as "You're really important to me."

The intensifying stage may also include formal dating. Sometimes, dating involves just the two people. At other times, it takes the form of "group dating," wherein several individuals socialize at once, allowing potential romantic partners the opportunity to interact with each other while still being surrounded by other friends. According to current research, college students report that group dates are just as common as traditional two-person dates.[41]

Research indicates that many college students are as likely to go on group dates as on traditional two-person dates. What's your preference?

Integrating. The **integrating stage** occurs when the partners have formed a deep commitment and they share a strong sense that the relationship has its own identity. At this stage, the partners' lives become integrated, and the two individuals begin to

Experimenting stage The stage of relationship development when partners have conversations to learn more about each other.

Intensifying stage The stage of relationship development when people move from being acquaintances to being close friends.

Integrating stage The stage of relationship development when a deep commitment has formed and there is a strong sense that the relationship has its own identity.

think of themselves as a pair—not just "you" and "me," but "we." Other people expect to see the two individuals together and begin referring to them as a couple.

The partners also take actions to demonstrate their relationship to other people, such as wearing matching rings, sending out joint holiday cards, or establishing a joint checking account. They may also begin to form friendships and socialize with other couples, as opposed to individuals. These types of behaviors symbolize the committed relationship the couple has developed.

Bonding. The final stage in Knapp's model of relationship development is the **bonding stage,** in which the partners make a public announcement of their commitment to each other. For many couples, this announcement takes the form of engagement or marriage. For others, it can involve moving in together or having a commitment ceremony. However they choose to do it, people who reach this stage are ready to announce to their social networks that they are committed to each other and to their relationship. They do so both to express their commitment in a public way and also to gain the support and approval of the people in their social networks.

A brief summary of the five stages of relationship development appears in the "At a Glance" box below.

As explained earlier, not every couple goes through these stages in the same way. Some couples may stay at the experimenting stage for a long time before moving into the intensifying stage. Others may progress through the stages very quickly. Still others may go as far as the integrating stage but put off the bonding stage for various reasons. Another important point is that these stages are not exclusive to opposite-sex romantic couples. Researchers have found that same-sex romantic relationships develop according to the same kinds of steps.[42]

Finally, keep in mind that the process of relationship formation is not necessarily the same in all cultures. In countries that practice arranged marriage, for instance, the process of forming a marital relationship would look much different. For one thing, it would include negotiation and decision making by the parents and less input (if any) from the children. In countries where polygamy is common, the integration and bonding stages probably look different, too, because one person may be joining multiple spouses at once. As we saw in the preceding section, cultures vary in their expectations about romantic relationships. As their expectations differ, their ways of forming relationships most likely do, as well.

Going further, even if people follow the same basic path toward developing their romantic relationships, they won't necessarily end up with the same type of relationship. Rather, research on marital relationships indicates that romantic couples embody distinct relational types. Communication researcher Mary Anne Fitzpatrick has spent many years studying patterns of marital communication. Her work suggests that people form and maintain marriages by relying on *marital schemata,* which represent their cognitive models for what marriage is and should be.[43] Fitzpatrick's research has found

Bonding stage The stage of relationship development when the partners publicly announce their commitment.

At a Glance: Stages of Relationship Development

According to Knapp's model, relationship development proceeds along five stages:

Initiating	Meeting and interacting with each other for the first time
Experimenting	Having conversations to learn more about the other person
Intensifying	Moving from being acquaintances to being close friends
Integrating	Forming a deep commitment and developing a relationship with its own identity
Bonding	Making a public announcement of commitment to each other

that three types of marriages are especially common: traditional, separate, and independent.[44]

Even if we form relationships according to the same basic stages, we don't necessarily end up with the same type of relationship. According to marriage expert Mary Anne Fitzpatrick, three fundamental types of marriage are especially common: traditional, separate, and independent.

- *Traditional couples* take a culturally conventional approach to marriage. They believe in gender-typical divisions of labor in which wives are in charge of housework and childrearing and husbands are responsible for home repair and auto maintenance. When conflict arises, spouses in traditional couples engage in it rather than avoid it.
- *Separate couples* are similar to couples in traditional marriages, except the spouses are autonomous rather than interdependent. They often have their own interests and their own social networks, and they think of themselves as separate individuals rather than as one couple. Because of their lack of interdependence, spouses in separate couples generally don't engage in conflict. Even when they disagree, they tend to ignore conflict rather than dealing with it directly.
- *Independent couples* see themselves as being independent of social expectations for marriage. They don't necessarily believe in conventional gender roles or divisions of labor, so the wife might support the family financially while the husband stays home with the children. Although these couples consider themselves to be independent of cultural norms, they are highly interdependent. As a result, they engage in conflict when it arises.

Fitzpatrick also found that in about half the couples she has studied, the husband and wife don't agree as to whether their marriage is traditional, separate, or independent. She refers to couples in which the two spouses have differing beliefs about their marriage as *mixed couples.* The most common type of mixed couple is one in which the wife's expectations match those of traditional couples and the husband's expectations match those of separate couples. Communication patterns in mixed couples most likely reflect the particular expectations each spouse holds.

Romantic relationships are as individual as the people who comprise them, and several of the ways they differ are related to communication behaviors. In the next section, we'll take a brief look at some of the different ways people communicate in their romantic relationships.

Interpersonal Communication in Romantic Relationships

We can learn a great deal about the quality of romantic relationships by looking at how the partners communicate with each other. Although couples engage in many forms of communication, four communication behaviors have particular influence on romantic partners' satisfaction with their relationship. These are:

- Conflict
- Privacy
- Emotional communication
- Instrumental communication

Romantic relationships vary in how they handle conflict. Conflict is a common characteristic of many romantic relationships. As we'll see in the next chapter, very often the way couples handle conflict—rather than the amount of conflict they experience—influences the success of their relationships. Much of what we know about how romantic partners handle conflict comes from research on marriage. For instance, social psychologist and marital therapist John Gottman has spent many years studying how spouses communicate during conflict episodes.[45] His work suggests marital couples can be classified into four groups, depending on how they handle conflict:[46]

- *Validating couples* talk about their disagreements openly and cooperatively. In such couples, spouses communicate respect for each other's opinions even when they disagree with them. They stay calm, even when discussing hotly contested topics. They also use humor and expressions of positive emotion to defuse the tension that conflict can create.
- *Volatile couples* also talk about their disagreements openly, but they do so in a way that is competitive rather than cooperative. That is, each spouse tries to persuade the other to adopt his or her point of view. Conflicts in such couples tend to be marked with expressions of negative emotion, rather than positive. These conflicts, however, are often followed by intense periods of affection and "making up."
- *Conflict-avoiding couples* deal with their disagreements indirectly, rather than openly. To avoid the discomfort of engaging in conflict directly, these couples try to defuse negative emotion and focus on their similarities. They feel there is little to be gained by engaging in conflict directly, believing that most problems will resolve themselves. They often "agree to disagree," which can side-step conflict but can also leave their points of disagreement unresolved.
- *Hostile couples* experience frequent and intense conflict. During conflict episodes, hostile couples use negative emotion displays, such as harsh tones of voice and facial expressions of anger or frustration. They also engage in personal attacks that include insults, sarcasm, name calling, blaming, and other forms of criticism.

Although Gottman developed his categories with reference to married couples, more recent work by researchers Thomas Holman and Mark Jarvis has indicated that the same categories also apply to unmarried heterosexual couples.[47] Less research has been conducted on the conflict communication of lesbian and gay couples. Gottman's studies have identified some differences in the conflict styles of homosexual and heterosexual couples, however. Specifically, his research has found that, compared with heterosexual couples, gay and lesbian couples:

- Use more humor and positive emotion during conflict conversations
- Are less likely to become hostile after a conflict
- Use fewer displays of dominance and power during a conflict episode
- Are less likely to take conflict personally
- Stay calmer emotionally and physiologically during conflict

It's unclear why these differences exist, but they may suggest that partners in same-sex couples have an easier time understanding each other during conflict episodes, perhaps because they *are* of the same sex.

For many romantic relationships, conflict is an unpleasant but unavoidable fact of life. We will learn more about successful strategies for managing conflict later in this chapter, and especially in Chapter 10, "Interpersonal Conflict."

Romantic relationships vary in how they handle privacy. People in every romantic relationship must choose for themselves how to manage information they consider to be private. When Kali and her husband, Neal, were having difficulty conceiving a child, for instance, they carefully considered whom they were going to tell. Neal felt the information was no one's business but theirs and therefore preferred to keep it private. By contrast, Kali wanted to tell her family and close friends because she needed their emotional support. Their problems conceiving were causing enough stress in their marriage already; disagreeing on whether to keep them private was only making matters more stressful.

Communication scientist Sandra Petronio believes we all experience tensions between disclosing certain information and keeping it private. She developed **communication privacy management (CPM) theory** to explain how individuals and couples manage those tensions.[48] CPM theory maintains that Kali and Neal *jointly own* the information about their problems. Because the information belongs to them, they must decide whether to keep it to themselves or share it with others. CPM theory further suggests that Kali and Neal have a theoretical *privacy boundary* around all the information they jointly own. If they decide to tell Kali's mother, for instance, about their difficulties conceiving a child, they expand the privacy boundary around that piece information to include her. Once she is included within the privacy boundary, Kali's mother becomes a co-owner of the information.[49]

Petronio's theory also explains that people within a privacy boundary are subject to rules regarding the maintenance of privacy. Some rules are explicit. For instance, Kali may say to her mother, "Please don't tell anyone else in the family about this." Other rules are implicit. If Kali tells her brother about her problems conceiving, for example, she may assume he recognizes that the information is to be kept private even though she doesn't say that directly.

According to CPM theory, relationships become distressed when implicit or explicit privacy rules are violated.[50] If Kali learns that her brother shared her information with others, for instance, she will likely feel that he violated her trust, particularly if he disclosed the information willingly. In such an instance, Kali and Neal may decide not to share private information with her brother in the future.

Individuals and couples vary in their approach to privacy. Some appear to be "open books" who are uninhibited about disclosing private information to others. By contrast, some are much more discreet, sharing private information only with a very select few. Perhaps you can

Communication privacy management (CPM) theory Theory developed by Sandra Petronio to explain how people manage the tension between privacy and disclosure.

Professor Sandra Petronio believes that one key to maintaining a satisfying relationship is keeping private information private. How do you feel when people share your private information with others without your permission?

think of people who fit both descriptions, as well as others who are in the middle. Research indicates that some of us are simply more prone than others to disclosing private information. In most cases, however, our decisions about sharing information are influenced by the people we are disclosing to, how much we trust them, and how disclosive they have been with us.[51] No matter what our reasons for disclosing to others, we should always be cognizant of information that a romantic partner expects us to keep private.

Romantic relationships vary in how they handle emotional communication. Emotional communication is an important part of most romantic relationships. Research indicates that the ways in which romantic partners express emotion to each other can tell us a great deal about the quality of their relationship.[52] Specifically, they indicate how satisfied the partners are with each other, as we'll see in this section.[53]

To illustrate the significance of emotional communication, let's consider two married couples who live across the street from each other. The first couple, Anita and Jonah, have been married for 8 years. They own a home together where they run a small pottery studio and raise Jonah's twin girls from his previous marriage. Like any couple, Anita and Jonah experience challenges in their marriage. Overall, however, they are both highly satisfied with their relationship. The second couple, Min-su and his wife, Jae-hwa, have been married for almost 10 years but have separated twice in that time. Their most recent separation lasted seven months and would have ended in divorce had Min-su's family not pressured the couple to work out their difficulties. Both spouses would describe their relationship as very unsatisfying.

According to research, one of the most noticeable differences in the communication patterns of these two couples will be in their expression of emotion. Over the course of several studies, social psychologists John Gottman and Robert Levenson have identified two patterns of emotional communication that differentiate happy from unhappy couples.

First, happy partners such as Anita and Jonah communicate more positive emotion and less negative emotion with each other than do unhappy partners such as Min-su and Jae-hwa.[54] In particular, people in satisfying relationships express more affection, use more humor, and communicate more assurances or verbal expressions of their commitment to the relationship. People in dissatisfying relationships tend to display the opposite pattern: They express more negative emotion in the form of anger, contempt, sadness, and hostility.[55]

You might already have guessed that happy couples communicate more positively than unhappy couples. Gottman and Levenson's research, however, has identified exactly *how much* more. According to several studies, people in satisfying couples maintain a ratio of approximately five positive behaviors for every one negative behavior.[56] Thus, for every instance when Anita speaks harshly to Jonah, she makes up for it with five positive behaviors, such as expressions of humor or affection. Significantly, Anita probably doesn't do this consciously. Rather, these behaviors are an intrinsic feature of their relationship. People in unsatisfying couples, by contrast, maintain a

According to Gottman's research, people in satisfying relationships enact five positive behaviors for every one negative behavior.

ratio closer to one positive behavior for every one negative behavior. Therefore, the number of times Min-su acts positively toward Jae-hwa would roughly equal the number of times he acts negatively toward her.

The second pattern of emotional communication Gottman and Levenson identified is that unhappy couples are more likely than happy couples to reciprocate expressions of negative emotion.[57] When Jae-hwa criticizes or expresses anger toward Min-su, for example, he often reciprocates her behavior by expressing criticism or anger back at her. Notice this pattern in the following exchange about the couple's finances:

Gottman has found that people in unsatisfying relationships enact only one positive behavior for every negative behavior.

Jae-hwa: Have you seen our credit card statement this month? Look at all these charges for golfing and dinners out! Are you trying to impress your hot-shot friends? I hope you know your kids are home eating macaroni and cheese while you're out throwing money around!

Min-su: Those are important business clients I'm taking out. You're the one who's always wasting money! Maybe if you stopped taking the car through that twelve-dollar car wash every other day, the kids would have something better to eat. Besides, I'm the one *making* the money in this family!

When Min-su reciprocates Jae-hwa's negativity in this manner, Jae-hwa usually becomes even more agitated. This type of response escalates the negativity in their conversation. As a result, they often find it difficult to address the issues underlying their conflict because they are so focused on the negative emotions they're communicating.

By comparison, happy couples are more likely to respond to negative expressions with positive or neutral ones. When Jonah gets frustrated and speaks harshly to Anita, for instance, Anita tries not to get angry herself. Instead, she attempts to reply in a calm way that acknowledges Jonah's feelings and keeps the focus on the issue they're discussing. Let's look at part of the conversation that ensued when Anita missed their children's dance recital at school:

Jonah: The kids were crushed that you weren't there! They danced their little hearts out and you couldn't even bother to show up! You know, these aren't just *my* children—they're *our* children. Maybe you'd understand that if you weren't so self-absorbed.

Anita: I know you're mad, and I'm really sorry I made you and the kids feel like you weren't a priority. I felt I needed to be with my sister last night; she's going through a hard time right now with her divorce. I'm sorry that came across as being self-absorbed. Maybe we should take the kids to the beach this weekend and spend some good time together as a family.

Notice how Anita begins by acknowledging Jonah's negative emotion and accepting responsibility for her part in causing it. This helps to de-escalate the negativity in the conversation. Then, instead of expressing negative emotion back to Jonah, the way Min-su does with Jae-hwa, Anita focuses on the problem (Jonah and the children feeling neglected) and offers a way of responding to it (spending the weekend at the beach). According to Gottman's research, failing to reciprocate negative emotion in this way is characteristic of a stable, happy couple.

Romantic relationships vary in how they handle instrumental communication. People in most romantic relationships communicate with each other about many mundane, instrumental topics, such as who's making dinner and who's taking the children to piano lessons or soccer practice.[58] Addressing such topics may not seem as significant as engaging in conflict, negotiating privacy boundaries, or managing emotional communication. Nevertheless, instrumental communication addresses the necessary day-to-day tasks couples face, which helps explain why it is one of the most common forms of communication between romantic partners.[59]

Although instrumental communication involves seemingly "minor" concerns, it can be one of the most contentious issues couples face, because romantic partners often disagree on how to divide responsibility for everyday tasks.[60] The ways in which partners negotiate the division of instrumental tasks can have a major impact on their relationship, for at least two reasons. First, day-to-day tasks such as cleaning, cooking, and caring for children need to be completed, so most couples cannot leave decisions about who will do them to chance.

Second, how partners divide mundane, everyday tasks often reflects the balance of power within their relationship.[61] If one partner assumes greater power and control than the other, then that partner is in a greater position to dictate how tasks will be divided. In contrast, if the two partners see themselves as equally powerful, then the division of instrumental tasks can be more equitable.[62]

Romantic relationships vary greatly in how the partners communicate about the division of day-to-day tasks. Among married couples, spouses who believe in traditional gender-role behaviors will often divide instrumental tasks along stereotypical gender lines.[63]

How partners divide mundane tasks, such as doing the laundry or maintaining the lawn, often reflects the balance of power in their relationship.

Thus, men perform tasks such as yard maintenance and auto repair, whereas women take responsibility for childcare and preparing meals. In such marriages, there may be little discussion or debate over how to divide such tasks. Rather, both partners simply may assume that each spouse will perform his or her gender-specific tasks. Spouses in traditional marriages often report high satisfaction with this division of domestic responsibilities.[64]

By contrast, spouses who do not necessarily adopt traditional gender-role behaviors frequently engage in conflict over how to divide instrumental tasks.[65] Specifically, women often wish their husbands would take greater responsibility for household tasks and childcare than they actually do.[66] Women are more likely than men to feel that the division of instrumental tasks is unfair. Significantly, these feelings often reduce women's satisfaction with the relationship.[67] Women are also more likely than men to express anger about the distribution of household responsibilities and to initiate discussion about dividing the tasks more equally.[68]

Although partners in opposite-sex relationships often divide instrumental tasks according to stereotypical sex roles, this method is not an option for partners in same-sex relationships. Recent research has speculated, therefore, that same-sex partners may divide tasks more equitably than opposite-sex partners, with each partner sharing in both stereotypically masculine and stereotypically feminine responsibilities. In a survey of more than 100 same-sex romantic couples from around the United States, communication researcher Justin Boren discovered that this pattern was common, particularly among couples who were highly satisfied with their relationships.[69]

Ending Romantic Relationships Is a Process

Just as romantic relationships develop over time, they also come apart over time. Communication researcher Mark Knapp, who identified the five stages of relationship for-

| 1 Differentiating | 2 Circumscribing | 3 Stagnating | 4 Avoiding | 5 Terminating |

Professor Mark Knapp suggests that relationships go through five distinct stages when they end.

mation we discussed earlier in this chapter, has similarly described five stages that relationships go through if they end: differentiating, circumscribing, stagnating, avoiding, and terminating.[70]

We'll look briefly at each of these five stages of relationship dissolution in this section.

Differentiating stage. Partners in a romantic relationship are similar to each other in some ways and different in other ways. In happy, stable relationships, partners see their differences as complementary. Perhaps your romantic partner is more outgoing, adventurous, and impulsive than you are, for instance. You might perceive these qualities as a good fit for your more introverted and reserved personality.

At the **differentiating stage,** however, partners begin to see their differences as undesirable or annoying. Whereas you may have valued your partner's impulsive, spontaneous ways when you first met, you might now find them to be impractical and irresponsible. This is how Miranda felt about her husband, Daniel, in *Mrs. Doubtfire,* which we discussed in Chapter 8. Many relationships experience differentiation from time to time, particularly during periods of stress. Differentiation becomes problematic, however, when it leads to later stages of relationship dissolution.

Differentiating stage The stage of relationship dissolution when partners begin to see their differences as undesirable or annoying.

Circumscribing stage The stage of relationship dissolution characterized by decreased quality and quantity of communication between partners.

Circumscribing stage. When romantic partners enter the **circumscribing stage,** the quality and the quantity of their communication with each other begin to decrease. This change occurs because the couple is trying to avoid dealing with conflicts in the relationship.[71] At the circumscribing stage, partners start spending more time apart from each other.[72] When they're together, they usually don't talk about problems, disagreements, or sensitive issues in their relationship. Rather, their conversations focus on "safe" topics and issues about which they agree. Couples in the circumscribing stage don't avoid each other completely, but they communicate less often and less effectively, especially about important issues.

Stagnating stage. If circumscribing progresses to the point where the partners are barely speaking to each other, the relationship enters the **stagnating stage.** This is the stage at which the relationship stops growing and partners feel they are merely "going through the motions" of their relationship. Partners avoid communicating about anything important because they fear it will only lead to conflict. Many relationships stay stagnant for long periods of time. Sometimes, this occurs because partners feel trapped, unsure of how to fix their relational problems. At other times, it's because the thought of leaving the relationship makes them too uncomfortable, so they conclude that even a stagnant relationship is better than no relationship at all.

Stagnating stage The stage of relationship dissolution when couples are barely communicating with each other.

In the circumscribing stages, romantic partners communicate less frequently and less effectively than usual. They may not avoid each other entirely, but they often don't interact even when they're together.

Avoiding stage. If partners decide they are no longer willing to live in a stagnant relationship, they enter the **avoiding stage.** At this stage, partners create physical and emotional distance from each other. Some partners take a direct route to creating distance, such as by moving out of the house or saying "I can't be around you right now." Others create distance indirectly. For example, they make up excuses for being apart ("I have company in town all next week, so I won't be able to see you"), or they curtail their availability to their partner by screening their phone calls or not responding to instant messages.

Clearly, a relationship that enters the avoiding stage is experiencing serious problems. Keep in mind, however, that avoidance does not, in itself, constitute the end of the relationship. In fact, even though many spouses separate for a period of time if they are contemplating divorce, not all couples who separate ultimately get divorced. Just the opposite, in some cases physical and emotional avoidance helps partners gain needed perspective on their relationship and increases or reinforces their commitment to each other. In other cases it helps the partners realize that their relationship is ending. In these cases the partners progress to the final stage of dissolution, known as terminating.

Avoiding stage The stage of relationship dissolution when partners create physical and emotional distance between them.

Terminating Stage. The last stage in Knapp's model of relationship dissolution is the **terminating stage,** at which point the relationship is officially deemed to be over. When nonmarital partners who have shared a residence terminate the relationship, one or both partners moves out. They also divide their property, announce to friends and family that the relationship has been terminated, and negotiate the rules of any future contact between them. At the end of a relationship, some partners choose to go their separate ways and never speak to each other again. Others elect to maintain a cordial relationship or even to remain friends after the breakup.[73]

Terminating stage The stage of relationship dissolution when the relationship is deemed to be officially over.

Divorce The legal termination of a marriage.

For partners who are legally married, relational termination involves getting a **divorce,** which is the legal discontinuation of the marriage. In the United States today, approximately 40% of all marriages end in divorce.[74] In fact, the U.S. divorce rate has been increasing fairly steadily since the end of the 19th century.

Researchers have uncovered several reasons for the increasing divorce rate.[75] One reason is that divorce is more socially acceptable now than it used to be. Put differently, being divorced doesn't seem to carry the stigma that it once did. In addition, obtaining a legal divorce is much easier today than in the past. States used to require spouses to show a specific harm (such as abuse or adultery) before granting a divorce. Today, however, nearly all U.S. states have a "no-fault divorce" law that allows spouses to divorce if they simply believe their marriage has failed, regardless of *why* it failed. A third reason why divorce may be on the rise is that women are increasingly less dependent on men economically, so they may find it easier to leave unsatisfying marriages.

The decision to divorce clearly is a significant one. The process of terminating a marriage often requires a substantial reorganization of the family, and it can take an enormous mental and emotional toll, particularly on children. Most former spouses struggle to adjust to life after divorce, and many children of divorced parents experience difficulties in their relationships with siblings, teachers, and peers.[76] Research shows that children, in particular, can be negatively affected by divorce well into their adulthood.[77]

Despite those problems, divorce doesn't always produce negative effects. When the marriage is highly conflicted, neglectful, or abusive, for instance, children and their parents are often better off after the divorce has occurred.[78] Regardless of its outcomes, divorce is one of the most significant events that a marriage and family can experience.[79]

A brief summary of the five stages of relationship dissolution appears in the "At a Glance" box.

At a Glance: Stages of Relationship Dissolution

According to Knapp, relationship dissolution proceeds along five stages:

Differentiating	Finding differences with your partner to be unpleasant and annoying
Circumscribing	Decreasing the quality and the quantity of communication with the partner
Stagnating	"Going through the motions" of a relationship that is no longer satisfying
Avoiding	Creating physical and emotional separation from the partner
Terminating	Formally ending the relationship

Learn It: What is relational infidelity? What are the stages of relationship development? How are validating, volatile, and conflict-avoiding couples different? What are the stages of relationship dissolution?

Try It: Pick a couple who has been together for at least 10 years, and ask the partners (together or separately) how their communication patterns have changed in the time they've been together. Ask them what advice they would give to others about communicating successfully in their relationship.

Reflect on It: To what extent do you expect your own romantic relationships to be permanent, or monogamous, or based on love? Has your privacy ever been violated by a romantic partner? If so, how did you feel? If not, how do you imagine you would respond?

3} Communicating in Families

As with romantic relationships, it's hard to overestimate the importance of families in our lives. For most of us, the first relationships we have in our lives are with our family members. Familial relationships can provide us with a sense of belonging, a sense of our own history, and a measure of unconditional love and support that we can't find anywhere else. As we discussed, growing up in a family also introduces us to the concept of relationships and can help us form mental models for how to engage in friendships and romantic relationships in adolescence and adulthood. Families can also be a source of great frustration and heartache—and many family relationships experience both peace and conflict. The depth of our engagement with

> *The family is one of nature's masterpieces.*
>
> —George Santayana (1863–1952)
> U.S. American philosopher

What makes a family a family? According to researchers, most family relationships have at least one of three fundamental characteristics: genetic ties, legal obligations, and role behaviors.

families, and the fact that they can be both so positive *and* so negative, make families one of our most important intimate relationships. In this section, we'll discuss:

- What makes a family a family, and what characteristics familial relationships often share
- What types of family structures exist
- How we can understand the family as a system
- What communication issues are common in families

What Makes a Family a Family?

If you were asked to draw a picture of your family, whom would you include? This question isn't as easy to answer as you might think. Some people might be obvious options, such as your parents, your spouse, your siblings, and your children. How about your grandparents, however? your nieces and nephews? your in-laws? What about your stepsiblings or your second cousins twice removed? Maybe there are close friends or longtime neighbors whom you think of as family: Would you include them as well?

If it's any consolation, even researchers have difficulty agreeing on exactly what makes a family a family. Many scholars agree, however, that most family relationships exhibit one or more of three fundamental elements: genetic ties, legal obligations, and role behaviors. Let's briefly examine each of these.

Genetic ties. Many family members are related "by blood," meaning they share a specified proportion of their genetic material. For instance, you share about 50% of your genes with your biological mother, your biological father, and each of your full biological siblings (or 100% if you're an identical twin or triplet). With your grandparents, aunts and uncles, and any half-siblings, you share about 25% of your genes; with cousins, it's about 12.5%.

Although most families include some genetic ties, many family relationships do not. For example, we typically share 0% of our genes with our spouses, steprelatives, and adopted relatives, yet we still consider them to be family. In addition, although sharing a genetic tie makes two people biological relatives, it does not necessarily mean they share a social or an emotional relationship. People who were adopted as infants, for example, may not even know their genetic parents. Rather, they may consider their adoptive parents to be their family. Clearly, then, a genetic tie is not the only element that defines family relationships. Rather, families share other characteristics as well.

Legal obligations. A second characteristic of many family relationships is that they involve legal bonds. Parents have many legal obligations toward their minor children, for instance, and neglecting their responsibilities to house, feed, educate, and care for their children is a crime in the United States and many other countries.[80] In fact, marriage is the most heavily regulated family relationship from a legal perspective. In the United States, for example, well over a thousand federal laws govern various aspects of marriage.[81] Adoptive relationships and domestic partnerships are also regulated by law, and even stepfamily relationships are affected by the laws regulating the stepparents' marriages.

Significantly, family members often believe they have responsibilities to one another even when there are no laws specifying those responsibilities. Laws formalize those responsibilities, however, and help to ensure that they are met.

Role behaviors. Regardless of whether a relationship is bound by genetic or legal ties, many believe the most important characteristic that defines it as familial is that the people in it *act* like family. According to this idea, there are certain behaviors or roles that family members are expected to enact. These roles can include living together, taking care of one another, loving one another, and representing themselves as a family to outsiders. According to this definition, people who do these things and who think of themselves as family are, in fact, family.

This definition provides you with flexibility in deciding who is—and isn't—part of your family, for two reasons. First, it allows you to include people with whom you have no genetic or legal ties, such as long-term friends or neighbors whom you have come to think of as "family." Perhaps you grew up calling your mother's best friend "Aunt Emma" or your next-door neighbor "Uncle Alan" even though those people weren't blood relatives.

Second, as we just saw, it confirms that sharing a genetic or a legal tie with someone doesn't necessarily make a relationship familial. If you were adopted, for instance, you may not think of your biological father as a part of your family, even though you're genetically related to him. The role element of family relationships focuses on how people feel and act toward one another rather than on legal or genetic bonds.

These elements—genetic, legal, and role—are not mutually exclusive, and some relationships include all three. How family scholars define family is important because it determines, in part, which relationships they choose to study. How *you* define family is also important, because it will influence whom you invite to participate in significant occasions in your life, whom you share resources with, and whom you will entrust with secrets or sensitive information.

Types of Families

Family of origin The family in which you grew up (often consisting of your parents and your siblings).

As we've seen, different elements play a part in defining family relationships. In turn, these elements give rise to a diverse set of family types. Indeed, one of the reasons that talking about families can be problematic is that families come in so many forms. In this section, we'll discuss some of the diversity of family types.

We begin this discussion by distinguishing between what researchers label your **family of origin** and your **family of procreation.** Your family of origin is the family you grew up in: It typically consists of your parents or stepparents and any siblings you

Family of procreation The family you start as an adult (often consisting of your spouse and your children).

In the 1950s television show *Leave It to Beaver*, the Cleavers were like most U.S. American families at the time: a legally married husband and wife and their biological children, all living together in the same household. For decades, people have referred to this arrangement as the "average American family," and in the 1950s, almost two-thirds of families in the United States fit this description. Is this arrangement still the average U.S. American family?

The answer is no. According to the U.S. Census Bureau, fewer than 50% of families in the United States are now headed by a married couple. This statistic doesn't mean that fewer people are marrying. Rather, it means more than half of U.S. American households are now headed by single adults, cohabiting opposite-sex couples, and cohabiting same-sex couples, more than at any point in U.S. history.

Typical family arrangements vary around the country too. According to the Census Bureau's American Community Survey, the highest percentage of households headed by a married couple is in Utah County, Utah, at nearly 70%. The lowest, at just 26%, is in Manhattan, New York.

Ask Yourself:

- Do you consider your family to be average or typical? In what ways?

- How do you think changes in family structure affect the ways family members communicate?

Source: U.S. Census Bureau. (2006). American community survey. Available online at: http://www.census.gov/acs/www/

have. Your family of procreation is the family you start as an adult: It consists of your spouse or romantic partner and/or any children you raise as your own. Most adults would assert that they belong to both a family of origin and a family of procreation. Others, however, may identify with only one type of family, such as young adults who have not had children of their own. Some may even identify with neither type.

Families of origin and families of procreation both develop in many forms. Perhaps the most traditional form consists of a married woman and man and their biological children. Researchers often call this family form a "nuclear family." Even though the nuclear family is the traditional family form in the United States, it is no longer the most common form. (See the "Fact or Fiction?" box on this page.)[82] An alternative family type that is becoming increasingly common is the "blended family," which consists of two adult partners—who may be married or living together unmarried and of the same or opposite sex—raising children who are not the biological offspring of both partners. The children may be adopted, or they may be the biological offspring of one of the parents and the stepchildren of the other.

A third family form that is becoming more common is the "single-parent family," which consists of one adult raising one or more children. As in blended families, the children may be the parent's biological offspring, or they may be adopted or stepchildren. There are more than 12 million single-parent families in the United States, and 10 million of these are headed by a single mother.[83] The final family form, "extended families," includes relatives such as grandparents, cousins, aunts and uncles, and other individuals whom you consider to be part of your family. We may or may not interact with our extended families on a regular basis, but research shows these relationships can be a significant part of our family experience.[84]

The Family as a System

Families come in many forms, and every family is different. Despite this diversity, all families share certain characteristics that influence how they communicate and interact. Researchers often define families as **systems** to emphasize that they consist of individual people and relationships that interact to form a complex whole. A system is any set of interdependent parts that work together to form an integrated whole. A piano, for example, consists of individual keys, metal strings, felt-padded hammers, gears, pedals, and a wood casing. None of these parts gives us music by itself. When these components of a piano work together as a system, however, they are capable of producing beautiful sounds.

System An arrangement of people (or other components) who interact with one another in complex, interdependent ways.

Similarly, no person constitutes a family by herself or himself. Rather, families comprise people who interact in interdependent ways. As systems, families tend to have several attributes in common.[85] To begin with, they are influenced by their environment, which means that communication outside the family affects interaction within the family. In addition, family members are interdependent, so each person's communication affects everyone else. Also, because families constitute more than the sum of their parts, each family has a collective personality and identity. Finally, family systems include smaller subsystems, each of which may communicate in distinct ways. Let's look at each of these attributes in greater detail.

Many family systems are composed of smaller subsystems, including the marital, parental, and sibling subsystems.

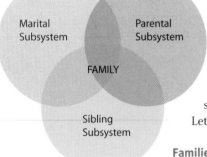

Marital Subsystem

Parental Subsystem

FAMILY

Sibling Subsystem

Families are influenced by their environments. The family is an example of what researchers call an *open system.* An open system is one that both affects and is affected by events that occur outside as well as inside the system. Spouses may be especially happy after receiving a large tax return, for example, so they decide to take their children on a much-desired vacation. The argument an unemployed mother has with her public assistance caseworker can make her so angry that she needlessly yells at her children when she gets home.

Likewise, events that occur within the family can affect how you communicate with other people. After staying up late hanging out with siblings you haven't seen in a long time, for instance, you may find it difficult to pay attention in class the next morning. Similarly, a man's conversation with his ailing grandmother may leave him so emotionally shaken that he becomes short-tempered with his co-workers. All these examples illustrate how family communication influences, and is influenced by, the environments in which families exist.

Family members are interdependent. As we discussed earlier in this chapter, interdependence means that each person in a relationship affects, and is affected by, every other person in that relationship. This characteristic is certainly true of families. Anything that happens to one person in the family has the potential to affect the entire family system.

Let's say, for example, that a father decides to go back to school to finish his degree. That decision can affect his family system in several ways. First, he's probably not home as often, which means he has fewer opportunities to interact with his

spouse and children. Second, because of the pressures of school, he may be feeling greater stress than usual, which could cause him to become more impatient with his family members. Third, there may be less money available because of his tuition bills, which could increase conflict over financial decisions. Fourth, once the father graduates, his new education may enable him to get a better job. Changing jobs could improve not only his professional satisfaction and sense of purpose but his family's quality of life as well. These are all examples of how, in an interdependent system such as a family, one person's actions have implications for everyone else in the system.

Families are more than the sum of their parts. Maybe you've noticed that each class you're in has its own "personality." Some classes are lively and talkative, others are more serious and subdued, but no two classes are exactly alike even if they have the same professor. That's because a class is more than just the identities of the individual people in it; it also has its own group identity. Families are the same way. We can't understand how a family communicates simply by looking at the spouses or the siblings, because a family is more than just the sum of its parts. To understand a family, we must see it as a system with its own collective identity.

Family systems include smaller subsystems. Many systems, including families, can be divided into smaller units called "subsystems." These units consist of specific relationships within the family, and many families are made up of several subsystems. For instance, the spousal subsystem consists of a relationship between romantic partners, and it is often the first subsystem to develop in a new family. The spousal subsystem may consist of a married husband and wife, but it can also involve an opposite-sex or same-sex couple who are cohabiting, or living together without being legally married.

The parental subsystem includes relationships between parents and children. It is created with the addition of the first child into the family, whether by birth, adoption, or other means. It isn't necessary to have a spousal subsystem in place before a parental subsystem is created; single adults who have or adopt children belong to a parental subsystem even though they aren't romantically partnered.

The addition of the second child into the family creates a sibling subsystem, made up of the relationships between and among brothers and sisters. The sibling subsystem is usually a child's first peer group. For that reason, sibling relationships provide a context for learning important social skills.[86] In some cases, such as the birth of twins or the adoption of two siblings, the parental subsystem and the sibling subsystem are created simultaneously.

Communication Issues in Families

As in all significant relationships, communication plays a big part in making or breaking family relationships. In this section, we'll examine four communication issues that families commonly deal with: roles, rituals, stories, and secrets.

Family roles. Family roles embody the functions you serve in the family system. One person may be the problem solver, for instance, whereas another is the family jokester or the family peacemaker. One sibling may be the troublemaker, whereas another is the caregiver or the helpless victim. Notice that roles are different from family positions, so we wouldn't talk about the role of the father, for instance, or the role of the daughter. Positions such as father or daughter are based on the structure of your relationships with others, whereas roles are based on the social and emotional functions your behavior serves within your family.

Family roles often become particularly relevant when the family is in conflict. Expert family therapist Virginia Satir has suggested that four roles become especially common during conflict episodes.[87] The first role is the "blamer," that is, the individual who holds others responsible for whatever goes wrong but accepts no responsibility for his or her own behaviors. A second role is the "placater," the peacemaker who will go to any lengths to reduce conflict. This person may simply agree with whatever anyone says to keep others from getting angry. A third role is the "computer," who attempts to use logic and reason (rather than emotion) to defuse the situation. Finally, there's the "distracter," who makes random, irrelevant comments to shift the family's attention away from the conflict situation. Can you identify which roles your family members and you tend to adopt during conflict situations?

Family roles can evolve over time. Early in the 2004 movie *Garden State*, Andrew Largeman (played by Zach Braff) avoids conflict to keep peace in his family. As the film progresses, however, he encourages others to express their feelings, even if they are negative. Can you think of ways in which your own family roles have evolved?

Significantly, each of these roles leads people to communicate in different ways. Some role behaviors, such as computing or placating, can be useful for resolving conflict or at least for preventing it from escalating. The behavior of blamers and distracters, in contrast, can intensify conflict by shifting attention away from the topic of the conflict, thereby making it less likely that the conflict will be addressed and resolved.

Family rituals. Many families have their own important traditions. One family's tradition might be to spend every Thanksgiving serving turkey dinners at a residence for injured homeless veterans. Another's might be to attend drag races every summer or to have dinner with the neighbors once a month. We call these traditions family **rituals,** or repetitive behaviors that have special meaning for a family. Can you think of any rituals that are important in your family?

Rituals
Repetitive behaviors that have special meaning for a group or relationship.

Rituals serve a variety of functions in family interactions, such as reinforcing a family's values and providing a sense of belonging. A family ritual such as an annual road trip isn't just about the trip but also about spending time together, creating memories, and emphasizing how important family relationships are.

According to communication scholars Dawn Braithwaite, Leslie Baxter, and Anneliese Harper, rituals can be especially important in blended families that consist of stepparents and stepchildren. Their research found that people often "import" rituals from their original family into their blended family.[88] Sometimes, the blended family retains or adapts these rituals; sometimes it does not.

For instance, Braithwaite and her colleagues described one family in which a widowed mother and her children would have a pizza "picnic" in the living room on a regular basis. The children would cuddle with the mother on the couch, eat pizza, and talk. Every family member considered this ritual to be a special time. When the mother remarried and acquired stepchildren, however, the ritual stopped, perhaps because the stepchildren would have been uncomfortable taking part.

In their research, Braithwaite and colleagues also found that it's important for blended families to develop their own unique rituals. In one family, for instance, a young man described how his new stepfather instituted a ritual of watching the Super Bowl with his brother and him. According to this young man, this ritual served as a means of promoting communication with his stepfather: "It gave us something in common and we could talk about sports. It gave us a link. We both understood things, so we could eventually talk about other things more freely. . . . I almost started thinking of him as my dad."[89]

Family stories. Many of us can think of particular stories we've heard over and over again from family members. Maybe your grandparents were fond of describing how they overcame hardships when they were first married. Perhaps your uncle enjoyed telling the story of how your parents first met, or your parents have a favorite story about your childhood antics. Even events that were stressful or unpleasant at the time but turned out well, such as fixing a flat tire while on vacation or finding a child after becoming separated in a department store, can serve a reassuring or cautionary function when they become part of the family lore and are talked about again and again.

Stories are common in families, and communication scholar Elizabeth Stone suggests that they do more than just provide entertainment. They also give families a sense of their history, express what family members expect of one another, and reinforce connections between and among different generations.[90]

Family stories are as varied as families are, but they all tend to share at least two characteristics. First, they're told and retold, often over long periods of time. In this way, they become part of a family's collective knowledge: Eventually almost everyone in the family has heard each story over and over. Second, family stories convey an underlying message about the family, such as "We are proud," "We overcome adversity," or "We stick together no matter what."

Family secrets. Many families have secrets they intentionally keep hidden from others. These secrets often contain information the family considers private and not appropriate for sharing with outsiders, such as religious practices, health or legal issues, family conflicts, and financial information. When you were growing up, for instance, you may remember your parents telling you not to talk about issues like these with people outside your family. Keeping family secrets doesn't just protect private family information, though. It also reinforces the family's identity and exclusivity, because only family members are allowed to know the secrets.[91]

Secrets can also be kept *within* families. For instance, Marco may not want his parents to know he has moved in with his girlfriend, so he swears his sister to secrecy. Erin and Tammy may not want their young children to know that Tammy has breast cancer, so they agree to keep it secret. Parents may decide not to tell their children they were adopted, at least until they have reached a certain age. People choose to keep secrets from other family members for many reasons, such as avoiding embarrassment or conflict, protecting another person's feelings, or maintaining a sense of autonomy and privacy.

Family rituals, such as decorating the house in support of a favorite sports team, can reinforce a family's values and provide a sense of belonging.

4} Improving Communication in Intimate Relationships

As we've seen in this chapter, romantic and familial relationships can be highly rewarding or extremely challenging—and many are both. They are always important to us, though. Therefore, it's in our best interests to communicate as competently as we can within them. In this section, we'll look at four strategies for improving communication within our intimate relationships: emphasizing excitement and positivity, handling conflict constructively, having realistic expectations, and managing dialectical tensions.

> *Love is a friendship set to music.*
>
> —E. Joseph Cossman (1918–2002)
> U.S. American entrepreneur

Emphasize Excitement and Positivity

You may have heard the saying "The family that plays together, stays together." It turns out this bit of folk wisdom has some truth to it. Research by social psychologist Art Aron and his colleagues has shown that spouses who engage in exciting forms of play together—such as rollerblading, riding a roller coaster, or going to a suspenseful movie—actually increase their level of relationship satisfaction.[92] Importantly, though, Aron's findings indicate that the play has to be something exciting or exhilarating. (See "How Do We Know?" on page 363.) Activities such as playing cards and going out to dinner, even if they are pleasant, don't have the same effect.

Why is this the case? Aron suggests that when partners engage in activities that elevate their physical arousal—the way riding a roller coaster or watching a suspenseful movie can—they may attribute their elevated arousal to one another instead of to the activity. Subconsciously, that is, people may notice that they feel physically aroused and may believe it's their partner, rather than the activity, that's causing their arousal. Sharing exhilarating play activities, therefore, can help partners maintain a level of positivity and freshness in their relationship that might otherwise fade with time. This isn't the only strategy for improving an intimate relationship, but research suggests it can be effective.

There are other ways to emphasize positivity in family relationships, as well. One important strategy is to use **confirming messages,** or behaviors that indicate how much we value another person. Sometimes, these are verbal statements, such as parents telling their children how special they are and how much they love them.

Confirming messages Behaviors that indicate how much we value another person.

In this chapter, you learned that one way to improve communication in intimate relationships is to engage in exciting and arousing activities with your partner. How do we know that this works?

In one study, social psychologists Art Aron, Christina Norman, Elaine Aron, and Colin McKenna invited 28 married and dating couples to their laboratory and asked them to provide self-reports of their relationship satisfaction and quality. They then assigned half of the couples to take part in a novel, arousing activity. These couples were bound to each other on one side at the wrist and ankle with

Velcro straps and were then instructed to move on their hands and knees through a makeshift obstacle course laid out on gymnasium mats while carrying a pillow between them. The other half of the couples took part in a mundane activity that involved rolling a ball to the center of the room.

After the activities, the couples reported again on their relationship quality and satisfaction. The researchers found that these scores increased for couples who took part in the arousing activity but not for those who did the mundane activity. Subsequent studies involving exciting or mundane activities that participants performed on their own, outside the laboratory, yielded the same pattern of results.

Ask Yourself:

- Why do you suppose that sharing exciting activities makes people feel more satisfied with the quality of their relationships?

- How might you use this information to improve your own relationships?

From Me to You:

- It may be difficult to see how rolling around on a gym mat while bound to your romantic partner could improve your relationship satisfaction. The activity itself isn't causing the improvement, however. Rather, it's the novel and physically arousing nature of the activity that produces the benefit. You can easily use this knowledge to improve your own relationships. With your romantic partner, your family members, or even your friends, make opportunities to share exciting and novel experiences. You may find that your relationships become closer as a result.

Source: Aron, A., Norman, C. C., Aron, E. N., McKenna, C., & Heyman, R. E. (2000). Couples' shared participation in novel and arousing activities and experienced relationship quality. *Journal of Personality and Social Psychology, 78,* 273–284.

Confirming messages can be nonverbal, too, such as focusing your attention on another person and really listening to what he or she is saying.[93]

Research shows that confirming messages are particularly important in marital relationships. Psychologist John Gottman has spent much of his career looking at why marriages succeed or fail. As we discussed earlier in this chapter, he has found that stable, satisfied couples have a 5:1 ratio of positive to negative communication. In other words, spouses who are happy with their marriages enact at least five positive behaviors (such as confirming messages) for every one negative behavior. Gottman has found that couples with lower positive-to-negative ratios have an elevated risk of divorce.[94]

Sharing novel and physically arousing activities, such as a long bike ride, can help romantic partners, family members, and even friends to feel closer and more appreciative of each other.

Handle Conflict Constructively

Even the happiest, most stable relationships experience conflict from time to time. Dealing with conflict is rarely fun, but as you'll learn in Chapter 10, conflict itself isn't necessarily bad for relationships. What matters to most relationships isn't the frequency or even the intensity of conflict—it's how the individuals involved handle the conflict.

Conflict arises when people in an interdependent relationship have competing goals. It's easy to imagine such a situation in a marriage or a family. People in these relationships often experience conflict over topics such as money, power and decision making, intimacy, and other issues that are easy to disagree about.[95]

When conflicts arise in intimate relationships, many people find it easiest to ignore them, minimize them, or pretend they don't exist. Avoiding conflict in these ways can serve important functions. For instance, it can help people calm down and gain composure so they can later address the topic of their conflict without becoming emotionally aroused. Avoidance can also help people keep small, inconsequential disagreements from escalating into large, unmanageable fights. In the opening vignette, for example, Ron kept his concerns about attending Meghan's family reunion to himself. In so doing, he prevented his concerns—which were unfounded—from turning into a conflict that may have hurt Meghan's feelings and produced stress within their relationship.

Research shows, however, that dealing with conflicts in an open and constructive manner is often better for intimate relationships in the long run. In Chapter 10, we will look at several specific ways to handle conflict positively. Suppose your spouse and you are in conflict over whether to let your mother-in-law move in with you. Let's say your spouse is in favor of this but you are not. As we'll learn in Chapter 10, one constructive strategy for dealing with this conflict is to accommodate, or acquiesce to the other person's wishes. Even if you're not keen on living with your mother-in-law, you may agree to it to please your spouse and keep harmony in your relationship. Another constructive strategy is to compromise, in which both parties give up something they want in order to arrive at a mutually acceptable solution. You and your spouse may decide, for instance, to provide a home for your mother-in-law for half of the year and to ask your spouse's brother to host her for the other half. We will learn much more about these and other strategies for dealing with relationship conflict in Chapter 10.

Have Realistic Expectations

Another way to improve communication in our intimate relationships is to make certain our expectations for those relationships are realistic. When our expectations are unrealistic, we are certain to find that our relationships fail to meet them, causing us to feel disappointed, hurt, or betrayed. It isn't enough that our expectations seem realistic to us, however. What matters is that they are realistic for everyone in the relationship. Only through open communication can we learn what everyone's expectations are and agree on how realistic they are.

Six months after marrying Carla, for instance, Gregory stopped spending time with his parents, his brother, and even his close friends. He wanted to spend *all* his time with Carla, and he began feeling anxious whenever they were apart. Eventually, Carla started to feel smothered, and she explained to Gregory that they both needed other people in their lives besides each other. She encouraged him to reconnect with his family and friends. Gregory, in turn, explained that spending time with Carla helped him feel secure about the status of their relationship. Eventually, they agreed on a new expectation for spending time together that seemed more reasonable to both of them. By communicating about their different expectations for their marriage and coming to agreement on what they both considered realistic, Carla and Gregory were able to strengthen their feelings of satisfaction with each other.

It's not uncommon for romantic partners to want to spend a great deal of time together, but it's important to be realistic about what we expect from each of our relationships. No one person—not even your spouse—can meet all your social and emotional needs. Expecting someone to do so places an unfair burden on that person and will eventually leave you disappointed.

A better approach is to appreciate each relationship individually and to remember that the important people in your life are *all* important to you, for different reasons. Maybe your mom is a great listener when you have a problem, but you go to your grandfather when you need to kick back and relax. You might talk to your romantic partner about most issues but feel more comfortable discussing your worries about your dad's health or your daughter's financial difficulties with your brother or sister. Keep in mind, too, that just as no single person can meet all *your* needs, neither can you meet someone else's every need. Being realistic about our expectations helps us appreciate the most positive aspects of each of our relationships.

Manage Dialectical Tensions

As we discussed earlier in this chapter, people in romantic and familial relationships often experience dialectic tensions, or conflicts between two opposing needs. Spouses may want predictability in their relationship, for example, but they may also long for novelty. Like conflict, dialectical tensions aren't necessarily bad for relationships. One way to improve communication in your intimate relationships, however, is to learn how to manage dialectical tensions when you experience them.

Researchers have identified eight strategies that people in intimate relationships use to manage dialectical tensions.[96] None of these strategies is inherently positive or negative. Rather, their effectiveness depends on your goals for the relationship and the context in which you are using them.

Like being on a see-saw, negotiating dialectical tensions in our relationships often requires us to go back and forth between two opposing desires.

To illustrate these strategies, let's suppose Moira has become engaged to marry Albee and she is experiencing the tension between autonomy and connection. She strongly desires to merge with Albee and be connected to him, yet she also strongly desires to retain her individuality and autonomy. Let's look at some strategies she might use to manage this tension:

- *Denial.* This strategy involves responding to only one side of the tension and ignoring the other. Were Moira to adopt this strategy, for instance, she might deny her desire for autonomy and focus all her attention on being connected with Albee.
- *Disorientation.* This strategy involves escaping the tension entirely by ending the relationship. Moira may feel so disoriented by the tension between her desires for autonomy and those for connection, for example, that she calls off her engagement.
- *Alternation.* Alternation means going back and forth between the two sides of a tension. On some days, for example, Moira might act in ways that enhance her autonomy and individuality, such as spending time alone. On other days, she might act in ways that enhance her connection to Albee, such as sharing activities they both enjoy.
- *Segmentation.* This strategy involves dealing with one side of a tension in some aspects, or segments, of your relationship and the other side of the tension in other segments. Were Moira to select this strategy, she might emphasize her connection to Albee by sharing intimate disclosures, but she might emphasize her autonomy by keeping her finances separate or retaining her own last name when they marry. Rather than going back and forth between the two sides of the tension, as in alternation, she is addressing one side of the tension in some segments of her relationship and the other side in other segments.
- *Balance.* People who use balance as a strategy try to compromise, or find a middle ground between the two opposing forces of a tension. For instance, Moira might disclose most of her feelings to Albee but keep some of her feelings to herself. This strategy might not make her feel as autonomous as she wants *or* as connected as she wants, but she might feel she is satisfying each desire to some degree.

- *Integration.* In this strategy, people try to develop behaviors that will satisfy both sides of a tension simultaneously. Moira feels connected to Albee when they spend their evenings together, but she also likes to choose how she spends her time. To integrate these needs, she often will read or do crossword puzzles while Albee watches television in the same room. This arrangement enables her to feel autonomous and connected at the same time. Unlike the balance strategy, which focuses on compromising each desire, integration focuses on finding ways to satisfy both desires without compromising either one.
- *Recalibration.* Adopting this strategy means "reframing" a tension so that the contradiction between opposing needs disappears. Instead of feeling conflicted by their competing needs for autonomy and connection, Moira and Albee could agree, through discussion, to treat autonomy and connection as equally desirable. As a result, they might come to see autonomy and connection as complementary needs rather than opposing ones.
- *Reaffirmation.* Finally, reaffirmation means simply embracing dialectical tensions as a normal part of life. Moira might come to realize that she will always feel torn between her needs for autonomy and connection. Instead of fighting the tension or struggling to resolve it, she simply accepts it as a normal feature of her relationship. Whereas reframing means eliminating the tension by seeing the opposing needs as complementary, reaffirmation means accepting the tension as normal.

It's not uncommon for people in families and romantic relationships to try several of these strategies. They may find some of these strategies to be more effective for them than others. Improving your communication in intimate relationships doesn't require you to adopt specific strategies and ignore others. Rather, if you're aware of the different options for managing dialectical tensions, then you can choose the ones that work best for you.

Learn It: What's an example of a confirming message? When is avoidance a useful strategy for managing conflict? Why are unrealistic expectations problematic for a relationship? How is alternation different from segmentation as a strategy for managing dialectical tensions?

Try It: Identify a dialectical tension you are currently experiencing in a romantic or familial relationship. Think about the two sides of the tension, and write a short paragraph describing how these two needs conflict with each other. Then, write a second paragraph describing how these two needs complement each other. That is, how do they work together to create a better relational experience than either need would on its own? Use this exercise to recalibrate the dialectical tension within the relationship. Finally, keep your new perception of the tension in mind as you communicate in your relationship.

Reflect on It: What role do excitement and positivity play in your intimate relationships? When do you have unrealistic expectations about your relationships?

Section 1} The Nature of Intimate Relationships (p. 333)

I. The Nature of Intimate Relationships

A. Intimate relationships require deep commitment	• Relational commitment involves emotional, social, legal, and financial responsibilities for another's well-being.
B. Intimate relationships foster interdependence	• Intimate relationships usually involve high degrees of interdependence.
C. Intimate relationships require continuous investment	• Intimate relationships also involve high degrees of investment.
D. Intimate relationships spark dialectical tensions	• Many dialectical tensions, including the tensions of autonomy-connection, openness-closedness, and predictability-novelty, are common in intimate relationships.

Section 2} Communicating in Romantic Relationships (p. 338)

II. Communicating in Romantic Relationships

A. Characteristics of romantic relationships

   1. Some romantic relationships are exclusive; others are not

   2. Some romantic relationships are voluntary; others are not

   3. Some romantic relationships are based on love; others are not

   4. Some romantic relationships involve opposite-sex partners; others do not

   5. Some romantic relationships are permanent; others are not

• Many romantic relationships are exclusive, voluntary, based on love, composed of opposite-sex partners, and permanent, but many others do not share these characteristics.

B. Forming romantic relationship is a process

   1. Initiating

   2. Experimenting

   3. Intensifying

   4. Integrating

   5. Bonding

• Forming a relationship is a process that involves at least five stages: initiating, experimenting, intensifying, integrating, and bonding.

C. Interpersonal communication in romantic relationships

   1. Romantic relationships vary in how they handle conflict

   2. Romantic relationships vary in how they handle privacy

   3. Romantic relationships vary in how they handle emotional communication

   4. Romantic relationships vary in how they handle instrumental communication

• Romantic relationships vary in how they handle communication issues such as conflict, privacy, emotional communication, and instrumental communication.

D. Ending romantic relationships is a process

1. Differentiating
2. Circumscribing
3. Stagnating
4. Avoiding
5. Terminating

- Ending a relationship is a process that involves at least five stages: differentiating, circumscribing, stagnating, avoiding, and terminating.

Section 3} Communicating in Families (p. 354)

III. Communicating in Families

A. What makes a family a family?

1. Genetic ties
2. Legal obligations
3. Role behaviors

- Genetic ties, legal obligations, and role behaviors all influence whether a given relationship is considered to be familial.

B. Types of families

- Families come in multiple forms, including natural families, blended families, single-parent families, and extended families.

C. The family as a system

1. Families are influenced by their environments
2. Family members are interdependent
3. Families are more than the sum of their parts
4. Family systems include smaller subsystems

- Families have several characteristics of systems.

D. Communication issues in families

1. Family roles
2. Family rituals
3. Family stories
4. Family secrets

- Several communication issues, including family roles, rituals, stories, and secrets, are important aspects of how families communicate.

Section 4} Improving Communication in Intimate Relationships (p. 362)

IV. Improving Communication in Intimate Relationships

A. Emphasize excitement and positivity

- Sending confirming messages is an important way of emphasizing positivity.

B. Handle conflict constructively

- Conflict isn't necessarily bad in intimate relationships, but it's important to handle conflict constructively.

C. Have realistic expectations

- Partners in good intimate relationships have realistic expectations about their relationships.

D. Manage dialectical tensions

- Dialectic tensions are common in relationships, and people have several strategies for managing them.

Key Terms

Avoiding stage
Bonding stage
Circumscribing stage
Commitment
Communication privacy management
   (CPM) theory
Confirming messages
Dialectical tensions
Differentiating stage

Divorce
Experimenting stage
Family of origin
Family of procreation
Infidelity
Initiating stage
Integrating stage
Intensifying stage
Interdependence

Investment
Monogamy
Polygamy
Rituals
Stagnating stage
Systems
Terminating stage

Discussion Questions

1. What are some of the ways you invest in your intimate relationships? In what ways do investments in romantic relationships differ from those in familial relationships?
2. When do you notice autonomy-connection, openness-closedness, and novelty-predictability tensions in your relationships? How do you see these tensions manifest themselves in your communication behaviors?
3. The chapter discussed five social expectations for romantic relationships. How much do you share those expectations? Which ones do you not share? Why?
4. What is your theory about why the divorce rate is higher in the United States than in the rest of the world?
5. How do you differentiate people in your family from people who are not in your family? How important are genetic ties, legal bonds, and role behaviors?
6. What roles did you play in your family while you were growing up? What roles would you say that you still play in your family?
7. Why do you think positivity is so important for stable, satisfying relationships?
8. What strategies do you tend to use to manage dialectical tensions in your own relationships?

Practice Quiz

Multiple Choice

1. The idea that our actions influence other people's lives as much as they influence our own is known as:
   a. independence
   b. dependence
   c. interdependence
   d. autonomy
2. Johann and his partner, Cris, go out to dinner and see a movie every Friday night. This routine is beginning to bore Johann but provides stability that Cris values. Which dialectical tension are Johann and Cris experiencing?
   a. openness-closedness
   b. connectedness-autonomy
   c. presence-absence
   d. predictability-novelty
3. The dialectical tension that captures the desire for disclosure and honesty as well as the desire for privacy is known as:
   a. openness-closedness
   b. connectedness-autonomy
   c. presence-absence
   d. predictability-novelty
4. The idea that romantic relationships occur between individuals who choose to be together is best described by which of the following characteristics?
   a. exclusivity
   b. voluntariness
   c. permanence
   d. love

5. Most potential relationships tend to end at which stage of Knapp's Relational Stage Model?
   a. initiating
   b. intensifying
   c. differentiating
   d. experimenting
6. According to Fitzpatrick's research, in which type of couple do spouses take a culturally conventional approach to marriage but are relatively autonomous?
   a. traditionals
   b. separates
   c. independents
   d. interdependents
7. According to Fitzpatrick's research, which type of couple is most likely to avoid conflict?
   a. traditionals
   b. separates
   c. independents
   d. interdependents
8. According to Gottman's research, which type of couple is characterized by engaging in frequent conflict episodes that include personal attacks and criticism?
   a. validating
   b. volatile
   c. conflict-avoiding
   d. hostile
9. Individuals in a satisfying romantic relationship maintain what ratio of positive to negative behaviors, according to Gottman?

a. 1:1
b. 1:2
c. 5:1
d. 2:5

10. Repetitive behaviors that have special meaning for a family are known as:
a. roles
b. rituals
c. responsibilities
d. systems

True/False

11. Obsessive relational intrusion (ORI) most often occurs in relationships in which the two partners are equally invested in each other.

12. Romantic relationships typically are characterized by lower interdependence than friendships.

13. Monogamy means being romantically or sexually involved with only one person at a time.

14. All marriages are based on love when they begin.

15. The circumscribing stage is characterized by a decrease in the quality and the quantity of communication in a romantic relationship.

Fill in the Blank

16. Novelty is in dialectical tension with _____.

17. Cognitive models of what a marriage is and should be are called marital _____.

18. According to Gottman, couples who talk openly about disagreements and stay calm throughout conflict episodes are called _____ couples.

19. According to _____ Theory, in a romantic relationship, partners jointly own information about their problems.

20. A romantic relationship is _____ when the partners are "going through the motions" of a relationship that is no longer satisfying.

Answers

Multiple Choice: 1 (c); 2 (d); 3 (a); 4 (b); 5 (d); 6 (b); 7 (b); 8 (d); 9 (c); 10 (b); **True/False:** 11 (F); 12 (F); 13 (T); 14 (F); 15 (T); **Fill in the Blank:** 16 (predictability); 17 (schemata); 18 (validating); 19 (communication privacy management); 20 (stagnating)

Research Library

Movies

She's the One (Drama; 1999; R)

This story focuses on how two adult brothers manage their relationships with their father, their wives, and a woman they both loved. Multiple family subsystems are portrayed in the film, including sibling relationships, parent-child relationships, and marital relationships. The story illustrates how rituals (such as the brothers' fishing trips with their father) can be important in families, and also how families enforce rules that can become problematic when they are violated.

Stepmom (Drama; 1998; PG-13)

In this film, two children experience the dissolution of their parents' marriage and the introduction of a new woman in their father's life, who becomes a stepmother to the children. Although the stepmother is committed to the children, she is also committed to her work. This fact draws criticism from the children's mother (who was a full-time mother), and tension between the two women mounts. The tension is complicated by the mother's cancer diagnosis. The movie illustrates the dissolution of one marital relationship and the formation of a new one. It also exemplifies how important family roles can be and how roles can be renegotiated.

When Harry Met Sally (Comedy; 1989; R)

This movie follows the process of relational development for Harry and Sally, casual acquaintances who move to New York at the same time and spend the majority of the movie as friends. Over the years, each one marries and divorces another person. Eventually, they realize their mutual attraction and they marry each other. The story portrays Harry and Sally at various stages of relational development, some in which they feel close to each other and some in which they feel separated. Their process of coming together illustrates the point that relationships don't always develop in a sequential, step-by-step manner.

Books

Baxter, L. A., & Montgomery, B. M. (1996). *Relating: Dialogues and dialectics*. New York: Guilford.

Fitzpatrick, M. A. (1988). *Between husbands and wives: Communication in marriage*. Newbury Park, CA: Sage.

Floyd, K., & Morman, M. T. (Eds.). (2006). *Widening the family circle: New research on family communication*. Thousand Oaks, CA: Sage.

Stone, E. (1989). *Black sheep and kissing cousins: How our family stories shape us*. New York: Penguin.

Journal Articles

Amato, P. R. (2000). The consequences of divorce for adults and children. *Journal of Marriage and the Family, 62,* 1269–1287.

Vangelisti, A. L., & Caughlin, J. P. (1997). Revealing family secrets: The influence of topic, function, and relationships. *Journal of Social and Personal Relationships, 14,* 679–705.

Web Sites

www.gottman.com

This is the Web site of the Gottman Institute, where psychologist and marital therapist John Gottman uses his research to help romantic couples and families improve their communication.

www.families.com

This site hosts blogs and forums on multiple issues related to families. It is not an academic site, but it provides one example of how people communicate about family issues and how they publicly portray their family relationships.

10

Interpersonal Conflict

What is interpersonal conflict?

What role does power play in conflict management?

How can we handle conflict to reach our interpersonal goals?

Laila and Annika

Laila and her six-year-old son, Olin, have been living with Laila's mother, Annika, for the past three months. During that time, Annika has come to feel that Laila is too permissive in the way she raises Olin. She lets him stay up late, she doesn't require him to do any chores, and she allows him to wear almost anything he wants to school, whether it's appropriate or not. These observations have bothered Annika ever since Laila and Olin arrived, but she has been hesitant to say anything.

One day, however, she can no longer hold her opinions in. "I just don't understand how you can raise my grandson this way!" she blurts out. "This is *not* the way I raised you!" Laila reacts to these words defensively, telling her mother to mind her own business. Her grandson *is* her business, Annika replies, and she's only looking out for him. "This has nothing to do with him! You just want to tell me how to run my life!" Laila responds. Annika is so upset by the conflict with her daughter that she leaves the house fuming and is gone all afternoon.

Almost every relationship experiences conflict from time to time. Even though Annika and Laila may have a close relationship, they still have different ideas about how Olin should be raised, and these gave rise to the conflict episode described here. Managing conflict can be productive, but it is also very challenging. As you'll see in this chapter, though, it's a normal part of the way we interact with other people. You can learn to manage conflict more constructively if you have the appropriate skills. Several features of this chapter will help you develop those skills.

This chapter focuses on the communication and the negotiation of conflict. Specifically, we'll discuss:

1} What interpersonal conflict is and how people think about it

2} How conflict operates in personal relationships and what commonly leads to conflict

3} How conflict is related to power and how we exercise power in relationships

4} What strategies we can use to manage conflict, and which conflict behaviors we should avoid

Conflict may not be pleasant, but it's largely inevitable. All personal relationships experience conflict now and then. What exactly is conflict, and what are those experiences like? In this section, we will examine the definition of conflict, and we will identify the characteristics all conflicts have in common. Then, we will take a look at some of the many ways people think about conflict in their relationships.

> *Conflict is the beginning of consciousness.*
> —Mary Esther Harding (1888–1971) British-born psychoanalyst

Defining Interpersonal Conflict

Interpersonal conflict An expressed struggle between interdependent parties who perceive incompatible goals, scarce resources, and interference.

What does it mean to experience conflict? Communication scholars William Wilmot and Joyce Hocker define **interpersonal conflict** as "an expressed struggle between at least two interdependent parties who perceive incompatible goals, scarce resources, and interference from the other party in achieving their goals."[1] According to Wilmot and Hocker, an interaction must have all these elements to qualify as interpersonal conflict. Let's take a closer look at the key elements in this definition.

Conflict is an expressed struggle. Having a conflict means more than just disagreeing. You may disagree with the president's foreign policies or your children's taste in music, but you don't really have a conflict until you've made the other person aware of your feelings. Conflict, therefore, is a *behavior*. Sometimes we express our disagreements verbally, but we can also express them through nonverbal behaviors such as a mean look or a harsh tone of voice.

Conflict occurs between interdependent parties. Although all conflicts involve disagreements, a disagreement becomes a conflict only if the parties depend on each other in some way—that is, if the actions of each party affect the well-being of the other. You may have noticed that conflict is particularly common in relationships with high degrees of interdependence, such as those you have with your parents, your children, your professors, your bosses, and your close friends. If two parties are completely independent of each other, then even though they may disagree, that disagreement isn't considered to be an interpersonal conflict.

It's possible to have conflicts within yourself, as well. For example, you might occasionally feel conflicted about how you spend your time. Perhaps part of you thinks you should spend more time with your friends and family, but another part of you thinks you should spend more time on your schoolwork. This is conflict, but it isn't interpersonal conflict. Rather, it's *intrapersonal,* because it is occurring within yourself. Therefore, it operates outside the realm of interpersonal conflict.

Conflict is about goals the parties see as incompatible. Conflict stems from perceiving that our goals are incompatible with another person's goals. Labeling goals as "incompatible" doesn't simply mean that they are *different.* Rather, two goals are incompatible when it's impossible to satisfy both of them. You want to change lanes on the freeway, but the driver next to you won't let you

Conflict is often communicated verbally, but it can also be conveyed with nonverbal behaviors that express anger, concern, or disappointment.

in. You want to spend your tax refund on a new flat-screen television, but your spouse wants to spend it on a family vacation.

Note that the first sentence in the previous paragraph explicitly refers to our *perceptions* that our goals are incompatible. In reality, it may be possible to resolve the conflict in a manner that allows both parties to achieve their goals. (See the discussion of conflict strategies later in the chapter.) The point here is that parties in a conflict *perceive* that their goals are mutually exclusive, even if that perception is not objectively true.

Conflict arises over perceived scarce resources. There's little sense in fighting over something that you have in abundance. People tend to have conflict over resources that they perceive to be limited. Many relational partners have conflict over money, for instance. When people feel they don't have enough money for everything they need and want, they can easily have conflict over how to spend the money they do have.

Time is another resource that people often perceive to be scarce. Therefore, people frequently engage in conflicts over how they should spend their time. Perhaps your romantic partner wants you to split your vacation time between hiking and being with his or her family. If you perceive that you don't have adequate time for both activities, then you can experience conflict over how you will spend your time.

In the chapter-opening story, the resource at the center of Annika and Laila's conflict was *power*—specifically, who had the power to make decisions affecting Olin. Annika and Laila both perceived this resource to be limited because the more power one of them had, the less the other felt she had.

Conflict includes interference. Two parties might have opposing goals with respect to some issue, but they won't have genuine conflict until they act in ways that prevent each other from achieving their goals. You might disapprove of your roommate's smoking habit, for instance, but you won't have true conflict until you behave in ways that interfere with his habit. Complaining about his smoking, for instance, might diminish the enjoyment he derives from it. Hiding his cigarettes or throwing them out would make it more difficult for him to smoke. In either case, you are interfering with your roommate's ability to achieve his goal.

Thinking About Interpersonal Conflict

When you think about your own experiences with interpersonal conflict, what words or images come to mind? It turns out that people often think about conflict using figurative language, such as metaphors.[2] Researchers have identified a number of metaphors people use to describe conflict. Some of the most common ones are listed next. How well does each of these metaphors reflect the way you think about your conflict experiences?

- *Conflict is a war:* Conflict is a series of battles, with winners and losers.
- *Conflict is an explosion:* Conflict is like hearing a time bomb ticking and then watching something blow up.
- *Conflict is a trial:* Each side presents its arguments and evidence, and whoever argues best wins the conflict.
- *Conflict is a struggle:* Conflict is a difficult and ongoing part of life.
- *Conflict is an act of nature:* Conflict simply happens to people; it cannot be prevented or controlled.
- *Conflict is an animal behavior:* Only the strong survive; conflict is a natural part of all creatures' lives.
- *Conflict is a mess:* Conflict is messy, and it contaminates other aspects of life.
- *Conflict is miscommunication:* Conflict is the result of misunderstanding and breakdowns in communication.
- *Conflict is a game:* Conflict is a fun competition wherein participants test their skills against each other.
- *Conflict is a heroic adventure:* Conflict is about taking risks and conquering new territory.
- *Conflict is a balancing act:* Engaging in conflict is like juggling or walking a tightrope; one wrong move can spell disaster.
- *Conflict is a bargaining table:* Conflict brings people together for a collective purpose.
- *Conflict is a tide:* Conflict ebbs and flows; on the basis of experience, we can predict when it is likely to occur.
- *Conflict is a dance:* Partners learn how to "move" with each other through their conflict episodes.
- *Conflict is a garden:* Experiences of conflict represent seeds for the future; if cared for, they will result in a worthwhile harvest.

Those are just some of the ways people describe conflict. As you can see, those metaphors represent a wide variety of ideas. Some images are inherently negative, but others could be considered neutral or even positive. Can you imagine how the way you think about conflict might affect your experience of it? For instance, if you think of conflict as a game, a dance, or a garden, might you experience it differently than if you think of it as a war, a struggle, or a mess?

Researchers have found that the way we interpret or "frame" a conflict can greatly affect the way we experience it and the communication choices we make to manage it.[3]

While arguing with his co-worker Madison over use of the company car, for instance, Russell suddenly realized that Madison was smiling in the midst of their heated discussion. Her smiling made him even angrier, because he felt she wasn't taking him seriously. The angrier he got, however, the more she smiled. Only during a conversation weeks later did they learn that they frame conflict quite differently: Russell frames conflict as a war, but Madison frames it as a game.

Two parties can be engaged in the same conflict but might frame the conflict quite differently. Do you think of conflict as a trial? As an animal behavior? As a dance? As a balancing act? As a war? As a game?

One result of this difference is that Madison probably experienced less stress over the conflict than Russell did. Because Madison sees conflict as a fun competition rather than as a battle between winners and losers, she doesn't necessarily feel threatened or distressed by what Russell said. Instead, she interprets his comments as challenges that test her interpersonal skills. In contrast, because Russell frames conflict as a war, he interprets every statement from Madison as an attempt to defeat him. As a result, he finds interpersonal conflict to be stressful and threatening in a way that Madison does not.

Because the way we frame a conflict can influence our experience of it, many therapists encourage people to "reframe" their conflicts. Reframing means changing the way you think about an interpersonal situation so that you adopt a more useful frame.[4] For instance, a therapist or a counselor could help Russell reframe his conflicts with his co-workers so that he sees them as an adventure, a balancing act, or a dance instead of as a war.

Learn It: What are the necessary elements of interpersonal conflict? What does it mean to reframe a conflict?

Try It: For a period of time (say, three to five days), make note of every conflict you observe, whether it includes you or not. Note what each conflict was about, who was involved in it, and how (if at all) it was resolved. For each conflict, identify the expressed struggle, the interdependent parties, the incompatible goals, the scarce resources, and the interference that made it an interpersonal conflict.

Reflect on It: With whom do you have conflict most frequently? Which metaphors for conflict seem the most accurate to you?

2} Conflict in Personal Relationships {

Conflict occurs at many social levels. Communities, organizations, and certainly nations have conflict with one another. Interpersonal conflict, however, often affects our lives in more direct and more intimate ways than conflicts at those broader levels.

In this section, we will examine several characteristics of interpersonal conflict and identify those topics most likely to spur conflict in our personal relationships. Next, we will address the ways that gender and culture influence conflict. We will conclude by considering why conflict seems to be especially common when we're communicating online.

> *Don't be afraid of opposition. Remember, a kite rises against—not with—the wind.*
>
> —Hamilton Mabie (1846–1916)
> U.S. American essayist

Characteristics of Interpersonal Conflict

Although we have conflicts over different issues with different people, we can make some general observations that apply to all interpersonal conflict. In this section, we'll look at five basic characteristics of conflict in personal relationships:

1. It's natural.
2. It has content, relational, and procedural dimensions.
3. It can be direct or indirect.
4. It can be harmful.
5. It can be beneficial.

Conflict is natural. Most of us would be hard-pressed to think of a single important relationship in which we don't have conflict from time to time. Conflict is a normal, natural part of relating to others. Maybe you enjoy listening to music at night, whereas your housemates prefer quiet. Perhaps you feel you've earned a raise at work, but your boss disagrees. Almost every significant relationship—especially those with close friends, relatives, and romantic partners—is bound to experience conflict once in a while.

Our conflicts with specific people vary, but conflict itself has five basic characteristics. It's natural. It has content, relational, and procedural dimensions. It can be direct or indirect. It can be harmful. And, it can be beneficial.

Having conflict with someone doesn't necessarily mean your relationship is unhealthy or distressed. Indeed, the presence of conflict indicates you have an interdependent relationship. It means you affect each other; if you didn't, you'd have no need for conflict in the first place. So, conflict itself isn't a bad thing. In fact, as we'll see later in this chapter, if we handle conflict productively, it can actually produce some positive outcomes. What matters is how people handle their conflicts. Later in this chapter, we'll learn about useful strategies for managing conflict.

Conflict has content, relational, and procedural dimensions. In personal relationships, conflicts often focus on a specific point of contention, but on a deeper level they also have broader implications for the relationship itself. To illustrate this point, let's suppose Marc finds out his teenage daughter, Amber, has been stealing his credit card out of his wallet to participate in online gambling. When Marc confronts her about it, they argue about the dishonesty of stealing and the risks of gambling. These are the

content dimensions of the conflict, the specific topics from which the conflict arose.

Even when Amber promises to change her behaviors, however, Marc doesn't feel completely satisfied with the outcome of their argument. The reason is that there are also *relational dimensions* to the conflict, which are the implications the conflict has for the relationship. Marc feels that Amber has shown disrespect by stealing from him and that he can no longer trust her. This dimension of the conflict is not so much about the content of their argument (Amber shouldn't steal or gamble) as it is about the nature of their relationship. Although Marc may be successful in changing Amber's behavior, repairing the damage to their mutual respect and trust may require much more time and a much greater effort.

Conflict also has *procedural dimensions,* which are the rules or expectations we follow for how to engage in conflict. Suppose Marc believes conflict should be dealt with straightforwardly through open and honest discussion, whereas Amber prefers to avoid conflict, hoping disagreements will resolve themselves. Marc and Amber may have a difficult time managing their conflict if they adopt such different procedures. In essence, they are attempting to play the same game by completely different rules.

When people adopt dramatically different procedures for managing conflict, they often wind up engaging in **meta-conflict,** which is conflict about conflict itself. "You always run away from disagreements," Marc might say to Amber. She might respond, "Well, you want to have a fight about every little issue—sometimes you just have to let things go!" Notice here that Marc and Amber are no longer arguing about Amber's stealing and gambling but about *how they engage in conflict in the first place.* Their meta-conflict is the result of approaching conflict with dramatically different expectations or rules. An illustration of the content, relational, and procedural dimensions of conflict appears in Figure 10.1.

Meta-conflict
Conflict about conflict.

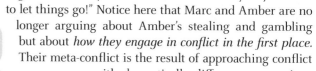

FIGURE 10.1 Interpersonal conflict has three distinct dimensions

Conflict can be direct or indirect. In many instances, people deal with their conflicts directly and openly. When Maria and Sofie disagree on where to spend the holidays, for example, they have a series of arguments in which each one tries to persuade the other to adopt her point of view. When Rosemary grounds her son for using drugs, they argue openly about the seriousness of his behavior and the severity of his punishment.

People can also express conflict indirectly. Instead of dealing with their conflicts openly, for instance, people may behave in ways that are hurtful or vengeful toward others. Jade is upset with her boyfriend, so she deliberately flirts with other men in front of him. Tamir is angry at his wife for inviting her parents to dinner, so he spends the whole evening playing solitaire on his computer. These behaviors express conflict, but in an indirect way that prevents the conflict from being resolved.

Which is better: to deal with conflict openly and directly, or to deal with it indirectly? That's a complex question, and the answer is that neither approach is better in every situation. Handling conflict directly can lead to quicker resolution, but it may also cause the conflict to escalate and become even more serious. Conversely, dealing with conflict indirectly may be easier and more comfortable, but it can also leave the conflict unresolved for a longer period of time. Which approach is better depends on the situation, what your goals are, whom you're having the conflict with, and how important the outcome of the conflict is to you. Later in this chapter, we'll discuss several strategies for engaging in conflict when you experience it.

Conflict can be harmful. Experiencing conflict doesn't usually feel good, so it may not surprise you to learn that conflict can actually be harmful to your well-being when you don't manage it properly. In one study, for instance, psychologists videotaped 150 healthy married couples discussing a contentious topic for six minutes. Two days later, they took a CT scan of each spouse's chest. They found that husbands who had been overly controlling and wives who had been overly hostile dur-

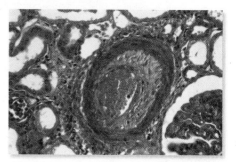

According to one study, husbands who are overly controlling and wives who are overly hostile during marital conflict experienced more hardening of the arteries than spouses who didn't engage in these conflict behaviors.

If you use alcohol, consider how it affects the way you think or feel about conflicts you're involved in.

ing the conflict episode exhibited a greater degree of hardening of the arteries than husbands and wives who didn't display these behaviors.[5]

Other studies have demonstrated that engaging in conflict often causes the body to produce a stress response by increasing the level of stress hormones[6] and natural killer cells[7] in the bloodstream. As one experiment illustrated, the stress created by conflict can even cause wounds to heal more slowly than they otherwise would, especially if the people in conflict behave in a negative, hostile way toward each other.[8] As these and other investigations show, the ways that people handle conflicts, particularly in their romantic relationships, have far-reaching implications for their health.[9]

Conflict is particularly harmful to personal well-being when it escalates into aggression and violence.[10] Researchers estimate that, over the past two decades, as many as half of all marital, cohabiting, and dating relationships have involved some combination of verbal, physical, and/or sexual aggression.[11] One study found that 12% of women and 11% of men had committed at least one violent act—such as slapping, kicking, or punching—against their romantic partner during a conflict episode *within the previous year.*[12]

In these relationships, aggression is often the result of one person's attempts to dominate an argument—and, by extension, to dominate the partner.[13] Although the victims of relational aggression are most likely to be women, men are also victimized, by both male and female romantic partners.[14] Research shows that violence during conflict is approximately as common in gay and lesbian relationships as in heterosexual ones.[15] Certain situations appear to give rise to aggression more often than others, such as when one partner is intoxicated. (See the "Dark Side" box on page 382.)

Managing conflict can be challenging under the best of circumstances, but it appears to be even more problematic when one partner is under the influence of alcohol. Research has shown that excessive alcohol use leads to more aggressive behaviors and elevates the chances of violence within close relationships. It is also a major public health risk. In fact, excessive use of alcohol is the third-leading preventable cause of death in the United States, after tobacco use and malnutrition. Alcohol consumption, then, not only can make conflict more likely but also can intensify existing conflicts. Can it also affect how people respond to conflict?

To answer that question, researchers in one study had participants recall a recent conflict from one of their personal relationships. They then served alcohol to half of the participants until they reached a point of legal intoxication. Finally, they asked all the participants to reflect on the conflict they had described and to indicate the following: (1) how negative their own feelings were, (2) how negative they thought their partners' feelings were, and (3) how much they blamed their partners for the conflict. Compared with their sober counterparts, the intoxicated participants rated their feelings and their perceptions of their partners' feelings as more negative. In addition, intoxicated participants who had low self-esteem were more likely than others to blame their partners for the conflict. These findings don't imply that drinking *causes* conflict. They do, however, suggest that alcohol use makes existing conflicts more negative and perhaps more difficult to deal with.

Ask Yourself:

- Why do you think alcohol affects people's experiences with conflict?

- If you've ever been engaged in a conflict with an intoxicated person, how did you handle it? Which strategies for handling the conflict were more successful or less successful?

From Me to You:

- If you use alcohol, consider how it affects the way you think or feel about conflicts you're involved in. Like the participants in the study just described, you may find that conflicts seem more intense or more negative when you're under the influence of alcohol. If that's the case, then when you use alcohol, you may find it helpful to avoid people with whom you are likely to have conflict.

Source: MacDonald, G., Zanna, M. P., & Holmes, J. G. (2000). An experimental test of the role of alcohol in relationship conflict. *Journal of Experimental Social Psychology, 36,* 182–193; Mokdad, A. H., Marks, J. S., Stroup, D. F., & Gerberding, J. L. (2004). Actual causes of death in the United States, 2000. *Journal of the American Medical Association, 291,* 1238–1245.

One of the most surprising findings concerning aggression is that it doesn't always lead to dissatisfaction in relationships.[16] In fact, people in abusive relationships often see their partners' physical aggression as a sign of love, and they are frequently quick to forgive their partners' aggressive behaviors or even to blame themselves.[17] This statement isn't suggesting that aggression is good for relationships. On the contrary, over time aggression frequently leads to an erosion of trust, happiness, and self-esteem among its victims.[18] Recipients of aggression, however, aren't always quick to end their relationships with the aggressors. Rather, they sometimes report relational satisfaction in spite of the aggression.[19]

Conflict can be beneficial. It's relatively easy to identify the negative features of conflict: It's stressful, it can damage our health, it can lead to aggression and violence. When conflict is managed well, however, it can actually have some benefits. Working through a conflict in a positive, constructive manner can help people learn more about each other and their relationship.[20] It may also lead them to a more satisfactory solution to the problem than either could have come up with alone. These benefits may depend on whether only one party in an interpersonal conflict—or both parties—has the skills to manage it well.

Managing conflict constructively can also help to prevent small problems from escalating into larger ones. Let's say your co-worker complains to you constantly about his girlfriend while you're trying to get your work done. Instead of addressing the problem, however, you just let it annoy you day after day until you finally explode at him, yelling, causing a scene, and eventually being reprimanded by your boss. Simply addressing the situation when it first arose would likely have alleviated much of your frustration and prevented this small annoyance from turning into a conflict with your co-worker.

When people manage their conflicts positively, they often gain greater confidence in their communication skills, and their relationships can benefit as a result.

Over time, the ability to handle conflicts positively may give people more confidence in their communication skills and in the strength of their interpersonal relationships. Research on married couples has shown that spouses who engage in constructive conflict behaviors, such as avoiding criticizing their spouses and being responsive to each other's concerns, are happier with their relationships[21] and more satisfied with the outcomes of their conflicts than spouses who don't.[22] It may be that handling conflict constructively makes couples satisfied, or that satisfied couples handle conflict in a constructive manner. In either case, relationship satisfaction and constructive conflict management are strongly connected.

Successful resolution of conflicts can be very beneficial, but can *every* conflict be resolved? Take a look at the "Fact or Fiction?" box on page 384 to find out.

The Most Common Sources of Conflict

Like relationships themselves, conflicts come in all shapes and sizes. What are some of the most common issues people fight about? In one study, communication scholar Larry Erbert asked spouses to report the most common sources of conflict in their marriages.[23] You might be surprised to learn that men and women identified the same three leading sources of conflict. The most common was *personal criticisms,* or spouses' complaints or criticisms of each other's undesirable behaviors or bad habits (such as smoking or excessive drinking). Almost 20% of the couples Erbert interviewed mentioned personal criticisms as a common source of conflict.

The second-most-frequent answer, at 13%, was *finances,* or conflicts about money. It's not uncommon for spouses to disagree about how their money should be spent, saved, or invested. Further, because money is a scarce resource for many people, conflicts over finances can be particularly difficult. Third on the list was *household chores,* or conflicts over the division of labor. Spouses have to negotiate how to divide up tasks such as cleaning, cooking, gardening, and car maintenance, and many couples find it easy to disagree about who should take on which responsibilities. Conflict can also emerge when spouses fail to meet their responsibilities, because both spouses suffer when the laundry doesn't get washed or the lawn doesn't get mowed.

In his study, Erbert found that personal criticisms, finances, and household chores together accounted for approximately 42% of all the conflict topics mentioned. Other common sources of conflict for married couples were their children, employment, in-laws, sex, how to spend holidays and vacations, how they should spend their time in general, and how they communicate with each other.[24] Studies have also shown that the major topics of conflict are nearly identical for gay, lesbian, and heterosexual couples.[25]

Personal criticisms, finances, and household chores are the three most common topics of marital conflict, according to research by Professor Larry Erbert.

Many studies have focused on conflict in romantic relationships because of the high degree of interdependence that characterizes these relationships. We experience conflict in a host of relationships, however. Many of us routinely have conflict with superiors or subordinates, neighbors, parents or children, co-workers, professors, and people with whom we are interdependent. Like conflicts with romantic partners, many of these conflicts center on issues of power, respect, and the distribution of resources such as money and time.[26] We will look specifically at the central role of power in the next section.

How Sex and Gender Affect Conflict

It's almost cliché to say that sex and gender play an important role in conflict. Indeed, many popular books, movies, television shows, poems, and songs have been based on the idea that women and men have difficulty understanding each other, thus creating situation after situation that is ripe for conflict. Although differences in their behaviors and ways of thinking can certainly be sources of conflict, women and men often have the added challenge of dealing with conflict in systematically different ways.

As we discussed in Chapter 2, "Culture and Gender," traditional gender socialization conflates sex and gender by teaching men to adopt masculine traits and behaviors and women to adopt feminine traits and behaviors. At least in North American societies, traditional gender socialization has encouraged women to "play nice" by avoiding conflict and sacrificing their own goals in order to accommodate the goals of others. Conversely, men are often encouraged to engage in conflict directly, using competitive or even aggressive behaviors to achieve victory. At the same time, however, men are often taught not to hurt women.[27]

These messages about gender can create challenges for both women and men when it comes to managing conflict. Some women may feel that engaging in conflict overtly is contrary to the feminine gender role, so they adopt more indirect tactics to achieve their goals. One such tactic is **passive aggression,** in which women "hide" their aggression in seemingly innocent behaviors.

Passive aggression A pattern of behaving vengefully while denying that one has aggressive feelings.

Consider the case of Chelsea, who becomes irritated when her boyfriend answers his cell phone whenever it rings, even while they're out to dinner. Instead of telling him how she feels, Chelsea expresses her irritation passively by sometimes failing to answer the phone when he calls. She then calls him back later and claims she hadn't heard the phone ring. In this way, Chelsea avoids overt conflict by behaving aggressively (ignoring her boyfriend's calls) but in a seemingly innocent manner (claiming she didn't hear the phone). As we'll see later in the chapter, however, women may also believe that they must fight for whatever resources are available to them, particularly when they feel they are in a less-powerful position than men.

How you handle conflict may depend partly on your sex. Research shows that men are more likely than women to engage in direct conflict behaviors, which sometimes include being physically aggressive. Women are more likely than men to engage in passive-aggressive behaviors, such as running up the balance on a family member's credit card.

In the demand-withdraw pattern, one partner makes demands about communicating and the other withdraws in response. Research indicates this is a common pattern in opposite-sex romantic relationships.

Society's messages to men about conflict may encourage them to engage in conflict overtly—possibly aggressively—even in situations when a subtler, more indirect approach could be just as effective. Because men are taught to engage in conflict directly but also not to hurt women, they may feel particularly conflicted about how to act during conflict episodes with women. Men often resolve this quandary by disengaging, thereby leaving the conflict unresolved. Psychologist John Gottman uses the term "stonewalling" to describe this pattern of withdrawal. As we'll learn later in this chapter, stonewalling can be a particularly problematic behavior for couples.

In opposite-sex romantic relationships, traditional gender messages often encourage partners to adopt a **demand-withdraw pattern** wherein one partner (typically the woman) makes demands ("We need to talk about the problems in our relationship") and the other partner (usually the man) responds by withdrawing ("I don't want to talk about it").[28] Even though this pattern of behavior largely conforms to typical North American gender roles, research indicates that these gender-related behavior differences are especially common in dissatisfied, distressed relationships.[29] One possible reason demand-withdrawal is particularly common in distressed relationships is that if one partner usually withdraws from the conversation, then the conflict is unlikely to be resolved. Over time unresolved conflict can lead to dissatisfaction.

Women and men appear to deal with conflict in much the same ways, whether they are heterosexual or homosexual. Research has found that lesbian and gay couples use strategies similar to those used by heterosexuals to deal with conflict.[30] As family communication researchers John Caughlin and Anita Vangelisti have suggested, however, gay and lesbian couples are also likely to experience potential sources of conflict that seldom afflict straight couples.[31] For one, lesbian and gay partners may have conflict over whom to tell, and how much to tell, about their sexual orientation.[32] If one partner is "out" to family and friends while the other partner conceals his or her sexual orientation, this discrepancy can lead to conflicts related to a couple's social relationships and their long-term plans. Gay and lesbian adults may also encounter discrimination and prejudice from their families, co-workers, or neighbors, which can cause considerable distress and make routine conflicts about other matters seem more substantial than they are.[33]

Demand-withdraw pattern A pattern of behavior wherein one party makes demands and the other party withdraws from the conversation.

How Culture Affects Conflict

Just as gender messages encourage people to handle conflicts in particular ways, so do cultural messages. That is, the values and norms we learn from our culture can shape the way we respond to conflict with members of our own culture. Some scholars believe the most important cultural factor is whether your culture is individualistic or collectivistic.[34] As you'll recall from Chapter 2, people raised in individualistic cultures are taught to value the rights, needs, and goals of the individual. They learn it's acceptable to disagree with others, and they are encouraged to "stand up for yourself" in the face of conflict.[35]

In individualistic cultures, people are encouraged to stand up for themselves and defend their point of view, even if it results in conflict.

By contrast, people raised in collectivistic cultures are taught that the group's priorities take precedence over the individual's and that maintaining group harmony takes precedence over pursuing individual success. Thus, they are more likely to manage conflict through avoiding the disagreement, yielding to the other person's wishes, or asking a neutral party to mediate the conflict, because these strategies can help preserve harmony.[36] They would probably consider the direct, overt behaviors that people in individualistic cultures often use to manage conflict to be insensitive or rude.

A second cultural dimension that influences how people manage conflict is whether the culture is low context or high context.[37] People in low-context cultures (such as the United States) value communication that is explicit, direct, and literal. When they engage in conflict with one another, therefore, they expect all parties to be clear about the source of the disagreement and up front about their suggestions for resolution.

By comparison, people in high-context cultures (such as Japan) value subtlety, deriving much of the meaning in their conversations from social conventions and nonverbal expressions. When they experience conflict with one another, they place a premium on "saving face" and not embarrassing the other party. As a result, they tend to discuss disagreements indirectly, without direct accusations or direct requests for action.[38]

Clearly, then, these cultural dimensions—individualism versus collectivism and high context versus low context—lead people to resolve conflicts in different ways. These differences are often magnified when conflicts arise between people from *different* cultures. Suppose that Gerry, who was raised in an individualistic culture, is having conflict with Kenan, who was raised in a collectivistic culture. Kenan will likely try to manage the conflict in a way that preserves harmony in the relationships and avoids offending or embarrassing Gerry. He may be distraught, therefore, if Gerry approaches the conflict in the direct, adversarial way that is common in his culture. Conversely, Gerry may feel that Kenan's more indirect way of engaging in conflict implies that Kenan doesn't care about the conflict or its outcome.

When two people approach a conflict with dramatically different values and norms, they are likely to misunderstand each other's behaviors, which can easily exacerbate the conflict.[39] By learning about the norms and behaviors of other cultures and interacting with people from different cultural backgrounds, however, we can improve our abilities to handle intercultural conflict in constructive ways.

Conflict Online

Conflict is common in face-to-face settings, but it can seem especially frequent when people communicate online. One reason is that computer-mediated communication has a **disinhibition effect,** meaning that it removes constraints and thus invites people to say or do things that they wouldn't in person.[40] Let's suppose Saika gets an e-mail from her supervisor saying he is rejecting her vacation request for next month. Saika feels angry, particularly because she worked overtime last month while her supervisor was on vacation. Because Saika reads her supervisor's words online instead of hearing them in person, she feels less inhibited about expressing her anger. As a result of her disinhibition, she sends her supervisor an e-mail reply filled with angry, inflammatory statements that she would never make to him in person. This causes her supervisor great distress and thus intensifies their conflict.

Disinhibition effect The tendency to say or do things in one environment (such as online) that one would not say or do in most other environments.

Researchers suggest several strategies for handling potential conflicts in online contexts. First, *don't respond right away.* Instead, give yourself several hours to calm down and collect your thoughts. Of course, this advice often applies to conflicts that occur in person as well. Because e-mail puts a person's words in print right in front

Online conflict frequently leads to flaming, which is the exchange of hostile and insulting messages.

of us, however, we may feel compelled to reply immediately when we really should give ourselves time to cool down first.

Second, *clarify anything that might be misunderstood,* instead of assuming you know what the other person meant by his or her statements. Third, *put yourself in the other person's shoes,* and think about how he or she would react to your response. Finally, *use emoticons to express your tone,* if it's appropriate, so that your reader knows when you're upset, when you're surprised, and when you're kidding.[41]

Learn It: In what ways can conflict be harmful? In what ways can it be beneficial? What are the most common topics of conflict in marital relationships? How do messages about gender affect us when we engage in conflict? Which cultural dimensions influence conflict behavior? What is the disinhibition effect?

Try It: The next time you receive an e-mail that's negative or aggressive, write a response right away, but then save it instead of sending it. Write a second response 24 hours later, and then compare it with the first response. Do you notice differences in your tone? Is your second response less aggressive and inflammatory? Which response would you choose to send? If it's the second one, then remember this lesson when you receive similar e-mails in the future.

Reflect on It: Why might you choose to engage in conflict indirectly, rather than directly? When are you most likely to have conflict online?

3} Power and Conflict

We have defined conflict as an expressed struggle between interdependent parties who perceive their goals as incompatible. Just because two parties are interdependent, however, doesn't mean they are equally powerful. Indeed, conflict often occurs in relationships in which one person—say, a parent or a supervisor—has more power than the other—say, a child or an employee. Conflict often involves a struggle for power between two parties, with each party trying to exercise as much influence or control over the situation as possible. Power and conflict are thus inextricably linked.

> *Power is a positive force if it is used for positive purposes.*
>
> —Elizabeth Dole (1936–)
> United States Senator

In this section, we will define power and then examine some of its characteristics, particularly as they relate to the experience of conflict. We will also consider various forms of power, and we'll discuss how gender and culture influence the expression of power in personal relationships.

Some Characteristics of Power

Power is the ability to manipulate, influence, or control other people or events.[42] Certain people have more power than others. Nevertheless, we all possess some power, and we exercise it whenever we find ourselves in conflict with others. In this section, we'll take a quick look at five characteristics of power that will help us understand its relationship to conflict.

Power The ability to manipulate, influence, or control other people or events.

Power is context-specific. Most forms of power are relevant only in specific situations. Your boss has power over you at work, for instance, but he doesn't have the right to tell you what to do when you're at home. His influence over you is confined to the work environment. Similarly, your doctor has the power to give you medical advice and prescribe medical treatments, but she doesn't have the right to advise you on your finances, your education, or your religious beliefs. These areas are outside her sphere of influence. As these examples illustrate, power is almost always confined to certain realms or contexts.

Power is always present. Even though power is context-specific, some form of power is relevant to every interpersonal interaction. When two people have roughly equal power in their relationship, such as friends, they have a **symmetrical relationship.** Conversely, when one person has more power than the other, such as a teacher and a student, the parties have a **complementary relationship.** The way people interact with each other depends, in part, on whether their relationship is symmetrical or complementary. For instance, you might say or do things with your friends that you wouldn't say or do with your teachers. Keep in mind, though that the power balance of a relationship can change over time. Parents and children usually have complementary relationships when the children are young, for example, but as the children become adults, these relationships often become more symmetrical.

Symmetrical relationship A relationship between parties of equal power.

Complementary relationship A relationship between parties of unequal power.

Power influences communication. The symmetrical or complementary nature of relationships often influences the way people communicate. Many years ago, communication researchers Philip Ericson and L. Edna Rogers proposed that relational power is reflected in three specific types of verbal messages people use.[43] A **one-up message** expresses dominance and an attempt to control the relationship. One-up messages often take the form of commands, such as "Do the dishes," "E-mail me your report," or "Stop making so much noise." A **one-down message** communicates submission or acceptance of another person's decision-making ability. Examples include questions such as "Where would you like to go for dinner?" and statements of assent, such as "Whatever you'd like is fine with me." Finally, a **one-across message,** which is neither dominant nor submissive, conveys a desire to neutralize relational control. One-across messages often take the form of statements of fact, such as "Dad needs a new lawnmower" and "There are many brands to choose from."

One-up message A verbal message through which the speaker attempts to exert dominance or gain control over the listener.

One-down message A verbal message that reflects acceptance of, or submission to, another person's power.

One-across message A verbal message that seeks to neutralize relational control and power.

Asking, "what would you like to have for dinner?" is an example of communicating a one-down message. Responding, "let's have spaghetti and meatballs" is an example of expressing a one-up message. The reply, "well, there are so many dishes to choose from" is an example of a one-across message.

People in symmetrical relationships often communicate using the same types of messages.[44] They might both use one-up messages ("Put away the groceries." "I'll put them away when I feel like it"). They might both use one-down messages ("Do you have any suggestions for what to wear tonight?" "I'm sure whatever you choose will look great"). Finally, they might both use one-across messages ("There are so many good movies showing in town right now." "And several good plays as well"). In each case, their communication reflects the fact that neither party exercises power over the other.

In contrast, people in complementary relationships frequently communicate using different types of statements. One person might use a one-up message ("Try searching for airfares online"), and the other might respond with a one-down message ("That's a great idea; thanks for the suggestion"). Alternatively, one partner might express a one-down message ("What should we get Grandma for her birthday?"), and the other might reply with a one-up message ("Let's get her some new DVDs"). In complementary relationships, one-up or one-down messages can also precede one-across messages. In response to a one-up message, for instance ("I think we should have pasta for dinner"), a partner might respond with a one-across message ("That's one option"). This move can signal that the partner doesn't wish to be dominated or controlled.

Power can be positive or negative. There's nothing inherently good or bad about power. Rather, as with conflict, the way people *handle* power makes it positive or negative. Even complementary relationships in which there is a large difference in power can be highly satisfying if they meet two conditions. First, the two parties must agree on the power arrangement. If the less-powerful person begins to question or challenge the other person's power (such as adolescents asserting their independence from their parents), the relationship can become dissatisfying. Second, the powerful person should exercise his or her power ethically and responsibly, in ways that benefit both parties. When people abuse their power by serving only their own needs or desires or improving their situation at the other person's expense, their actions can easily lead to resentment and dissatisfaction within the relationship.

Power and conflict influence each other. At their core, many conflicts are struggles for power. Annika and Laila's conflict, described at the beginning of this chapter, was about how Olin should be raised. On another level, however, it was also a disagreement about *who has the power to decide* how Olin is raised. Siblings who fight over control of the television remote, neighbors who fight over their property boundaries, and drivers fighting for the few remaining spaces in a parking lot are all clashing over power: Who has the right to control resources?

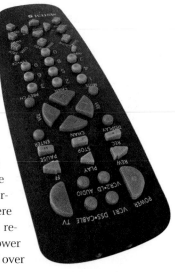

Just as power influences conflict, conflict can also influence the balance and exercise of power. Let's say that after Shawn turns 15, he has conflict with his parents over household rules. As a result, his parents give him a later curfew and greater flexibility in deciding where he goes and with whom. This development—which was the direct result of Shawn's conflict with his parents—changed the balance of power in the parent-child relationship, with Shawn acquiring more control over his own life.

So far, we've talked about power as if it were a singular thing. In fact, power comes in many forms, as we'll see next.

Forms of Power

People exercise influence or control over others in many ways. In a now-classic study, social psychologists John French and Bertram Raven classified power into five specific forms: reward, coercive, referent, legitimate, and expert power.[45] As we take a closer look at these forms, remember that they aren't mutually exclusive; rather, one person may exercise multiple forms of power in a given situation.

Reward power. As its name implies, **reward power** operates when one party has the ability to reward the other in some way. Your supervisor has power over you, for instance, because she pays you and can promote you for doing what she says. In this case, your

Reward power
Power that derives from the ability to reward.

Many of us tend to comply with requests made by people we like, admire, or find attractive. This is what French and Raven referred to as *referent power*.

pay and the possibility for advancement are the rewards. If your supervisor loses the ability to pay or promote you (if the company goes bankrupt or she leaves her job, for instance), then she loses her power over you.

Coercive power. The opposite of reward power is **coercive power,** or power that derives from the ability to punish. When you go to court, for example, the judge has power over you because he can punish you with fines or imprisonment for not doing as he says. Significantly, parents and employers often have both reward power and coercive power over their children or their employees; they can provide rewards for good behavior and issue punishments for bad behavior.

Coercive power Power based on the ability to punish.

Referent power. French and Raven used the term **referent power** to refer to the power of attraction: We tend to comply with requests made by people we like, admire, or find attractive in some way. For instance, you might find that you work harder for professors you like than for professors you dislike. Similarly, many of us are persuaded to buy products if they are endorsed by celebrities we admire. These examples involve complementary relationships. Referent power can also operate in symmetrical relationships, however. For instance, we might comply with requests from our friends because we like them and want to please them.

Referent power Power that derives from one's attraction to or admiration for another.

Legitimate power Power based on one's legitimate status or position.

Legitimate power. People exercise **legitimate power** when their status or position gives them the right to make requests with which others must comply. If a police officer signals you to pull your car over, you comply because you perceive that the officer has a legitimate right to make you do so. When you travel by air, you follow the instructions of the airport screeners, flight attendants, and pilots because you perceive that their positions give them certain authorities over you in that context.

Expert power Power that derives from one's expertise, talent, training, specialized knowledge, or experience.

Expert power. The last form on French and Raven's list is **expert power,** which operates when we comply with the directions of people we perceive to be experts in a particular area. We follow the advice of a doctor, a professor, a stockbroker, a fashion expert, or an electrician because we recognize that their training and experience give them expertise we ourselves don't have. Like other forms of power, expert power is context-specific. You consult your stockbroker for financial advice, for example, but you wouldn't ask him how to fix your sink, because that goes beyond his expertise.

As we explained earlier, different forms of power often operate together. We've seen that parents have both reward and coercive power over their children, for instance, but they often have other forms as well. They have referent power if their children obey them out of respect or admiration. They have legitimate power when they exercise control on the basis of their position. ("Because I'm your mother, that's why!") Finally, they have expert power when they teach their children how to drive or balance a checkbook. The "At a Glance" box on page 392 provides a quick reference to help you

Expert power is the power of one's training or expertise. We follow the advice of experts because we trust that the advice is sound.

remember French and Raven's five forms of power.

Sex, Gender, and Power

Few factors influence the experience of power more than sex and gender. Across cultures and time periods, societies have defined male-female relationships largely in terms of men's power over women. The virtually universal practice of *patriarchy,* which structures social units such as families and communities so that men control the resources, has allowed men throughout history to exercise political, religious, and economic power over women.[46] As a result, women historically have experienced more limited access to education, lower-quality health care, fewer economic opportunities, and more limited political involvement than men have.[47]

These inequities persist in many parts of the world, including the United States. According to the United Nations, only 12% of elected political representatives in the United States are women. Worldwide, the number is only slightly higher: 14%.[48] Women and men have equal employment rates in fewer than half the world's countries, and they have equal literacy rates in only a third of the countries. Finally, in a large majority of countries, women earn less than 70% of what men in comparable jobs earn.[49]

Traditional gender roles reinforce the inequitable division of power between women and men. As we saw in Chapter 2, stereotypical femininity emphasizes characteristics such as passiveness, submissiveness, and accommodation, whereas stereotypical masculinity prizes strength, control, and dominance. To the extent that men and women identify strongly with masculine and feminine gender roles, the inequitable distribution of power may be reflected in their interpersonal behavior. For instance, men may take for granted that what they say at work or in the home will matter to those around them. They may also express dominance through *verbal aggression,* using words to attack or demean those around them.[50]

By contrast, if women have or perceive they have less power than men, they may be less likely to assume that other people will take their words or ideas seriously.[51] They may also be inclined to exercise power in more covert ways, such as through passive-aggressive behavior.

As women gain positions of power and influence, gender inequities in power may be eroded. As of 2008, several nations had a female head of state, including Ireland, New Zealand, South Korea, Mozambique, Finland, Latvia, and the Philippines. (See Table 10.1.) In the U.S. government, women have assumed unprecedented positions of power in the past three decades, including Attorney General (Janet Reno), Secretary of State (Madeleine Albright, Condoleeza Rice), and Speaker of the House of Representatives (Nancy Pelosi).

At a Glance: Forms of Power

According to French and Raven, these are the five principal types of power that people exercise in their relationships with others:

Reward	Power based on the ability to reward for compliance
Coercive	Power based on the ability to punish for noncompliance
Referent	Power based on liking, admiring, and being attracted to the powerful party
Legitimate	Power based on rightfully granted status or position
Expert	Power based on special knowledge, training, experience, and/or expertise

Patriarchial social units are structured so that men control the most important resources. Patriarchy is common around the world.

Table 10.1: Countries with Female Heads of State

Country	Head of State	Title
Chile	Michelle Bachelet	President
New Zealand	Helen Clark	Prime Minister
Mozambique	Luisa Diogo	Prime Minister
Finland	Tarja Halonen	President
South Korea	Myeong Sook Han	Prime Minister
Liberia	Ellen Johnson-Sirleaf	President
The Philippines	Gloria Macapagal-Arroyo	President
Ireland	Mary McAleesse	President
Germany	Angela Merkel	Chancellor
Latvia	Vaira Vike-Freiberga	President

Note: This table includes elected or appointed heads of state but excludes monarchs. Information current as of March 2008.

People who have studied the association between conflict and health have concluded that power affects women and men differently. In one study, a team of researchers led by human ecology professor Timothy Loving took a novel approach to measuring power relations in married couples.[52] The researchers selected 72 couples and instructed each spouse to complete measures indicating how much he or she loved the other. They then checked how closely each person's response matched that of his or her spouse. To determine the spouses' relative power, the researchers applied the *principle of least interest*. This principle states that the partner who is less invested in the relationship is the more powerful partner, because he or she has less to lose by leaving the relationship.[53]

In this study, the researchers used love as the measure of investment. If the wife and husband reported relatively equal love scores, the researchers considered them to have equal power. When the husband's love score was significantly higher than his wife's, the researchers concluded that the wife had more power. Conversely, when the wife's love score was significantly higher than her husband's, then the husband was more powerful.

The researchers then instructed each couple to engage in a conflict conversation while they monitored the stress hormone levels of all the participants. The results indicated that being in a power-balanced marriage benefited women and men by protecting them against an increase in the stress hormone ACTH. The same pattern was observed in marriages in which the wife was deemed more powerful. In marriages in which the husband was deemed more powerful, however, women's ACTH levels rose significantly, indicating increased stress. Among this same group, however, men's ACTH levels *dropped* significantly, indicating reduced stress.

In sum, then, men experienced no increase in stress as a result of marital conflict under any circumstances. Moreover, when men argued with less-powerful wives, their stress actually decreased. One possible explanation for these results is that because men historically have enjoyed power in social affairs and relationships, they may subconsciously not perceive marital conflict to be threatening and stressful, even when they have less power in the relationship.

Like men, women didn't experience increased stress as a result of conflict when they had equal power with or more power than their spouse. Unlike men, however, they did react stressfully to conflict when they had less

According to one study, spouses' stress hormones were not elevated during conflict if the spouses had a power-balanced marriage or one in which the wife was deemed more powerful. In marriages in which the husband was deemed more powerful, conflict elevated women's stress hormones but reduced men's.

power. Because of their less-powerful position, the wives in the study may have felt more threatened and insecure as a result of conflict, causing their stress to elevate. ACTH is only one hormone that reacts to stress, however, so the results might have been different had the researchers utilized other indicators of stress.

Culture and Power

Cultural practices and beliefs also affect the ways in which people exercise power in personal relationships. As you learned in Chapter 2, one dimension along which cultures differ is their *power distance.* High-power-distance cultures are characterized by an uneven distribution of power. In these cultures, certain social groups (royalty, the aristocracy or "upper class," the ruling political party) have considerably more power than the average citizen. Moreover, people in high-power-distance cultures are socialized to view the unequal distribution of power as normal or even desirable. Upper-class citizens are treated with respect and privilege, whereas citizens of lesser status are taught to behave humbly.[54] In particular, lower-status citizens are not expected to question or challenge the decisions, opinions, or directions of the ruling class. When all social groups accept this arrangement, then the society can avoid many potential conflicts.[55] One example of this type of power division is India's caste system, wherein people are born into social groups, or castes, that largely dictate with whom they can associate.

People in low-power-distance cultures are more likely to question authority than people in high-power-distance cultures.

By contrast, low-power-distance cultures exhibit a more equal distribution of power among social groups. Although some social groups may have somewhat more power than others, the prevailing belief among citizens is that all people are inherently equal and that power differences between groups should be small. One result of this cultural belief is that people from low-power-distance cultures are more likely than their counterparts in high-power-distance cultures to question authority and to engage in conflict with teachers, supervisors, politicians, and other people who exercise power over them.

Another difference is that people in low-power-distance cultures often believe they have greater control over the course of their lives. Whereas people in high-power-distance cultures are often raised to believe their life course is determined by their social class, many people in low-power-distance cultures are socialized to believe they can achieve whatever they set their minds to. In the United States, for instance, there are many examples of people, such as Bill Clinton and Oprah Winfrey, who have risen from humble beginnings into positions of great power and influence. As politician Adlai Stevenson, former U.S. ambassador to the United Nations, once noted, "In America, anyone can become president." To the extent they believe their social class doesn't dictate their lives, people in low-power-distance cultures may be more likely than their counterparts in high-power-distance cultures to engage in conflict with anyone they perceive to be oppressive.

Learn It: What is the difference between a symmetrical relationship and a complementary one? What are French and Raven's five forms of power? What is patriarchy? How do cultural messages influence the exercise of power?

Try It: Conflicts that seem to be about one thing, such as what to watch on TV, are often really about power, as in who gets to decide what we watch on TV. The next time you're in conflict with someone, analyze the conflict to identify the power struggle, if any, it involves. As you make decisions about how to communicate during the conflict, try to recognize the underlying power struggle and not just the obvious topic of the disagreement. Also, notice how the power struggle may be different in a symmetrical relationship as opposed to a complementary one.

Reflect on It: When do you view the exercise of power as positive? Who has referent power over you?

4} Managing Interpersonal Conflict

There are almost as many ways to handle conflict as there are things to disagree about. When we experience conflicts in our personal relationships, we need to make choices about how to manage and resolve them. Sometimes we choose our behaviors wisely and sometimes we choose poorly, but our choices almost always have an effect on our relationships. We'll begin this section by looking at some particularly problematic conflict behaviors. We'll then examine five general strategies we can use to manage conflict successfully.

> *You can't shake hands with a clenched fist.*
> —Indira Gandhi (1917–1984)
> Prime Minister of India

Problematic Behaviors During Conflict

Earlier in this chapter, we learned that it isn't the presence of conflict itself that is necessarily damaging to our relationships; rather, it's the way we handle conflict that matters. Whereas some relational partners manage conflict in a mature, constructive way, others deal with it so poorly that it jeopardizes the relationship itself. Which behaviors are the problematic ones?

To find out, psychologist John Gottman has spent years studying how spouses and partners interact with each other during conflict episodes. Conventional wisdom might suggest that couples who fight frequently are most likely to split up. In fact, Gottman's research has found otherwise. According to Gottman, *how* couples argue, and not how frequently they argue, predicts their chances for staying together.[56] Gottman's work has identified four specific behaviors that are warning signs for separation or divorce: criticism, contempt, defensiveness, and stonewalling. Gottman refers to these behaviors as the "Four Horsemen of the Apocalypse" to indicate that they signal distress.[57] Let's take a closer look at each of these problematic behaviors.

Criticism
The expression of complaints about another party.

Criticism. According to Gottman, the first warning sign occurs when partners engage in **criticism** or complaints about each other. Criticism isn't always bad, but it becomes counterproductive when it focuses on people's personality or character rather than on their behavior. Statements such as "You always have to be right" or "You never listen" focus on attacking the person and assigning blame.

Criticisms also tend to be global statements about a person's value or virtue instead of specific critiques about the topic of the conflict. Instead of saying "You should be more attentive when I describe my feelings to you," for instance, a distressed partner might say "You never think of anyone but yourself." Because criticisms so often come across as personal attacks instead of as accurate descriptions of the sources of conflict, they tend to inflame conflict situations. At that point, criticism becomes a sign of a distressed relationship.

Criticism can also be counterproductive when partners engage in *gunnysacking*—that is, privately "saving up" their past grievances and then bringing them up all at once.[58] When Enrique criticized his wife, Sonja, for spending too much money on their children's school clothes, for example, Sonja responded by criticizing Enrique for past offenses she had not previously discussed with him. "You think *I'm* wasteful?" she replied. "What about all the money you wasted on that stupid fishing trip last year? And while we're on the subject, don't think I didn't notice that money you transferred out of our savings account last month without asking me. What'd you waste that on? Another piece of overpriced art for your office? You expect me to be careful with money while you've been wasting it ever since we got married!"

Each of Sonja's grievances may have merit. Nevertheless, her response to Enrique's criticism is unproductive. By bringing up all her criticisms at once, Sonja is deflecting attention from their current conflict, which is likely to leave that conflict unresolved.

Contempt
The expression of insults and attacks on another's self-worth.

Contempt. A second warning sign occurs when partners show **contempt** for each other by insulting each other and attacking each other's self-worth. This behavior can include calling each other names ("you stupid idiot"), using sarcasm or mockery to make fun of the other person, and using nonverbal behaviors that suggest a low opinion of the other person, such as rolling your eyes or sneering. It can also include ridiculing the person in front of others and encouraging others to do the same.

Regardless of its form, however, contempt functions to put down and degrade the other person. Research indicates that responding to conflict with this type of hostile behavior often increases physical stress in the partners, which can impair their health.[59]

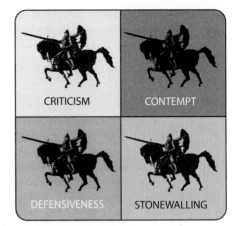

Psychologist John Gottman has called criticism, contempt, defensiveness, and stonewalling the *Four Horsemen of the Apocalypse* because these behaviors signal distress for couples in conflict.

Gunnysacking, which involves remembering past grievances and then bringing them up all at once, is unproductive. When you criticize a relational partner, focus your criticism only on the issue at hand.

Defensiveness. A third danger sign is that partners become defensive during their conflict. **Defensiveness** means seeing yourself as a victim and denying responsibility for your behaviors. Instead of listening to their partners' concerns and acknowledging that they need to change certain behaviors, defensive people whine ("It's not fair"), make excuses ("It's not my fault"), and respond to complaints with complaints ("Maybe I spend too much money, but you never make time for the kids and me"). People are particularly prone to feel defensive about criticisms when they recognize that the criticisms have merit but they don't want to accept the responsibility for changing their behaviors.

Stonewalling. The last of Gottman's "Four Horsemen" is **stonewalling**, or withdrawing from the conversation. As we discussed earlier, people who engage in stonewalling will often act as though they are "shutting down"; that is, they stop looking at their partners, they stop speaking, and they stop responding to what their partners are saying. In some cases, they even physically leave the room to end the conversation. The reason for this departure isn't to calm down, which might be an effective strategy. Rather, it is to shut off the conversation entirely.

Gottman's research has suggested that people stonewall when they feel emotionally and psychologically "flooded," or incapable of engaging in the conversation any longer. Unfortunately, when one partner stonewalls, it becomes almost impossible for the couple to resolve their disagreements. Research has also shown that when husbands stonewall during a conflict, their wives often experience significant increases in the stress hormones cortisol and norepinephrine.[60]

Why does Gottman assert that these four conflict behaviors can predict the collapse of a relationship? The "How Do We Know?" box on page 398 addresses this question.

Defensiveness The tendency to deny the validity of criticisms directed at the self.

Stonewalling The behavior of withdrawing from a conversation or an interaction.

Strategies for Managing Conflict Successfully

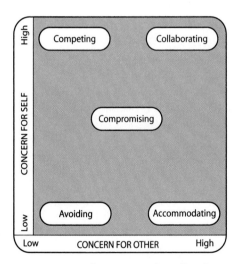

FIGURE 10.2 When concern for self and concern for other are juxtaposed, they give rise to five strategies for engaging in conflict: competing, avoiding, accommodating, collaborating, and compromising.

We know from Gottman's work that criticizing, showing contempt, becoming defensive, and engaging in stonewalling aren't productive ways of handling conflict. Because we can't escape conflict, what alternatives do we have for managing it properly? According to researchers Robert Blake and Jane Mouton, our options for dealing with conflict are based on two underlying dimensions: our concern for our own needs and desires, and our concern for the other party's needs and desires.[61] When plotted on a graph (see Figure 10.2), these dimensions give rise to five major strategies for engaging in conflict: competing, avoiding, accommodating, compromising, and collaborating.

In this section, we take a quick look at each strategy in this section. As we do so, recall from earlier in the chapter that conflict itself is neither inherently positive nor inherently negative. Rather, it is neutral. What determines whether it good or bad is the strategy we adopt for handling it. Some of the strategies we discuss in this section might seem more constructive to you than others, but none of them is the right choice in every situation. Instead, each strategy can be the best option in particular circumstances.

In his research on couples in conflict, John Gottman has identified four particular behaviors—criticism, contempt, defensiveness, and stonewalling—that indicate that a couple is at increased risk of separating or divorcing. How did he arrive at this conclusion?

In a typical study, Gottman invites spouses to his laboratory and seats them across from each other in specially designed chairs that are equipped to record their movements and measure basic physiological processes such as heart rate and blood pressure. In addition, he uses video cameras to record each partner's words and facial expressions. In this setting, Gottman asks the couple to discuss a point of contention in their relationship, such as money, parenting styles, and the division of household labor. Before long, the discussion itself becomes a conflict episode, which enables Gottman to observe how each partner behaves in the conflict.

After the discussion has been concluded, Gottman examines the words, facial expressions, and tone of voice of each participant to look for signs of criticism, contempt, defensiveness, and stonewalling. He also contacts the couple at regular intervals to see whether the partners are still together. Using this method, Gottman has determined that couples who use criticism, contempt, defensiveness, and/or stonewalling when they fight are more likely to separate or divorce than are couples who stay away from these behaviors.

Ask Yourself:

- How easily would you recognize criticism, contempt, defensiveness, or stonewalling if someone used these behaviors with you? if you used these behaviors with someone else?

- Do you think the most problematic conflict behaviors would be different for nonromantic relationships than for romantic ones? if so, which behaviors would you predict are most problematic for nonromantic relationships?

From Me to You:

- Even if you know which behaviors to avoid during conflict, it's difficult to avoid them when you are physiologically aroused, as we often are during conflict episodes. The next time you're in conflict with someone, try your best to remain calm and stay composed. If you can avoid excessive physiological arousal, you'll be better able to think clearly and respond to the conflict in constructive ways.

Source: Gottman, J. M. (1994). *What predicts divorce? The relationship between marital processes and marital outcomes.* Hillsdale, NJ: Lawrence Erlbaum Associates.

Competing. The **competing** style represents a high concern for your own needs and desires and a low concern for those of the other party. Your goal is to win the conflict while the other person loses. Engaging conflict in this style is much like playing football. There are no "tie games"—one team's win is the other team's loss. This style might be appropriate in situations when there is a concrete outcome that cannot be shared, such as when two people are competing for the same job. Ongoing competition can also enhance relationships, as long as relational partners view competition as a positive aspect of their relationships rather than a negative one.[62] Competition becomes problematic when it starts leading to feelings of resentment or desires to get even with the other person.[63]

Competing
A strategy for managing conflict wherein your goal is to win while the other party loses.

Avoiding. A very different approach to conflict is the **avoiding** style, which involves a low concern for both the self and the other. Adopting this style means ignoring the conflict and hoping it will go away on its own. Whereas stonewalling means withdrawing from the conversation in the middle of a conflict episode, avoiding means failing to engage the conflict in the first place. Often, however, conflicts that are avoided simply become worse. Some people choose avoidance because they are uncomfortable engaging in conflict; others choose it because they don't care enough about the outcome of the conflict to bother. Avoiding conflict isn't always the wrong choice; many people in satisfying relationships choose to ignore or avoid certain points of contention in order to maintain harmony.[64] When avoidance becomes the primary way of managing conflict, however, it often leaves important conflicts unresolved, leading to dissatisfying relationships.[65]

Avoiding A strategy for managing conflict that involves ignoring or failing to deal with the conflict.

Avoiding conflict isn't always a poor strategy, but it can lead to dissatisfying relationships when it becomes the primary means of managing conflict.

Accommodating. **Accommodating** is the opposite of competing. This style involves demonstrating a high concern for the other party but a low concern for the self. In the accommodating style, your goal is to sacrifice so that the other party wins and you lose. Sometimes people accommodate to "keep the peace" in their relationships. This strategy may work well in the short term. In the long term, continually accommodating the other party can make you feel resentful.

Accommodating A strategy for managing conflict that involves giving in to the other party's needs and desires while subordinating one's own.

Culture plays an important role in the use of accommodation. In collectivistic societies (such as many Asian societies), accommodating in response to conflict is often expected and is viewed as respectful or noble.[66] By contrast, people in individualistic societies (such as the United States) may be seen as weak or "spineless" if they consistently accommodate others.

Compromising A strategy for managing conflict in which both parties give up something they want so that both can receive something they want.

Compromising. **Compromising** involves a moderate concern for everyone's needs and desires. In this strategy, both parties give up something in order to gain something. Neither party gets exactly what he or she wants, but all parties leave the conflict having gained something valuable.

Let's say you're negotiating a job offer and you want a higher salary than the employer wants to pay. Through your negotiation, you agree to accept a lower salary than you originally wanted, and the employer agrees to give you an extra week of vacation in return. Neither of you got exactly what you wanted, but you each got something you valued in return for giving up something else. Compromising takes time and patience, but it often leads to better outcomes than competing, avoiding, or accommodating.

Collaborating A strategy for managing conflict that involves working toward a solution that meets both parties' needs.

Collaborating. The **collaborating** style represents a high concern for both your partner's needs and your own. The goal is to arrive at a *win-win* situation that maximizes both parties' gains. After they had their first child,

Amateur golfers usually don't require opponents to putt again when the ball is close to the hole. By accommodating their opponents in this way, many golfers demonstrate more concern for the relationship than for winning.

At a Glance: Five Approaches to Conflict

Carla and Ben are siblings who have each saved $1,500 to put toward a car. Their parents can add only enough money to buy one car, not two, so Carla is in conflict with Ben over who should get that money. Here are examples of five different approaches she might take when engaging this conflict:

Competing	Carla tries to get her parents to give all their saved-up money to her and none of it to Ben.
Avoiding	Carla doesn't bring up the conflict, hoping her parents will figure out a way to resolve it on their own.
Accommodating	Carla encourages her parents to give their saved-up money to Ben instead of to her.
Compromising	Carla suggests that she and Ben pool their money with their parents' money and buy one car that they will share.
Collaborating	Carla works with Ben and their parents to try to figure out how she and Ben can each get a car.

for instance, Mick and Laura felt the strain of paying for day care while Mick worked and Laura went to school. Their collaborative solution was for Mick to reduce his work hours and for Laura to enroll in online courses so at least one of them would be home every day. The money they saved in day care more than made up for the income they lost because of Mick's reduced hours. Moreover, both Laura and Mick felt better because they were able to care for their child themselves.

Collaborating probably sounds like the ideal way to handle conflict—and in many situations, it is. It can also require a great deal of energy, patience, and imagination. Although it might seem like the best approach, it can also be the most difficult.

How might each of these strategies operate in real life? "At a Glance" above highlights one conflict—two siblings fighting over who is going to get a new car—and illustrates how each of these approaches can be employed when engaging in the conflict.

Learn It: How are criticism and contempt different? When might avoidance be a better conflict management strategy than accommodating?

Try It: Many people manage conflicts using a preferred set of tactics and skills. To find out what your preferred strategy is, fill out the short questionnaire in the "Getting to Know You" box on the next page.

Reflect on It: How do you feel when someone stonewalls during a conflict with you? When do you find collaborating a challenge?

Getting to Know You
What's My Conflict Style?

Although every conflict episode is unique, many of us have a preferred style for dealing with all conflicts. What's your style? To find out, take a look at the statements below, and put a check mark next to the ones you agree with. The style with the most check marks is the style you prefer when handling conflict. If your score results in a tie between two or more styles, then you have more than one preference.

Competing

1. _____ In a conflict, I usually focus on my side of the issue.
2. _____ I use whatever means I have to win.
3. _____ I use my resources to make sure I get what I want.
4. _____ My focus is on winning the argument.

Avoiding

1. _____ I try to stay away from topics of disagreement.
2. _____ When I disagree with others, I usually keep it to myself.
3. _____ My tendency is to avoid situations that will lead to conflict.
4. _____ I try to avoid conflicts whenever I can.

Accommodating

1. _____ In a conflict, my goal is to make the other person happy.
2. _____ I usually give in to what the other person wants.
3. _____ It's important to me that the other person is satisfied.
4. _____ I usually do whatever the other person suggests.

Compromising

1. _____ I think everyone in the conflict has to give up something to find an acceptable solution.
2. _____ I try to find a solution that will be close to what everyone wants, but not exactly what anyone wants.
3. _____ I believe compromising is essential to managing conflict.
4. _____ I don't expect to get exactly what I want in a conflict but something that is close to what I want.

Collaborating

1. _____ My goal in a conflict is to find a solution that everyone likes.
2. _____ I usually try to find a "win-win" solution to the conflict.
3. _____ I share information and ideas so an acceptable solution can be found.
4. _____ I prefer to come up with a resolution that everyone is pleased with.

Source: Some items adapted from Rahim, M. A., & Mager, N. R. (1995). Confirmatory factor analysis of the styles of handling interpersonal conflict: First-order factor model and its invariance across groups. *Journal of Applied Psychology, 80*, 122–132.

Master the Chapter

Section 1} What is Interpersonal Conflict? (p. 375)

I. What is Interpersonal Conflict?

  A. Defining interpersonal conflict
- Conflict is an expressed struggle between two or more interdependent parties who perceive incompatible goals, scarce resources, and interference.

    1. Conflict is an expressed struggle

    2. Conflict occurs between interdependent parties

    3. Conflict is about goals the parties see as incompatible

    4. Conflict arises over perceived scarce resources

    5. Conflict includes interference

  B. Thinking about interpersonal conflict
- People often think about conflict using a variety of metaphors such as a trial, a game, a balancing act, and a garden.

Section 2} Conflict in Personal Relationships (p. 378)

II. Conflict in Personal Relationships

  A. Characteristics of interpersonal conflict
- Conflict is natural. It has content, relational, and procedural dimensions, and it can be direct or indirect. Conflict can be harmful, and it can also be beneficial.

    1. Conflict is natural

    2. Conflict has content, relational, and procedural dimensions

    3. Conflict can be direct or indirect

    4. Conflict can be harmful

    5. Conflict can be beneficial

  B. The most common sources of conflict
- People have conflict about a range of issues. Some issues, such as personal criticism, finances, and household chores, are especially common in personal relationships.

  C. How sex and gender affect conflict
- Conflict is influenced by sex and gender role orientations, encouraging men to be competitive and women to be accommodating.

  D. How culture affects conflict
- How people manage conflict is affected by whether their culture is individualistic or collectivistic, and also by whether it is high-context or low-context.

  E. Conflict online
- Conflict is especially prevalent in online settings, because of the disinhibition effect.

Section 3} Power and Conflict (p. 388)

III. Power and Conflict

  A. Some characteristics of power
- Power is the ability to manipulate, influence, or control other people or events.

    1. Power is context-specific
    2. Power is always present
- Power is context-specific but always present. It can be positive or negative, depending on how it is exercised. Power and conflict influence each other.

    3. Power influences communication
    4. Power can be positive or negative
    5. Power and conflict influence each other

  B. Forms of power
- People exercise five general forms of power: reward, coercive, referent, legitimate, and expert.

    1. Reward power
    2. Coercive power
    3. Referent power
    4. Legitimate power
    5. Expert power

  C. Sex, gender, and power
- Power is influenced by sex and gender roles.

  D. Culture and power
- The way people think about power is affected by whether they come from a high-power-distance culture or a low-power-distance one.

Section 4} Managing Interpersonal Conflict (p. 395)

IV. Managing Interpersonal Conflict

  A. Problematic behaviors during conflict
- In romantic relationships, four conflict behaviors are reliable predictors of relationship dissolution: criticism, contempt, defensiveness, and stonewalling.

    1. Criticism
    2. Contempt
    3. Defensiveness
    4. Stonewalling

  B. Strategies for managing conflict successfully
- People use five general strategies for managing conflict: competing, avoiding, accommodating, collaborating, and compromising. Which conflict management strategy is best depends on the situation and on the goals of the participants.

    1. Competing
    2. Avoiding
    3. Accommodating
    4. Compromising
    5. Collaborating

Key Terms

Accommodating	Criticism	One-up message
Avoiding	Defensiveness	Passive aggression
Coercive power	Demand-withdraw pattern	Power
Collaborating	Disinhibition effect	Referent power
Competing	Expert power	Reward power
Complementary relationship	Legitimate power	Stonewalling
Compromising	Meta-conflict	Symmetrical relationship
Conflict	One-across message	
Contempt	One-down message	

Discussion Questions

1. With whom do you have the most troublesome conflicts? What are your conflicts with these parties about?
2. How might the particular metaphor you use to think about conflict affect how you approach conflict?
3. Why does conflict usually make people so uncomfortable?
4. What have you noticed about the different ways in which men and women engage in conflict?
5. What are some examples of the positive use of power? The negative use?
6. Why is referent power so influential? Why are we so eager to follow those whom we admire or find attractive?
7. Which of Gottman's four horsemen would you find the most distressing if enacted in your own relationships? Why?
8. When are avoiding and accommodating the best strategies for dealing with conflict?

Practice Quiz

Multiple Choice

1. Which of the following is *not* one of the defining characteristics of interpersonal conflict?
   a. Conflict is an expressed struggle.
   b. Conflict occurs between independent parties.
   c. Conflict is about goals that are perceived as incompatible.
   d. Conflict arises over scarce resources.
2. Which of the following metaphors is best described by the statement "Conflict is a fun competition wherein participants test their skills against one another"?
   a. Conflict is a war.
   b. Conflict is a heroic adventure.
   c. Conflict is a bargaining table.
   d. Conflict is a game.
3. The "Dark Side" box described a study of the conflict experiences of intoxicated and sober participants. Which of the following was *not* one of its findings?
   a. Intoxicated individuals rated their feelings as more negative.
   b. Intoxicated individuals rated their partners' feelings as more negative.
   c. Intoxicated individuals with low self-esteem were more likely to blame their partners for the conflict.
   d. Intoxicated individuals with low self-esteem were more likely to blame themselves for the conflict.
4. According to research by Larry Erbert, the three most common sources of marital conflict, in order, are:
   a. finances, household chores, personal criticism
   b. household chores, personal criticism, finances
   c. personal criticism, finances, household chores
   d. money, sex, in-laws
5. An imbalance of power, wherein one person in a relationship has more power than the other, is known as:
   a. symmetrical relationship
   b. complementary relationship
   c. equitable relationship
   d. none of the above
6. Which of the following refers to the power of attraction, wherein people tend to comply with requests made by those they like, admire, or find attractive?
   a. reward
   b. coercive
   c. referent
   d. legitimate
7. According to Gottman, the "Four Horsemen of the Apocalypse" are:
   a. conflict, criticism, defensiveness, stonewalling
   b. defensiveness, contempt, complaining, conflict
   c. criticism, contempt, defensiveness, stonewalling
   d. stonewalling, debate, criticism, contempt
8. Seeing yourself as victim and denying responsibility for your own behavior are characteristics of:
   a. defensiveness
   b. stonewalling
   c. contempt
   d. complaining
9. Which approach to conflict is characterized by a moderate concern for others' needs?
   a. competing
   b. avoiding
   c. collaborating
   d. compromising
10. Which of the following is *not* one of the approaches to managing conflict?
    a. competing
    b. compromising
    c. avoiding
    d. circumventing

True/False

11. It is not natural for individuals to experience conflict within the context of a relationship.
12. It is always best to deal with conflict directly.
13. If you have the right skills and try hard enough, you can resolve any conflict.
14. People raised in low-context cultures value communication that is explicit, direct, and literal.
15. Low-power-distance cultures display a more equal distribution of power among social groups than do high-power-distance cultures.

Fill in the Blank

16. The _____ dimension of conflict relates to the specific topics that the conflict is about.

17. The _____ pattern is characterized by one partner making requests and the other partner pulling away.

18. People raised in _____ cultures are taught to consider the group's priorities and maintain group harmony, making them likely to manage conflict through avoidance.

19. In computer-mediated communication, the _____ effect invites people to say or do things they would not do in person.

20. Because of their status or position, individuals with _____ power have the right to make requests with which others must comply.

Research Library

Movies

American Beauty (Drama; 1999; R)

This drama stars Kevin Spacey as Lester, whose life is a series of tensions and disappointments. He feels increasingly estranged from his career-obsessed wife (played by Annette Bening) and his angry, confused teenage daughter. In response to these tensions, Lester quits his job, buys a sports car, and begins lifting weights to attract the attention of his daughter's attractive friend. The movie includes many scenes of conflict, both enacted and avoided, including one climactic scene at the family dinner table. This film won the Academy Award for best picture in 1999.

The Brothers McMullen (Drama; 1995; R)

This film begins with three Irish Catholic brothers dealing with their father's recent death. The story then fast-forwards several years to portray the brothers dealing with the dramas in their own lives. One brother, Jack, is carrying on an affair that is discovered by his wife, Molly. Another brother, Pat, is dumped by his fiancée, Susan, whose Jewish background raises her concerns about entering into an interfaith marriage. Several examples of relational conflict are depicted in this drama.

Ordinary People (Drama; 1980; R)

This classic film focuses on communication in an upper-middle-class family in the wake of the older son's tragic death. Younger son Conrad (played by Timothy Hutton) has recently been released from a psychiatric hospital after attempting suicide. His older brother, Buck, had excelled at athletics and academics and was clearly his parents' favorite child. Now, with his brother gone, Conrad struggles to connect with his father, Calvin (played by Donald Sutherland), and his mother, Beth (played by Mary Tyler Moore), both of whom are emotionally distant and resentful that Conrad was partially responsible for his brother's death. The film, which won the Academy Award for best picture, includes many excellent scenes of family conflict.

Books

Gottman, J. M. (1993). *What predicts divorce? The relationship between marital processes and marital outcomes.* Mahwah, NJ: Lawrence Erlbaum Associates.

Oetzel, J. H., & Ting-Toomey, S. (Eds.). (2006). *The SAGE handbook of conflict communication: Integrating theory, research, and practice.* Thousand Oaks, CA: Sage.

Weeks, D. (1994). *The eight essential steps to conflict resolution.* Los Angeles: Tarcher.

Journal Articles

Erbert, L. A. (2000). Conflict and dialectics: Perceptions of dialectical contradictions in marital conflict. *Journal of Social and Personal Relationships, 17,* 638–659.

Kiecolt-Glaser, J. K., Malarkey, W. B., Chee, M., Newton, T., Cacioppo, J. T., Mao, H.-Y., & Glaser, R. (1993). Negative behavior during marital conflict is associated with immunological down-regulation. *Psychosomatic Medicine, 55,* 395–409.

Web Sites

www.drnadig.com/conflict.htm

This Web site is sponsored by Dr. Larry Nadig, a clinical psychologist and marriage and family therapist. It focuses on healthy conflict resolution and details some of the common mistakes couples and families make when dealing with conflict.

www.iacm-conflict.org/links/

This page, sponsored by the International Association for Conflict Management, offers links to several online resources relevant to conflict and conflict management.

11

Deceptive Communication

What is interpersonal deception, and is it ever justified?

Why do people attempt to deceive others?

How can we detect deception?

Kendra and Andy

When Kendra first met her husband, Andy, he was heavily in debt. Over the next six years, she helped him restructure his finances and pay off all his credit card balances. He then admitted he owed nearly $13,000 on an additional credit card she didn't know about. Kendra refinanced their house to pay off this debt, but she informed Andy in no uncertain terms that if he ever lied to her again about his debts, she would leave him. Yesterday Kendra found a credit card statement with a balance of almost $6,000 under the passenger's seat in Andy's car. She felt betrayed. It was bad enough that Andy was jeopardizing their family's financial health by continuing to accrue debt. The fact that he was also lying to Kendra about it made her feel as though he had completely violated her trust.

No one likes being lied to. Like Kendra, when we find out someone has deceived us, we feel angry and taken advantage of. Although these feelings of betrayal and violation can occur in all relationships, they can be particularly strong—and painful—when the deception occurs in the context of a close relationship. Deception hurts us emotionally, and it erodes our trust in others.[1]

Yet, are you completely honest all the time? For instance, do you ever pretend you're happy to see someone, just to avoid hurting that person's feelings? How about saying "Sorry, I have plans" when you don't really have plans but you've been invited to do something you don't want to do? Most of us would have to admit we don't always tell "the truth, the whole truth, and nothing but the truth." But being polite, tactful, or discreet isn't really the same thing as lying. Is it?

In this chapter, we explore the concept of deception by looking at several issues:

1} What deception is and what it means to be deceptive

2} Why people lie and what forms of deception they use

3} How deception is related to behavior

4} What strategies you can use to improve your ability to detect deception by others

> A lie can run around the world before the truth can get its boots on.
>
> —James Watt (1736–1819)
> Scottish inventor

Whatever our personal feelings may be about the value of honesty, the reality is that most people conceal the truth, in one form or another, on a regular basis.[2] To respect the privacy of a co-worker who is in treatment for alcohol addiction, for instance, you may tell her clients that she's away from work on a "special assignment." By the same token, you may tell your 12-year-old nephew that he did a "wonderful job" performing in his school musical, even though he can barely carry a tune, because you want to encourage him. Sometimes, in fact, we actually reprimand people for telling the truth. When children make straightforward comments about other people ("You smell funny," "Your teeth are really yellow"), we usually teach them it is impolite to say such things, even though they are honest opinions.

We might agree that lying is wrong if we do it to hurt someone, but what if we do it to *avoid* hurting someone?[3] We may choose not to think of politeness or discretion as examples of lying, because words such as *lying* and *deception* have negative connotations. Even when their intentions are admirable, however, people often misrepresent the truth to achieve them.[4] When we think of lying as a misrepresentation of the truth—no matter what the intention—we realize that deception is often a part of everyday social interaction, as the "Dark Side" box on page 410 points out.

Throughout this chapter, it's important to keep an open mind and think of deception as just one of many communication processes you're learning about in this class. That doesn't mean you should check your morals or beliefs at the door. On the contrary, how we think about the value of honesty, reliability, and integrity helps to define who we are as human beings. Many people believe honesty is truly the best policy. Nearly all the major world religions promote the virtue of honesty and condemn deceptive behavior.

Remember, though, that *studying* something isn't the same as *condoning* it. Whether or not you are ethically or morally opposed to lying, understanding deception helps you to become a better communicator.[5] In fact, the more you know about deception, the better you may become at detecting it.

Most of us would probably define deception as "making statements that aren't true," and we might associate it with actions such as fibbing, misleading, exaggerating, stretching the truth, concealing the truth, and telling white lies. None of those types of deception, however, represents a fully adequate definition. After all, people can be deceptive by leaving out parts of a story or by giving vague, ambiguous answers to questions. Neither of those scenarios requires saying anything that technically isn't true.

The Girl Scout Law

I will do my best to be
  honest and fair,
  friendly and helpful,
  considerate and caring,
  courageous and strong, and
  responsible for what I say and do,
and to
  respect myself and others,
  respect authority,
  use resources wisely,
  make the world a better place, and
  be a sister to every Girl Scout.

The Dark Side of Interpersonal Communication
How Common Is Lying?

You don't have to look very hard to see some high-profile examples of deception. Marion Jones forfeited her Olympic medals after admitting she lied about taking performance-enhancing drugs. Martha Stewart was sentenced to prison for lying to investigators. Contestants on reality shows such as *Survivor*, *The Apprentice*, and *Big Brother* often lie to gain an advantage over their competitors. Is deception really that common in everyday life, or do these high-profile examples simply make us think it is? Consider the following:

- In a 2004 survey of 3,000 adults, 71% of participants reported they had lied to friends or relatives to spare their feelings; 63% had faked an illness to get out of work; 32% had lied to their spouse about a purchase; and 28% had lied to their spouse about their relationship with someone else.

- After conducting 3.8 million background checks in April 2005, Automatic Data Processing, Inc., found that 52 percent of job applicants had lied on their resumes. A different survey by the Gillette Corporation found that, for men, the number was 86 percent.

- In a study conducted in 2004, researchers at Cornell University asked college students to keep a diary on every social interaction they had for a week. The results? Students reported lying in 26% of their interactions. Deception was the most common in telephone conversations, followed by face-to-face interaction, instant messages, and e-mail.

Some people may be surprised at how high these figures are. Others may be surprised at how *low* they are. In either event, there's no question that we encounter deception regularly in our day-to-day interactions with people. That is all the more reason why it's smart for us to understand deception—and in particular, why it's useful to know the reliable clues to deception.

Ask Yourself:

- Do you think lying is more common today than it used to be? If so, why do you think that is?

- In what situations do you believe lying is justified?

Sources: Hancock, J., Thom-Santelli, J., & Ritchie, T. (2004, April). *Deception and design: The impact of communication on lying behavior.* Paper presented to Computer-Human Interaction (CHI) scientific meeting, Vienna, Austria; Kalish, N. (2004, January). How honest are you? *Reader's Digest*, pp. 114–119; Kanner, B. (2005). *When it comes to guys, what's normal?* New York: St. Martin's Press.

What Is Deception?

According to communication researchers, **deception** occurs when a speaker *transmits information knowingly and intentionally for the purpose of creating a false belief in the receiver.* In other words, if you communicate in a way that is meant to make someone believe a fact or form an impression you know to be untrue, then you are engaging in deception.

We can think of deceptive acts as falling along a continuum from "high-stakes" lies to "low-stakes" lies. High-stakes lies are those for which the penalties for getting

Deception
The knowing and intentional transmission of information to create a false belief in the hearer.

caught are severe.[6] Many high-stakes lies are forms of *fraud,* which means they are misrepresentations of facts for the sake of material gain. Some types of fraudulent lies are (1) misrepresenting your identity by forging someone else's signature on checks or other documents; (2) impersonating a physician, a police officer, or some other licensed professional; (3) engaging in insider trading by using privileged information to make stock sales or purchases; (4) underreporting your income on your tax returns; and (5) filing false insurance claims. Each of those actions is a high-stakes lie because the penalty for getting caught can include steep fines and imprisonment. The same can be said for *perjury,* or lying under oath, which constitutes a felony.

In addition to carrying legal penalties, high-stakes lies can also carry significant *personal* penalties. For example, lying to your spouse to cover up an affair or lying to your boss about a substantial mistake you made would also qualify as a high-stakes lie because you could destroy your marriage or lose your job if your lie were to be revealed.[7]

On the other end of the continuum are low-stakes lies, for which the penalties for getting caught are comparatively mild. These lies, which people sometimes call *little white lies,* often serve to avoid embarrassing people and hurting their feelings. Some examples of low-stakes lies are (1) telling a friend you "love the graduation gift" she gave you when you actually don't like it; (2) assuring your brother and sister-in-law that helping them move "is no problem," even though it's inconvenient for you; (3) claiming that you arrived late to your haircut appointment because you "ran into heavy traffic on the way," when in fact you left your house late; and (4) saying "nice to meet you" to your newest co-worker even though he makes a bad first impression on you.

Deception means knowingly trying to create a false impression in someone else's mind.

Some forms of deception might be called "high-stakes" lies because the penalties for getting caught are severe. These can include losing your job, destroying your marriage, or even being sentenced to prison.

In many cases, the only real penalty for being caught in a low-stakes lie is emotional discomfort. If your hairdresser discovers you actually weren't late for your appointment because of traffic, for instance, you'll probably feel slightly guilty for having told the lie and slightly embarrassed at being discovered. Those emotions will probably be temporary, though, and it's unlikely that more serious consequences will follow.

Many other deceptive acts fall somewhere along the continuum between high-stakes and low-stakes lies. Suppose, for instance, that while taking the midterm exam in your marketing class, you notice your friend Soren cheating on the test. After reading Soren's exam, the professor suspects him of cheating but doesn't have direct proof. She contacts several students—including you—to ask if you witnessed anyone cheating on the test. Because Soren is your friend, you say no. What penalties do you suffer if you are caught in this lie? Perhaps the professor gives you a failing grade on the exam, making it impossible for you to earn a higher grade than C in the class. This penalty is certainly more severe than just feeling guilty or embarrassed, but it isn't as severe as losing your job, your marriage, or your freedom. Lies of this sort might therefore be considered "middle-stakes" lies.

The Basic Elements of Deception

In summary, to qualify as deception, a communicative act must have three basic elements:

- The sender must know the information is false.
- The sender must be transmitting the information on purpose.
- The sender must be attempting to make the receiver believe the information.

Importantly, a behavior must exhibit all three characteristics to be considered deceptive.

Our definition of deception excludes certain situations, which we now consider. You probably encounter these situations from time to time in your social interactions.

You aren't lying if you believe what you're saying is true. Suppose you ask me how long a nautical mile is and I tell you it's 1,920 meters. This answer reflects what I honestly think. It's also untrue—a nautical mile is actually 1,852 meters. (You should know better than to ask a communication professor such questions.) So, I gave you false information. Did I transmit the information on purpose? Yes; you asked and I answered. Did I intend for you to believe the information? Of course. Nevertheless, according to our definition I wasn't being deceptive because I didn't know the information was false.

You aren't lying if you don't intend for others to believe what you're saying. Quite often, we make statements we don't mean for other people to take literally, such as "I'm so hungry I could eat a horse," or "I'm so tired I could sleep 'til Tuesday." Chances are, you've never *actually* been that hungry or that tired—and if you say something like this, most people who hear you will understand that you don't literally mean what you're saying. If we say "it's raining cats and dogs," we know that felines and canines aren't actually falling from the sky; thus, the literal information is false. Nevertheless, we aren't being deceptive in this situation, because when we use such idioms we're not trying to make others believe the false information. Many forms of teasing and sarcasm also are not meant to be taken literally. We can usually tell by people's facial expressions or tone of voice when they are joking and don't expect us to believe them.

You cannot lie to yourself. From time to time, we may try to make ourselves believe facts or ideas that we know aren't really true. When we realize it didn't work, we may say, "I was just deceiving myself." According to our definition, however, it is impossible for people to deceive themselves. We certainly attempt to change our opinions or beliefs on various issues; sometimes we're successful and sometimes not. Recall, however, that for a communicative act to qualify as deception, the sender—knowing the information is false—must attempt to make the receiver believe it is true. The problem with trying to deceive yourself is that the sender and the receiver are the same person—you—and you can't logically believe something is true while at the same time knowing it is false. The moment you believe your lie, in other words, it stops being a lie, because the sender now believes the information to be true. We might try to trick ourselves from time to time; for example, we might set all our clocks 10 minutes fast so we're never late. The process of deception actually requires, however, that the sender and the receiver be different people.

Two additional characteristics of our definition of deception deserve your attention. First, deception involves the transmission of *information,* and not just the transmission of words. Words convey information, of course, but, as we have discussed, so do nonverbal behaviors. Thus, it is possible to be deceptive without ever saying a word.

Imagine, for instance, that David and Aileen are living together as romantic partners but haven't yet told Aileen's family. Whenever her parents come to visit, therefore, David and Aileen must alter the appearance of their apartment to give the impression that they are simply roommates. Thus, they take down any photos showing the two of them together. They put away any souvenirs or mementos that would provide clues to their relationship. David moves out of the master bedroom and into the guest room, which is referred to as "his" room. Through these actions, Aileen and David give the impression that they are simply two friends sharing an apartment. Even though they don't specifically *say* they aren't romantic partners, their actions convey that deceptive message.

The other characteristic of the definition of deception is that it doesn't mention anything about motive. *The reason* someone is deceiving another person has nothing to do with *whether* that person is being deceptive. This point is important because we sometimes think deception isn't really deception if we do it for the "right" reasons. While treating an adolescent in critical condition after a car crash, for instance, a physician may choose not to tell him that his friend died in the crash because she's worried the stress and grief will compromise the victim's recovery. Similarly, a police officer may give a homicide victim's relatives only a vague description of the crime, omitting details he believes they would find upsetting. In other circumstances, you may have deceived other people to help them—or, at least, to avoid hurting them—and felt justified in doing so.

From time to time, we all try to make ourselves believe things we know aren't true. According to our definition of deception, however, you cannot lie to yourself.

In fact, people have several motives for engaging in deception, many of which are altruistic. Deception is deception, however, whether we consider it justified or not. Lying, even to save someone's life, is still lying.

Sometimes we think deception isn't really deception if we do it for the "right" reasons. Why people lie, however, has nothing to do with whether they are lying.

Interpersonal Deception Is Common

Whether we like it or not, deception is relatively common in interpersonal communication. Research indicates that it is especially frequent when we are attempting to be polite and when we are communicating online. Let's take a closer look at each of these situations.

Deception is a common component of politeness. As several of our examples of deception have illustrated, one of the most common reasons people lie is to be polite and to avoid hurting other people.[8] An important component of being polite, after all, is making others feel appreciated, whether you genuinely appreciate them or not.[9] Behaving in a polite manner therefore means trying not to cause offense.

In their attempts to be polite, people frequently make statements that express appreciation and steer clear of offense, even if those statements are misleading. Ally is unimpressed on her first date with Rich, for example, but she doesn't want to hurt his feelings, so she says, "I had fun; we should do this again," even though she doesn't mean it. Carma feels uncomfortable attending church with her mother-in-law whenever she visits, but she doesn't want to offend her, so she says, "I'd love to go," even though she doesn't want to.

Deceptions committed in the service of politeness help maintain social harmony and avoid disruptions in relationships. Imagine for a minute what interpersonal communication would be like if everyone told the complete, unedited truth about everything. People would no longer hold back their opinions about you or your behavior, no matter how hurtful those opinions would be to you. It's easy to imagine that such a situation would do more to damage relationships than to enhance them.

Even if we have moral objections to lying, some researchers believe deception can serve as a "social lubricant" by decreasing friction between people and helping them get along.[10] Psychologist Leonard Saxe believes that people who are obsessed with being totally honest might become socially isolated because others would see them as impolite and lacking in social skill.[11]

Mild deception often acts as a social lubricant, helping people get along. Someone who is blatantly honest all the time would be considered impolite.

Deception is especially common when communicating online. Research suggests that deception also occurs more frequently when we're engaged in computer-mediated communication. One possible explanation for this tendency is that online communication doesn't involve face-to-face contact and the communicators can hide their identities, particularly if they use screen names. This anonymity protects our privacy, but it also enables us to exaggerate or falsify aspects of our online identities, such as age, educational level, ethnicity, and income.[12] Some people even engage in "gender switching" in which they pretend to be members of the other sex.[13]

A striking example of online deception occurs on dating Web sites, where subscribers post personal information with the hope of attracting potential romantic partners. Profiles on dating sites typically ask for information about the subscriber's height, weight, personal appearance, profession, education, hobbies, interests, and what he or she is looking for in a prospective partner. It may not surprise you to learn that deception is common on these sites. In fact, research has found that as many as 20% of online daters admit to lying about some aspect of their personal profile. When people are asked how many *other* people they believe are being deceptive, however, that figure jumps to nearly 90%.[14]

What do online daters lie about? For women, the major areas of deception are age, weight, and physical appearance. For men, they are educational level, income, height, age, and even marital status. (Research suggests that at least 13% of men on dating Web sites are married.)[15] Why is this lying so common? The answer is that online daters are looking for a partner and they want their profile to be as attractive as possible, even if it isn't entirely accurate. Unfortunately, their belief that being completely truthful would hurt their chances may be justified. At least one study found that the more honest people were in describing themselves, the less success they had in finding dates online.[16]

Why, exactly, might someone choose to lie, either online or in person? We'll take a look at some of the most common reasons for deception in the next section.

2} Deceptive Acts Are Diverse

> *Who lies for you will lie against you.*
> —Bosnian proverb

We've already seen that we can't lie by accident. Whenever people attempt to deceive others, therefore, they must have a reason. In the examples we have seen thus far, people practiced deception for a number of reasons. Communication research confirms that people have many motivations for lying. You may consider some of these motivations to be reprehensible—for example, lying to hurt someone. You may find others to be acceptable under some circumstances—for example, lying to avoid hurting someone.[17] To assess your attitudes about deception, complete the exercise contained in the "Getting to Know You" activity on page 416.

Some Reasons Why People Deceive

In this section, we consider some of the most common reasons why people engage in deception, and we examine an example of each one. Can you think of any other motives to add to this list?[18]

- *Some lies benefit the hearer:* To make your friend feel good, you say you like her new haircut even though you don't because it doesn't match her overall style.[19]
- *Some lies help you get to know someone:* You invent an excuse to interact with someone just so you can get to know him or her.
- *Some lies protect your privacy:* Your co-worker asks how you are, and even though you're having problems at home, you say "fine" because you don't want to discuss your domestic situation with her.
- *Some lies help you avoid conflict:* Your romantic partner asks if you want to go with him to a party and you say that you do—even though you don't—to avoid a fight.
- *Some lies make you look better:* At your class reunion, you exaggerate facts about your education and income level to appear more successful.[20]
- *Some lies help you avoid punishment:* You are stopped for speeding and tell the officer you didn't know what the speed limit was—when you actually did—hoping you won't get a ticket.
- *Some lies help you protect yourself from distress:* When your aunt invites you to Thanksgiving dinner, you make up a story about having other plans so you don't have to listen to your uncle's inevitable criticisms of you.

{ Getting to Know You }
Attitudes About Deception

What are your attitudes about lying? For each of the statements below, record your level of agreement by writing in the appropriate number on each line, according to this scale:

5 = Strongly Agree

4 = Somewhat Agree

3 = Neither Agree nor Disagree

2 = Somewhat Disagree

1 = Strongly Disagree

A. _____ Lying is wrong under any conditions.

B. _____ I have lied when I felt the situation called for it.

C. _____ Sometimes you have to know when to stretch the truth.

D. _____ Honesty is always the best policy.

E. _____ I rarely, if ever, lie to others.

F. _____ There are justifiable reasons for lying.

Now, go back to items B, C, and F, and reverse your scores. That is, change scores of 5 to 1, 4 to 2, 2 to 4, and 1 to 5. Then, add up your scores for all six items. Your total score should be between 6 and 30.

The higher your score, the more negative your attitude toward deception. You believe honesty is an important virtue and that lying is rarely, if ever, the right thing to do.

The lower your score, the more pragmatic your attitude toward deception. You think lying is sometimes necessary and that there are valid reasons for being deceptive.

If you scored in the middle of the range (14–22), your attitude toward deception is a mixture of these two positions. You likely take a situational attitude about lying, believing it is sometimes wrong and sometimes justifiable, depending on the circumstances.

- *Some lies help you get revenge on someone:* To get back at a former romantic partner for cheating on you, you spread false rumors about that person to his or her friends.
- *Some lies help you hurt someone for no reason:* Out of boredom one night, you make up a rumor about one of your classmates and begin posting it on various class listservs.
- *Some lies protect you or your livelihood:* For fear of social rejection or employment discrimination, you deny having a mental illness even though you are currently being treated for one.
- *Some lies amuse you:* During a conversation with your neighbor on a long flight, you tell her completely made-up stories about yourself.[21]

Whatever our motives for lying, there are many ways to deceive beyond simply making up information that is entirely untrue. For instance,

dental floss

100 YD (91.4 m)

One of the many reasons people deceive is to make themselves look better in front of others. Are you ever less than honest with your dentist about how often you floss? If so, why do you do that?

telling your dentist you have been flossing regularly when in fact you haven't is one way to lie, but there are others as well. In fact, deceptive acts fall into two categories: acts of simulation and acts of dissimulation. Let's take a closer look at each one.

Some Deceptive Acts Are Acts of Simulation

When people provide information that isn't true, they are engaging in **acts of simulation.** Making up an excuse to break a date, telling a potential employer you have a master's degree when you actually don't, and telling a friend you like his new car when you really think it's quite unattractive are all acts of simulation. In each of these examples, you're conveying a message you know isn't true for the purpose of getting your listener to believe it. People can engage in simulation through two different kinds of behaviors: falsification and exaggeration.

People can lie through falsification. Falsification is outright lying—in other words, communicating false information as though it were true. Suppose, for example, that Ramón is applying for an apartment and he indicates on his application that he has rented before, when in fact he never has. In this case, Ramón has falsified his application; he has presented information that he knows to be false as though it were true. Similarly, if Sarah tells Annette that she is excited about the concert to which she is taking Annette for her birthday when she is actually dreading it, she is also falsifying. Even though Sarah lied to benefit Annette—whereas Ramón lied to benefit himself—they have both used falsification.

Studies have shown that falsification is one of the most common ways that people deceive others. In a diary study, for instance, communication scientist Sandra Metts found that people used falsification in almost half (48%) of their deception attempts.[22]

Job candidates sometimes exaggerate the details of their work history to appear more desirable to prospective employers. Research shows that exaggeration is a fairly common form of deception.

People can lie through exaggeration. Another act of simulation is **exaggeration,** in which a person takes a fact that is true in principle and overstates it. Suppose, for example, you're interviewing for a job and you exaggerate the level of responsibility you had at your last job to make it seem as though you're more qualified than you are. In this example, you may give completely true statements about *what your responsibilities were,* but you may overstate *the level of those responsibilities* to create a more favorable impression.[23] You may be tempted to think exaggeration isn't a form of deception. In fact, it does intentionally mislead others, so it is deceptive.

Some Deceptive Acts Are Acts of Dissimulation

When we engage in acts of simulation, we make statements or convey ideas that aren't true. By contrast, in **acts of dissimulation** we *fail to convey* information that, if known, would change the nature of our story. People can engage in dissimulation in two ways: through omission and through equivocation.

People can lie through omission. Omission simply means leaving out particular details of a story to create a false impression. Suppose Lukas is a salesperson who is attempting to sell a used car to Martha, an elderly woman living on a fixed income. While going over the details of the sale, Lukas tells Martha that "this car has 11,425 miles on it, it comes with a one-year limited warranty, and your car payment will be $185." He then indicates where she should sign to accept the agreement. Martha signs and takes the car home, only to discover later that her car payment is $185 *every two weeks.* When Lukas said her payment would be $185, she assumed that meant per month. Martha quickly realized she could not afford to keep the car, and she felt angry with Lukas for deceiving her.

Strictly speaking, everything Lukas told Martha was true—the car payment was, in fact, $185. Therefore, was Lukas being deceptive? Absolutely, because in all likelihood he knew Martha would assume he was quoting the amount of her monthly payment and not her bi-weekly payment. Therefore, he knowingly created a false impression in Martha's mind, not by what he said, but by what he did *not* say. In this instance, Lukas may have told the truth, but he did not tell the *whole truth,* and the end effect was deceptive.

People can lie through equivocation. Equivocation means expressing information that is so vague or ambiguous that it creates the impression it has communicated a message it hasn't actually conveyed. Suppose Rajani asks her assistant whether he likes the newly hired sales manager and, in response, he smiles and says, "He's quite a guy!" Rajani interprets this response to mean he likes the new manager. In fact, he never actually said that, did he?

Instead of answering Rajani's question directly, her assistant gave an ambiguous response that he knew she would interpret as positive, even though he actually doesn't like the new manager very much. This is an example of equivocation. Just like omission, equivocation deliberately creates a false impression, so it qualifies as a form of deception. A brief review of the four primary forms of deception appears in the "At a Glance" box.

Equivocation A form of deception that involves giving vague, ambiguous answers to a question to give the false impression that one has answered it.

At a Glance: Forms of Deception

There are four primary ways to construct lies:

Falsification	Passing off false or fabricated statements as though they were true
Exaggeration	Inflating or overstating information that is true in principle
Omission	Leaving out consequential pieces of information in one's story
Equivocation	Giving vague or ambiguous answers to avoid actually answering a question

Even though people engage in deception frequently, finding out you've been lied to can be a distressing experience. You may feel as though the other person has violated your trust and irreparably harmed your relationship with him or her. You may also feel angry at being lied to and perhaps even embarrassed that you believed the lie. Those negative feelings are probably magnified when the deceiver is someone you are emotionally close to, such as a family member, a good friend, or a romantic partner. In the chapter opening story, for instance, we saw that Kendra was upset not only because of the debt Andy had incurred but also because he violated her trust by lying about it.

The distress generated by discovering you've been lied to makes many people eager to learn how to detect deception in others. Can you really tell when you're being lied to? What are the best behaviors to look for as clues to deception? What makes certain people better liars than others? We'll explore each of these questions in the next section.

3} Communication Behaviors and Deception {

How good are you at distinguishing truth from deception? Before you answer, consider the following experiment. I put two average students, Machiko and Jody, in separate rooms. I go into the first room and tell Machiko how I spent my summer vacation. Meanwhile, Jody is alone in another room, doing nothing. Afterward, we all come back together and I ask both Machiko and Jody whether I'm lying about my summer vacation. Machiko could hear everything I said, listen to my tone of voice, and watch my body language to evaluate the believability of my story. Jody, however, was in another room and has no idea what I have said. Who will be more accurate in determining whether I have lied? Machiko, right? After all, Jody has no clue as to what I said and might as well flip a coin—at least that would provide a 50% chance of being right.

> *The mouth may lie, but the face it makes nonetheless tells the truth.*
>
> —Friedrich Nietzsche (1844–1900) German philosopher

The truth is that Machiko *would* be more accurate, but not by much. Whereas Jody had a 50% chance of being right just by flipping a coin, Machiko's chance of being right—even after being in the room, hearing my story, and watching my body language—is only 55%, *just slightly better than if Machiko hadn't been there at all.* Research has shown that under normal conditions, the average person can detect deception about 55% of the time.[24] Even police interrogators, psychiatrists, customs officials, and polygraph examiners, whom you might expect to be good at detecting deception, typically do little better than the average person.[25]

One reason many of us aren't that good at detecting deception is that we want to believe that others are being honest with us. Unless we have a specific reason not to, we tend to believe most of what other people tell us.

Detecting Deception Is Difficult

Why don't we do any better than chance at detecting deception? One reason is that we often look for the wrong clues. How many times have you heard, for instance, that a lack of eye contact is the surest sign you're being lied to? In fact, this saying isn't true, as we'll see shortly. Obviously, the more attention we focus on the wrong clues to deception, the less we focus on the *right clues.* Paying attention to the wrong clues will keep us from being accurate much of the time.[26]

A second reason we're not very good lie detectors is that most of us *want* to believe most of what we hear. Unless we have a reason not to, we tend to believe what other people tell us. Researchers call this the **truth bias.**[27] Why do we have this tendency as our default position? One reason is that we generally expect our communication with others to be pleasant, and being lied to can be very unpleasant.[28] Another reason is that it takes a great deal of mental energy to question everything we hear, so it's much easier for us to believe what we're told, unless we have a specific reason not to.[29]

Even though the average ability to detect deception is around 55%, we might do better if we know what to look for and what *not* to look for in people's behaviors. What are the clues that best indicate someone is lying? We address this question in the next section.

Truth bias
The tendency to believe what someone says, in the absence of a reason not to.

Some Behaviors Are Common During Acts of Deception

For a long time, scientists in various disciplines tried to discover a foolproof method for detecting lies. So far, research has identified only a small number of behaviors that show any consistent relationship with deception, and none of them characterizes every lie or every liar.[30] In this section, we'll take a look at some of the verbal and nonverbal behaviors that show reliable associations with lying. We'll also identify some behaviors that do not.

False information is often inconsistent. One of the most straightforward clues to deception is inconsistency in the information presented. Let's say you call in sick to work on Friday so you can leave town early for a weekend beach trip. While you're swimming on Saturday, however, your sunscreen washes off and your boss sees you back at work on Monday with an obvious sunburn. This situation creates information inconsistency: The visual information provided by your appearance contradicts your story about being sick at home. Moreover, because it's hard to fake a sunburn, your boss correctly infers that you faked your illness.

Sometimes liars betray themselves with information inconsistency, and sometimes other people betray them. In fact, research has concluded that information provided by third parties is one of the most common ways people find out they've been lied to.[31] Referring back to our previous example, suppose you didn't get sunburned but your boss's daughter also happened to be at the beach and later innocently mentioned to your boss that she had seen you. Clearly, she wasn't trying to get you into trouble. Her information, however, will still be inconsistent with your story about being sick, implying that you did not tell the truth. The "How Do We Know?" box on the next page examines third-party information in more detail.

Deceivers often commit speech errors. When people are telling lies, they often make more speech errors than usual. Speech errors include behaviors such as taking excessively long pauses in the middle of a conversation (while thinking up a story), using numerous vocal fillers such as "um" or "uh," starting to speak but then stopping abruptly, and taking an extra long time to respond to people's questions.[32] Why are deceivers more prone to making these errors? The answer is that people often feel guilty or nervous (or both) when they are lying, and these emotions can cause their speech patterns to become less fluent than normal.[33] The key is knowing how smooth

In this chapter, you learned that one of the most common ways people discover they have been lied to is through third-party information. How do we know this?

Communication scholars Hee Sun Park, Timothy Levine, Steven McCornack, Kelly Morrison, and Merissa Ferrara asked 200 undergraduates to describe a recent instance in which they discovered that someone had lied to them. In particular, they asked the participants to recall *how* they discovered they had been deceived. More than half of the participants reported that they had discovered the lie through information provided by a third party and not through the actual deceiver. Following third-party information, the most common methods of discovering deception were through physical evidence (e.g., a sunburn when someone claimed to be ill), a confession on the part of the deceiver, or some combination of these methods.

Ask Yourself:

- The last time you discovered you had been lied to, how did you find out?

- What other methods do you think people commonly use to detect deception?

From Me to You:

- If you know that a friend has been lied to by someone else, should you tell your friend, even if it will hurt him or her to find out? Many people who find themselves in this situation face an ethical dilemma. On one hand, you don't want to see your friend misled; on the other hand, you don't want to cause him or her pain. If you find yourself in this situation, my advice is to weigh the pros and cons of each option carefully before deciding how to act. Sometimes, informing your friend of the lie is in his or her best interests. At other times, the best thing you can do for your friend is to be discreet and keep what you know to yourself.

Source: Park, H. S., Levine, T. R., McCornack, S. A., Morrison, K., & Ferrara, M. (2002). How people really detect lies. *Communication Monographs, 69,* 144–157.

and fluent a person's speech *usually* is, so you can discern when that person is making more speech errors than he or she typically does.

Deception often increases vocal pitch. As we discussed in Chapter 6, "Nonverbal Communication," vocal pitch describes how high or low your voice is. Sometimes, such as when you wake up in the morning, your pitch is lower than normal, and your voice sounds deeper than usual. When you feel nervous, excited, or agitated, the opposite occurs: Your pitch sounds higher than normal.[34] As you might guess, because people often become stressed or nervous when they're being deceptive, their pitch tends to rise.[35] Moreover, they may not even be aware they are speaking in a higher pitch than normal, which can make increased vocal pitch a particularly good clue to deception. A study by communication researchers Joyce Bauchner, Elyse Kaplan, and

Gerald Miller found that vocal characteristics such as pitch are more reliable clues to deception than any other nonverbal behavior.[36]

Two eye behaviors are associated with lying. We've already mentioned that although many people consider lack of eye contact to be a reliable clue to deception, it actually is a very poor clue (see the "Fact or Fiction?" box above). In fact, eye blinking and pupil dilation are much better indicators. On average, a person blinks about 15–20 times per minute to keep a consistent layer of moisture on the surface of the eyes.[37] When you feel nervous or anxious, however—the way you might if you were lying to someone—you begin to blink more often, as a way for your body to expend your nervous energy.[38] In addition, your pupils dilate, or open up wider, when you get nervous or aroused.[39] Several studies have demonstrated that when people are telling lies their pupils dilate more than usual.[40]

Liars often use false smiles. On average, people don't smile any more or any less than normal when lying.[41] What does tend to change, however, is the *type* of smile people

When people try to be deceptive, they are less likely to display genuine smiles, such as the smile portrayed here. Research indicates that deceivers are more likely than truth-tellers to use false smiles.

use during deception. Specifically, deceivers are more likely than truth tellers to use a false smile, which is the kind of smile you wear when you want to look happier than you really are.[42] One of the distinctive features of genuine smiles is that they cause the skin at the sides of your eyes to wrinkle. By contrast, false smiles don't, so the upper and lower halves of the face seem inconsistent with each other. People often use false smiles when they're feeling distressed but are trying to hide it, as they might if they feel nervous or guilty about lying.

Many liars use minimal body movement. When we get nervous, many of us move around more—we may fidget or pace back and forth more than usual. This is our body's way of getting rid of nervous energy, so it might seem reasonable to expect that people exhibit more of this random movement when they're lying than when they're telling the truth. Surprisingly, research tells us just the opposite: Deceivers exhibit *fewer* body movements than truth tellers do. In particular, communication studies have found that, compared with truth tellers, deceivers display fewer hand and finger movements,[43] fewer forward leans,[44] fewer gestures,[45] and fewer leg and foot movements.[46]

Why do deceivers move less, rather than more? One possible explanation is that to avoid getting caught, deceivers may try so hard to prevent themselves from pacing or fidgeting that they end up appearing rigid or tense. Another possible reason is that there are so many things to think about while lying (such as whether the story is believable and whether the hearer seems suspicious) that people simply don't pay as much attention to their nonverbal behaviors as they normally do.

The "At a Glance" box summarizes what research tells us about communication behaviors people use while lying.

Before we move on, it's important to remember two things about this list of behaviors. The first is that these are not the only behaviors related to deception. Rather, they're just some of the behaviors that communication research has identified as reliable clues to lying. Second, none of these clues is foolproof. Even though people *tend* to make more speech errors, use more false smiles, blink more frequently, exhibit a higher vocal pitch, and move less when they lie, they may do all these things for other reasons as well. Communication scientists have not yet discovered any foolproof clues to deception, and chances are good that they never will.[47]

Now that you know some of the behaviors to look for to detect deception, such as information inconsistency, and some to ignore, such as eye contact, let's take a look in the next section at the various factors that influence our skill at detecting lies when we communicate interpersonally.

At a Glance: Communication While Lying

Here's a review of how several behaviors tend to be affected by one's attempts to deceive. A "+" sign means the behavior usually increases during deception; a "−" sign means it usually decreases. "NC" means the behavior usually doesn't increase or decrease during deceptive acts.

Behavior	Typical Change, If Any
Information inconsistency	+
Speech errors	+
Blinking rate	+
Eye contact	NC
Pupil dilation	+
False smiles	+
Genuine smiles	NC
Vocal pitch	+
Body movement	−

4} Detecting Lies in Different Contexts

Many characteristics of people or communication situations can make it either harder or easier for us to tell we're being lied to. Two examples are how familiar we are with the other person and how interactive our conversation is. We'll review a number of these characteristics in this section. I hope you can use this information in your interpersonal communication to improve your skill at detecting deceit.

> *Falsehood is invariably the child of fear.*
>
> —Aleister Crowley (1875–1947) British author

Familiarity Affects Detection Success

Is it easier to detect deception when you are talking to strangers or to friends? On one hand, you might be tempted to say "friends" because you know them better. You know how they normally speak and act, so it's easier to tell when they're not being themselves. On the other hand, because the truth bias is stronger for friends than for strangers,[48] we are more likely to believe what we hear from a friend than from a stranger. Thus, we are more likely to scrutinize strangers than friends for signs of deception. Depending on our perspective, then, both answers are feasible. So, which one is correct?

To try to solve this puzzle, communication scientists conducted an experiment in which participants made false or misleading statements to another individual.[49] Half of the participants were paired with a close friend, and the other half with a stranger. After the conversations were concluded, the friends and the strangers were asked to report how truthful they thought the participants were being. The results showed that people were more accurate at detecting deception by strangers than by friends. In other words, the participants lied more successfully to their friends than they did to strangers. The researchers concluded that the truth bias prevented friends from noticing when they were being deceived.

Expressive People Are Better Liars

You probably know people who are very expressive; they tend to be outgoing, uninhibited, and very demonstrative of their emotions. According to several studies, expressive people are more successful at deception than unexpressive people are, for at least two reasons.[50] First, expressive people tend to be more aware and in better control of their own communication behaviors than unexpressive people. Therefore,

the conversational style they adopt when they are lying may appear to be more fluent and normal.[51]

Second, expressive communicators tend to be more aware of other people's behaviors, so they may be more skilled at anticipating a hearer's suspicion and correcting their behavior to allay those suspicions.[52] This doesn't necessarily mean that expressive people lie *more often* than unexpressive people.[53] It does mean they tend to be better at it when they do lie.

Culture Matters, but Only Sometimes

We've seen that the average person detects deception only about 55% of the time. Most studies of detection ability, however, have involved speakers and listeners who share the same cultural background. What if you're listening to someone whose culture is different from yours? Would that make it harder to detect deception? Common sense suggests it would, because you may not be familiar with another culture's communication practices. If you're not familiar with the way a person behaves when communicating under normal circumstances, then how can you identify changes in those behaviors when the person is lying? In line with this assumption, an early research study concluded that people are, in fact, much more accurate at detecting deception *within* cultures than *between* cultures.[54]

In this study, however, participants were required to judge deception solely on the basis of visual cues. They watched videotapes of two people in a conversation, but they were unable to hear what these people were saying. As a result, they were unable to detect information inconsistency or listen for vocal cues. Rather, they had to base their judgments entirely on the behaviors they could see.

The researchers later repeated the study, but this time they allowed the participants to hear what the speakers were saying. When they did so, they discovered that the participants were equally able to detect deception by speakers of their own culture and speakers of other cultures.[55] We can likely conclude from these results that cultural differences can affect our ability to detect deception, but only when we have limited access to what the speaker is saying. In normal face-to-face conversation, culture appears to matter less.

Motivation Doesn't Always Help

Suppose you felt you had to lie but the consequences of getting caught were severe (such as being expelled from school or going to jail). You'd probably be highly motivated to lie successfully—but would that help or hurt you? We often perform better when we're highly motivated. According to social psychologist Bella DePaulo, however, this observation doesn't apply to lying. Her hypothesis, called the **motivation impairment effect,** maintains that when people are engaged in high-stakes lies, their motivation to succeed will backfire by making their nonverbal performance less believable than normal.[56]

Motivation impairment effect A perspective offering that motivation to succeed in a lie will impair a deceiver's verbal performance, making the lie less likely to be believed.

Why does this happen? The answer is that when the consequences of getting caught in a lie are severe, we experience a great deal of nervous energy, which we have to control if we are to succeed in being deceptive. The harder we try to control our nervous energy, however, the more rigid, insincere, and unnatural we can end up looking and sounding. Put simply, when people tell high-stakes lies, their motivation to succeed ultimately will impair their success.[57] By contrast, because low-stakes lies don't produce the same degree of nervous arousal, DePaulo's theory does not predict that motivation to succeed will backfire when people attempt a low-stakes lie.

The motivation impairment effect explains that when people attempt high-stakes lies, their motivation to succeed can backfire, causing them to behave nervously and therefore appear dishonest.

Suspicion May Not Improve Detection Ability

When we feel suspicious about what someone is telling us, we tend to scrutinize that person's behavior and message more than usual. Therefore, it seems logical to assume we are better able to detect deception when we're suspicious than when we aren't. That doesn't seem to be the case, however. Research tells us that even though suspicion causes people to *think* they're being lied to, it doesn't always make them any better at spotting deception.[58] In fact, some studies have shown that suspicion can actually make people *worse* at detecting lies, not better.[59]

One reason suspicion might impair our detection ability is suggested by interpersonal deception theory, proposed by scholars David Buller and Judee Burgoon.[60] Interpersonal deception theory argues that skilled liars can detect when people are suspicious and then adapt their behavior to appear more honest. Suppose, for instance, that Eliah's new doctor asks him how often he exercises. To make a good impression, Eliah exaggerates, saying he swims at least four times a week. He can immediately tell his doctor is suspicious of his answer, so he adapts his behavior to make himself appear honest. He makes certain he is speaking with a normal vocal pitch and without committing excessive speech errors. He avoids nervous laughter, false smiles, and excessive blinking. He makes sure he is moving and gesturing normally. Because he noticed his doctor's suspicion, that is, he could make certain he was communicating in ways that signal honesty rather than deception. As a result, his doctor eventually believed Eliah, even though he was being dishonest.

Some deceivers are skilled at detecting suspicion and then adapting their behavior to avoid detection. In the 2002 film, *Catch Me If You Can*, Leonardo DiCaprio plays Frank Abagnale, a con man who impersonated a doctor, airline pilot, attorney, and teacher before being captured by authorities.

Another reason why suspicion can reduce our ability to detect deception is what researchers call the *Othello error.* This error occurs when a listener's suspicion makes a truthful speaker appear to be lying even though she or he isn't. Let's say Maggie is explaining to her nurse practitioner that her four-year-old son bruised the side of his face by falling off his bed. Because the nurse treats physically abused children frequently, she has suspicions about the truthfulness of Maggie's account. Maggie senses the nurse's suspicions and gets nervous and flustered. She begins to fidget, to make speech errors, and to use false smiles. Noticing these behaviors, the nurse concludes that Maggie is lying.

Maggie, however, is being completely truthful. She looks and sounds deceptive only because the nurse's obvious suspicion has made her nervous. In this instance, the nurse has been inaccurate in detecting deception—not by believing a lie, but by failing to believe the truth.[61]

Noninteractive Contexts Are Best for Detection

Suppose Stan's regional manager directed him to file a report about the company's quarterly earnings with the state auditor's office. He told Stan that the report wasn't due for six weeks, but that it needed to be filed by the deadline or the company would incur financial penalties. With so much time before the deadline, Stan kept putting the assignment aside, focusing on more pressing projects. By the time he remembered it, it was three days overdue.

Interactive context A context for communicating in which participants can see and/or hear each other and react to each other in real time (e.g., face-to-face conversation, telephone conversation).

Fearing that his negligence might cost him his job, Stan chooses to lie to his manager about why the report was late. He has several options for how to deliver his lie: He could do it in person, over the telephone, by leaving a voice mail message, or by sending an e-mail. Which option gives him the best chance for success? On the one hand, we might say that an **interactive context,** such as a face-to-face or telephone conversation, helps Stan the most, because he can watch and listen for signs of suspicion from his manager and then adapt his behavior accordingly. On the other hand, a **noninteractive context,** such as voice mail or e-mail, may be best, because it gives Stan the most control over his message.

Noninteractive context A context for communicating in which the participants cannot react to each other in real time (e.g., voice mail message, e-mail message).

Communication researchers have found that lies are more likely to succeed in an interactive context than in a noninteractive one—but only when the speaker is lying to a stranger.[62] Apparently, interacting directly with speakers makes people more likely to believe what those speakers are saying. One possible explanation for this finding is that interactivity helps create a sense of connection with someone else that is lacking in noninteractive contexts. In addition, when people are engaged in conversations, they pay more attention to their own communication behaviors than to the behaviors of

When people communicate with strangers, they are less likely to be caught lying if they're talking face to face than if they're exchanging e-mail messages. Interactivity heightens our truth bias, but only with strangers. With friends, the mode of communication doesn't matter.

others. Consequently, listeners might be less likely to notice any signs of deception displayed by the speaker.[63]

If the speaker and the hearer are already friends, however, then the interactivity of the context doesn't seem to matter. In these cases, lies are equally successful in interactive and noninteractive contexts. Perhaps if friends already feel an emotional connection with each other, then communicating in interactive contexts no longer provides an advantage.

Familiarity, expressiveness, culture, motivation, suspicion, and interactivity certainly aren't the only characteristics that influence our detection skills, but each of these factors can play an important role in our ability to detect deception successfully.

Although deception is relatively common in interpersonal communication, it can sometimes cause great distress, just as it did for Kendra in the chapter opening story. When deception is discovered in a personal relationship, it can lead to conflict and to feelings of anger and betrayal. We often find it difficult to forgive people who have lied to us, let alone to trust them again.

In this chapter, you've been introduced to many skills for detecting interpersonal deception, and previous chapters have introduced you to skills for managing conflict and maintaining your interpersonal relationships. Armed with these skills, you may find it easier to respond to the emotional distress of deception and to repair the emotional damage it can cause.

Learn It: Is it easier to detect deception from strangers or from friends? Why are expressive people better at lying than unexpressive people? How do cultural differences affect our ability to detect deception? What is the motivation impairment effect? How does suspicion affect our ability to detect deception? Are lies easier to detect in interactive or noninteractive contexts?

Try It: Sharpen your deception-detection skills by adopting an attitude of cautiously accepting information, particularly when it comes from highly expressive people. Train yourself to look beyond their expressive behaviors and to question the credibility of what you're hearing.

Reflect on It: When do you feel suspicious of others? With whom would you find it the most difficult to be deceptive?

} Master the Chapter {

Section 1} The Nature of Interpersonal Deception (p. 409)

I. The Nature of Interpersonal Deception
   A. What is deception?

- Deception occurs when a speaker knowingly and intentionally transmits false information to create a false belief in the hearer.

B. **The basic elements of deception**
1. You aren't lying if you believe what you're saying is true
2. You aren't lying if you don't intend for others to believe what you're saying
3. You cannot lie to yourself

- Deceptive acts have three basic elements: the speaker knows the information is false, the speaker transmits the information on purpose, and the speaker tries to make the hearer believe that the information is true.

C. **Interpersonal deception is common**
1. Deception is a common component of politeness
2. Deception is especially common when communicating online

- Deception is especially common in the service of politeness and in computer-mediated communication.

Section 2} Deceptive Acts Are Diverse (p. 415)

II. **Deceptive Acts Are Diverse**
A. **Some reasons why people deceive**
1. Some lies benefit the hearer
2. Some lies help you get to know someone
3. Some lies protect your privacy
4. Some lies help you avoid conflict
5. Some lies make you look better
6. Some lies help you avoid punishment
7. Some lies help you protect yourself from distress
8. Some lies help you get revenge on someone
9. Some lies help you hurt someone for no reason
10. Some lies protect you or your livelihood
11. Some lies amuse you

- People have several motives for lying, some of which are benevolent, some of which are malicious, and some of which are benign.

B. **Some deceptive acts are acts of simulation**
1. People can lie through falsification
2. People can lie through exaggeration

- Some deceptive acts are acts of simulation; these include falsification and exaggeration.

C. **Some deceptive acts are acts of dissimulation**
1. People can lie through omission
2. People can lie through equivocation

- Some deceptive acts are acts of dissimulation; these include omission and equivocation.

Section 3} Communication Behaviors and Deception (p. 419)

III. **Communication Behaviors and Deception**
A. **Detecting deception is difficult**

- Detecting deception is often very difficult, partly because we often have a truth bias.

B. **Some behaviors are common during acts of deception**
1. False information is often inconsistent
2. Deceivers often commit speech errors
3. Deception often increases vocal pitch
4. Two eye behaviors are associated with lying
5. Liars often use false smiles
6. Many liars use minimal body movement

- Behaviors common during deceptive attempts include information inconsistency, speech errors, increased blinking, pupil dilation, false smiles, increased vocal pitch, and decreased body movement.

IV. Detecting Lies in Different Contexts

A. Familiarity affects detection success

- We are more accurate at detecting deception from strangers than from friends, on average.

B. Expressive people are better liars

- Expressive people are often more successful at lying than unexpressive people.

C. Culture matters, but only sometimes

- Cultural differences appear to matter only when the hearer has limited access to what the speaker is saying.

D. Motivation doesn't always help

- Motivation to succeed at lying doesn't always help, and in the case of high-stakes deception it can actually impair our ability to succeed.

E. Suspicion may not improve detection ability

- Suspicion does not necessarily improve our detection ability.

F. Noninteractive contexts are best for detection

- Detection is higher in noninteractive contexts than in interactive ones, but only for strangers.

Key Terms

Acts of dissimulation

Acts of simulation

Deception

Equivocation

Exaggeration

Falsification

Interactive context

Motivation impairment effect

Noninteractive context

Omission

Truth bias

Discussion Questions

1. Why is it so distressing to find out someone has lied to you?
2. Being polite often involves being deceptive; is deception justified if it is done to spare someone's feelings? What if it is done to spare someone's life?
3. Why can you technically not deceive yourself?
4. In what professions do you think people lie the most? the least?
5. How do you feel when you lie to someone? In what situations are you the most likely to feel nervous? How about guilty?
6. Why do you think most people do so poorly at detecting deception?
7. With which people in your life do you have the strongest truth bias? Is there anyone you would believe *no matter what*?
8. What do you think are the most common things for people to lie about?

Practice Quiz

Multiple Choice

1. Which of the following is *not* a communicative element of deception?
   a. The sender must know the information is false.
   b. The receiver must believe the information is true.
   c. The sender must be transmitting the information on purpose.
   d. The sender must be attempting to make the receiver believe the information.
2. Communicating false information as though it were true is known as which of the following?
   a. · acts of dissimulation
   b. omission
   c. exaggeration
   d. falsification
3. Which of the following is an act of dissimulation?
   a. falsification
   b. exaggeration
   c. equivocation
   d. truth telling
4. Deceivers are more likely than truth tellers to engage in which of the following behaviors?
   a. speech errors
   b. increased vocal pitch
   c. use of false smiles
   d. all of the above
5. The two eye behaviors associated with lying are which of the following?
   a. lack of eye contact and blinking
   b. lack of eye contact and pupil dilation
   c. blinking and pupil dilation
   d. none of the above
6. Which of the following is the best definition of the motivation impairment effect?
   a. a hypothesis that predicts that when individuals are engaged in high-stakes lies, their motivation to succeed backfires by making their nonverbal performance less believable than normal
   b. a situation in which a listener's suspicion makes a truthful speaker appear to be lying even though she or he is not
   c. a hypothesis that predicts that when skilled liars can tell when people are suspicious, they adapt their behavior accordingly
   d. none of the above

7. Which of the following is the best definition of the Othello error?
   a. a hypothesis that predicts that when individuals are engaged in high-stakes lies, their motivation to succeed backfires by making their nonverbal performance less believable than normal
   b. a situation in which a listener's suspicion makes a truthful speaker appear to be lying even though he or she is not
   c. a hypothesis that predicts that when skilled liars can tell when people are suspicious, they adapt their behavior accordingly
   d. none of the above

8. Which of the following is an act of simulation?
   a. exaggeration
   b. omission
   c. equivocation
   d. none of the above

9. Kyra stayed out late and did not finish her report. To avoid being fired, she told her boss that her computer crashed and she lost the report. This is an example of which of the following reasons that people deceive?
   a. to amuse herself
   b. to help her get to know someone
   c. to help her avoid punishment
   d. to protect her privacy

10. Research indicates that when people discover they have been lied to, they are most likely to find out in which of the following ways?
    a. through information provided by a third party
    b. from the deceiver
    c. through physical evidence
    d. none of the above

True/False

11. Deception occurs when a speaker transmits information knowingly and unintentionally for the purpose of creating a false belief in a receiver.
12. You can lie to yourself by making yourself believe information that is not true.
13. A lack of eye contact is a reliable cue for detecting deception.
14. When lying, a person is likely to use minimal body movement.
15. Expressive people are better at deceiving than less expressive people.

Fill in the Blank

16. Lies that have severe penalties for getting caught are known as _____.
17. On average, people can detect lies _____ percent of the time.
18. The _____ occurs because we tend to believe what others tell us.
19. Compared to between cultures, people are much _____ accurate at detecting deception within cultures.
20. Lies are more likely to succeed in _____ contexts, especially when communicating with a stranger.

Answers
Multiple Choice: 1 (b); 2 (d); 3 (c); 4 (d); 5(c); 6 (a); 7 (b); 8 (a); 9 (c); 10 (a); **True/False:** 11 (F); 12 (F); 13(F); 14 (T); 15 (T); **Fill in the Blank:** 16 (high-stakes lies); 17 (55); 18 (truth bias); 19 (more); 20 (noninteractive)

Research Library

Movies

Breach (Drama; 2007; PG-13)

Breach *is based on the true story of Robert Hanssen, a former senior agent for the Federal Bureau of Investigation currently serving a life sentence for selling U.S. intelligence secrets to the former Soviet Union. The movie stars Ryan Phillippe as Eric O'Neill, a computer specialist assigned to work for Hanssen and collect evidence of his illegal activities. In dramatic fashion, the film portrays the consequences of high-stakes deception.*

Liar, Liar (Comedy; 1997; PG-13)

This comedy stars Jim Carrey as Fletcher Reed, a successful attorney and habitual liar whose five-year-old son wishes for his birthday that his father would have to tell nothing but the truth for the next 24 hours. As if his son's wish cast a curse on him, Reed soon discovers he is physically incapable of lying, and his unedited, brutally honest comments offend many. In a humorous way, the movie illustrates how deception often functions as an important social lubricant.

Secrets & Lies (Drama; 1996; R)

This movie follows the story of a black optometrist who decides to locate her birth mother after her adoptive mother passes away. She finally locates her birth mother and discovers that she is timid, neurotic, and white. She also has two grown children, an obstinate daughter and a son with a compulsive and abrasive wife. The theme of the movie is that maintaining a façade of happiness, even if it is deceptive, can be an important defense mechanism in a dysfunctional family.

Books

Ford, C. V. (1999). *Lies! Lies!! Lies!!! The psychology of deceit.* Washington, DC: American Psychiatric Press.

Lieberman, D. J. (1999). *Never be lied to again: How to get the truth in 5 minutes or less in any conversation or situation.* New York: St. Martin's Griffin.

Smith, D. L. (2004). *Why we lie: The evolutionary roots of deception and the unconscious mind.* New York: St. Martin's Press.

Journal Articles

Buller, D. B., & Burgoon, J. K. (1996). Interpersonal deception theory. *Communication Theory, 6,* 203–242.

McCornack, S. A. (1992). Information manipulation theory. *Communication Monographs, 59,* 1–16.

Web Sites

www.truthaboutdeception.com
This Web site offers commentary and advice on how to deal with deception in personal and social relationships.

deception.crimepsychblog.com
This blog, which focuses on applications of psychological research on deception, provides a broad-ranging discussion of interesting deception studies.

12

Emotion

What are emotions?

How do emotions affect interpersonal communication?

In what ways can we manage emotions constructively?

Chan and Jesse

When Chan found out he had lung cancer, he and his best friend, Jesse, were overcome with emotion. Chan felt terrified of what the outcome might be, angry at himself for smoking for so long, and guilty at the thought of leaving Jesse. These emotions took a toll on him physically by making him feel stressed and unable to sleep. Jesse felt overwhelming sadness and anxiety at the possibility of losing a loved one. When Chan's doctor brought them encouraging news about his prognosis, their feelings of anxiety and fear were replaced by relief and optimism, and they both realized that sharing their emotions had brought them closer.

Emotion is a powerful force. When we experience intense emotions, such as the profound sorrow of losing a loved one or the profound joy of reuniting with one, it can seem as though our emotions consume us. In some respects, that's exactly what happens: Our emotions are so connected to our bodies, our minds, and our behaviors that they practically overtake us. Understanding this powerful and often mysterious force can therefore help us to appreciate the enormous role it plays in the way we relate to others.

In this chapter, we'll explore the nature of emotion and examine its relationship to interpersonal communication. We'll discuss:

1} What emotion is and what types of emotion are particularly relevant for interpersonal communication

2} What the defining attributes of emotions are

3} What factors influence the experience and the expression of emotion

4} How you can improve your emotional communication skills

So much of what we say, think, and do is affected by our emotions; yet, we seldom stop to consider what emotions are. We realize that emotions cause us to feel and act in certain ways, but why? In this section, we'll discuss what emotions are, and we'll consider how they are related to moods. We'll then examine specific forms of emotions that are joyful and affectionate, hostile, or sad and anxious, considering their applications to interpersonal communication as we do.

> *There can be no knowledge without emotion.*
>
> —Arnold Bennett (1867–1931)
> British writer

What Is an Emotion?

Emotion
The body's multidimensional response to any event that enhances or inhibits one's goals.

Emotion might seem like the kind of phenomenon you can't really define, but when you feel it, you certainly recognize it. Most of us know that emotions can be powerful, even life-changing, experiences, but what kind of experiences are they, exactly? According to researchers, an **emotion** is *your body's multidimensional response to any event that either enhances or inhibits your goals.*[1] For example, you feel nervous before a final exam because the possibility of failing interferes with your goal of passing it. Doing well on the exam makes you happy because your goal has been met; doing poorly makes you angry or disappointed because your goal has been inhibited. You feel sad when a cherished pet dies because your goal of maintaining a relationship with that pet has been thwarted. You feel jealous when you think your romantic partner has become interested in another person because your goal of having an exclusive relationship with your partner is being hampered. Basically speaking, emotion is your mind and body's way of reacting so that meeting your goals feels good and failing to meet them feels bad.

An emotion is your body's multidimensional response to any event that enhances or inhibits your goals.

Emotion is different from mood. Many people refer to emotions as moods (and vice versa), but moods and emotions are actually different experiences. Whereas an emotion is a response to a specific event (such as passing an exam or losing a pet), a **mood** is a feeling that has no specific identifiable cause.[2] You might feel as though you're in a good or a bad mood for no obvious reason. If you can identify the reason you feel good or bad, then you're probably experiencing an emotion, rather than a mood. Moods also are more persistent, often lasting for days or weeks at a time.[3] In contrast, most emotions are relatively short-lived.

Mood A feeling, often prolonged, that has no identifiable cause.

Communication scientist Laura Guerrero suggests that most emotions fit one of three categories: those that are joyful or affectionate, those that are hostile, and those that are sad or anxious.

Emotions come in many forms. Communication scientist and emotion expert Laura Guerrero has suggested that we can understand many emotions by placing them in one of three categories: (1) joyful and affectionate, (2) hostile, or (3) sad and anxious.[4] Let's take a look at some of the specific emotions that constitute each category.

Joyful/Affectionate Emotions: Happiness, Love, Passion, and Liking

What makes you happy? If you're like most people, your personal relationships are high on the list.[5] Feeling connected to others is a source of profound joy for many people, and emotional experiences of joy and happiness play an important role in making those relationships rewarding. In this section, we will look at the emotions of happiness, love, passion, and liking to understand some of the functions they serve in interpersonal communication.

Happiness motivates us to reconnect with people. When we feel happy, many of us want to be around others and share our happiness with them.

Happiness. Of all human emotions, happiness is one of the most easily and universally recognized.[6] **Happiness** is a state of contentment, pleasure, and cheer. People in all known cultures display happiness by smiling, laughing, and being energetic, and they all interpret those behaviors as indicating happiness.[7]

To some extent, happiness begins as an individual experience. When we feel happy, however, our tendency is to approach and reconnect with people.[8] In other words, when people feel happy, they tend to share their joy with others by seeking contact and being emotionally expressive in their interactions.[9] Those behaviors,

Happiness
A state of contentment, joy, pleasure, and cheer.

in turn, often make the other party happy, so that happiness becomes a truly social experience. Research indicates that happiness also contributes to our health and well-being by helping us recover from the harmful effects of stress.[10]

Love and passion. Love can be easier to recognize than to define. One reason is that we experience so many forms of love, including romantic love, love for friends, love for family members, love for God, and love for the self. Love is a remarkably powerful emotion that motivates people to behave in ways they otherwise would not. Love for a romantic partner, for instance, can cause people to quit their jobs, sell their homes, and even move thousands of miles to be together. Likewise, people make extraordinary sacrifices out of love for their children or love for God. **Love,** therefore, means caring for, feeling attached to, and feeling committed to someone else.[11]

Love The emotion of caring for, feeling attached to, and feeling committed to someone.

Some forms of love are accompanied by **passion,** an emotion that mixes feelings of joy and surprise with experiences of excitement and attraction for the target of our passion.[12] People often feel passion in the early stages of a romantic or sexual relationship, when behaviors such as kissing, hand-holding, saying "I love you," and interacting sexually are novel. Because passion is partially based on surprise, it is fueled by the novelty of these behaviors.

Passion A secondary emotion consisting of joy and surprise, plus experiences of excitement and attraction for another.

Passion mixes the emotions of joy and surprise with feelings of excitement and attraction. In this way, it helps bring people together at the start of a romantic relationship. It often fades over time, however, as it's replaced with feelings of long-term love.

For the same reason, however, passion also tends to fade as people get to know each other better.[13] In this way, passion acts to bring people together initially so they can discover and explore whatever feelings they have for each other. If they develop genuine love for each other, their relationship can develop and grow even after the experience of passion has faded away.[14]

Love and passion are examples of *social emotions,* which means they typically arise out of our social interactions. That is, social emotions are usually directed at specific people or other social entities (such as a pet or a deity). When you love, you love *someone* in particular. When you feel passion, it is for *someone* specific. Another example of a social emotion is liking, which we'll learn about next.

Liking. You might consider liking to be simply a less intense form of love but liking and loving actually are different emotions. Is there anyone you would say you love but don't really like? If so, then you already have an understanding of the difference in these experiences.

Whereas love means feeling attachment, caring, and commitment to someone, **liking** is a product of your overall evaluation of another person.[15] If you enjoy being around someone and generally view her personality and behavior positively, then you probably like that person even if you wouldn't say you love her. Likewise,

Liking A positive overall evaluation of another person.

if there's someone you love and feel a sense of commitment to but don't really enjoy spending time with, then you probably love that person even though you don't particularly like him.

When we feel liking for others, we often display that emotion using high immediacy behaviors such as smiling, touch, and standing or sitting close to them. We also tend to share activities, such as going to movies, playing sports, or shopping together, and we make an effort to spend time with them because we enjoy their company.[16]

Happiness, love, passion, and liking are different emotions, but they all motivate us to seek the company of other people.

Although happiness, love, passion, and liking are distinct emotions, they often have similar effects on interpersonal communication. Specifically, they all motivate us to seek the company of others.[17] When we feel happy, we often want to share our happiness with friends and family members by interacting with them. When we like, love, or feel passionate about someone, we enjoy being around that person, and we often feel unsatisfied when we're apart. In this way, joyful, affectionate emotions all act to enhance interpersonal communication by drawing us closer to the people we care about.

Hostile Emotions: Anger, Contempt, Disgust, Jealousy, and Envy

Joyful, affectionate emotions are positive experiences. As we all know from experience, however, there are occasions in our relationships when more unpleasant emotions become aroused. In this section, we'll look at five hostile emotions that are common in interpersonal relationships and can be destructive if they aren't managed properly: anger, contempt, disgust, jealousy, and envy.

Anger. **Anger** is an emotional response to perceiving that you have been wronged in some way. If another driver cuts you off in traffic, if you get a lower final grade than you feel you deserve, or if your spouse forgets your anniversary, you'll likely feel some measure of anger, whether it be mild annoyance or outright rage. When we feel angry, our tendency is to attack or enact revenge on whoever we perceive has wronged us.[18] That's why the communication of anger includes behaviors such as yelling, throwing objects, making unpleasant facial expressions, or even physically attacking the other person.[19]

Anger An emotional response to being wronged.

A particularly dangerous situation arises when the motivation to attack strikes someone while he or she is driving. This emotional response can lead to aggressive, violent behaviors that researchers call *road rage.* (See the "Dark Side" box on page 439.) As you might imagine, such behaviors are not the most productive ways of managing anger. We will discuss some skills for managing and expressing emotions productively later in this chapter.

Just as experiencing happiness can enhance our well-being, research indicates that anger can be harmful to our health. Several studies have shown that the stress of feeling and expressing anger puts people at elevated risk for coronary heart disease,[20] other heart problems,[21] circulatory disorders,[22] and stroke.[23] Other research has reported that people who are unable to control their anger have weakened immune systems[24] and take longer to heal from wounds[25] compared with people who manage their anger in more positive ways.

Not only do we experience anger toward others, but we also feel angry with ourselves at times. In the chapter opening story, Chan was angry with himself for having smoked for so many years, because he believed his smoking habit contributed to his lung cancer. Self-directed anger can be frustrating and can cause us to punish ourselves or put

The Dark Side of Interpersonal Communication
Anger on the Highway: The Problem of Road Rage

We all get angry from time to time. In most cases, anger doesn't lead to violent behavior. If we become violent while we are behind the wheel of a car, however, the results can be devastating. Researchers use the term *road rage* to describe aggressive or violent behavior by drivers, including excessive speeding, cutting others off in traffic, making threats against or obscene gestures to other drivers, and, in extreme cases, shooting other drivers or hitting them with your car. Some scientists believe that people are more likely to respond to anger with aggressive behavior when they're driving a car than when they're doing other activities because of the stresses of driving and because we may subconsciously think of other drivers' behaviors as personal threats against or insults to us.

Who engages in road rage? It might surprise you to learn that women and men do so equally often. It's most common among drivers under the age of 25, but it's not uncommon among middle-aged people. In the United States,

incidents of road rage are more common in the South and the West than in other parts of the country, but they occur to some extent almost everywhere. Experts believe that more vigilant law enforcement and driver education programs focusing on road rage may help to address the problem.

Road rage interacts with interpersonal communication in several ways. First, behaving aggressively while driving can spark interpersonal conflict with your passengers, especially if they perceive that you're overreacting or putting them in danger. Second, if you have relatives or close friends in the car with you, they can help you stay calm during situations when you might feel road rage. Finally, people often share their stories as victims of road rage with others in social contexts, providing them a way to bond through their similar experiences.

Ask Yourself:

- Why do people frequently seem more prone to anger

when they're driving than at other times?

- Have you ever experienced rage from another driver? If so, how did you react?

From Me to You:

- When another driver's behavior makes you angry, responding aggressively can feel very satisfying in the moment. Acting on your rage is almost never your best option, however, particularly when you're behind the wheel. If another driver is behaving aggressively toward you, take a deep breath and resist the temptation to fight back. Think of your loved ones and how they would feel if you were hurt. Remember that your anger is only temporary and will quickly disappear if you focus your attention on something more positive.

Sources: James, L. (2000). Congressional testimony (1997). Aggressive driving and road rage: Dealing with emotionally impaired drivers. Available online at: http://www.aloha.net/~dyc/testimony.html; Overberg, P. (1999, March/April). Debunking a 'trend.' *Columbia Journalism Review*, 37.

ourselves down. Self-anger can also be useful, however, if it motivates us to change our behaviors for the better.

Contempt. Contempt leads you to feel that you're better than someone else. As you might expect, it is one of the most harmful emotions for personal relationships.[26] People express contempt by insulting or mocking others, putting others down, belittling or making fun of others, and signaling that the other person is stupid or incompetent.[27] Those actions send messages of judgment, disapproval, and disrespect. Research shows that they can trigger a cycle of negative behavior within relationships. Studies by psychologist John Gottman have found that expressions of contempt from one romantic partner often lead the other to withdraw and become distant, which can leave conflicts unresolved and put the couple at increased risk of breaking up.[28]

Jon Stewart is known for using sarcasm and contempt in a humorous way. In personal relationships, however, contempt often triggers a cycle of negative behavior and distress.

Disgust a feeling of revulsion in reaction to something offensive.

Disgust. **Disgust** is the feeling of revulsion you experience when confronted with something you find offensive or repellent.[29] Perhaps it's a foul odor that causes your stomach to churn, or perhaps it's a message or an image that profoundly offends you. In either case, disgust provokes a strong emotional and physical reaction that motivates you to avoid, reject, or expel whatever is disgusting you.[30] Many researchers believe disgust developed as an instinctive reaction to prevent us from consuming food that is rancid or unclean.[31] If you feel disgusted at the thought of drinking sour milk or eating bacteria-ridden meat, for instance, that emotional response probably protects you from the physical harm that could result if you ate those foods.

How is this relevant to interpersonal communication? The answer is that people can feel the same type of repulsion when they are confronted with others whose values, beliefs, or behaviors they abhor.[32] Their disgust often causes them to avoid interacting with such people and even to avoid artifacts they feel represent them. Researchers have found, for instance, that most U.S. Americans are unwilling to put on a sweater if they believe it was once worn by a convicted murderer.[33] The connection between people's disgust for the murderer and their rejection for his or her sweater is so strong, in fact, that most people remain unwilling to wear the sweater even if it has been completely unraveled and re-knit.[34]

Jealousy. Many people use the term *jealousy* interchangeably with the term *envy*, or they say that they're jealous when they really mean they're envious. Jealousy and envy actually are two different emotions. We experience envy when we want what another person has. For instance, you might feel envious of a friend's new condo or your brother's new motorbike. **Jealousy** occurs when people feel that the existence or the quality of an important relationship is threatened by a third party.[35] You might feel jealous when you see your romantic partner flirting with someone else, for example.

Jealousy The perception that the existence or the quality of an important relationship is being threatened by a third party.

The experience of jealousy mixes three emotions: fear (that your relationship is being threatened), anger (at the people who are threatening it), and sadness (at the thought of losing your relationship). Although we may associate jealousy primarily with romantic relationships, we can experience it within the context of other important relationships as well. For instance, we may feel jealous if a close friend begins spending time with a new friend, even though we don't usually think of friendship as an exclusive relationship.[36] What matters in that situation is that we consider our relationship with our friend to be important. We tend not to react with jealousy when unimportant relationships are threatened.

Envy. As we just discussed, **envy** occurs when we want what another person has.[37] You may be envious of the attention your sibling gets from your family, the kind of car your manager drives, or the great job your friend has. We may envy one person's wealth, another person's intelligence, and another person's physical attractiveness

Envy The desire for something another person has.

because we want those attributes for ourselves. As these examples illustrate, envy involves comparing ourselves with others and perceiving that we come up short in the comparison.[38] As you might guess, however, and as research confirms, we feel envious only when the object of our comparison is highly relevant to us. You'll envy another person's car, for instance, only if having a nice car is important to you.[39]

By itself, envy isn't always negative. It can, in fact, be a good motivator. Envying another person's physique might motivate you to exercise more often. Envying someone else's income could motivate you to do well in school or start your own business.[40] The problem is that we sometimes harm or impede the people we envy. For instance, Collette's envy at her roommate's new promotion and higher salary leads her to try to get her roommate in trouble at work. She frequently calls and stops by the bank where her roommate works because she knows these actions annoy the bank manager and reflect poorly on her roommate. Instead of trying to improve her own work performance, Collette tries to sabotage her roommate's career. As this example illustrates, envy can cause people to harm other people, and in the process they can harm their relationships with those people.

Like joyful, affectionate emotions, hostile emotions influence the ways we communicate interpersonally. In contrast to joyful emotions, hostile emotions are often unpleasant and challenging for relationships. Anger leads us to attack or to seek revenge. Contempt leads us to put others down, and disgust motivates us to avoid them. Jealousy motivates us to attack a perceived rival, and envy can encourage us to harm those we envy. Regardless of their negative outcomes for relationships, however, these emotions are normal aspects of the human experience. Just as it is normal to feel joy or love, it is also entirely normal to feel anger, contempt, disgust, jealousy, and envy from time to time. What matters for interpersonal communication is how we manage these emotions when we feel them. We will address constructive ways of managing emotions in Section Four of this chapter.

Sad/Anxious Emotions: Sadness, Depression, Grief, Fear, and Social Anxiety

Hostile emotions are unpleasant and often motivate people to hurt others in some way. Sad and anxious emotions are no less unpleasant than hostile emotions. In contrast to hostile emotions, however, they typically prompt us to withdraw instead of attack. That is, when we experience sad, anxious emotions we often shut ourselves off from other people. In this sense, then, sad and anxious emotions can be just as problematic for relationships as hostile emotions. In this section, we will look at five types of sad/anxious emotions: sadness, depression, grief, fear, and social anxiety.

Sadness and depression. **Sadness,** which means feeling unhappy, sorrowful, and discouraged, is most often the result of some form of loss. Indeed, two of the most common causes of sadness are the loss of a person and the termination of a relationship.[41] For instance, we would feel sad about the death of a close friend but also about losing our relationship with a loved one because of Alzheimer's disease. We sometimes even feel sadness at the thought of a *potential* loss, as Jesse did in the chapter opening story. Like our displays of happiness, expressions of sadness are highly similar across cultures. They tend to include frowning, crying, disengaging from routine activities, and speaking quietly, slowly, and without energy.[42]

Sadness
Emotion involving feeling unhappy, sorrowful, and discouraged, usually as a result of some form of loss.

Sad and anxious emotions often motivate us to withdraw from social interaction and shut others out.

Some people think of depression as simply an extreme state of sadness, but the two are quite different. Sadness is a normal emotional response to loss, and although it is often painful, it is relatively short-lived. By contrast, clinical **depression** is a medically diagnosed physical illness that can linger for months or even years and is associated with symptoms such as excessive fatigue, insomnia, significant changes in weight, feelings of worthlessness, and recurring thoughts of suicide or death.[43] Whereas people are typically sad about specific events, they can be depressed for no apparent reason.

Suffering from clinical depression can be profoundly debilitating and can lead to job loss, divorce, social isolation, and strained relationships with family and friends.[44] Fortunately, there are several ways of treating depression, including antidepressant medications and various forms of counseling and psychotherapy.[45] Exercising[46] and keeping a journal[47] have also been shown to help individuals suffering from depression.

Grief. When a loss is profound (such as the loss of a loved one), we experience sadness as **grief.** According to researchers, grief is not an isolated emotional experience so much as it is an emotional *process* of dealing with a terrible loss.[48] Therapists have suggested that the grieving process is made up of five steps. The first step, *denial,* means pretending the loss didn't occur and everything is fine. In the next step, *anger,* the grieving person is furious with whoever inflicted the loss, even if that person has passed away. The third step, *bargaining,* means offering deals with a higher power to restore what was lost (such as promising to live differently if God will take away the loss). The fourth step is called *depression,* and although it does not necessarily mean suffering from clinical depression, it entails feeling withdrawn or "numb." The final step, *acceptance,* occurs when the anger, sadness, and mourning have tapered off and the person accepts the reality of the loss.[49] Although each of these steps is a normal part of the grieving process, not every grieving person experiences all five steps or goes through them in order.

Fear. **Fear** is your mind and body's reaction to perceived danger. Many people fear heights, enclosed spaces, snakes, or guns, for instance, because of the perceived dangers of falling, being trapped, being bitten, or being shot.[50] Fear causes immediate changes in our body that are largely controlled by a cluster of neurons in the brain called the *amygdala.*[51] When we experience fear, the amygdala causes our heart rate and breathing rate to go up, the pupils of our eyes to dilate, and our stress hormones to be elevated.[52] These physiological changes make us more aware of the potential threat and give us extra energy to respond to it.[53] The amygdala sometimes also causes us to become tense, or "freeze up." This response temporarily immobilizes the body, giving us a chance to assess the danger before reacting to it.[54] The purpose of fear, therefore, is to keep us safe from harm. When we experience fear, our tendency is usually to withdraw from the situation and protect ourselves, at least long enough to figure out what the danger is and how we can best deal with it.

Depression A physical illness involving excessive fatigue, insomnia, changes in weight, feelings of worthlessness, and/or thoughts of suicide.

Grief The emotional process of dealing with profound loss.

Fear The mind and body's reaction to perceived danger.

Amygdala

Fear causes immediate changes in our body that are largely controlled by a cluster of neurons in the brain called the amygdala.

Social anxiety Fear of not making a good impression on others.

Social anxiety. From time to time, many people experience **social anxiety,** which is, the fear of not making a good impression on others.[55] Perhaps you're meeting your romantic partner's family for the first time and you worry that they won't like you; or, you fret about the impression you'll make on your first day at a new job. Maybe you're just afraid you might mess up on a presentation you have to give in class. Each of those situations is a form of social anxiety, and the behavioral tendency associated with social anxiety is to hide or avoid the situation. Feeling social anxiety from time to time is normal. When it becomes more chronic and starts to interfere with daily life, it may be a mental health condition known as *social anxiety disorder.*[56] Unlike routine social anxiety, social anxiety disorder often requires some combination of psychotherapy and medication to treat.

Experiencing sadness, depression, grief, fear, or social anxiety often makes us want to withdraw from social interaction, for at least two reasons. In the cases of sadness, depression, and grief, we may avoid others—or, at least, limit our interactions with others—because we need time alone to deal with our emotion. By contrast, when we feel fearful or socially anxious, withdrawing from others can help us feel protected and safe. When we perceive that others are experiencing sad or anxious emotions, however, we often want to interact with them *more,* to convey our care and concern. In such cases, it's important to remember that others may need time to themselves, just as we might if we were in the same situation.

Emotions are indeed powerful and complex experiences that affect us both personally and interpersonally. In this chapter, we'll explore the many factors that influence how we feel and express emotions. We'll also learn how to manage our emotions in a productive manner.

Learn It: What is an emotion, and how is it different from a mood? How are love and liking different? What's the difference between jealousy and envy? When do people experience grief?

Try It: Interacting with someone who is depressed can be challenging if you don't understand the nature of depression. The next time you encounter someone you know has been diagnosed with clinical depression, resist the urge to ask *why* the person is depressed or to encourage him or her to "get over it." Remember that depression isn't just a bad mood. Rather, it's a physical illness and should be treated as such.

Reflect on It: When do you feel contempt or disgust? What experiences cause you fear?

2} The Nature of Emotion

We humans experience a broad range of emotions. Although every emotion is distinct, we can understand emotions better by examining their common characteristics. In this section, we'll learn that:

- Emotions are multidimensional.
- Emotions vary in valence and intensity.
- Emotions come in primary and secondary forms.
- Sometimes emotions are meta-emotions.

Emotions Are Multidimensional

We call emotions multidimensional because every emotion has several components. Specifically, there are physiological, cognitive, social, and behavioral elements to each emotion. In this section, we will look briefly at each of these elements.

Emotions are physiological. Suppose you're at home waiting for your friend Simone, whom you've invited for dinner, to arrive. When she's 15 minutes late, you start to wonder if she's okay, but you conclude that the rush-hour traffic is slowing her down. After an additional half hour passes, you begin to fidget and feel tense, so you try calling her on her cell phone. When she doesn't answer, you start getting a sick feeling in your stomach, and you notice that you're breathing more heavily than normal. Then, when you finally see her pull into your driveway, you immediately begin to feel relaxed as your body returns to its normal state.

When we experience emotions, particularly intense ones, our physiological systems react in patterned, predictable ways. Fear, for instance, usually causes your heart to beat faster, your breathing rate to increase, and your pupils to dilate. Your adrenal gland elevates the stress hormone cortisol, which increases your blood sugar and suppresses bodily systems (such as your digestive and reproductive systems) that aren't essential for fighting the source of your fear.[57] These physiological responses all put you in a state of "high alert" so you can deal with whatever is causing you fear. Indeed, the main reason emotions such as fear, joy, sadness, and jealousy feel so distinct from one another is that they cause different changes to occur in our bodies.[58]

The specific bodily changes that accompany each emotion serve a purpose. In particular, each emotion causes physiological responses that help the body first to deal with that specific emotion and then to restore itself to a natural, balanced state. The physiological component of emotion is so strong, in fact, that it can be difficult to separate it from the emotion itself. That is, most of us wouldn't be able to say we're truly experiencing joy or surprise or disgust unless we were also experiencing the physiological changes those emotions bring about.

Emotions are cognitive. Although each emotion feels distinct in some ways, different emotions can share some of the same physiological components. For instance, both

passion and fear cause increases in heart rate, breathing rate, and blood pressure. When we experience those reactions, how do we know whether we're feeling fear, passion, or some other emotion entirely? We can identify the true emotion because our mind steps in and puts an emotional "label" on what we're feeling.[59] Emotions, therefore, also have a strong cognitive component.

You probably know this to be true if you've ever found yourself confused about which emotion you're feeling. Let's say you're sitting at the dinner table with your family and find yourself unable to concentrate because you're perspiring, your heart is pounding, and you can barely sit still. There's no obvious reason why you should be feeling this way. You don't feel upset or nervous or especially excited. So your mind begins searching for an explanation. Perhaps you think about how you argued with a co-worker the day before and you think to yourself, "I must be more upset about that than I thought I was." Maybe you wonder if you're anxious about an upcoming job interview and decide for yourself, "I'm obviously feeling stressed about that." Those are just two examples of how your mind makes inferences about your emotions. You notice how you're feeling physically, and your mind uses the available information to identify the emotion you must be feeling.

Action tendencies
Biologically based motives toward specific behavioral responses to emotions.

Emotions are behavioral. In addition to being physiological and cognitive events, emotions include a behavioral component. Specifically, they have **action tendencies,** which are the specific behaviors each emotion motivates us to engage in.[60] For example, the action tendency associated with fear is self-protection. Therefore, feeling afraid causes us either to withdraw from a frightening situation or to defend ourselves against a threat.[61] If we successfully withdraw from or fight off the source of our fear, then we no longer feel afraid. When we feel angry, our action tendency is to attack or to enact revenge on the party that has wronged us.[62] When we feel joyful, our action tendency is to interact with the people we care about.[63]

Action tendencies relate to the specific behavioral pattern that an emotion motivates us to engage in, but that doesn't mean we'll *always* engage in it. If you feel frightened, for example, you aren't always able to fight the source of your fear or to withdraw from it, even though those are the action tendencies associated with fear. As another example, regardless of how worried you are concerning your upcoming mid-year review with your supervisor, you may not be able to avoid it even if you want to.

Most emotions have action tendencies, which are the behavior patterns they motivate. For instance, fear motivates self-protection, love motivates approach, and anger motivates attack.

Emotions are social and cultural. The emotions we feel in a given situation are shaped, in many ways, by our society's beliefs about that situation.[64] For instance, many people in the U.S. American culture would feel disgust at the thought of eating dogs, cats, snails, snakes, camels, guinea pigs, or rats, even though these animals are routinely eaten in societies around the world.[65] People raised as Hindus would feel similar disgust at the thought of eating hamburger—a staple of the U.S. American diet—because cows are considered sacred in the Hindu religion.[66] There's nothing *inherently* more disgusting about eating one type of animal rather than another. What causes some people to feel disgust and others to feel delight are the social practices and messages they grew up with.

Social differences in emotions can translate into dramatically different behaviors. Suppose you applied to several universities but didn't get into your top choice. If you grew up in a North American society, you'd probably experience feelings of disappointment at being turned down, or maybe even anger at yourself for not having prepared yourself better for the admissions test. In response to those emotions, you might retake the admissions test the following year (in hopes of reapplying to the college of your choice), or accept admission to a less desirable school.

In contrast, if you grew up in Japan, your primary emotion in this situation would likely be shame at the dishonor or disgrace you have brought upon yourself and your family by failing to achieve admission. In fact, one way some people in Japan deal with severe shame is by committing suicide, because the action tendency for shame is to hide or disappear from others.[67] Japan has one of the highest suicide rates in the world, partly because shame is such a large part of Japan's emotional repertoire.[68]

A concise summary of the four basic components of emotion appears in this "At a Glance" box.

At a Glance: Components of Emotion

According to research, emotions share four primary characteristics. This table provides a brief explanation of each one.

Physiological	Emotions cause changes in physiological outcomes, such as blood pressure, breathing rate, and hormone levels.
Cognitive	We cognitively label the physiological outcomes of emotion to identify a particular emotional state.
Behavioral	Emotions have action tendencies that cause us to behave in particular ways.
Social and Cultural	The emotions we experience and express are partially determined by the social and cultural messages and practices we have learned.

Emotions Vary in Valence and Intensity

We now understand that all emotions are multidimensional: An emotional experience is simultaneously physiological, cognitive, behavioral, and sociocultural. Emotions are not, however, composed of the same exact combinations of these four dimensions. In this section, we will look at two variables that make each emotional experience distinctive: valence and intensity.

Emotions vary in valence. Perhaps the most fundamental way to classify emotions is by their **valence,** which means how positive or negative they are. Many emotions, such as joy and love, have a positive valence. As a result, we generally enjoy experiencing them. Other emotions, such as anger, fear, and contempt, have a negative valence. We find these emotional experiences generally unpleasant.

In both cases, the physiological processes that go along with these emotions are largely responsible for *why* they feel good or bad to us. For instance, a positively valenced emotion such as love promotes relaxation, reduces stress, and increases the production of feel-good hormones such as oxytocin or dopamine.[69] In contrast, a negatively valenced

Valence The positivity or negativity of an emotion.

Look at this photograph for a moment and imagine yourself there. Do you feel calm? relaxed? happy? Positive emotions often have the same effect by promoting relaxation, reducing stress, and increasing the production of feel-good hormones.

emotion such as anger promotes anxiety, increases blood pressure, and elevates levels of stress hormones such as cortisol.[70]

We can classify *most* emotions as either positively or negatively valenced, but not all. An exception is the emotion of surprise, which is generally considered to have a neutral valence.[71] When we are happy about a surprise, such as an unexpected gift or a generous raise, we experience surprise positively. When we are unhappy about a surprise, such as a lower grade than we expected or a disappointing movie we had looked forward to, we experience it negatively. In either case, though, it is the *topic* of our surprise—the raise or the bad movie—and not the emotion of surprise itself that creates the positive or negative valence.

Emotions vary in intensity. Besides varying in valence, emotions vary in their intensity or strength. For instance, when Jerome received several voice mail messages from the loan officer at his bank, he felt anxious about what it might mean, because he had missed a couple of payments on his mortgage. When he called the loan officer and was asked to come back in right away, Jerome felt worried about what the news would be. Finding out that the bank had decided to foreclose on his home made Jerome feel genuinely terrified about where he was going to live. Anxiety, worry, and terror are all forms of the same emotion—fear—but they differ from one another in their intensity. Anxiety is a mildly intense form of fear, worry is a moderately intense form, and terror is a very intense form. Similarly, some experiences might make you annoyed, others might make you mad, and still others might make you furious. Those are all forms of anger, but they differ in their intensity, just as anxiety, worry, and terror do.

When emotional experiences become overly intense, they can be debilitating. That means they impair our ability to function. When you're terrified or furious, for instance, the intensity of your emotions can make it difficult for you to think or behave rationally. It can also inhibit your ability to communicate clearly with others, because your emotions may be overwhelming you. When you find yourself debilitated by the intensity of your emotions, it's important to recognize that you may not be in control of your thoughts or behaviors. In those cases, you should ask for help from someone you trust. The good news is that extreme emotional intensity rarely lasts for very long, so if you have someone who can help you through the emotional experience, you'll soon find that you are no longer debilitated.

Emotions Come in Primary and Secondary Forms

Perhaps you can think of times when you haven't been certain of which emotions you were feeling. One reason you might have been uncertain is that some emotional experiences are mixtures of other emotions. You might have learned about the primary colors—red, yellow, and blue—when you were a child. They're called *primary* because they are not derived from other colors. When you combine them, however, you get secondary colors: Red and blue make purple; blue and yellow make green; yellow and red make orange. In some ways, emotions are the same. Researchers consider particular emotions to be **primary emotions,** meaning they are distinct emotional experiences, not combinations of other emotions.[72]

Primary emotions
Distinct emotional experiences not consisting of combinations of other emotions.

People in every known culture experience joy in response to positive events, such as being reunited with a loved one. Cultural similarity in this and other emotional experiences suggests that emotion is not strongly influenced by culture, but may be more innate.

One important feature of primary emotions is that people experience and express them in fundamentally the same way across cultures. Psychologist Paul Ekman has proposed that six of the emotions we have discussed thus far in this chapter are primary emotions: joy, sadness, anger, fear, surprise, and disgust.[73] How does he know? Because people in a wide range of cultures—including preliterate cultures minimally influenced by the Western world—encode and decode these emotions similarly. (See the "How Do We Know?" box on page 449.)[74] In every known society, for instance, smiling means joy, frowning means sorrow, and a scowl means anger. Researchers have also found that the primary emotions have fundamentally the same causes everywhere.[75] For example, people in all cultures feel surprised when unexpected events happen, joy when good results happen, fear when they believe something bad is about to happen, and sorrow when bad events do occur.

The fact that people experience and express primary emotions similarly across cultures suggests that primary emotions are not strongly influenced by culture. Rather, they may be more innate, which means we're born with the tendency to experience and express primary emotions in particular ways. If so, then primary emotions are likely to be directly affected by biological structures. The body's *limbic system* coordinates how the brain and nervous system regulate emotion and motivation. When you experience a primary emotion, the limbic system—and particularly the amygdala—is actively engaged.[76]

There is *some* cultural variation about which emotions are considered to be primary. Traditional Hindu beliefs propose nine primary emotions, including amusement, sorrow, fear, anger, wonder, perseverance, disgust, serenity, and sexual passion.[77] Traditional Chinese culture also recognizes shame and "sad love" (love for former partners) as primary. For the most part, however, the primary emotions are more similar than different across human cultures.

Primary emotions can combine in various ways to produce **secondary emotions.** A good example is the emotion of jealousy. Let's say you suspect your romantic partner of secretly dating another person. When we perceive that an important relationship is threatened, we tend to feel jealous—but what does jealousy feel like? It is actually a combination of three primary emotions: *anger* directed at your rival or at your partner's behavior, *fear* that your relationship is being threatened, and *sadness* about the possibility of losing your relationship.[78] Many other emotions are also combinations of primary emotions, including remorse (a combination of sadness and disgust), contempt (disgust and anger), and awe (surprise and fear).[79]

Secondary emotions
Emotions composed of combinations of primary emotions.

Referring to these and other emotions as *secondary* doesn't mean they are any less important than the primary emotions. We'll discuss later in the chapter how many secondary emotions play central roles in the ways people communicate within personal relationships. Calling an emotion *secondary* means only that it is made up

{ **How Do We Know?**
Cultural Consistency in Interpreting Emotion Displays }

People around the world interpret facial displays of the basic emotions (happiness, sadness, anger, fear, surprise, disgust) quite similarly. How do we know this? Let's take a look at the efforts of one research team.

Psychologists Paul Ekman and Wallace Friesen have been pioneers in the area of nonverbal communication and emotion. In two studies, they surveyed people from multiple Western and non-Western literate and preliterate cultures, including New Guinea, Sumatra, Turkey, Scotland, Estonia, Hong Kong, Italy, and the United States. They showed participants from each culture photographs of adults performing posed and spontaneous expressions of emotion, and they asked them to indicate which emotion was being displayed in each picture. The researchers found that people from these very diverse cultures interpreted the facial displays of emotion more similarly than would be expected by chance alone.

Ask Yourself:

- On the basis of these findings, would you expect cultures to think and talk about emotion in the same ways, as well as to express it similarly?

- How does your culture reinforce the way you express emotions?

Sources: Ekman, P., & Friesen, W. V. (1975). *Unmasking the face: A guide to recognizing emotions from facial clues.* Englewood Cliffs, NJ: Prentice-Hall; Ekman, P., Friesen, W. V., O'Sullivan, M., Chan, A., Diacoyanni-Tarlatzis, I., Heider, K., Krause, R., LeCompte, W. A., Pitcairn, T., Ricci-Bitti, P. E., Scherer, K., Tomita, M., & Tzavaras, A. (1987). Universals and cultural differences in the judgments of facial expressions of emotion. *Journal of Personality and Social Psychology, 53,* 712–717.

of a combination of primary emotions, just as a secondary color such as purple is composed of a combination of primary colors (red and blue).

Sometimes Emotions Are Meta-Emotions

Do you enjoy watching scary movies? Have you ever been embarrassed because you felt jealous of someone else? Have you felt excited about being in love, or guilty that you don't feel sad enough when tragedy struck? If your answer to any of those questions is yes, then you can recall experiencing meta-emotions. You might recall from earlier chapters that meta-communication is communication *about* communication. Similarly, when researchers use the term **meta-emotion,** they are referring to emotion *about* emotion.[80] If you experience joy because of the controlled fear induced by a scary movie, for instance, you are feeling one emotion (joy) about another (fear). Your joy, therefore, is a meta-emotion. If you feel embarrassed about your jealousy, excited about your love, or guilty about your lack of sadness, then your embarrassment, excitement, and guilt are all meta-emotions.[81]

Meta-emotion includes how we feel about other people's emotions as well as our own. Perhaps you've been surprised at a co-worker's anger, worried about a friend's depression, or happy about a child's joy. Your surprise, worry, and happiness are meta-emotions, too, even though they are feelings about someone else's emotions rather than your own.

Meta-emotions are important because they help us understand and reflect on the emotions that we or others are experiencing or not experiencing. If I feel guilty about not being sad when a tragic event occurs, then I evidently think I *should* feel sad even though I don't. My guilt, therefore, can cause me to reflect on what the tragedy

Meta-emotion
An emotion about emotion.

means to me, why I'm not feeling sadder about it, and why I believe I should feel sad. In the process, I can come to understand my own emotions better. Similarly, if I feel surprised by a co-worker's anger, my surprise can lead me to consider what emotion I expected the co-worker to have and why he or she reacted with anger instead. As a result of reflecting on my meta-emotions, I may become better attuned to the emotional experiences of others as well as my own.[82]

Learn It: What are examples of the physiological, cognitive, behavioral, and sociocultural dimensions of emotion? What is the difference between an emotion's valence and its intensity? How do you know if an emotion is primary or secondary? What are some examples of meta-emotions?

Try It: The ability to interpret the valence and intensity of emotion displays is important when it comes to interacting with others. Go through some photos in magazines or newspapers that capture expressions of different emotions. For each, determine whether the emotion is positive or negative, and whether it is mild, moderately intense, or very intense. Compare your assessments of valence and intensity with those made by others. This type of practice will help you to recognize emotion displays you encounter in other people.

Reflect on It: When do you have difficulty labeling an emotion you're feeling? What physical changes do you notice when you experience an intensely positive emotion?

3} Influences on Emotional Experience and Expression

Several variables affect how we experience and express emotions. In this section, we'll focus on the influences of cultural background, display rules, technology, emotional contagion, sex and gender, personality, and emotional intelligence.

> *Don't be afraid to feel as angry or as loving as you can, because when you feel nothing, it's just death.*
>
> —Lena Horne (1917–)
> U.S. American singer

Culture

Even though people around the world experience the same range of emotions, cultural practices shape the ways in which we express some emotions. For instance, collectivistic cultures such as India and Japan discourage people from expressing negative emotions toward members of their own culture, but they often condone negative emotions directed at people from other cultures.[83] That pattern is reversed in individualistic cultures such as the United States and Canada, which sometimes discourage the expression of negative emotion toward people from other cultures but often allow it when directed at "insiders."[84]

Even within the United States, cultural groups vary in how they express emotions. For example, Chinese Americans often reflect the traditional Chinese values of moderation and emotional control by being less demonstrative of their positive and negative emotions than Americans of European decent.[85] By contrast, traditional Mexican culture encourages people to express emotions openly, so Mexican Americans

Montesquieu proposed that people are more emotionally expressive in warm climates than in cold climates, and contemporary research has supported this idea. What do you think about this research?

tend to be more demonstrative of emotion, on average, than European Americans.[86]

Geography. One factor that curiously appears to influence cultural differences in emotional expression is geography. In 1748, the French political thinker Charles de Secondat Montesquieu proposed that living in a warm climate would make people more expressive of their emotions than would living in a cold climate.[87] Contemporary research has found that to be the case. In a survey of nearly 3,000 college students from 26 countries, psychologists James Pennebaker, Bernard Rimé, and Virginia Blankenship found that people from southern parts of countries are more emotionally expressive than those from northern regions.[88] Other research has found that, within the United States, people from the South touch each other more frequently than do people from the North.[89]

How do we account for this tendency? Montesquieu explained that warm weather causes the skin to relax, allowing nerve endings to become more exposed to pain, pleasure, and other sensations. He believed this heightened sensitivity made people more attentive to what they were feeling and, therefore, more likely to express it. By contrast, cold weather inhibits the sensitivity of nerves, causing people to be less attentive to various sensations and, therefore, less expressive of what they feel.

Co-cultures. Co-cultures can also affect how we deal with emotions. Some co-cultures encourage people to examine their emotions directly and express them freely. For example, artistic co-cultures, such as a theater group or a community of sculptors, would likely encourage the ability to express and respond to emotions for its value in creating and appreciating these forms of art.

Other co-cultures, however, can discourage people from dealing openly with their emotions. As one example, many military personnel returning from active combat duty avoid seeking treatment for posttraumatic stress disorder because they perceive that the military co-culture stigmatizes such treatment. Posttraumatic stress disorder (PTSD) is an anxiety disorder that some people develop after experiencing severely troubling events, such as combat. In a recent study of soldiers returning to the United States from combat in Iraq and Afghanistan, medical researchers found that as many as 77% of soldiers with signs of PTSD refused to seek treatment, citing their fear of being stigmatized by the military as one of their primary concerns.[90] These results are significant because when PTSD is untreated, it frequently leads to other problems, including drug and alcohol abuse.

Display Rules

Display rules Unwritten codes that govern the ways people manage and express emotions.

Another factor influencing the expression of emotion is what psychologists Paul Ekman and Wallace Friesen call **display rules.**[91] Display rules comprise five unwritten codes that govern the ways people manage and express their emotions, and they vary according to the individual's social situation. The first display rule, *intensification*, means exaggerating your emotion to appear as though you are experiencing it more intensely than you are. For example, you may pretend to be overjoyed about seeing an old acquaintance at an event, when you really find it only mildly pleasant. In that case, you intensify your emotion to make your acquaintance feel good.

The second rule, *de-intensification,* means just the opposite of intensification: downplaying an emotion to appear as though you are experiencing it less intensely than you are. For example, you may be extremely angry with a co-worker for missing a deadline, but in the presence of your supervisor you may decide it's best to seem only mildly annoyed. In that situation, you de-intensify your emotion to be polite or to avoid damaging your colleague's reputation.

The third display rule, *simulation,* means acting as though you're feeling an emotion that you actually aren't experiencing. You may not really care about your neighbor's good news, for instance, but you act happy anyway when you hear about it because you want to appear sensitive and supportive. *Inhibition,* the fourth display rule, is the opposite of simulation: It means acting as though you're indifferent or emotionless when you're actually experiencing an emotion. For example, it may make you jealous to see your romantic partner flirting with someone else, but you choose to act as though it doesn't bother you because you don't want to appear vulnerable in front of the other person.

At a Glance: Emotion Display Rules

Ekman and Friesen proposed that the expression of emotion is partially governed by five display rules. An example of each rule appears below.

Intensification	Acting as though you're furious when you're only mildly annoyed.
De-intensification	Acting as though you're mildly annoyed when you're actually furious.
Simulation	Acting as though you're furious when you are really indifferent.
Inhibition	Acting as though you're indifferent when you are actually furious.
Masking	Acting as though you're furious when you're actually sad.

Finally, the fifth display rule is *masking,* or expressing one emotion when you are actually experiencing a completely different one. You may be sad and nervous when your child leaves home for college, for instance, but you behave as though you're happy, so as not to spoil your child's excitement.

A brief review of Ekman and Friesen's display rules is provided in the "At a Glance" box.

Technology

Many people use technological creations—including an iPod, a Blackberry, or a Facebook page—so often that they may not even realize how these technologies affect the way they experience and express emotions. In fact, technology affects our emotional behaviors, in at least three ways.

First, as we discussed in Chapter 6, text-based communication technologies, such as e-mail and text messaging, don't allow us to see or hear the other person's nonverbal signals of emotion. That is, we can't use his or her facial expressions or tone of voice to figure out what he or she is feeling. As a result, we have created other means of representing emotions within the text. These methods include using emoticons, which are text-based representations of facial expressions, such as :) for a happy face or :/ for a confused face. They also include embedding statements about one's own emotion into the text. Sometimes we do this in abbreviated form, such as writing "j/k," which stands for "just kidding," to convey that we are joking or being sarcastic. In these ways, we compensate for the limitations of channel-lean forms of communication on the expression of emotion.

A second way technology affects our experience and expression of emotion is by increasing our opportunities for sharing emotions. Social networking Web sites, such as Facebook and MySpace, allow us to stay in contact with current friends or to reestablish contact with old ones. In that way, technology provides us with ongoing opportunities to share positive and negative experiences in our lives with others.

In addition, when we go through emotionally challenging experiences, the Internet provides multiple opportunities to discuss those experiences with people who have also gone through them. We can find online chat rooms and support groups for a wide range of emotional experiences, including losing a loved one, dealing with a significant job loss or a serious illness, or having to provide care for an elderly relative. In these sites, people express emotions about their situation to others whom they know can relate to them, and they listen to the experiences of other people. In these ways, the Internet creates many opportunities to share our emotions with other people.

Finally, we experience emotions about technology itself. Perhaps you can recall feeling anxiety or frustration when your computer malfunctioned or your cell phone lost its signal. You may also remember feelings of excitement and joy the first time you encountered a new technology, such as a plasma TV or an iPhone. Research confirms that many people experience intense and genuine emotions when they are interacting with technology.[92] Sometimes, these emotions even affect our relationships with others. You may be able to think of times when you've felt closer to someone while watching television or playing a video game together, for instance.[93] In all these ways, technology influences how we experience emotions and also how we communicate them to others.

Emotional Contagion

Emotional contagion
The tendency to mimic the emotional experiences and expressions of others.

The emotions we feel and express are influenced not only by the culture in which we're raised but also by the emotions being felt and expressed by the individuals around us in any given situation. This process, called **emotional contagion,** involves the tendency to mimic other people's experiences and expressions.[94] Maybe you've noticed, for instance, that when there's one unhappy person in your group, it's not long before *everyone* is unhappy. That's because emotions are "socially contagious." Therefore, being around a cheerful person can make you more cheerful, and being around an anxious person can lead you to feel nervous.[95] Some research has suggested that the emotional contagion effect is more powerful for negative emotions than for positive ones, but other studies have found that positive and negative emotions are equally contagious.[96]

Sex and Gender

Biological sex and gender roles influence both the experience and the expression of emotions. Research shows, for instance, that men are more likely than women to report feeling hostile emotions such as anger across a range of cultures. Conversely, women are more likely than men to report feelings of fear, sadness, shame, and guilt.[97] The consistency of these findings across cultures suggests that these sex differences in emotional experience may have a biological cause.[98]

Women and men also differ in how they express several emotions. Several studies have shown, for example, that women are more likely than men to express positive emotions such as joy[99] and affection.[100] Women are also more likely than men to express sadness and depression.[101] Some studies have found that men are more likely than women to express anger when they feel it,[102] but other research has failed to find such a difference.[103]

Sexual differences in jealousy? One emotion for which women and men may differ in both their experience and their expression is jealousy. Several studies have found

Women and men often differ in their experiences of jealousy. According to several studies, women are more likely to feel jealous when their partners are emotionally unfaithful, but men are more likely to feel jealous when their partners are sexually unfaithful.

that in personal relationships, men are more likely than women to experience *sexual jealousy* (stemming from their partners' sexual interaction with another person), whereas women are more likely than men to experience *emotional jealousy* (stemming from their partners' emotional connection with another person).[104] Research finds this sex difference across cultures,[105] and also indicates that women and men have distinctly different patterns of brain activity when imagining sexual and emotional infidelity.[106] Other research has found that men are more likely than women to express their jealousy through behaviors such as confronting the rival, becoming sexually aggressive or promiscuous with others, wooing the partner back with gifts, or breaking off the relationship.[107] Women, by contrast, tend to express their jealousy through behaviors such as improving their own physical appearance, seeking support from others, demanding increased commitment from the partner, and trying to make the partner jealous himself.[108]

Not all research has supported these sex differences in jealousy, however. Some studies have suggested that they reflect flawed methods of measuring jealousy.[109] Other studies have shown that both sexes experience more anger over sexual infidelity but more hurt over emotional infidelity.[110] Still other research has found that women and men differ from each other when they imagine how they *would feel* if a partner were unfaithful but not when they recall how they *did feel* during an actual experience of infidelity.[111] Researchers are likely to continue studying and debating sex differences in jealousy for some time.[112]

Gender roles and emotional expression. Emotional expression is influenced by gender roles as well as by biological sex. Research indicates that individuals who classify themselves as androgynous (meaning they have both feminine and masculine traits) are more emotionally expressive than are individuals who classify themselves as only highly masculine. This finding appears to be true regardless of the type of emotion being displayed. Androgynous people have also been shown to be more expressive than people who are only highly feminine when it comes to certain emotions, such as happiness, sadness, and disgust.[113]

Why might gender role affect the expression of emotion? Some scholars believe that traditional femininity encourages women to express emotions that help them form relationships (such as happiness) and make them appear vulnerable (such as sadness) but to suppress emotions that make them appear dominant (such as anger). Conversely, traditional masculinity is thought to encourage men to express anger but discourage them from expressing most other emotions.[114] These observations don't mean that women and men always communicate in these ways. They do suggest, however, that traditional gender roles may encourage this type of differentiation.

There is evidence that gender roles affect not only the expression of emotion but the experience of it as well. In one study, for instance, highly feminine women were more likely than highly masculine women to experience negative emotions, including guilt, sadness, pessimism, and self-dislike. By comparison, highly masculine men were more likely than highly feminine men to report experiencing social withdrawal, dissatis-

The experience of emotion is affected by gender as well as sex. One study found that highly masculine men were more likely to experience social withdrawal, dissatisfaction, and suicidal thoughts than highly feminine men were.

A common stereotype, at least in North American cultures, is that women experience emotions more intensely than men do and are more likely to express their emotions than men are. Is this stereotype true?

The answer is yes, and no. In a pair of experiments, psychologists Ann Kring and Albert Gordon looked at whether women and men differ from each other on how emotionally expressive they are and what their physiological responses were to emotional situations. Participants in their studies watched movie clips designed to evoke strong emotional reactions.

Consistent with the stereotype, women in both studies expressed more emotion than men did. They did *not* experience their emotions more intensely than men did, however, which is contrary to the stereotype. In fact, men were more physiologically reactive than women, but only to the emotion of fear—reactions to other emotions did not differ between women and men. It appears, therefore, that women *are* more emotional than men when it comes to expressing emotion, but *not* when it comes to how intensely they experience emotions.

Ask Yourself:

- In what ways do you see the stereotype of emotionally expressive women and inexpressive men portrayed in mainstream media?

- Kring and Gordon's study focused on basic emotions, such as joy, sadness, fear, and disgust. Do you suppose their results would have been different if they had studied relationship-focused emotions such as love, passion, and jealousy?

From Me to You:

- Because men usually aren't as emotionally expressive as women, the media often portray them as emotionally *deficient*. They aren't, though. There are certainly benefits to expressing your emotions, a skill at which many women excel. There is also benefit to controlling your emotions, however, a point that is often lost in pop psychology books and talk-show discussions. Controlling emotions may give people an advantage in social situations. By not letting others know how they feel, those who control their expressions may avoid having their emotions exploited by others. Therefore, don't think of men's lesser expressiveness as a deficit but, rather, as a characteristic that can be advantageous in some circumstances.

Source: Kring, A. M., & Gordon, A. H. (1998). Sex differences in emotion: Expression, experience, and physiology. *Journal of Personality and Social Psychology, 74,* 686–703.

faction, and suicidal thoughts.[115] In both instances, that is, masculine women and feminine men reported more positive emotions.

Personality

In Chapter 3, "Communication and the Self," we explained how personality profoundly influences many aspects of your life. The experience of emotion is no exception. Research suggests that three particular aspects of your personality affect how you experience emotion: agreeableness, extroversion, and neuroticism.[116]

Agreeableness relates to how pleasant, accommodating, and cooperative you are. Compared with the average person, highly agreeable people are happier and are better at managing both stress and emotions in general.[117] They're also more likely than others to use constructive styles for managing conflict and are more willing to "lose" an argument to preserve a relationship with someone else.[118]

Extroversion refers to how sociable and outgoing you are. Extroverted people enjoy social interaction and are often talkative, assertive, and enthusiastic. Extroverted people tend to focus on the positive aspects of other people or situations.[119] Perhaps as a result, extroverted people are happier, on average, than the typical person.[120]

Finally, *neuroticism* is the tendency to think negative thoughts about oneself. Unlike extroverted people, people who are highly neurotic tend to see the worst in situations and to focus much of their attention on negative events.[121] As you might imagine, therefore, they are more likely than others to experience negative emotions such as anger, guilt, anxiety, and depression, and are less likely to report being happy.[122] They also manage their emotions less successfully than do their less neurotic counterparts.[123]

Because they tend to focus on the positive aspects of people or situations, extraverted people are often happier than the average person.

Emotional Intelligence

Emotional intelligence refers to a person's ability to "perceive and accurately express emotions, to use emotion to facilitate thought, to understand emotions, and to manage emotions for emotional growth."[124] A person with high emotional intelligence, therefore, is someone who is aware of her own emotions as well as the emotions of others, and who pays attention to her emotions when making decisions about how to act.[125] Few studies have investigated the association between emotional intelligence and emotional expressiveness. Those that have tend to report that individuals with high emotional intelligence are more likely than those with lower levels to express warmth, affection, and other prosocial emotions.[126] Given what we know about sex differences in emotional expression, it may not surprise you to learn that women score higher than men on measures of emotional intelligence.[127] How emotionally intelligent are you? Take the short quiz in the "Getting to Know You" activity on page 457 to find out.

Emotional intelligence The ability to perceive and understand emotions, use emotions to facilitate thought, and manage emotions constructively.

Several studies have also found that emotional intelligence is an asset not only in personal relationships but also in business. For instance, salespeople with high emotional intelligence generate more sales than those with lower emotional intelligence, regardless of whether they are selling insurance,[128] cosmetics,[129] or consulting services.[130] Using emotional intelligence as a criterion for hiring or promoting people to managerial positions appears to increase their success.[131] Moreover, research suggests that training existing managers to be more emotionally intelligent can improve productivity and decrease employee complaints.[132]

One condition that inhibits emotional intelligence is *alexithymia,* a personality trait characterized by a relative inability to understand, process, and describe emotions.[133] Studies indicate that the prevalence of alexithymia in the general population is approximately 5–9% and that it is equally common among women and men.[134] Those with alexithymia do not understand their own emotions and often seem stone-faced, distant, and unconcerned with other people's feelings.[135] As a result, they may avoid developing emotionally close interpersonal relationships.[136] For people in established

Getting to Know You
How Emotionally Intelligent Are You?

Take a look at the following statements, and indicate how much you agree or disagree with each statement by writing a number between 1 and 10. 1 means you completely disagree, and 10 means you completely agree. When you're done, add up your scores.

1. _____ I think about and reflect on my emotions.
2. _____ I can express my emotions to others.
3. _____ I understand the causes and effects of my emotions.
4. _____ I use my emotions to improve my relationships.
5. _____ I am able to experience both positive and negative feelings.
6. _____ I can accurately identify the emotions other people are feeling.
7. _____ I know the difference between emotions and moods.
8. _____ I can reorganize my thoughts on the basis of what I'm feeling.
9. _____ I understand how emotions change over time.
10. _____ I can manage my own emotions effectively.

Your total score should range from 10 to 100. If you scored between 10 and 40, then you probably can improve your emotional intelligence. Learning more about this topic may help you. If your score was 41–70, you are moderately emotionally intelligent, meaning you have the skills to express and perceive emotions accurately but you can also improve this ability. If you scored between 71 and 100, you have high emotional intelligence, which probably benefits your interpersonal communication with others. Are you surprised by your score? Why or why not? How do you think your score reflects how you deal with emotions?

Source: Adapted from Mayer, J. D., & Salovey, P. (1997). What is emotional intelligence? In P. Salovey & J. D. Sluyter (Eds.), *Emotional development and emotional intelligence* (pp. 3–31). New York: Basic Books.

relationships, alexithymia can impair relationship satisfaction by making it difficult for partners to understand what the other is feeling.[137]

Learn It: How do people from individualistic and collectivistic cultures differ in their expression of negative emotions? What are the five display rules for emotion? What is emotional contagion? How do women and men differ in their emotional expression? Which aspects of personality influence emotion? How is emotional intelligence affected by alexithymia?

Try It: To identify how gender roles might influence the communication of emotion, spend five minutes with a few other classmates brainstorming about which emotions women are encouraged and discouraged from expressing. Now, do the same for men's emotions. What patterns do you see?

Reflect on It: In what situations do you intensify or de-intensify your emotional expressions? In what ways does your gender role influence your experience and expression of emotion?

As is the case for many communicative behaviors, we can manage the expression of our emotions in either positive or negative ways. Denying and suppressing our emotions isn't healthy. In fact, medical research shows it can actually contribute to a host of health problems, including asthma, heart disease, and cancer.[138] At the other extreme, overreacting to your emotions isn't good for you, either.[139] The best strategy for dealing with emotions is to find a balance between these two extremes. This section will offer some suggestions for improving your ability to manage your emotional expression in productive ways.

> *The sign of an intelligent people is their ability to control their emotions by the application of reason.*
>
> —Marya Mannes (1904–1990)
> U.S. American writer

Identifying Emotions

Perhaps the most important emotional communication skill you can develop is the ability to recognize and identify the emotions you're experiencing.[140] Research shows that people who can accurately identify which emotion they're feeling—whether it's anger, nervousness, sadness, shame, or guilt, for instance—are best equipped to manage emotions in productive ways.[141]

To illustrate this point, let's say that a new co-worker has joined your team and is receiving a great deal of praise and attention from your supervisor. As a result, you begin to feel jealousy, which, as we discussed, is a combination of anger, sadness, and fear. What would happen, though, if you only recognized that you were feeling anger and not sadness and fear as well? In that situation, you'd respond only to your anger, perhaps by speaking harshly to your supervisor or co-worker. You wouldn't also deal with your fear of losing your supervisor's favor or your sadness that others might like or respect your co-worker more than you. As a result, your sadness and fear would go unaddressed, and your expressions of anger would likely be counterproductive.

If you find it difficult to identify your emotions in a given situation, there are at least three techniques that might help: Listen to your body, pay attention to your thoughts, and take stock of the situation. Let's take a closer look at each one.

Listen to your body. First, try paying attention to what your body is doing. Emotions cause physiological changes. Although different emotions can have similar effects on the body, thinking about how your body is reacting to the situation may help you determine which emotion you're experiencing. On the basis of your experiences, for instance, you probably know that jealousy causes your body to feel differently than anger, joy, disgust, and surprise do. Reflecting on how you feel physically can therefore help you determine which emotional experiences you are going through.

Pay attention to your thoughts. Emotions affect our minds as well as our bodies, so paying attention to your thoughts can help you clarify the emotional experiences you're having. Let's say you're questioning whether a particular situation is making you angry or sad. If you're feeling angry, your thoughts most likely are focused on hurting or punishing whomever is the source of your anger. For instance, if you notice that you're imagining yelling or speaking sternly to the person, these thoughts probably arise out of anger. In contrast, if you're feeling sad, your thoughts

When you're uncertain about which emotion you're feeling, pay attention to how your body is reacting to the situation.

probably are focused on whatever you feel you're losing, whether it's a cherished friendship, an enjoyable time in your life, or a job you enjoy.

Take stock of the situation. Earlier in this chapter, you learned that emotions are reactions to events that you perceive to interfere with your goals. Unlike a mood, therefore, every emotion has a cause. A third strategy you can use to identify your emotions is to try to determine what is happening in your situation that you're reacting to.

Suppose, for example, you're feeling upset, but you can't figure out if you're anxious or envious. Take stock of what's occurring in your environment. Has a recent illness caused you to fall behind in your schoolwork? If so, that situation might make you anxious because it's interfering with your goal of completing your work. From a different perspective, has a close friend recently become engaged? Although that situation might make you happy, it might also make you envious if you perceive that your friend has a better romantic relationship than you do, which interferes with your goal of having the relationship you want. Often, we can identify which emotion we're experiencing by considering what might be interfering with our goals.

Taking stock of the situation can also help us identify the emotions that other people are experiencing. Let's say you notice that your brother seems unusually quiet and reserved, but you can't tell if he's angry or worried or just a little tired. Take stock of the situation he's in and what he might be reacting to in his environment. Then consider how you would feel under the same circumstances. If you know some of his wife's co-workers have recently been laid off because of budget cuts, for instance, then he might be worried about how to provide for his family if his wife loses her job. You can then engage in perception checking by saying to your brother, "You seem like you're worried about something; are you?" He might reply that he is, or he might instead say, "No, I'm actually mad at my neighbor for letting his children leave their toys in my yard." Taking stock of your brother's situation can give you an idea about what he might be feeling, and perception checking can help you determine if you're correct.

Are you ever unsure of why you're feeling the way you do? Take stock of what's happening in your environment that might be enhancing or inhibiting your goals.

Reappraising Negative Emotions

When you experience a negative emotion, a productive strategy for dealing with it is to engage in **emotional reappraisal.** Emotional reappraisal involves changing the way you think about the situation that gave rise to the negative emotion so that the effect of the emotion is reduced.[142] Let's say you're upset with the grade you received on a research paper. Whereas you felt your work was highly original and well written, your instructor's evaluation didn't reflect that opinion. Going to your instructor's office while you're angry and distraught, however, may cause you to say or do things that will inflame the situation.

Instead, you could wait until you're less upset to reappraise the situation and then consider the best way to express your thoughts. For example, you might think more analytically about your paper and what you might have done to make it better reflect the assignment. You can remind yourself that your grade isn't your instructor's evaluation of you as a person but, rather, of your performance. You might also remind yourself that your instructor was just doing his or her job by grading you or that this grade will have only a modest effect on your overall academic record. Exercises such as these, all of which help you reappraise an emotional situation, will enable you to consider the situation from a broader perspective. Adopting this strategy can reduce your negative emotions and help you communicate more effectively.[143]

Emotional reappraisal The process of changing how you think about the situation that gave rise to an emotion so that the effect of the emotion is diminished.

Accepting Responsibility for Emotions

In Chapter 5, "Language," you learned about the importance of "owning" your thoughts and feelings. In other words, you acknowledge that you determine your own thoughts and emotions by describing them with I-statements (*I feel angry*) rather than you-statements (*You are making me angry*). Accepting responsibility for our emotions is challenging because emotions are, after all, *reactions* to events that affect you. When someone teases or insults you, for instance, you probably feel hurt. You don't *choose* to feel hurt, however. Instead, you're simply reacting to that person's behavior.

The problem with describing your emotions with you-statements is that they fail to acknowledge the part you play in determining how you feel. Instead, they simply blame the other person for your emotions, without any prescription for change.[144] A more productive approach is to say *I feel hurt when you insult me.* This statement acknowledges that your emotions are your own (*I feel hurt . . .*), but it also identifies the specific event that causes them (. . . *when you insult me*), making it clear to the recipient which behaviors you are asking him or her to change.

Separating Emotions from Actions

As we've seen in this chapter, emotion and behavior go hand in hand, and most emotions have specific action tendencies associated with them. Experiencing an emotion, however, doesn't mean you have to act on it. Feeling angry with someone, for example, doesn't necessarily mean you must yell at that person. Likewise, feeling love for someone doesn't necessarily mean you must express it. Just as you "own" your emotions, you also "own" your behaviors. Part of being a competent interpersonal communicator, therefore, is being able to determine the most appropriate and effective way for you to act on your emotions.

Before you act on your emotions, it's generally best to stop and think about the possible effects of your actions. Let's say Gerard is worried about how much weight his brother-in-law Magnus has gained in the last year. Because of his fear, Gerard feels he should talk to Magnus about the health dangers of obesity and encourage him to exercise and adopt a lower-calorie diet. Before Gerard does so, however, he weighs the pros and cons of acting on his fear in this way.

Most emotions motivate us to act in certain ways. Just because you're experiencing an emotion, however, that doesn't necessarily mean you have to act on it.

From a positive perspective, Magnus may appreciate knowing how much Gerard cares about him. He may also be motivated to reduce his weight, saving himself from potentially life-threatening health problems. From the opposite perspective, however, Magnus may resent Gerard's interference. He may tell Gerard to mind his own business and refuse to change his behaviors, which would put his health at even greater risk.

Although Gerard's primary concern is for Magnus's health, he also does not want to embarrass Magnus or jeopardize their relationship. In the end, Gerard decides to share his concerns with Magnus's wife, in the hope that she might be better able to persuade Magnus to lose weight.

Identifying and reappraising emotions, accepting responsibility for emotions, and separating emotions from actions are all skills we can learn. The more we practice these skills, the more adept we'll become at managing our emotional communication.

Learn It: How can you identify emotions accurately? When is it helpful to re-appraise an emotion? What does it mean to accept responsibility for your emotions? Why should we separate emotions from actions?

Try It: Emotional reappraisal is very useful, but it takes practice. The next time you experience a strong negative emotion, force yourself to stop and reappraise the situation before you act. This will give your emotion time to cool down, and it will help you to understand the situation differently. You'll then be in a much better position to decide how best to act.

Reflect on It: When do you tend to blame other people for your emotions? For which emotions do you have the hardest time accepting responsibility?

} Master the Chapter {

Section 1} Emotion in Interpersonal Communication (p. 435)

I. Emotion in Interpersonal Communication
  A. What is an emotion?
    1. Emotion is different from mood
  B. Joyful/affectionate emotions: happiness, love, passion, and liking
    1. Happiness
    2. Love and passion
    3. Liking
  C. Hostile emotions: anger, contempt, disgust, jealousy, and envy
    1. Anger
    2. Contempt
    3. Disgust
    4. Jealousy
    5. Envy
  D. Sad/anxious emotions: sadness, depression, grief, fear, and social anxiety
    1. Sadness and depression
    2. Grief
    3. Fear
    4. Social anxiety

- An emotion is your body's reaction to any event that enhances or inhibits your goals.

- Three classes of emotion are particularly relevant for interpersonal communication: joyful/affectionate emotions, hostile emotions, and sad/anxious emotions. Joyful/affectionate emotions include happiness, love, passion, and liking.

- Hostile emotions include anger, contempt, disgust, jealousy, and envy.

- Sad/anxious emotions include sadness, depression, grief, fear, and social anxiety.

Section 2} The Nature of Emotion (p. 443)

II. The Nature of Emotion
  A. Emotions are multidimensional
    1. Emotions are physiological
    2. Emotions are cognitive
    3. Emotions are behavioral
    4. Emotions are social and cultural
  B. Emotions vary in valence and intensity
    1. Emotions vary in valence
    2. Emotions vary in intensity
  C. Emotions come in primary and secondary forms
  D. Sometimes emotions are meta-emotions

- Emotions have physiological, cognitive, social, and behavioral components.

- Emotions vary in valence and intensity.

- Emotions come in primary and secondary forms.

- Emotions can be meta-emotions.

Section 3} Influences on Emotional Experience and Expression (p. 450)

III. Influences on Emotional Experience and Expression

A. Culture
- 1. Geography
- 2. Co-cultures

- People across cultures experience the same range of emotions, but cultural practices and messages affect how those emotions are communicated.

B. Display rules

- Five display rules influence which emotions people express and how intensely they express them.

C. Technology

- Technology affects how we experience emotions and how we communicate them to others.

D. Emotional contagion

- According to the emotional contagion effect, people have a tendency to mimic the emotional experiences and expressions of those around them.

E. Sex and gender
- 1. Sexual differences in jealousy?
- 2. Gender roles and emotional expression

- Women and men differ in their tendencies to experience emotion, but not in the intensity of their experiences. Women are also more expressive than men. Androgynous adults are more emotionally expressive than masculine men or feminine women.

F. Personality

- Three characteristics of personality—neuroticism, extroversion, and agreeableness—influence the experience and expression of emotion.

G. Emotional intelligence

- Emotionally intelligent people are attuned to which emotions they are experiencing, and they use their emotions to make decisions about behavior.

Section 4} Emotional Communication Skills (p. 458)

IV. Emotional Communication Skills

A. Identifying emotions
- 1. Listen to your body
- 2. Pay attention to your thoughts
- 3. Take stock of the situation

- Accurately identifying emotions in yourself and others is an important emotional communication skill.

B. Reappraising negative emotions

- Reappraising negative emotions means changing the way you think about the situation that caused the emotions, which can lessen their negative effects.

C. Accepting responsibility for emotions

- Competent communicators accept responsibility for their own emotions instead of blaming others for how they feel.

D. Separating emotions from actions

- Although emotions motivate us toward particular behaviors, we are not obligated to act on every emotion we experience.

Key Terms

Action tendencies
Anger
Contempt
Depression
Disgust
Display rules
Emotion
Emotional contagion
Emotional intelligence

Emotional reappraisal
Envy
Fear
Grief
Happiness
Jealousy
Liking
Love
Meta-emotion

Mood
Passion
Primary emotions
Sadness
Secondary emotions
Social anxiety
Valence

Discussion Questions

1. How does it feel, physically, to be sad? How about disgusted? joyful? angry? surprised? In what ways are the physical experiences of these emotions the same? In what ways are they different?
2. Besides joy, sadness, anger, fear, surprise, and disgust, do you think there are any other "primary" emotions (i.e., emotions that are distinctive, not combinations of other emotions)? If so, what are they?
3. We normally think of passion as being romantic in nature, but can you experience passion for others that is not romantic? What are some examples?

4. Research shows that contempt is one of the most destructive emotions for personal relationships. Why do you suppose it is so much more destructive than other emotions?
5. Why are women more emotionally expressive than men, on average? What accounts for this difference?
6. Why is the emotional contagion effect influential? That is, why do we mimic the emotional experiences and expressions of those around us?
7. When do you have difficulty identifying your own emotional experiences?
8. Can you think of an instance when you have reappraised a negative emotion? If so, what was the outcome?

Practice Quiz

Multiple Choice

1. Which of the following is the best definition of liking?
   a. feelings of contentment, pleasure, and cheer
   b. feelings of joy, and surprise with experiences of excitement and attraction
   c. the overall evaluation of another person
   d. caring for, feeling attached to, and feeling committed to someone else
2. Which of the following is an emotional response to the perception that you have been wronged in some way?
   a. envy   c. contempt
   b. jealousy   d. anger
3. The expression of which of the following has been shown to trigger a cycle of negative behavior in relationships that can lead to one partner withdrawing?
   a. envy   c. disgust
   b. contempt   d. anger
4. Which of the following is the correct order of the five steps in the grieving process?
   a. sadness, anger, denial, bargaining, acceptance
   b. depression, anger, denial, bargaining, acceptance
   c. denial, anger, bargaining, depression, acceptance
   d. anger, bargaining, denial, depression, acceptance
5. Annika hates going to parties, and tends to socialize only with her family and closest friends. Annika's fear of not making a good impression on others is best described as which of the following?

a. depression   c. grief
b. social anxiety   d. loneliness

6. Which of the four primary characteristics of emotions is best described by the body's changes in blood pressure, breathing rate, and hormone levels?
   a. social and cultural   c. physiological
   b. cognitive   d. behavioral
7. Which of the following is *not* a secondary emotion?
   a. disgust   c. contempt
   b. remorse   d. awe
8. Shayne's partner forgot his birthday. Even though Shayne did not really care because he has one every year, he put on quite a show and acted furious just to make his partner feel bad. Which of the following emotion display rules did Shayne use?
   a. inhibition   c. masking
   b. simulation   d. de-intensification
9. Which of the following aspects of personality tend(s) to be associated with how emotion is experienced?
   a. agreeableness   c. neuroticism
   b. extroversion   d. all of the above
10. Someone who is able to perceive and accurately express emotions and use emotions to facilitate thought, to understand emotions, and to manage emotions for emotional growth is considered to have which of the following?
    a. emotional intelligence   c. emotional reappraisal
    b. intelligence quotient   d. none of the above

True/False

11. Men engage in road rage more often than women.
12. Sadness is a medically diagnosed physical illness that can linger for months or years.
13. Emotions are valenced, meaning they range from positive to negative.
14. Regardless of culture, people tend to accurately identify facial displays of primary emotion.
15. The tendency to mimic the experiences and the expression of others is known as emotional contagion.

Fill in the Blank

16. The motivation of an angry person to attack another person while driving is known as _____.

17. _____ occurs when someone feels that the existence or the quality of his or her relationship is threatened by a third party; whereas _____ occurs when someone wants what someone else has.
18. The behavioral components of emotions are called _____, which are specific behaviors that each emotion motivates us to engage in.
19. The emotion of _____ is generally considered to have a neutral valence.
20. A productive strategy for dealing with negative feelings is _____, by changing the way one thinks about the situation to reduce the effect it has.

Research Library

Movies

Hotel Rwanda (Drama; 2004; PG-13)

This movie is a historical drama about a hotel manager in Rwanda who uses his resources and political connections to save people during a 1994 civil war between two rival native Rwandan groups, Hutu and Tutsi. The manager himself is conflicted because he is Hutu but his wife is Tutsi. The film presents many powerfully emotional scenes. For instance, the manager's wife expresses a profound sense of fear when she and her children are separated from her husband. The manager also expresses great relief at being reunited with his family and with his two young nieces at the end of the film.

The Kite Runner (Drama; 2007; PG-13)

This film depicts the friendship between two Afghan boys: Amir, who is well-to-do, and Hassan, the son of Amir's father's servant. Hassan, who is brave, frequently stands up to bullies on Amir's behalf. At one point, however, bullies attack Hassan while Amir secretly watches, too afraid to intervene. The characters in the film experience a wide range of emotions. Over the course of the story, Amir struggles to come to terms with the guilt and shame he feels at not having defended his friend. Amir and his father also deal with their anger at the Soviet occupation of Afghanistan, and Amir deals with his joy at finding a wife and his sadness at losing his father.

What's Love Got to Do with It (Drama; 1993; R)

This biographical drama portrays the career of rock singer Tina Turner and her turbulent marriage to her producer and mentor Ike Turner. Ike expresses pride in having discovered Tina and establishing her career, but then her fame causes him to become jealous and eventually highly abusive. Tina's emotions range from excitement and joy at her new career to fear of Ike and his temper. In one particularly emotional scene, Tina checks into a hotel after a brutal confrontation with Ike and tries to maintain her composure while overwhelmed with sadness, fear, and anger.

Books

Andersen, P. A., & Guerrero, L. K. (Eds.). (1998). *Handbook of communication and emotion: Research, theory, applications, and contexts.* San Diego, CA: Academic Press.

Hatfield, E., Cacioppo, J. T., & Rapson, R. L. (1994). *Emotional contagion.* New York: Cambridge University Press.

Izard, C. E. (1991). *The psychology of emotions.* New York: Plenum.

Lewis, M., & Haviland, J. M. (Eds.). (1993). *Handbook of emotions* (2nd ed.). New York: Guilford.

Journal Articles

Bippus, A. M., & Young, S. L. (2005). Owning your emotions: Reactions to expressions of self- versus other-attributed positive and negative emotions. *Journal of Applied Communication Research, 33,* 26–45.

Kring, A. M., & Gordon, A. H. (1998). Sex differences in emotion: Expression, experience, and physiology. *Journal of Personality and Social Psychology, 74,* 686–703.

Mayne, T. J. (1999). Negative affect and health: The importance of being earnest. *Cognition and Emotion, 13,* 601–635.

Web Sites

www.paulekman.com

This is the home page of psychologist Paul Ekman, a pioneer in the study of emotion. The site details Professor Ekman's research and offers resources for learning more about the communication of emotion.

www.griefnet.org

This Web site hosts multiple support groups for adults and children suffering grief and sadness in the wake of a major loss.

Glossary

Accommodating: A strategy for managing conflict that involves giving in to the other party's needs and desires while subordinating one's own.

Action tendencies: Biologically based motives toward specific behavioral responses to emotions.

Acts of dissimulation: Forms of deception that involve omitting or avoiding certain details that would change the nature of the story if they were known.

Acts of simulation: Forms of deception that involve fabricating information or exaggerating facts for the purpose of misleading others.

Adaptor: Gesture used to satisfy a personal need.

Affect display: Gesture that communicates emotion.

Ambiguous language: Having more than one possible meaning.

Anchor-and-contrast: A form of persuasion in which you initially make a large request that is rejected and then follow it with a smaller, more reasonable request.

Androgyny: A gender role characterized by a combination of masculine and feminine traits.

Anger: An emotional response to being wronged.

Approach behaviors: Communication behaviors that signal your interest in getting to know someone.

Artifact: Object or visual feature of an environment with communicative value.

Asexuality: A sexual orientation characterized by a general lack of interest in sex.

Attribution: An explanation for an observed behavior.

Autonomy face: The need to avoid being imposed upon by others.

Avoidance behaviors: Communication behaviors that signal your lack of interest in getting know someone.

Avoiding: A strategy for managing conflict that involves downplaying or failing to deal with the conflict.

Avoiding stage: Stage of relationship dissolution when partners create physical and emotional distance between them.

Bisexuality: A sexual orientation characterized by sexual interest in both women and men.

Bonding stage: Stage of relationship development when the partners publicly announce their commitment.

Breadth: The range of topics about which one person self-discloses to another.

Channel: Pathway through which messages are conveyed.

Channel-lean context: Communication context involving few channels at once.

Channel-rich context: Communication context involving many channels at once.

Chronemics: Use of time.

Circumscribing stage: Stage of relationship dissolution characterized by decreased quality and quantity of communication between partners.

Closed-mindedness: Tendency not to listen to anything with which you disagree.

Co-cultures: Groups of people who share values, customs, and norms related to a mutual interest or characteristic.

Coercive power: Power based on the ability to punish.

Cognitive complexity: Ability to understand a given situation in multiple ways.

Collaborating: A strategy for managing conflict that involves working toward a solution that meets both parties' needs.

Collectivistic culture: A culture that places greater emphasis on loyalty to the family, workplace, or community than on the needs of the individual.

Commitment: A desire to stay in a relationship.

Communication codes: Verbal and nonverbal behaviors, such as idioms and gestures, that characterize a culture and distinguish it from other cultures.

Communication competence: Communicating in ways that are effective and appropriate for a given situation.

Communication privacy management (CPM) theory: Theory developed by Sandra Petronio to explain how people manage the tension between privacy and disclosure.

Comparison level: Your realistic expectation of what you think you deserve from a relationship.

Comparison level for alternatives: Your assessment of how good your current relationship is, compared to your other options.

Competence face: The need to be respected and viewed as competent and intelligent.

Competing: A strategy for managing conflict wherein your goal is to win while the other party loses.

Competitive interrupting: Using interruptions to take control of a conversation.

Complementary relationship: A relationship between parties of unequal power.

Compromising: A strategy for managing conflict in which both parties give up something they want in order that both can receive something they want.

Confirmation bias: The tendency to seek information that supports our values and beliefs, while discounting or ignoring information that doesn't.

Confirming messages: Behaviors that indicate how much we value another person.

Connotative meaning: A word's implied or secondary meaning, in addition to its literal meaning.

Contempt: The expression of insults and attacks on another's self-worth.

Content dimension: Literal information that is communicated by a message.

Context: Physical or psychological environment in which communication occurs.

Credibility: The extent to which others find our words and actions trustworthy.

Critical listening: Listening with the goal of evaluating or analyzing what we hear.

Criticism: The expression of complaints about another party.

Culture: The learned, shared symbols, language, values, and norms that distinguish one group of people from another.

Deception: The knowing and intentional transmission of information in order to create a false belief in the hearer.

Decode: To interpret or give meaning to a message.

Defensiveness: The tendency to deny the validity of criticisms directed at the self.

Demand-withdraw pattern: A pattern of behavior wherein one party makes demands and the other party withdraws from the conversation.

Denotative meaning: A word's literal meaning or dictionary definition.

Depression: A physical illness involving excessive fatigue, insomnia, changes in weight, feelings of worthlessness, and/or thoughts of suicide.

Depth: The intimacy of the topics about which one person self-discloses to another.

Dialectical tensions: Conflicts between two important but opposing needs or desires.

Differentiating stage: Stage of relationship dissolution when partners begin to see their differences as undesirable or annoying.

Disgust: a feeling of revulsion in reaction to something offensive.

Disinhibition effect: The tendency to say or do things in one environment (such as online) that one would not say or do in most other environments.

Display rules: Unwritten codes that govern the ways people manage and express emotions.

Divorce: The legal termination of a marriage.

Dyad: A pair of people.

Egocentric: A state of inability to take another person's perspective.

Emblem: Gesture with a direct verbal translation.

Emotion: The body's multi-dimensional response to any event that enhances or inhibits one's goals.

Emotional contagion: The tendency to mimic the emotional experiences and expressions of others.

Emotional intelligence: Ability to perceive and understand emotions, use emotions to facilitate thought, and manage emotions constructively.

Emotional reappraisal: The process of changing how you think about the situation that gave rise to an emotion, so the effect of the emotion is diminished.

Empathic listening: Listening in order to experience what another person is thinking or feeling.

Empathy: Ability to think and feel as others do.

Encode: To put an idea into language or gesture.

Envy: The desire for something another person has.

Equity theory: A theory predicting that a good relationship is one in which your ratio of costs and rewards is equal to your partner's.

Equivocation: A form of deception that involves giving vague, ambiguous answers to a question in order to give the false impression that one has answered it.

Ethics: A code of morality or a set of ideas about what is right.

Euphemism: A vague, mild expression that symbolizes something more blunt or harsh.

Exaggeration: A form of deception that involves inflating or overstating facts.

Experimenting stage: Stage of relationship development when partners have conversations to learn more about each other.

Expert power: Power that derives from one's expertise, talent, training, specialized knowledge, or experience.

Explicit rule: Rule about behavior that has been clearly articulated.

Expressive talk: Verbal communication whose purpose is to express emotions and build relationships.

Face: A person's desired public image.

Face needs: Components of one's desired public image.

Face-threatening act: Any behavior that threatens one or more face needs.

Facework: The behaviors we use to maintain our desired public image to others.

Facial display: Use of facial expression for communication.

Falsification: A form of deception that involves presenting false, fabricated information as though it were true.

Family of origin: The family in which you grew up (often consisting of your parents and your siblings).

Family of procreation: The family you start as an adult (often consisting of your spouse and your children).

Fear: The mind and body's reaction to perceived danger.

Feedback: Verbal and nonverbal responses to a message.

Fellowship face: The need to have others like and accept you. See also *Need for inclusion*.

Femininity: A gender role, typically assigned to women, that emphasizes expressive, nurturant behavior.

Fundamental attribution error: The tendency to attribute others' behaviors to internal rather than external causes.

Gender role: A set of expectations for appropriate behavior that a culture typically assigns to an individual based on his or her biological sex.

Gesticulation: Use of arm and hand movements to communicate.

Glazing over: Daydreaming with the time not spent listening.

Gossip: The sharing of an individual's personal information with a third party without the individual's consent.

Grief: Emotional process of dealing with profound loss.

Happiness: A state of contentment, joy, pleasure, and cheer.

Haptics: Study of how we use touch to communicate.

Hate speech: A form of profanity meant to degrade, intimidate, or dehumanize groups of people.

Heterosexuality: A sexual orientation characterized by sexual interest in members of the other sex.

High-contact culture: Culture in which people frequently touch and maintain little personal distance with one another.

High-context culture: A culture in which verbal communication is often ambiguous and meaning is drawn from contextual cues, such as facial expressions and tone of voice.

High-power-distance culture: A culture in which much or most of the power is concentrated in a few people, such as royalty or a ruling political party.

Homosexuality: A sexual orientation characterized by sexual interest in members of one's own sex.

HURIER model: A model of effective listening that involves hearing, understanding, remembering, interpreting, evaluating, and responding.

I-statement: A statement that claims ownership of one's thoughts or feelings.

Identity: See *Self-concept*.

Illustrator: Gesture that enhances or clarifies a verbal message.

Image: The way one wishes to be seen or perceived by others.

Image management: The process of projecting one's desired public image. See also *Facework*.

Immediacy behavior: Nonverbal behavior that conveys attraction or affiliation.

Implicit rule: Rule about behavior that has not been clearly articulated but is nonetheless understood.

Individualistic culture: A culture that emphasizes individuality and responsibility to oneself.

Infidelity: Being sexually involved with someone other than your spouse.

Information overload: Being overwhelmed by the amount of information one takes in.

Informational listening: Listening in order to learn something.

In-groups: Groups of people with which one identifies.

Initiating stage: Stage of relationship development when people meet and interact for the first time.

Instrumental needs: Practical, everyday needs.

Instrumental talk: Verbal communication whose purpose is to convey information.

Integrating stage: Stage of relationship development when a deep commitment has formed and there is a strong sense that the relationship has its own identity.

Intensifying stage: Stage of relationship development when people move from being acquaintances to being close friends.

Interactive context: A context for communicating in which participants can see and/or hear each other and react to each other in real time (e.g., face-to-face conversation, telephone conversation).

Interdependence: A state in which each a person's behaviors affect everyone else in the relationship.

Interpersonal attraction: Any force that draws people together to form a relationship.

Interpersonal communication: Communication that occurs between two people within the context of their relationship and that, as it evolves, helps them to negotiate and define their relationship.

Interpersonal conflict: An expressed struggle between interdependent parties who perceive incompatible goals, scarce resources, and interference.

Interpretation: The process of assigning meaning to information that has been selected for attention and organized.

Intrapersonal communication: Communication that occurs with oneself.

Investment: The resources we put into our relationships.

Jealousy: Perception that the existence or quality of an important relationship is being threatened by a third party.

Johari Window: A visual representation of components of the self that are known or unknown to the self and to others.

Kinesics: Study of movement.

Language: A structured system of symbols used for communicating meaning.

Legitimate power: Power based on one's legitimate status or position.

Libel: A defamatory statement made in print or some other fixed medium.

Liking: A positive overall evaluation of another person.

Listening: The active process of making meaning out of another person's spoken message.

Loaded language: Terms that carry strongly positive or negative connotations.

Love: The emotion of caring for, feeling attached to, and feeling committed to someone.

Low-contact culture: Culture in which people touch infrequently and maintain relatively high levels of personal distance with one another.

Low-context culture: A culture in which verbal communication is expected to be explicit and is often interpreted literally.

Low-power-distance culture: A culture in which power is not highly concentrated in specific groups of people.

Masculinity: A gender role, typically assigned to men, that emphasizes strength, dominance, competition, and logical thinking.

Mass communication: Communication in which one source speaks to a large audience.

Message: Verbal and nonverbal elements of communication to which people give meaning.

Meta-communication: Communication about communication.

Meta-conflict: Conflict about conflict.

Meta-emotion: An emotion about emotion.

Model: A formal description of a process.

Monochronic: A concept that treats time as a finite commodity that can be earned, saved, spent, and wasted.

Monogamy: Being in only one romantic relationship at a time and avoiding romantic or sexual involvement with others outside the relationship.

Mood: A feeling, often prolonged, that has no identifiable cause.

Motivation impairment effect: A perspective offering that motivation to succeed in a lie will improve a deceiver's verbal performance but simultaneously impair his or her nonverbal performance, making the lie less likely to be believed.

Need for affection: One's need to give and receive expressions of love and appreciation.

Need for control: One's need to maintain a degree of influence in one's relationships.

Need for inclusion: One's need to belong to a social group and be included in the activities of others. See also *Fellowship face.*

Need to belong: A hypothesis that says each of us is born with a fundamental drive to seek, form, maintain, and protect strong social relationships.

Negativity bias: The tendency to focus heavily on a person's negative attributes when forming a perception.

Noise: Anything that interferes with the encoding or decoding of a message.

Noninteractive context: A context for communicating in which the participants cannot react to each other in real time (e.g., voice mail message, email message).

Nonverbal channels: The various forms that nonverbal communication takes.

Nonverbal communication: Those behaviors and characteristics that convey meaning without the use of words.

Norm of reciprocity: A social expectation, articulated by Alvin Gouldner, that resources and favors provided to one person in a relationship should be reciprocated by that person.

Oculesics: Study of eye behavior.

Olfactics: Study of the sense of smell.

Omission: A form of deception that involves leaving consequential details out of one's story.

One-across message: A verbal message that seeks to neutralize relational control and power.

One-down message: A verbal message that reflects acceptance of, or submission to, another person's power.

One-up message: A verbal message through which the speaker attempts to exert dominance or gain control over the listener.

Onomatopoeia: A word formed by imitating the sound associated with its meaning.

Organization: The process of categorizing information that has been selected for attention.

Out-groups: Groups of people with which one does not identify.

Overattribution: The tendency to attribute a range of behaviors to a single characteristic of a person.

Over-benefited: The state in which your relational rewards exceed your relational costs.

Passion: A secondary emotion consisting of joy and surprise, plus experiences of excitement and attraction for another.

Passive aggression: A pattern of behaving vengefully while denying that one has aggressive feelings.

Peer: Someone of similar power or status.

Perception: The ongoing process of making meaning from the things we experience in the environment.

Perceptual set: A predisposition to perceive only what we want or expect to perceive.

Personality: The pattern of behaviors and ways of thinking that characterize a person.

Physical attraction: Attraction to someone's physical appearance.

Polychronic: A concept that treats time as an infinite resource rather than a finite commodity.

Polygamy: A practice in which one person is married to two or more spouses at once.

Positivity bias: The tendency to focus heavily on a person's positive attributes when forming a perception.

Power: The ability to manipulate, influence, or control other people or events.

Predicted outcome value theory: A theory predicting that we form relationships when we think the effort will be worth it.

Primacy effect: The tendency to emphasize the first impression over later impressions when forming a perception.

Primary emotions: Distinct emotional experiences not consisting of combinations of other emotions.

Profanity: A form of language considered vulgar, rude, or obscene in the context in which it is used.

Proportionality: Size of facial features relative to one another.

Proxemics: Study of spatial use.

Pseudolistening: Using feedback behaviors to give the false impression that one is listening.

Rebuttal tendency: Tendency to debate a speaker's point and formulate a reply while the person is still speaking.

Receiver: The party who interprets a message.

Recency effect: The tendency to emphasize the most recent impression over earlier impressions when forming a perception.

Reference groups: The groups of people to whom one compares oneself in the process of social comparison.

Referent power: Power that derives from one's attraction to or admiration for another.

Reflected appraisal: The process whereby people's self-concept is influenced by their beliefs concerning what other people think of them.

Regulator: Gesture that controls the flow of conversation.

Relational dimension: Signals about the relationship in which a message is being communicated.

Relational maintenance behaviors: Behaviors used to maintain and strengthen personal relationships.

Reward power: Power that derives from the ability to reward.

Rituals: Repetitive behaviors that have special meaning for a group or relationship.

Sadness: Emotion involving feeling unhappy, sorrowful, and discouraged, usually as a result of some form of loss.

Sapir-Whorf hypothesis: The idea that language influences the ways that members of a culture see and think about the world.

Secondary emotions: Emotions composed of combinations of primary emotions.

Selection: The process of attending to a stimulus.

Selective attention: Listening only to what you want to hear.

Self-concept: The set of perceptions a person has about who he or she is; also known as identity.

Self-disclosure: The act of giving others information about oneself that one believes they do not already have.

Self-esteem: One's subjective evaluation of one's value and worth as a person.

Self-fulfilling prophecy: An expectation that gives rise to behaviors that cause the expectation to come true.

Self-monitoring: Awareness of one's behavior and how it affects others.

Self-serving bias: The tendency to attribute one's successes to internal causes and one's failures to external causes.

Sexual orientation: A characteristic determining the sex or sexes to which someone is sexually attracted.

Skepticism: The practice of evaluating the evidence for a claim.

Slander: A defamatory statement made aloud.

Slang: Informal, unconventional words that are often understood only by others in a particular subculture.

Small group communication: Communication occurring within small groups of three or more people.

Social anxiety: Fear of not making a good impression on others.

Social attraction: Attraction to someone's personality.

Social comparison: The process of comparing oneself to others.

Social exchange theory: A theory predicting that people seek to form and maintain relationships in which the benefits outweigh the costs.

Social penetration theory: A theory, developed by Irwin Altman and Dalmas Taylor, that predicts that as relationships develop, communication increases in breadth and depth.

Social validation principle: The prediction that people will comply with requests if they believe others are also complying.

Societies: Groups of people who share symbols, language, values, and norms.

Source: The originator of a thought or idea.

Stagnating stage: Stage of relationship dissolution when couples are barely communicating with each other.

Stereotypes: Generalizations about groups of people that are applied to individual members of those groups.

Stigma: A characteristic that discredits a person, making him or her be seen as abnormal or undesirable.

Stonewalling: The behavior of withdrawing from a conversation or interaction.

Symbol: A representation of an idea.

Symmetrical relationship: A relationship between parties of equal power.

Symmetry: Similarity between left and right sides of the face or body.

System: An arrangement of people (or other components) who interact with each other in complex, interdependent ways.

Task attraction: Attraction to someone's talents, abilities, or dependability.

Terminating stage: Stage of relationship dissolution when the relationship is deemed to be officially over.

Truth bias: The tendency to believe what someone says, in the absence of a reason not to.

Turn-taking signal: Nonverbal behavior that indicates when a person's speaking turn begins and ends.

Uncertainty avoidance: The degree to which people find novel, unfamiliar situations problematic.

Uncertainty reduction theory: A theory suggesting that people are motivated to reduce their uncertainty about others.

Underbenefited: The state in which your relational costs exceed your relational rewards.

Valence: The positivity or negativity of an emotion.

Vividness effect: The tendency for dramatic, shocking events to distort our perception of reality.

Vocalics: Characteristics of the voice.

You-statement: A statement that shifts responsibility for one's own thoughts or feelings to the listener.

Notes for Chapter 1

[1] Bonta, J., & Gendreau, P. (1995). Re-examining the cruel and unusual punishment of prison life. In T. J. Flanagan (Ed.), *Long-term imprisonment: Policy, science, and correctional practice* (pp. 75–84). Thousand Oaks, CA: Sage.

[2] See, e.g., Ray, E. B. (Ed.). (1996). *Communication and disenfranchisement: Social health issues and implications.* Mahwah, NJ: Lawrence Erlbaum Associates; Takahashi, L. M. (1998). *Homelessness, AIDS, and stigmatization: The NIMBY syndrome in the United States at the end of the Twentieth Century.* New York: Oxford University Press.

[3] Perry, B. D. (2002). Childhood experience and the expression of genetic potential: What childhood neglect tells us about nature and nurture. *Brain and Mind, 3,* 79–100.

[4] Field, T. (2001). *Touch.* Cambridge, MA: MIT Press.

[5] Cacioppo, J. T., Ernst, J. M., Burleson, M. H., McClintock, M. K., Malarkey, W. B., Hawkley, L. C., Kowalewski, R. B., Paulsen, A., Hobson, J. A., Hugdahl, K., Spiegel, D., & Berntson, G. G. (2000). Lonely traits and concomitant physiological processes: The MacArthur Social Neuroscience Studies. *International Journal of Psychophysiology, 35,* 143–154; Narem, R. (1980). Try a little TLC. *Science, 80,* 15; Ruberman, R. (1992). Psychosocial influences on mortality of patients with coronary heart disease. *Journal of the American Medical Association, 267,* 559–560.

[6] Cohen, S., Doyle, W. J., Skoner, D. P., Rabin, B. S., & Gwaltney, J. M. (1997). Social ties and susceptibility to the common cold. *Journal of the American Medical Association, 277,* 1940–1944; Kiecolt-Glaser, J. K., Loving, T. J., Stowell, J. R., Malarkey, W. B., Lemeshow, S., Dickinson, S. L., & Glaser, R. (2005). Hostile marital interactions, proinflammatory cytokine production, & wound healing. *Archives of General Psychiatry, 62,* 1377–1384.

[7] Goffman, E. (1963). *Stigma: Notes on the management of spoiled identity.* Englewood Cliffs, NJ: Prentice-Hall.

[8] Welch Cline, R. J., & McKenzie, N. J. (1996). "Stripping you of everything you ever held dear to your heart": The many losses of women with HIV/AIDS. In E. B. Ray (Ed.), *Case studies in communication and disenfranchisement: Applications to social health issues* (pp. 195–213). Mahwah, NJ: Lawrence Erlbaum Associates.

[9] See, e.g., Takahashi, L. M. (1998). *Homelessness, AIDS, and stigmatization: The NIMBY syndrome in the United States at the end of the Twentieth Century.* New York: Oxford University Press.

[10] Rubin, R. B., Perse, E. M., & Barbato, C. A. (1988). Conceptualization and measurement of interpersonal communication motives. *Human Communication Research, 14,* 602–628.

[11] Yingling, J. (1994). Constituting friendships in talk and metatalk. *Journal of Social and Personal Relationships, 11,* 411–426.

[12] Parks, M. R., & Floyd, K. (1996). Making friends in cyberspace. *Journal of Communication, 46,* 80–97.

[13] See, e.g., Usita, P. M., & Blieszner, R. (2002). Immigrant family strengths: Meeting communication challenges. *Journal of Family Issues, 23,* 266–286.

[14] Lane, H. (1975). *The Wild Boy of Aveyron.* Cambridge, MA: Harvard University Press.

[15] Baumeister, R. F., & Leary, M. R. (1995). The need to belong: Desire for interpersonal attachments as a fundamental human motivation. *Psychological Bulletin, 117,* 497–529.

[16] Diener, E., & Seligman, M. E. P. (2002). Very happy people. *Psychological Science, 13,* 81–84.

[17] Popenoe, D. (2007). *The state of our unions: The social health of marriage in America.* Piscataway, NJ: The National Marriage Project. See also Glenn, N. D., & Weaver, C. N. (1981). The contribution of marital happiness to global happiness.

Journal of Marriage and the Family, 43, 161–168.

[18] Weissman, M. M. (1987). Advances in psychiatric epidemiology: Rates and risks for major depression. *American Journal of Public Health, 77,* 445–451; Renne, K. S. (1971). Health and marital experience in an urban population. *Journal of Marriage and the Family, 23,* 338–350.

[19] Cooley, C. H. (1983). *Human nature and the social order.* Edison, NJ: Transaction Publishers.

[20] Higher Education Research Institute, University of California, Los Angeles. (2005). *The spiritual life of college students: A national study of college students' search for meaning and purpose.* Los Angeles: Author. Retrieved April 20, 2006, from: www.spirituality.ucla.edu

[21] Maslow, A. H. (1970). *Motivation and personality* (2nd ed.). New York: Harper & Row.

[22] Trevino, L. K., Draft, R. L., & Lengel, R. H. (1990). Understanding managers' media choices: A symbolic interactionist perspective. In J. Fulk & C. Steinfield (Eds.), *Organizations and communication technology* (pp. 71–94). Newbury Park, CA: Sage.

[23] Watzlawick, T., Beavin, J., & Jackson, D. (1967). *The pragmatics of human communication.* New York: Norton.

[24] Motley, M. T. (1990). On whether one can(not) communicate: An examination via traditional communication postulates. *Western Journal of Speech Communication, 54,* 1–20.

[25] This position is usually attributed to Watzlawick, Beavin, & Jackson, 1967.

[26] See Motley, M. T. (1990). On whether one can(not) not communicate: An examination via traditional communication postulates. *Western Journal of Communication, 54,* 1–20.

[27] Buck, R., & VanLear, C. A. (2002). Verbal and nonverbal communication: Distinguishing symbolic, spontaneous and pseudo-spontaneous nonverbal

behavior. *Journal of Communication, 52,* 522–541.

[28] Shimanoff, S. B. (1980). *Communication rules: Theory and research.* Beverly Hills, CA: Sage.

[29] National Communication Association. (1999). *How Americans communicate* [online]. Retrieved April 16, 2006, from http://www.natcom.org/research/Roper/how_americans_communicate.htm

[30] Brownell, J. (1990). Perceptions of listening behavior: A management study. *Journal of Business Communication, 27,* 401–416; Peterson, M. S. (1997). Personnel interviewers' perceptions of the importance and adequacy of applicants' communication skills. *Communication Education, 46,* 287–291.

[31] Gottman, J. M., & Silver, N. (1999). *The seven principles for making marriage work.* New York: Crown.

[32] For a classic text, see Katriel, T., & Philipsen, G. (1981). "What we need is communication": "Communication" as a cultural category in some American speech. *Communication Monographs, 48,* 300–317.

[33] McDaniel, S. H., Beckman, H. B., Morse, D. S., Silberman, J., Seaburn, D. B., & Epstein, R. M. (2007). Physician self-disclosure in primary care visits: Enough about you, what about me? *Archives of Internal Medicine, 167,* 1321–1326.

[34] Baxter, L. A., & Bullis, C. (1986). Turning points in developing romantic relationships. *Communication Research, 12,* 469–493.

[35] National Communication Association, 1999.

[36] See Jones, D. C. (1991). Friendship satisfaction and gender: An examination of sex differences in contributors to friendship satisfaction. *Journal of Social and Personal Relationships, 8,* 167–185; Noller, P., & Callan, V. J. (1990). Adolescents' perceptions of the nature of their communication with parents. *Journal of Youth and Adolescence, 19,* 349–362.

[37] Kiecolt-Glaser, J. K., & Newton, T. L. (2001). Marriage and health: His and hers. *Psychological Bulletin, 127,* 472–503.

[38] Wing, R. R., & Jeffrey, R. W. (1999). Benefits of recruiting participants with friends and increasing social support for weight loss and maintenance. *Journal of Consulting and Clinical Psychology, 67,* 132–138.

[39] Beatty, M. J., Marshall, L. A., & Rudd, J. E. (2001). A twins study of communicative adaptability: Heritability of individual differences. *Quarterly Journal of Speech, 87,* 366–377; Beatty, M. J., McCroskey, J. C., & Heisel, A. D. (1998). Communication apprehension as temperamental expression: A communibiological paradigm. *Communication Monographs, 65,* 197–219.

[40] Spitzberg, B. H. (2000). What is good communication? *Journal of the Association for Communication Administration, 29,* 103–119.

[41] Spitzberg, B. H., & Cupach, W. (1989). *Handbook of interpersonal competence research.* New York: Springer-Verlag.

[42] Chen, G. M., & Starosta, W. J. (1996). Intercultural communication competence: A synthesis. In B. R. Burleson & A. W. Kunkel (Eds.), *Communication yearbook 19* (pp. 353–383). Thousand Oaks, CA: Sage.

[43] Schraw, G. (1998). Promoting general metacognitive awareness. *Instructional Science, 26,* 113–125; Sypher, B. D., & Sypher, H. E. (1983). Perceptions of communication ability: Self-monitoring in an organizational setting. *Personality and Social Psychology Bulletin, 9,* 297–304.

[44] Goleman, D. (2006). *Social intelligence: The new science of human relationships.* New York: Bantam Books; Goleman, D. (1996). *Emotional intelligence: Why it can matter more than IQ.* New York: Bantam Books.

[45] Stamp, G. H. (1999). A qualitatively constructed interpersonal communication model: A grounded theory analysis. *Human Communication Research, 25,* 531–547.

[46] Ifert, D. E., & Roloff, M. E. (1997). Overcoming expressed obstacles to compliance: The role of sensitivity to the expressions of others and ability to modify self-presentation. *Communication Quarterly, 45,* 55–67.

[47] Burleson, B. R., & Caplan, S. E. (1998). Cognitive complexity. In J. C. McCroskey, J. A. Daly, M. M. Martin, & M. J. Beatty (Eds.), *Communication and personality: Trait perspectives* (pp. 233–286). Cresskill, NJ: Hampton Press.

Notes for Chapter 2

[1] Tajfel, H., & Turner, J. C. (1986). The social identity theory of intergroup behavior. In S. Worchel & W. G. Austin (Eds.), *The psychology of intergroup relations* (pp. 7–24). Chicago: Nelson-Hall.

[2] Levitt, M. J., Lane, J. D., & Levitt, J. (2005). Immigration stress, social support, and adjustment in the first postmigration year: An intergenerational analysis. *Research in Human Development, 2,* 159–177.

[3] Öhman, L., Bergdahl, J., Nyberg, L., & Nilsson, L-G. (2007). Longitudinal analysis of the relation between moderate long-term stress and health. *Stress and Health, 23,* 131–138.

[4] See, e.g., Rushton, J. P. (2005). Ethnic nationalism, evolutionary psychology and Genetic Similarity Theory. *Nations and Nationalism, 11,* 489–507.

[5] McConnell, A. R., & Leibold, J. M. (2001). Relations among the Implicit Association Test, discriminatory behavior, and explicit measures of racial attitudes. *Journal of Experimental Social Psychology, 37,* 435–442.

[6] Suransky-Polakov, S. (2002). Denmark: Rebuffing immigrants. Retrieved July 27, 2007, from: http://www.worldpress.org/Europe/642.cfm

[7] Gordon, R. G. (Ed.). (2005). *Ethnologue: Languages of the world* (15th ed.). Dallas, TX: SIL International.

[8] Office of the New York State Comptroller: http://www.osc.state.ny.us/

[9] Foundation for Endangered Languages: http://www.ogmios.org/home.htm

[10] See Williams, R. M. (1970). *American society: A sociological interpretation* (3rd ed.). New York: Knopf.

[11] Padden, C., & Humphries, T. (1988). *Deaf in America: Voices from a culture.* Cambridge, MA: Harvard University Press.

[12] Holcomb, R. K., Holcomb, S. K., & Holcomb, T. K. (1995). *Deaf culture our way* (3rd ed.). San Diego, CA: DawnSign Press.

[13] See Lane, H., Hoffmeister, R., & Bahan, B. (1996). *A journey into the deaf world.* San Diego, CA: DawnSign Press.

[14] Leathers, D. G. (1997). *Successful nonverbal communication: Principles and applications* (3rd ed.). Boston: Allyn & Bacon.

[15] Triandis, H. C. (1990). Cross-cultural studies of individualism and collectivism. In J. Berman (Ed.), *Nebraska symposium on motivation* (pp. 41–133). Lincoln: University of Nebraska Press.

[16] Hofstede, G. (2003). *Culture's consequences: Comparing values, behaviors, institutions, and organizations across nations* (2nd ed.). Thousand Oaks, CA: Sage.

[17] Piot, C. (1999). *Remotely global: Village modernity in West Africa.* Chicago: University of Chicago Press.

[18] Hofstede, 2003.

[19] Cai, D. A., & Fink, E. L. (2002). Conflict style differences between individualists and collectivists. *Communication Monographs, 69,* 67–87.

[20] See Andersen, P. A. (1999). *Nonverbal communication: Forms and functions.* Palo Alto, CA: Mayfield.

[21] Hall, E. T. (1959). *Beyond culture.* New York: Doubleday.

[22] Ambady, N., Koo, J., Lee, F., & Rosenthal, R. (1996). More than words: Linguistic and nonlinguistic politeness in two cultures. *Journal of Personality and Social Psychology, 70,* 996–1011.

[23] Hofstede, 2003.

[24] Hofstede, G., & Hofstede, G. J. (2004). *Cultures and organizations: Software of the mind* (2nd ed.). Boston: McGraw-Hill.

[25] Andersen, P. (1991). Explaining intercultural differences in nonverbal communication. In L. A. Samovar & R. E. Porter (Eds.), *Intercultural communication: A reader* (6th ed., pp. 286–296). Belmont, CA: Wadsworth.

[26] Yook, E. L., & Albert, R. D. (1998). Perceptions of the appropriateness of negotiation in educational settings: A cross-cultural comparison among Koreans and Americans. *Communication Education, 47,* 18–29.

[27] Hofstede & Hofstede, 2004.

[28] Hofstede & Hofstede, 2004.

[29] Hall, E. T., & Hall, M. R. (1990). *Understanding cultural differences: Germans, French, and Americans.* Boston: Intercultural Press.

[30] Hall, E. T. (1990). *The silent language.* New York: Anchor Books.

[31] Hilton, B. A. (1994). The Uncertainty Stress Scale: Its development and psychometric properties. *Canadian Journal of Nursing Research, 26,* 15–30.

[32] Hofstede, G. (1986). Cultural differences in teaching and learning. *International Journal of Intercultural Relations, 10,* 301–320.

[33] Lee, W. S. (1994). On not missing the boat: A processual method for intercultural understanding of idioms and lifeworld. *Journal of Applied Communication Research, 22,* 141–161.

[34] Pease, A., & Pease, B. (2004). *The definitive book of body language: The secret meaning behind people's gestures.* London: Orion Books.

[35] Maccoby, E. E. (1998). *The paradox of gender.* Cambridge, MA: Harvard University Press.

[36] Pratto, F. (1996). Sexual politics: The gender gap in the bedroom, the cupboard, and the cabinet. In D. M. Buss & N. M. Malamuth (Eds.), *Sex, power, conflict: Evolutionary and feminist perspectives* (pp. 179–230). New York: Oxford University Press.

[37] See, e.g., Kimmel, M. (1996). *Manhood in America.* New York: Free Press.

[38] Courtenay, W. (2000). Constructions of masculinity and their influence on men's well-being: A theory of gender and health. *Social Science and Medicine, 50,* 1385–1401.

[39] U.S. Department of Justice, Bureau of Justice Statistics. Victim characteristics. Downloaded June 10, 2006, from: http://www.ojp.usdoj.gov/bjs/cvict_v.htm

[40] Kimmel, 1996; see also Williamson, P. (November 29). Their own worst enemy. *Nursing Times, 91*(48), 24–27.

[41] Spence, J. T. (1984). Gender identity and its implications for the concepts of masculinity and femininity. *Nebraska Symposium on Motivation, 32,* 59–95.

[42] American Psychiatric Association Work Group on Eating Disorders. (2000). Practice guideline for the treatment of patients with eating disorders (revision). *American Journal of Psychiatry, 157*(1 Suppl), 1–39; Regier, D. A., Narrow, W. E., Rae, D. S., Manderscheid, R. W., Locke, B. Z., & Goodwin, F. K. (1993). The de facto mental and addictive disorders service system: Epidemiologic catchment area prospective 1-year prevalence rates of disorders and services. *Archives of General Psychiatry, 50,* 85–94.

[43] See, e.g., Martin, D., & Walker, L. E. (1979). What keeps a woman captive in a violent relationship? The social context of battering. In D. M. Moore (Ed.), *Battered women* (pp. 33–58). Beverly Hills, CA: Sage.

[44] Bem, S. L. (1974). The measurement of psychological androgyny. *Journal of Consulting and Clinical Psychology, 43,* 155–162.

[45] Simpson, M. (1994, November 5). Here come the mirror men. *The Independent* (London), p. 22.

[46] Segall, M. H., Dasen, P. R., Berry, J. W., & Poortinga, Y. H. (1990). *Human behavior in global perspective: An introduction to cross-cultural psychology.* New York: Pergamon.

[47] Hofstede, G. H. (1997). *Cultures and organizations: Software of the mind.* New York: McGraw-Hill.

[48] Human Rights Campaign Foundation. (2004). *Transgender issues in the workplace: A tool for managers.* Washington, DC: Author.

[49] Clements-Nolle, K., Marx, R., Guzman, R., & Katz, M. (2001). HIV prevalence, risk behaviors, health care use, and mental health status of transgender persons: Implications for public health intervention. *American Journal of Public Health, 91,* 915–921.

[50] Gagné, P., Tewksbury, R., & McGaughey, D. (1997). Coming out and crossing over: Identity formation and proclamation in a transgender community. *Gender and Society, 11,* 478–508.

51 Blackless, M., Charuvastra, A., Derryck, A., Fausto-Sterling, A., Lauzanne, K., & Lee, E. (2000). How sexually dimorphic are we? Review and synthesis. *American Journal of Human Biology, 12,* 151–166.

52 Grumbach, M. M., & Conte, F. A. (1998). Disorders of sex differentiation. In J. D. Wilson, D. W. Foster, H. M. Kronenberg, & P. R. Larsen (Eds.), *Williams textbook of endocrinology* (pp. 1303–1425). Philadelphia: W. B. Saunders.

53 Dreger, A. D. (1998). *Hermaphrodites and the medical invention of sex.* Cambridge, MA: Harvard University Press.

54 See, e.g., Australian Research Centre in Health, Sex, and Society. (2003). Sex in Australia: The Australian Study of Health and Relationships. *Australian and New Zealand Journal of Public Health, 27*(2); Bagley, C., & Tremblay, P. (1998). On the prevalence of homosexuality and bisexuality in a random community survey of 750 men aged 18 to 27. *Journal of Homosexuality, 36,* 1–18; King, A. J. C., Beasley, R. P., Warren, W. K., Hankins, C. A., Robinson, A. S., & Radford, J. L. (1989). Highlights from the Canada Youth and AIDS Study. *Journal of School Health, 59,* 139.

55 Embrick, D. G., Walther, C. S., & Wickens, C. M. (2007). Working class masculinity: Keeping gay men and lesbians out of the workplace. *Sex Roles, 56,* 757–766; Herek, G. M. (1992). The social context of hate crimes: Notes on cultural heterosexism. In G. H. Herek & K. Berrill (Eds.), *Hate crimes* (pp. 89–104). Thousand Oaks, CA: Sage; Peel, E. (2001). Mundane heterosexism: Understanding incidents of the everyday. *Women's Studies International Forum, 24,* 541–554.

56 Foucault, M. (1990). *The history of sexuality. Vol. 1: An introduction* (Robert Hurley, Trans.) New York: Vintage.

57 Rotundo, E. A. (1993). *American manhood: Transformations in masculinity from the revolution to the modern era.* New York: Basic Books.

58 See Vilain, E. (2000). Genetics of sexual development. *Annual Review of Sex Research, 11,* 1–25.

59 Mosher, W. D., Chandra, A., & Jones, J. (2005, September 15). Sexual behavior and selected health measures: Men and women 15–44 years of age, United States, 2002. Atlanta, GA: Centers for Disease Control and Prevention. Retrieved July 27, 2007, from: http://www.cdc.gov/nchs/data/ad/ad362.pdf

60 Rieger, G., Chivers, M. L., & Bailey, J. M. (2005). Sexual arousal patterns of bisexual men. *Psychological Science, 16,* 579–584; Rodriguez, P. C. (Ed.). (1999). *Bisexuality in the United States: A social science reader.* New York: Columbia University Press.

61 Burleson, B. E. (2005). *Bi America: Myths, truths, and struggles of an invisible community.* Binghamton, NY: Haworth Press.

62 Mosher et al., 2005.

63 Bogaert, A. F. (2004). Asexuality: Prevalence and associated factors in a national probability sample. *Journal of Sex Research, 41,* 279–287.

64 Gray, J. (1992). *Men are from Mars, women are from Venus: A practical guide to improving communication and getting what you want in your relationships.* New York: HarperCollins.

65 Gray, 1992, p. 5.

66 Tannen, D. (1990). *You just don't understand: Women and men in conversation.* New York: Morrow; Wood, J. T. (2000). Relational culture: The nucleus of intimacy. In J. T. Wood (Ed.), *Relational communication: Continuity and change in personal relationships* (2nd ed., pp. 76–100). Belmont, CA: Wadsworth.

67 Bate, B., & Bowker, J. (1997). *Communication and the sexes* (2nd ed.). Prospect Heights, IL: Waveland Press; Johnson, F. L. (2000). *Speaking culturally: Language diversity in the United States.* Thousand Oaks, CA: Sage.

68 Burleson, B. R., & Kunkel, A. (2006). Revisting the different cultures thesis: An assessment of sex differences and similarities in supportive communication. In K. Dindia & D. J. Canary (Eds.), *Sex differences and similarities in communication* (2nd ed., pp. 137–159). Mahwah, NJ: Lawrence Erlbaum Associates.

69 See, e.g., MacGeorge, E. L., Feng, B., & Butler, G. L. (2003). Gender differences in the communication values of mature adults. *Communication Research Reports, 20,* 191–199; Parks, M. R., & Floyd, K. (1996). Meanings for closeness and intimacy in friendship. *Journal of Social and Personal Relationships, 13,* 85–107; Xu, Y., & Burleson, B. R. (2001). Effects of sex, culture, and support type on perceptions of spousal social support: An assessment of the "support gap" hypothesis in early marriage. *Human Communication Research, 27,* 535–566.

70 Burleson & Kunkel, 2006.

71 Dindia, K. (2006). Men are from North Dakota, women are from South Dakota. In K. Dindia & D. J. Canary (Eds.), *Sex differences and similarities in communication* (2nd ed., pp. 3–20). Mahwah, NJ: Lawrence Erlbaum Associates.

72 Canary, D. J., & Hause, K. S. (1993). Is there any reason to research sex differences in communication? *Communication Quarterly, 41,* 129–144; Wright, P. H. (1988). Interpreting gender differences in friendship: A case for moderation and a plea for caution. *Journal of Social and Personal Relationships, 5,* 367–373.

73 Wood, J. T., & Inman, C. C. (1993). In a different mode: Masculine styles of communicating closeness. *Journal of Applied Communication Research, 21,* 279–295.

74 See Wood, J. T. (1998). *But I thought you meant . . . : Misunderstandings in human communication.* Mountain View, CA: Mayfield.

75 Wood, J. T. (2007). *Gendered lives: Communication, gender, and culture* (7th ed.). Belmont, CA: Wadsworth.

76 Neppl, T. K., & Murray, A. D. (1997). Social dominance and play patterns among preschoolers: Gender comparisons. *Sex Roles, 36,* 381–393.

77 See, e.g., Clark, R. A. (1998). A comparison of topics and objectives in a cross section of young men's and women's everyday conversations. In D. Canary & K. Dindia (Eds.), *Sex differences and similarities in communication: Critical essays and empirical investigations of sex and gender interaction* (pp. 303–319). Mahwah, NJ: Lawrence Erlbaum Associates; Martin, C., Fabes, R., Evans, S.,

& Wyman, H. (2000). Social cognition on the playground: Children's beliefs about playing with girls versus boys and their relations to sex segregated play. *Journal of Social and Personal Relationships, 17,* 751–771.

[78] Lippa, R. A. (2000). Gender-related traits in gay men, lesbian women, and heterosexual men and women: The virtual identity of homosexual-heterosexual diagnosticity and gender diagnosticity. *Journal of Personality, 68,* 899–926.

[79] Henley, N. (1977). *Body politics: Power, sex, and nonverbal communication.* Englewood Cliffs, NJ: Prentice-Hall; Henley, N. (1995). Body politics revisited: What do we know today? In P. Kalbfleisch & M. Cody (Eds.), *Gender, power, and communication in human relationships* (pp. 27–61). Hillsdale, NJ: Lawrence Erlbaum Associates.

[80] Kalbfleisch, P. J., & Herold, A. L. (2006). Sex, power, and communication. In K. Dindia & D. Canary (Eds.), *Sex differences and similarities in communication* (2nd ed., pp. 299–313). Mahwah, NJ: Lawrence Erlbaum Associates.

[81] Mehl, M. R., Vazire, S., Ramírez-Esparza, N., Slatcher, R. B., & Pennebaker, J. W. (2007). Are women really more talkative than men? *Science, 317,* 82.

[82] Athenstaedt, U., Haas, E., & Schwab, S. (2004). Gender role self-concept and gender-typed communication behavior in mixed-sex and same-sex dyads. *Sex Roles, 50,* 37–52; Brownlow, S., Rosamond, J. A., & Parker, J. A. (2003). Gender-linked linguistic behavior in television interviews. *Sex Roles, 49,* 121–132.

[83] Mehl, M., & Pennebaker, J. (2002, January). *Mapping students' natural language use in everyday conversations.* Paper presented at the third annual meeting of the Society for Personality and Social Psychology, Savannah, GA; Redeker, G., & Maes, A. (1996). Gender differences in interruptions. In D. Slobin, J. Gerhardt, A. Kyratzis, & J. Guo (Eds.), *Social interaction, social context, and language* (pp. 579–612). Mahwah, NJ: Lawrence Erlbaum Associates.

[84] Basow, S., & Rubenfeld, K. (2003). "Trouble talk": Effects of gender and gender-typing. *Sex Roles, 48,* 183–187.

[85] House, A., Dallinger, J., & Kilgallen, D. (1998). Androgyny and rhetorical sensitivity: The connection of gender and communication style. *Communication Reports, 11,* 11–20.

[86] Gay, W. C. (1999). Linguistic violence. In R. Litke & D. Curtin (Eds.), *Institutional violence* (pp. 13–35). Amsterdam: Rodopi.

[87] Gay, W. C. (1997). The reality of linguistic violence against women. In L. O'Toole & J. Schiffman (Eds.), *Gender violence: Interdisciplinary perspectives* (pp. 467–473). New York: New York University Press.

[88] Wessler, S. (2005). *Discrimination against gay, lesbian, bisexual, and transgender individuals in Maine.* Portland, ME: The Center for the Prevention of Hate Violence.

[89] Mulac, A., Bradac, J. J., & Gibbons, P. (2001). Empirical support for the gender-as-culture hypothesis: An intercultural analysis of male/female language differences. *Human Communication Research, 27,* 121–152.

[90] Mulac, A. (2006). The gender-linked language effect: Do language differences really make a difference? In K. Dindia & D. Canary (Eds.), *Sex differences and similarities in communication* (2nd ed., pp. 219–239). Mahwah, NJ: Lawrence Erlbaum Associates.

[91] Lumby, M. E. (1976). Code switching and sexual orientation: A test of Bernstein's sociolinguistic theory. *Journal of Homosexuality, 1,* 383–399.

[92] Major, B., Schmidlin, A. M., & Williams, L. (1990). Gesture patterns in social touch: The impact of setting and age. *Journal of Personality and Social Psychology, 58,* 634–643.

[93] Leathers, 1997. (See note 14.)

[94] Eakins, B. W., & Eakins, R. G. (1978). *Sex differences in human communication.* Boston: Houghton Mifflin.

[95] Uzzell, D., & Horne, N. (2006). The influence of biological sex, sexuality and gender role on interpersonal distance. *British Journal of Social Psychology, 45,* 579–597.

[96] Newport, F. (2001, February 21). Americans see women as emotional and affectionate, men as more aggressive. Retrieved July 23, 2007, from: http://www.galluppoll.com/content/?ci=1978&pg=1

[97] Burgoon, J. K., & Bacue, A. E. (2003). Nonverbal communication skills. In J. O. Greene & B. R. Burleson (Eds.), *Handbook of communication and social interaction skills* (pp. 179–219). Mahwah, NJ: Lawrence Erlbaum Associates.

[98] LaFrance, M., Hecht, M. A., & Levy Paluck, E. (2003). The contingent smile: A meta-analysis of sex differences in smiling. *Psychological Bulletin, 129,* 305–334.

[99] Hall, J. A., & Friedman, G. (1999). Status, gender, and nonverbal behavior: A study of structured interactions between employees. *Personality and Social Psychology Bulletin, 25,* 1082–1091; LaFrance, M., & Hecht, M. A. (2000). Gender and smiling: A meta analysis. In A. H. Fischer (Ed.), *Gender and emotion: Social psychological perspective* (pp. 118–142). Cambridge, England: Cambridge University Press.

[100] Witmer, D. F., & Katzman, S. (1997). On-line smiles: Does gender make a difference in the use of graphic accents? *Journal of Computer-Mediated Communication, 2*(4). Retrieved June 24, 2006, from http://jcmc.indiana.edu/vol2/issue4/witmer1.html

[101] A sex difference in anger expression was reported in Coats, E. J., & Feldman, R. S. (1996). Gender differences in nonverbal correlates of social status. *Personality and Social Psychology Bulletin, 22,* 1014–1022. One study that failed to report such a difference was Burrowes, B. D., & Halberstadt, A. G. (1987). Self- and family-expressiveness styles in the experience and expression of anger. *Journal of Nonverbal Behavior, 11,* 254–268.

[102] White, G. L., & Mullen, P. E. (1989). *Jealousy: Theory, research, and clinical strategies.* New York: Guilford.

[103] Harris, I. D., & Howard, K. I. (1987). Correlates of depression and anger in adolescence. *Journal of Clinical and Adolescent Psychotherapy, 4,* 199–203; Stapley, J. C., & Haviland, J. M. (1989). Beyond depression: Gender differences in normal

adolescents' emotional experiences. *Sex Roles, 20,* 295–308.

[104] Kring, A. M., & Gordon, A. H. (1998). Sex differences in emotion: Expression, experience, and physiology. *Journal of Personality and Social Psychology, 74,* 686–703; see also Gross, J. J., & John, O. P. (1998). Mapping the domain of expressivity: Multimethod evidence for a hierarchical model. *Journal of Personality and Social Psychology, 74,* 170–191.

[105] Kring & Gordon, 1998.

[106] Gottman, J. M., Levenson, R. W., Gross, J., Frederickson, B. L., McCoy, K., Rosenthal, L., Ruef, A., & Yoshimoto, D. (2003). Correlates of gay and lesbian couples' relationship satisfaction and relationship dissolution. *Journal of Homosexuality, 45,* 23–43.

[107] For a review, see Floyd, K. (2006). *Communicating affection: Interpersonal behavior and social context.* Cambridge, England: Cambridge University Press.

[108] Floyd, K., & Voloudakis, M. (1999). Affectionate behavior in adult platonic friendships: Interpreting and evaluating expectancy violations. *Human Communication Research, 25,* 341–369; Shuntich, R. J., & Shapiro, R. M. (1991). Explorations of verbal affection and aggression. *Journal of Social Behavior and Personality, 6,* 283–300.

[109] Floyd, K. (1997). Knowing when to say "I love you": An expectancy approach to affectionate communication. *Communication Research Reports, 14,* 321–330.

[110] Floyd, K., & Morman, M. T. (2000). Reacting to the verbal expression of affection in same-sex interaction. *Southern Communication Journal, 65,* 287–299.

[111] See Taylor, S. E., Klein, L. C., Lewis, B. P., Gruenwald, T. L., Guring, R. A. R., & Updegraff, J. A. (2000). Biobehavioral responses to stress in females: Tend-and-befriend, not fight-or-flight. *Psychological Review, 107,* 411–429.

[112] Floyd, K., & Morman, M. T. (2000). Affection received from fathers as a predictor of men's affection with their own sons: Tests of the modeling and compensation hypotheses. *Communication Monographs,*

67, 347–361; Floyd, K., & Tusing, K. J. (2002, July). *"At the mention of your name": Affect shifts induced by relationship-specific cognitions.* Paper presented at annual meeting of the International Communication Association, Seoul, South Korea; Morman, M. T., & Floyd, K. (1999). Affectionate communication between fathers and young adult sons: Individual- and relational-level correlates. *Communication Studies, 50,* 294–309.

[113] Kurdek, L. A. (2006). Differences between partners from heterosexual, gay, and lesbian cohabiting couples. *Journal of Marriage and Family, 68,* 509–528.

[114] Floyd, K. (2001). Human affection exchange: I. Reproductive probability as a predictor of men's affection with their sons. *Journal of Men's Studies, 10,* 39–50; Floyd, K., Sargent, J. E., & Di Corcia, M. (2004). Human affection exchange: VI. Further tests of reproductive probability as a predictor of men's affection with their fathers and their sons. *Journal of Social Psychology, 144,* 191–206.

Notes for Chapter 3

[1] Luft, J., & Ingham, H. (1955). The Johari window: A graphic model of interpersonal awareness. *Proceedings of the Western Training Laboratory in Group Development.* Los Angeles: UCLA.

[2] Reported in Myers, D. G. (1980). *The inflated self.* New York: Seabury Press.

[3] Brown, J. D., & Mankowski, T. A. (1993). Self-esteem, mood, and self-evaluation: Changes in mood and the way you see you. *Journal of Personality and Social Psychology, 64,* 421–430; Campbell, J. D. (1990). Self-esteem and clarity of the self-concept. *Journal of Personality and Social Psychology, 59,* 538–549.

[4] Tarlow, E. M., & Haaga, D. A. F. (1996). Negative self-concept: Specificity to depressive symptoms and relation to positive and negative affectivity. *Journal of Research in Personality, 30,* 120–127.

[5] Swann, W. B., Rentfrow, P. J., & Guinn, J. S. (2003). Self-

verification: The search for coherence. In J. P. Tangney & M. R. Leary (Eds.), *Handbook of self and identity* (pp. 367–383). New York: Guilford Press.

[6] Greenwald, A. G. (1995). Getting (my) self into social psychology. In G. G. Brannigan & M. R. Merrens (Eds.), *The social psychologists: Research adventures* (pp. 3–16). New York: McGraw-Hill.

[7] Block, J., & Robins, R. W. (1993). A longitudinal study of consistency and change in self-esteem from early adolescence to early childhood. *Child Development, 64,* 909–923.

[8] Woodgate, R. (2005). A different way of being: Adolescents' experiences with cancer. *Cancer Nursing, 28,* 121–128.

[9] van der Meulen, M. (2001). Developments in self-concept theory and research: Affect, context, and variability. In H. A. Bosma & E. S. Kunnen (Eds.), *Identity and emotion: Development through self-organization* (pp. 10–38). New York: Cambridge University Press.

[10] Rosenblith, J. F. (1992). *In the beginning: Development from conception to age two.* Newbury Park, CA: Sage.

[11] Wright, W. (1998). *Born that way: Genes, behavior, personality.* New York: Knopf.

[12] Bouchard, T. J., Lykken, D. T., McGue, M., & Segal, N. L. (1990). Sources of human psychological differences: The Minnesota Study of Twins Reared Apart. *Science* (October 12), 223–228.

[13] Kagan, J. (1989). *Unstable ideas: Temperament, cognition, and self.* Cambridge, MA: Harvard University Press; Schwartz, C. E., Wright, C. I., Shin, L. M., Kagan, J., & Rauch, S. L. (2003). Inhibited and uninhibited infants "grown up": Adult amygdalar response to novelty. *Science* (June 20), 1952–1953.

[14] Gudykunst, W. B., & Ting-Toomey, S. (1988). *Culture and interpersonal communication.* Newbury Park, CA: Sage.

[15] Holstein, J. A., & Gubrium, J. F. (2000). *The self we live by: Narrative identity in a postmodern world.* New York: Oxford University Press.

[16] See McIntyre, L. (2006). *The practical skeptic: Core*

concepts in sociology. New York: McGraw-Hill; Yeung, K.-T., & Martin, J. L. (2003). The looking glass self: An empirical test and elaboration. *Social Forces, 81,* 843–879.

[17] Hergovitch, A., Sirsch, U., & Felinger, M. (2002). Self-appraisals, actual appraisals and reflected appraisals of pre-adolescent children. *Social Behavior and Personality, 30,* 603–612.

[18] See Beatty, M. J., & Dobos, J. A. (1993). Adult males' perceptions of confirmation and relational partner communication apprehension: Indirect effects of fathers on sons' partners. *Communication Quarterly, 41,* 66–76.

[19] Han, M. (2003). Body image dissatisfaction and eating disturbance among Korean female college students: Relationships to media exposure, upward comparison, and perceived reality. *Communication Studies, 34,* 65–78.

[20] "Skinny models banned from catwalk." (2006, September 13). Available online at: http://www.cnn.com/2006/WORLD/europe/09/13/spain.models/index.html?section=cnn_latest

[21] "N.Y. considers banning ultra-thin fashion models." (2007, February 3). Available online at: http://www.cnn.com/2007/US/02/01/skinny.models/index.html

[22] Flegal, K. M., Carroll, M. D., Ogden, C., & Johnson, C. L. (2002). Prevalence and trends in obesity among U.S. adults, 1999–2000. *Journal of the American Medical Association, 288,* 1723–1727.

[23] Carr, D., & Friedman, M. A. (2005). Is obesity stigmatizing? Body weight, perceived discrimination, and psychological well-being in the United States. *Journal of Health and Social Behavior, 46,* 244–259.

[24] Hamachek, D. (1992). *Encounters with the self* (3rd ed.). Fort Worth, TX: Holt, Rinehart & Winston.

[25] Hamachek, 1992.

[26] Centers for Disease Control and Prevention. (2007). Prevalence of the autism spectrum disorders in multiple areas of the United States, surveillance years 2000 and 2002. Down-loaded August 13, 2007, from: http://www.cdc.gov/ncbddd/dd/addmprevalence.htm

[27] Kolligan, J. (1990). Perceived fraudulence as a dimension of perceived incompetence. In R. J. Sternberg & J. Kolligan (Eds.), *Competence considered* (pp. 261–285). New Haven, CT: Yale University Press; Downey, G., & Feldman, S. I. (1996). Implications of rejection sensitivity for intimate relationships. *Journal of Personality and Social Psychology, 70,* 1327–1343.

[28] MacIntyre, P. D., & Thivierge, K. A. (1995). The effects of speaker personality on anticipated reactions to public speaking. *Communication Research Reports, 12,* 125–133.

[29] Rosenthal, R., & Jacobson, L. (1968). *Pygmalion in the classroom.* New York: Holt, Rinehart & Winston.

[30] Ridge, R. D., & Reber, J. S. (1998, August). *Women's responses to men's flirtations in a professional setting: Implications for sexual harassment.* Paper presented at the annual meeting of the American Psychological Society, Washington, DC.

[31] Rosenthal & Jacobson, 1968.

[32] Campbell, J. D., & Lavallee, L. F. (1993). Who am I? The role of self-concept confusion in understanding the behavior of people with low self-esteem. In R. F. Baumeister (Ed.), *Self-esteem: The puzzle of low self-regard* (pp. 3–20). New York: Plenum Press.

[33] Tafarodi, R. W., & Vu, C. (1997). Two-dimensional self-esteem and reactions to success and failure. *Personality and Social Psychology Bulletin, 23,* 626–635.

[34] Buhrmester, D., Furman, W., Wittenberg, M. T., & Reis, H. T. (1988). Five domains of interpersonal competence in peer relations. *Journal of Personality and Social Psychology, 55,* 991–1008; Murray, S. L., Rose, P., Bellavia, G., Holmes, J. G., & Kusche, A. (2002). When rejection stings: How self-esteem constrains relationship-enhancement processes. *Journal of Personality and Social Psychology, 83,* 556–573.

[35] Bishop, J., & Inderbitzen-Nolan, H. M. (1995). Peer acceptance and friendship: An investigation of their rela-tion to self-esteem. *Journal of Early Adolescence, 15,* 476–489; Rusbult, C. E., Morrow, G. D., & Johnson, D. J. (1987). Self-esteem and problem solving behavior in close relationships. *British Journal of Social Psychology, 26,* 293–303.

[36] Baumeister, R. F. (2001). Violent pride: Do people turn violent because of self-hate, or self-love? *Scientific American, 284*(4), 96–101; Olweus, D. (1994). *Bullying at school: What we know and what we can do.* Malden, MA: Blackwell.

[37] McGee, R. O., & Williams, S. M. (2000). Does low self-esteem predict health compromising behaviours among adolescents? *Journal of Adolescence, 23,* 569–582.

[38] Baumeister, R. F., Campbell, J. D., Krueger, J. I., & Vohs, K. D. (2003). Does high self-esteem cause better performance, interpersonal success, happiness, or healthier lifestyles? *Psychological Science in the Public Interest, 4,* 1–44.

[39] Lyubomirsky, S., Tkach, C., & DiMatteo, M. R. (2005). What are the differences between happiness and self-esteem? *Social Indicators Research, 52,* 1–43.

[40] Diener, E., & Diener, M. (1995). Cross-cultural correlates of life satisfaction and self-esteem. *Journal of Personality and Social Psychology, 68,* 653–663.

[41] Baumeister et al., 2003.

[42] Mesmer-Magnus, J., Viswesvaran, C., Deshpande S., & Joseph, J. (2006). Social desirability: The role of overclaiming, self-esteem, and emotional intelligence. *Psychology Science, 48,* 336–356.

[43] Baumgardner, A. H., Kaufman, C. M., & Levy, P. E. (1989). Regulating affect interpersonally: When low esteem leads to greater enhancement. *Journal of Personality and Social Psychology, 56,* 907–921.

[44] Ybarra, O. (1999). Misanthropic person memory when the need to self-enhance is absent. *Personality and Social Psychology Bulletin, 25,* 261–269.

[45] Amabile, T. M. (1983). *The social psychology of creativity.* New York: Springer-Verlag.

[46] McGee, R., Williams, S., & Nada-Raja, S. (2001). Low

self-esteem and hopelessness in childhood and suicidal ideation in early adulthood. *Journal of Abnormal Child Psychology, 29,* 281–291.

[47] Lewinsohn, P. M., Rohde, P., & Seeley, J. R. (1994). Psychosocial risk factors for future adolescent suicide attempts. *Journal of Consulting and Clinical Psychology, 62,* 297–305.

[48] For additional examples, see Twenge, J. (2006). *Generation me: Why today's young Americans are more confident, assertive, entitled—and more miserable than ever before.* New York: Free Press.

[49] Swygert, K. (2005, January 28). Spelling the end of spelling bees. *Number 2 Pencil,* retrieved August 15, 2007, from: http://www.kimberlyswygert.com/archives/002605.html

[50] See, e.g., Pottebaum, S. M., Keith, T. Z., & Ehly, S. (1986). Is there a causal relation between self-concept and academic achievement? *Journal of Educational Research, 79,* 140–144.

[51] Gabriel, M. T., Critelli, J. W., & Ee, J. S. (1994). Narcissistic illusions in self-evaluations of intelligence and attractiveness. *Journal of Personality, 62,* 143–155.

[52] Forsyth, D. R., & Kerr, N. A. (1999, August). *Are adaptive illusions adaptive?* Paper presented at the annual meeting of the American Psychological Association, Boston, MA.

[53] Baumeister et al., 2003. (See note 38.)

[54] Wallace, H. M., & Baumeister, R. F. (2002). The performance of narcissists rises and falls with perceived opportunity for glory. *Journal of Personality and Social Psychology, 82,* 819–834.

[55] Baumeister, R. F., Heatherton, T. F., & Tice, D. M. (1993). When ego threats lead to self-regulation failure: Negative consequences of high self-esteem. *Journal of Personality and Social Psychology, 64,* 141–156.

[56] Myers, D. G. (2001). *Psychology* (6th ed.). New York: Worth Publishers.

[57] Twenge, J. M., & Crocker, J. (2002). Race and self-esteem: Meta-analyses comparing whites, blacks, Hispanics, Asians, and American Indians and comment on Gray-Little and Hafdahl (2000). *Psychological*

Bulletin, 128, 371–408; see also Gray-Little, B., & Hafdahl, A. R. (2000). Factors influencing racial comparisons of self-esteem: A quantitative review. *Psychological Bulletin, 126,* 26–54.

[58] Twenge & Crocker, 2002.

[59] Crocker, J., & Major, B. (1989). Social stigma and self-esteem: The self-protective properties of stigma. *Psychological Review, 89,* 608–630.

[60] American Association of University Women. (1992). *The AAUW report: How schools shortchange girls.* Washington, DC: Author.

[61] Twenge & Crocker, 2002.

[62] Sidanius, J., & Pratto, F. (1999). *Social dominance.* Cambridge, England: Cambridge University Press.

[63] Kuijer, R. G., Buunk, B. P., Ybema, J. F., & Wobbes, T. (2002). The relation between perceived inequity, marital satisfaction and emotions among couples facing cancer. *British Journal of Social Psychology, 41,* 39–56.

[64] Judge, T. A., Erez, A., Bono, J. E., & Thoresen, C. J. (2002). Are measures of self-esteem, neuroticism, locus of control, and generalized self-efficacy indicators of a common core construct? *Journal of Personality and Social Psychology, 83,* 693–710.

[65] Baumeister, R. F., & Leary, M. R. (1995). The need to belong: Desire for interpersonal attachments as a fundamental human motivation. *Psychological Bulletin, 117,* 497–529.

[66] Robins, R. W., Tracy, J. L., Trzesniewski, K., Potter, J., & Gosling, S. D. (2001). Personality correlates of self-esteem. *Journal of Research in Personality, 35,* 463–482.

[67] For review, see Floyd, K. (2006). *Communicating affection: Interpersonal behavior and social context.* Cambridge, England: Cambridge University Press.

[68] Floyd, K. (2002). Human affection exchange: V. Attributes of the highly affectionate. *Communication Quarterly, 50,* 135–154.

[69] McAdams, D. P. (1996). Personality, modernity, and the storied self: A contemporary framework for studying

persons. *Psychological Inquiry, 7,* 295–321.

[70] Butler, L. M., Elliott, D., & Gunther, J. (Eds.). (2001). *Strategies to overcome oppression and discrimination for marginalized groups.* Lewiston, NY: Edwin Mellen.

[71] Meyer, I. H. (2003). Prejudice, social stress, and mental health in lesbian, gay, and bisexual populations: Conceptual issues and research evidence. *Psychological Bulletin, 129,* 674–697.

[72] Cole, S. W., Kemeny, M. E., Taylor, S. E., & Visscher, B. R. (1996). Elevated physical health risk among gay men who conceal their homosexual identity. *Health Psychology, 15,* 243–251.

[73] Cole, S., Kemeny, M., Taylor, S., Visscher, B., & Fahey, J. (1996). Accelerated course of HIV infection in gay men who conceal their homosexual identity. *Psychosomatic Medicine, 58,* 219–231.

[74] Hidaka, Y., & Operario, D. (2006). Attempted suicide, psychological health and exposure to harassment among Japanese homosexual, bisexual or other men questioning their sexual orientation recruited via the internet. *Journal of Epidemiology and Community Health, 60,* 962–967.

[75] Russell, S. T., & Joyner, K. (2001). Adolescent sexual orientation and suicide risk: Evidence from a national study. *American Journal of Public Health, 91,* 1276–1281.

[76] Huebner, D. M., & Davis, M. C. (2005). Gay and bisexual men who disclose their sexual orientations in the workplace have higher workday levels of salivary cortisol and negative affect. *Annals of Behavioral Medicine, 30,* 260–267.

[77] Lewis, R. J., Derlega, V. J., Griffin, J. L., & Krowinski, A. C. (2003). Stressors for gay men and lesbians: Life stress, gay-related stress, stigma consciousness, and depressive symptoms. *Journal of Social and Clinical Psychology, 22,* 716–729.

[78] Goldschmidt, M. M. (2004). Good person stories: The favor narrative as a self-presentation strategy. *Qualitative Research Reports in Communication, 5,* 28–33.

[79] See Ting-Toomey, S., Oetzel, J. G., & Yee-Jung, K. (2001). Self-

construal types and conflict management styles. *Communication Reports, 14,* 87–104; Ting-Toomey, S., & Oetzel, J. G. (2001). *Managing intercultural conflict effectively.* Thousand Oaks, CA: Sage.

[80] Goffman, E. (1959). *The presentation of the self in everyday life.* New York: Doubleday; see also Brown, P., & Levinson, S. C. (1987). *Politeness: Some universals in language usage.* Cambridge, England: Cambridge University Press.

[81] Lim, T. S., & Bowers, J. W. (1991). Facework: Solidarity, approbation, and tact. *Human Communication Research, 17,* 415–449.

[82] Cupach, W. R., & Metts, S. (1994). *Facework.* Thousand Oaks, CA: Sage.

[83] Brocklehurst, J., & Dickinson, E. (1996). Autonomy for elderly people in long-term care. *Age and Aging, 25,* 329–332.

[84] See, e.g., Takahashi, L. M. (1998). *Homelessness, AIDS, and stigmatization: The NIMBY syndrome in the United States at the end of the Twentieth Century.* New York: Oxford University Press.

[85] VanLear, C. A. (1991). Testing a cyclical model of communicative openness in relationship development: Two longitudinal studies. *Communication Monographs, 58,* 337–361.

[86] See Qian, H., & Scott, C. R. (2007). Anonymity and self-disclosure on weblogs. *Journal of Computer-Mediated Communication, 12*(4), article 14. http://jcmc.indiana.edu/vol12/issue4/qian.html

[87] Sproull, L., & Kiesler, S. (1991). *Connections: New ways of working in the networked organization.* Cambridge: MIT Press.

[88] We, G. (1993, April). *Cross-gender communication in cyberspace.* Unpublished manuscript, Department of Communication, Simon Frasier University, Canada [Online], 8 pp. Available: ftp://cpsr.org/cpsr/gender/we_cross_gender (April 26, 1995).

[89] Walther, J. B. (1996). Computer-mediated communication: Impersonal, interpersonal, and hyperpersonal interaction. *Communication Research, 23,* 3–43.

[90] Gouldner, A. W. (1960). The norm of reciprocity: A preliminary statement. *American Sociological Review, 25,* 161–178.

[91] Miller, L. C., & Kenny, D. A. (1986). Reciprocity of self-disclosure at the individual and dyadic levels: A social relations analysis. *Journal of Personality and Social Psychology, 50,* 713–719.

[92] Derlega, V. J., Metts, S., Petronio, S., & Margulis, S. T. (1993). *Self-disclosure.* Newbury Park, CA: Sage.

[93] See Wood, J. T. (2007). *Gendered lives: Communication, gender, and culture* (7th ed.). Belmont, CA: Wadsworth.

[94] See, e.g., Triandis, H. C. (1989). The self and social behavior in differing cultural contexts. *Psychological Review, 96,* 506–520.

[95] Dindia, K. (2000). Sex differences in self-disclosure, reciprocity of self-disclosure, and self-disclosure and liking: Three meta-analyses reviewed. In S. Petronio (Ed.), *Balancing the secrets of private disclosures* (pp. 21–35). Mahwah, NJ: Lawrence Erlbaum Associates.

[96] Lippert, T., & Prager, K. J. (2001). Daily experiences of intimacy: A study of couples. *Personal Relationships, 8,* 283–298.

[97] Chelune, G. J., Rosenfeld, L. B., & Waring, E. M. (1985). Spouse disclosure patterns in distressed and nondistressed couples. *American Journal of Family Therapy, 13,* 24–32.

[98] Dindia, K. (2002). Self-disclosure research: Knowledge through meta-analysis. In M. Allen & R. W. Preiss (Eds.), *Interpersonal communication research: Advances through meta-analysis* (pp. 169–185). Mahwah, NJ: Lawrence Erlbaum Associates.

[99] Kelly, A. E., Klusas, J. A., von-Weiss, R. T., & Kenny, C. (2001). What is it about revealing secrets that is beneficial? *Personality and Social Psychology Bulletin, 27,* 651–665.

[100] See Kacewicz, E., Slatcher, R. B., & Pennebaker, J. W. (2007). Expressive writing: An alternative to traditional methods. In L. L'Abate (Ed.), *Low-cost approaches to promote physical and mental health: Theory, research, and practice* (pp. 271–284). New York: Springer.

[101] Helgeson, V. S., & Gottlieb, B. H. (2000). Support groups. In S. Cohen, L. G. Underwood, & B. H. Gottlieb (Eds.), *Social support measurement and intervention* (pp. 221–245). New York: Oxford University Press.

[102] Agne, R., Thompson, T. L., & Cusella, K. P. (2000). Stigma in the line of face: Self-disclosure of patients' HIV status to health care providers. *Journal of Applied Communication Research, 28,* 235–261.

[103] Parks, M. R. (1982). Ideology in interpersonal communication: Off the couch and into the world. In M. Burgoon (Ed.), *Communication yearbook 5* (pp. 79–107). New Brunswick, NJ: Transaction.

[104] Derlega et al., 1993. (See note 92.)

[105] Suler, J. (1996). The psychology of cyberspace. Available online at: http://www.rider.edu/~suler/psycyber/psychber.html

[106] Whittle, D. B. (1997). *Cyberspace: The human dimensions.* New York: W. H. Freeman and Company.

Notes for Chapter 4

[1] See Kenny, D. A. (1994). *Interpersonal perception: A social relations analysis.* New York: Guilford.

[2] Schermerhorn, J. R., Hunt, J. H., & Osborn, R. N. (2003). *Organizational behavior* (8th ed.). New York: John Wiley & Sons.

[3] Goldstein, E. B. (2007). *Sensation and perception* (7th ed.). Pacific Grove, CA: Wadsworth.

[4] Floyd, K., Ramirez, A., & Burgoon, J. K. (2008). Expectancy violations theory. In L. K. Guerrero, J. A. DeVito, & M. L. Hecht (Eds.), *The nonverbal communication reader: Classic and contemporary readings* (3rd ed., pp. 503–510). Prospect Heights, IL: Waveland.

[5] Zajonc, R. B. (2001). Mere exposure: A gateway to the subliminal. *Current Directions in Psychological Science, 10,* 224–228.

[6] Goldstein, 2007.

[7] Andersen, P. A. (1998). *Nonverbal communication: Forms and functions.* New York: McGraw-Hill.

8 Sowa, J. F. (2000). *Knowledge representation: Logical, philosophical, and computational foundations.* Pacific Grove, CA: Brooks/Cole.

9 Funder, D. C. (1999). *Personality judgment: A realistic approach to person perception.* San Diego: Academic Press.

10 Fiske, S. T., & Taylor, S. E. (1991). *Social cognition* (2nd ed.). New York: McGraw-Hill.

11 Kelley, H. H. (1967). Attribution theory in social psychology. In D. Levine (Ed.), *Nebraska Symposium on Motivation* (Vol. 15, pp. 192–238). Lincoln: University of Nebraska Press.

12 Jones, E. E., & Davis, K. E. (1965). From acts to dispositions: The attribution process in person perception. In L. Berkowitz (Ed.), *Advances in experimental social psychology* (Vol. 2, pp. 219–266). New York: Academic Press.

13 See, e.g., Manusov, V. (1993). It depends on your perspective: Effects of stance and beliefs about intent on person perception. *Western Journal of Communication, 57,* 27–41.

14 Andersen, 1998.

15 See, e.g., Bruce, V., Georgeson, M. A., & Green, P. R. (2003). *Visual perception: Physiology, psychology and ecology* (4th ed.). New York: Psychology Press.

16 Miró, E., Cano, M. C., Espinoza-Fernández, L., & Beula-Casal, G. (2003). Time estimation during prolonged sleep deprivation and its relation to activation measures. *Human Factors, 45,* 148–159.

17 Alaimo, K., Olson, C. M., & Frongillo, E. A. (2001). Food insufficiency and American school-aged children's cognitive, academic, and psychosocial development. *Pediatrics, 108,* 44–53.

18 See Bartoshuk, L. (1980, September). Separate works of taste. *Psychology Today, 14,* 48–63.

19 Touitou, Y. (1998). Biological clocks: Mechanisms and application. *Proceedings of the International Congress on Chronobiology.* New York: Elsevier Science.

20 Larson, J. H., Crane, D. R., & Smith, C. W. (1991). Morning and night couples: The effect of wake and sleep patterns on marital adjustment. *Journal of Marital and Family Therapy, 17,* 53–65.

21 Ji, L. K., Peng, K., & Nisbett, R. E. (2000). Culture, control, and perception of relationships in the environment. *Journal of Personality and Social Psychology, 78,* 943–955; Knowles, E. D., Morris, M. W., Chiu, C -Y., & Hong, Y -Y. (2001). Culture and the process of person perception: Evidence for automaticity among East Asians in correcting for situational influences on behavior. *Personality and Social Psychology Bulletin, 27,* 1344–1356.

22 Hall, E. T. (1959). *The silent language.* Garden City, NY: Doubleday.

23 Luszcz, M. A., & Fitzgerald, K. M. (1986). Understanding cohort differences in cross-generational, self, and peer perceptions. *Journal of Gerontology, 41,* 234–240.

24 Argyle, M. (1993). *The psychology of social class.* New York: Routledge.

25 Farwell, L., & Weiner, B. (2000). Bleeding hearts and the heartless: Popular perceptions of liberal and conservative ideologies. *Personality and Social Psychology Bulletin, 26,* 845–852.

26 See Butler, L. M., Elliott, D., & Gunther, J. (Eds.). (2001). *Strategies to overcome oppression and discrimination for marginalized groups.* Lewiston, NY: Edwin Mellen.

27 Edmondson, C. B., & Conger, J. C. (1995). The impact of mode of presentation on gender differences in social perception. *Sex Roles, 32,* 169–183.

28 Littrell, M. A., & Berger, E. A. (1986). Perceiver's occupation and client's grooming: Influence on person perception. *Clothing and Textiles Research Journal, 4,* 48–55; Maeder, E. M., Wiener, R. L., & Winter, R. (2007). Does a truck driver see what a nurse sees? The effects of occupation type on perceptions of sexual harassment. *Sex Roles, 56,* 801–810.

29 Lepore, L., & Brown, R. (1997). Category and stereotype activation: Is prejudice inevitable? *Journal of Personality and Social Psychology, 72,* 275–287.

30 Buttney, R. (1997). Reported speech in talking race on campus. *Human Communication Research, 23,* 477–506; Nelson, T. D. (2005). Ageism: Prejudice against our featured future self. *Journal of Social Issues, 61,* 207–221.

31 See, e.g., Hendrix, K. G. (2002). "Did being Black introduce bias into your study?" Attempting to mute the race-related research of black scholars. *Howard Journal of Communication, 13,* 153–171; Hughes, P. C., & Baldwin, J. R. (2002). Communication and stereotypical impressions. *Howard Journal of Communication, 13,* 113–128.

32 Aronson, J., Lustina, M. J., Good, C., & Keough, K. (1999). When white men can't do math: Necessary and sufficient factors in stereotype threat. *Journal of Experimental Social Psychology, 35,* 29–46.

33 Snyder, M., & Uranowitz, S. (1978). Reconstructing the past: Some cognitive consequences of person perception. *Journal of Personality and Social Psychology, 36,* 941–950.

34 Allen, M. (1998). Methodological considerations when examining a gendered world. In D. J. Canary & K. Dindia (Eds.), *Handbook of sex differences and similarities in communication* (pp. 427–444). Mahwah, NJ: Lawrence Erlbaum Associates.

35 Fyock, J., & Stangor, C. (1994). The role of memory biases in stereotype maintenance. *British Journal of Social Psychology, 33,* 331–343.

36 Lee, Y -T., Jussim, L. J., & McCauley, C. R. (1996). *Stereotype accuracy: Toward appreciating group differences.* Washington, DC: American Psychological Association.

37 Tetlock, P. E. (1983). Accountability and the perseverance of first impressions. *Social Psychology Quarterly, 46,* 285–292.

38 Asch, S. (1946). Forming impressions of personality. *Journal of Abnormal and Social Psychology, 41,* 258–290.

39 Parsons, C. K., Liden, R. C., & Bauer, T. N. (2001). Personal perception in employment interviews. In M. London (Ed.), *How people evaluate others in organizations* (pp. 67–90). Mahwah, NJ: Lawrence Erlbaum Associates.

40 Luchins, A. (1957). Primacy-recency in impression forma-

tion. In C. Hovland (Ed.), *The order of presentation in persuasion* (pp. 33–61). New Haven, CT: Yale University Press.

[41] Ybarra, O. (2001). When first impressions don't last: The role of isolation and adaptation processes in the revision of evaluative impressions. *Social Cognition, 19,* 491–520.

[42] Baddeley, A. D., & Hitch, G. (1993). The recency effect: Implicit learning with explicit retrieval? *Memory and Cognition, 21,* 146–155.

[43] McCann, C. D., Higgins, E. T., & Fondacaro, R. A. (1991). Primacy and recency in communication and self-persuasion: How successive audiences and multiple encodings influence subsequent evaluative judgments. *Social Cognition, 9,* 47–66.

[44] Schyns, P. G., & Oliva, A. (1999). Dr. Angry and Mr. Smile: When categorization flexibly modifies the perception of faces in rapid visual presentations. *Cognition, 69,* 243–265.

[45] Stern, M., & Karraker, K. H. (1989). Sex stereotyping of infants: A review of gender labeling studies. *Sex Roles, 20,* 501–522.

[46] Mondloch, C. J., Lewis, T. L., Budreau, D. R., Maurer, D., Dannemiller, J. L., Stephens, B. R., & Kleiner-Gathercoal, K. A. (1999). Face perception during early infancy. *Psychological Science, 10,* 419–422; Morton, J., & Johnson, M. H. (1991). CONSPEC and CONLERN: A two-process theory of infant face recognition. *Psychological Review, 98,* 164–181.

[47] King, D. E., & Bushwick, B. (1994). Beliefs and attitudes of hospital inpatients about faith healing and prayer. *Journal of Family Practice, 39,* 349–352.

[48] Floyd, K. (2000). Affectionate same-sex touch: Understanding the influence of homophobia on observers' perceptions. *Journal of Social Psychology, 140,* 774–788.

[49] Gregory, R. L., & Gombrich, E. H. (Eds.). (1973). *Illusion in nature and art.* New York: Charles Scribner's Sons.

[50] Lapsley, D. K., Milstead, M., Quintana, S. M., Flannery, D., & Buss, R. R. (1986). Adolescent egocentrism and formal operations: Tests of a theoreti-

cal assumption. *Developmental Psychology, 22,* 800–807.

[51] Piaget, J. (1930). *The child's conception of physical causality.* London: Routledge & Kegal Paul; Piaget, J. (1932). *The moral judgment of the child.* New York: Harcourt, Brace & World.

[52] Kelley, C. M. (1996). Adult egocentrism: Subjective experience versus analytic bases for judgment. *Journal of Memory and Language, 35,* 157–175.

[53] Cummins, R. A., & Nistico, H. (2002). Maintaining life satisfaction: The role of positive cognitive bias. *Journal of Happiness Studies, 3,* 37–69.

[54] Hendrick, C., & Hendrick, S. S. (1988). Lovers wear rose colored glasses. *Journal of Social and Personal Relationships, 5,* 161–183.

[55] Murray, S. L., Holmes, J. G., & Griffin, D. W. (1996). The benefits of positive illusions: Idealization and the construction of satisfaction in close relationships. *Journal of Personality and Social Psychology, 70,* 79–98; see also Fisher, H. (2004). *Why we love: The nature and chemistry of romantic love.* New York: Henry Holt.

[56] Lupfer, M. B., Weeks, M., & Dupuis, S. (2000). How pervasive is the negativity bias in judgments based on character appraisal? *Personality and Social Psychology Bulletin, 26,* 1353–1366.

[57] Webster, E. (1964). *Decision making in the employment interview.* Montreal, Canada: Industrial Relations Centre, McGill University.

[58] Anderson, N. (1981). *Foundations of information integration theory.* New York: Academic Press.

[59] Bradbury, T. N., & Fincham, F. D. (1990). Attributions in marriage: Review and critique. *Psychological Bulletin, 107,* 3–33.

[60] Manusov, V., & Harvey, J. H. (Eds.). (2001). *Attribution, communication behavior, and close relationships.* Cambridge, England: Cambridge University Press.

[61] Weiner, B. (2000). Intrapersonal and interpersonal theories of motivation from an attributional perspective. *Educational Psychology Review, 12,* 1–14.

[62] Pascarella, E. T., Edison, M., Hagedorn, L. S., Nora, A., & Terenzini, P. T. (1996). Influences on students' internal locus of attribution for academic success in the first year of college. *Research in Higher Education, 37,* 731–756.

[63] Weiner, B. (1985). An attributional theory of achievement motivation and emotion. *Psychological Review, 92,* 548–573.

[64] Hooley, J. M., & Campbell, C. (2002). Control and controllability: Beliefs and behaviour in high and low expressed emotion relatives. *Psychological Medicine, 32,* 1091–1099.

[65] Block, J., & Funder, D. C. (1986). Social roles and social perception: Individual differences in attribution and error. *Journal of Personality and Social Psychology, 51,* 1200–1207.

[66] Sedikides, C., Campbell, W. K., Reeder, G. D., & Elliott, A. J. (1998). The self-serving bias in relational context. *Journal of Personality and Social Psychology, 74,* 378–386.

[67] See, e.g., Bradbury & Fincham, 1990; Sillars, A., Roberts, L. J., Dun, T., & Leonard, K. (2001). Stepping into the stream of thought: Cognition during marital conflict. In V. Manusov & J. H. Harvey (Eds.), *Attribution, communication behavior, and close relationships* (pp. 193–210). Cambridge, England: Cambridge University Press.

[68] Trower, P., & Chadwick, P. (1995). Pathways to defense of the self: A theory of two types of paranoia. *Clinical Psychology: Science and Practice, 2,* 263–278.

[69] Ross, L. (1977). The intuitive psychologist and his shortcomings: Distortions in the attribution process. In L. Berkowitz (Ed.), *Advances in experimental social psychology* (Vol. 10, pp. 173–220). New York: Academic Press; Tetlock, P. E. (1985). Accountability: A social check on the fundamental attribution error. *Social Psychology Quarterly, 48,* 227–236.

[70] Napolitan, D. A., & Goethals, G. R. (1979). The attribution of friendliness. *Journal of Experimental Social Psychology, 15,* 105–113.

[71] Corneille, O., Leyens, J.-P., Yzerbyt, V. Y., & Walther, E.

(1999). Judgeability concerns: The interplay of information, applicability, and accountability in the overattribution bias. *Journal of Personality and Social Psychology, 76,* 377–387; Webster, D. M. (1993). Motivated argument and reduction of the overattribution bias. *Journal of Personality and Social Psychology, 65,* 261–271.

[72] Leyens, J -P., Yzerbyt, V. Y., & Corneille, O. (1996). The role of applicability in the emergence of the overattribution bias. *Journal of Personality and Social Psychology, 70,* 219–229.

[73] Schweinle, W. E., Ickes, W., & Bernstein, I. H. (2002). Empathic inaccuracy in husband to wife aggression: The overattribution bias. *Personal Relationships, 9,* 141–158.

[74] Schweinle, W. E., & Ickes, W. (2007). The role of men's critical/rejecting overattribution bias, affect, and attentional disengagement in marital aggression. *Journal of Social and Clinical Psychology, 26,* 173–198.

[75] See, e.g., Alicke, M. D., Zerbst, J. I., & LoSchiavo, F. M. (1996). Personal attitudes, constraint magnitude, and correspondence bias. *Basic and Applied Social Psychology, 18,* 211–228.

[76] See Woolfolk, R. L., Doris, J. M., & Darley, J. M. (2006). Identification, situational constraint, and social cognition: Studies in the attribution of moral responsibility. *Cognition, 100,* 283–301.

[77] Bursik, K. (1992). Perceptions of sexual harassment in an academic context. *Sex Roles, 27,* 401–412; Katz, R. C., Hannon, R., & Whitten, L. (1996). Effects of gender and situation on the perception of sexual harassment. *Sex Roles, 34,* 35–42; Marks, M. A., & Nelson, E. S. (1993). Sexual harassment on campus: Effects of professor gender on perception of sexually harassing behaviors. *Sex Roles, 28,* 207–217.

Notes for Chapter 5

[1] Christensen, M., & Kirby, S. (Eds.). (2003). *Language evolution.* New York: Oxford University Press.

[2] Jenkins, L. (2000). *Biolinguistics: Exploring the biology of language.* Cambridge, England: Cambridge University Press.

[3] Hockett, C. F. (1958). *A course in modern linguistics.* New York: Macmillan.

[4] See, e.g., Shetter, W. Z. (2002). Your mouse just went "click": Speech sounds imitating natural ones. Retrieved September 9, 2006, from http://home .bluemarble.net/~langmin/ miniatures/onomato.htm; Trask, R. L. (1999). *Language: The basics.* New York: Routledge.

[5] Pinker, S. (2007). *The stuff of thought: Language as a window into human nature.* New York: Viking.

[6] Ogden, C. K., & Richards, I. A. (1927). *The meaning of meaning: A study of the influence of language upon thought and of the science of symbolism* (2nd ed.). Orlando, FL: Harcourt Brace.

[7] British Council. (2004). Mum's the word: British Council announces results of 70 most beautiful words survey. Retrieved online September 23, 2006, from: http://www .britishcouncil.de/e/about/ 70words.htm

[8] Garlinger, P. P. (2004). "In all but name": Marriage and the meaning of homosexuality. *Discourse, 26,* 41–72.

[9] Garlinger, 2004.

[10] Bryson, B. (1990). *The mother tongue: English and how it got that way.* New York: William Morrow.

[11] Paul, J., & Strbiak, C. A. (1997). The ethics of strategic ambiguity. *The Journal of Business Communication, 34,* 149–159.

[12] Hayakawa, S. I., & Hayakawa, A. R. (1991). *Language in thought and action.* San Diego, CA: Harcourt.

[13] Gudykunst, W., & Lee, C. (2002). Cross-cultural communication theories. In W. Gudykunst & B. Mody (Eds.), *The handbook of international and intercultural communication* (2nd ed., pp. 25–50). Thousand Oaks, CA: Sage.

[14] Giles, H., & Franklyn-Stokes, A. (1989). Communicator characteristics. In M. K. Asante & W. Gudykunst (Eds.), *Handbook of international and intercultural communication* (pp. 117–144). Newbury Park, CA: Sage.

[15] Schultz, E. A. (1990). *Dialogue at the margins: Whorf, Bakhtin, and linguistic relativity.* Madison: University of Wisconsin Press; Whorf, B. L. (1956). The relation of habitual thought and behavior to language. In J. B. Carroll (Ed.), *Language, thought, and reality; Selected writings of Benjamin Lee Whorf* (pp. 134–159). Cambridge: MIT Press.

[16] Gumperz, J. J., & Levinson, S. C. (Eds.). (1996). *Rethinking linguistic relativity.* New York: Cambridge University Press.

[17] For more detail on the Sapir-Whorf hypothesis, see Hoijer, H. (1988). The Sapir-Whorf hypothesis. In L. A. Samovar & R. E. Porter (Eds.), *Intercultural communication: A reader* (5th ed., pp. 225–232). Belmont, CA: Wadsworth.

[18] Moore, C. J. (2004). *In other words: A language lover's guide to the most intriguing words around the world.* New York: Walker & Co.

[19] Marcus, M. G. (1976, October). The power of a name. *Psychology Today, 9,* 75–77, 106.

[20] Steele, K. M., & Smithwick, L. E. (1989). First names and first impressions: A fragile relationship. *Sex Roles, 21,* 517–523.

[21] Garwood, S. G., Cox, L., Kaplan, V., Wasserman, N., & Sulzer, J. L. (1980). Beauty is only "name" deep: The effect of first-name on ratings of physical attraction. *Journal of Applied Social Psychology, 10,* 431–435.

[22] U. S. Social Security Administration. Popular baby names. Retrieved September 17, 2006, from http://www.ssa.gov/OACT/ babynames/

[23] Foss, K. A., & Edson, B. A. (1989). What's in a name? Accounts of married women's name choices. *Western Journal of Speech Communication, 53,* 356–373.

[24] Parigoris, C. G. (2002). Marital surnames and gender roles of contemporary women. *Dissertation Abstracts International, 62,* 3851; Twenge, J. M. (1997). "Mrs. His Name": Women's preferences for married names. *Psychology of Women Quarterly, 21,* 417–429.

[25] Stafford, L., & Kline, S. L. (1996). Married women's name choices and sense of self. *Communication Reports, 9,* 85–92.

[26] Goodman, R. J., Morris, J. D., Sutherland, J., & Huckeba, J.

(2006, August). *Is beauty a joy forever? Young women's emotional responses to varying types of beautiful advertising models.* Paper presented at the annual conference of the Association for Education in Journalism and Mass Communication, San Francisco.

27 Burger, J. M. (1986). Increasing compliance by improving the deal: The that's-not-all technique. *Journal of Personality and Social Psychology, 31,* 277–283.

28 Cialdini, R. B. (1994). Interpersonal influence. In S. Shavitt & T. C. Brock (Eds.), *Persuasion: Psychological insights and perspectives* (pp. 195–218). Boston: Allyn & Bacon.

29 Cody, M. J., Seiter, J., & Montagne-Miller, Y. (1995). Women and men in the marketplace. In P. Kalbfleisch & M. J. Cody (Eds.), *Gender, power, and communication in human relationships* (pp. 305–328). Hillsdale, NJ: Lawrence Erlbaum Associates.

30 Giles, H., & Wiemann, J. M. (1987). Language, social comparison and power. In C. R. Berger & S. H. Chaffee (Eds.), *The handbook of communication science* (pp. 350–384). Newbury Park, CA: Sage.

31 Bavelas, J. B., Black, A., Bryson, L., & Mullett, J. (1988). Political equivocation: A situational explanation: *Journal of Language and Social Psychology, 7,* 137–145; Bavelas, J. B., Black, A., Chovil, N., & Mullett, J. (1990). *Equivocal communication.* Newbury Park, CA: Sage.

32 Hamilton, M. A., & Mineo, P. J. (1998). A framework for understanding equivocation. *Journal of Language and Social Psychology, 17,* 3–35.

33 Daly, J. A., Diesel, C. A., & Weber, D. (1994). Conversational dilemmas. In W. R. Cupach & B. H. Spitzberg (Eds.), *The dark side of interpersonal communication* (pp. 127–156). Mahwah, NJ: Lawrence Erlbaum Associates.

34 Bradac, J. J., Wiemann, J. M., & Schaefer, K. (1994). The language of control in interpersonal communication. In J. A. Daly & J. M. Wiemann (Eds.), *Strategic interpersonal communication* (pp. 102–104). Hillsdale, NJ: Lawrence Erlbaum Associates.

35 Hosman, L. A. (1989). The evaluative consequences of hedges, hesitations, and intensifiers: Powerful and powerless speech styles. *Human Communication Research, 15,* 383–406.

36 Huston, T. L., Caughlin, J. P., Houts, R. M., Smith, S. E., & George, L. J. (2001). The connubial crucible: Newlywed years as predictors of marital delight, distress, and divorce. *Journal of Personality and Social Psychology, 80,* 237–252.

37 Jorm, A. F., Dear, K. B. G., Rodgers, B., & Christensen, H. (2003). Interaction between mother's and father's affection as a risk factor for anxiety and depression symptoms. *Social Psychiatry and Psychiatric Epidemiology, 38,* 173–179; Schwartz, G. E., & Russek, L. G. (1998). Family love and lifelong health? A challenge for clinical psychology. In D. K. Routh & R. J. DeRubeis (Eds.), *The science of clinical psychology: Accomplishments and future directions* (pp. 121–146). Washington, DC: American Psychological Association.

38 See Floyd, K. (2006). *Communicating affection: Interpersonal behavior and social context.* Cambridge, England: Cambridge University Press.

39 Floyd, K., & Morman, M. T. (2000). Reacting to the verbal expression of affection in same-sex interaction. *Southern Journal of Communication, 65,* 287–299.

40 ASD/AMD Merchandise Group. (2006). Greeting card marketers and retailers struggle. Retrieved September 18, 2006, from: http://www.merchandisegroup.com/merchandise/newsletter/newsletter_display.jsp?vnu_content_id=1001306530

41 www.bluemountain.com

42 See, e.g., Zunin, L. M., & Zunin, H. S. (1992). *The art of condolence: What to write, what to say, and what to do at a time of loss.* New York: Harper.

43 See Pennebaker, J. W. (Ed.). (1995). *Emotion, disclosure, and health.* Washington, D.C.: American Psychological Association.

44 Floyd, K., Mikkelson, A. C., Tafoya, M. A., Farinelli, L., La Valley, A. G., Judd, J., Haynes, M. T., Davis, K. L., & Wilson, J. (2007). Human affection exchange: XIII. Affectionate communication accelerates neuroendocrine stress recovery. *Health Communication, 22,* 123–132.

45 Wiseman, R. (2002). *Laughlab: The scientific search for the world's funniest joke.* London, England: Random House.

46 Mobbs, D., Greicius, M. D., Abdel-Azim, E., Menon, V., & Reiss, A. L. (2003). Humor modulates the mesolimbic reward centers. *Neuron, 40,* 1041–1048.

47 Norrick, N. R. (1993). *Conversational joking: Humor in everyday talk.* Indianapolis: Indiana University Press.

48 Keller, K. (1984). *Humor as therapy.* Wauwatosa, WI: MedPsych.

49 Feingold, A. (1992). Gender differences in mate selection preferences: A test of the parental investment model. *Psychological Bulletin, 112,* 125–139.

50 Alberts, J. K. (1992). Teasing and sexual harassment: Double bind communication in the workplace. In L. A. Perry, H. Sterk, & L. Turner (Eds.), *Constructing and reconstructing gender* (pp. 150–120). Albany: SUNY Press.

51 Makin, V. S. (2004). Face management and the role of interpersonal politeness variables in euphemism production and comprehension. *Dissertation Abstracts International, 64,* 4077; McGlone, M. S., & Batchelor, J. A. (2003). Looking out for number one: Euphemism and face. *Journal of Communication, 53,* 251–264.

52 Gladney, G. A., & Rittenburg, T. L. (2005). Euphemistic text affects attitudes, behavior. *Newspaper Research Journal, 26,* 28–41.

53 McGlone, M. S., Beck, G., & Pfiester, A. (2006). Contamination and camouflage in euphemisms. *Communication Monographs, 73,* 261–282.

54 Deans, B. (1991). The sanitized lexicon of modern war. *Newspaper Research Journal, 12,* 11–12.

55 Lutz, W. (1987). *Doublespeak: From "revenue enhancement" to "terminal living": How government, business, advertisers, and others use language to deceive you.* New York: Harper & Row.

56 Gladney & Rittenburg, 2005.

57 Bandura, A. (1999). Moral disengagement in the perpetration of inhumanities. *Personality and Social Psychology Review, 3,* 193–209.

58 See Spacks, P. M. (1985). *Gossip.* New York: Knopf.

59 Butler, J. (1997). *Excitable speech: A politics of the performative.* New York: Routledge.

60 Abelson, R. (2001, April 20). Online message boards getting nasty. *Raleigh News and Observer,* pp. E1, E3.

61 Bryant, S. (2006). Feds retrieve Google records after Gmail used for hate speech. Retrieved September 6, 2006, from: http://googlewatch.eweek .com/blogs/google_watch/ archive/2006/07/27/11852.aspx

62 Bernstein, E. D. (2003). "You can't say that": Canadian thought police on the march. Retrieved September 6, 2006, from: http:// www.nationalreview.com

63 Emanuel, E. J. (1994). The history of euthanasia debates in the United States and Britain. *Annals of Internal Medicine, 121,* 793–802.

64 Hurst, S. A., & Mauron, A. (2006). The ethics of palliative care and euthanasia: Exploring common values. *Palliative Medicine, 20,* 107–112.

65 Kubany, E. S., Richard, D. C., Bauer, G. B., & Muraoka, M. Y. (1992). Impact of assertive and accusatory communication of distress and anger: A verbal component analysis. *Aggressive Behavior, 18,* 337–347.

Notes for Chapter 6

1 Nierenberg, G. (1990). *How to read a person like a book.* New York: Pocket Books.

2 Calero, H. H. (2005). *The power of non-verbal communication: What you do is more important than what you say.* Lansdowne, PA: Silver Lake Publishing.

3 Mehrabian, A. (1968). Communication without words. *Psychology Today, 2,* 51–52.

4 Birdwhistell, R. L. (1970). *Kinesics and context.* Philadelphia: University of Pennsylvania Press; see also Philpott, J. S. (1983). *The relative contribution to meaning of verbal and nonverbal channels of communication: A meta-analysis.*

Unpublished master's thesis, University of Nebraska, Lincoln.

5 Burgoon, J. K. (1985). Nonverbal signals. In M. L. Knapp & G. R. Miller (Eds.), *Handbook of interpersonal communication* (pp. 344–390). Beverly Hills, CA: Sage.

6 See Hall, J. A. (2006). How big are nonverbal sex differences? The case of smiling and nonverbal sensitivity. In K. Dindia & D. J. Canary (Eds.), *Sex differences and similarities in communication* (2nd ed., pp. 59–81). Mahwah, NJ: Lawrence Erlbaum Associates.

7 Ekman, P., & Friesen, W. V. (1975). *Unmasking the face: A field guide to recognizing emotions from facial clues.* Englewood Cliffs, NJ: Prentice-Hall.

8 Ekman, P. (1972). Universals and cultural differences in facial expressions of emotion. In J. Cole (Ed.), *Nebraska symposium on motivation, 1971* (Vol. 19, pp. 207–282). Lincoln: University of Nebraska Press.

9 Boucher, J. D., & Carlson, G. E. (1980). Recognition of facial expression in three cultures. *Journal of Cross-Cultural Psychology, 11,* 263–280; Cüceloglu, D. M. (1970). Perception of facial expressions in three cultures. *Ergonomics, 13,* 93–100; Ekman, P., Friesen, W. V., O'Sullivan, M., Chan, A., Diacoyanni-Tarlatzis, I., Heider, K., Krause, R., LeCompte, W. A., Pitcairn, T., Ricci-Bitti, P. E., Scherer, K., Tomita, M., & Tzavaras, A. (1987). Universals and cultural differences in the judgments of facial expressions of emotion. *Journal of Personality and Social Psychology, 53,* 712–717; Izard, C. E. (1971). *The face of emotion.* New York: Appleton-Century-Crofts; McAndrew, F. T. (1986). A cross-cultural study of recognition thresholds for facial expression of emotion. *Journal of Cross-Cultural Psychology, 17,* 211–224; Niit, T., & Valsiner, J. (1977). Recognition of facial expressions: An experimental investigation of Ekman's model. *Acta et Commentationes Universitatis Tarvensis, 429,* 85–107.

10 Elfenbein, H. A., & Ambady, N. (2002). On the universality and cultural specificity of emotion recognition: A meta-analysis. *Psychological Bulletin, 128,* 203–235.

11 Kappas, A., Hess, U., & Scherer, K. R. (1991). Voice and emotion. In R. S. Feldman & B. Rime (Eds.), *Fundamentals of nonverbal communication* (pp. 200–237). Cambridge, England: Cambridge University Press.

12 Scherer, K. R., Banse, R., & Wallbott, H. G. (2001). Emotion inferences from vocal expression correlate across languages and cultures. *Journal of Cross-Cultural Psychology, 32,* 76–92.

13 Knapp, M. L. (1978). *Nonverbal communication in human interaction* (2nd ed.). New York: Holt.

14 Ellis, H. D., & Young, A. W. (1989). Are faces special? In A. W. Young & H. D. Ellis (Eds.), *Handbook of research on face processing* (pp. 1–26). Amsterdam: North-Holland.

15 Grammer, K., & Thornhill, R. (1994). Human (*homo sapiens*) facial attractiveness and sexual selection: The role of symmetry and averageness. *Journal of Comparative Psychology, 108,* 233–242; Scheib, J. E., Gangestad, S. W., & Thornhill, R. (1999). Facial attractiveness, symmetry, and cues to good genes. *Proceedings of the Royal Society of London, Series B, 266,* 1913–1917.

16 http://www.aafprs.org/patient/ procedures/rhinoplasty.html

17 Ekman, P., Friesen, W. V., & Ellsworth, P. (1972). *Emotion in the human face: Guidelines for research and an integration of findings.* New York: Pergamon Press.

18 Rosenthal, R., & DePaulo, B. M. (1979). Sex differences in accommodation in nonverbal communication. In R. Rosenthal (Ed.), *Skill in nonverbal communication: Individual differences* (pp. 68–103). Cambridge, MA: Oelgeschlager, Gunn & Hain.

19 Eagly, A. H., & Crowley, M. (1986). Gender and helping behavior: A meta-analytic review of the social psychological literature. *Psychological Bulletin, 100,* 283–308.

20 Akert, R. M., & Panter, A. T. (1988). Extraversion and the ability to decode nonverbal communication. *Personality & Individual Differences, 9,* 965–972.

21 Smith, C., Lentz, E. M., & Mikos, K. (1988). *Signing natu-*

rally. San Diego, CA: DawnSign Press.

22 Matsumoto, D. (2006). Culture and nonverbal behavior. In V. Manusov & M. L. Patterson (Eds.), _The SAGE handbook of nonverbal communication_ (pp. 219–236). Thousand Oaks, CA: Sage.

23 Iizuka, Y. (1994). Gaze during speaking as related to shyness. _Perceptual and Motor Skills, 78,_ 1259–1264; Larsen, R. J., & Shackelford, T. K. (1996). Gaze avoidance: Personality and social judgments of people who avoid direct face-to-face contact. _Personality and Individual Differences, 21,_ 907–917.

24 Iverson, J. M., Tencer, H. L., Lany, J., & Goldin-Meadow, S. (2000). The relation between gesture and speech in congenitally blind and sighted language-learners. _Journal of Nonverbal Behavior, 24,_ 105–130.

25 Burgoon, J. K., Le Poire, B. A., Beutler, L. E., Bergan, J., & Engle, D. (1992). Nonverbal behaviors as indices of arousal: Extension to the psychotherapy context. _Journal of Nonverbal Behavior, 16,_ 159–178; Vrij, A. (2006). Nonverbal communication and deception. In V. Manusov & M. L. Patterson (Eds.), _The SAGE handbook of nonverbal communication_ (pp. 341–359). Thousand Oaks, CA: Sage.

26 Floyd, K. (2006). _Communicating affection: Interpersonal behavior and social context._ Cambridge, England: Cambridge University Press.

27 Field, T. M. (Ed.). (1995). _Touch in early development._ Mahwah, NJ: Lawrence Erlbaum Associates.

28 Harlow, H. F., & Zimmermann, R. R. (1958). The development of affectionate responses in infant monkeys. _Proceedings of the American Philosophical Society, 102,_ 501–509.

29 Del Prete, T. (1997). Hands off? A touchy subject. _The Education Digest, 62,_ 59–61. (Quote in text is from p. 59.)

30 Field, T. (2001). _Touch._ Cambridge, MA: MIT Press. (Quote in text is from p. 5.)

31 For review, see Field, 2001.

32 Burgener, S., Bakas, T., Murray, C., Dunahee, J., & Tossey, S. (1998). Effective caregiving approaches for patients with Alzheimer's disease. _Geriatric Nursing, 19,_ 121–126; Gadow, S. (1984). Touch and technology: Two paradigms of patient care. _Journal of Religion and Health, 23,_ 63–69.

33 See, e.g., Tjaden, P., & Thoennes, N. (1998). Prevalence, incidence, and consequences of violence against women: Findings from the National Violence Against Women Survey. Washington, DC: National Institute of Justice, NCJ 172837.

34 For example, see Kneidinger, L. M., Maple, T. L., & Tross, S. A. (2001). Touching behavior in sport: Functional components, analysis of sex differences, and ethological considerations. _Journal of Nonverbal Behavior, 25,_ 43–62.

35 Puts, D. A., (2005). Mating context and menstrual phase affect women's preferences for male voice pitch. _Evolution and Human Behavior, 26,_ 388–397; Riding, D., Lonsdale, D., & Brown, B. (2006). The effects of average fundamental frequency and variance of fundamental frequency on male vocal attractiveness to women. _Journal of Nonverbal Behavior, 30,_ 55–61.

36 Feinberg, D. R., Jones, B. C., DeBruine, L. M., Moore, F. R., Law Smith, M. J., Cornwell, R. E., Tiddeman, B. P., Boothroyd, L. G., & Perrett, D. I. (2005). The voice and face of women: One ornament that signals quality? _Evolution and Human Behavior, 26,_ 398–408.

37 Dabbs, J. M., & Mallinger, A. (1999). High testosterone levels predict low pitch among men. _Personality and Individual Differences, 27,_ 801–804.

38 Zuckerman, M., & Miyake, K. (1993). The attractive voice: What makes it so? _Journal of Nonverbal Behavior, 17,_ 119–135.

39 Zuckerman & Miyake, 1993.

40 Wolvin, A., & Coakley, C. (1996). _Listening._ Dubuque, IA: Brown & Benchmark.

41 Buller, D. B., Le Poire, B. A., Aune, R. K., & Eloy, S. V. (1992). Social perceptions as mediators of the effect of speech rate: Similarity on compliance. _Human Communication Research, 19,_ 286–311.

42 See, e.g., Burgoon, J. K., Birk, T., & Pfau, M. (1990). Nonverbal behaviors, persuasion, and credibility. _Human Communication Research, 17,_ 140–169.

43 Morley, J. (1996). Second language speech/pronunciation: Acquisition, instruction, standards, variation, and accent. In J. E. Alatis (Ed.), _Georgetown University roundtable on languages and linguistics_ (pp. 140–160). Washington, DC: Georgetown University Press.

44 Kleiner-Fisman, G., & Kott, H. S. (1998). Myasthenia gravis mimicking stroke in elderly patients. _Mayo Clinic Proceedings, 73,_ 1077–1078.

45 Burgoon, J. K., Guerrero, L. K., & Floyd, K. (in press). _Nonverbal communication._ Boston: Allyn & Bacon.

46 Williams, K. D., Shore, W. J., & Grahe, J. E. (1998). The silent treatment: Perceptions of its behaviors and associated feelings. _Group Processes and Intergroup Relations, 1,_ 117–141.

47 For further discussion, see Kamakura, W. A., Basuroy, S., & Boatwright, P. (2006). Is silence golden? An inquiry into the meaning of silence in professional product evaluations. _Quantitative Marketing and Economics, 4,_ 119–141.

48 Field, T. M. (1999). American adolescents touch one another less and are more aggressive toward their peers as compared with French adolescents. _Adolescence, 34,_ 753–758.

49 Hall, E. T. (1959). _The silent language._ Garden City, NY: Doubleday; Hall, E. T. (1963). System for the notation of proxemic behavior. _American Anthropologist, 65,_ 1003–1026.

50 Keyton, J. (2006). _Communicating in groups: Building relationships for group effectiveness_ (3rd ed). New York: Oxford University Press.

51 Braithwaite, D. O., & Braithwaite, C. A. (2000). Understanding communication of persons with disabilities as cultural communication. In L. A. Samovar & R. E. Porter (Eds.), _Intercultural communication: A reader_ (9th ed., pp. 136–145). Belmont, CA: Wadsworth.

52 Heinemann, W., Pellander, F., Antje, V., & Wojtek, B. (1981). Meeting a deviant person: Subjective norms and affective reactions. _European Journal of Social Psychology, 11,_ 1–25;

Park, J. H., Faulkner, J., & Schaller, M. (2003). Evolved disease-avoidance processes and contemporary anti-social behavior: Prejudicial attitudes and avoidance of people with physical disabilities. *Journal of Nonverbal Behavior, 27,* 65–87.

[53] Dion, K. K., Berscheid, E., & Walster, E. (1972). What is beautiful is good. *Journal of Personality and Social Psychology,* 24, 285–290; Eagley, A. E., Ashmore, R. D., Makhijani, M. G., & Longo, L. C. (1991). What is beautiful is good, but . . . : A meta-analytic review of research on the physical attractiveness stereotype. *Psychological Bulletin, 110,* 109–139; Kuhlenschmidt, S., & Conger, J. C. (1988). Behavioral components of social competence in females. *Sex Roles, 18,* 107–112.

[54] Curran, J. P., & Lippold, S. (1975). The effects of physical attraction and attitude similarity on attraction in dating dyads. *Journal of Personality, 43,* 528–539; O'Grady, K. E. (1989). Physical attractiveness, need for approval, social self-esteem, and maladjustment. *Journal of Social and Clinical Psychology, 8,* 62–69.

[55] Efran, M. G. (1974). The effect of physical appearance on the judgment of guilt, interpersonal attraction, and severity of recommended punishment in a simulated jury task. *Journal of Experimental Research in Personality, 8,* 45–54; Efran, M. G., & Patterson, E. (1974). Voters vote beautiful: The effect of physical appearance on a national debate. *Canadian Journal of Behavioral Science, 6,* 352–356; West, S. G., & Brown, T. J. (1975). Physical attractiveness, the severity of the emergency and helping: A field experiment and interpersonal simulation. *Journal of Experimental Social Psychology, 11,* 531–538.

[56] Howard, P. N. (2003). Digitizing the social contract: Producing American political culture in the age of new media. *The Communication Review, 6,* 213–245.

[57] Werner, C. M., Peterson-Lewis, S., & Brown, B. B. (1989). Inferences about homeowners' sociability: Impact of Christmas decorations and other cues. *Journal of Environmental Psychology, 9,* 279–296.

[58] Pointer, M. R., & Attridge, G. G. (1998). The number of discernible colours. *Color Research and Application, 23,* 52–54.

[59] Davidoff, J. (1991). *Cognition through color.* Cambridge: MIT Press.

[60] Lüscher, M., & Scott, I. (1969). *The Lüscher Color Test.* New York: Random House.

[61] Wegner, D. M., & Vallacher, R. R. (1977). *Implicit psychology: An introduction to social cognition.* New York: Oxford University Press.

[62] See, e.g., Eagley, A. H., Ashmore, R. D., Makhijani, M. G., & Longo, L. C. (1991). What is beautiful is good, but . . . : A meta-analytic review of research on the physical attractiveness stereotype. *Psychological Bulletin, 110,* 109–138.

[63] Burgoon, J. K., Buller, D. B., & Woodall, W. G. (1996). *Nonverbal communication: The unspoken dialogue* (2nd ed.). New York: McGraw-Hill.

[64] Bavelas, J. B., Coates, L., & Johnson, T. (2002). Listener responses as a collaborative process: The role of gaze. *Journal of Communication, 52,* 566–580.

[65] Drummond, K., & Hopper, R. (1993). Acknowledging tokens in series. *Communication Reports, 6,* 47–53.

[66] Knapp, M. L., Hart, R. P., Freidrich, G. W., & Shulman, G. M. (1973). The rhetoric of goodbye: Verbal and nonverbal correlates of human leave-taking behavior. *Speech Monographs, 40,* 182–198.

[67] Knapp et al., 1973; see also O'Leary, M. J., & Gallois, C. (1985). The last ten turns: Behavior and sequencing in friends' and strangers' conversational findings. *Journal of Nonverbal Behavior, 9,* 8–27.

[68] Fridlund, A. J., & Russell, J. A. (2006). The functions of facial expressions: What's in a face? In V. Manusov & M. L. Patterson (Eds.), *The SAGE handbook of nonverbal communication* (pp. 299–319). Thousand Oaks, CA: Sage.

[69] Sroufe, L. A. (1984). The organization of emotional development. In K. R. Scherer & P. Ekman (Eds.), *Approaches to emotion* (pp. 109–128). Hillsdale, NJ: Lawrence Erlbaum Associates.

[70] Fox, N., & Davidson, R. (1988). Patterns of brain electrical activity during facial signs of emotion in 10-month-old infants. *Developmental Psychology, 24,* 230–236.

[71] See Floyd, K. (2006). An evolutionary approach to understanding nonverbal communication. In V. Manusov & M. L. Patterson (Eds.), *The SAGE handbook of nonverbal communication* (pp. 139–157). Thousand Oaks, CA: Sage.

[72] Scherer, K. (1995). Expression of emotion in voice and music. *Journal of Voice, 9,* 235–248.

[73] Murray, I. R., & Arnott, J. L. (1993). Toward the simulation of emotion in synthetic speech: A review of the literature on human vocal emotion. *Journal of the Acoustical Society of America, 93,* 1097–1108.

[74] Johnson, W. F., Emde, R. N., Scherer, K. R., & Klinnert, M. D. (1986). Recognition of emotion from vocal cues. *Archives of General Psychiatry, 43,* 280–283.

[75] Murray & Arnott, 1993.

[76] Fónagy, I. (1981). Emotions, voice and music. In J. Sundberg (Ed.), *Research aspects on singing* (pp. 51–79). Stockholm, Sweden: Royal Swedish Academy of Music; Öster, A., & Risberg, A. (1986). The identification of the mood of a speaker by hearing impaired listeners. *Quarterly Professional Status Report (QPSR), 4,* 79–90.

[77] Guerrero, L. K., & Floyd, K. (2006). *Nonverbal communication in close relationships.* Mahwah, NJ: Lawrence Erlbaum Associates.

[78] Moore, M. M. (1985). Nonverbal courtship patterns in women: Context and consequences. *Ethology and Sociobiology, 6,* 237–247; Moore, M. M. (2002). Courtship communication and perception. *Perceptual and Motor Skills, 94,* 97–105.

[79] Givens, D. B. (1978). The nonverbal basis of attraction: Flirtation, courtship, and seduction. *Psychiatry, 41,* 346–359.

[80] Floyd, K. (2006). *Communicating affection: Interpersonal behavior and social context.* Cambridge, England: Cambridge University Press.

[81] Spain, D. (1992). *Gendered spaces.* Chapel Hill: University of North Carolina Press.

[82] Chapman, A. J. (1975). Eye contact, physical proximity and laughter: A re-examination of the equilibrium model of social intimacy. *Social Behavior and Personality, 3,* 143–155; Kimble, C. E., Forte, R. A., & Yoshikawa, J. C. (1981). Nonverbal concomitants of enacted emotional intensity and positivity: Visual and vocal behavior. *Journal of Personality, 29,* 271–283; Siegman, A. W. (1978). The telltale voice: Nonverbal messages of verbal communication. In A. W. Siegman & S. Feldstein (Eds.), *Nonverbal behavior and communication* (pp. 183–243). Hillsdale, NJ: Lawrence Erlbaum Associates.

[83] Burgoon, J. K., & Koper, R. J. (1984). Nonverbal and relational communication associated with reticence. *Human Communication Research, 10,* 601–626; Cappella, J. N., & Greene, J. O. (1984). The effects of distance and individual differences in arousability on nonverbal involvement: A test of discrepancy-arousal theory. *Journal of Nonverbal Behavior, 8,* 259–286; Kemper, T. D. (1984). Power, status, and emotions: A sociological contribution to a psychophysiological domain. In K. R. Scherer & P. Ekman (Eds.), *Approaches to emotion* (pp. 369–383). Hillsdale, NJ: Lawrence Erlbaum Associates.

[84] Burgoon, J. K., Buller, D. B., Hale, J. L., & deTurck, M. A. (1984). Relational messages associated with nonverbal behaviors. *Human Communication Research, 10,* 351–378; Patterson, J. L., Jordan, A., Hogan, M. B., & Frerker, D. (1981). Effects of nonverbal intimacy on arousal and behavioral adjustment. *Journal of Nonverbal Behavior, 5,* 184–198.

[85] American Psychiatric Association. (2000). *Diagnostic and statistical manual of mental disorders* (4th ed. text revision). Washington, DC: Author.

[86] Troisi, A., & Moles, A. (1999). Gender differences in depression: An ethological study of nonverbal behavior during interviews. *Journal of Psychiatric Research, 33,* 243–250.

[87] Burgoon et al., in press. (See note 45.)

[88] Guerrero & Floyd, 2006. (See note 77.)

[89] Carroll, L., & Gilroy, P. J. (2002). Role of appearance and nonverbal behavior in the perception of sexual orientation among lesbians and gay men. *Psychological Reports, 91,* 115–122.

[90] Douglas Creed, W. E., Scully, M. A., & Austin, J. R. (2002). Clothes make the person? The tailoring of legitimating accounts and the social construction of identity. *Organization Science, 13,* 475–496.

[91] McGlone, R. E., & Hollien, H. (1963). Vocal pitch characteristics of aged women. *Journal of Speech and Hearing Research, 6,* 164–170.

[92] Schötz, S. (2003). Towards synthesis of speaker age: A perceptual study with natural, synthesized and resynthesized stimuli. *PHONUM, 9,* I-X.

[93] Mendoza, E., Valencia, N., Muñoz, J., & Trujillo, H. (1996). Differences in voice quality between men and women: Use of the long-term average spectrum (LTAS). *Journal of Voice, 10,* 59–66.

[94] Günzburger, D. (1984). Perception of some male-female voice characteristics. *Progress Report Institute of Phonetics Utrecht, 9,* 15–26.

[95] Bennett, S., & Montero-Diaz, L. (1982). Children's perceptions of speaker sex. *Journal of Phonetics, 10,* 113–121.

[96] Linville, S. E. (1998). Acoustic correlates of perceived versus actual sexual orientation in men's speech. *Folia Phoniatrica et Logopaedica, 50,* 35–48; Munson, B., McDonald, E. C., DeBoe, N. L., & White, A. R. (2006). The acoustic and perceptual bases of judgments of women and men's sexual orientation from read speech. *Journal of Phonetics, 34,* 202–240; Smyth, R., Jacobs, G., & Rogers, H. (2003). Male voices and perceived sexual orientation: An experimental and theoretical approach. *Language in Society, 32,* 329–350.

[97] Pierrehumbert, J., Bent, T., Munson, B., Bradlow, A. R., & Bailey, M. (2004). The influence of sexual orientation on vowel production. *Journal of the Acoustical Society of America, 116,* 1905–1908.

[98] Linville, 1998.

[99] Avery, J. D., & Liss, J. M. (1996). Acoustic characteristics of less-masculine-sounding male speech. *Journal of the Acoustical Society of America, 99,* 3738–3748; Rogers, H., & Smyth, R. (2003, August). *Phonetic differences between gay- and straight-sounding male speakers of North American English.* Paper presented at the 15th International Congress of Phonetic Sciences, Barcelona, Spain.

[100] Xue, S. A., Neeley, R., Hagstrom, F., & Hao, J. (2001). Speaking F_0 characteristics of elderly Euro-American and African-American speakers: Building a clinical comparative platform. *Clinical Linguistics and Phonetics, 15,* 245–252.

[101] Knapp, M. L. (1978). *Nonverbal communication in human interaction* (2nd ed.). New York: Holt, Rinehart & Winston.

[102] Paek, S. L. (1986). Effect of garment style on the perception of personal traits. *Clothing and Textiles Research, 5,* 10–16.

[103] Pratt, M. G., & Rafaeli, A. (2004). Organizational dress as a symbol of multilayered social identities. In M. J. Hatch & M. Schultz (Eds.), *Organizational identity: A reader* (pp. 275–312). New York: Oxford University Press.

[104] Buckley, H. M., & Roach, M. E. (1974). Clothing as a nonverbal communicator of social and political attitudes. *Family and Consumer Sciences Research Journal, 3,* 94–102.

[105] See Burgoon et al., in press. (See note 45.)

[106] Burgoon et al., in press.

[107] Kramsch, C. (1998). *Language and culture.* New York: Oxford University Press.

[108] O'Neal, G. S., & Lapitsky, M. (1991). Effects of clothing as nonverbal communication on credibility of the message source. *Clothing and Textiles Research Journal, 9,* 28–34.

[109] Bickman, L. (1974). The social power of a uniform. *Journal of Applied Social Psychology, 4,* 47–61; Cha, A., Hecht, B. R., Nelson, K., & Hopkins, M. P. (2004). Resident physician attire: Does it make a difference to our patients? *American Journal of Obstetrics and Gynecology, 190,* 1484–1488.

[110] Bickman, L. (1971). The effect of social status on the honesty of others. *Journal of Social Psychology, 85,* 97–82.

[111] Street, R. L., & Brady, R. M. (1982). Speech rate acceptance ranges as a function of evaluative domain, listener speech rate, and communication context. *Communication Monographs, 49,* 290–308.

[112] Kimble, C. E., & Seidel, S. D. (1991). Vocal signs of confidence. *Journal of Nonverbal Behavior, 15,* 99–106.

[113] Burgoon, J. K., Birk, T., & Pfau, M. (1990). Nonverbal behaviors, persuasion, and credibility. *Human Communication Research, 17,* 140–169.

[114] Linkey, H. E., & Firestone, I. J. (1990). Dyad dominance composition effects, nonverbal behaviors, and influence. *Journal of Research in Personality, 24,* 206–215.

[115] See Walker, D., & Dubitsky, T. M. (1994). Why liking matters. *Journal of Advertising Research, 3,* 9–18.

[116] Floyd, K., & Burgoon, J. K. (1999). Reacting to nonverbal expressions of liking: A test of interaction adaptation theory. *Communication Monographs, 66,* 219–239.

[117] Wetzel, C. G., & Crusco, A. H. (1984). The Midas touch: The effects of interpersonal touch on restaurant tipping. *Personality and Social Psychology Bulletin, 10,* 512–517.

[118] Kleinke, C. L. (1977). Compliance to requests made by gazing and touching experimenters in field settings. *Journal of Experimental Social Psychology, 13,* 218–223; Paulsell, S., & Goldman, M. (1984). The effect of touching different body areas on prosocial behavior. *Journal of Social Psychology, 122,* 269–273.

[119] Burgoon, J. K., Stern, L. A., & Dillman, L. (1995). *Interpersonal adaptation: Dyadic interaction patterns.* New York: Cambridge University Press.

[120] Lutz-Zois, C. J., Bradley, A. C., Mihalik, J. L., & Moorman-Eavers, E. R. (2006). Perceived similarity and relationship success among dating couples: An idiographic approach. *Journal of Social and Personal Relationships, 23,* 865–880; Morry, M. M.

(2007). The attraction-similarity hypothesis among cross-sex friends: Relationship satisfaction, perceived similarities, and self-serving perceptions. *Journal of Social and Personal Relationships, 24,* 117–138.

[121] Buller, D. B., & Aune, R. K. (1988). The effects of vocalics and nonverbal sensitivity on compliance: A speech accommodation theory explanation. *Human Communication Research, 14,* 301–332; Buller, D. B., & Aune, R. K. (1992). The effects of speech rate similarity on compliance: Application of communication accommodation theory. *Western Journal of Communication, 56,* 37–53; Buller, D. B., & Burgoon, J. K. (1986). The effects of vocalics and nonverbal sensitivity on compliance: A replication and extension. *Human Communication Research, 13,* 126–144.

[122] Kahle, L. R., & Homer, P. A. (1985). Physical attractiveness of the celebrity endorser: A social adaptation perspective. *Journal of Consumer Research, 11,* 954–961.

[123] Dion, K. K., & Stein, S. (1978). Physical attractiveness and interpersonal influence. *Journal of Experimental Social Psychology, 14,* 97–108; Krapfel, R. E. (1988). Customer complaint and salesperson response: The effect of the communication source. *Journal of Retailing, 64,* 181–198; Pallak, S. R. (1983). Salience of a communicator's physical attractiveness and persuasion: A heuristic versus systematic processing interpretation. *Social Cognition, 2,* 158–170.

[124] Bettinghaus, E. P., & Cody, M. J. (1987). *Persuasive communication.* New York: Holt, Rinehart and Winston.

[125] Watkins, L. M., & Johnston, L. (2000). Screening job applicants: The impact of physical attractiveness and application quality. *International Journal of Selection and Assessment, 8,* 76–84.

[126] Hamermesh, D. S., & Biddle, J. E. (1994). Beauty and the labor market. *American Economic Review, 84,* 1174–1194.

[127] Shahani-Denning, C., Dipboye, R. L., & Gehrlein, T. M. (1993). Attractiveness bias in the interview: Exploring the boundaries of an effect. *Basic*

and Applied Social Psychology, 14, 317–328.

[128] West, S. G., & Brown, T. J. (1975). Physical attractiveness, the severity of the emergency and helping: A field experiment and interpersonal simulation. *Journal of Experimental Social Psychology, 11,* 531–538.

[129] Aune, R. K. (1999). The effects of perfume use on perceptions of attractiveness and competence. In L. K. Guerrero, J. A. DeVito, & M. L. Hecht (Eds.), *The nonverbal communication reader: Classic and contemporary readings* (2nd ed., pp. 126–132). Prospect Heights, IL: Waveland Press.

[130] Collins, S. A., & Missing, C. (2003). Vocal and visual attractiveness are related in women. *Animal Behavior, 65,* 997–1004; Feinberg et al., 2005 (see note 36).

[131] Ekman, P., Friesen, W. V., & O'Sullivan, M. (1997). Smiles when lying. In P. Ekman & E. L. Rosenberg (Eds.), *What the face reveals: Basic and applied studies of spontaneous expression using the facial action coding system (FACS)* (pp. 201–214). New York: Oxford University Press.

[132] Ekman, P., Friesen, W. V., & Scherer, K. R. (1976). Body movement and voice pitch in deceptive interaction. *Semiotica, 16,* 23–27.

[133] Ekman, P., O'Sullivan, M., Friesen, W. V., & Scherer, K. R. (1991). Face, voice, and body in detecting deceit. *Journal of Nonverbal Behavior, 15,* 125–135.

[134] Davis, M., & Hadiks, D. (1995). Demeanor and credibility. *Semiotica, 106,* 5–54.

[135] Köhnken, G. (1989). Behavioral correlates of statement credibility: Theories, paradigms and results. In H. Wegener, F. Löwel, & J. Haisch (Eds.), *Criminal behavior and the justice system: Psychological perspectives* (pp. 271–289). New York: Springer-Verlag; Vrij, A., Semin, G. R., & Bull, R. (1996). Insight into behavior displayed during deception. *Human Communication Research, 22,* 544–562.

[136] Buller, D. B., & Aune, R. K. (1987). Nonverbal cues to deception among intimates, friends, and strangers. *Journal of*

Nonverbal Behavior, 11, 269–290; Vrij, A. (1995). Behavioral correlates of deception in a simulated police interview. *Journal of Psychology, 129,* 15–29.

[137] DePaulo, B. M. (1992). Nonverbal behavior and self-presentation. *Psychological Bulletin, 111,* 203–243.

[138] Burgoon, J. K., Kelley, D. L., Newton, D. A., & Keeley-Dyreson, M. P. (1989). The nature of arousal and nonverbal indices. *Human Communication Research, 16,* 217–255.

[139] See, e.g., Hall, J. A. (2006). How big are nonverbal sex differences? The case of smiling and nonverbal sensitivity. In K. Dindia & D. J. Canary (Eds.), *Sex differences and similarities in communication* (2nd ed., pp. 59–81). Mahwah, NJ: Lawrence Erlbaum Associates.

[140] Ekman, P., & Friesen, W. V. (1982). Felt, false, and miserable smiles. *Journal of Nonverbal Behavior, 6,* 238–252.

[141] Riggio, R. E. (2005). The Social Skills Inventory (SSI): Measuring nonverbal and social skills. In V. Manusov (Ed.), *The sourcebook of nonverbal measures: Going beyond words* (pp. 25–34). Mahwah, NJ: Lawrence Erlbaum Associates.

[142] Riggio, R. E. (2006). Nonverbal skills and abilities. In V. Manusov & M. L. Patterson (Eds.), *The SAGE handbook of nonverbal communication* (pp. 79–96). Thousand Oaks, CA: Sage.

[143] Riggio, R. E. (1986). Assessment of basic social skills. *Journal of Personality and Social Psychology, 51,* 649–660.

[144] See Friedman, H. S., & Riggio, R. E. (1981). Effects of individual differences in nonverbal expressiveness on transmission of emotion. *Journal of Nonverbal Behavior, 6,* 96–102.

[145] Friedman, H. S., Prince, L. M., Riggio, R. E., & DiMatteo, M. R. (1980). Understanding and assessing nonverbal expressiveness: The Affective Communication Test. *Journal of Personality and Social Psychology, 39,* 333–351.

[146] Carlson, J. (2005). *Family therapy techniques: Integrating and tailoring treatment.* New York: Routledge.

Notes for Chapter 7

[1] See Spitzberg, B. H. (1994). The dark side of (in)competence. In W. R. Cupach & B. H. Spitzberg (Eds.), *The dark side of interpersonal communication* (pp. 25–50). Hillsdale, NJ: Lawrence Erlbaum Associates.

[2] Emmert, P. (1996). President's perspective. *ILA Listening Post, 56,* 2–3.

[3] Dindia, K., & Kennedy, B. L. (2004, November). *Communication in everyday life: A descriptive study using mobile electronic data collection.* Paper presented at the annual conference of the National Communication Association, Chicago, IL.

[4] Barker, L., Edwards, R., Gaines, C., Gladney, K., & Holley, F. (1980). An investigation of proportional time spent in various communicating activities by college students. *Journal of Applied Communication Research, 8,* 101–109; Hargie, O., Saunders, C., & Dickson, D. (1994). *Social skills in interpersonal communication* (3rd ed.). New York: Routledge.

[5] Windsor, J. L., Curtis, D. B., & Stephens, R. D. (1997). National preferences in business and communication education: An update. *Journal of the Association for Communication Administration, 3,* 170–179.

[6] Wolvin, A. D. (1984). Meeting the communication needs of the adult learner. *Communication Education, 33,* 267–271.

[7] See, e.g., Prager, K. J., & Buhrmester, D. (1998). Intimacy and need fulfillment in couple relationships. *Journal of Social and Personal Relationships, 15,* 435–469.

[8] Brownell, J. (1990). Perceptions of effective listeners: A management study. *Journal of Business Communication, 27,* 401–415.

[9] Carrell, L. J., & Willmington, S. C. (1996). A comparison of self-report and performance data in assessing speaking and listening competence. *Communication Reports, 9,* 185–191.

[10] See Lane, K., Balleweg, B. J., Suler, J. R., Fernald, P. S., & Goldstein, G. S. (2000). Acquiring skills—Undergraduate students. In M. E. Ware & D. E. Johnson (Eds.), *Handbook of demonstrations and activities in the teaching of psychology: Vol. 3. Personality, abnormal, clinical-counseling, and social* (2nd ed., pp. 109–124). Mahwah, NJ: Lawrence Erlbaum Associates.

[11] Spinks, N., & Wells, B. (1991). Improving listening power: The payoff. *Bulletin of the Association for Business Communication, 54,* 75–77.

[12] Broome, B. J. (1991). Building shared meaning: Implications of a relational approach to empathy for teaching intercultural communication. *Communication Education, 40,* 235–249.

[13] Wolvin, A. D. (1987, June). *Culture as a listening variable.* Paper presented at the summer conference of the International Listening Association, Toronto, Ontario.

[14] Chen, G.-M., & Chung, J. (1997). The "Five Asian Dragons": Management behaviors and organization communication. In L. A. Samovar & R. E. Porter (Eds.), *Intercultural communication: A reader* (pp. 317–328). Belmont, CA: Wadsworth.

[15] Brownell, J. (2002). *Listening attitudes, principles, and skills* (2nd ed.). Boston: Allyn & Bacon.

[16] Macrae, C. N., & Bodenhausen, G. V. (2001). Social cognition: Categorical person perception. *British Journal of Psychology, 92,* 239–255.

[17] Thomas, L. T., & Levine, T. R. (1994). Disentangling listening and verbal recall: Separate but related constructs? *Human Communication Research, 21,* 103–127.

[18] Benoit, S. S., & Lee, J. W. (1986). Listening: It can be taught. *Journal of Education for Business, 63,* 229–232.

[19] Bellezza, F. S., & Buck, D. K. (1988). Expert knowledge as mnemonic cues. *Applied Cognitive Psychology, 2,* 147–162.

[20] Duncan, S., & Fiske, D. W. (1977). *Face-to-face interaction: Research, methods, and theory.* New York: Wiley.

[21] Egan, G. (1998). *The skilled helper* (6th ed.). Pacific Grove, CA: Brooks/Cole.

[22] Kuhn, J. L. (2001). Toward an ecological humanistic psychology. *Journal of Humanistic Psychology, 41,* 9–24.

23 Duan, C., & Hill, C. E. (1996). The current state of empathy research. *Journal of Counseling Psychology, 43,* 261–274.

24 Stiff, J. B., Dillard, J. P., Somera, L., Kim, H., & Sleight, C. (1988). Empathy, communication, and prosocial behavior. *Communication Monographs, 55,* 198–213.

25 See Armstrong, B. G., Boiarsky, G. A., & Mares, M. L. (1991). Background television and reading performance. *Communication Monographs, 58,* 235–253.

26 Haider, M. (1970). Neuropsychology of attention, expectation, and vigilance. In D. I. Mostofsky (Ed.), *Attention: Contemporary theory and analysis* (pp. 419–432). New York: Appleton-Century-Crofts.

27 Ball, S. A., & Zuckerman, M. (1992). Sensation seeking and selective attention: Focused and divided attention on a dichotic listening task. *Journal of Personality and Social Psychology, 63,* 825–831.

28 Media Dynamics, Inc. (2007, February 15). Our rising ad dosage: It's not as oppressive as some think. *Media Matters, XXI*(3), 1–2.

29 Toffler, A. (1970). *Future shock.* New York: Random House.

30 Keller, E. (2007, July 19). Why you can't get any work done: Workplace distractions cost U.S. business some $650 billion a year. Retrieved online November 23, 2007, from: http://www.businessweek.com/careers/content/jul2007/ca20070719_880333.htm

31 American Psychiatric Association (1994). *Diagnostic and statistical manual of mental disorders* (4th ed.). Washington, DC: Author.

32 Attention-deficit hyperactivity disorder: ADHD in adults. Retrieved online March 8, 2008, from: http://www.webmd.com/add-adhd/guide/adhd-adults

33 Versfeld, N. J., & Dreschler, W. A. (2002). The relationship between the intelligibility of time-compressed speech and speech-in-noise in young and elderly listeners. *Journal of the Acoustical Society of America, 111,* 401–408; Wolvin, A., & Coakley, C. (1996). *Listening.*

Dubuque, IA: Brown & Benchmark.

34 Golen, S. (1990). A factor analysis of barriers to effective listening. *Journal of Business Communication, 27,* 25–36.

35 Golen, 1990.

36 Watson, K. W., & Smeltzer, L. R. (1984). Barriers to listening: Comparisons between students and practitioners. *Communication Research Reports, 1,* 82–87.

37 Golen, 1990.

38 James, D., & Clarke, S. (1993). Women, men, and interruptions: A critical review. In D. Tannen (Ed.), *Gender and conversational interaction* (pp. 231–267). New York: Oxford University Press.

39 Redeker, G., & Maes, A. (1996). Gender differences in interruptions. In D. Slobin, J. Gerhardt, A. Kyratzis, & J. Guo (Eds.), *Social interaction, social context, and language* (pp. 579–612). Mahwah, NJ: Lawrence Erlbaum Associates.

40 Gilovich, T. (1997, March/April). Some systematic biases of everyday judgment. *Skeptical Inquirer,* 31–35.

41 Taylor, S. E., & Thomson, S. C. (1982). Stalking the elusive "vividness" effect. *Psychological Review, 89,* 155–181.

42 http://www.planecrashinfo.com/rates.htm

43 Glassman, J. K. (1998, May 29). Put shootings in proper perspective. *San Jose Mercury News,* p. B7.

44 Ruggeiro, V. (1988). *Teaching thinking across the curriculum.* New York: Harper & Row.

45 Tannen, D. (1990). *You just don't understand: Women and men in conversation.* New York: Ballentine.

46 Pollak, K. I., Arnold, R. M., Jeffreys, A. S., Alexander, S. C., Olsen, M. K., Abernethy, A. P., Skinner, C. S., Rodriguez, L. K., & Tulsky, J. A. (2007). Oncologist communication about emotion during visits with patients with advanced cancer. *Journal of Clinical Oncology, 25,* 5748–5752.

47 Floyd, K. (2006). *Communicating affection: Interpersonal behavior and social context.* Cambridge, England: Cambridge University Press.

Notes for Chapter 8

1 Parks, M. R. (2007). *Personal relationships and personal networks.* Mahwah, NJ: Lawrence Erlbaum Associates. Quote is from page 1.

2 See Fiske, A. P. (1992). The four elementary forms of sociality: Framework for a unified theory of social relations. *Psychological Review, 99,* 689–723.

3 Baumeister, R. F., & Leary, M. R. (1995). The need to belong: Desire for interpersonal attachments as a fundamental human motivation. *Psychological Bulletin, 117,* 497–529.

4 See Bonta, J., & Gendreau, P. (1995). Re-examining the cruel and unusual punishment of prison life. In T. J. Flanagan (Ed.), *Long-term imprisonment: Policy, science, and correctional practice* (pp. 75–84). Thousand Oaks, CA: Sage.

5 Schumm, W. R., Bell, D. B., Knott, B., & Rice, R. E. (1996). The perceived effect of stressors on marital satisfaction among civilian wives of enlisted soldiers deployed to Somalia for Operation Restore Hope. *Military Medicine, 161,* 601–606.

6 Dykstra, P. A., van Tilburg, T. G., & De Jong-Gierveld, J. (2005). Changes in older adult loneliness: Results from a seven-year longitudinal study. *Research on Aging, 27,* 725–747; Sorkin, D., Rook, K. S., & Lu, J. L. (2002). Loneliness, lack of emotional support, lack of companionship, and the likelihood of having a heart condition in an elderly sample. *Annals of Behavioral medicine, 24,* 290–298; Tijhuis, M. A., De Jong-Gierveld, J., Feskins, E. J., & Kromhout, D. (1999). Changes in and factors related to loneliness in older men: The Zutphen Elderly Study. *Age and Ageing, 28,* 491–495.

7 Parks, M. R., & Floyd, K. (1996). Making friends in cyberspace. *Journal of Communication, 46,* 80–97.

8 See, e.g., Halsen, M., Wollebergh, W., & Meeus, W. (2000). Social support from parents and friends and emotional problems in adolescence. *Journal of Youth and Adolescence, 29,* 319–335.

9 Rawlins, W. K. (1992). *Friendship matters: Communication,*

dialectics, and the life course. New York: Aldine de Gruyter.

[10] Cohen, S., Doyle, W. J., Turner, R., Alper, C. M., & Skoner, D. P. (2003). Sociability and susceptibility to the common cold. *Psychological Science, 14,* 389–395.

[11] Ruberman, W., Weinblatt, E., Goldberg, J. D., & Chaudhary, B. S. (1984). Psychosocial influences on mortality after myocardial infarction. *New England Journal of Medicine, 311,* 552–559.

[12] House, J. S., Landis, K. R., & Umberson, D. (1988). Social relationships and health. *Science, 241,* 540–545.

[13] See, e.g., Schnurr, P. P., & Green, B. L. (Eds.). (2004). *Trauma and health: Physical health consequences of exposure to extreme stress.* Washington, DC: American Psychological Association.

[14] Jackson, P. B. (1992). Specifying the buffering hypothesis: Support, strain, and depression. *Social Psychology Quarterly, 55,* 363–378.

[15] Cohen, S., & Wills, T. A. (1985). Stress, social support, and the buffering hypothesis. *Psychological Bulletin, 98,* 310–357; Landerman, R., George, L. K., Campbell, R. T., & Blazer, D. G. (1989). Alternative models of the stress buffering hypothesis. *American Journal of Community Psychology, 17,* 625–642.

[16] Sallis, J. F., Grossman, R. M., Pinski, R. B., Patterson, T. L., & Nader, P. R. (1987). The development of scales to measure social support for diet and exercise behaviors. *Preventive Medicine 16,* 825–836.

[17] Berkanovic, E., & Telesky, C. (1982). Social networks, beliefs, and the decision to seek medical care: An analysis of congruent and incongruent patterns. *Medical Care, 20,* 1018–1026.

[18] Brassington, G. S., Atienza, A. A., Perczek, R. E., DiLorenzo, T. M., & King, A. C. (2002). Intervention-related cognitive versus social mediators of exercise adherence in the elderly. *American Journal of Preventive Medicine, 23,* 80–86; Duncan, T. E., & McAuley, E. (1993). Social support and efficacy cognitions in exercise adherence:

A latent growth curve analysis. *Journal of Behavioral Medicine, 16,* 199–218.

[19] Gallant, M. P. (2003). The influence of social support on chronic illness self-management: A review and directions for research. *Health Education & Behavior, 30,* 170–195.

[20] McCroskey, J. C., & McCain, T. A. (1974). The measurement of interpersonal attraction. *Speech Monographs, 41,* 261–266.

[21] Adams, G. R., & Roopnarine, J. L. (1994). Physical attractiveness, social skills, and same-sex peer popularity. *Journal of Group Psychotherapy, Psychodrama and Sociometry, 47,* 15–35; Speed, A., & Gangestad, S. W. (1997). Romantic popularity and mate preferences: A peer-nomination study. *Personality and Social Psychology Bulletin, 23,* 928–936.

[22] Barber, N. (1995). The evolutionary psychology of physical attractiveness: Sexual selection and human morphology. *Ethology and Sociobiology, 16,* 395–424; Hume, D. K., & Montgomerie, R. (2001). Facial attractiveness signals different aspects of "quality" in women and men. *Evolution and Human Behavior, 22,* 93–112.

[23] Dion, K. K., Berscheid, E., & Walster, E. (1972). What is beautiful is good. *Journal of Personality and Social Psychology, 24,* 285–290; Mehrabian, A., & Blum, J. S. (2003). Physical appearance, attractiveness, and the mediating role of emotions. In N. J. Pallone (Ed.), *Love, romance, sexual interaction: Research perspectives from current psychology* (pp. 1–29). New Brunswick, NJ: Transaction.

[24] For an extended discussion, see Guerrero, L. K., & Floyd, K. (2006). *Nonverbal communication in close relationships.* Mahwah, NJ: Lawrence Erlbaum Associates.

[25] Dutilleux, J. P. (1994). *L'indien blanc: Vingt ans de sortilege amazonien* [The white Indian: Twenty years of the Amazonian curse]. Paris: R. Laffont.

[26] Thesander, M. (1997). *The feminine ideal.* London: Reaktion Books.

[27] Singh, D., & Luis, S. (1995). Ethnic and gender consensus

for the effect of waist-to-hip ratio on judgments of women's attractiveness. *Human Nature, 6,* 51–65; Singh, D., & Young, R. K. (1995). Body weight, waist-to-hip ratio, breasts, and hips: Role in judgments of female attractiveness and desirability for relationships. *Ethology and Sociobiology, 16,* 483–507.

[28] Singh, D. (1995). Female judgment of male attractiveness and desirability for relationships: Role of waist-to-hip ratio and financial status. *Journal of Personality and Social Psychology, 69,* 1089–1101.

[29] Workman, L., & Reader, W. (2004). *Evolutionary psychology: An introduction.* Cambridge, England: Cambridge University Press.

[30] Rubenstein, A. J., Kalakanis, L., & Langlois, J. H. (1999). Infant preferences for attractive faces: A cognitive explanation. *Developmental Psychology, 35,* 848–855.

[31] Larose, H., & Standing, L. (1998). Does the halo effect occur in the elderly? *Social Behavioral and Personality, 26,* 147–150; Mulford, M., Orbell, J., Shatto, C., & Stockard, J. (1998). Physical attractiveness, opportunity, and success in everyday exchange. *American Journal of Sociology, 103,* 1565–1592; Staffieri, J. R. (1967). A study of social stereotype of body image in children. *Journal of Personality and Social Psychology, 7,* 101–104.

[32] See, e.g., Aboud, F. E., & Mendelson, M. J. (1998). Determinants of friendship selection and quality: Developmental perspectives. In W. M. Bukowski & A. F. Newcomb (Eds.), *The company they keep: Friendship in childhood and adolescence* (pp. 87–112). New York: Cambridge University Press.

[33] Festinger, L., Schachter, S., & Back, K. W. (1963). *Social pressures in informal groups: A study of human factors in housing.* Stanford, CA: Stanford University Press.

[34] Parks & Floyd, 1996 (see note 7); Parks, M. R., & Roberts, L. D. (1998). "Making MOOsic": The development of personal relationships online and a comparison to their off-line counterparts. *Journal of Social*

and *Personal Relationships, 15,* 517–537.

[35] Urberg, K. A., Degirmencioglu, S. M., & Tolson, J. M. (1998). Adolescent friendship selection and termination: The role of similarity. *Journal of Social and Personal Relationships, 15,* 703–710.

[36] See Byrne, D. (1997). An overview (and underview) of research and theory within the attraction paradigm. *Journal of Social and Personal Relationships, 14,* 417–431.

[37] Hamilton, W. D. (1964). The genetical evolution of social behavior. I & II. *Journal of Theological Biology, 7,* 1–52.

[38] Daly, M., & Wilson, M. (1995). Discriminative parental solicitude and the relevance of evolutionary models to the analysis of motivational systems. In M. S. Gazzaniga (Ed.), *The cognitive neurosciences* (pp. 1269–1286). Cambridge: MIT Press.

[39] See Floyd, K., & Morman, M. T. (2001). Human affection exchange: III. Discriminative parental solicitude in men's affectionate communication with their biological and nonbiological sons. *Communication Quarterly, 49,* 310–327.

[40] Nowicki, S., & Manheim, S. (1991). Interpersonal complementarity and time of interaction in female relationships. *Journal of Research in Personality, 25,* 322–333.

[41] Berger, C. R., & Calabrese, R. J. (1975). Some explorations in initial interaction and beyond: Toward a developmental theory of interpersonal communication. *Human Communication Research, 1,* 99–112.

[42] Sunnafrank, M. (1986). Predicted outcome value during initial interactions: A reformulation of uncertainty reduction theory. *Human Communication Research, 13,* 3–33; Sunnafrank, M. (1986). Predicted outcome values: Just now and then? *Human Communication Research, 13,* 39–40.

[43] Sunnafrank, M. (1988). Predicted outcome value in initial conversations. *Communication Research Reports, 5,* 169–172.

[44] Sunnafrank, M. (1990). Predicted outcome value and uncertainty reduction theories: A test

of competing perspectives. *Human Communication Research, 17,* 76–103.

[45] Gergen, K. J., Greenbert, M. S., & Willis, R. H. (1980). *Social exchange: Advances in theory and research.* New York: Plenum Press; Thibaut, J. W., & Kelley, H. H. (1959). *The social psychology of groups.* New York: Wiley.

[46] See, e.g., Lloyd, S. A., Cate, R. M., & Henton, J. M. (1984). Predicting premarital relationship stability: A methodological refinement. *Journal of Marriage and the Family, 46,* 71–76.

[47] Messick, R. M., & Cook. K. S. (Eds.) (1983). *Equity theory: Psychological and sociological perspectives.* New York: Prager.

[48] Stafford, L., & Canary, D. J. (1991). Maintenance strategies and romantic relationship type, gender, and relational characteristics. *Journal of Social and Personal Relationships, 8,* 217–242.

[49] Canary, D. J., & Stafford, L. (1992). Relational maintenance strategies and equity in marriage. *Communication Monographs, 59,* 243–268.

[50] See Hecht, M. L., Shepard, T., & Hall, T. J. (1979). Multivariate indices of the effects of self-disclosure. *Western Journal of Speech Communication, 43,* 235–245.

[51] Argyle, M., & Henderson, M. (1984). The rules of friendship. *Journal of Social and Personal Relationships, 1,* 211–237.

[52] Milardo, R. M. (1986). Personal choice and social constraint in close relationships: Application of network analysis. In V. J. Derlega & B. A. Winstead (Eds.), *Friendship and social interaction* (pp. 145–166). New York: Springer-Verlag.

[53] Coltrane, S. (1996). *Family man.* New York: Oxford University Press.

[54] Floyd, K., & Morman, M. T. (1997). Affectionate communication in nonromantic relationships: Influences of communicator, relational, and contextual factors. *Western Journal of Communication, 61,* 279–298.

[55] Wright, P. H. (1984). Self-referent motivation and the intrinsic quality of friendship. *Journal of Social and Personal Relationships, 1,* 115–130.

[56] See Shimanoff, S. B. (1980). *Communication rules: Theory and research.* Beverly Hills, CA: Sage.

[57] Argyle & Henderson, 1984.

[58] Parks, M. R., & Floyd, K. (1996). Meanings for closeness and intimacy in friendship. *Journal of Social and Personal Relationships, 15,* 517–537.

[59] Floyd, K. (1995). Gender and closeness among friends and siblings. *Journal of Psychology, 129,* 193–202; see also Morman, M. T., & Floyd, K. (1998). "I love you, man": Overt expressions of affection in male-male interaction. *Sex Roles, 38,* 871–881.

[60] Sapadin, L. A. (1988). Friendship and gender: Perspectives of professional men and women. *Journal of Social and Personal Relationships, 5,* 387–403.

[61] Rawlins, 1992. (See note 9.)

[62] Kaplan, D. L., & Keys, C. B. (1997). Sex and relationship variables as predictors of sexual attraction in cross-sex platonic friendships between young heterosexual adults. *Journal of Social and Personal Relationships, 14,* 191–206; Sapadin, L. A. (1988). Friendships and gender perspectives of professional men and women. *Journal of Social and Personal Relationships, 5,* 387–403.

[63] Egland, K. I., Spitzberg, B. G., & Zormeier, M. M. (1996). Flirtation and conversational competence in cross-sex platonic and romantic relationships. *Communication Reports, 9,* 105–118.

[64] Fuiman, M., Yarab, P., & Sensibaugh, C. (1997, July). *Just friends? An examination of the sexual, physical, and romantic aspects of cross-gender friendships.* Paper presented at the biennial meeting of the International Network on Personal Relationships, Oxford, OH.

[65] Afifi, W. A., & Faulkner, S. L. (2000). On being 'just friends': The frequency and impact of sexual activity in cross-sex friendships. *Journal of Social and Personal Relationships, 17,* 205–222.

[66] Werking, K. J. (1997). *We're just good friends: Women and men in nonromantic relationships.* New York: Guilford.

[67] Messman, S. J., Canary, D. J., & Hause, K. S. (2000). Motives to remain platonic, equity, and

the use of maintenance strategies in opposite-sex friendships. *Journal of Social and Personal Relationships, 17,* 67–94.

[68] Rose, S. M. (1985). Same- and cross-sex friendships and the psychology of homosociality. *Sex Roles, 12,* 63–74.

[69] Rawlins, W. K. (1981). *Friendship as a communicative achievement: A theory and an interpretive analysis of verbal reports.* Unpublished doctoral dissertation, Temple University, Philadelphia, PA.

[70] Rose, S. M. (1984). How friendships end: Patterns among young adults. *Journal of Social and Personal Relationships, 1,* 267–277.

[71] See Bleske-Rechek, A. L., & Buss, D. M. (2001). Opposite-sex friendship: Sex differences and similarities in initiation, selection, and dissolution. *Personality and Social Psychology Bulletin, 37,* 1310–1323.

[72] Rose, 1984; see also Argyle & Henderson, 1984.

[73] See Feld, S. L. (1997). Structural embeddedness and the stability of interpersonal relations. *Social Networks, 19,* 91–95.

[74] Sias, P. M., Krone, K. J., & Jablin, F. M. (2002). An ecological systems perspective on workplace relationships. In M. L. Knapp & J. A. Daly (Eds.), *Handbook of interpersonal communication* (3rd ed., pp. 615–642). Thousand Oaks, CA.

[75] Sias, P. M., & Cahill, D. J. (1998). From co-worker to friends: The development of peer friendships in the workplace. *Western Journal of Communication, 62,* 273–300.

[76] Marks, S. R. (1994). Intimacy in the public realm: The case of coworkers. *Social Forces, 72,* 843–858.

[77] Winstead, B. A., Derlega, V. J., Montgomery, M. J., & Pilkington, C. (1995). The quality of friendships at work and job satisfaction. *Journal of Social and Personal Relationships, 12,* 199–215.

[78] Zorn, T. E. (1995). Bosses and buddies: Constructing and performing simultaneously hierarchical and close friendship relationships. In J. T. Wood & S. Duck (Eds.), *Under-studied relationships: Off the beaten track* (pp. 122–147). Thousand Oaks, CA: Sage.

[79] Largent, R. N. (1987). *The relationship of friendship with a supervisor to job satisfaction and satisfaction with the supervisor.* Unpublished master's thesis, University of North Dakota, Grand Forks, ND.

[80] See Fiedler, F. E. (1957). A note on leadership theory: The effect of social barriers between leaders and followers. *Sociometry, 20,* 87–94.

[81] Zorn, 1995.

[82] Adelman, M. B., Ahuvia, A., & Goodwin, C. (1994). Beyond smiling. In R. T. Rust & R. L. Oliver (Eds.), *Service quality: New directions in theory and practice* (pp. 139–171). Thousand Oaks, CA: Sage; Locke, K. (1996). A funny thing happened! The management of consumer emotions in service encounters. *Organizational Science, 7,* 40–59.

[83] Gwinner, K. P., Gremler, D. D., & Bitner, M. J. (1998). Relational benefits in service industries: The customer's perspective. *Journal of the Academy of Marketing Science, 26,* 101–114.

[84] American College of Physicians. *Ethics manual.* Retrieved February 9, 2008, from: http://www.acponline.org/running_practice/ethics/

Notes for Chapter 9

[1] Hecht, M. L., Marston, P. J., & Larkey, L. K. (1994). Love ways and relationship quality in heterosexual relationships. *Journal of Social and Personal Relationships, 11,* 25–44.

[2] Baxter, L. A., & Montgomery, B. M. (1996). *Relating: Dialogues and dialectics.* New York: Guilford.

[3] Peterson, G. W., & Bush, K. R. (1999). Predicting adolescent autonomy from parents: Relationship connectedness and restrictiveness. *Sociological Inquiry, 69,* 431–457.

[4] Blacker, L. (1999). The launching phase of the life cycle. In B. Carter & M. McGoldrick (Eds.), *The expanded family life cycle: Individual, family, and social perspectives* (3rd ed., pp. 287–306). Boston: Allyn & Bacon.

[5] U.S. Census Bureau. (2007). Marriage and divorce. Downloaded January 19, 2007, from: http://www.census.gov/population/www/socdemo/marr-div.html

[6] Kaplan, R. M., & Kronick, R. G. (2006). Marital status and longevity in the United States population. *Journal of Epidemiology and Community Health, 60,* 760–765; Manzoli, M., Villarti, P., Pirone, G. M., & Boccia, A. (2007). Marital status and mortality in the elderly: A systematic review and meta-analysis. *Social Science & Medicine, 64,* 77–94.

[7] Macintyre, S. (1992). The effects of family position and status on health. *Social Science & Medicine, 35,* 453–464.

[8] Goldman, N. (1993). Marriage selection and mortality patterns: Inferences and fallacies. *Demography, 30,* 189–208.

[9] Booth, A., & Johnson, D. R. (1994). Declining health and marital quality. *Journal of Marriage and the Family, 56,* 218–223.

[10] Duncan, G., Wilkerson, B., & England, P. (2006). Cleaning up their act: The effects of marriage and cohabitation in licit and illicit drug use. *Demography, 43,* 691–710.

[11] Bachman, J. G., Wadsworth, K. N., O'Malley, P. M., Johnston, L. D., & Schulenberg, J. E. (1997). *Smoking, drinking, and drug use in young adulthood: The impacts of new freedoms and new responsibilities.* Mahwah, NJ: Lawrence Erlbaum Associates.

[12] Kim, H. K., & McKenry, P. (2002). The relationship between marriage and psychological well-being. *Journal of Family Issues, 23,* 885–911; Lamb, K. A., Lee, G. R., & DeMaris, A. (2003). Union formation and depression: Selection and relationship effects. *Journal of Marriage and Family, 65,* 953–962.

[13] See Kiecolt-Glaser, J. K., & Newton, T. L. (2001). Marriage and health: His and hers. *Psychological Bulletin, 127,* 472–503.

[14] Waldron, I., Hughes, M. E., & Brooks, T. L. (1996). Marriage protection and marriage selection—Prospective evidence for reciprocal effects of marital

status and health. *Social Science & Medicine, 43,* 113–123.

[15] Bringle, R. G., & Buunk, B. P. (1991). Extradyadic relationships and sexual jealousy. In K. McKinney & S. Sprecher (Eds.), *Sexuality in close relationships* (pp. 135–153). Mahwah, NJ: Lawrence Erlbaum Associates.

[16] Mazur, R. M. (2000). *The new intimacy: Open-ended marriage and alternative lifestyles.* Boston: iUniverse.com Inc.

[17] Rust, P. C. (2003). Monogamy and polyamory: Relationship issues for bisexuals. In L. Garnets and D. Kimmel (Eds.), *Psychological perspectives on lesbian, gay, and bisexual experiences* (pp. 475–495). New York: Columbia University Press.

[18] Bettinger, M. (2004). Polyamory and gay men: A family systems approach. *Journal of GLBT Family Studies, 1,* 97–116; Blasband, D., & Peplau, L. A. (1985). Sexual exclusivity versus openness in gay male couples. *Archives of Sexual Behavior, 14,* 395–412.

[19] Munson, M., & Stelbourn, J. P. (Eds.). (1999). *The lesbian polyamory reader: Open relationships, non-monogamy, and casual sex.* Binghamton, NY: The Haworth Press.

[20] Bringle & Buunk, 1991.

[21] Priambodo, N. (2006, April 17). Dating trends jump on the technological train. *University of La Verne Campus Times,* available online at: http://www.ulv.edu/ctimes/web_exclusives_stories/datingtrends.htm

[22] Dion, K. K., & Dion, K. L. (1996). Cultural perspectives on romantic love. *Personal Relationships, 3,* 5–17.

[23] Amato, P. R., & Previti, D. (2003). People's reasons for divorcing. *Journal of Family Issues, 24,* 602–626.

[24] Levine, R. B. (1993). Is love a luxury? *American Demographics, 15,* 27–28.

[25] Hsu, F. L. K. (1981). The self in cross-cultural perspective. In A. J. Marsella, B. De Vos, & F. L. K. Hsu (Eds.), *Culture and self* (pp. 24–55). London: Tavistock. Quote is from p. 50.

[26] Coontz, S. (2006). *Marriage, a history: How love conquered marriage.* New York: Penguin.

[27] Kurdek, L. A. (2004). Are gay and lesbian cohabiting couples *really* different from heterosexual married couples? *Journal of Marriage and Family, 66,* 880–900.

[28] Kurdek, L. A. (1998). Relationship outcomes and their predictors: Longitudinal evidence from heterosexual married, gay cohabiting, and lesbian cohabiting couples. *Journal of Marriage and the Family, 60,* 553–568.

[29] Kurdek, L. A. (1994). Conflict resolution styles in gay, lesbian, heterosexual nonparent, and heterosexual parent couples. *Journal of Marriage and the Family, 56,* 705–722.

[30] Kurdek, L. A. (1994). Areas of conflict for gay, lesbian, and heterosexual couples: What couples argue about influences relationship satisfaction. *Journal of Marriage and the Family, 56,* 923–934.

[31] Kurdek, L. A., & Schmitt, J. P. (1987). Perceived emotional support from family and friends in members of homosexual, married, and heterosexual cohabiting couples. *Journal of Homosexuality, 14,* 57–68.

[32] Kurdek, L. A. (1993). The allocation of household labor in gay, lesbian, and heterosexual married couples. *Journal of Social Issues, 49,* 127–139.

[33] Balsam, K. F., Beauchaine, T. P., Rothblum, E. D., & Solomon, S. E. (2008). Three-year follow-up of same-sex couples who had civil unions in Vermont, same-sex couples not in civil unions, and heterosexual married couples. *Developmental Psychology, 44,* 102–116; Roisman, G. I., Clausell, E., Holland, A., Fortuna, K., & Elieff, C. (2008). Adult romantic relationships as contexts of human development: A multimethod comparison of same-sex couples with opposite-sex dating, engaged, and married dyads. *Developmental Psychology, 44,* 91–101.

[34] Barker, L. A., & Emery, R. E. (1993). When every relationship is above average: Perceptions and expectations of divorce at the time of marriage. *Law and Human Behavior, 17,* 439–450.

[35] United States General Accounting Office. Available online: http://www.gao.gov/archive/1997/og97016.pdf

[36] Knapp, M. L. (1978). *Social intercourse: From greeting to good-bye.* Boston: Allyn & Bacon; see also Knapp, M. L., & Vangelisti, A. L. (2000). *Interpersonal communication and human relationships* (4th ed.). Boston: Allyn & Bacon.

[37] Avtgis, T. A., West, D. V., & Anderson, T. L. (1998). Relationship stages: An inductive analysis identifying cognitive, affective, and behavioral dimensions of Knapp's relational stages model. *Communication Research Reports, 15,* 280–287.

[38] Rabby, M. K., & Walther, J. B. (2003). Computer-mediated communication effects on relationship formation and maintenance. In D. J. Canary & M. Dainton (Eds.), *Maintaining relationships through communication: Relational, contextual, and cultural variations* (pp. 141–162). Mahwah, NJ: Lawrence Erlbaum Associates.

[39] Cegala, D., Waldro, V., Ludlum, J., McCabe, B., Yost, S., & Teboul, B. (1988, March). *A study of interactants' thoughts and feelings during conversation.* Paper presented at the Ninth Annual Conference on Discourse Analysis, Philadelphia, PA.

[40] Parks, M. R., & Floyd, K. (1996). Making friends in cyberspace. *Journal of Communication, 46,* 80–97; Parks, M. R., & Roberts, L. D. (1998). "Making MOOsic": The development of personal relationships online and a comparison to their offline counterparts. *Journal of Social and Personal Relationships, 15,* 517–537.

[41] Mongeau, P. A., Shaw, C., & Bacue, A. (2000, February). *Dating norms on one college campus.* Paper presented at annual meeting of Western States Communication Association, Sacramento, CA.

[42] Peplau, L. A. (2003). Lesbian and gay relationships. In L. Garnets and D. Kimmel (Eds.), *Psychological perspectives on lesbian, gay, and bisexual experiences* (pp. 395–419). New York: Columbia University Press.

[43] Fitzpatrick, M. A. (1988). *Between husbands and wives: Communication in marriage.* Newbury Park, CA: Sage.

44 Fitzpatrick, M. A., Fey, J., Segrin, C., & Schiff, J. L. (1993). Internal working models of relationships and marital communication. *Journal of Language and Social Psychology, 12,* 103–131.

45 Gottman, J. M., & Levenson, R. W. (1992). Marital processes predictive of later dissolution: Behavior, physiology, and health. *Journal of Personality and Social Psychology, 63,* 221–233.

46 Gottman, J. M. (1994). *What predicts divorce?* Hillsdale, NJ: Lawrence Erlbaum Associates.

47 Holman, T. B., & Jarvis, M. O. (2003). Hostile, volatile, avoiding, and validating couple-conflict types: An investigation of Gottman's couple-conflict types. *Personal Relationships, 10,* 267–282.

48 Petronio, S. (2002). *Boundaries of privacy.* Albany: SUNY Press.

49 Petronio, S. (2000). The boundaries of privacy: Praxis of everyday life. In S. Petronio (Ed.), *Balancing the secrets of private disclosures* (pp. 37–49). Mahwah, NJ: Lawrence Erlbaum Associates.

50 Petronio, S. (1991). Communication boundary management: A theoretical model of managing disclosures of private information between marital couples. *Communication Theory, 1,* 311–335.

51 See Dindia, K., Fitzpatrick, M. A., & Kenny, D. A. (1997). Self-disclosure in spouse and stranger interaction: A social relations analysis. *Human Communication Research, 23,* 388–412.

52 Cordova, J. V., Gee, C. B., & Warren, L. Z. (2005). Emotional skillfulness in marriage: Intimacy as a mediator of the relationship between emotional skillfulness and marital satisfaction. *Journal of Social and Clinical Psychology, 24,* 218–235.

53 Mirgain, S. A., & Cordova, J. V. (2007). Emotion skills and marital health: The association between observed and self-reported emotion skills, intimacy, and marital satisfaction. *Journal of Social and Clinical Psychology, 26,* 983–1009.

54 Gottman, J. M., & Levenson, R. W. (1986). Assessing the role of emotion in marriage. *Behavioral Assessment, 8,* 31–48.

55 Carstensen, L. L., Gottman, J. M., & Levenson, R. W. (1995). Emotional behavior in long-term marriage. *Psychology and Aging, 10,* 140–149.

56 Gottman, 1994.

57 Gottman, 1994.

58 Kluwer, E. S., Heesink, J. A. M., & Van de Vliert, E. (1997). The marital dynamics of conflict over the division of labor. *Journal of Marriage and the Family, 59,* 635–653; Perry-Jenkins, M., & Folk, K. (1994). Class, couples, and conflict: Effects of the division of labor on assessments of marriage in dual-earner families. *Journal of Marriage and the Family, 56,* 165–180.

59 Alberts, J. K., Yoshimura, C. G., Rabby, M., & Loschiavo, R. (2005). Mapping the topography of couples' daily conversation. *Journal of Social and Personal Relationships, 22,* 299–322.

60 Kluwer, E. S., Heesink, J. A. M., & Van de Vliert, E. (1996). Marital conflict about the division of household labor and paid work. *Journal of Marriage and the Family, 58,* 958–969.

61 Coltrane, S. (2000). Research on household labor: Modeling and measuring the social embeddedness of routine family work. *Journal of Marriage and the Family, 62,* 1208–1233; Coltrane, S., & Adams, M. (2001). Men's family work: Child-centered fathering and the sharing of domestic labor. In R. Hertz & N. L. Marshall (Eds.), *Working families: The transformation of the American home* (pp. 72–99). Berkeley: University of California Press.

62 Zvonkovic, A. M., Schmiege, C. J., & Hall, L. D. (1994). Influence strategies used when couples make work-family decisions and their importance for marital satisfaction. *Family Relations, 43,* 182–188.

63 Zvonkovic et al., 1994.

64 Baxter, J. (2000). The joys and justice of housework. *Sociology, 34,* 609–631; Dempsey, K. C. (1999). Attempting to explain women's perceptions of the fairness of the division of housework. *Journal of Family Studies, 5,* 3–24.

65 Mannino, C. A., & Deutsch, F. M. (2007). Changing the division of household labor: A negotiated process between partners. *Sex Roles, 56,* 309–324.

66 Johnson, E. M., & Huston, T. L. (1998). The perils of love, or why wives adapt to husbands during the transition to parenthood. *Journal of Marriage and the Family, 60,* 195–204; Kluwer, E. S., Heesink, J. A. M., & Van de Vliert, E. (2000). The division of labor in close relationships: An asymmetrical conflict issue. *Personal Relationships, 7,* 263–282.

67 Kluwer, E. S. (1998). Responses to gender inequality in the division of family work: The status quo effect. *Social Justice Research, 11,* 337–357.

68 Deutsch, F. M. (1999). *Halving it all: How equally shared parenting works.* Cambridge, MA: Harvard University Press; Risman, B. J., & Johnson-Sumerford, D. (1998). Doing it fairly: A study of postgender marriages. *Journal of Marriage and the Family, 60,* 23–40.

69 Boren, J. P. (2007, November). *Negotiating the division of household labor in same-sex romantic partnerships.* Paper presented at the annual meeting of the National Communication Association, Chicago.

70 Knapp, 1978; Knapp & Vangelisti, 2000. (See note 36.)

71 Duck, S. (1987). How to lose friends without influencing people. In M. E. Roloff & G. R. Miller (Eds.), *Interpersonal processes: New directions in communication research* (pp. 278–298). Beverly Hills, CA: Sage.

72 Kellerman, K., Reynolds, R., & Chen, J. B. (1991). Strategies of conversational retreat: When parting is not sweet sorrow. *Communication Monographs, 58,* 362–383.

73 Metts, S., Cupach, W. R., & Bejllovec, R. A. (1989). "I love you too much to ever start liking you": Redefining romantic relationships. *Journal of Social and Personal Relationships, 6,* 259–274.

74 Kreider, R. M. (2005). *Number, timing, and duration of marriages and divorces, 2001.* Washington, DC: U.S. Census Bureau; Munson, M. L., & Sutton, P. D. (2004, June 10). Births, marriages, divorces, and

deaths: Provisional data for 2003. *National Vital Statistics Report, 52*(22). Hyattsville, MD: National Center for Health Statistics.

[75] Furstenberg, F. F., & Cherlin, A. (1991). *Divided families: What happens to children when parents part.* Cambridge, MA: Harvard University Press; Popenoe, D. (1993). American family decline, 1960–1990: A review and appraisal. *Journal of Marriage and the Family, 55,* 527–555.

[76] Hetherington, E. M. (2003). Intimate pathways: Changing patterns in close personal relationship across time. *Family Relations, 52,* 318–331; Kelly, J. B. (2003). Changing perspectives on children's adjustment following divorce: A view from the United States. *Childhood, 10,* 237–254.

[77] Amato, P. R. (2000). The consequences of divorce for adults and children. *Journal of Marriage and the Family, 62,* 1269–1287.

[78] Hetherington, E. M., & Stanley-Hagen, M. (1999). The adjustment of children with divorced parents: A risk and resiliency perspective. *Journal of Child Psychology and Psychiatry, 40,* 129–140.

[79] Wallerstein, J. S., & Blakeslee, S. (1989). *Second chances: Men, women, and children a decade after divorce.* New York: Ticknor & Fields.

[80] American Bar Association. (1996). *Guide to family law.* New York: Times Books.

[81] General Accounting Office. (1997). Memo B-275860. Retrieved online at: http://www.gao.gov/archiva/1997/og97016.pdf

[82] Satir, V. (1972). *Peoplemaking.* Palo Alto, CA: Science and Behavior Books.

[83] U.S. Census Bureau. (2005). *Living arrangements of children: 2001* (Current Population Reports, P70-104). Washington, DC.

[84] Floyd, K., & Morman, M. T. (Eds.). (2006). *Widening the family circle: New research on family communication.* Thousand Oaks, CA: Sage.

[85] Whitchurch, G. C., & Constantine, L. L. (1993). Systems theory. In P. G. Boss, W. J. Doherty, R. LaRosa, W. R. Schumm, &

S. K. Steinmetz (Eds.), *Source book of family theories and methods: A conceptual approach* (pp. 325–352). New York: Plenum Press.

[86] Anderson, S. A., & Sabatelli, R. M. (2007). *Family interaction: A multigenerational developmental perspective* (4th ed.). Boston: Allyn & Bacon.

[87] Satir, 1972.

[88] Braithwaite, D. O., Baxter, L. A., & Harper, A. M. (1998). The role of rituals in the management of dialectical tensions of "old" and "new" in blended families. *Communication Studies, 49,* 105–120.

[89] Braithwaite et al., 1998; quote is from page 113.

[90] Stone, E. (1989). *Black sheep and kissing cousins: How our family stories shape us.* New York: Penguin.

[91] Vangelisti, A. L., & Caughlin, J. P. (1997). Revealing family secrets: The influence of topic, function, and relationships. *Journal of Social and Personal Relationships, 14,* 679–705.

[92] Aron, A., Norman, C. C., Aron, E. N., McKenna, C., & Heyman, R. E. (2000). Couples' shared participation in novel and arousing activities and experienced relationship quality. *Journal of Personality and Social Psychology, 78,* 273–284.

[93] Ellis, K. (2002). Perceived parental confirmation: Development and validation of an instrument. *Southern Communication Journal, 67,* 319–334.

[94] Gottman, J. (2003). Why marriages fail. In K. M. Galvin & P. J. Cooper (Eds.), *Making connections: Readings in relational communication* (pp. 258–266). Los Angeles: Roxbury.

[95] Napier, A. Y., & Whitaker, C. A. (1989). *The family crucible: The intense experience of family therapy.* New York: HarperTrade.

[96] Baxter & Montgomery, 1996.

Notes for Chapter 10

[1] Wilmot, W. W., & Hocker, J. L. (2001). *Interpersonal conflict.* New York: McGraw-Hill.

[2] Adapted from Hocker, J. L., & Wilmot, W. W. (1995). *Interpersonal conflict.* Madison, WI: Brown & Benchmark.

[3] Orbe, M. P., & Warren, K. T. (2000). Different standpoints, different realities: Race, gender, and perceptions of intercultural conflict. *Communication Quarterly, 48,* 51–57.

[4] Mayer, B. (2000). *The dynamics of conflict resolution.* San Francisco: Jossey-Bass.

[5] Smith, T. W., Berg, C., Uchino, B. N., Florsheim, P., & Pearce, G. (2006, March). *Marital conflict behavior and coronary artery calcification.* Paper presented at annual meeting of the American Psychosomatic Society, Denver, CO.

[6] Kiecolt-Glaser, J. K., Glaser, R., Cacioppo, J. T., & Malarkey, W. B. (1998). Marital stress: Immunologic, neuroendocrine, and autonomic correlates. *Annals of the New York Academy of Sciences, 840,* 656–663.

[7] Dopp. J. M., Miller, G. E., Myers, H. F., & Fahey, J. L. (2000). Increased natural killer-cell mobilization and cytotoxicity during marital conflict. *Brain, Behavior, and Immunity, 14,* 10–26.

[8] Kiecolt-Glaser, J. K., Loving, T. J., Stowell, J. R., Malarkey, W. B., Lemeshow, S., Dickinson, S. L., & Glaser, R. (2005). Hostile marital interactions, proinflammatory cytokine production, and wound healing. *Archives of General Psychiatry, 62,* 1377–1384.

[9] See, e.g., Kiecolt-Glaser, J. K., Glaser, R., Cacioppo, J. T., MacCallum, R. C., Snydersmith, M., Kim, C., & Malarkey, W. B. (1997). Marital conflict in older adults: Endocrinological and immunological correlates. *Psychosomatic Medicine, 59,* 339–349; Kiecolt-Glaser, J. K., Malarkey, W. B., Chee, M., Newton, T., Cacioppo, J. T., Mao, H.-Y., & Glaser, R. (1993). Negative behavior during marital conflict is associated with immunological down-regulation. *Psychosomatic Medicine, 55,* 395–409.

[10] Cahn, D., & Floyd, S. (Eds.). (1996). *Family violence from a communication perspective.* Thousand Oaks, CA: Sage; Gottman, J. M. (1994). *What predicts divorce?* Hillsdale, NJ: Lawrence Erlbaum Associates.

[11] Lloyd, S. A., & Emery, B. C. (2000). The context and dynamics of intimate aggression against women. *Journal of So-*

cial and Personal Relationships, 17, 503–521.

[12] See Barnett, O. W., Miller-Perrin, C. L., & Perrin, R. D. (1997). *Family violence across the life-span: An introduction.* Thousand Oaks, CA: Sage.

[13] Lloyd, S. A., & Emery, B. C. (2000). *The dark side of courtship: Physical and sexual aggression.* Thousand Oaks, CA: Sage.

[14] Island, D., & Letellier, P. (1991). *Men who beat the men who love them: Battered gay men and domestic violence.* New York: Haworth Press; McLeod, M. (1984). Women against men: An examination of domestic violence based on an analysis of official data and national victimization data. *Justice Quarterly, 1,* 171–193.

[15] Peplau, L. A., & Spaulding, L. R. (2000). The close relationships of lesbians, gay men and bisexuals. In C. Hendrick & S. S. Hendrick (Eds.), *Close relationships: A sourcebook* (pp. 111–123). Thousand Oaks, CA: Sage.

[16] Cate, R. M., Henton, J. M., Koval, J. E., Christopher, F. S., & Lloyd, S. A. (1982). Premarital abuse: A social psychological perspective. *Journal of Family Issues, 3,* 79–90; Henton, J. M., Cate R. M., Koval, J. E., Lloyd, S. A., & Christopher, F. S. (1983). Romance and violence in dating relationships. *Journal of Family Issues, 3,* 467–482.

[17] Lloyd & Emery, 2000.

[18] Rogge, R. D., & Bradbury, T. N. (1999). Till violence does us part: The differing roles of communication and aggression in predicting adverse marital outcomes. *Journal of Consulting and Clinical Psychology, 67,* 340–351.

[19] Lloyd, S. A. (1996). Physical aggression and marital distress: The role of everyday marital interaction. In D. D. Cahn & S. A. Lloyd (Eds.), *Family violence from a communication perspective* (pp. 177–198). Thousand Oaks, CA: Sage.

[20] Canary, D. J., Weger, H., & Stafford, L. (1991). Couples' argument sequences and their associations with relational characteristics. *Western Journal of Speech Communication, 55,* 159–179.

[21] Gottman, J. M. (1982). Emotional responsiveness in marital conversations. *Journal of Communication, 32,* 108–120.

[22] Koren, P., Carlton, K., & Shaw, D. (1980). Marital conflict: Relations among behaviors, outcomes, and distress. *Journal of Consulting and Clinical Psychology, 48,* 460–468.

[23] Erbert, L. A. (2000). Conflict and dialectics: Perceptions of dialectical contradictions in marital conflict. *Journal of Social and Personal Relationships, 17,* 638–659.

[24] Canary, D. J. (2003). Managing interpersonal conflict: A model of events related to strategic choices. In J. O. Greene & B. R. Burleson (Eds.), *Handbook of communication and social interaction skills* (pp. 515–550). Mahwah, NJ: Lawrence Erlbaum Associates.

[25] Kurdek, L. A. (1994). Areas of conflict for gay, lesbian, and heterosexual couples: What couples argue about influences relationship satisfaction. *Journal of Marriage and the Family, 56,* 923–934.

[26] See Canary, D. J., Cupach, W. R., & Messman, S. J. (1995). *Relationship conflict: Conflict in parent-child, friendship, and romantic relationships.* Thousand Oaks, CA: Sage.

[27] Wood, J. T. (1998). *But I thought you meant . . . : Misunderstandings in human communication.* Mountain View, CA: Mayfield.

[28] Klinetob, N. A., & Smith, D. A. (1996). Demand-withdraw communication in marital interaction: Tests of inter-spousal contingency and gender role hypotheses. *Journal of Marriage and Family, 58,* 945–958.

[29] Caughlin, J. P., & Vangelisti, A. L. (1999). Desire for change in one's partner as a predictor of the demand/withdraw pattern of marital communication. *Communication Monographs, 66,* 66–89.

[30] Kurdek, L. A. (1994). Conflict resolution styles in gay, lesbian, heterosexual nonparent, and heterosexual parent couples. *Journal of Marriage and the Family, 56,* 705–722.

[31] Caughlin, J. P., & Vangelisti, A. L. (2006). Conflict in dating and marital relationships. In J. G. Oetzel & S. Ting-Toomey (Eds.), *The SAGE handbook of conflict communication: Integrating theory, research, and practice* (pp. 129–157). Thousand Oaks, CA: Sage.

[32] Patterson, C. J. (2000). Family relationships of lesbians and gay men. *Journal of Marriage and the Family, 62,* 1052–1069.

[33] Peplau, L. A., & Beals, K. P. (2004). The family lives of lesbians and gay men. In A. L. Vangelisti (Ed.), *Handbook of family communication* (pp. 233–248). Mahwah, NJ: Lawrence Erlbaum Associates.

[34] Ting-Toomey, S. (1997). Managing intercultural conflicts effectively. In L. A. Samovar & R. F. Porter (Eds.), *Intercultural communication: A reader* (pp. 392–403). Belmont, CA: Wadsworth.

[35] Ting-Toomey, S. (1985). Toward a theory of conflict and culture. In W. B. Gudykunst, L. P. Stewart, & S. Ting-Toomey (Eds.), *Communication, culture, and organizational processes* (pp. 71–86). Beverly Hills, CA: Sage.

[36] Gudykunst, W. B., & Kim, Y. Y. (2003). *Communicating with strangers: An approach to intercultural communication* (4th ed.). New York: McGraw-Hill.

[37] Ting-Toomey, S. (1988). Rhetorical sensitivity style in three cultures: France, Japan, and the United States. *Central States Speech Journal, 39,* 28–36.

[38] Okabe, K. (1987). Indirect speech acts of the Japanese. In L. Kincaid (Ed.), *Communication theory: Eastern and Western perspectives* (pp. 127–136). San Diego, CA: Academic Press.

[39] Ting-Toomey, S., & Kurogi, A. (1998). Facework competence in intercultural conflict: An updated face-negotiation theory. *International Journal of Intercultural Relations, 22,* 187–225.

[40] Suler, J. R. (1996). The psychology of cyberspace. Available online at: http://www.rider.edu/-suler/psycyber/ psycyber.html

[41] Suler, J. R. (2004). The online disinhibition effect. *CyberPsychology and Behavior, 7,* 321–326.

[42] See Donahue, W. A., & Kolt, R. (1992). *Managing interpersonal conflict.* Newbury Park, CA: Sage.

[43] Ericson, P. M., & Rogers, L. E. (1973). New procedures for ana-

lyzing relational communication. *Family Process, 12,* 245–267.

[44] Erchul, W. P., Sheridan, S. M., Ryan, D. A., Grissom, P. F., Killough, C. E., & Mettler, D. W. (1999). Patterns of relational communication in conjoint behavioral consultation. *School Psychology Quarterly, 14,* 121–147.

[45] French, J. P. R., & Raven, B. (1959). The bases of social power. In D. Cartwright & A. Zander (Eds.), *Group dynamics* (pp. 607–623). New York: Harper and Row.

[46] Brown, R. (1991). *Human universals.* Philadelphia: Temple University Press.

[47] Mies, M. (1991). *Patriarchy and accumulation on a world scale: Women in the international division of labor.* London: Zed Books.

[48] United Nations Inter-Agency Network on Women and Gender Equality. (2002, March). *Gender equality and the millennium development goals (MDG): Assessing progress in achieving gender equality.* Washington, DC: Author.

[49] United Nations Inter-Agency Network on Women and Gender Equality, 2002.

[50] Schumacher, J. A., & Leonard, K. E. (2005). Husbands' and wives' marital adjustment, verbal aggression, and physical aggression as longitudinal predictors of physical aggression in early marriage. *Journal of Consulting and Clinical Psychology, 73,* 28–37.

[51] Spender, D. (1990). *Man made language.* London: Pandora Press.

[52] Loving, T. J., Heffner, K. I., Kiecolt-Glaser, J. K., Glaser, R., & Malarkey, W. B. (2004). Stress hormone changes and marital conflict: Spouses' relative power makes a difference. *Journal of Marriage and Family, 66,* 595–612.

[53] Sprecher, S., Schmeeckle, M., & Felmlee, D. (2006). The principle of least interest: Inequality in emotional involvement in romantic relationships. *Journal of Family Issues, 27,* 1255–1280.

[54] Ting-Toomey, S. (1999). *Communicating across cultures.* New York: Guilford.

[55] Bochner, S., & Hesketh, B. (1994). Power distance, individualism/collectivism, and job related attitudes in a culturally diverse work group. *Journal of Cross-Cultural Psychology, 25,* 233–257.

[56] Gottman, J. M. (1993). A theory of marital dissolution and stability. *Journal of Family Psychology, 7,* 57–75.

[57] Gottman, J. M. (1994). *What predicts divorce? The relationship between marital processes and marital outcomes.* Hillsdale, NJ: Lawrence Erlbaum Associates.

[58] Payne, K., & Cangemi, J. (2001). Gender differences in leadership. In K. E. Payne (Ed.), *Different but equal: Communication between the sexes* (pp. 145–162). Westport, CT: Praeger.

[59] Kiecolt-Glaser, J. K., Glaser, R., Cacioppo, J. T., & Malarkey, W. B. (1998). Marital stress: Immunologic, neuroendocrine, and autonomic correlates. *Annals of the New York Academy of Sciences, 840,* 656–663.

[60] Kiecolt-Glaser, J. K., Newton, T., Cacioppo, J. T., MacCallum, R. C., Glaser, R., & Malarkey, W. B. (1996). Marital conflict and endocrine function: Are men really more physiologically affected than women? *Journal of Consulting and Clinical Psychology, 64,* 324–332; Kiecolt-Glaser, Loving et al., 2005 (see note 8).

[61] Blake, R. R., & Mouton, J. S. (1984). *The managerial grid III* (3rd ed.). Houston, TX: Gulf Publishing.

[62] Messman, S. J., & Mikesell, R. L. (2000). Competition and interpersonal conflict in dating relationships. *Communication Reports, 13,* 21–34.

[63] Olson, L. N., & Braithwaite, D. O. (2004). "If you hit me again, I'll hit you back": Conflict management strategies of individuals experiencing aggression during conflicts. *Communication Studies, 55,* 271–285.

[64] Cahn, D. D. (1992). *Conflict in intimate relationships.* New York: Guilford.

[65] Wilmot, W. W., & Hocker, J. L. (2007). *Interpersonal conflict* (7th ed). New York: McGraw-Hill.

[66] Oetzel, J. G., & Ting-Toomey, S. (2003). Face concerns in interpersonal conflict: A cross-cultural empirical test of the face negotiation theory. *Communication Research, 30,* 599–625.

Notes for Chapter 11

[1] Tyler, J. J., Feldman, R. S., & Reichert, A. (2006). The price of deceptive behavior: Disliking and lying to people who lie to us. *Journal of Experimental Social Psychology, 42,* 69–77.

[2] Smith, D. L. (2004). *Why we lie: The evolutionary roots of deception and the unconscious mind.* New York: St. Martin's Press.

[3] Gordon, A. K., & Miller, A. G. (2000). Perspective differences in the construal of lies: Is deception in the eye of the beholder? *Personality and Social Psychology Bulletin, 26,* 163–170.

[4] Adler, K. (2007). *The lie detectors: The history of an American obsession.* New York: Free Press.

[5] Plante, T. G. (2004). *Do the right thing: Living ethically in an unethical world.* Oakland, CA: New Harbinger.

[6] See Levine, T. R., Asada, K. J. K., & Lindsey, L. L. M. (2003). The relative impact of violation type and lie severity on judgments of message deceitfulness. *Communication Research Reports, 20,* 208–218.

[7] Cole, T. (2001). Lying to the one you love: The use of deception in romantic relationships. *Journal of Social and Personal Relationships, 18,* 107–129.

[8] Kornet, A. (1997, May/June). The truth about lying. *Psychology Today, 30*(3), p. 53.

[9] Martin, J. (1999). *Miss Manners' basic training: The right thing to say.* New York: Random House/Crown.

[10] Saxe, L. (1991). Lying: Thoughts of an applied social psychologist. *American Psychologist, 46,* 409–415.

[11] Saxe, 1991.

[12] See Garfinkel, S. (1995). *PGP: Pretty good privacy.* Sebastopol, CA: O'Reilly and Associates.

[13] Turkle, S. (1995). *Life on the screen: Identity in the age of the Internet.* New York: Simon & Schuster.

[14] See Frost, J. (2006). *Impression formation in the information age: A study of and design for online dating.* Unpublished doctoral dissertation, Massachusetts Institute of Technology. Dissertation Abstracts International: Section B: The Sciences

and Engineering. Vol. 67(5-B), pp. 2875.

[15] Epstein, R. (2007, February/March). The truth about online dating. *Scientific American Mind,* 28–35.

[16] Gibbs, J. L., Ellison, N. B., & Heino, R. D. (2006). Self-presentation in online personals: The role of anticipated future interaction, self-disclosure, and perceived success in Internet dating. *Communication Research, 33,* 152–177.

[17] See Johnson, C. E. (2001). *Meeting the ethical challenges of leadership.* Thousand Oaks, CA: Sage.

[18] Knapp M. L. (2008). *Lying and deception in human interaction.* Boston: Pearson/Allyn & Bacon.

[19] Stengel, R. (2000). *(You're too kind) A brief history of flattery.* New York: Simon & Shuster.

[20] Feldman, R. S., Forrest, J. A., & Happ, B. R. (2002). Self-presentation and verbal deception: Do self-presenters lie more? *Basic and Applied Social Psychology, 24,* 163–170.

[21] Ekman, P. (2001). *Telling lies: Clues to deceit in the market-place, politics, and marriage.* New York: Norton; Seiter, J. S., Bruschke, J., & Bai, C. (2002). The acceptability of deception as a function of perceivers' culture, deceiver's intention, and deceiver-deceived relationship. *Western Journal of Communication, 66,* 158–180.

[22] Metts, S. (1989). A preliminary investigation of deception in close relationships. *Journal of Social and Personal Relationships, 6,* 159–179.

[23] Shulman, D. (2007). *From hire to liar: The role of deception in the workplace.* Ithaca, NY: Cornell University Press.

[24] DePaulo, B. M., & Morris, W. L. (2004). Discerning lies from truths: Behavioural cues to deception and the indirect pathway of intuition. In P. A. Granhag & L. A. Strömwall (Eds.), *The detection of deception in forensic contexts* (pp. 15–40). New York: Cambridge University Press; Malone, B. E., & DePaulo, B. M. (2001). Measuring sensitivity to deception. In J. A. Hall & F. J. Bernieri (Eds.), *Interpersonal sensitivity: Theory and measurement* (pp. 103–124). Mahwah, NJ: Lawrence Erlbaum Associates;

Park, H. S., Levine, T. R., Harms C. M., & Ferrara, M. H. (2002). Group and individual accuracy in deception detection. *Communication Research Reports, 19,* 99–106; Vrij, A. (2000). *Detecting lies and deceit: The psychology of lying and the implications for professional practice.* New York: Wiley.

[25] Vrij, A. (2000). *Detecting lies and deceit: The psychology of lying and the implications for professional practice.* New York: Wiley.

[26] See Kaufmann, G., Drevland, G. C. B., Wessel, E., Goverskeid, G., & Magnussen, S. (2003). The importance of being earnest: Displayed emotions and witness credibility. *Applied Cognitive Psychology, 17,* 21–34; O'Sullivan, M. (2003). The fundamental attribution error in detecting deception: The boy-who-cried-wolf effect. *Personality and Social Psychology Bulletin, 29,* 1316–1327.

[27] Buller, D. B., & Hunsaker, F. (1995). Interpersonal deception: XIII. Suspicion and the truth-bias of conversational participants. In J. Aitken (Ed.), *Intrapersonal communication process reader* (pp. 239–251). Westland, MI: Hayden-McNeil.

[28] Buller, D. B., & Burgoon, J. K. (1996). Interpersonal deception theory. *Communication Theory, 6,* 203–242.

[29] Gilbert, D. T. (1991). How mental systems believe. *American Psychologist, 46,* 107–119; Gilbert, D. T., Krull, D. S., & Malone, P. S. (1990). Unbelieving the unbelievable: Some problems in the rejection of false information. *Journal of Personality and Social Psychology, 59,* 601–613.

[30] DePaulo, B. M., Lindsay, J. J., Malone, B. E., Muhlenbruck L., Charlton, K., & Cooper, H. (2003). Cues to deception. *Psychological Bulletin, 129,* 74–118.

[31] Park, H. S., Levine, T. R., McCornack, S. A., Morrison, K., & Ferrara, M. (2002). How people really detect lies. *Communication Monographs, 69,* 144–157.

[32] Guerrero, L. K., & Floyd, K. (2006). *Nonverbal communication in close relationships.* Mahwah, NJ: Lawrence Erlbaum Associates; see also deTurck, M. A., & Miller, G. R. (1985).

Deception and arousal: Isolating the behavioral correlates of deception. *Human Communication Research, 12,* 181–201; Feeley, T. H., & deTurck, M. A. (1998). The behavioral correlates of sanctioned and unsanctioned deceptive communication. *Journal of Nonverbal Behavior, 22,* 189–204.

[33] Guerrero & Floyd, 2006; Zuckerman, M., DePaulo, B. M., & Rosenthal, R. (1986). Humans as deceivers and lie-detectors. In P. D. Blanck, R. Buck, & R. Rosenthal (Eds.), *Nonverbal communication in the clinical context* (pp. 13–35). University Park: Pennsylvania State University Press.

[34] DePaulo et al., 2003; Ekman, P., Friesen, W. V., & Scherer, K. R. (1976). Body movement and voice pitch in deceptive interaction. *Semiotica, 16,* 23–27.

[35] Ekman, P., O'Sullivan, M., Friesen, W. V., & Scherer, K. R. (1991). Face, voice, and body in detecting deceit. *Journal of Nonverbal Behavior, 15,* 125–135.

[36] Bauchner, J. E., Kaplan, E. P., & Miller, G. R. (1980). Detecting deception: The relationship of available information to judgmental accuracy in initial encounters. *Human Communication Research, 6,* 251–264.

[37] Tecce, J. J. (1992). Psychology, physiology, and experimental psychology. In Staff (Ed.), *McGraw-Hill yearbook of science and technology* (pp. 375–377). New York: McGraw-Hill.

[38] DePaulo et al., 2003; DePaulo, B. M., Stone, J. I., & Lassiter, G. D. (1985). Deceiving and detecting deceit. In B. R. Schlenker (Ed.), *The self and social life* (pp. 323–370). New York: McGraw-Hill; Zuckerman, M., & Driver, R. E. (1985). Telling lies: Verbal and nonverbal correlates of deception. In A. W. Siegman & S. Feldstein (Eds.), *Multichannel integrations of nonverbal behavior* (pp. 129–148). Hillsdale, NJ: Lawrence Erlbaum Associates.

[39] Jomier, J., Rault, E., & Aylward, S. R. (2004). Automatic quantification of pupil dilation under stress. *IEEE International Symposium on Biomedical Imaging, 1,* 249–252.

[40] Lubow, R. E., & Fein, O. (1996). Pupillary size in response to a visual guilty knowledge test: New techniques for

the detection of deception. *Journal of Experimental Psychology: Applied, 2,* 164–177; Zuckerman & Driver, 1985.

[41] Guerrero & Floyd, 2006; see also Greene, J. O., O'Hair, H. D., Cody, M. J., & Yen, C. (1985). Planning and control of behavior during deception. *Human Communication Research, 11,* 335–364; Riggio, R. E., & Friedman, H. S. (1983). Individual differences and cues to deception. *Journal of Personality and Social Psychology, 45,* 899–915.

[42] Ekman, P. (2003). Darwin, deception, and facial expression. *Annals of the New York Academy of Sciences, 1000,* 205–221; Ekman, P., Friesen, W. V., & O'Sullivan, M. (1988) Smiles when lying. *Journal of Personality and Social Psychology, 54,* 414–420; Scharlemann, J. P. W., Eckel, C. C., Kacelnik, A., & Wilson, R. K. (2001). The value of a smile: Game theory with a human face. *Journal of Economic Psychology, 22,* 617–640.

[43] Vrij, A. (1995). Behavioral correlates of deception in a simulated police interview. *Journal of Psychology, 129,* 15–29.

[44] Buller, D. B., & Aune, R. K. (1987). Nonverbal cues to deception among intimates, friends, and strangers. *Journal of Nonverbal Behavior, 11,* 269–290.

[45] Ekman, P., & Friesen, W. V. (1974). Detecting deception from body or face. *Journal of Personality and Social Psychology, 29,* 288–298.

[46] Greene et al., 1985.

[47] Buller & Burgoon, 1996 (see note 28); but see Frank, M. G., & Ekman, P. (2004). Appearing truthful generalizes across different deception situations. *Journal of Personality and Social Psychology, 86,* 486–495.

[48] Burgoon, J. K., Buller, D. B., Ebesu, A., & Rockwell, P. (1994). Interpersonal deception: V. Accuracy in deception detection. *Communication Monographs, 61,* 303–325.

[49] Burgoon, J. K., & Floyd, K. (2000). Testing for the motivation impairment effect during deceptive and truthful interaction. *Western Journal of Communication, 64,* 243–267; see also Millar, M., & Millar, K. (1995). Detection of deception in familiar and unfamiliar persons: The effects of information restriction. *Journal of Nonverbal Behavior, 19,* 69–84.

[50] Feldman, R. S., Tomasian, J. C., & Coats, E. J. (1999). Nonverbal deception abilities and adolescents' social competence: Adolescents with higher social skills are better liars. *Journal of Nonverbal Behavior, 23,* 237–249; see also Burgoon, J. K., Buller, D. B., & Guerrero, L. K. (1995). Interpersonal deception: IX. Effects of social skill and nonverbal communication on deception success and detection accuracy. *Journal of Language and Social Psychology, 14,* 289–311; DePaulo, B. M., Blank, A. L., Swaim, G. W., & Hairfield, J. G. (1992). Expressiveness and expressive control. *Personality and Social Psychology Bulletin, 18,* 276–285.

[51] Riggio, R. E., Tucker, J., & Widaman, K. F. (1987). Verbal and nonverbal cues as mediators of deception ability. *Journal of Nonverbal Behavior 11,* 126–145.

[52] Buller & Burgoon, 1996. (See note 28.)

[53] For an exception, see Feldman, R. S., Forrest, J. A., & Happ, B. R. (2002). Self-presentation and verbal deception: Do self-presenters lie more? *Basic and Applied Social Psychology, 24,* 163–170.

[54] Bond, C. F., Omar, A., Mahmoud, A., & Bonser, R. N. (1990). Lie detection across cultures. *Journal of Nonverbal Behavior, 14,* 189–204.

[55] Bond, C. F., & Atoum, A. O. (2000). International deception. *Personality and Social Psychology Bulletin, 26,* 385–395.

[56] For review, see Burgoon, J. K., & Floyd, K. (2000). Testing for the motivation impairment effect during deceptive and truthful interaction. *Western Journal of Communication, 64,* 243–267; see also DePaulo, B. M., & Kirkendol, S. E. (1989). The motivational impairment effect in the communication of deception. In J. Yuille (Ed.), *Credibility assessment* (pp. 51–70). Deurne, Belgium: Kluwer.

[57] Bond, C. F., & DePaulo, B. M. (2006). Accuracy of deception judgments. *Personality and Social Psychology Review, 10,* 214–234.

[58] Burgoon, Buller, Ebesu, & Rockwell, 1994 (see note 48);

Toris, C., & DePaulo, B. M. (1984). Effects of actual deception and suspiciousness of deception on interpersonal perceptions. *Journal of Personality and Social Psychology, 47,* 1063–1073; but see McCornack, S. A., & Levine, T. R. (1990). When lovers become leery: The relationship between suspicion and accuracy in detecting deception. *Communication Monographs, 57,* 219–230.

[59] Burgoon, Buller, Ebesu, & Rockwell, 1994. (See note 48.)

[60] Buller & Burgoon, 1996. (See note 28.)

[61] See Bond, C. F., Thomas, B. J., & Paulson, R. M. (2004). Maintaining lies: The multiple-audience problem. *Journal of Experimental Social Psychology, 40,* 29–40; Ekman, P., & Yamey, G. (2004). Emotions revealed: Recognising facial expressions. *British Medical Journal, 328,* 75–76.

[62] Burgoon, J. K., Buller, D. B., & Floyd, K. (2001). Does participation affect deception success? A test of the interactivity principle. *Human Communication Research, 27,* 503–534.

[63] Dunbar, N. E., Ramirez, A., & Burgoon, J. K. (2003). The effect of participation on the ability to judge deceit. *Communication Reports, 16,* 23–33.

Notes for Chapter 12

[1] Frijda, N. H. (1993). Moods, emotion episodes, and emotions. In M. Lewis & J. M. Haviland (Eds.), *Handbook of emotions* (2nd ed., pp. 381–403). New York: Guilford.

[2] Morris, W. N. (1992). A functional analysis of the role of mood in affective systems. In M.S. Clark (Ed.), *Emotion* (pp. 256–293). Newbury Park, CA: Sage.

[3] Thayer, R. E. (1989). *The biopsychology of mood and arousal.* New York: Oxford University Press.

[4] Guerrero, L. K., & Floyd, K. (2006). *Nonverbal communication in close relationships.* Mahwah, NJ: Lawrence Erlbaum Associates.

[5] Sheldon, K. M., Elliott, A. J., Kim, Y., & Kasser, T. (2001). What is satisfying about satisfying events? Testing 10 candidate

psychological needs. *Journal of Personality and Social Psychology, 80,* 325–339.

[6] Russell, J. A. (1994). Is there universal recognition of emotion from facial expression? *Psychological Bulletin, 115,* 102–141.

[7] Scherer, K. R., & Walbott, H. G. (1994). Evidence for universality and cultural variation of differential emotion response patterning. *Journal of Personality and Social Psychology, 66,* 310–328.

[8] Lazarus, 1991. *Emotion and adaptation.* New York: Oxford University Press.

[9] Rimé, B., Mesquita, B., Philippot, B., & Boca, S. (1991). Beyond the emotional event: Six studies of the social sharing of emotions. *Cognition and Emotion, 5,* 435–465.

[10] Fredrickson, B. L., Tugade, M. M., Waugh, C. E., & Larkin, G. R. (2003). What good are positive emotions in crisis? A prospective study of resilience and emotions following the terrorist attacks on the United States on September 11th, 2001. *Journal of Personality and Social Psychology, 84,* 365–376; Tugade, M. M., & Fredrickson, B. L. (2004). Resilient individuals use positive emotions to bounce back from negative emotional experiences. *Journal of Personality and Social Psychology, 86,* 320–333.

[11] See Marston, P. J., & Hecht, M. L. (1994). Love ways: An elaboration and application to relational maintenance. In D. J. Canary & L. Stafford (Eds.), *Communication and relational maintenance* (pp. 187–202). Orlando, FL: Academic Press.

[12] Berscheid, E. (2002). Emotion. In H. H. Kelley, E. Berscheid, A. Christensen, J. Harvey, T. L. Huston, G. Levinger, E. McClintock, L. A. Peplau, & D. R. Peterson, (Eds.), *Close relationships* (2nd ed., pp. 110–168). Clinton Corners, NY: Percheron Press.

[13] Sprecher, S., & Regan, P. C. (1998). Passionate and companionate love in courting and young married couples. *Sociological Inquiry, 68,* 163–185.

[14] See Hatfield, E., Traupmann, J., & Sprecher, S. (1984). Older women's perceptions of their intimate relationships. *Journal of Social and Clinical Psychology, 2,* 108–124.

[15] Rubin, Z. (1970). Measurement of romantic love. *Journal of Personality and Social Psychology, 16,* 265–273.

[16] See, e.g., Ray, G. B., & Floyd, K. (2006). Nonverbal expressions of liking and disliking in initial interaction: Encoding and decoding perspectives. *Southern Communication Journal, 71,* 45–65; Andersen, P. A., & Guerrero, L. K. (1998). The bright side of relational communication: Interpersonal warmth as a social emotion. In P. A. Andersen & L. K. Guerrero (Eds.), *Handbook of communication and emotion: Research, theory, applications, and contexts* (pp. 303–329). San Diego, CA: Academic Press.

[17] Cacioppo, J. T., Gardner, W. L., & Berntson, G. G. (1999). The affect system has parallel and integrative processing components: Form follows function. *Journal of Personality and Social Psychology, 76,* 839–855.

[18] Haidt, J., & Sabini, J. (2000). *What exactly makes revenge sweet?* Unpublished manuscript, University of Virginia; Lazarus, 1991 (see note 8).

[19] Roseman, I. J., Wiest, C., & Swartz, T. S. (1994). Phenomenology, behaviors, and goals differentiate discrete emotions. *Journal of Personality and Social Psychology, 67,* 206–221.

[20] Player, M. S., King, D. E., Mainous, A. G., & Greesey, M. E. (2007). Psychosocial factors and progression from prehypertension to hypertension or coronary heart disease. *Annals of Family Medicine, 5,* 403–411; see also Kawachi, I., Sparrow, D., Spiro, A., Vokonas, P., & Weiss, S. T. (1996). A prospective study of anger and coronary heart disease. *Circulation, 94,* 2090–2095.

[21] Eaker, E. D., Sullivan, L. M., Kelly-Hayes, M., D'Agostino, R. B., & Benjamin, E. J. (2004). Anger and hostility predict the development of atrial fibrillation in men in the Framingham Offspring Study. *Circulation, 109,* 1267–1271.

[22] Bleil, M. E., McCaffery, J. M., Muldoon, M. F., Sutton-Tyrell, K., & Manuck, S. B. (2004). Anger-related personality traits and carotid artery atherosclerosis in untreated hypertensive men.
Psychosomatic Medicine, 66, 633–639; Raikkonen, K., Matthews, K. A., Sutton-Tyrell, K., & Kuller, L. H. (2004). Trait anger and the metabolic syndrome predict progression of carotid atherosclerosis in healthy middle-aged women. *Psychosomatic Medicine, 66,* 903–908.

[23] Eng, P. M., Fitzmaurice, G., Kubzansky, L. D., Rimm, E. B., & Kawachi, I. (2003). Anger expression and risk of stroke and coronary heart disease among male health professionals. *Psychosomatic Medicine, 65,* 100–110.

[24] Wilcox, S., King, A. C., Vitaliano, P. P., & Brassington, G. S. (2000). Anger expression and natural killer cell activity in family caregivers participating in a physical activity trial. *Journal of Health Psychology, 5,* 431–440.

[25] Gouin, J. P., Kiecolt-Glaser, J. K., Malarkey, W. B., & Glaser, R. (in press). The influence of anger expression on wound healing. *Brain, Behavior, and Immunity.*

[26] Gottman, J. M. (1994). *What predicts divorce? The relationship between marital processes and marital outcomes.* Hillsdale, NJ: Lawrence Erlbaum Associates.

[27] Izard, C. E. (1991). *The psychology of emotions.* New York: Plenum.

[28] Gottman, 1994.

[29] Rozin, P., Haidt, J., & McCauley, C. (2000). Disgust. In M. Lewis & J. Haviland (Eds.), *Handbook of emotions* (2nd ed., pp. 637–653). New York: Guilford.

[30] Haidt, J. (2003). The moral emotions. In R. J. Davidson, K. R. Scherer, & H. H. Goldsmith (Eds.), *Handbook of affective sciences* (pp. 852–870). Oxford, England: Oxford University Press.

[31] Haidt, J., Koller, S., & Dias, M. (1993). Affect, culture, and morality, or is it wrong to eat your dog? *Journal of Personality and Social Psychology, 65,* 613–628.

[32] Rozin, P., Haidt, J., McCauley, C., Dunlop, L., & Ashmore, M. (1999). Individual differences in disgust sensitivity: Comparisons and evaluations of paper-and-pencil versus behavioral measures. *Journal of Research in Personality, 33,* 330–351.

33 Rozin, P., Markwith, M., & McCauley, C. R. (1994). The nature of aversion to indirect contacts with other persons: AIDS aversion as a composite of aversion to strangers, infection, moral taint, and misfortune. *Journal of Abnormal Psychology, 103,* 495–504.

34 Nemeroff, C., & Rozin, P. (1994). The contagion concept in adult thinking in the United States: Transmission of germs and of interpersonal influence. *Ethos, 22,* 158–186.

35 Schützwohl, A. (2008). The intentional object of romantic jealousy. *Evolution and Human Behavior, 29,* 92–99; see also Guerrero, L. K., & Andersen, P. A. (1998). The experience and expression of romantic jealousy. In P. A. Andersen & L. K. Guerrero (Eds.), *Handbook of communication and emotion: Research, theory, applications, and contexts* (pp. 155–188). San Diego, CA: Academic Press

36 Parker, J. G., Low, C. M., Walker, A. R., & Gamm, B. K. (2005). Children's friendship jealousy: Assessment of individual differences and links to sex, self-esteem, aggression, and social adjustment. *Developmental Psychology, 41,* 235–250.

37 Parrott, W. G. (1991). The emotional experiences of envy and jealousy. In P. Salovey (Ed.), *The psychology of jealousy and envy* (pp. 3–30). New York: Guilford.

38 Guerrero, L. K., & Andersen, P. A. (1998). The dark side of jealousy and envy: Desire, delusion, desperation, and destructive communication. In B. H. Spitzberg & W. R. Cupach (Eds.), *The dark side of close relationships* (pp. 33–70). Mahwah, NJ: Lawrence Erlbaum Associates.

39 Salovey, P., & Rothman, A. J. (1991). Envy and jealousy: Self and society. In P. Salovey (Ed.), *The psychology of jealousy and envy* (pp. 271–286). New York: Guilford.

40 Smith, R. H. (1991). Envy and the sense of injustice. In P. Salovey (Ed.), *The psychology of jealousy and envy* (pp. 79–99). New York: Guilford.

41 Shaver, P. R., Schwartz, J., Kirson, D., & O'Connor, C. (1987). Emotion knowledge: Further explorations of a prototype approach. *Journal of Personal-ity and Social Psychology, 52,* 1061–1086.

42 Guerrero, L. K., & Reiter, R. L. (1998). Expressing emotion: Sex differences in social skills and communicative responses to anger, sadness, and jealousy. In D. J. Canary & K. Dindia (Eds.), *Sex differences and similarities in communication* (pp. 321–350). Mahwah, NJ: Lawrence Erlbaum Associates; Scherer, K. R. (1986). Vocal affect expression: A review and model for future research. *Psychological Bulletin, 99,* 143–165.

43 American Psychiatric Association. (1994). *Diagnostic and statistical manual of mental disorders* (4th ed.). Washington, DC: Author.

44 See, e.g., Klein, D. F., & Wender, P. H. (1993). *Understanding depression: A complete guide to its diagnosis and treatment.* New York: Oxford University Press.

45 Melfi, C. A., Chawla, A. J., Croghan, T. W., Hanna, M. P., Kennedy, S., & Sredl, K. (1998). The effects of adherence to antidepressant treatment guidelines on relapse and recurrence of depression. *Archives of General Psychiatry, 55,* 1128–1132.

46 Babyak, M., Blumenthal, J. A., Herman, S., Khatri, P., Doraiswamy, M., Moore, K., Craighead, W. E., Baldewicz, T. T., & Krishnan, K. R. (2000). Exercise treatment for major depression: Maintenance of therapeutic benefit at 10 months. *Psychosomatic Medicine, 62,* 633–638.

47 Keepman, C., Ismailji, T., Holmes, D., Classen, C. C., Palesh, O., & Wales, T. (2005). The effects of expressive writing on pain, depression and posttraumatic stress disorder symptoms in survivors of intimate partner violence. *Journal of Health Psychology, 10,* 211–221.

48 See, e.g., Najib, A., Lorberbaum, J. P., Kose, S., Bohning, D. E., & George, M. S. (2004). Regional brain activity in women grieving a romantic relationship breakup. *American Journal of Psychiatry, 161,* 2245–2256.

49 Kübler-Ross, E. (1997). *On death and dying* (reprint edition). New York: Scribner.

50 Curtis, G. C., Magee, W. J., Eaton, W. W., Wittchen, H. U., & Kessler, R. C. (1998). Specific fears and phobias: Epidemiology and classification. *British Journal of Psychiatry, 173,* 212–217.

51 LeDoux, J. (2003). The emotional brain, fear, and the amygdala. *Cellular and Molecular Neurobiology, 23,* 727–738; see also Adolphs, R., Tranel, D., Damasio, H., & Damasio, A. R. (1995). Fear and the human amygdala. *Journal of Neuroscience, 15,* 5879–5891.

52 Amunts, K., Kedo, O., Kindler, M., Pieperhoff, P., Mohlberg, H., Shah, N. J., Habel, U., Schneider, F., & Zilles, K. (2005). Cytoarchitectonic mapping of the human amygdala, hippocampal region and entorhinal cortex: Intersubject variability and probability maps. *Anatomy and Embryology, 210,* 343–352.

53 Adolphs, R., Gosselin, F., Buchanan, T., Tranel, D., Schyns, P., & Damasio, A. (2005). A mechanism for implied fear recognition in amygdala damage. *Nature, 433,* 68–72.

54 Davis, M. (1992). The role of the amygdala in fear and anxiety. *Annual Review of Neuroscience, 15,* 353–375.

55 Leary, M. R., & Kowalski, R. M. (1995). *Social anxiety.* New York: Oxford University Press.

56 Ruscio, A. M., Brown, T. A., Chiu, W. T., Sareen, J., Stein, M. B., & Kessler, R. C. (2008). Social fears and social phobia in the USA: Results from the National Comorbidity Survey Replication. *Psychological Medicine, 38,* 15–28; see also Belzer, K. D., McKee, M. B., & Liebowitz, M. R. (2005). Social anxiety disorder: Current perspectives on diagnosis and treatment. *Primary Psychiatry, 12,* 40–53.

57 Hubert, W., Möller, M., & de Jong-Meyer, R. (1993). Film-induced amusement changes in saliva cortisol levels. *Psychoneuroendocrinology, 18,* 265–272; Kirschbaum, C., & Hellhammer, D. H. (1994). Salivary cortisol in psychoneuroendocrine research: Recent developments and applications. *Psychoneuroendocrinology, 19,* 313–333.

58 Albert, F. (1953). The physiological differentiation between fear and anger in humans. *Psychosomatic Medicine, 15,* 433–442.

[59] Valins, S. (1966). Cognitive effects of false heart-rate feedback. *Journal of Personality and Social Psychology, 4,* 400–408.

[60] Lazarus, R. S. (1991). (See note 8.)

[61] Frijda, 1993. (See note 1.)

[62] Haidt, 2003. (See note 30.)

[63] Robbins, B. D. (2003, May). *Joy, awe, gratitude and compassion: Common ground in a will-to-openness.* Paper presented at the conference Works of Love: Scientific and Religious Perspectives on Altruism, Philadelphia, PA.

[64] Goddard, C. (2002). Explicating emotions across languages and cultures: A semantic approach. In S. R. Fussell (Ed.), *The verbal communication of emotions* (pp. 19–53). Mahwah, NJ: Lawrence Erlbaum Associates.

[65] Woody, S. R., & Teachman, B. A. (2000). Intersection of disgust and fear: Normative and pathological views. *Clinical Psychology: Science and Practice, 7,* 291–311; see also Schwabe, C. W. (1988). *Unmentionable cuisine.* Charlottesville: University of Virginia Press.

[66] Bhaskarananda, S. (2002). *The essentials of Hinduism: A comprehensive overview of the world's oldest religion* (2nd ed.). Seattle, WA: Viveka Press.

[67] Elison, J., Pulos, S., & Randy, L. (2006). Shame-focused coping: An empirical study of the compass of shame. *Social Behavior and Personality, 34,* 161–168; Elster, J. (1996). Rationality and the emotions. *The Economic Journal, 106,* 1386–1397.

[68] Young, J. (2002). Morals, suicide, and psychiatry: A view from Japan. *Bioethics, 16,* 412–424.

[69] Grewen, K. M., Girdler, S. S., Amico, J., & Light, K. C. (2005). Effects of partner support on resting oxytocin, cortisol, norepinephrine, and blood pressure before and after warm partner contact. *Psychosomatic Medicine, 67,* 531–538.

[70] Solomon, G. F., & Benton, D. (2000). Immune functions, their physiological correlates, and health. In Manuck, S. B., Jennings, R., Rabin, B. S., & Baum, A. (Eds.), *Behavior, health, and aging* (pp. 109–117).

Mahwah, NJ: Lawrence Erlbaum Associates.

[71] Sugimoto, F., Yazu, K., Murakami, M., & Yoneyama, M. (2004). A method to classify emotional expressions of text and synthesize speech. *Control, Communications, and Signal Processing, 2004,* 611–614.

[72] Rainville, P., Bechara, A., Naqvi, N., & Damasio, A. R. (2006). Basic emotions are associated with distinct patterns of cardiorespiratory activity. *International Journal of Psychophysiology, 61,* 5–18; see also Damasio, A. (2003). Feelings of emotion and the self. *Annals of the New York Academy of Sciences, 1001,* 253–261.

[73] Ekman, P. (1972). Universals and cultural differences in facial expressions of emotion. In J. R. Cole (Ed.), *Nebraska symposium on motivation, Vol. 19* (pp. 207–283). Lincoln: University of Nebraska Press.

[74] For a review of this work, see Matsumoto, D. (2006). Culture and nonverbal behavior. In V. Manusov & M. L. Patterson (Eds.), *The SAGE handbook of nonverbal communication* (pp. 219–235). Thousand Oaks, CA: Sage.

[75] Scherer, K. R. (1997). Profiles of emotion-antecedent appraisal: Testing theoretical predictions across cultures. *Cognition and Emotion, 11,* 113–150.

[76] Adolphs, R., & Tranel, D. (2004). Impaired judgments of sadness but not happiness following bilateral amygdala damage. *Journal of Cognitive Neuroscience, 16,* 453–462; Kipps, C. M., Duggins, A. J., McCusker, E. A., & Calder, A. J. (2007). Disgust and happiness recognition correlate with anteroventral insula and amygdala volume respectively in preclinical Huntington's disease. *Journal of Cognitive Neuroscience, 19,* 1206–1217; Stein, M. B., Goldin, P. R., Sareen, J., Zorrilla, L. T., & Brown, G. G. (2002). Increased amygdala activation to angry and contemptuous faces in generalized social phobia. *Archives of General Psychiatry, 59,* 1027–1034.

[77] Shweder, R. A. (1993). The cultural psychology of the emotions. In M. Lewis & J. M. Haviland (Eds.), *Handbook of emotions* (pp. 417–431). New York: Guilford.

[78] Guerrero, L. K., & Andersen, P. A. (1998). Jealousy experience and expression in romantic relationships. In P. A. Andersen & L. K. Guerrero (Eds.), *Handbook of communication and emotion: Research, theory, applications, and contexts* (pp. 155–188). San Diego, CA: Academic Press.

[79] Plutchik, R. (1993). Emotions and their vicissitudes: Emotions and psychopathology. In M. Lewis & J. M. Haviland (Eds.), *Handbook of emotions* (pp. 53–66). New York: Guilford.

[80] Hakim-Larson, J., Parker, A., Lee, C., Goodwin, J., & Voelker, S. (2006). Measuring parental meta-emotion: Psychometric properties of the emotion-related parenting styles self-test. *Early Education and Development, 17,* 229–251.

[81] Gottman, J. M. (1997). *Meta-emotion: How families communicate emotionally.* Mahwah, NJ: Lawrence Erlbaum Associates.

[82] Gottman, J. M., Katz, L. F., & Hooven, C. (1996). Parental meta-emotion philosophy and the emotional life of families: Theoretical models and preliminary data. *Journal of Family Psychology, 10,* 243–268.

[83] Gallois, C. (1993). The language and communication of emotion: Universal, interpersonal, or intergroup? *American Behavioral Scientist, 36,* 309–338.

[84] Triandis, H. C. (1994). *Culture and social behavior.* New York: McGraw-Hill.

[85] Tsai, J. L., & Levenson, R. W. (1997). Cultural influences of emotional responding: Chinese American and European American dating couples during interpersonal conflict. *Journal of Cross-Cultural Psychology, 28,* 600–625.

[86] Soto, J. A., Levenson, R. W., & Ebling, R. (2005). Cultures of moderation and expression: Emotional experience, behavior, and physiology in Chinese Americans and Mexican Americans. *Emotion, 5,* 154–165.

[87] Montesquieu, C. de S. (1989). *The spirit of the laws.* Cambridge, England: Cambridge University Press. (Original work published 1748.)

[88] Pennebaker, J. W., Rimé, B., & Blankenship, V. E. (1996). Stereotypes of emotional expressiveness of northerners and

southerners: A cross-cultural test of Montesquieu's hypothesis. *Journal of Personality and Social Psychology, 70,* 372–380.

[89] Andersen, J. E., Andersen, P. A., & Lustig, M. W. (1987). Opposite-sex touch avoidance: A national replication and extension. *Journal of Nonverbal Behavior, 2,* 89–109.

[90] Hoge, C. W., Castro, C. A., Messer, S. C., McGurk, D., Cotting, D. I., & Koffman, R. L. (2004). Combat duty in Iraq and Afghanistan, mental health problems, and barriers to care. *The New England Journal of Medicine, 351,* 13–22.

[91] Ekman, P., & Friesen, W. V. (1975). *Unmasking the face: A guide to recognizing emotions from facial clues.* Englewood Cliffs, NJ: Prentice-Hall.

[92] Stelmaszewska, H., Fields, B., & Blandford, A. (2005, September). *Emotion and technology: An empirical study.* Paper presented at the Workshop on the Role of Emotion in Human-Computer Interaction, Edinburgh, Scotland.

[93] Stelmaszewska et al., 2005.

[94] Hatfield, E., Cacioppo, J. T., & Rapson, R. L. (1994). *Emotional contagion.* New York: Cambridge University Press.

[95] Sy, T., Côté, S., & Saavedra, R. (2005). The contagious leader: Impact of the leader's mood on the mood of group members, group affective tone, and group processes. *Journal of Applied Psychology, 90,* 295–305.

[96] Barsade, S. G. (2000, October). *The ripple effect: Emotional contagion in groups.* Yale School of Management Working Paper No. OB-01. Available from Social Science Research Network: http://ssrn.com/abstract=250894

[97] Fisher, A. H., Rodriguez Mosquera, P. M., van Vianen, A. E. M., & Manstead, A. E. R. (2004). Gender and culture differences in emotion. *Emotion, 4,* 87–94.

[98] See, e.g., Guerrero, L. K., Jones, S. M., & Boburka, R. R. (2006). Sex differences in emotional communication. In K. Dindia & D. J. Canary (Eds.), *Sex differences and similarities in communication* (2nd ed., pp. 241–261). Mahwah, NJ: Lawrence Erlbaum Associates.

[99] Burgoon, J. K., & Bacue, A. E. (2003). Nonverbal communication skills. In J. O. Greene & B. R. Burleson (Eds.), *Handbook of communication and social interaction skills* (pp. 179–219). Mahwah, NJ: Lawrence Erlbaum Associates; Coats, E. J., & Feldman, R. S. (1996). Gender differences in nonverbal correlates of social status. *Personality and Social Psychology Bulletin, 22,* 1014–1022.

[100] Floyd, K. (2006). *Communicating affection: Interpersonal behavior and social context.* Cambridge, England: Cambridge University Press; Owen, W. F. (1987). The verbal expression of love by women and men as a critical communication event in personal relationships. *Women's Studies in Communication, 10,* 15–24.

[101] Blier, M. J., & Blier-Wilson, L. A. (1989). Gender differences in sex-rated emotional expressiveness. *Sex Roles, 21,* 287–295; Nolen-Hoeksema, S. (1987). Sex differences in unipolar depression: Evidence and theory. *Psychological Bulletin, 101,* 259–282.

[102] Coats & Feldman, 1996. (See note 99.)

[103] Burrowes, B. D., & Halberstadt, A. G. (1987). Self- and family-expressiveness styles in the experience and expression of anger. *Journal of Nonverbal Behavior, 11,* 254–268.

[104] Buss, D. M., Larsen, R. J., & Westen, D. (1996). Sex differences in jealousy: Not gone, not forgotten, and not easily explained by alternative hypotheses. *Psychological Science, 7,* 373–375; Buss, D. M., Larsen, R. J., Westen, D., & Semmelroth, J. (1992). Sex differences in jealousy: Evolution, physiology, and psychology. *Psychological Science, 3,* 251–255; Mathes, E. W. (2003). Are sex differences in sexual vs. emotional jealousy explained better by differences in sexual strategies or uncertainty of paternity? *Psychological Reports, 93,* 895–906; Mathes, E. W. (2005). Men's desire for children carrying their genes and sexual jealousy: A test of paternity uncertainty as an explanation of male sexual jealousy. *Psychological Reports, 96,* 791–798.

[105] Fernandez, A. M., Vera-Villarroel, P., Sierra, J. C., & Zubeidat, I. (2007). Distress in response to emotional and sexual infidelity: Evidence of evolved gender differences in Spanish students. *Journal of Psychology, 141,* 17–24; see also Buss, D. M., Shackelford, T. K., Kirkpatrick, L. E., Choe, J. C., Hang, K. L., Hawegawa, M., Hawegawa, T., & Bennett, K. (1999). Jealousy and the nature of beliefs about infidelity: Tests of competing hypotheses about sex differences in the United States, Korea, and Japan. *Personal Relationships, 6,* 125–150.

[106] Takahashi, H., Matsuura, M., Yahata, N., Koeda, M., Suhara, T., & Okubo, Y. (2006). Men and women show distinct brain activations during imagery of sexual and emotional infidelity. *Neuroimage, 32,* 1299–1307.

[107] Buss, D. M. (1988). From vigilance to violence: Tactics of mate retention in American undergraduates. *Ethology and Sociobiology, 9,* 291–317.

[108] White, G. L., & Mullen, P. E. (1989). *Jealousy: Theory, research, and clinical strategies.* New York: Guilford.

[109] DeSteno, D., Bartlett, M. Y., Braverman, J., & Salovey, P. (2002). Sex differences in jealousy: Evolutionary mechanism or artifact of measurement. *Journal of Personality and Social Psychology, 83,* 513–518; Harris, C. R. (2003). A review of sex differences in sexual jealousy, including self-report data, psychophysiological responses, interpersonal violence, and morbid jealousy. *Personality and Social Psychology Review, 7,* 102–128.

[110] Green, M. C., & Sabini, J. (2006). Gender, socioeconomic status, age, and jealousy: Emotional responses to infidelity in a national sample. *Emotion, 6,* 330–334.

[111] Berman, M. I., & Frazier, P. A. (2005). Relationship power and betrayal experience as predictors of reactions to infidelity. *Personality and Social Psychology Bulletin, 31,* 1617–1627; Harris, C. R. (2002). Sexual and romantic jealousy in heterosexual and homosexual adults. *Psychological Science, 13,* 7–12.

[112] Sagarin, B. J. (2005). Reconsidering evolved sex differences

in jealousy: Comment on Harris (2003). *Personality and Social Psychology Review, 9,* 62–75.

[113] Kring, A. M., & Gordon, A. H. (1998). Sex differences in emotion: Expression, experience, and physiology. *Journal of Personality and Social Psychology, 74,* 686–703.

[114] Floyd, K., & Morman, M. T. (2000). Reacting to the verbal expression of affection in same-sex interaction. *Southern Communication Journal, 65,* 287–299.

[115] Oliver, S. J., & Toner, B. B. (1990). The influence of gender role typing on the expression of depressive symptoms. *Sex Roles, 22,* 775–790.

[116] Pervin, L. A. (1993). Affect and personality. In M. Lewis & J. M. Haviland (Eds.), *Handbook of emotions* (2nd ed., pp. 301–311). New York: Guilford.

[117] Lopes, P. N., Salovey, P., Cote, S., & Beers, M. (2005). Emotion regulation abilities and the quality of social interaction. *Emotion, 5,* 113–118.

[118] Jensen-Campbell, L. A., & Graziano, W. G. (2001). Agreeableness as a moderator of interpersonal conflict. *Journal of Personality, 69,* 323–361.

[119] Larsen, R. J., & Ketelaar, T. (1991). Personality and susceptibility to positive and negative emotional states. *Journal of Personality and Social Psychology, 61,* 132–140.

[120] Myers, D. (1992). *The pursuit of happiness.* New York: Avon Books.

[121] Larsen & Ketelaar, 1991.

[122] Matthews, G., & Deary, I. J. (1998). *Personality traits.* Cambridge, England: Cambridge University Press.

[123] Lopes et al., 2005.

[124] Brackett, M. A., Mayer, J. D., & Warner, R. M. (2004). Emotional intelligence and its relation to everyday behavior. *Personality and Individual Differences, 36,* 1387–1402. (Quote is from p. 1389.)

[125] Mayer, J. D., Roberts, R. D., & Barsade, S. G. (2008). Human abilities: Emotional intelligence. *Annual Review of Psychology, 59,* 507–536.

[126] Mayer, J. D., Caruso, D. R., & Salovey, P. (1999). Emotional intelligence meets traditional standards for an intelligence. *Intelligence, 27,* 267–298; Rice, C. L. (1999). *A quantitative study of emotional intelligence and its impact on team performance.* Unpublished masters thesis, Pepperdine University, Malibu CA.

[127] Bracket et al., 2004.

[128] Goleman, D. (1998). *Working with emotional intelligence.* New York: Bantam; Seligman, M. E. P. (1990). *Learned optimism.* New York: Knopf.

[129] Spencer, L. M. J., McClelland, D. C., & Kelner, S. (1997). *Competency assessment methods: History and state of the art.* Boston: Hay/McBer.

[130] Boyatzis, R. (1982). *The competent manager: A model for effective performance.* New York: John Wiley and Sons.

[131] McClelland, D. C. (1999). Identifying competencies with behavioral-event interviews. *Psychological Science, 9,* 331–339.

[132] Pesuric, A., & Byham, W. (1996, July). The new look in behavior modeling. *Training and Development,* 25–33.

[133] Parker, J. D. A., Taylor, G. J., & Bagby, R. M. (2001). The relationship between emotional intelligence and alexithymia. *Personality and Individual Differences, 30,* 107–115.

[134] Taylor, G. J., Bagby, R. M., & Parker, J. D. A. (1997). *Disorders of affect regulation: Alexithymia in medical and psychiatric illness.* Cambridge, England: Cambridge University Press; see also Fukunishi, I., Berger, D., Wogan, J., & Kuboki, T. (1999). Alexithymic traits as predictors of difficulties with adjustment in an outpatient cohort of expatriates in Tokyo. *Psychological Reports, 85,* 67–77; Salminen, J. K., Saarijärvi, S., Aärelä, E., Toikka, T., & Kauhanen, J. (1999). Prevalence of alexithymia and its association with sociodemographic variables in the general population of Finland. *Journal of Psychosomatic Research, 46,* 75–82.

[135] Luminet, O., Rimé, B., Bagby, R. M., & Taylor, G. J. (2004). A multimodel investigation of emotional responding in alexithymia. *Cognition and Emotion, 18,* 741–766.

[136] Vanheule, S., Desmet, M., Meganck, R., & Bogaerts, S. (2007). Alexithymia and interpersonal problems. *Journal of Clinical Psychology, 63,* 109–117.

[137] Yelsma, P., & Marrow, S. (2003). An examination of couples' difficulties with emotional expressiveness and their marital satisfaction. *Journal of Family Communication, 3,* 41–62.

[138] Mayne, T. J. (1999). Negative affect and health: The importance of being earnest. *Cognition and Emotion, 13,* 601–635.

[139] Siegman, A. W., & Snow, S. C. (1997). The outward expression of anger, the inward experience of anger and CVR: The role of vocal expression. *Behavioral Medicine, 1,* 29–45.

[140] Grewal, D., & Salovey, P. (2005). Feeling smart: The science of emotional intelligence. *American Scientist, 93,* 330–339.

[141] Barrett, L. F., Gross, J., Christensen T., & Benvenuto, M. (2001). Knowing what you're feeling and knowing what to do about it: Mapping the relation between emotion differentiation and emotion regulation. *Cognition and Emotion, 15,* 713–724.

[142] Jackson, D. C., Malmstadt, J. R., Larson, C. L., & Davidson, R. J. (2000). Suppression and enhancement of emotional responses to unpleasant pictures. *Psychophysiology, 37,* 515–522.

[143] John, O. P., & Gross, J. J. (2004). Healthy and unhealthy emotion regulation: Personality processes, individual differences, and lifespan development. *Journal of Personality, 72,* 1301–1334.

[144] Bippus, A. M., & Young, S. L. (2005). Owning your emotions: Reactions to expressions of self-versus other-attributed positive and negative emotions. *Journal of Applied Communication Research, 33,* 26–45.

} Credits {

Photo Credits:

Chapter 1
Page 2: © Simon Jarratt/Corbis; **4:** Goodshoot/PictureQuest; **5:** © John Birdsall/The Image Works; **8:** © Erik Freeland/Corbis SABA; **9:** (left to right) © Digital Vision/Getty Images, © David Young-Wolff/ PhotoEdit, Inc., The McGraw-Hill Companies, Inc./Christopher Kerrigan, Photographer, (bottom) Liquidlibrary/Dynamic Graphics/ Jupiter Images; **11:** Brand X Pictures/ PunchStock; **13:** Flying Colours Ltd/ Getty Images; **14:** © Image 100/ PunchStock; **15:** (left to right) Brand X Pictures, © David Young-Wolff/ PhotoEdit, Inc.; **16:** © Warner Bros. Television/Courtesy Everett Collection; **17:** Photodisc; **19:** © Paramount/Courtesy Everett Collection; **21:** Royalty-Free/Corbis; **22:** © Image Source/PunchStock; **25:** © Jeff Greenberg/The Image Works; **26:** (left to right) © Lee Snider/The Image Works, Scott Garfield/© ABC/ Courtesy Everett Collection, © Richard Lord/The Image Works; **28:** © David Young-Wolff/PhotoEdit, Inc.; **30:** Imagesource; **31:** (top) © Bill Aron/PhotoEdit, Inc., (bottom) © Monika Graff/The Image Works

Chapter 2
38: © Chloe Johnson/Alamy; **40:** © Fujifotos/The Image Works; **41:** © Alexander Farnsworth/The Image Works; **42:** AP Images; **43:** AFP/ Getty Images; **44:** Brand X Pictures; **45:** © Corbis; **46:** AP Photo/Joanne Carole; **48:** (left) © Topham/The Image Works, (right) © Lisa Anne Corbis/Corbis; **51:** © DPA/The Image Works; **52:** © Philadelphia Museum of Art/Corbis; **54:** (top) © Jim Craigmyle/Corbis, (bottom) © Kelly-Mooney Photography/ Corbis; **57:** © BananaStock/Picture-Quest; **59:** © Private Collection/The Stapleton Collection/The Bridgeman Art Library; **60:** The National Human Genome Research Institute; **62:** © Bill Aron/PhotoEdit, Inc.; **64:** © Digital Vision/PunchStock; **65:** © Sonda Dawes/The Image Works; **67:** © David Young-Wolff/PhotoEdit, Inc.; **68:** AP Photo/Mark J. Terrill; **70:** Courtesy of the Family Violence Prevention Fund; **72:** AP Photo/ Marcio Jose Sanchez

Chapter 3
80: © Brand X Pictures/Jupiter-images; **82:** Luc Choquer/Getty Images; **84:** (middle) © Getty Images; (clockwise from top) PhotoLink/ Getty Images, © Photodisc/Punch-Stock, ©BananaStock/PunchStock, © Jupiter Images, The McGraw-Hill Companies, Inc./John Flournoy, photographer, C Squared Studios/ Getty Images; **86:** © Robin Nelson/ PhotoEdit, Inc.; **87:** © Kayoco/zefa/ Corbis; **89:** © Digital Vision/Punch-Stock; **90:** Rob Melnychuk/Getty Images; **91:** (top) Reuters/L'Equipe Agence, (bottom) altrendo images/ Getty Images; **92:** Camera Press, Lt/Retna, Ltd.; **96:** © Rubberball Productions/Getty Images; **97:**

© Bloomimage/Corbis; **99:** © moodoard/Corbis; **101:** Universal/ Courtesy Everett Collection; **104:** © Michael Newman/PhotoEdit, Inc.; **105:** © LWA-Dann Tardif/Corbis; **107:** Siri Stafford/Getty Images; **110:** Ryan McVay/Getty Images; **111:** Commercial Eye/Getty Images; **113:** © Randy Faris/Corbis; **114:** Loungepark/Getty Images

Chapter 4
120: © Millennium Images/Glasshouse; **122:** Monica Lau/Getty Images; **124:** AFP/Getty Images; **125:** Michael Germana/Everett Collection; **127:** Jon Bradley/Getty Images; **129:** (top) © Herb Watson/Corbis, (bottom) © Kelly Redinger/Design Pics/Corbis; **132:** Digital Vision/ PunchStock; **133:** Kent Mathews/ Getty Images; **134:** BananaStock/ JupiterImages; **136:** © LWA/Dann Tardif/Blend Images/Corbis; **138:** (left) AP Photo/NASA, (right) Courtesy of NASA; **142:** © DLILLC/Corbis; **144:** Thomas Northcut/Getty Images; **146:** C Squared Studios/Getty Images; **148:** © Brand X Pictures/ PunchStock; **149:** © Joel Sartore/ Getty Images; **152:** (top) © Aaron Farley/Getty Images, (bottom) © Image Source Black; **153:** Courtesy Everett Collection; **157:** Izabela Habur/iStockphoto

Chapter 5
162: © Buzzshotz/Alamy; **164:** © Image Source/PunchStock; **165:** Steven Peterson; **167:** (top) © Transtock/Corbis, (bottom) © Mitsuaki Iwago/Getty Images; **168:** © David Frazier/The Image Works; **169:** (top) © Photodisc/PunchStock; (bottom) ©BananaStock/PunchStock; **170:** (left to right) American Images Inc./ Getty Images, © Fabio Cardoso/ Corbis, AP Photo/Steven Senne; **172:** © Gerville Hall/iStockphoto; **174:** James Woodson/Getty Images; **175:** (left to right) © Reuters/Corbis, © Reuters/Corbis, AP Photo/Chris Pizzello; **177:** AP Photo/Rusty Kennedy; **178:** Getty Images; **180:** AP Photo/ Ted S. Warren; **181:** Stockbyte/Getty Images; **182:** © Brooke Fasani/ Corbis; **184:** © Shoot/zefa/Corbis; **186:** © Robert Glenn/Getty Images; **187:** © Joe Raedle/Getty Images; **189:** © Rick Doyle/Corbis; **190:** © Jim West/The Image Works; **194:** © Romilly Lockyer/Getty Images; **195:** © Westend61/Getty Images; **199:** © Chris Ware/The Image Works; **200:** (left and right) Chris Haston/© NBC/Courtesy Everett Collection, (center) Mitchell Haaseth/© NBC/Courtesy Everett Collection

Chapter 6
206: © PhotoAlto/Glasshouse; **208:** (top) Digital Vision/Alamy, (bottom) Blend Images Photography/Veer; **209:** Supplied by Capital Pictures/ drr.net; **210:** CSU/Everett Collection; **214:** Getty Images; **215:** © Li-Hua Lan/Syracuse Newspapers/The Image Works; **216:** Nacivet/Getty Images; **219:** Courtesy Martin Gruendl; **221:** Courtesy of the author; **222:** Masterfile Royalty Free; **223:** (left to right)

© Topham/The Image Works; AP Photo/Tony Tribble, © Bloomimage/ Corbis; **224:** © Julian Winslow/ Corbis; **225:** Michel Touraine/Jupiter-images; **227:** AP Images; **228:** © Castle Rock Entertainment/Courtesy Everett Collection; **230:** Corbis Photography/Veer; **231:** Peter Samuels/Jupiterimages; **232:** (both) © The McGraw-Hill Companies/ Suzie Ross, Photographer; **234:** ML Harris/Getty Images; **236:** © Brand X Pictures/PunchStock; **237:** Pixland/ Jupiterimages; **239:** (left to right) Jupiterimages, Tatjana Alvegard/Ju-piterimages, AP Photo/Seth Perlman; **241:** © Brand X Pictures/PunchStock; **243:** Comstock Images/Jupiterimag-es; **245:** About-Face: www.about-face. org; **248:** Fancy Photography/Veer; **249:** Robert Harding Library

Chapter 7
256: © Digital Vision/Veer; **258:** Collage Photography/Veer; **259:** Fancy Photography/Veer; **260:** Alloy Photography/Veer; **261:** ©Image 100/Corbis; **262:** Andersen Ross/ Digital Vision/Getty Images; **263:** Masterfile Royalty Free; **265:** © Royalty-Free/Corbis; **266:** HBO/ The Kobal Collection; **268:** Masterfile Royalty Free; **269:** Ingram Publishing/Alamy; **270:** Masterfile Royalty Free; **271:** Fosten/Veer; **272:** (left) Garry Black/Masterfile, (right) Masterfile; **275:** © Bettmann/ Corbis; **276:** Jerzyworks/Masterfile; **278:** Nick Koudis/Getty Images; **279:** Frazer Harrison/Getty Images; **280:** Cliff Lipson/© CBS/Courtesy Everett Collection; **281:** The McGraw-Hill Companies Inc./Ken Cavanagh, Photographer; **283:** DMH Images/ Getty Images

Chapter 8
290: © Andrew Rubtsov/Alamy; **292:** Masterfile Royalty Free; **293:** (left) Department of Defense, photo by Staff Sgt. James L. Harper Jr., U.S. Air Force, (right) AP Photo/ Ted S. Warren; **295:** The McGraw-Hill Companies Inc./Ken Cavanagh Photographer; **296:** (top) © The Estate of Keith Haring, (bottom) © Randy Faris/Corbis; **298:** Masterfile Royalty Free; **300:** © Warner Bros./Courtesy Everett Collection; **302:** (top) © Cultura/ Corbis, (bottom) © Comstock/ PunchStock; **304:** (top) Masterfile Royalty Free, (bottom) Heath Robbins/Getty Images; **306:** © THE CW/Courtesy Everett Collection; **307:** (left) © Ingram Publishing/ Fotosearch; (right) © Digital Vision; **309:** Tim Mantoani/Masterfile; **310:** Masterfile Royalty Free; **312:** WireImageStock/Masterfile; **313:** Comstock Images/Alamy; **315:** (left to right) © Mark Karrass/Corbis, © Artiga Photo/Corbis, © Bob Daemmrich/The Image Works; **316:** Corbis; **317:** © Chet Gordon/The Image Works; **320:** Digital Vision/ Alamy; **321:** Comstock Images/ Alamy; **322:** © BananaStock Ltd.

Chapter 9
330: © Corbis Premium RF/Alamy; **333:** Tony Cordoza/Jupiterimages;

334: Min Roman/Masterfile; **335:** Jupiterimages; **336:** Jon Feingersh Photography, Inc./drr.net; **337:** © JJM Stock Photography/Food/Alamy; **338:** (left to right) © Thomas Cockrem/ Alamy, Steve Raymer/Jupiterimages, Maria Teijeiro/age fotostock; **340:** (top) © Hulton-Deutsch Collection/ Corbis, (bottom) © Reza/Webistan/ Corbis; **341:** (top) © Raquel Ramirez/ PhotoEdit, Inc., (bottom) Hisham F. Ibrahim/Getty Images; **342:** © Ju-piter Images; **344:** Rob Melnychuk/ Getty Images; **346:** © image100/ Alamy; **347:** Erich Geduldig/Jupi-terimages; **348:** Jeff Kauck/Jupiter-images; **349:** (left) Photomondo/ Getty Images; (right) ©Image Source/PunchStock; **350:** (left) Photomondo/Getty Images, (right) ©Image Source/PunchStock; **351:** BananaStock/Jupiter Images; **352:** ©Royalty-Free/Corbis; **353:** © Stock-byte/Alamy; **355:** © Kevin Dodge/ Corbis; **357:** Everett Collection; **359:** FOX/Photofest; **360:** Camelot Pictures/The Kobal Collection/Baily, K C; **361:** AP Photo/Alex Brandon; **363:** Courtesy of Professor Art Aron; **364:** © David P. Hall /Masterfile; **366:** © Leland Bobbe/Getty Images

Chapter 10
372: © Mike Hill/Alamy; **375:** © Royalty-Free/Corbis; **376:** (top) Stockbyte, (bottom) © Think-stock Images/Jupiterimages; **377:** Comstock Images/Alamy; **379:** (top) PhotoAlto Photography/Veer, (bottom) Masterfile Royalty Free; **380:** The McGraw-Hill Companies, Inc./Al Telser, photographer; **381:** Masterfile; **383:** © Russell Monk/ Radius Images; **384:** Jupiterimages; **385:** (left) Masterfile Royalty Free, (right) Susan Findlay/Masterfile; **386:** (top) © Dynamic Graphics/ PictureQuest, (bottom) © Banana-Stock/PunchStock; **387:** Image Source Photography/Veer; **389:** Mark Thomas/Jupiterimages; **390:** Comstock Images/Alamy; **391:** (top) Tim Boyle/Getty Images, (bottom) Barbara Nitke/© Bravo/Courtesy Everett Collection; **392:** BananaStock/ Jupiterimages; **393:** © Streetstock Images/CORBIS; **394:** AP Photo/ Dave Martin; **396:** Gary S Chapman/ Getty Images; **399:** (top) © isifa Image Service s.r.o./Alamy, (bottom) © Getty Images/Photodisc; **400:** LWA Dann Tardif/Corbis

Chapter 11
406: © Marco Di Lauro/Getty Images; **408:** © Digital Vision/Alamy; **409:** (top) © John Giustina/Getty Images, (bottom) Masterfile Royalty Free; **410:** CBS-TV/The Kobal Collection; **411:** (top) Susan Findlay/ Masterfile, (bottom) © Stockbyte/ Getty Images; **412:** © Stockbyte/ Getty Images; **413:** (top) Masterfile, (bottom) Thomas Dannenberg/ Masterfile; **414:** Masterfile Royalty Free; **416:** Royalty-Free/Corbis; **417:** Masterfile; **419:** © Simon Jarratt/ Corbis; **420:** © Kelvin Murray/Getty Images; **421:** © Ian Sanderson/Getty Images; **423:** (top) Peter Ciresa Cires/Index Stock; **425:** ABC/Photo-fest; **426:** Jerzyworks/Masterfile;

427: (top) © Dreamworks/Courtesy Everett Collection, (bottom) Photo-Alto Photography/Veer

Chapter 12

432: Blend Images/Ariel Skelley/drr.net; **434:** Fancy Photography/Veer; **435:** Somos Photography/Veer; **436:** (left to right) Bryan F. Peterson/CORBIS, Masterfile, James Darell/Getty Images, (bottom) Fancy Photography/Veer; **437:** Eyecandy Images/drr.net; **438:** (top) Helen King/CORBIS, (bottom) © Paramount. Courtesy Everett Collection; **440:** Comedy Central/Mad Cow Productions/The Kobal Collection; **441:** © Jeff Greenberg/The Image Works; **444:** © Royalty-Free/Corbis; **445:** (left to right) © Rob Wilkinson/Alamy, Alistair Berg/Getty Images, Somos Photography/Veer; **447:** (top) Guy Crittenden/Getty Images, (bottom) © David J. Green - people/Alamy; **448:** © Image Source Pink/Alamy; **451:** © Brand X Pictures; **452:** © Andreas Kuehn/Getty Images; **454:** (top) Digital Vision Photography/Veer, (bottom) Fancy Photography/Veer; **456:** Digital Vision/Alamy; **458:** © CMCD/Getty Images; **459:** © Brand X Pictures; **460:** © LWA-Stephen Welstead/Corbis; **461:** © Caspar Benson/Getty Images

Text Credits

Chapter 1

Page 23: From "Blurring Boundaries? Linking technology use, spillover, individual distress, and family satisfaction" by N. Chesley from JOURNAL OF MARRIAGE AND THE FAMILY (2005), Vol. 67, pp. 1237–1248. Reprinted by permission of Blackwell Publishing; **28:** "Effects of social networks on 10-yeasr survival in very old Australians: The Australian Longitudinal Study of Aging" by L.C. Giles, G.F. Glonek, M.A. Luszcz and G.R. Andrews from JOURNAL OF EPIDEMIOLOGY AND COMMUNITY HEALTH (2005), Vol. 59, pp. 574–579. Reprinted by permission of BMJ Publishing Group Ltd.; **32:** Items adapted from "A measure of emotional empathy" by A. Mehrabian and N. Epstein in JOURNAL OF PERSONALITY (1972), Vol. 40, pp. 525–543. Reprinted by permission of Blackwell Publishing.

Chapter 2

Page 42: "Muslims face discrimination and intolerance" by M. Kerr from THE STONY BROOK STATESMAN (February 19, 2003); **56:** "The development and validation of the intercultural sensitivity scale" by G.M. Chen and W.J. Starosta from HUMAN COMMUNICATION (2000), Vol. 3, pp. 1–14. Reprinted by permission of the author; **66:** Sources: Bem, S. L. (1974). The measurement of psychological androgyny. Journal of Consulting and Clinical Psychology, 42, 155–162; see also Ballard-Reisch, D., & Elton, M. (1992). Gender orientation and the Bem Sex Role Inventory: A psychological construct revisited. Sex Roles, 27, 291–306; **66:** Reproduced by special permission of the Publisher, MIND GARDEN, Inc., 855 Oak Grove Ave., Suite 215, Menlo Park,CA 94025 USA www.mindgarden.com from the BEM Sex Role Inventory 1978 Consulting Psychologists Press, 1978 Sandra Bem. Further reproduction is prohibited without the Publisher's written consent; **69:** "Are women really more talkative than men?" by M.R. Mehl, S. Vazire, N. Ramirez-Esparza and R.B. Slatcher from SCIENCE, 2007, Vol. 317, p. 82. Used by permission.

Chapter 3

Page 88: "Sources of human psychological differences: The Minnesota Study of Twins Reared Apart" by T.J. Bouchard, D.T. Lykken, M. McGue, N.L.Segal and A. Tellegen from SCIENCE, (October 12, 1990), pp. 223–228. Used by permission; **95:** Rosenberg, Morris. 1989. *Society and the Adolescent Self-Image.* Revised edition. Middletown, CT: Wesleyan University Press; **96:** "Cross-cultural correlates of life satisfaction and self-esteem" by E. Diener and M. Diener from JOURNAL OF PERSONALITY AND SOCIAL PSYCHOLOGY (1995), Vol. 68, pp. 653–663. Used by permission of American Psychological Association; **103:** "HIV-infected persons' attributions for the disclosure and nondisclosure of the seropositive diagnosis to significant others" by V.J. Derlega and B.A. Winstead from ATTRIBUTION, COMMUNICATION BEHAVIOR AND CLOSE RELATIONSHIPS ed. By V. Manusov and J.H. Harvey, pp. 266–284. Reprinted by permission of Cambridge University Press.

Chapter 4

Page 139: "Illusion and culture" by J.B. Deregowski from ILLUSION IN NATURE AND ART ed. By R.L. Gregory & E.H. Gombrich, pp. 165; **149:** "Empathic inaccuracy in husband to wife aggression: The overattribution bias" by W.E. Schweinle, W. Ickes and I.H. Bernstein from PERSONAL RELATIONSHIPS (2002), Vol. 9, pp. 141–158. Reprinted by permission of Blackwell Publishing; **157:** "A room with a cue: Personality judgements based on offices and bedrooms" by S.D. Gosling, S.J. Ko, T. Mannarelli and M. E. Morris from JOURNAL OF PERSONALITY AND SOCIAL PSYCHOLOGY (2002), Vol. 82, pp. 379–398. Used by permission of American Psychological Association.

Chapter 5

Page 174: From THE LANGUAGE INSTINCT by Steven Pinker. Copyright © 1994 by Steven Pinker. Reprinted by permission of HarperCollins Publishers; **183:** "The connubial crucible: Newlywed years as predictors of marital delight, distress and divorce" by T.H. Huston, J.P. Caughlin, R.M. Houts, S.E. Smith and L.J. George from JOURNAL OF PERSONALITY AND SOCIAL PSYCHOLOGY (2001), Vol. 80, pp. 237–252. Used by permission of American Psychological Association.

Chapter 6

Page 217: Scherer, K. R., Banse, R., & Wallbott, H. G. (2001). Emotion inferences from vocal expression correlate across languages and cultures. Journal of Cross-Cultural Psychology, 32, 76–92. Used by permission of Sage Publications; **251:** Riggio, R.E. (1986). Assessment of basic social skills. Journal of Personality and Social Psychology, 51, 649–660.

Chapter 7

Page 260: Communication in everyday life: A descriptive study using mobile electronic data collection by K. Dinidia and B.L. Kennedy. Paper presented at the annual conference of the National Communication Association, Chicago, IL Reprinted by permission of Kathryn Dindia, Ph.D.; **261:** Windsor, J.L., Curtis, D.B., & Stephens, R.D. (1997). National preferences in business and communication education: A survey update. Journal fo the Association for Communication Administration, 3, 170–179. Material is adapted from Table 4, p. 176; **270:** Sources: Imhof, M. (2004). Who are we as we listen? Individual listening profiles in varying contexts. International Journal of Listening, 18, 36–45; Watson, K. W., Barker, L. L., & Weaver, J. B. (1995). The listening styles profile (LSP-16): Development and validation of an instrument to assess four listening styles. International Journal of Listening, 9, 1–13; **276:** Sargent, S. L. & Weaver, J. B. (2003). Listening styles: Sex differences in perceptions of self and others. International Journal of Listening, 17, 5–18. Used by permission of International Listening Association; **284:** Adapted from St. Mary's College Counseling Center Grief and Loss Guidelines

Chapter 8

Page 295: Cohen, S., Doyle, W.J., Turner, R., Alper C.M., & Skoner, D.P. (2003). Sociability and susceptibility to the common cold. Psychological Science, 14, 389–395. Reprinted by permission of Wiley-Blackwell; **301:** Neimeyer, R.A., & Mitchell, K.A. (1988) Similiarity and attraction: A longitudinal study. Journal of Social and Personal Relationships, 5, 131–148. Reprinted by permission of Sage Publications Ltd.; **313:** Argyle, M., & Henderson, M. (1984). The rules of friendship. Journal of Social and Personal Relationships, I, 211–237. Reprinted by permission of Sage Publications Ltd.; **318:** Items adapted from McCroskey, J.C. & McCain, T.A. (1974). The measurement of interpersonal attraction. Speech Monographs, 41, 261–266.

Chapter 9

Page 334: Sources: Cupach, W. R., & Spitzberg, B. H. (2004). *The dark side of relationship pursuit: From attraction to obsession and stalking.* Mahwah, NJ: Lawrence Erlbaum Associates; Spitzberg, B. H., & Hoobler, G. (2002). Cyberstalking and the technologies of interpersonal terrorism. *New Media & Society, 4,* 71–92; **341:** Source: Human Rights Campaign; **363:** Source: Aron, A., Norman, C. C., Aron, E. N., McKenna, C., & Heyman, R. E. (2000). Couples' shared participation in novel and arousing activities and experienced relationship quality. *Journal of Personality and Social Psychology, 78,* 273–284. Copyright © 2000, APA. Reprinted by permission.

Chapter 10

Page 382: Source: MacDonald, G., Zanna, M. P., & Holmes, J. G. (2000). An experimental test of the role of alcohol in relationship conflict. *Journal of Experimental Social Psychology, 36,* 182–193; Mokdad, A. H., Marks, J. S., Stroup, D. F., & Gerberding, J. L. (2004). Actual causes of death in the United States, 2000. *Journal of the American Medical Association, 291,* 1238–1245; **398:** Source: Gottman, J. M. (1994). *What predicts divorce? The relationship between marital processes and marital outcomes.* Hillsdale, NJ: Lawrence Erlbaum Associates. Reprinted by permission; **401:** Source: Some items adapted from Rahim, M. A., & Mager, N. R. (1995). Confirmatory factor analysis of the styles of handling interpersonal conflict: First-order factor model and its invariance across groups. *Journal of Applied Psychology, 80,* 122–132. Copyright © 1995, APA. Reprinted by permission.

Chapter 11

Page 410: Sources: Hancock, J., Thom-Santelli, J., & Ritchie, T. (2004,April). Deception and Design: The Impact of Communication on Lying Behavior. Paper presented to Computer-Human Interaction (CHI) Scientific Meeting, Vienna, Austria; Kalish, N. (2004, January). How Honest Are You? *Reader's Digest,* pp. 114–119; Kanner, B. (2005). *When it Comes to Guys, What's Normal?* New York: St. Martin's Press; **421:** Source: Park, H. S., Levine, T. R, McCornack, S. A., Morrison, K., & Ferrara, M. (2002). How people really detect lies. *Communication Monographs, 69,* 144–157. Reprinted by permission; **422:** Source: Zuckerman, M., & Driver, R. E. (1985). Telling lies: Verbal and nonverbal correlates of deception. In A. W. Siegman & S. Feldstein (Eds.), *Multichannel integrations of nonverbal behavior* (pp. 128–148). Hillsdale, NJ: Lawrence Erlbaum Associates. Reprinted by permission.

Chapter 12

Page 439: Sources: James, L. (2000). Congressional testimony (1997) Aggressive driving and road rage: Dealing with emotionally impaired drivers. Available online at: http://www.aloha.net/-dyc/testimony.html; Overberg, P. (1999, March/April). Debunking a 'trend'. *Columbia Journalism Review, 37;* **449:** Sources: Ekman, P., & Friesen, W. V. (1975). *Unmasking the face: A guide to recognizing emotions from facial clues.* Englewood Cliffs, NJ: Prentice-Hall; Ekman, P., Friesen, W. V., O'Sullivan, M., Chan, A., Diacoyanni-Tarlatzis, I., Heider, K., Krause, R., LeCompte, W. A., Pitcairn, T., Ricci-Bitti, P. E., Scherer, K., Tomita, M., & Tzavaras, A. (1987). Universals and cultural differences in the judgments of facial expressions of emotion. *Journal of Personality and Social Psychology, 53,* 712–717; **455:** Source: Kring, A. M., & Gordon, A. H. (1998). Sex differences in emotion: Expression, experience, and physiology. *Journal of Personality and Social Psychology, 74,* 686–703. Copyright © 1998, APA. Reprinted by permission; **457:** Source: Adapted from Mayer, J. D., & Salovey, P. (1997). What is emotional intelligence? In P. Salovey & J. D. Sluyter (Eds.), *Emotional development and emotional intelligence* (pp. 3–31). New York: Basic Books.